PENGUIN BOOKS

INVITATION TO AN INQUEST

Walter Schneir is a free-lance writer interested in politics, the law, and science. Articles by him have appeared in numerous magazines, including the *Nation,* the *Reporter, Liberation,* and the *New York Times Magazine.* After the 1968 Democratic Convention, he edited *Telling It Like It Was: The Chicago Riots.* At present, he is at work on a study of class conflict in the United States.

Miriam Schneir is the editor of *Feminism: The Essential Historical Writings,* an anthology. She has written on education, politics, and women's history for various national publications, among them the *New York Times Magazine, Ms.,* and *Liberation.* She is currently working on a history of colonial and revolutionary America, as seen from a feminist point of view.

INVITATION
TO AN INQUEST

Reopening the
Rosenberg
"Atom Spy" Case

WALTER & MIRIAM SCHNEIR

Penguin Books Inc
Baltimore · Maryland

Penguin Books Inc, 7110 Ambassador Road,
Baltimore, Maryland 21207, U.S.A.
Penguin Books Ltd, Harmondsworth,
Middlesex, England
Penguin Books Australia Ltd, Ringwood,
Victoria, Australia
Penguin Books Canada Ltd,
41 Steelcase Road West, Markham,
Ontario, Canada

First published by Doubleday & Co., Inc., New York, 1965
Published by Penguin Books Inc, 1973
Reprinted 1974 (twice)
Published by Penguin Books Ltd, 1974

Printed in the United States of America by
Murray Printing Co., Forge Village, Massachusetts

ACKNOWLEDGMENTS
Letter by Jacques Monod, from the *Bulletin of the
Atomic Scientists*, October 1953. Copyright 1953
by the Educational Foundation for Nuclear Science.
Letter by A. B. Martin, from the *Bulletin of the
Atomic Scientists*, December 1953. Copyright 1953
by the Educational Foundation for Nuclear Science.
Reprinted by permission of the *Bulletin of the
Atomic Scientists*.
Tapes and other material on Harry Gold, re-
printed by permission of Harry Gold.
. Excerpts from "The Atomic Bomb and Those
Who Stole It" by Bill Davidson, from *Look*, Octo-
ber 29, 1957. Reprinted by permission of *Look*
magazine.
Excerpts from letters by Morton Sobell, reprinted
by permission of Helen L. Sobell.
Letters by Julius and Ethel Rosenberg, reprinted
by permission of the Rosenberg estate.
Excerpts from the William H. Taylor brief, reprinted by permission of Byron N. Scott, Esq.
Excerpt from "Problem in Security," *Time*, March
19, 1951. Copyright 1951 by Time, Inc. Reprinted
by permission of TIME The Weekly Newsmagazine.

"To be writing an opinion in a case affecting two lives after the curtain has been rung down upon them has the appearance of pathetic futility. But history also has its claims."

Justice FELIX FRANKFURTER

Written three days after the execution of the Rosenbergs

CONTENTS

Foreword   ix
Preface—An Unanswered Question   xvii
   1   A Capsule View   1

THE BOMB
   2   The World Is Headed for Grief   7
   3   Why the United States Was First   14
   4   The Manhattan Project   20
   5   A Feeling of Profound Responsibility   27

SHOCK WAVES
   6   Security Through Secrecy   35
   7   A Blurring of Vision   41
   8   The Monopoly Ends   52

ATOM SPIES
   9   Klaus Fuchs Confesses   59
  10   Capture of an Accomplice   70
  11   More Arrests   76
  12   Blueprints from a Cellar Closet   90
  13   An "Extraordinarily Selfless Person"   107

UNITED STATES VS. ROSENBERGS AND SOBELL
  14   The Trial   119
  15   While the Jury Is Out   157
  16   Judgment Day   168

FINAL APPEALS
  17   The Campaign and the Courts   175
  18   New Evidence   196
  19   Death House Letters   213
  20   Eleventh-Hour Fight   237
  21   Post-Mortem Dialogues   254

THE INQUEST OPENS

22 The Crime in Perspective   261
23 In Search of a Spy Ring   283

A REASONABLE DOUBT

24 Elizabeth Bentley   309
25 Morton Sobell   323
26 David and Ruth Greenglass   344
27 Harry Gold   363

JUNE 3, 1945

28 The Scene of the Crime   371
29 The Hilton Hotel Card   378
30 Money from the Russians   391
31 Voices from the Past   397

SUMMATION

32 Putting the Pieces Together   405
Epilogue   426
Postscript—1967   427
Sources   455
Index   476

Illustrations   *following page* 228

FOREWORD
TO THE 1973 PENGUIN EDITION

Over seven years have passed since the first edition of *Invitation to an Inquest* was published. We had set ourselves the task of reconstructing a fragment of the domestic history of America in the Fifties. How well we succeeded depends in large measure on the genuineness of the fragment.

The reader should be aware, therefore, that after considerable public scrutiny this study of the Rosenberg-Sobell case still stands intact. Scores of critics, both favorable and adverse, have had a go at us; the FBI and the Department of Justice have been challenged repeatedly by the media to refute our new evidence, but none of our discoveries has been discredited. Afforded an opportunity now to make corrections or deletions, we find no need for any. (However, this third edition, like the second, includes a chapter we added to bring the story of the case up to date.)

The year 1973 is the twentieth anniversary of the executions of Ethel and Julius Rosenberg by the United States government. The occasion is being marked by a number of mass media enterprises that will reach millions of people and doubtlessly influence many of them. Louis Nizer—who takes the position that the accused "atom spies" were guilty—has written a book on the case and also a screenplay, which is being filmed by Otto Preminger.

Meanwhile, inevitably, the actual events are suffering a sea change; they are being transmuted into art. Most recently we have seen the novels of E. L. Doctorow, *The Book of Daniel*, and Helen Yglesias, *How She Died*. The case had earlier been employed as background by Sylvia Plath in *The Bell Jar* and also had inspired many poems and several plays, the latter performed over the years in Eastern Europe, France, and Israel. An American play, *Inquest* by Donald Freed (based in part on our book), was staged in New York City in 1970.

The real Rosenberg-Sobell case, however, belongs to history rather than art. The themes that intrigue the novelist—the betrayed kinships and friendships out of which the case was woven; the mysterious ability of ordinary people to withstand intense efforts by the state to "break" them—are of only peripheral concern to the historian. The big questions for us were what *really* happened and why. In fact, some of the details of the real case are far too crude, too melodramatic, for serious fiction.

For example, it was widely reported at the time of the executions that a telephone line had been kept open in a last dreadful effort to squeeze a confession out of the condemned couple. François Mauriac, in a commentary in *Figaro* titled "Torture by Hope," referred scathingly to the "simple telephone wire which the day before the Sabbath linked the White House and Sing Sing and which will link them forever." Now specific details of the episode have become available. James V. Bennett, retired Director of the Federal Bureau of Prisons, has written in his memoirs: "The evening of the execution, I joined the deathwatch in FBI Director J. Edgar Hoover's office. For two hours we waited beside an open telephone line, hoping to the end that the Rosenbergs would talk. They had been told for the last time that, if they spoke out, they might get a stay. In the White House, President Eisenhower was on hand, waiting to the end for any word from us."

Some observers of post-World War II America have tended to explain the political repression of the times as the product of national hysteria and paranoia. But to dwell too heavily on the psychopathology of the period—to see events in terms of emotional illness—is to miss an important point. The ambitious politicians and obedient police bureaucrats who conjured up these political shows were inspired more by a sense of purpose. True, most of the lesser "cases" exhibited to the public contained only slight content; but they were never altogether without meaning even though it might be simply a bit of homespun, an anti-Communist homily. By contrast, individuals selected from the available pool of alleged dissidents by investigating committees, prosecutors, and the media and accorded prolonged attention were those whose biographies and "crimes" lent themselves to some ideological point considered highly relevant at the moment. The Rosenbrg-Sobell trial became a great *cause célèbre* precisely because it was so rich in symbolic meanings. Every aspect of the case, including the death penalty, communicated overtones to the sensitive ear.

Thus, European intellectuals interpreted the executions of the Rosenbergs as a message that America was prepared to be relentless in pursuit of its aims. Even Eisenhower understood this, and in a letter to a friend who had appealed to him for clemency, he said that such a course would confirm the Communists in their belief that we are "weak and fearful."

We now can begin to discern that the Rosenberg-Sobell case may have served as part of the ideological trappings of a number of vital national policy decisions. One of these, which we discuss in this book, was the determination, in January, 1950, that the U.S. should build a thermonuclear or H-bomb—as a response to the first Soviet test of an A-bomb. But bits of data have become available on another even more important decision that also was made in the period preceding the "atom spy" case and may well have influenced its coming into being.

In the early months of 1950, the American government, without reference to the consent of the governed, reached the conclusion that it should increase military spending massively. This judgment, which was arrived at by the State Department and Pentagon, and concurred in by President Truman, was nothing less than the beginning of what we today know as the "arms race."

The basic document describing this portentous decision and the reasoning behind it, National Security Council-68, remains classified, but we have some knowledge of its contents from several sources, including the memoirs of Secretary of State Dean Acheson. We know, therefore, that in Spring, 1950, those who supported NSC-68 faced a difficult political question: how would it be possible to implement such an enormously costly program? Though NSC-68 is still secret, it is no secret that the classic way to persuade people to spend money for armaments is to stir fear.

Acheson did just this. All that year he travelled about the country preaching a simplistic doctrine—which he later characterized as "clearer than truth"—about the menace to the United States from an aggressive, expansionist Soviet Communism. The urgent need of the hour, as Acheson saw it, was to arouse and unify Americans so that they would support a quadrupling of the existing military budget. No doubt other top administration leaders also felt called to help sound the tocsin. Thus, the atmosphere within the government may have motivated the FBI to develop cases demonstrating the dangers of Russian Communism. But this is speculation. Until more information is released from the archives, or a Daniel Ellsberg comes along to give us such documents as NSC-68, much of the true history of the post-World War II decades will remain hidden.

Growing up politically in the Fifties, one had little choice but to fashion a consciousness from what was essentially a montage of *Daily News* headlines. Starting in 1960, however, a number of shocking public happenings occurred, and Americans began to get educated. When Francis Gary Powers had the misadventure to crash in his U-2 and be captured (disloyally ignoring the poisoned needle); when the Bay of Pigs invasion failed and Adlai Stevenson was left holding a bagful of lies at the UN; when someone talked about My Lai and someone else had actual photographs; when Daniel Ellsberg spilled the beans; when the Watergate bugging incident ended ignominiously; we had a glimpse of the nether world of contemporary politics. Such glimpses may be inadequate, but they do help us to get our bearings.

In addition, a wide array of books and articles that probe American society have become available over the past decade, revealing the past and analyzing the present. Today, anyone who wants to can circumvent the inadequacies and distortions of the mass media, the educational system, and official propaganda. The inquisitive citizen has to show some initiative if he wishes to orient himself in the Seventies, but it is nowhere near as difficult as it was for confused and frightened Americans in the Fifties.

Where were the intellectuals in the Fifties who might have pointed the way out of that dark age of American politics? Where were the books? The magazine articles? The whole counter-culture, which did not emerge until the worst was over? Some few oases of rationality and dissent existed, of course, but for every Edward R. Murrow there were ten Walter Winchells; for every publication like the *Nation*, the *Progressive*, or the *National Guardian* there were dozens of conformist journals. In the book field, a few firms known as "left-wing" or "progressive" continued to publish, but the volumes they put out were rarely reviewed and were carried by very few bookstores.

In this connection, it may be of interest to recount a bit of the background of the publication of *Invitation to an Inquest*. We all know that there was no official censorship in the United States during the Fifties and early Sixties. But there was censorship of an informal, unofficial nature—and it was very effective. Unlike state-imposed censorship—which reveals itself unmistakably through statutes, edicts, and a bureaucratic apparatus—the unofficial variety is difficult to detect. Information about it is hard to come by. We offer the following, therefore, as a sort of sample case study of how a book may be gently, but firmly, suppressed.

The year was 1962. The movement to end atmospheric testing of atomic weapons—precursor of the peace movement—had been attacked by a Senate committee but was nevertheless gaining in influence. The Freedom Riders were on the move in the South. Slowly but perceptibly the political atmosphere was beginning to change. The research that we had begun in 1959 on the Rosenberg case was mostly finished and about half the writing had been completed. We set out to find a publisher, pleased that the times seemed more propitious than they previously had been for a book on a sensitive, controversial subject. We knew we needed one of the major commercial houses if the book was to receive any critical attention. The search took over a year.

At one firm, a senior editor wanted to buy the book. He said that ordinarily he could make this decision on his own but in the case of our book he had to get the OK of management. He held the manuscript for months while he waited for word from (as we referred to him privately) the man who signs the checks. Finally, the editor decided to have an expert look over our material and give an opinion. The writer Fred J. Cook was selected to do the critique, and he praised the manuscript highly. Soon after, the book was summarily turned down by someone who had not read it, strictly as a matter of policy. The editor quit his job in disgust.

Another firm returned our manuscript with what we considered an unusual letter of rejection. It seemed that, without asking our permission, they had turned over our work-in-progress to a lawyer who was, in their words, "peculiarly fitted to go over the case and study your manuscript." This lawyer advised the publishers that we had not "sufficiently proved" our claims and then, somewhat contradictorily, made the suggestion that our material ought to be submitted to the Department of Justice: "Otherwise, won't you be withholding something that should not be withheld?" Later, we learned that what had "peculiarly fitted" this man to judge our book was that he had been a prosecutor for the federal government in cases against Communists.

Next, we encountered another publishing phenomenon of that period, the "house leftist." This was an individual who, after being pilloried by congressional or other investigating committees, or black-listed, or villified in the press, had been fortunate enough to find a safe harbor in a publishing office. The "house leftist" assigned by his firm to deal with us was a man of about sixty, whose own writings on the Soviet Union had once been highly regarded. After he read our manuscript, he met with us. He was sorry, he said, but he had to question our approach in the section on science at the beginning of the book. We assured him that could easily be taken care of. But what about the main body of the book? What about the Rosenbergs? Oh, he responded, all that was fine. No problem. We waited for some further comment. None came. Then we looked into his tired eyes that had been avoiding ours. They seemed to say, Look here, I've been through the political wars; why are you trying to complicate my life? We took pity and left.

Two young editors who today are executives in large publishing firms wanted to buy the manuscript for the house they then worked for. However, they told us, a policy decision would have to be made by the owner. When the answer came, they were so dismayed by the reasons he gave that they showed his memorandum to us. The owner had not commented at all on the manuscript; in fact, there was no indication that he had looked at it. Instead, he noted that he was Jewish and would not care to see the Rosenberg case revived. Moreover, he had checked with the American Civil Liberties Union, and they informed him that the ACLU at the time had not seen any civil liberties issues in the matter.

One of the last editors with whom we discussed our book and some of its conclusions advised that he didn't think any commercial publisher in the country would do it. He regretted this state of affairs, sympathized with our plight, but did not offer to push the book in his own firm. Why not try England, he suggested.

When Ken McCormick of Doubleday agreed to publish *Invitation to an Inquest*, we had almost given up believing that it ever would appear in print in the United States. Our ebullience was such that it could not be dimmed—not even when a Doubleday managing editor phoned and inquired shamefacedly as to our politics. We told him we were not now and never had been members of the Communist Party and he breathed an audible sigh of relief. Our contract arrived shortly afterward. And when the FBI asked Doubleday for advance galleys, they were good enough to report the request to us. We said no, and our decision was honored.

Such was publishing in America a decade ago—at least where works of political or social criticism were involved. If, however, a writer's perceptions jibed with establishment views, his or her way would be a good deal smoother. Many found it prudent to look away when anything nasty was in sight. But this "see no evil" attitude was clumsy to maintain while wearing the mask of an intellectual and led some of the leading cultural figures of the Fifties into stupendous blunders.

In October 1953 *Encounter* magazine published an essay by the liberal anti-Communist literary critic Leslie A. Fiedler, "Afterthoughts on the Rosenbergs." Fiedler termed the case of the then recently executed pair an "open-and-shut" one; the evidence "overwhelming"; their lies "flagrant"; their guilt "clearly established," "palpable," and "beyond doubt." His essay is founded, as he himself indicates, entirely on "an assumption . . . of guilt."

Fiedler's dogmatic assumption of guilt—couched in such astonishingly absolutist terms—did not arise from any special knowledge of the case or even from a reading of the trial record. He describes himself (accurately it would seem) as an "indifferent researcher." Clearly, then, his was not a reasoned opinion but a matter of faith. Leslie Fiedler, who surely knew better, had chosen to take as the *sine qua non* of his thinking about the Rosenberg case the proposition that the American judicial system is infallible. Whatever his other motivations, Fiedler's act of faith was absolutely essential if he wished his article on this subject to appear in *Encounter*.

Relieved of the troublesome question of guilt or innocence, Fiedler discoursed at length about a host of subsidiary matters such as the nature of popular-front Communism and the alleged opportunism of the campaign to save the Rosenbergs. This technique for avoiding substantive issues by debating ersatz issues instead is, as Gore Vidal has recently noted, one of the commonest and most pernicious characteristics of American politics.

(This discussion of Fiedler deserves a brief footnote: In 1967, Professor Fiedler himself became a defendant in a criminal case, along with his wife, son, and daughter-in-law. He was a faculty advisor at the State

University in Buffalo, New York, to a student group advocating legalization of marijuana, when his house was raided and he was arrested for possession of the drug. The outraged Fiedler charged what he could not bring himself so much as to consider a decade earlier—a conscious governmental frame-up.)

Another liberal anti-Communist intellectual of the Fifties was Irving Kristol, who held high staff positions on three influential and respected publications: he was managing editor of *Commentary*, co-founder and co-editor (with Stephen Spender) of *Encounter*, and editor of the *Reporter*. One of us wrote for the *Reporter* at the time he was an editor there and found him a competent and considerate person to work with. Later, he became chief editor of a publishing firm, and we submitted *Invitation to an Inquest* to him. When we came to his office to discuss the manuscript—by then about two-thirds complete—he persisted in small talk, avoiding any reference to the pages of our book sitting on his desk. Finally impatience overcame us. "Well, Irving," we asked, "are you going to publish it?" He smiled. "If I published this book, none of my friends would ever speak to me again." "Then you're rejecting it?" No answer. More small talk. Then: "Listen, I knew Julius Rosenberg when we were both students at City College, and he always looked like a spy to me." Long silence. He paced a bit. "I'll tell you what. I'd like to show this to an expert. Make me up a list of people you would suggest sending it to for an opinion." (That we agreed to this gambit a second time was merely a sign of our desperation in the search for a publisher.)

We promptly sent Kristol a long list of "experts"—mostly eminently respectable liberals. Weeks became months, and he never got in touch with us. A few times we managed to reach him by phone. He said he was trying to decide on the "right" person to show it to, but had not done anything yet. We asked that he take some action and suggested that he simply reject it. He refused. At last he wore us down. We reclaimed our unrejected manuscript and went our way.

Kristol was every bit as eager as Fiedler had been to skirt the crucial issues of the Rosenberg case. The total response of both was to accept blindly the official story, even to the point of foolishness ("he always looked like a spy"), and to avoid any other perspective. When we thrust a conflicting point of view into Irving Kristol's unwilling hands, he fell into a state of virtual paralysis.

Then, in 1967, *Ramparts* magazine published an exposé disclosing that the Central Intelligence Agency had been bankrolling an organization called the Congress for Cultural Freedom, which in turn had subsidized several magazines, among them *Encounter*. Kristol, who had never looked like a spy to us, had, it appeared, been on the CIA payroll. Fiedler's intemperate attack on the Rosenbergs had been published in a CIA publication.

Two very gullible individuals had been duped by the government in which they confidently had placed their trust. More than that, they had been conned, and, as with most victims of con games, their own ambition and pride had been the basis of their undoing.

It must, at the least, have been embarrassing. Perhaps a show of bravado, Kristol made the inane comment that he has the same neutral feelings towards the CIA as towards the post office—a comparison that might strike the peasants of Laos as a bit grotesque.

It would be unfair, however, to single out *Encounter* as the recipient of CIA largesse. The intelligence agency also had been bestowing its favors on the National Student Association, labor unions, and various academic research, journalism, business, and legal organizations. No doubt the entire story has not yet been told.

When the full history of the Fifties is written, it should make interesting reading!

PREFACE
AN UNANSWERED QUESTION

The train from Huancayo to Lima travels over the highest standard-gauge railroad track in the world. Along the aisle hurried a squat, barrel-chested physician, observing passengers for signs of mountain sickness. An Indian assistant carried a large leather bladder, filled with oxygen.

In the coach seat facing us, an energetic Franciscan friar kept up an enthusiastic conversation. He was boundlessly curious about America. His English was imperfect; our Spanish was halting, but we communicated.

It was the summer of 1959. We had come to Peru from New York on a vacation, to indulge a hobby—archaeology.

Our traveling companion seemed pleased that we had journeyed so far to see his country. Did we like Peru? Where had we been? What had we seen? Where were we going? He was returning to his parish in a small isolated desert town, far south near the Chilean border.

The loose folds of the padre's brown, cowled cloak fluttered as he gestured animatedly. Had we, he asked, visited the Franciscan catacombs in Lima? No? What a pity! They were *magnífico!* He kissed the tips of five fingers with a loud smacking sound to express the wonders of the catacombs. Immediately, he found a pencil and began drawing a map of their location.

The train was pulling into Galera Station, highest point on the line. A sign told us we were at 15,673 feet. The railroad physician was administering a few whiffs of oxygen to a pallid-faced passenger across the aisle. On the platform, several Indian women wrapped in faded blankets huddled around a charcoal brazier, selling llama heads and other medicinal charms. One of the women scurried after her derby hat, blown off by the strong wind.

The padre handed us his penciled map of the route to the catacombs. They were located beneath the Church of San Francisco, not far from the cathedral on Plaza de Armas.

He inquired: "Are you Catholic?"

"No, Jewish."

His instantaneous response startled us.

"Tell me," he asked, "do you think the Rosenbergs were guilty?"

We stared at each other incredulously. A few months before, we had decided to write a book about the Rosenberg case. We had already started our research, but it was still in an early stage. The padre's simple, direct question challenged us; we felt frustrated by our inability to give him an answer.

Seeing our hesitation, he tried to be helpful. In any event, he said, they should not have been killed. The sentence was too harsh. The Pope had appealed for clemency.

Finally, we admitted that we could not answer his question. We did not know whether the Rosenbergs were guilty or not. We agreed that the sentence was very severe.

The padre appeared disappointed, but he was polite. He changed the subject and did not mention the Rosenbergs again for the rest of the trip.

Later, back in our own country, the unanswered question continued to haunt us. Setting to work to uncover the truth—whatever it might be—we plumbed every publicly available source, then searched out new facts. Often, we thought of our brown-cowled traveling companion from the distant desert parish. For us, he came to stand for those millions of other unknown questioners, in many lands, whose doubts about the Rosenberg-Sobell case never have been resolved.

The purpose of this book is to provide an unequivocal and final answer to the lingering question posed by the Peruvian padre: Were the Rosenbergs guilty and, we would add, if so, guilty of what?

CHAPTER 1

A CAPSULE VIEW

"On August 6, 1945, a split atom sent waves of destruction circling out over Hiroshima—an explosion whose implications still batter against the institutions of our time. On June 19, 1953, two people, charged with having transmitted the secrets of this destruction to a foreign power, were executed after judgment by their fellow citizens."

Thus the *Columbia Law Review* began a critique of what it called "the outstanding 'political' trial of this generation."

The awesome enormity of the crime for which Julius and Ethel Rosenberg were condemned was made clear by Judge Irving R. Kaufman when he pronounced the death sentence on April 5, 1951.

". . . by your betrayal," he told the Rosenbergs, "you undoubtedly have altered the course of history to the disadvantage of our country."

Two co-conspirators in the case, Morton Sobell and David Greenglass, received prison terms of thirty and fifteen years respectively.

So ended a trial whose implications, like those of the split atom, "still batter against the institutions of our time."

For fourteen days in New York City's federal courthouse at Foley Square, the drama of United States *vs.* Rosenbergs and Sobell held the stage, pitting brother against sister; friend against friend. The charge was conspiracy to commit espionage; the defendants were all alleged to have been participants in a plot aimed at obtaining national defense information for the benefit of the Soviet Union.

But the crux of the matter was the accusation that the Rosenbergs—in the language of the government prosecutor—had stolen "through David Greenglass this one weapon, that might well hold the key to the survival of this nation and means the peace of the world, the atomic bomb." The motive for this crime was said to be ideological: Communism.

In the face of deeply incriminating testimony, the accused husband and wife had repeatedly denied any involvement in the conspiracy. Morton Sobell (whose alleged espionage role was not related to the atomic bomb) also claimed his innocence.

Testifying against Julius and Ethel Rosenberg was Ethel's younger brother, David Greenglass, who pleaded guilty and appeared as the principal prosecution witness. David, a machinist who had been stationed at

Los Alamos as an enlisted man during World War II, told the court how he divulged the secrets of the atom bomb at the request of his brother-in-law and sister. His wife, Ruth, confirmed her husband's story and added to it.

Chief prosecution witness against Morton Sobell was Max Elitcher, Sobell's boyhood chum, neighbor, and co-worker, who provided the only testimony linking his former friend to the espionage conspiracy.

Finally, the major *dramatis personae* included the curious little Philadelphia chemist, Harry Gold (already under sentence of thirty years), who had skyrocketted to sudden notoriety some ten months before when FBI Director J. Edgar Hoover revealed him as the confessed American accomplice of British spy Klaus Fuchs. A man who appeared to have tiptoed through life with downcast eyes, Gold shed his cocoon of self-effacement on the witness stand and told his story in robust tones, frequently jabbing his right forefinger at the jurors to make a point.

About him, the federal prosecutor had said: "Harry Gold, who furnished the absolute corroboration of the testimony of the Greenglasses, forged the necessary link in the chain that points indisputably to the guilt of the Rosenbergs."

All seven of these individuals were alleged, either during the trial or in press reports, to have been sympathetic to or active in radical left-wing politics. All seven were Jews (as were the Judge and two of the main prosecuting attorneys in the case, Irving H. Saypol and Roy M. Cohn).

Julius and Ethel Rosenberg, David and Ruth Greenglass, Morton Sobell and Max Elitcher were all in their late twenties or early thirties, married and the parents of young children. The Rosenbergs and the Greenglasses were related and had lived in the same New York City lower East Side neighborhood all their lives. The Rosenberg, Sobell, and Elitcher families were acquainted socially; Julius, Morton, and Max had been classmates together at the College of the City of New York, where they studied engineering. In a sense, the outsider in this group was Harry Gold, a forty-year-old bachelor, who—except for an alleged espionage meeting with the Greenglasses—did not claim to have known or met any of the other principals.*

The day after Judge Kaufman sentenced the Rosenbergs to death, a brief item in a New York *Post* column suggested that the government was prepared to barter the lives of the condemned couple for information. Soon the choice facing the Rosenbergs was widely known and publicly discussed. The refusal of the prisoners to proffer a *mea culpa* was cited frequently in the press as conclusive evidence of their political fanaticism, disregard for their children, and overweening wish to become Marxist

---

* Similarly, prosecution witness Elizabeth Bentley never had met any of those against whom she testified.

martyrs. The apparent use of a death sentence for coercion was generally accepted without criticism.

In the United States, a small but persistent minority, its ranks buttressed by the presence of a few scientific notables, was acutely troubled by the case. In part, this response was conditioned by the distrust some people felt for any trial with wide political implications conducted in an atmosphere of hostility and tension. The constant questioning of the Rosenbergs as to their political ideas, opinions, reading habits, and affiliations made the trial seem suspect.

Students of history were well aware that, in times of stress, any judicial system may fail. Juries may be wrong and judges biased; the innocent may be convicted. Hearing the Rosenbergs' repeated assertions of innocence, some were reminded painfully of the injustices visited on Dreyfus, on Mooney and Billings, on Sacco and Vanzetti.

But a claim of innocence is no proof of innocence, though such claims, persisted in over a very long time and even under extreme duress, may make us uneasy. And knowledge of previous miscarriages of justice can at best serve as a warning of caution, nothing more.

Nor did a reading of the trial record provide any *positive* answer for most people as to the guilt or innocence of the Rosenbergs, though many who studied the trial record came away with gnawing uncertainties as to the validity of the verdict. In the United States, some Rosenberg partisans undoubtedly were completely convinced of the innocence of the pair; others believed that there was more than a reasonable doubt as to their guilt. A third point of view was that the Rosenbergs were probably guilty of "something," but that the importance of their crime had been greatly exaggerated for political purposes.

Not surprisingly, many of the comparatively small band who sought clemency for the Rosenbergs—particularly members of the clergy—completely bypassed the thorny issue of guilt or innocence, concentrating their efforts instead on the severity of the sentence.

In particular, one unique aspect of the Rosenberg case served to discourage support for the couple: All previous cases which American liberals and radicals had assailed as judicial errors or outright frameups had been tried in state courts; the Rosenbergs were tried by the federal judiciary. To cry frameup here was a far more serious matter; it was, in effect, to accuse high officials of the United States government itself of perpetrating a vicious hoax.

Such an accusation would not be an easy one to make under any circumstances. But in 1952 and 1953, the tide of McCarthyism was at its crest. The far left was no longer a force in American politics; the ranks of the liberals were badly split—former New Deal supporters were shaken and confused by the barrage of Congressional charges regarding Communists in government. After the conviction of Alger Hiss in early 1950, many American liberals vowed total abstinence from any further dalliance with the radical left; while some few were seduced from their resolves by the Rosenberg case, most reacted to the affair by hurriedly snapping shut their political chastity belts and tossing away the keys.

Later, sociologists David Riesman and Nathan Glazer commented aptly in the *Partisan Review*: "The Sacco-Vanzetti case united the liberals; the Rosenberg case divided them."

If the campaign for the Rosenbergs achieved only modest mass appeal in the United States and practically no support from the press, in many other nations the case became a *cause célèbre* with impressive popular backing. Undoubtedly, Communist parties played a considerable role in this protest movement. What nettled and bewildered knowledgeable Americans, however, was the inexplicable depth and extent of pro-Rosenberg sentiment among non-Communists abroad, particularly in Western Europe.

Far more than in the United States, many influential Europeans— often after studying the facts of the case and reading the trial record— were convinced of the Rosenbergs' innocence. Their statements on the case shaped the views of millions. In France, the campaign to save the doomed couple produced an astonishing unanimity among all factions of that nation's polychrome political spectrum. The Rosenberg case was, in fact, the single issue about which disputatious Frenchmen had been able to unite since the war.

For the vast majority of Americans, the world-wide outcry over the Rosenbergs was puzzling, even infuriating. For had not the Rosenbergs been tried and convicted in an American court of law? Was not the case officially closed when the jury brought in its verdict and the reviewing courts let that verdict stand? Some of the most distinguished newspapers had editorially congratulated Judge Kaufman after the sentencing. Why then this frenzied effort in behalf of two spies who had outrageously betrayed their country and showed no signs of contrition?

In fine, the only mystery about the case for most Americans was a general bafflement about the great clamor being raised by millions over the fate of the Rosenbergs. Both the press and public opinion in the United States generally ascribed this uproar to abysmal duplicity on the part of Rosenberg partisans who willfully distorted the truth. At the very least, supporters of the couple were said to be the foolish dupes of Communist Machiavellism. In Europe, however, the Rosenberg case was seen by many as a dispiriting symptom of the deterioration of traditional democratic freedoms in the United States.

As the movement for clemency grew, the Rosenbergs' refusal to admit their guilt and cooperate with the government became the central issue in determining their life or death. For twenty-six months, the colloquy between the government and the Rosenbergs proved futilely repetitious.

Confess or die, said the government. And, from their death house cells, the prisoners replied: We are innocent. Toward the end, the macabre spectacle was watched by a vast audience. Surely this was one of the strangest tests of will ever staged in an international arena by a great and powerful nation and two of its more obscure citizens.

Those who had bet that the two would break lost their gamble. The Rosenbergs died in the electric chair at Sing Sing Prison, still asserting their innocence. They were the only Americans in United States history ever executed for espionage by judgment of a civil court. Also a first for the federal judiciary was the double execution of a husband and wife. Before the electrocution of Ethel Rosenberg, the last woman put to death by the United States government was Mary Surratt, condemned nearly ninety years before for alleged complicity in the assassination of Abraham Lincoln.

Of the principal prosecution witnesses, neither Ruth Greenglass, Max Elitcher, nor Harry Gold was indicted in the case. (Gold is at Lewisburg Penitentiary serving the sentence received at an earlier trial for his espionage activities with Klaus Fuchs.) David Greenglass is free today after serving ten years of his fifteen-year term.

Morton Sobell is presently imprisoned at a federal penitentiary, serving his thirty-year sentence. Like the Rosenbergs, he could certainly have mitigated his punishment by confession and cooperation; even today he could probably gain his freedom in this way at any time. After fifteen years behind bars (more than five of them in Alcatraz), he continues to affirm his innocence.

THE BOMB

•

CHAPTER 2
THE WORLD IS HEADED FOR GRIEF

During the winter of 1896, men and women throughout the world were still marveling over the astonishing discovery made a few months earlier by a German physicist, Wilhelm Roentgen. Scientists, in particular, were intensely curious as to the source and nature of Roentgen's mysterious x-rays that permitted one to take pictures through solid matter.

At that moment, from a French laboratory, came word of a second momentous discovery—made quite by accident—whose reverberations added to those produced by Roentgen's find.

The French scientist, Henri Becquerel, had stored in a desk drawer a sample of the heaviest metal known to man, uranium, along with a sensitive photographic plate, wrapped to protect it from light.

When Becquerel chanced to develop the plate, he was perplexed to find that it was badly fogged. How could this be explained? Perhaps the wrapping was faulty. Again and again he placed the uranium rock close to a carefully covered photographic plate. The results were always the same. Some hitherto unknown and invisible ray from within the uranium rock penetrated the wrapping and fogged the plate.

In reporting his research to his fellow scientists, Becquerel coined the word "radioactive" to describe this strange property of uranium.

Pierre Curie was a colleague of Becquerel's. Like scientists in many lands, he and his Polish-born wife Marie were intrigued and challenged by the meaning of the recent discoveries. The ordinary objects of daily life appeared to the senses to be cold, inert, solid, and stable. Clearly this appearance was only a façade behind which nature hid profound secrets. Where did Roentgen's x-rays come from? What was the source of the radioactivity revealed by Becquerel? This unknown energy must come from somewhere deep within the very atoms of a substance.

Pierre and Marie Curie wondered if there were other naturally radioactive elements, like uranium. Within the black pitchblende rock from which uranium was extracted, the Curies detected the presence of a far more powerful and rare radioactive substance. They announced their

7

findings in 1898; not until four years later were they able to separate a few specks of radium from a ton of pitchblende which they toiled over devotedly in a crude, unheated shed.

Now the world of science was indeed in ferment. It was as if all the known physical laws were being turned topsy turvy. The proof was there for anyone to see. Using a photographic film, for example, one could easily detect the energy coming from the radioactive rock. A week later; a month later; a year later, the energy was still being emitted. The rock must contain a fabulous quantity of energy.

A twenty-six-year-old Swiss patent office clerk named Albert Einstein confirmed this supposition in 1905 when he published his Special Theory of Relativity, which provided a mathematical formula that could be used to calculate the incredible amount of energy stored in the atom. The now well-known formula, $E=mc^2$, has been called a "scientist's poem." What it says is that all matter is a dormant form of energy. Einstein suggested that one proof of his equation might be obtained from a study of the newly discovered radioactive substances.

So scientists began to explore the atom, to imagine what an atom looked like, and to try to learn what cosmic glue held one together. The story of the men and women who arduously and lovingly built the edifice of modern physics in the early part of this century is one of the most fascinating chapters in man's intellectual history.

Soon the mathematical calculations and soaring imaginations of dedicated scientists in many lands gave form and order to the atom. Such greats as Ernest Rutherford in England, Max Planck in Germany and Niels Bohr in Denmark supplied the needed ideas and theories to guide others. They pictured the atom itself as a miniature solar system and disclosed that the powerhouse of the atom is at its center, or nucleus.

During the Twenties, brilliant young men all over the world were attracted to the study of atomic physics. A whole new science was being built before their eyes and they wanted to be a part of it. A few centers of research and learning flowered—at Cambridge, where Rutherford worked; in Paris, at Madame Curie's Radium Institute; in Copenhagen, home of Niels Bohr; and, in Germany, at the old university town of Göttingen. To each of these centers flocked scientists of many nationalities, to see, hear, study, and exchange ideas.

While some of these youthful pioneers may occasionally have dreamed of finding a way to release the atom's power, such thoughts did not concern most of the scientists. There was glory and satisfaction enough in pure research—in laying claim to a new atomic particle, a new element, a new piece of equipment, a newly revealed law of nature.

Still, from the beginning, the possible practical implications of the infant science stirred the imaginations of some. At the University of Vienna, Professor Hans Thirring read Einstein's formula and said: "It takes one's breath away to think of what might happen in a town, if the dormant energy of a single brick were to be set free, say in the form of an explosion. . . . This, however, will never happen. . . ."

In 1922, the director of the Soviet State Radium Institute in Leningrad, V. I. Vernadskii, predicted:

"We are approaching a tremendous revolution in human life with which nothing hitherto experienced can be compared. It will not be long before man will receive atomic energy for his disposal. . . ."

Soon after, Vernadskii left the Soviet Union for extended visits to the world centers of the new physics in Western Europe. Before returning to Leningrad, he spent considerable time in Paris, where he worked at Madame Curie's Radium Institute.

Such visits—by a scientist from one country to a laboratory in another country—were not at all unusual. Secrecy and security regulations were unknown; free exchange of information was regarded as the lifeblood of science.

Both American and Soviet scientists came to work and study with their colleagues in the Western European centers. Among the dozens of American physicists and chemists at Göttingen during the Twenties were Karl T. Compton, J. Robert Oppenheimer, Edward U. Condon, and Linus Pauling. At least three leading Soviet scientists—Peter Kapitza, Yulii Khariton, and Kyrill Sinel'kinov—served for long periods on the research staff of Rutherford's Cavendish Laboratory, while the great Abram Joffe and Lev Landau both visited or taught at Göttingen.

The world of physics was a truly cosmopolitan community. The major figures had read each other's papers, met at international meetings, studied and worked together, and often were acquainted socially. The principal scientific journals were similarly international in character. It was not unusual for a paper by an Italian or Hungarian scientist to appear in the German *Zeitschrift für Physik*, for a paper by a Japanese or Soviet researcher to be published in the American *Physical Review*, or for a paper by a Frenchman or Dane to be printed in the British *Nature*. Until 1947, all scientific papers published in the Soviet Union bore both titles and abstracts in Russian, English, and German, and the Soviet *Journal of Physics* was published in all three languages.

Wherever an important paper appeared, it soon was being discussed throughout the world.

As might be expected, the greatest quantity of first-class research in the new physics before World War II was accomplished by the more numerous scientists of the major industrial powers—England, France, Germany, Italy, the United States, the Soviet Union, and Japan. But excellent contributions were also being made by physicists in Denmark, Sweden, Holland, Austria, Switzerland, and Belgium, as well as Canada, Australia, New

Zealand, Ireland, China, India, Rumania, Hungary, Poland, Portugal, and Brazil.

Thus, diligent scientists in more than a score of nations were constantly adding bits to man's growing knowledge of the atomic universe. While the United States hardly reigned supreme in the international world of physics, the contributions of her scientists were substantial and noteworthy. The pioneering studies of A. A. Michelson, R. A. Millikan, and Arthur Compton were known and respected everywhere, as was the later work of Carl Anderson and Harold Urey.

It was the inventive genius of two Americans—Ernest O. Lawrence and M. S. Livingston—that created the cyclotron, one of a number of new and revolutionary tools for studying the heart of the atom. The invention drew scientists from all over the world to the Radiation Laboratory at Berkeley, California. And, perhaps as a portent, the second nation in the world to put a cyclotron into operation was the Soviet Union.

But, despite much outstanding work in both countries, neither the United States nor the Soviet Union was the focus of attention for physicists during the Thirties. The reason was an extraordinary series of scientific discoveries in Western Europe; in a period of six years, the spotlight moved from England, to France, to Italy, to Germany.

In 1932, from England came a discovery that offered man a possible key to the atom's tightly locked door. James Chadwick—following up the earlier work of German and French colleagues—announced the identification of a previously unknown atomic particle, the neutron. The find was immediately hailed as one of the most important in the short history of atomic physics.

Much of the experimental work of physicists is done by emulating diamond cutters. As those ingenious craftsmen use a diamond to cut a diamond, so physicists use parts of the nucleus of the atom as projectiles with which to transmute the atom itself, as medieval alchemists had dreamed of doing.

Previously, the atomic particle had to be hurled at its hard target with such force that far more energy was utilized by the physicists than was released from the atom. The neutron, however, was an electrically neutral particle and so could enter the nucleus rather easily, without being repelled by the powerful forces within the atom. One of the first to take advantage of the neutron as a new tool for exploring the atom was a young Italian physicist, Enrico Fermi. At his laboratory in Rome in 1934, Fermi read of an epochal experiment performed by the daughter of Madame Curie, Irène Curie, and her husband, Frédéric Joliot-Curie. The two had managed to produce artificially radioactive substances, opening up a vast new field of research.

Fermi wondered if neutrons also might be used to make substances they hit radioactive. He and his co-workers began bombarding every known element with neutrons. When Fermi tried the experiment with uranium, the results were confusing—but it was clear that something highly unusual was happening. The Italian scientist reported that he had probably created a brand new element, but he could not be sure. A few other scientists also were uncertain, but most went along with Fermi's tentative explanation.

For four years, Fermi's experiment with uranium was repeated and discussed by scientists everywhere—and understood by no one. Then, in late 1938, the Fermi experiment was repeated for the thousandth time by two outstanding German chemists, Otto Hahn and Fritz Strassmann.

Using the very latest methods of chemical analysis, the two scientists meticulously studied the microscopic bits of uranium metal that had been struck by neutrons. They found something that no one ever had noticed before. Instead of the new, unknown element that Fermi had predicted, Hahn and Strassmann detected a number of old, familiar elements in place of the original uranium. The elements they found were approximately half the weight of the uranium atoms. It was as if the atoms of uranium had been split into two unequal pieces by the bombarding neutrons. But such a nuclear reaction was unheard of! The two chemists went over and over their findings, but they could find no flaw. Their results seemed both certain and impossible.

An indication of their perplexity is this qualifying sentence which they cautiously added to their final report: "It is yet possible that a series of strange and deceptive accidents could have produced the results we obtained." With great trepidation, they sent their report to a German scientific journal on December 22, 1938.

Then, seeking reassurance, the two uneasy men mailed a copy of their paper to an old colleague, Lise Meitner, whose opinion they both respected. Lise Meitner was an example of what had happened to the apolitical world of physics after the rise to power of Mussolini and Hitler. A mass exodus of Central European scientists had begun: Many of the refugees were Jews; others simply refused to live under the anti-intellectual gangster regime established in Berlin.

Lise Meitner, an Austrian Jew, had worked at the Kaiser Wilhelm Institute in Berlin for over thirty years when she was forced to flee Germany to escape the terror of Nazi racial decrees. Her long scientific collaboration with Otto Hahn was well-known in the world of physics, where she was a luminary in her own right. With the aid of sympathetic Dutch scientists, she managed a hasty escape and finally reached the haven of Sweden. There, a lonely exile, she received over the Christmas holiday the letter sent by her former colleagues.

The meaning of the news from Hahn and Strassmann was soon apparent to the agile-minded Meitner. She knew that the careful analytic techniques employed by the two scientists made a "series of strange and deceptive accidents" extremely unlikely. There was only one possible conclusion to be drawn: Something hitherto unknown to physics had occurred—the heavy uranium atom had been split into two separate parts.

Excitedly, she discussed the report with her nephew, Otto Frisch, a young refugee physicist working in Niels Bohr's laboratory in Copenhagen. What made their heads swim was the knowledge that the uranium atom is held together by a fantastic amount of energy. If uranium atoms could indeed be split, this energy would be released in the process.

Frisch quickly informed Bohr of the probable splitting of the uranium atom by neutrons. The great Danish physicist was just preparing to leave for America, where he had planned a sojourn of several months at Princeton with the best-known of the refugee scientists—Albert Einstein. According to one story, when Bohr heard the news of the Hahn-Strassmann discovery, he slapped himself on the forehead and exclaimed: "How could we have missed it all this time!"

While Bohr was en route to America, Frisch set up a simple experiment and confirmed that uranium atoms are split in two when hit by neutrons. By long-distance telephone between Copenhagen and Stockholm, he and his aunt composed a short scientific report and dispatched it to England for publication in *Nature*. To describe the splitting of the atom, they borrowed a word from biology: fission.

On January 16, 1939, Laura and Enrico Fermi went to the pier of the Swedish Line in New York to meet Bohr. Laura Fermi recalled later: "He talked of one subject only: the danger of war in Europe." It was a subject of more than passing interest to the Fermi family; they themselves had arrived in America as refugees from Fascist Italy only two weeks before, after a brief stopover in Stockholm, where Enrico received the Nobel Prize.

Bohr informed colleagues at Princeton and Columbia of the Hahn-Strassmann experiment and the interpretation of it by Meitner and Frisch. The news quickly spread by word of mouth. Shortly afterward, Bohr formally reported the discovery at a scientific meeting in Washington, D.C.*

But the real bombshell at that meeting was dropped by Enrico Fermi. The imaginative Italian physicist startled his colleagues when he suggested that each time a uranium atom was split a few spare neutrons might be freed from the atom in the process. These neutrons could then strike and split other uranium atoms, liberating still more neutrons. A chain reaction would be set up. Each split atom would release energy. The implications were stupendous.

One of the refugee scientists at Columbia, Leo Szilard, a Hungarian, also had concluded that a chain reaction might be possible. Szilard's immediate concern was that the discovery of fission might provide Germany

---

* The Fifth Washington Conference on Theoretical Physics, held on January 26, 1939.

with a horrible weapon in the impending European war. In early February 1939, in a letter to Joliot-Curie in Paris, Szilard broached the subject that was already haunting him:

"When Hahn's paper reached this country about a fortnight ago, a few of us at once got interested in the question whether neutrons are liberated in the disintegration of uranium. Obviously, if more than one neutron were liberated, a sort of chain reaction would be possible. In certain circumstances this might then lead to the construction of bombs which would be extremely dangerous in general and particularly in the hands of certain governments."

Actually, the idea that neutrons might be freed in the splitting of the uranium atom had occurred independently to Joliot-Curie in Paris, as it had to Fermi and to Szilard in New York, and also to at least two Soviet scientists, Rusinov and Flerov, in Leningrad. Within a matter of a few weeks of each other, four research teams in three different countries were all able to prove the possibility of a chain reaction.

A description of the work of one of these teams is provided by Szilard, who, together with Canadian-born Walter Zinn, performed the experiment on March 3, 1939, on the seventh floor of Pupin Hall at Columbia University:

"After two days of preparation, everything was ready and all we had to do was to turn a switch, lean back and watch the screen of a television tube.

"If flashes of light appeared on the screen, that would mean that neutrons were emitted in the fission process of uranium, and this, in turn, would mean that the large-scale liberation of atomic energy was just around the corner.

"We turned the switch and we saw the flashes.

"We watched them for a little while and then we switched everything off and went home.

"That night there was little doubt in my mind the world was headed for grief."

CHAPTER 3

WHY THE UNITED STATES WAS FIRST

By a tragic coincidence of history, scientists were preparing the way for the release of the energy of the atom at the very moment that the great nations were moving relentlessly toward war.

Goaded by terror that atomic bombs might provide the Nazis with a weapon for global conquest, a small group of refugee scientists—led by Leo Szilard*—sought to convince the American government of the need to build the bomb first. Their initial attempt met with failure. A letter to the Navy was written by an American colleague, Dean George B. Pegram of Columbia University. It requested an appointment for Enrico Fermi to explain "the possibility that uranium might be used as an explosive that would liberate a million times as much energy per pound as any known explosive." The meeting was arranged but accomplished nothing.

Ironically, the letter was sent on March 16, 1939, the very day Nazi legions goose-stepped into and annexed the last of Czechoslovakia. That nation's Joachimsthal mines—origin of the pitchblende ore from which the Curies first had extracted radium nearly forty years before—were the richest known source of uranium in Europe. Soon after, seemingly ominous news reached the ears of the foreign-born scientists: The Germans had embargoed the sale of Czech uranium.

As the months passed, additional bits of information filtering out of Germany led the anxious scientists to assume that the Nazis had launched a crash program to build an atomic bomb. Backed by Niels Bohr, Szilard and a few others proposed that physicists in the United States and Western Europe voluntarily restrict publication of their atom-splitting experiments, in the hope of impeding the progress of the German scientists. Reaction was mixed; papers were published freely for another year.

In the summer of 1939, Szilard and several colleagues turned for help to Albert Einstein, believing they might use his great prestige to gain access to high government officials. The former pacifist, who had gained some firsthand knowledge of Nazi barbarism, listened to their story and agreed to sign a letter to President Roosevelt alerting him to the possible danger. The now famous letter informed the President that "it may become pos-

* Others were Enrico Fermi, Eugene Wigner, Victor F. Weisskopf, and Edward Teller.

sible to set up a nuclear chain reaction in a large mass of uranium by which vast amounts of power . . . would be generated."

The letter warned: "This new phenomenon" might lead to the construction of "extremely powerful bombs of a new type. . . ."

Even with the Einstein letter, the refugee scientists required two more months to reach the White House; they had enlisted the aid of an unofficial presidential adviser, Alexander Sachs, and it was he who finally delivered the message. According to an apocryphal account of the event, FDR read the letter and accompanying memo from Szilard and immediately ordered the expenditure of two billion dollars. His actual response was more modest. A three-man committee—with two members from the Armed Forces—was set up to look into the matter. Over the next seven or eight months, a grand total of about six thousand dollars was made available for research. Progress was minimal.

Eventually, the slow pace of research activity alarmed a number of prominent members of the American scientific community, where interest in the military potentialities of atomic energy was growing. In the summer of 1940, a new and enlarged committee—this time composed almost entirely of civilian scientists—was established and the situation improved. Even so, the government's investment in the work was meager: Over the next eighteen months approximately three hundred thousand dollars was allocated for some sixteen small research projects.

The scientists soon learned that the uranium with which an atom bomb might be made is an extremely rare form of the metal, called U-235. Separating U-235 from ordinary uranium on a large scale would be a herculean task. The other possible explosive ingredient for an atomic bomb was a totally new metal, plutonium, which physicists thought they might be able to create in an as yet only-theoretical chain-reacting machine.

To produce substantial amounts of either U-235 or plutonium would require the construction of huge and costly manufacturing plants of novel design. Obviously, only a great industrial nation might vie for the power of the atom.

Within a year after the Hahn-Strassmann discovery, over a hundred scientific papers on atom-splitting experiments had been published all over the world. The implications of this research were clear to scientists everywhere: A nation willing to pay an astronomical price could *probably* learn to utilize atomic energy.

The word *probably* was important. For no competent scientist could guarantee to his government that some insurmountable obstacle might not be encountered, perhaps after many millions of dollars had been expended. Neither could anyone estimate with reasonable accuracy the time required to make an atomic bomb, nor what the ultimate cost might be.

The failure of FDR to have ordered immediate and massive backing for so dubious and revolutionary a proposal is hardly surprising. The fact that any atomic energy project would at best be a gamble, beset by many uncertainties, was well-known in other nations—Japan, Germany, France, the Soviet Union, and England—whose scientific and industrial resources were sufficient to give them an atomic potential.

The theoretical work of Japanese physicists, for example, was running roughly parallel to that of physicists in the United States. They possessed first-class laboratory facilities and equipment. The important research of Hideki Yukawa and other Japanese physicists was respected by scientists throughout the world. But the Japanese economy was already strained by war and preparation for war. The scientists could hardly recommend that their nation's limited resources be heavily invested in such a long-range and problematical proposition.

More difficult to explain is the fact, learned at the end of the war, that the Nazi government had accorded a comparatively minor status to atomic research. A special American intelligence mission in Europe in 1945 found that the Germans had been building a uranium chain-reacting machine, but the device was still in a rather rudimentary state. Germany had lost many top physicists as a result of religious and political persecutions and at least some of the more eminent scientists who remained were unenthusiastic about the regime. The attitude of many Nazi leaders toward science, heavily influenced by mysticism and opportunism, was an even more serious impediment; pet projects of *Der Führer* himself or other nonscientists were allocated dwindling resources.

Then too, Hitler had counted on a short war and so was not interested in new weapons that would not be available quickly. By the time his miscalculation became evident, the severe drain on the economy of the Third Reich caused by the Russian campaign and the heavy Allied air bombardments made any substantial atomic program impossible. German scientists reassured their government leaders that the task of building an atomic bomb was so difficult that the United States also would be unable to accomplish it during the war.

French scientists had played a leading role throughout the history of atomic physics and, in 1939 and 1940, they performed some of the most important atom-splitting experiments. With help from the French government, Joliot-Curie headed a team working on a chain-reacting machine. All work was abruptly terminated, however, in June 1940, when German armies swiftly overran France. Five of the nation's leading physicists escaped to England, where they aided the atomic program in progress there.

In the Soviet Union, where interest in the practical release of atomic energy had long been great, physicists greeted the news of the splitting of the uranium atom with a burst of research effort directed toward a greater understanding of nuclear fission. At scientific seminars and meetings, as

16

well as in popular publications, the Russians discussed and evaluated the new discovery.

During 1939, Soviet physicists duplicated much of the work then being performed in the West and made a number of outstanding contributions of their own. For example, two Soviet physicists, Georgii Flerov and Konstantin Petrzhak, proved the existence of spontaneous fission in an ingenious experiment that succeeded where several devised by an American physicist, Willard F. Libby, had failed.

By spring 1940, the Soviet Academy of Sciences had set up a Special Committee for the Problem of Uranium, including as members fourteen of the nation's leading scientists. A comprehensive plan called for a scientific research program for the study of uranium, and the development of methods for separating U-235 from ordinary uranium and controlling the chain reaction. An expedition headed by a top Soviet geologist was organized to prospect for uranium.

None of this activity was secret; results of research and plans for the future were freely published, though they were noted by only a few Western scientists. Years later, the RAND Corporation surveyed some of these publicly available Soviet sources for the United States Air Force and concluded: "The problem of separating uranium isotopes was being studied at about the same rate in the United States and the USSR, except that in the theoretical exploration of some of these methods the Russians may have been somewhat in the lead."

With the German invasion of Russia in June 1941, the Soviet atomic energy program was slowed or halted for at least a year or two; the leader of Soviet atomic research, Igor Kurchatov, temporarily abandoned his work and departed for the Black Sea area to devise methods for protecting ships from German mines. But Soviet scientists, like their colleagues in other parts of the world, remained aware of the military potential of atomic energy. On October 13, 1941, for example, both *Pravda* and *Izvestia* carried excerpts from a speech on explosives made by physicist Peter Kapitza to a gathering of scientific workers:

". . . recent years have seen the opening up of still newer possibilities—that is, the utilization of internal atomic energy. Theoretical calculations show that, whereas a modern high-explosive bomb can destroy an entire city block, an atom bomb, even one of small size, if it can be manufactured, could easily destroy a major capital city with several million inhabitants."

Probably no other nation has made more fundamental contributions to nuclear physics than Great Britain; the science rests on the work of such men as Rutherford, J. J. Thomson, Chadwick, and John D. Cockcroft and his Irish co-worker, E. T. S. Walton. Yet the atomic energy program in Great Britain, as in the United States, was first incited by refugee scientists—particularly Rudolph Peierls and Otto Frisch—though some native British scientists, including Chadwick, were independently thinking along the same lines.

The government provided substantial financial aid and, once the war had begun, the scientists concentrated all their work on a direct military objective: An atomic bomb. Though aware of the possibility of a plutonium bomb, the British decided not to divide their effort and so focused attention entirely on a bomb made from U-235.

The latter part of 1941 was a time of decision for the American atomic project. Some of the leading men on the government committee, believing that the project was too speculative and long-range, wanted to drop it in favor of work more immediately related to national defense. Others argued for an all-out push. A special committee headed by physicist Arthur Compton was assigned to draw up a report that would recommend a course of action.

At this stage, the then more advanced British program had an important and probably decisive influence. Despite a system for censoring scientific journals that had been voluntarily established in the United States in 1940, American and British scientists had frequently exchanged information on their atomic energy research, with the knowledge and approval of their respective governments. As a result, the British made known in mid-1941 that the amount of U-235 required for a bomb would be many times less than earlier American work had indicated. Furthermore, copies of a highly optimistic British report on the prospects for making a U-235 bomb were sent to the leaders of the American project, James B. Conant and Vannevar Bush.

When Bush reviewed the substance of the British report with President Roosevelt, the latter gave the signal to go ahead. Four or five million dollars from a special presidential fund were made available immediately. If and when the stage for the construction of giant installations was reached, the Army would take over. Meanwhile, the project remained in the hands of the scientists.

The Compton committee submitted its own report in early November 1941 and, though some of its estimates of the explosive force of the bomb were more conservative than those in the British report, its conclusions were similarly favorable.

A small group of scientific leaders, including Compton, met in Washington on December 6, 1941, to hear the decision and begin organizing the work. Next day, a Sunday, Compton was on his way by train from Washington to New York to discuss the project with Fermi, Szilard, and other Columbia scientists, when a passenger boarding at Wilmington told him of the attack on Pearl Harbor.

At that moment in history, the United States—alone among the major powers—had the immediate potential of producing an atomic bomb. England, whose project had progressed faster than the one in the United

States, soon would abandon all thought of a construction program of its own and place its scientists at the disposal of the American endeavor.

By a twist of fate, the United States, enriched by the arrival of scores of brilliant foreign scientists, possessed of industrial resources vast enough to support simultaneously both a major war and a huge and uncertain atomic project, and relatively invulnerable to air attack or invasion, would be the first to unleash the power of the atom.

Ironically, it had been the civilian scientists, not the military or the politicians, who had promoted the project and rallied support for the decision to go ahead. It was they, stirred by nightmares of possible Nazi triumph, who had taken the initiative. Long years afterward, some would still search their consciences and ponder the correctness of their action.

Nearly three years had passed since Hahn and Strassmann had sent their startling report to Lise Meitner. Now, unknown to all but a few inhabitants of the planet, momentous developments were in the offing.

CHAPTER 4

THE MANHATTAN PROJECT

The principal problem of the entire wartime atomic bomb project can be stated with rather deceptive simplicity: To find a way to produce some hundreds of pounds of either of two fissionable elements—uranium 235 or plutonium. Based on their mathematical calculations and experiments, scientists were reasonably certain that if a large enough chunk (the exact amount was then unknown) of either substance could be accumulated, it would explode spontaneously in a runaway chain reaction.

Actually, of course, the task was far from simple. In December 1941 no one had ever even seen either of the metals, though delicate laboratory tests had confirmed their existence. Today we know that—in appearance at least—U-235 and plutonium are innocent enough; despite their unique destructive potential, they closely resemble other, familiar elements. Both are bright, easily tarnished metals, similar in color to silver or nickel, and half again as heavy as lead; a fifty-pound sphere of plutonium or U-235 would be only about the size of a softball.

But here their likeness to any other substance known to man ends; this amount of fissionable material would be far more than enough to incinerate the population of a large city.

The project planners would have preferred to direct their total effort to the production of either plutonium or uranium 235, both equally suitable as the explosive core of an atomic bomb. But the scientists were on an untrod path; unforeseen difficulties might arise. In the midst of what was thought to be a deadly race with Nazi Germany, no one dared risk the success or failure of the entire atomic project on a single untried production process. As a form of insurance, therefore, two completely separate programs were set in motion—one aimed at producing plutonium; the other, U-235.

Headquarters for the plutonium program—code-named the Metallurgical Project—was established by Arthur Compton at the University of Chicago. The plan was to build a chain-reacting machine, or atomic pile, in which ordinary uranium would be transmuted into the totally new metal—plutonium. Enrico Fermi and his colleagues had first attempted to set up an atomic pile at Columbia; now this pioneer team moved to Chicago and began assembling what was literally a large pile of black graphite bricks, regularly interspersed with hundreds of lumps of ordinary uranium metal.

Thousands of Met Lab employees soon were tackling an enormous range of arduous research tasks. Every step revealed formidable barriers to success: The single job of obtaining large amounts of ordinary uranium and graphite, both of previously unheard-of purity, engaged the efforts of scores of scientists and technicians. Some of the problems facing the Met Lab could be solved in a few months by a small team of scientists; others—often of labyrinthine complexity—were entirely new areas of research that might be studied profitably for years.

In all, more than seventy research organizations throughout the country participated in the plutonium program. During the year 1942 alone, Met Lab employees turned out over four hundred scientific papers on their highly varied findings. According to a reliable estimate, a complete report of all research conducted under the auspices of the Laboratory would require no less than thirty volumes.

Meanwhile, at scores of other laboratories, researchers sought ways to obtain the required quantity of U-235. The two centers of activity were Columbia, where Harold Urey was the leading figure, and the Radiation Laboratory at the University of California, where Ernest Lawrence directed operations.

The job was fantastically difficult. Uranium 235 is always completely intermixed with far larger amounts of common uranium—a hundred-pound rock of common uranium (U-238) would contain only about ten ounces of U-235. The crux of the problem is that the two metals are identical in every respect save one: As the numbers indicate, U-235 is just a trifle lighter than U-238. This minute difference in weight is what makes possible their separation.

Scientists all over the world had long been familiar with at least four methods that could be used to separate submicroscopic amounts of U-235 from ordinary uranium. The problem facing the atomic project scientists was to select one or more of these existing methods which might be expanded several millionfold to produce U-235 on a relatively large scale.

The choice was not easy—every method had at least a number of serious drawbacks and all would be enormously costly. The two most promising were the gaseous diffusion and the electromagnetic processes and eventually both were used. Another, the thermal diffusion process, was developed on a limited scale.

At first, estimates of the critical amount of material needed to effect a chain reaction were imprecise, ranging all the way from two to two hundred pounds. A piece of fissionable material smaller than this critical size would be stable and harmless; no chain reaction would occur.

This widely known fact of nature—that a certain specific minimum amount of material was necessary for a sustained chain reaction—was in

no way an American secret and neither, therefore, were the basic requirements for the detonation of an atomic bomb: Take two or more small
pieces of U-235 or plutonium which, *when combined*, exceed the deadly
critical size. Bring them together quickly. Result—a fiery chain reaction
with unprecedented release of energy.

Initially, the actual job of designing a bomb that would utilize this
principle was assigned secondary priority by project leaders, as compared
with the primary task of producing the material from which the bomb
could be made. Nevertheless, the work was not neglected. At several
dozen universities, a relatively small number of experimental physicists
were collecting some of the enormous store of technical data essential
for the bomb design. By mid-1942, this work was placed under the direction of J. Robert Oppenheimer, a thirty-eight-year-old physics professor
at the University of California.

As the plutonium and U-235 programs both approached a stage calling
for construction of the gargantuan production plants, the scientists relinquished their management of the project to the United States Army
Engineers. Placed in charge of the sprawling enterprise—now designated
the Manhattan District—was Brigadier General Leslie R. Groves. Soon the
massive industrial phase of the work would begin.

On December 2, 1942, Enrico Fermi and his colleagues at the University
of Chicago achieved a signal success that marks a milestone of the atomic
age. Four years after scientists throughout the world had foreseen a chain
reaction as a theoretical possibility, Fermi slowly pulled a control rod out
of a carefully arranged pile of graphite bricks and ordinary uranium and
transformed the possibility into a reality. Within the weirdly silent pile,
neutrons from split U-235 atoms bounced around like billiard balls, some
splitting additional U-235 atoms and releasing more neutrons to sustain the
chain reaction, others striking the atoms of ordinary uranium and trans-
muting them into plutonium.

Immediately, an elated Compton telephoned one of the top project
officials, James B. Conant at Harvard, to give him the news. Speaking
cryptically to preserve secrecy, Compton reported: ". . . the Italian navi-
gator has just landed in the new world."

Fortified by the knowledge that they could initiate a *controlled* self-
sustaining chain reaction, Manhattan Project leaders now forged ahead
confidently with plans to create the world's first *uncontrolled* chain reaction: An atomic bomb. Leading American scientists were already engaged
in the effort, working side by side with distinguished foreign colleagues—
including four Nobel Prize winners—from Italy, Denmark, Germany,
Hungary, Canada, Australia, and, particularly, Britain. Now giant corporations and their key personnel were recruited for the job that lay ahead.
Over the next few years, vast resources and some two billion dollars
would be expended. Hundreds of thousands of people—perhaps as many

as half a million—would contribute to the final outcome, yet all but a few would be ignorant of the purpose of their labors.

By spring of 1943, three secret cities were being carved out of the American wilderness in Washington state, Tennessee, and New Mexico. On the west bank of the Columbia River in south-central Washington, thousands of workmen swarming over the sagebrush plains hastily assembled a sprawling construction camp that eventually housed a population of sixty thousand. Soon the first of three elephantine atomic piles took shape against a desolate landscape of dark, barren hills. The construction of the Hanford Engineer Works—production center for the plutonium program—was under way.

The scientists had built the first atomic pile on the University of Chicago campus, but this small pile would have taken hundreds of years to create a single pound of plutonium. The design and construction of the huge pile and other facilities at Hanford was primarily a job for engineers, with scientists relegated to an advisory capacity. Building a $350 million industrial complex so soon after the achievement of the first chain reaction was a daring venture. The engineers completed their unique assignment with amazing dispatch—by fall of 1944 the first atomic pile at Hanford went into operation, followed early the next year by the other two.

Now began the actual creation of the plutonium destined to destroy the city of Nagasaki less than a year later. Each of the three box-shaped, two-story-high graphite piles, or reactors, enclosed with a thick concrete and lead wall to shield workmen against lethal radioactivity, was honeycombed straight through with hundreds of tunnels about the diameter of a silver dollar. At loading time, technicians mechanically inserted thousands of small uranium slugs into the holes in the graphite.

Once the chain reaction was kindled, billions of splitting atoms within the reactor released tremendous heat, requiring constant cooling if the entire structure were not to melt or burst apart, spewing deadly radioactivity over a wide area. When the reactors were functioning, fear of such a disaster caused the abandonment of the original workers' city at Hanford and the building of a new city at Richland, some fifteen or more miles downriver. Cooling the reactors required Bunyanesque measures: Power in enormous amounts from the Grand Coulee Dam was employed to pump a goodly portion of the Columbia River through thousands of tiny crevices in the graphite pile.

After "cooking" in the reactor for months, the uranium slugs—each now impregnated with a tiny amount of plutonium—were pushed completely through the graphite pile and out the other side, dropping into a deep, water-filled canal to cool. Then the minute bits of newly formed plutonium were chemically extracted from the uranium slugs—a highly complex process in itself—by technicians who performed every step of their potentially hazardous work with specially designed periscopes, mechanical arms, and other elaborate remote control equipment.

Laboriously, speck by speck, the metal was gathered. All through the spring and into the summer of 1945, armed guards carried mysterious Lilliputian cargoes from Hanford to a secret installation in New Mexico, where the plutonium was purified and fabricated into shapes suitable for the core of an atomic bomb.

The site selected for the large-scale separation of U-235 from ordinary uranium was an area of wooded ridges and remote valleys in eastern Tennessee, conveniently located near an ample supply of cooling water, the Clinch River, and an abundant source of power, TVA.

Oak Ridge was even bigger, costlier, and more complex than Hanford. Alternately slogging through seas of mud or choking in clouds of dust, tens of thousands of workers—the peak population at Oak Ridge was eighty thousand—erected a $500 million gaseous diffusion plant and a $350 million electromagnetic plant to produce U-235 for atomic bombs.

If a mixture of two gases diffuses through an extremely fine sieve, or porous barrier, the lighter of the two gases moves through faster. This is the general principle of gaseous diffusion, known to scientists everywhere since 1896, when it was discovered by a renowned English physicist, Lord Rayleigh. Using this principle to separate the slightly lighter U-235 from ordinary uranium 238 was a formidable task.

First, the uranium had to be reduced to a gas—no mean feat in itself. Then some of this uranium gas was pumped into a chamber and half of it was allowed to strain through the sieve-like barrier into a second chamber. The strained portion of the gas was a trifle enriched with the lighter U-235; the remainder of the gas was pumped back to the first stage to be recirculated. The process was incredibly arduous and time-consuming. Only a little progress was made at each stage. To produce relatively pure U-235 suitable for atomic bombs, any given quantity of gas had to pass through literally thousands of stages over a period of many weeks. Eventually, of course, the gas had to be converted back to a solid.

Staggering problems faced the engineers and scientists: The entire gaseous diffusion system had to be leakproof; thousands of specially designed pumps were required; the intense corrosiveness of the uranium gas necessitated the development of unique plastics, oils, and waxes. Particularly difficult was the production of literally acres of porous barriers, with billions of minuscule holes that would not clog up or enlarge.

Not surprisingly, the U-shaped gaseous diffusion plant—three stories high, a quarter of a mile wide, and half a mile long—was the largest continuous process plant in the world. Each day this hungry giant consumed as much electric power as all of New York City; more water than the city of Washington, D.C.; and great quantities of steam, supplied by one of the biggest steam power plants ever built.

While not as large as the gaseous diffusion plant, the electromagnetic separation plant at Oak Ridge was, by any standard, a tremendous undertaking that cost as much as the entire Hanford project. Engineers from five large industrial corporations handled the planning, construction, and operation, while the scientific research was centered at the University of California in Berkeley.

A single example reveals the scale of the work: Used in the electromagnetic plant were gigantic magnets—the world's largest—that required far more copper for windings than could possibly be provided by the war-strained economy. This temporary emergency was met by borrowing an equivalent amount of silver from the United States Treasury—fifteen thousand tons of the metal was needed.

Actually, the single most expensive enterprise of the entire Manhattan Project, the gaseous diffusion plant, was not fully operative until the summer of 1945—too late to contribute much of its deadly product to the war effort. It was the electromagnetic process that supplied most of the core of U-235 for the Hiroshima bomb. However, the process was a comparatively inefficient one and, soon after the war, the electromagnetic plant was closed and its elaborate equipment dismantled.

Simultaneously with the first burgeoning of activity in Washington and Tennessee, J. Robert Oppenheimer led a group of scientists over a winding mountain road about thirty miles from Santa Fe, New Mexico to a stark barracks-like town surrounded by barbed wire. Here, at Los Alamos—a former boys' ranch school—Oppenheimer planned to gather several dozen scientists for work on the design of an atomic bomb. He miscalculated the size of the job: Two years later, six thousand people were living in the secret city on the mesa, almost completely isolated from the outside world.

Carloads of ponderous physics equipment, borrowed from America's leading universities, soon were shipped to Los Alamos—or Site Y, as it was called—providing the scientific Shangri-La with the best-equipped physics research laboratory in the world. The laboratory facilities were located within the sacrosanct Technical Area—a thin strip of mesa fenced off with chicken wire—where only persons with special badges could gain admittance. Within this Technical Area, working full time or visiting for consulations, were such scientific luminaries as Niels Bohr, James Chadwick, Enrico Fermi, Harold Urey, Otto Frisch, and Hans Bethe, as well as dozens of other outstanding scientists.

Available to assist the scientists in a variety of jobs were more than two thousand young soldiers in a Special Engineer Detachment, brought into the project because of the wartime shortage of civilian labor. Their jobs ranged from junior scientific positions—for those who had some college training—to technicians and mechanics; they wore intermediate badges entitling them to learn just enough to do their work, but not to know what the purpose of the project was.

The assignment of the Los Alamos staff was to design and put together atomic bombs that would utilize the plutonium and U-235 being produced at Hanford and Oak Ridge. The main problem was to find ways to bring together rapidly two or more lumps of the fissionable material in such a way that an *efficient* explosion would result. It was essential that the two lumps not fly apart before the chain reaction had consumed much of the material, or the bomb would be a partial dud. The aim of the scientists, in short, was to get the biggest explosion they could from the smallest possible amount of the rare fissionable material.

Within a relatively few months, two different designs for the bomb were settled on. One was for a gun-type device in which two pieces of fissionable material were placed at either end of a closed tube. The bomb was detonated with a conventional explosive charge that shot one piece of fissionable material against the other, forming a critical mass and an almost instantaneous chain reaction. This was the design of the bomb used at Hiroshima.

The second design was for an implosion or compression bomb. This was a spherical device with the fissionable material inside. The outer shell of the ball was composed of dozens of specially shaped conventional explosive charges; when all of these explosives were detonated simultaneously, part of their force was directed inward, toward the center of the sphere. The implosion squeezed the fissionable material within the sphere into a critical mass, producing a chain reaction. This was the design of the bomb used at Nagasaki.

Of course, the actual design of the bomb was a far more complex task than this brief description indicates: Thousands of abstruse calculations and intricate and often hazardous experiments were required. Yet despite innumerable novel and difficult problems—and without in the slightest disparaging the scope or importance of the work at Los Alamos—one can fairly say that the design of the bomb was, comparatively speaking, the easiest and certainly the least expensive part of the entire Manhattan Project. Probably no important scientist familiar with the problem doubted for a moment that *if* sufficient fissionable material could be obtained from the great production plants, a workable bomb could be made. This was by far the most certain aspect of the whole project.

The plutonium and U-235 accumulated with agonizing slowness. From each ton of crude uranium-bearing ore that started down the long Manhattan Project production line, only a fraction of an ounce of fissionable metals was ultimately obtained. But by December 30, 1944, General Groves was able to dispatch a memorandum to the Army Chief of Staff, General George C. Marshall, with a firm prediction as to the date when a bomb would be completed.

"It is now reasonably certain," the top-secret message read, that the first atomic bomb *"should be ready about 1 August 1945."*

CHAPTER 5

A FEELING OF PROFOUND RESPONSIBILITY

While the great manufacturing plants of the secret cities in Washington and Tennessee worked round the clock, some of the scientists who had helped to set the whole fantastic project in motion began to experience anxious forebodings. For a short time, they had had at least the illusion of being actors and prime movers in an epic drama; now they awaited the inevitable advent of the atomic bomb as frightened spectators.

These men had lived with the atomic project for years; they were intimately acquainted with its history; they had thought deeply about the ominous possibilities of its future development. Lacking any decision-making power themselves, they felt an urgent need to communicate their ideas to the nation's leaders. But the all-embracing secrecy regulations of the project made it difficult to approach anyone or to know when or how to take action or even to have any clear idea as to what was going on.

Ironically, it was the scientists themselves who had first willingly sacrificed their cherished ideal of free exchange of information to keep any militarily useful technical data from reaching the Nazis. But the system of censorship established by the scientists in 1940 was a voluntary one, proposed and administered by scientists, depending on the free cooperation of editors and authors, and enforced through the integrity and honor of the individual. Those in charge were experts, well acquainted with the material with which they dealt, and therefore qualified to make decisions on a rational rather than an arbitrary basis. Nevertheless, at least one top scientist, Arthur Compton, has noted in retrospect that even this "self-imposed secrecy was . . . a substantial barrier to progress" during the early days of the project.

General Leslie R. Groves was a career Army officer with almost twenty-five years of service at the time he was placed in charge of the Manhattan District. A practical engineer with no knowledge of nuclear physics, he suddenly found himself guardian to hundreds of scientists who, temporarily, had become extremely valuable property of the United States Army. Viewing the erudite scientists with a somewhat jaundiced eye, Groves clearly regarded them as a potentially untrustworthy "collection of crackpots." But the General was both patriotically and ambitiously devoted to his assigned mission: To build an atom bomb. Since this strange crew was apparently essential to the success of the project, they had to be encouraged, humored, and carefully controlled.

One way of achieving this last objective was through rigid compartmentalization of information; Groves was absolutely adamant about the need to prevent any one scientist from knowing too much about the total project. Scientists were forbidden to discuss their work with colleagues on the project, except within certain sharply defined and rather narrow confines.

Under the rule of the Army, the top scientists were assigned one or more false names and personal bodyguards, had their backgrounds and particularly their politics and associations investigated, and were sometimes shadowed by intelligence agents. At Los Alamos, mail was censored, phone calls monitored, and travel severely restricted. Scientists and their families were not permitted to associate with residents of nearby communities; all through the area, undercover agents abounded in train and bus terminals, bars and hotels.

Ostensibly, these far-reaching security precautions were aimed at keeping news of the project from the Germans; actually, Army Intelligence spent considerable time minutely observing any scientists who might possibly be sympathetic to the Soviet Union and, on occasion, excluding them from the project. General Groves's feelings about the Soviet Union were frank and clear-cut: ". . . there was never from about two weeks from the time I took charge of this project," he has recalled, "any illusion on my part but that Russia was our enemy and that the project was conducted on that basis. I didn't go along with the attitude of the country as a whole that Russia was a gallant ally."

In addition, Groves was most unhappy about the presence in the United States of a rather sizable contingent of distinguished British scientists, despite the fact that they served and buttressed a number of important areas of the bomb project.

Groves later admitted:

". . . I was not responsible for our close cooperation with the British. I did everything to hold back on it. . . . I did not carry out the wishes of our Government with respect to cooperation with the British. . . ."

However, whatever illusions the somewhat xenophobic General may have harbored about the possibility of a long-term American monopoly of the new weapon, they were not shared by the men who had initiated the project. The scientists knew that other nations, and particularly the Soviet Union, would be able to make atomic bombs. They suffered under a heavy burden of knowledge that the world—unknown to most of its inhabitants—was about to undergo a historic change, carrying with it tremendous perils for the survival of civilization. After years of rather docilely accepting rigorous restrictions on their personal freedom, they restlessly chafed at their enforced passivity.

In late summer 1944, Niels Bohr—in a personal meeting with FDR—had presented a memorandum to the President referring to "the terrifying prospect of a future competition between nations" and implying that other countries might develop simpler methods for producing fissionable material for bombs. Bohr was one of several influential scientists who believed the Soviet Union should be told about the atomic bomb while the war was in progress and the alliance still in effect.

At the Metallurgical Laboratory in Chicago, where many of the top priority tasks were completed by late 1944, scientists had increasing time to meditate over the effects of their work. Concern gradually centered on questions of war and peace. In March 1945, one of the Chicago scientists, Leo Szilard—who nearly six years before had helped to draft the Einstein letter to Roosevelt—once again took a personal initiative and composed a thoughtful memorandum for the President. Before the Szilard memorandum could be delivered, Roosevelt was dead and Harry S. Truman became the thirty-third President of the United States.

The aura of secrecy surrounding the Manhattan Project was so pervasive that most high government officials, top military officers, and Congressional leaders had little or no inkling of a development that would soon alter all political, diplomatic, and strategic thinking. Among those kept in the dark was the Vice President of the United States; during his nearly three months in office no one had told Harry Truman a word about the atomic bomb.

Immediately after taking the oath of office on April 12, 1945, the new President held a brief Cabinet meeting. Then, as the bereaved members of the Cabinet rose and filed slowly out of the room, Secretary of War Henry L. Stimson lingered behind. Later, Truman recounted:

"He asked to speak to me about a most urgent matter. Stimson told me that he wanted me to know about an immense project that was under way—a project looking to the development of a new explosive of almost unbelievable destructive power. . . . It was the first bit of information that had come to me about the atomic bomb, but he gave me no details."

The impending San Francisco Conference to organize the United Nations made some of the scientists more anxious than ever about the intense secrecy of the atomic project; they knew that almost all of the Conference delegates would be completely ignorant of the great changes in the world situation soon to be wrought by the atomic bomb. One of the Chicago scientists, James Franck, a Nobel Prize-winning physicist and refugee from Nazi Germany, prepared a memorandum on April 21 explaining that atomic bombs would be made by other nations and warning of the terrible dangers of an atomic armaments competition. Accompanied by Arthur Compton, Franck presented his memorandum to Secretary of Commerce Henry A. Wallace during a brief breakfast meeting in Washington.

Referring to secrecy rules imposed by the Army, Franck commented with rather bitter irony:

"None of the scientists objects to these regulations as long as they only bring about personal inconveniences and restrictions in mutual information which would be useful for the work. These regulations become intolerable if a conflict is brought about between our conscience as citizens and human beings and our loyalty to the oath of secrecy. . . .

"How is it possible that the statesmen are not informed that the aspect of the world and its future is entirely changed by the knowledge that atomic energy can be tapped, and how is it possible that the men who know these facts are prevented from informing the statesmen about the situation?"

On April 25, the day the San Francisco Conference convened, one of the world's most powerful statesmen, Harry S. Truman, was receiving his first full briefing on the atomic bomb from Secretary Stimson and General Groves. Stimson left behind a memorandum for the President in which he stated soberly:

"Within four months we shall in all probability have completed the most terrible weapon ever known in human history, one bomb of which could destroy a whole city."

The seventy-seven-year-old Secretary of War had followed the progress of the atomic project closely from its inception; no other man in the Administration was more aware of its fateful implications. Stimson pointed out in his memorandum that other nations would be able to make atomic bombs and might very likely discover methods for producing them more cheaply and easily than the United States had.

With the surrender of Germany on May 8 and the obvious inevitability of the defeat of Japan, more and more scientists began to discuss the morality and expediency of delivering the *coup de grâce* to the beleaguered island empire with an atomic bomb. One of the main justifications for the extraordinary degree of secrecy imposed on the Manhattan Project was supposedly the very real fear of a German atomic bomb. Now that the end of the European War had removed that fear, some of the scientists hoped that the more onerous regulations might be eased somewhat to permit freer debate on such pressing questions as the potential use of the bomb against Japan. However, rather than any policy shift toward the relaxation of stringent wartime measures, scientists were soon given a rather dramatic demonstration of the determination of the Army to continue its secrecy regulations in full force.

Shortly after V-E Day, a group of American scientists was preparing to fly to Moscow on United States government planes to attend the celebration of the 220th anniversary of the Soviet Academy of Sciences. When General Groves heard of this, he immediately forbade any of the Manhattan Project scientists to go. He also tried to prevent the departure of two prominent scientists who formerly had done work on the project—Edward U. Condon of Westinghouse and Irving Langmuir of General Electric. Both men were making the trip with top officials of their corporations; Langmuir, who had had only a slight connection with the atomic project, was finally permitted to go, but Condon, despite his very strong protests, had his passport withdrawn at the insistence of Groves. The incident, which distressed and alarmed many scientists, was later described before a Senate committee by Langmuir, a winner of a Nobel Prize for chemistry:

"The day before we were scheduled to leave two Army officers, who did not know on what grounds the request was based, asked me to decline to go to Russia. . . . Since there appeared to be direct conflict between the War Department and the State Department, I refused to withdraw my acceptance at the request of the War Department and demanded that the matter be taken up with the State Department cancelling my passport if necessary. . . . When . . . the War Department was made to realize how little I knew of the atomic energy project, I was finally allowed to go. Other Americans, however, who had been invited, were not permitted to go after having accepted.

"This, of course, the Russian Embassy knew. They knew also that no physicists were among those who accepted the invitations.

"When I reached Russia I was told by the English group that eight British physicists who had accepted the Russian invitation, had had their passports cancelled after they had reached the airport ready to fly to Moscow. . . . I also heard the opinion expressed that this action must have been taken at the request of the American Government because no one outside of the American Army could be so stupid. . . .

"I believe that these attempts to maintain secrecy resulted in giving to the Russians the very information which the Army most wished to keep from them. Any sensible Russian scientist knowing of these facts would have believed that we were developing an atomic bomb and were keeping it secret from the Russians."

On May 28, Leo Szilard—who for more than a month had been seeking a way to bring his memorandum to the attention of the new President—met with James F. Byrnes in the latter's home town of Spartanburg, South Carolina. The visit had been suggested by President Truman, in a message conveyed through his appointments secretary. Szilard presented to Byrnes the memorandum originally prepared for FDR, warning that the use of the bomb against Japanese cities would start an atomic arms race with Russia. The memorandum raised the question as to whether the possibility of avoiding such an arms race might not be more important than the immediate goal of knocking Japan out of the war a little sooner.

The meeting was not a fruitful one; Szilard and the two scientists who accompanied him—Walter Bartky and Harold Urey—felt that Byrnes had not really grasped the tremendous significance of the release of atomic energy. As for the scientists' assertions that the Soviet Union also would be able to make atomic bombs, Byrnes apparently was not convinced. According to Szilard, Byrnes—who at the time had no official position but was soon after appointed Secretary of State—told the scientists that "Groves had informed him that Russia had no uranium."

Three days after the visit from the scientists, Byrnes went to Washington to attend what was probably the most important meeting of the Interim Committee, a group of prominent civilians appointed earlier by Truman at Stimson's suggestion. Committee members considered the question of the use of the bomb against Japan with the understanding that, without atomic weapons, the final demise of Japan would require a bloody invasion of the home islands—an assumption that many military analysts today do not accept. On June 1, the Committee recommended that the atomic bomb be used against a Japanese city with both military and civilian targets without any prior warning as to the nature of the new weapon.

Whether the Interim Committee, and its advisory scientific panel—consisting of Oppenheimer, Fermi, A. H. Compton, and Lawrence—actually played an important part in the decision to drop the atomic bomb, or whether they merely confirmed a decision already foreordained by a complex of events, is a question for historians to argue. The fact remains that the final decision was reserved for the President and he, in his own words, "regarded the bomb as a military weapon and never had any doubt that it should be used."

Unaware of the recommendations of the Interim Committee and the thinking of the President, some of the scientists still sought ways to influence the government against use of the atomic bomb on Japanese cities. Their concern was deeply felt. Physicist Eugene Rabinowitch later recalled:

"It was unbearably hot in Chicago at that time. As I walked through the streets of the city, I was overcome by a vision of crashing skyscrapers under a flaming sky. Something had to be done to warn humanity."

Rabinowitch was one of seven Chicago scientists* who served on the Metallurgical Laboratory's Committee on Social and Political Implications of Atomic Energy. The title speaks for itself as to how far scientists had already moved from the prevalent prewar ivory tower attitude of disengagement from the social and political issues of their day. On June 11, a report—addressed by the seven scientists to the Secretary of War—was taken to Washington and left there for Stimson's attention.

Briefly, the report (which has since come to be called the Franck Report) emphasized that atomic weapons could not possibly remain an ex-

---

* Others were James Franck, Leo Szilard, Donald Hughes, Glenn Seaborg, J. J. Nickson, and Joyce Stearns.

clusive American monopoly for more than a few years, that the United States with its heavy concentrations of industry was particularly vulnerable to atomic warfare, and that an unannounced atomic attack on Japan would trigger an atomic armaments race and lessen the likelihood of a postwar international agreement on the control of atomic weapons.

The report made clear that other nations would be able to develop atomic bombs after the war:

"In Russia, too, the basic facts and implications of nuclear power were well understood in 1940, and the experience of Russian scientists in nuclear research is entirely sufficient to enable them to retrace our steps within a few years, even if we should make every attempt to conceal them."

As for when other nations would have the bomb, the report predicted:

". . . it might take other nations three or four years to overcome our present head start, and eight or ten years to draw even with us if we continue to do intensive work in this field."

Well into July, the Chicago scientists continued to register their ideas through petitions, polls, and panel discussions, though the latter were finally banned by the Army. Unknown even to many of the scientists, on July 16—a few days after sufficient plutonium for a bomb had arrived at Los Alamos from Hanford—an awesome ball of fire from man's first uncontrolled chain reaction lit the early morning darkness of the desert at Alamogordo, New Mexico. Immediately, a coded message was cabled to Stimson, in Germany with the President awaiting the start of the Potsdam Conference.

A few days later, a detailed report of the test arrived at Potsdam. The unexpected enormity of the explosion had obviously shaken Groves. Interspersed in his report was the stark comment: "I no longer consider the Pentagon a safe shelter from such a bomb."

Accompanying Groves's report to Potsdam were some supplementary impressions by Groves's chief assistant, Brigadier General Thomas F. Farrell. Describing the reactions of the observers after the explosion, Farrell wrote:

"All seemed to feel that they had been present at the birth of a new age—The Age of Atomic Energy—and felt their profound responsibility to help in guiding into right channels the tremendous forces which had been unlocked for the first time in history."

Despite this feeling of "profound responsibility," the die had already been cast for the first use of atomic energy in war. The project was ticking away like some cosmic alarm clock, set to waken the world on August 6, 1945. Twenty-one days after the revelation at Alamogordo, a mushroom cloud rose over the ruins of Hiroshima. Three days later, the light brighter than the midday sun was seen briefly by the inhabitants of Nagasaki.

Surveying the casualty figures of hundreds of thousands of killed and maimed, one might have commented that the treasure house of energy within the atom that had tantalized scientists for fifty years had proved, on closer inspection, to be a charnel house.

SHOCK WAVES

•

CHAPTER 6
SECURITY THROUGH SECRECY

Immediately after Hiroshima, the American people were avid for information on the fearful and mysterious genie that the scientists had unbottled. The scientists, clothed in newly acquired prestige, emerged from their enforced obscurity into a spotlight of public attention.

Determined to tell their still somewhat dazed fellow citizens the sober truths about the new atomic age, the men of the Manhattan Project quickly organized the Atomic Scientists of Chicago, as well as groups at Los Alamos, Oak Ridge, and New York City. Relieved at the long-awaited opportunity to speak out more freely—though Army censors continued to pass on their statements for many weeks—they approached their educational mission enthusiastically. Scientists who formerly had spoken only at scholarly meetings or written exclusively for learned journals now mounted the lecture platform two or three times a week, prepared popular articles for magazines and newspapers, and held countless talks with community leaders.

Over and over again, they asserted that no amount of secrecy would enable the United States to retain an atomic bomb monopoly (though carried to extremes such secrecy might seriously hamstring American scientific progress). Thus, any large future war would be an atomic war, thousands of times more terrible in its consequences than anything mankind had hitherto experienced. Most important, they were convinced that only by seeing the *real* alternatives—peace or the destruction of civilization—might ordinary citizens and politicians make the radical changes in attitude and outlook necessary if man were to abolish war.

But though the primary interest of the scientists was in an international agreement leading to the elimination of atomic weapons, their efforts were soon diverted to a bitter domestic struggle between adherents of military and civilian control over atomic energy. A bill to have the Army retain control over atomic energy was prepared by the War Department and quietly introduced by Andrew J. May, chairman of the House Military

Affairs Committee. An attempt was made to slip this important measure through the committee with a single day's hearing, at which only proponents of military control were heard.

The overwhelming majority of the scientists strongly opposed continued military domination of atomic energy. However, some of the most influential scientists—including J. Robert Oppenheimer—privately counseled their colleagues that the then current political atmosphere in Washington made any fight against military control futile. Ignoring this practical advice, many of the younger scientists launched an attack on the May-Johnson bill and sent representatives from their ranks to Washington; they were joined by a few "oldsters" in their forties, including Szilard, Condon, and Urey.

Scores of scientists sacrificed precious research time to the task of acquainting Congressional and Administration leaders with the hard facts of the atomic age, through off-the-record dinners, tea parties, luncheons, informal briefings, and even classes. The scientists' "crusade," as it came to be called, was an amazing improvisation, slapped together by inspired political amateurs. Commented *Newsweek*: "One of the curious by-products of atom splitting is a lobby wholly unlike any Washington has ever seen."

While the fight over military vs. civilian control of atomic energy raged in Congress, the Army remained in charge of the atomic installations. To the utter surprise of the scientists, one of the first postwar acts of General Groves had been the official release of a book called *Atomic Energy for Military Purposes* by Henry De Wolf Smyth, containing a large assortment of data classified top secret only the day before.

Smyth, an eminent physicist who had written the book at the General's request, called it "a semi-technical report which it is hoped men of science in this country can use to help their fellow citizens in reaching wise decisions." As for the atomic scientists, they found the Smyth Report useful as a means of gaining a fuller picture of the total work of the Manhattan Project, but the succinct message they were trying to impart to the American people did not require any technical knowledge for understanding.

After releasing a book dealing with the *military* uses of atomic energy—a book which had a first edition of thirty thousand in the Soviet Union—the Army took various contradictory and inexplicable actions, impeding scientific research that was devoid of any military application at all.

In Japan, for example, the Tokyo Institute of Physical and Chemical Research—headed by Yoshio Nishina, a well-known physicist who had worked in both the United States and Western Europe—was granted permission by the Army to operate its two cyclotrons for studies in the fields of biology and medicine. About a month later, the Army suddenly rescinded its permission to operate the research machines and, without explanation, ordered their destruction. Perhaps some completely misinformed person had decided that the cyclotrons might somehow be used by the Japanese to discover the "secret" of the atom bomb, or even to build bombs, though this was nonsense.

Whatever the reasons, engineers of the American Eighth Army, working around the clock, accomplished the demolition of the intricate machines —representing a dozen years of toil by scores of scientists—in five days. The two cyclotrons were the only ones in the entire Far East; the larger one had been completed only the previous year. Seven years would pass before a replacement was available from the United States.

American physicists heard the news with horror. Having produced a weapon of vast destructive force by an act of supreme rationality, they must have felt a foreboding chill at this display of wanton irrationality in response to fear. Scientists at Oak Ridge called the deed "a crime against mankind" that was "as disreputable and ill considered as would be the burning of Japanese libraries or the smashing of Japanese printing presses."

But the destruction of the cyclotrons was only the most blatant of many incidents involving suppression of non-military research in the immediate postwar months. During the fall of 1945, Edwin McMillan, a young American physicist, reported the invention of an important new research device called the synchrotron. Soon after, it became known that a Soviet physicist, Vladimir Veksler, had described the same device in a Russian scientific journal as early as April 1944. This sort of occurrence— simultaneous discovery—had happened many times previously in physics. What followed, however, was something new to American science.

McMillan graciously acknowledged the prior discovery by the Soviet physicist and proceeded to build the machine at the University of California with funds provided by the Manhattan Project. Shortly thereafter, an MIT physicist decided to construct a synchrotron for research at that school and asked McMillan for his magnet design, an important element in the machine. McMillan was forced to inform his colleague that the Army had invoked secrecy regulations and would not permit release of information on the magnet.

Incidents such as these angered and worried the scientists. Their own attitude toward secrecy had been expressed soon after the war by Selig Hecht, a biophysics professor at Columbia:

"We have all heard about the secrets of the atomic bomb, how they were guarded, and how important it is to keep or not to keep them to ourselves. . . . If there was one great secret, we gave it away in July 1945. It was that a chain reaction *is* possible and that it can be used to make a bomb. . . . Of course there have been—and still are—many technical and engineering secrets. They cannot involve anything fundamental. Most likely they are the kind that competing motor-car manufacturers keep from one another. In a short time competent engineers and inventors can duplicate them and probably improve them."

How long would it be before "competent engineers and inventors" in the Soviet Union could make atomic bombs? In September 1944, Vannevar Bush and James Conant had estimated the time as three or four years. During the early postwar period, many former Manhattan Project scientists offered similar predictions that were widely publicized and accepted. Summing up the latter judgments, Robert M. Hutchins, President of the University of Chicago, said: "The concensus of the scientists who made the bomb is that the Russians can make them in five years or less."

Nevertheless, the general public, much of the press, and a good deal of the Congress continued to *think* about the bomb as though it were an American secret weapon that could not be made by any other nation—without help from the United States—for an indeterminately long time, if ever. Thus, when a freshman Senator from Connecticut, Brien McMahon, introduced a bill for civilian control of atomic energy that reflected some of these misapprehensions, the scientists were pleased but by no means totally satisfied with its contents. Bernice Brode, wife of a scientist, described the reaction at Los Alamos:

"We called a mass meeting at the Lodge, which was jammed, to hear the reading of the first draft of the new bill. There were many 'bugs' in the bill, which precipitated much argument. The Congressmen, as well as the military, seemed obsessed with 'keeping the secrets' and did not believe that any other scientist except an American could discover anything. Even General Groves testified that the Russians, for example, could not make an atomic bomb before 20 years. In this first draft there was a clause which could be interpreted as providing the death penalty for inadvertently giving away any 'secrets.' This was eventually thrown out, but a lot of secrecy was kept in."

Why was it that outcries about preserving American atomic secrets were increasingly sounded during the postwar years, despite the repeated admonitions of so many scientists and others about the limited nature and ephemeral life of these "secrets"? How to explain the fact that, before long, influential politicians—such as Senator Bourke B. Hickenlooper—were beating their breasts over the shipment to Europe for research purposes of radioisotopes, which had no more military value than the Japanese cyclotrons?

Simple ignorance, of course, was one reason. Another was a pervasive fear of atomic attack on the United States, perhaps sown by American guilt over the deaths of so many thousands of civilians at Hiroshima and Nagasaki. Then too, the political pendulum in the United States after the war swung rather rapidly away from the left-of-center New Deal toward the right. Conservative politicians soon discovered—particularly after the Canadian spy cases—that charges of laxness regarding atomic security were a convenient club with which to beat the opposition.

Even more instrumental in promoting the obsession with secrecy, however, was the widely held wish—contrary to all rational knowledge or understanding—that the United States might retain its atomic monopoly indefinitely. The wish was father to the ostrich-like fantasy that somehow, through absolute secrecy regarding atomic energy, we might prevent other nations from developing atomic bombs. In a period of frightening Cold War tensions, it was a comforting belief.

In this context, the destruction of a cyclotron or the suppression of information about a synchrotron was not just an act of ludicrous stupidity, but also a pathetic ritual—reflecting the difficulty many people experienced in facing the unpleasant truths about the new atomic age. The very realistic fear of the atomic bomb was displaced by the fear that America might lose the "secret."

Not surprisingly, many of the events in the postwar history of atomic energy in the United States had an Alice-in-Wonderland quality. For example, some ardent partisans of strict military control of atomic energy, embarrassed by the existence of the Smyth Report, soon were claiming that the scientists—and not the Army—had actually been responsible for its release. Retorted Eugene Rabinowitch, editor of the *Bulletin of the Atomic Scientists:*

"The suggestion . . . that the Army was 'lambasted' into its publication by the scientists is ridiculous. The scientists were dumbfounded by the sudden publicity given to the industrial aspects of the atomic bomb project. Furthermore, they were not interested in it. The firms which have participated in the immense enterprise, may have had an understandable desire to publicize their achievement, and the Manhattan District was anxious to show what it did with two billion dollars. . . . It is ironical that scientists are accused of a desire to reveal 'atomic secrets' because they want to publish the properties of a new uranium compound, the nuclear characteristics of a new isotope, or clinical observations of the effects of radiation; while the only important—and from the point of view of scientific progress, unnecessary—revelations concerning the military and industrial aspects of atomic energy, have come from the professed 'guardians of atomic security.'"

The McMahon-Douglas Atomic Energy Act became law in the summer of 1946 and, soon after, the newly appointed Atomic Energy Commission took over from the Army. The scientists had won their battle for civilian control and, in a second victory, had helped to insure the confirmation of a liberal, David E. Lilienthal, as the first chairman of the AEC.

By then, the scientists' "crusade" was largely over. After many months of time-consuming work, men who had been away from their laboratories for too long felt the need to resume their careers. Furthermore, scientists were hardly of one mind politically; united in their "crusade" only by a set of general propositions, they held widely differing opinions regarding the developing Cold War.

Equally important in discouraging political activity among scientists was the fact that a growing number of them—including men working at universities—were receiving most or all of their research funds from the Armed Forces. This totally new economic situation for scientists developed rapidly after the war. While much excellent research has unquestionably been accomplished under such grants, the recipients quite naturally may have felt a certain timidity in risking their precious security clearance by opposing orthodoxy. Particularly vulnerable were the younger scientists, who had not yet established reputations and so were most expendable.

During their sojourn into politics, the scientists had received a hearing for their message from millions of Americans. They had outspokenly ridiculed the concept of security through absolute secrecy as a perilous illusion, which kept people from facing the real task of trying to avoid an atomic war. Their labors would have a number of important effects—some of them quite unexpected—on the nation's political life in the coming years.

For exposing people's illusions is always a risky business. Along with many friends, the scientists as a group had acquired powerful and vindictive enemies. Perhaps sensing this, Edward U. Condon warned in a magazine article titled "An Appeal to Reason," published in 1946:

"The laws of nature, some seem to think, are ours exclusively, and that we can keep others from learning by locking up what we have learned in the laboratory. . . .

"It is sinister indeed how one evil step leads to another. Having created an air of suspicion and mistrust, there will be persons among us who think other nations can know nothing except what is learned by espionage. So, when other countries make atom bombs, these persons will cry 'treason' at our scientists, for they will find it inconceivable that another country could make a bomb in any other way except by aid from Americans."

CHAPTER 7

A BLURRING OF VISION

A few days after the formal end of World War II, a young man by the name of Igor Gouzenko walked out of the Soviet Embassy at Ottawa, a bunch of papers relating to his work hidden beneath his shirt. Gouzenko was a code clerk on the staff of the Soviet Military Attaché and, as such, had knowledge of some aspects of Soviet intelligence activity in Canada. He turned the papers over to the authorities and requested permission to remain in Canada.

Canadian officials had been rather neatly handed a part of the Soviet intelligence operation in Canada—how important or effective a part is impossible to judge. The ring consisted of the Military Attaché and his staff (whose offices in an isolated wing of the Embassy were barred to the Ambassador), aided by a group of amateur helpers who were largely Canadian nationals. During the later years of the war, these "helpers" had proffered a mixed bag of technical, political, and economic information, apparently motivated by political sympathy for the Soviet Union and also, perhaps, by money which, in any event, was accepted by some of them.

For five months, the Canadian government studied the Gouzenko papers and pondered what to do with their embarrassment of riches. As would be true of any nation, the decision was bound to be a political one—dictated by both national and international considerations. Within a matter of weeks, Canadian Prime Minister Mackenzie King personally informed both President Truman and British Prime Minister Clement Attlee about the affair. Finally, on February 15, 1946, a muted official statement revealed "disclosures of secret and confidential information to unauthorized persons, including some members of the staff of a foreign mission in Ottawa."

Far less circumspect were newspaper accounts that identified the country involved as Russia and "authoritatively" stated that the information concerned atomic energy. Immediately, the Soviet intelligence operation uncovered in Canada was fashioned by the headline writers into an "atom spy network."

Five days after the Canadian statement, the Soviet government replied with a note admitting the essentials of the story, blaming the Military Attaché (who had been recalled "in view of the inadmissibility of acts of members of his staff"), and belittling the importance of the material obtained: ". . . the information in question could be found in published works on radio location, etc., and also in the well-known brochure of the American, J. D. Smyth, *Atomic Energy*. It would, therefore, be ridiculous to affirm that delivery of insignificant secret data of this kind could create any threat to the security of Canada."

Complaining of "the unbridled anti-Soviet campaign which began in the Canadian press and on the Canadian radio simultaneously with the publication of the Canadian Government's statement," the note asserted that the Canadian government "was pursuing some other ends having no relation to the security interests of Canada."

In the United States, the Canadian spy case stirred great interest; press accounts undoubtedly led millions of Americans to conclude that their northern neighbors had discovered a Soviet "atomic spy ring." An opportunity to evaluate this widely held belief was soon afforded by the publication of a voluminous official report of the Canadian investigation, including translations of the papers brought out by Gouzenko. These revealed that, while Soviet intelligence was certainly interested in atomic energy data, the Military Attaché's communications—written only a few months before Hiroshima—contain only the most rudimentary information on the subject and show no awareness at all of the imminence of the testing and use of an atomic bomb. Only one informant, Allan Nunn May, provided any material on atomic energy; nevertheless, the myth of an atomic espionage ring persists tenaciously.

This point was emphasized many years later by the Joint Congressional Committee on Atomic Energy: "The wartime Canadian spy ring is primarily associated, in many minds, with divulgement of atomic secrets; but Allan Nunn May is the only member of the ring who gave Russia information in this category."

May, a thirty-four-year-old British physicist, had worked during the war at the Montreal Laboratory of the National Research Council of Canada, where atomic energy research not directly related to the production of the bomb was carried on. On a number of occasions in 1944, May had visited the Manhattan Project's Metallurgical Laboratory in Chicago.

Tried in London May 1, 1946, he admitted (in a confession read in court) that the year before he had turned over to a man in Montreal "whose identity I decline to divulge" two microscopic-size samples of uranium and also "a written report on atomic research as known to me. This information was mostly of a character which has since been published or is about to be published." (At least one bit of information that has never been published was apparently given by May immediately after Hiroshima: Production estimates—of unknown accuracy—for U-235 and plutonium.)

May had accepted money from his contact, "against my will," but stressed that "I certainly did not do it for gain." Scheduled to return to England after the war, he was given specific instructions for meeting an agent in London, but failed to keep the appointment because "I decided to wash my hands of the whole business."

May's sentence of ten years' imprisonment for violation of the British Official Secrets Act (he subsequently served six and a half) was by far the most severe punishment meted out to any defendant in the Canadian cases.

Following the first disclosures of the Canadian "atomic spy ring," hints were heard of possible ramifications in the United States. Revealed a March 8 story in the New York *Times*:

"Sufficient evidence of attempts to obtain information concerning the atomic bomb by foreign agents in the United States has been accumulated by the House Committee Investigating un-American Activities to send its chairman, Rep. John S. Wood, Democrat, of Georgia, out of town tonight for a ten-day trip. . . .

"He (Wood) said that his committee was working closely with other government agencies, including the War Department, in its present spy hunt, and added that he was not yet sure whether the trails he was following had any connection with the leaks recently disclosed in Canada."

Later that month, FBI Director J. Edgar Hoover announced the arrest on espionage charges of a twenty-nine-year-old Russian naval lieutenant, Nicolai Redin, assigned to the Soviet Purchasing Commission in Seattle, Washington. Noting that this was the first espionage arrest in American history of a uniformed officer of a friendly power, *Newsweek* commented: "The arrest of Lieutenant Redin at least indirectly reflects the Administration's new policy of getting tough with Russia. . . ."

Hoover's announcement stated that Redin had "induced another to obtain plans, documents and writings relating to the *Yellowstone*, a U.S. destroyer tender." Some, who apparently found this charge unimpressive, immediately speculated as to whether Redin was really connected with an atomic spy ring, perhaps the Canadian ring. Observed the New York *Times*:

"One source close to the [Un-American Activities] committee told a reporter tonight that the committee was familiar with some of Lieutenant Redin's activities.

"The committee announced several weeks ago that it was checking reports that a foreign spy ring was attempting to steal this nation's atomic bomb secrets."

In a similar vein, the *Times* reported a few days later:

"As one of the first reactions to the arrest came the question whether Lieutenant Redin's purported activities might relate in any way to atomic energy secrets. This resulted not only from the furore over the Soviet

Union's alleged spy ring in Canada, but over the fact that the Pacific Northwest is the home of the Hanford (Wash.) plutonium production plant, which played a role in the development of the atomic bomb."

In late June, when Redin was tried, it developed that the case was not linked to the Canadian one, had nothing whatsoever to do with atomic energy, and—to the disappointment of some people—did, in fact, concern allegations regarding the *Yellowstone*. Furthermore, the evidence against Redin was apparently exceedingly flimsy. Despite prosecution warnings that "if you come back with a verdict of not guilty, you will be branding your Federal Bureau of Investigation . . . witnesses as perjurers," a Seattle jury acquitted Redin. Said *Newsweek*: ". . . the Redin affair fell flatter than a dud bomb. . . ."

November 1946 was the first postwar American election and the Congress that convened in Washington the following January was the first Republican Congress since the days of Herbert Hoover. One of the victors was J. Parnell Thomas, a New Jersey Republican who, while serving on the House Military Affairs Committee, had strongly opposed the scientists in their fight for civilian control of atomic energy. He was particularly anxious about possible loss of American atomic "secrets" and still hoped for "the transfer of the atomic bomb development back to the military."

Now Thomas became chairman of the House Committee on Un-American Activities. Soon after he assumed the chairmanship, he announced a program that included: "Investigation of those groups and movements which are trying to dissipate our atomic bomb knowledge for the benefit of a foreign power."

Several months later, Edward U. Condon, who had actively campaigned for civilian control of atomic energy, was suddenly attacked in several stories in the Washington *Times-Herald* for alleged association with left-wing organizations. The stories hinted that serious charges were pending against Condon—an atomic scientist, an outspoken liberal, and a member of the Truman Administration (Director of the National Bureau of Standards)—and indicated that he soon would be called before the Un-American Activities Committee.

Condon was not called by the committee, but in June, in an article in *American* magazine titled "Russia Grabs Our Inventions," J. Parnell Thomas himself stated that the National Bureau of Standards Director would shortly be subpoenaed. Later that month, Condon and other scientists came in for renewed attention from Thomas in the chairman's article in *Liberty* magazine titled "Reds in Our Atom-Bomb Plants." Illustrated with a large hammer and sickle superimposed over an American atomic installation, the article's subhead stated: "A congressman who has dug out the facts warns that our atomic-energy secrets may be secrets no longer."

After vainly awaiting the subpoena he had been informed of via *American* magazine, Condon wrote Thomas requesting an opportunity to appear before the committee. No reply was received, but soon after another *Times-Herald* story—based on a committee press release—struck at the scientist again. Condon settled down to await the next attack.

For the next few months, however, the Un-American Activities Committee had little time for scientists or atomic espionage; they were on the trail of even bigger game—at least so far as publicity was concerned. The Hollywood hearings staged in October 1947 were undoubtedly one of the greatest spectaculars ever served up by a Congressional committee. Eventually, ten Hollywood writers were jailed for contempt of Congress and scores of others were blacklisted from the studios. (An ironical turn was that later, after their appeals had been denied, several of the writers found themselves prisonmates at Danbury Federal Correctional Institution with their erstwhile accuser, J. Parnell Thomas, who by then had himself been jailed for accepting "kickbacks" from the salaries of his office staff.)

However, even the most star-studded extravaganza may lag a bit toward the end. Apparently to avoid this prospect, for several days before the conclusion of the hearings the committee had proclaimed that waiting in the wings were a number of "mystery" witnesses who would give "sensational" testimony regarding espionage. On the final day of the hearings (shortly after the testimony of Berthold Brecht), a single "mystery" witness appeared. He was none other than the committee's own investigator, Louis Russell, who spoke at some length about alleged wartime atomic espionage at the University of California's Radiation Laboratory in Berkeley.

Understandably, the press was somewhat confused by the combining of motion picture industry celebrities and atom spies in the same hearing. Some of the headlines the next day were a weird mélange; a rambling *Times* headline read: "Film Inquiry Reveals Move By Soviet Agents To Obtain Atom Research Data In 1942—Expert Balked It—Dr. Oppenheimer Called Step 'Treasonable' Investigator Says—Two More Writers Hit—Lardner, Jr. and Lester Cole Face Contempt Action as Hearings Halt Abruptly."

During the latter half of 1947 and early 1948, Americans were given new cause to shudder at the possible loss of their country's atomic secrets. In July 1947 the FBI arrested two former Army sergeants who, according to a Department of Justice announcement, "had stolen vital atomic secrets from the heart of the atomic bomb project at Los Alamos."

Some members of Congress and many newspapers reacted with predictable shock—and vivid headlines. Artfully ignoring the fact that the alleged thefts had occurred while Los Alamos was under Army control, J. Parnell Thomas stated: "What I feared is happening. Under the Atomic

Energy Commission there is very little security. The A-bomb secrets are no longer safe."

Eventually, a total of six former GI's were arrested by the FBI (charges were dropped against one) and, as the facts emerged, all fears regarding America's security proved groundless. Guilty of nothing more than souvenir-hunting, the men had foolishly made off with some classified negatives and documents. Only two received prison sentences—one for six and the other for eighteen months.

About a year after the first "trial balloon" attacks on Condon, the Un-American Activities Committee—then awaiting action on a large budgetary request—lashed out at the Director of the National Bureau of Standards in a special report, charging that "from the evidence at hand, it appears that Dr. Condon is one of the weakest links in our atomic security." To back up this somewhat indistinct if damning indictment, the report contained what Representative Chet Holifield later termed "regurgitations of the charges made in the Washington *Times-Herald*" the summer before.

Capping this offering of warmed-over innuendo was the conclusion that "the situation as regards Dr. Condon is not an isolated one, but that there are other Government officials in strategic positions who are playing Stalin's game. . . ." The evidence "indicates very strongly that there is in operation at the present time in the United States an extensive Soviet espionage ring, and to permit this ring to continue, in view of the high atomic prizes which they are seeking, is folly, and can only lead to ultimate disaster."

Edward U. Condon, the man thus pilloried, was forty-six years old at the time and had earned a high reputation during a varied career as a professor, an internationally renowned theoretical physicist, an industrial scientist, and a government official. He was one of the scientific consultants for the government in the early days of the atomic bomb project.

The Condon case rapidly became a *cause célèbre*. Condon himself charged "an undercover attempt to smear civilian control of atomic energy by smearing the scientists who assisted the development of the Atomic Energy Act. . . ." Scientific organizations and individual scientists rose to his defense with letters to Congress and public statements; editorials were written in his behalf. But if Condon eventually emerged from his ordeal with some measure of moral victory, he was hardly unscathed; to millions of Americans he was "the weakest link" and, as many people were discovering, such charges, once made, had a tendency to stick.

Smarting under the criticisms brought on by the Condon report, the committee continued to snipe at the scientist. On August 2, 1948, the New York *Mirror* carried this headline across an entire page: "Atom Aide Linked to Red Spy Ring." The story began: "Dr. Edward U. Condon . . . whose dealings with citizens of Soviet-dominated countries led the

House un-American Activities Committee to call him 'the weakest link in our atomic security chain,' was accused today of 'associating' with members of [a] Communist espionage syndicate headed by Elizabeth T. Bentley. A source close to the House Committee said Condon knew Nathan Gregory Silvermaster and others who, Miss Bentley swore, were key operatives in her capital spy web."

This story, which all but calls Condon an atom spy, and others like it which appeared in hundreds of American newspapers, was not based on any testimony or statement of Miss Bentley's (she had not mentioned Condon)—but solely on "a source close to the House Committee."

The time was summer 1948, less than three months before a Presidential election. Congress was in the midst of a special session, announced by President Truman at the Democratic National Convention. In this highly charged political atmosphere, dozens of former New Deal employees—including Harry Dexter White, William W. Remington, and Lauchlin Currie—were being accused by Miss Bentley of having been members or close associates of a Soviet espionage organization.

At the same time, similar charges were being leveled by another ex-Communist, Whittaker Chambers, who testified that he had been a member of a Communist "underground" in Washington during the Thirties. His accusations against Alger Hiss soon led to a heated public controversy, a libel suit by Hiss, the production of the so-called Pumpkin Papers and other material by Chambers, and the two trials and eventual conviction and imprisonment of Hiss for perjury.

All through August 1948, Americans read about New Deal officials accused of espionage by Miss Bentley while, simultaneously, the Hiss-Chambers drama unfolded. On September 1, the committee's activities assumed the dimensions of a three-ring circus with the announcement of still another investigation. The subject: Atomic espionage by United States scientists.

The committee promised open hearings with sensational revelations. Actually, all of the hearings were closed. The headlines about "atom spies" that filled the nation's newspapers that month were all based on the outpourings of a high-powered publicity campaign by the committee. As for sensational revelations, much of the material released by the committee was a rehash of testimony about atomic espionage at Berkeley offered the year before at the conclusion of the Hollywood hearings; some was even older, having been reported by the Hearst press in December 1945.

Periodically during the "investigation," the committee issued blatantly political statements. Typical was one, quoted in a Washington *Post* story, that promised that "in spite of Mr. Truman, Mr. Lilienthal and a few misguided scientists, the American people will continue to get the facts from this committee and in the next few days, we shall reveal a shocking chapter in Communist espionage in the atomic field."

Some additional details on the alleged espionage were contained in a loudly heralded committee report, released in late September. The committee was mainly concerned with two "cases," both apparently gleaned from the wartime files of Army Intelligence. One, the Hiskey-Adams case, involved one Clarence F. Hiskey, a Manhattan District scientist who had worked at both Columbia University and the Metallurgical Laboratory in Chicago. Army Intelligence was said to have determined that Hiskey was in touch with an alleged Soviet agent, Arthur Adams; as a result, in 1944, Hiskey, a reserve officer, was called to active duty in the Army.

A surreptitious search of Adams's room was said to have revealed "highly secret information regarding the atomic bomb plant at Oak Ridge, Tenn., as well as other vital information regarding the development of atomic energy in other countries." However, Adams had left the country in 1945 and the source, nature, and importance of this alleged material has never been stated.

Before departing for the Army, Hiskey was said to have asked another Metallurgical Laboratory scientist, John H. Chapin, to meet with Adams. Chapin admitted to one such meeting but resolutely denied having given Adams information of any kind and the committee apparently accepted his story.

The second incident of major interest to the committee was the so-called Scientist X or Nelson-Weinberg case. Scientist X, as the committee persisted in calling him, was Joseph W. Weinberg, a research chemist employed during the war at the Radiation Laboratory in Berkeley. According to the testimony of a former Army Intelligence agent, in March 1943 Scientist X had gone to the home of a Communist Party functionary, Steve Nelson, late at night and had given him a "complicated formula" from the Radiation Laboratory. Nelson was said to have later met with the Soviet vice-consul in San Francisco "in the middle of an open park" and transferred to the Soviet official "an envelope or package." This story was said to have come to Army Intelligence from a "highly confidential informant" who was unable to identify either the scientist involved or the material allegedly passed. Supposedly, Army Intelligence had eventually "narrowed it down" to Weinberg.

However, most of the testimony in the Scientist X case concerned not espionage but a Communist meeting at Weinberg's Berkeley apartment in summer 1943 at which Nelson was said to have been present. Three Army Intelligence agents allegedly spotted Nelson in the Weinberg apartment by peeking through a window from a vantage point on a nearby rooftop.

The entire story, including the meeting, was completely denied on a number of occasions by Weinberg, who asserted that he did not even know Nelson. Subsequently tried for perjury for denying Communist Party membership, Weinberg was acquitted.

A third "case" that provided headlines for a time was that of Martin Kamen, a distinguished chemist. In the summer of 1944, while employed at Berkeley, he had openly dined with two Soviet consular officials at Bernstein's Fish Grotto in San Francisco. Army Intelligence agents at a nearby table allegedly overheard parts of the conversation of the three during their meal in the noisy restaurant; the agents' report of the conversation is said to have shown that Kamen apparently mentioned some classified topics while shucking his oysters. Ten days later, without explanation, he was asked to resign from the Radiation Laboratory, where he had worked for eight years. After the war, he discovered that he was unable to obtain a passport.

Testifying before the committee, Kamen made clear that, at worst, he had been somewhat indiscreet, nothing more. The committee itself concluded that "there appears to be little if any evidence at this time that his revealing of classified information was willful and deliberate."

When details of these three widely publicized incidents were later included in the Joint Congressional Committee on Atomic Energy publication, *Soviet Atomic Espionage*, they appeared in a section headed: "Charges Not Proven in a Court of Law." This was appropriate, inasmuch as not a single espionage indictment ever resulted from any of the Un-American Activities Committee's investigations. But in the halls of Congress and in the press, men were accused openly of wartime espionage, a crime punishable by death.

Hearings on these "atomic espionage cases" continued intermittently for several years, with the committee calling various colleagues of the principal accused; the relationship of these witnesses to the investigation was often difficult to discern. In June 1949, when the committee heard Frank Oppenheimer, a former Radiation Laboratory scientist, and his wife, no evidence was presented even remotely connecting them with the alleged subject of the inquiry—atomic espionage. A fair inference was that the scientist had been called as a means of embarrassing his famous brother, J. Robert Oppenheimer, whose prestige was then so great that the committee would hardly have risked a frontal assault. (Few would have believed at the time that in the America of five years hence Oppenheimer, the former hero-scientist, would be tried in a loyalty proceeding and denied security clearance for access to the nation's atomic "secrets.")

Frank Oppenheimer and his wife were questioned largely about their politics. They discussed their own former membership in the Communist Party, eight years earlier while students, but refused the committee's importuning to name others. Before coming to Washington to testify, Frank Oppenheimer had offered his resignation as an assistant professor at the University of Minnesota; during the hearing he received word that the resignation had been accepted.

49

Four years after the end of World War II, incidents such as this were commonplace. At times, one might have concluded that the major themes of postwar American life were disloyalty, subversion, espionage, and treason. Some students of history saw these events as a mere repetition of the hysterical anti-Red campaigns that followed upon World War I; others wondered fearfully whether they presaged a drastic long-term shift in the nation's political values and ideals.

State and federal anti-subversive committees, blacklisting organizations, and teachers' loyalty oaths were being fastened firmly upon the nation as guardians of right-wing orthodoxy. For some, this was a time of personal tragedies—shattered careers and unemployment, isolation from the community, imprisonment, broken marriages, suicides. Yet only a comparatively few were affected so directly by these postwar events; for most others, the effects were far less easily discernible—but nonetheless real.

Soon after Hiroshima, millions of Americans had been educated—with the help of the scientists—to some of the facts of life in the atomic age. In the following four years, much of this education was erased as every literate citizen was exposed to a massive barrage of stories about "atomic secrets" and "atomic espionage." Press sensation followed press sensation in endless procession. So thick and fast did the headlines come that it is unlikely most newspaper readers could possibly have distinguished one espionage "case" from another. They all tended to meld into one odious whole—part of what some called "the mess in Washington."

The Hollywood hearings were mixed together with atomic espionage charges—incredibly, the very same headline mentioned Ring Lardner, Jr., and J. Robert Oppenheimer. The Bentley accusations and the Hiss-Chambers controversy were scrambled together and then tossed into the same stew pot with the Condon case, the Hiskey-Adams case, the Kamen case, and the Nelson-Weinberg case—all "cases" never tried in any American court of law. How could one possibly separate these accusations, pick out the innocent from any who might be guilty, or decide soberly whether the alleged crimes truly imperiled the safety of the nation?

Group guilt—as opposed to the time-honored concept of individual guilt for a *specific* crime—was becoming an *idée fixe* among the American body politic. Increasingly, a charge of possible wrongdoing against a single individual was being regarded, symbolically, as a charge against everyone else—New Dealers, scientists, college professors, Communists—in the group the accused was said to represent.

Gradually, the credibility threshold of Americans was lowered to the point where large numbers of people seemed able to accept any allegation by a demagogic politician—no matter how fantastic and unsubstantiated it might be. Possible errors of judgment or stupidity by government officials were being cited retrospectively as evidence of treasonable intent. At times, the real world and the comic strip world merged as headlines and stories told of stolen "secret formulas" and an overheard conversation in a fish grotto, and presented the latest episode of the "weakest link," the "spy queen," or "Scientist X."

It was as if some insidious disease were destroying the thinking faculties of Americans, blurring their vision, eliminating all-important subtle differences, reducing every situation to the gross appositiveness of good guys and bad guys. Step by step, the ability of Americans to deal rationally and wisely with the terrible problems posed by atomic weapons was inexorably diminished.

CHAPTER 8

THE MONOPOLY ENDS

United States Naval Research Laboratory scientists first noticed in early 1948 that whenever rain fell their radiation instruments throughout the Northern Hemisphere registered sharply increased levels of radiation. An investigation soon revealed that the falling rain was picking up tiny radioactive particles blown high into the air by earlier United States atomic bomb tests in the Pacific. The scientists had stumbled upon a simple method for detecting atomic explosions.

All during the spring and summer of 1949, rainwater from several locations was analyzed routinely, but no fission products were found. Then, in early September of that year, the Navy scientists' vigil paid off. Radioactive fallout was detected in rainwater from Kodiak, Alaska, and Washington, D.C. Immediately, Air Force planes were sent aloft for other samples. The fresh radioactivity was not difficult to date or trace. On or about August 29, 1949, an atomic explosion had taken place in the Soviet Union. The American atomic bomb monopoly had ended.

On September 23, 1949, President Truman made public the discovery. The President's statement read, in part:

"We have evidence that within recent weeks an atomic explosion occurred in the U.S.S.R.

"Ever since atomic energy was first released by man, the eventual development of this new force by other nations was to be expected. This probability has always been taken into account by us.

"Nearly four years ago I pointed out that 'scientific opinion appears to be practically unanimous that the essential theoretical knowledge upon which the discovery is based is already widely known. There is also substantial agreement that foreign research can come abreast of our present theoretical knowledge in time.'"

Some, like General Eisenhower, unexcitedly took the announcement in stride. Said he:

". . . the news we have been given by the President merely confirms scientific predictions. I see no reason why a development that was anticipated years ago should cause any revolutionary change in our thinking or in our actions."

Along similar lines, the New York *Times* commented:

". . . there is no valid reason for surprise at this development. . . . Only those Americans who failed to pay attention to what was said of the atomic bomb by the men who knew most about it—namely, the men who made it—could ever have believed that we possessed a permanent and exclusive monopoly of this destructive weapon."

Others, however, reacted to the news with shock and fear. Editorialized *Atomics*, a scientific periodical:

"Though the announcement is but a few days old, the news has already rocked the nation; it is being screamed from banner headlines in every newspaper from Los Angeles to Portland, Maine, and radio commentators have worked themselves into a minor panic, many of them have the country practically at war with Russia."

In an astute observation on the national mood, the *Times* suggested: ". . . while we were intellectually prepared, perhaps we were not for the most part emotionally prepared."

Unfortunately, the cries of alarm that filled the press soon after Truman's announcement indicated that many politicians and journalists were neither emotionally nor intellectually prepared for the news. They quickly deduced that America's atomic "secrets" had been stolen and, as Edward U. Condon had predicted three and a half years earlier, they cried "treason" and looked around for someone to blame. Culpability was freely assigned to past and present Democratic Administrations.

Charged Senator Karl Mundt:

"It now appears that earlier and prevailing laxity in safeguarding this country against Communist espionage has permitted what were once the secrets of our atomic bomb to fall into the hands of America's only potential enemy."

Even more partisan were the remarks of Representative Richard M. Nixon, as reported in the New York *Journal-American*:

"Representative Nixon . . . member of the House Un-American Activities Committee, said today Russia's atomic know-how was 'hastened' by the Truman Administration's failure to act against Red spies in the United States.

"'If the President says the American people are entitled to know all the facts—I feel the American people are also entitled to know the facts about the espionage ring which was responsible for turning over information on the atom bomb to agents of the Russian government,' said Nixon."

While this public clamor resounded throughout the nation, behind the scenes—on the highest echelons of government—not everyone was nearly so calm and matter of fact about the Soviet accomplishment as might have been inferred from the tone of the Truman announcement. The sad truth was that the nearly unanimous public estimates of the scientists in 1945— that Russia would have the bomb in five years or less—had been taken with a generous grain of salt by American policymakers. Many top officials

—possibly influenced by their fervent wish that the United States retain exclusive possession of the bomb—had relied heavily in their thinking on far more conservative secret predictions.

Later, physicist Karl T. Compton explained the reasoning behind one such prediction that the Russians probably would require ten years to make a bomb:

". . . the predominant factor was not scientific information, because we realized that the Russians could get that as well as we could, but it had to do with industrial capacity—machine tools, to make tools, production of electronic control equipment, capacity to produce certain chemicals with the desired degree of purity, and things of that sort."

Obviously, many Americans were badly informed as to the state of Soviet technology and industry. On September 24, 1948—less than one year before the Soviet bomb was exploded—Secretary of Defense James V. Forrestal conferred with Walter Bedell Smith, then Ambassador to the Soviet Union, on when the Russians might produce an atomic bomb. In his diary, Forrestal summarized the opinions of Smith (who later became chief of the CIA):

"The Russians cannot possibly have the industrial competence to produce the atomic bomb now, and it will be five or even ten years before they could count on manufacture of it in quantity. They may well now have the 'notebook' know-how, but not the industrial complex to translate that abstract knowledge into concrete weapons."

That such thinking was more or less widespread in Washington at the time of Truman's announcement later was made clear by John Foster Dulles:

"I was in a position to know, in the spring of 1949, that our top official experts were then convinced that it would probably be five years or more before the Russians would be able to make atomic bombs. . . .

"There seemed in official quarters to be a 'superiority' complex. . . ."

Unfortunately, many of the postwar military and diplomatic policies of the United States had been based on the assumption that the Russians would not have atomic weapons in the foreseeable future. Now, perplexed government leaders wondered: What do we do next? According to Joseph and Stewart Alsop, a frequent answer to this question heard from stunned Pentagon strategists was: "Well, the Soviets have the A-bomb but we'll just get the H-bomb, and then everything will still be all right."

The theoretical possibility of a fantastically powerful super or "hydrogen" bomb that would use an A-bomb as a trigger was rather widely known in the American scientific community in 1949, but only a few guarded mentions of it had ever appeared in the public prints. J. Robert Oppenheimer had discussed such a bomb with Arthur Compton as early as the summer of 1942. Noted Compton: ". . . time and again throughout the war period men on the project would think of the idea independently and bring it to our attention."

After the explosion of the first Soviet A-bomb, Edward Teller and other scientists—almost certainly a small minority—felt strongly that an immediate crash program to build the super was indicated. Other scientists believed with equal conviction that such a program would be a terrible mistake.

On October 29, 1949, the Atomic Energy Commission's General Advisory Committee, headed by J. Robert Oppenheimer, met and voted unanimously against a crash program. In part, their decision was founded on various political and military considerations, including the fact that no one knew whether or not a "hydrogen" bomb could be made. Enormous resources would have to be diverted from the "conventional" atomic program to sustain an effort whose ultimate success was highly uncertain.

But, of course, in the foreground of much, if not all, of the opposition to the super was an overwhelming moral question: Did scientists have the right to develop a weapon with the potential for destroying all life on earth? Faced with this terrifying problem, the members of the General Advisory Committee hoped that America would, in the words of Enrico Fermi, "try to outlaw the thing before it was born."

While vital decisions about the super were being discussed secretly in government circles, the attention of many citizens was increasingly directed to the question of who was to "blame" for the loss of the nation's atomic monopoly. Ten weeks after the first news of the Soviet bomb, Americans were reading startling accusations of treason leveled against a number of former New Deal leaders. The source of these charges, an ex-Army Air Force major named George Racey Jordan, later described his reaction to Truman's September announcement:

"I was shocked and stunned to the depths of my being. American policy had suffered a stupendous defeat. There was evidence in my possession, I was convinced, proving that the disaster was chargeable not only to spies but to actual members of the Federal hierarchy."

Appearing before the House Committee on Un-American Activities (in December 1949), Jordan testified that in 1943 and 1944, while serving at Great Falls, Montana, as a Lend-Lease expediter of wartime air-freight shipments from the United States to the Soviet Union, he had seen secret data on atomic research—as well as quantities of uranium—being shipped to Russia. He recalled particularly finding material concerning Oak Ridge, including a map that was accompanied by a handwritten note on White House stationery—imprinted with Harry L. Hopkins's name— that read: "Had a hell of a time getting these away from Groves. H.H."

Former Vice President Henry A. Wallace's name was soon drawn into the matter as the person who allegedly had overruled Groves on the uranium shipments, a charge that Wallace angrily denied. Jordan's story tended to grow with each telling: One of his later recollections was of a sealed suitcase that had broken open, revealing folders filled with State Department documents "and in the front would be a white piece of paper with 'From Hiss' . . . and so on."

Publicly unknown at the time was that a meticulous investigation of the accusations, quietly ordered by the Joint Congressional Committee on Atomic Energy, had refuted any inference of wrongdoing regarding several completely open, legal, and harmless wartime shipments of uranium and had discredited or failed to substantiate all of Jordan's other charges.

That many Americans were taken in by such charges as those of Jordan was a reflection of the growing national mood of bewilderment and dissatisfaction with the developing course of world events. Increasingly, the prevalent belief was that things were not going well for the United States and people wanted to know why. Even the most irrational and self-serving explanations were accorded a serious hearing.

Thus, when Alger Hiss was convicted of perjury, Richard M. Nixon inferred that the former second-echelon State Department official had been the cause of vast changes in the political complexion of the world. Nixon told the House of Representatives:

"Five years ago, at the time of the Dumbarton Oaks Conference in 1944, when Alger Hiss served as director of our secretariat, the number of people in the world in the Soviet orbit was 180,000,000. . . . in 1944, before Dumbarton Oaks, Teheran, Yalta, and Potsdam, the odds were 9 to 1 in our favor. Today, since those conferences, the odds are 5 to 3 against us."

Nixon's statement typifies the tendency of many politicians during the postwar years to simplify and personify historical events in the most naïvely parochial terms. Complex happenings, like the Soviet development of the atomic bomb or even the Communist victory in the Chinese Civil War, were attributed to the malfeasance or perfidy of individuals in the State Department or Democratic party. The assumption underlying this thinking was, apparently, that all history was made and manipulated in the United States; the other 94 per cent of the planet's population did not exist. It was not necessary to formulate policy skillfully so as to deal successfully with a fast-changing world; all that was required was to "clean out the traitors in our midst." Many gave up the difficult search for sensible answers and spent their energies running with the pack in the hunt for scapegoats.

Completely unknown to the public, all during the final months of 1949, the secret debate on the super-bomb continued. The General Advisory Committee report against a crash program did not settle the matter, nor did the concurring opinions of four of the five Atomic Energy Commissioners (the dissenter was Lewis L. Strauss). President Truman appointed a special three-man subcommittee of the National Security Council to render further advice.

On January 31, 1950, the President's subcommittee voted two to one for a crash program, with Secretary of State Dean Acheson and Secretary of Defense Louis Johnson opposing AEC chairman David Lilienthal. That same day, President Truman—again in the most matter-of-fact terms—made his second momentous announcement in four months:

". . . I have directed the Atomic Energy Commission to continue its work on all forms of atomic weapons, including the so-called hydrogen or super-bomb."

Then and only then did the American people learn that the United States was going to try to build a bomb a thousand times more powerful than the one that had decimated Hiroshima. One may surmise that, for many, the news was as stunning as that earlier revelation, on August 6, 1945, of the advent of the atomic age.

ATOM SPIES

•

CHAPTER 9
KLAUS FUCHS CONFESSES

While Americans still were absorbing the impact of President Truman's H-bomb announcement a few days before—and the first voices of protest were being heard—the nation was rocked anew. Klaus Fuchs, a member of the British scientific team that worked on the Manhattan Project during World War II, had been arrested as a Soviet agent. Headlined the New York *Times:* "British Jail Atom Scientist As A Spy After Tip By F.B.I.; He Knew Of Hydrogen Bomb."

In much of the press, the news of Fuchs's reported treachery was juxtaposed with references to the President's decision to build the super-bomb, though a White House statement immediately denied any connection.

A story from London, where the arrest had taken place, offered little concrete information other than the legal charge—violation of the British Official Secrets Act—and a few meager details indicating that Fuchs had communicated atomic energy information "to a person unknown" in Britain and in the United States.

During a brief formal court proceeding on February 3, 1950, the accused scientist (he had been arrested the day before) made no answer to the charge and a preliminary hearing was set for one week later.

Somewhat more information on the alleged crime emanated from Washington, where J. Edgar Hoover was testifying before a Senate appropriations subcommittee regarding the FBI's request for increased funds and personnel in the coming fiscal year. According to a front-page *Times* story based on leaks from this closed-door hearing, Hoover "told a group of Senators that the evidence indicated that Dr. Fuchs had transmitted both hydrogen and atomic bomb information to the Soviet Union." One of those present at the hearing, Senator Styles Bridges, called Hoover's story of Fuchs's activities "one of the most shocking things I have ever listened to."

At the time of his arrest, Klaus Emil Julius Fuchs held a responsible post as head of the Theoretical Physics division at Harwell, a British atomic energy installation. Starting around 1941, the German-born refugee scientist had been employed on the British atomic program. From December 1943 to June 1946, he served on the British mission to the Manhattan Project, working first for about seven months in New York City on the gaseous diffusion process and, afterward, at Los Alamos, where he was assigned theoretical problems relating to the design and construction of an atomic weapon.

During this period, Fuchs could have obtained little information from American sources about the H-bomb (the general scientific theory of which was not a secret). He had participated in a few discussions on the subject at Los Alamos in 1945 or 1946, but American scientists did not know how to make an H-bomb then—nor did they know how to make one at the time of Fuchs's arrest.

As for the A-bomb, Fuchs was obviously a scientist who had knowledge of a number of important areas of weapons research. Immediately, speculation began as to how many months or years Fuchs's betrayal had saved the Soviet Union in their development of an atomic bomb. According to *U.S. News & World Report*, for example, Fuchs had "given the Russians enough information to advance their own atomic progress by at least a year." Lost in the excitement of the moment was the simple fact that such estimates are meaningless unless firmly based on precise knowledge of the material turned over by Fuchs, as well as the state of related Soviet research—and no such information was available.

The British press and officialdom were relatively subdued in their statements on the Fuchs affair, as compared with the United States. Commented *Time* magazine:

"Fuchs's arrest hit Washington between the eyes. A member of the Atomic Energy Commission said: 'We realized that this was one of the blackest days in the history . . . of the security of this country. We are treating this as the biggest problem we ever had.' In consternation, President Truman's Cabinet met to discuss the case. One of those who attended the session said: 'You can't overemphasize the seriousness of this development.'"

A commentary by Arthur Krock was headlined: "Atomic Spy Case Brings Quick Capital Reaction—A Political Issue Is Handed to Those Who Have Attacked Administration Attitude on Security and Spying." Krock observed that the arrest "had an impact and a powerful one on the entire Government of the United States for reasons which stretch far beyond the interests of national security."

The Fuchs case was widely cited as additional justification for an all-out effort to make the H-bomb, enhanced atomic secrecy, and increased vigilance against Communist spies and traitors in the United States. Evaluating the effect of the case on the public, *Newsweek* said: ". . . the fantastic is beginning to be accepted as fact. There are men like Fuchs and Hiss."

In this atmosphere, on February 9, 1950, a little-known United States Senator, perhaps feeling that the tide of his destiny was at the flood, launched one of the most extraordinary careers in American politics with a speech before the Women's Republican Club of Wheeling, West Virginia. Probably declaiming a phrase that was soon his trademark—"I hold here in my hand"—Joseph R. McCarthy waved at his wide-eyed audience a list of 205 (or 57 or 81; the exact number is lost to history) names of State Department employees "who have been named as members of the Communist Party and members of a spy ring," and repeated similar charges over the next few days in Salt Lake City and Reno—with growing effect.

At ten-thirty in the morning on February 10, police guards cleared a path through dozens of reporters crowded into London's tiny Bow Street court for a slim, mild-looking prisoner, whose ascetic, egg-shaped face was dominated by expressionless eyes rimmed with large spectacles.

Commander Leonard J. Burt, chief of Scotland Yard's special branch, who had arrested Fuchs the week before, came up to him, smiled, and took him by the shoulders. "How do you feel? All right?"

"Yes, thank you," replied Fuchs, smiling back. These were the only words spoken by the scientist in court that day.

The accused man was a thirty-eight-year-old bachelor, the son of a German Protestant clergyman—known for his anti-Nazi and pacifist views. Seventeen years before, in 1933, young Fuchs had fled to England as a political refugee and, during the war years, had become a British citizen. His personal life had been touched with tragedy—his mother had died a suicide, as had one of his sisters. He had no close relatives in Britain. Now, the paleness of his face accentuated by the color of his wrinkled brown suit, khaki shirt, and dark red tie, Klaus Fuchs appeared impassive as three witnesses for the prosecution testified at his preliminary hearing.

The first, Wing Commander Henry Arnold, security officer at Harwell and a friend of Fuchs, observed that he always had regarded the scientist as "an exceptionally security-conscious person." Arnold related how Fuchs had come to him, in October 1949, to report that his seventy-five-year-old father was planning to move from Frankfurt, in the American Zone of Germany, to Leipzig, in the Soviet Zone, to accept a post there as professor of theology. Fuchs had been anxious as to whether this action by his father would pose any security problem at Harwell so far as his own job was concerned and had thought he might have to resign. The scientist's motives for approaching Arnold on this matter were obscure.

At the time, British security officials were apparently in possession of information from the United States suggesting a possible leak of atomic energy information. Not clear from Arnold's testimony is whether Fuchs was already a suspect or whether his own disclosure regarding his father had first called him to the attention of the authorities.

The prosecution's principal witness, William J. Skardon, a thoughtful-looking, pipe-smoking, mustached man who looked every inch the part of the experienced police investigator, told the court of his many conversations with Fuchs, starting on December 21, 1949. Portions of the prosecutor's questioning of Skardon were reported in the New York *Times*:

"At a later stage did you make it clear that you suspected him [Fuchs] of passing information to the Soviet authorities?"

"Yes."

"What was his first reaction?"

"He seemed surprised and said, 'I don't think so.'"

"Did you make it clear to him that you were in possession of precise information on this matter?"

"Yes."

"What did he say?"

"He again replied, 'I do not think so.' I told him that that was an ambiguous reply and he said, 'I do not understand. Perhaps you will tell me what the evidence is. I have not done any such thing.'"

Skardon then told of going to Fuchs's private residence on January 24 —at Fuchs's own request. The prosecutor asked:

"What did you say to him?"

"I said, 'you asked to see me and here I am.' He replied, 'Yes, it is rather up to me now.'"

"Did he once again tell you the story of his life but with no admission of these offenses?"

"Yes."

"What seemed to be his mental condition?"

"He was under considerable mental stress."

"What did you say to him?"

"I suggested that he should unburden his mind and clear his conscience by telling me the full story. It seemed to me that whereas he had told a long story providing a motive for his acts he had told me nothing about the acts themselves."

"What did he say to that?"

"He said, 'I will never be persuaded by you to talk.' There was then an interval for lunch and after lunch Dr. Fuchs said to me suddenly and voluntarily that he had decided it would be in the best interests to answer questions. He added that he had a clear conscience at present, but was very worried about the effect of his behavior upon the friendships which he had contracted at Harwell."

Fuchs then told Skardon that he had been engaged in espionage from mid-1942 to about 1949 and had passed information relating to atomic energy at irregular but frequent meetings. He had taken the initiative himself in this activity and had spoken with an individual* who had arranged the first meeting.

Skardon recounted the story told him by Fuchs:

"For a long time the defendant confined his information to the product of his own brain. But as time went on this developed into something more." The meetings "were sometimes certainly with Russians, but others were with persons of unknown nationality. . . . He said there was a prearranged rendezvous, and recognition signals were exchanged. The association continued through 1944 in New York, for a period at Los Alamos and in London again on his return to England. Generally the meetings were of short duration and consisted of his passing documentary information and with the other party arranging the next rendezvous. At times he was questioned, but the defendant thought it to have been inspired from some other quarter than his contact. For the last two years of his association with the Russians there was a gradual reduction in the flow of information which he imparted since he was beginning to have doubts as to the propriety of his actions."

Rather astonishingly, after confessing this espionage activity to Skardon, Fuchs seemed quite unaware that he faced punishment for his crime and was primarily concerned about his career. Skardon related:

". . . he said that since he was under suspicion he might, upon reflection, think it impossible to continue to work at Harwell and that if he came to that conclusion he would offer his resignation. He thought it would be perfectly simple for him to obtain a university post. He also foresaw that there would be no particular disadvantage in his doing so. It seemed to me to be quite clear that his great interest was in the work upon which he was then engaged."

As for Fuchs's motive for suddenly confessing, no explanation was offered except this testimony by Skardon:

"He said he still believed in communism, but not as practiced in Russia today. In this form he thinks it is something to fight against. He said he had never been a member of the British Communist Party. He said that he had decided fairly recently that he could only settle in England and that he had been terribly worried about the impact of his behavior upon his friendship with various people and in particular with Wing Commander Arnold at Harwell."

Skardon then related how two days after receiving this confession he had again seen Fuchs, on January 26—once more at the scientist's own request. Fuchs had continued his story, telling Skardon about three or four meetings in New York City—following the first which had been arranged before he left England—and further meetings between the time

---

* In a subsequent written confession, Fuchs said he "established contact through a member of the Communist Party."

he went to Los Alamos and his return to England. He noted that there was only one person at each contact.

Fuchs still showed no awareness that he was facing arrest and Skardon humored him for a while longer. Skardon testified:

"He was anxious that his position should be resolved as quickly as possible. He wondered whether the authorities would clearly understand his position and I asked him whether he would like to make a written statement, incorporating any details which he thought ought to be borne in mind."

The next day, January 27, Fuchs came down to London, alone, and Skardon met him at Paddington Station. The two men then went to the War Office and, after cautioning Fuchs as to his rights, Skardon wrote down a statement at Fuchs's dictation. Fuchs's lack of comprehension as to the import of his actions persisted. Said Skardon:

"After making the statement Dr. Fuchs said he was most anxious to discover what his future was to be. He said he did not want to waste any time in getting the matter cleared up."

Fuchs then offered to give all technical information about his espionage to a technical expert. Three days later, he again came down to London, without escort, and met Skardon at Paddington Station. Once more the two went to the War Office, where Fuchs met with Michael Perrin, who had served on the British atomic bomb project.

At the hearing, Perrin testified briefly. Asked if the information Fuchs said he had passed was "of value to a potential enemy," he said: "It was."

Fuchs's technical confession to Perrin never has been made public, but portions of his signed confession to Skardon were read during the preliminary hearing and later reported in the press. The Fuchs confession was found fascinating by almost all who read it. *Time* magazine called it "a remarkable psychological document of warped, brilliant intelligence and twisted morality." *Newsweek* stated: "The mind of Klaus Fuchs . . . was a strange, almost a surrealistic thing. The man was half genius, half imbecile."

These comments, and the prosecution's reference to Fuchs as a "Dr. Jekyll and Mr. Hyde" personality, were inspired primarily by this passage in Fuchs's written confession:

"In the course of this work [at Harwell] I began naturally to form bonds of personal friendship and I had to conceal from them my own thoughts. I used my Marxian philosophy to conceal my thoughts in two separate compartments. One side was the man I wanted to be. I could be free and easy and happy with other people without fear of disclosing myself because I knew the other compartment would step in if I reached the danger point. It appeared to me at the time I had become a free man because I succeeded in the other compartment in establishing myself completely independent of the surrounding forces of society. Looking back on it now the best way is to call it a controlled schizophrenia."

Fuchs's claim of using Marxian philosophy to establish himself "independent of the surrounding forces of society" is, of course, complete gibberish and the antithesis of Marxism. Similarly, on close reading, other of his statements are difficult to comprehend or lack internal logic. Describing the breaking off of his espionage activities, Fuchs said:

"In the postwar period I had doubts about Russian policy, but eventually I came to the point when I knew I disapproved of many actions of the Russians. I still believed Russia would build a new world and that I would take part in it. During this time I was not sure I could give all the information I had, however. It became more and more evident that the time when Russia would spread influence all over Europe was far away. I had to decide whether I could continue to hand over information without being sure I was doing right. I decided I could not do so. I did not go to one rendezvous because I was ill at the time and I decided not to go to the following one."

Fuchs then recounted his odd action in October 1949, when he had spoken to Arnold, the Harwell security officer, about his father:

"Shortly afterward my father told me he might be going to the eastern zone of Germany. He disapproved of many things in Eastern Europe and had always done so, and he knew that when he went there he would stay there. I could not bring myself to stop my father from going there. However, it made me face at least some of the facts about myself. I suppose I did not have the courage to fight it out myself, and therefore took it out of my hands by informing the authorities that my father was going to the eastern zone.

"A few months passed and I became more and more convinced that I had to leave Harwell. I was then confronted with the fact that there was evidence I had given away information in New York. I at first denied the allegations made against me. I decided I would have to leave Harwell, but it became clear that in leaving Harwell in these circumstances I would deal a great blow to Harwell and all the work I had loved and also leave suspicions against friends whom I had loved and people who thought I was their friend. . . . I know that all I can do now is to try. . . . to make sure that Harwell will suffer as little as possible."

A few days after completing his two confessions, Fuchs—still a free man—had been asked to come to London once more to see Perrin. Unsuspecting, he made the journey and was apparently astonished when, while waiting in Perrin's office, a police inspector placed him under arrest. He is said to have cried out in surprise and dismay: "You realize what this will mean at Harwell?"

At the end of Fuchs's preliminary hearing, trial was set for Old Bailey and the magistrate asked Fuchs if he wished to make a statement. His attorney replied: "He has nothing to say at this stage and will call no evidence in this court."

The publication of Fuchs's confession elicited a curious comment from his seventy-five-year-old father, who had become Professor of Theology at Leipzig University only two weeks before his son's arrest. Professor Emil Fuchs told the Associated Press by telephone: "There are things in it [the confession] that are just impossible." He declined to elaborate but said he would like to be a defense witness at his son's trial.

No witness appeared for the defense, however, at the trial on March 1 of Klaus Fuchs in the rather ostentatious, oak-lined, windowless Number One Court at London's famed Old Bailey. The prisoner stood in the great glass-walled dock, across the courtroom from the bewigged, scarlet-robed Lord Chief Justice of England, while the clerk intoned the indictment.

Asked the clerk: "Are you guilty or not guilty?"

Striking a seemingly casual pose, with one hand in his pocket, Fuchs replied in a low voice: "Guilty."

Commented *Life* magazine: "It was the expected plea in one of the most unexpected criminal actions in Anglo-Saxon legal history."

The Attorney General opened for the prosecution by stating that communism was the motive in the case. He presented no evidence as to the precise nature or importance of the material Fuchs had passed, but said:

"There were, of course, many fields of atomic research and of the general experimental and developmental work in regard to atomic energy which were being carried on and which were unknown to him, and those fields were consequently protected.

"On the other hand he was a scientist of the highest standing in his own particular field, and although, according to his statement, he did not disclose the whole of his knowledge in that field, information he had admittedly disclosed would undoubtedly have been of the greatest assistance as to that particular field."

The Attorney General noted that Fuchs's statement, so far as the police had been able to check it, was believed to be true.

Fuchs's defense counsel tried to extenuate his client's crimes by placing them in their historic setting. Most important, he called to the stand William Skardon, who revealed that before he took the statement from Fuchs there was no evidence upon which the scientist could have been prosecuted. The only evidence now offered against the prisoner had been provided by himself.

Portions of this evidence—Fuchs's confession—were read once again while the scientist, possibly thinking of the life at Harwell now lost to him forever, fingered the dozen or so pencils and pens in his vest pocket —the tools of his trade as a theoretical physicist. During his entire trial, he spoke only once after his guilty plea; the single statement made by him in his three brief court appearances. According to press reports, he read his enigmatic statement in a barely intelligible voice:

"There are also some other crimes which I have committed, other than the ones with which I am charged. When I asked my counsel to put certain facts before you I did so in order to atone for these crimes. They are not crimes in the eyes of the law. . . . I have had a fair trial and I wish to thank you, My Lord, my counsel, and the governor and staff of Brixton Prison for their considerate treatment."

After delivering a stern rebuke to the prisoner for his crime—characterized by next day's New York *Times* as "one of the most monstrous betrayals in human history"—the Chief Justice imposed the maximum sentence for the offense allowable under English law—a term of fourteen years.

Reported *Time* magazine: "For a moment Fuchs stood still in the dock, then a warder tapped him on the back and he turned, mechanically tapping his yellow note sheets into a neat pile which he slipped into his coat pocket."

After one hour and twenty-seven minutes, the trial of Klaus Fuchs was over.

Several days later, Tass, the official Soviet news agency, wrote a postscript to the case by repudiating Fuchs's confession, stating: "Fuchs is unknown to the Soviet Government and no 'agents' of the Soviet Union had any connection with Fuchs."

Soon after the trial, copies of Fuchs's confessions to Skardon and Perrin were made available by the British to the United States government, and the complete texts were read in closed session of the Joint Committee on Atomic Energy. Despite the suggestion of some committee members that both documents be made public, this has never been done. A committee statement explained: ". . . there is no proof positive . . . that every last shred of the information was effectively and accurately delivered. . . ."

Raising this same point, *Time* magazine commented:

". . . As a trusted insider in both U.S. and British atom-bomb laboratories, Fuchs had an enormous amount of secret and vital information. He insists that he transmitted his knowledge to the Russians. If he did, the secrets might as well be published openly, with benefit to all Western scientists.

"But did he? Who can be sure? Fuchs was a theoretical physicist (one of the best), and the matters he dealt with were abstract and difficult. It is hard to transmit such knowledge from one qualified scientific mind to another, even with plenty of time and many face-to-face conversations. There is an excellent chance that much of Fuchs's information never reached Russian physicists in a form they can use.

"Besides, the authorities reason, Fuchs may still be trying to help the Russians from his prison cell. He may be confessing to have told more than he actually did—in hope that publication will finally transmit all his knowledge to the Russians. So the authorities figure that it is best to keep their mouths tight shut, act as if Traitor Fuchs had told the Russians nothing."

The question of how Klaus Fuchs first came under suspicion by the British authorities has intrigued many writers and, following the trial, some suggestions were made that the first clues had come from the Canadian investigation of the Gouzenko affair. As part of this investigation, Canadian police had seized dozens of calendar pads, diaries, telephone number finders, letters, notebooks, and address books. In one of these— a book belonging to a Canadian mathematics professor, Israel Halperin (who was acquitted)—the name of Klaus Fuchs appeared.

Why his name was there has never been fully explained, but it has been reported that in 1940, while Fuchs was interned in a Canadian camp for German aliens, Halperin had sent him magazines—apparently at the request of a relative of Fuchs. After Fuchs's arrest, some people tried to attach great significance to the appearance of his name in the Halperin address book. However, there is no evidence of any connection between Fuchs and the Canadian spy ring, nor is there any reason for believing that the address book picked up in 1945 led the British to Fuchs five years later.

Also widely reported was that Fuchs had been apprehended through information supplied to the British by the FBI. Some clarification of this supposition was provided by Prime Minister Attlee, who told Commons: "In the autumn of last year [1949] information came from the United States suggesting there had been some leakage while the British mission, of which Fuchs was a member, was in the United States. *This information did not point to any individual.* The security services got to work with great energy and were, as the House knows, successful." (Emphasis added.)

Thus, all that can be said at present about the apprehension of Fuchs is that in the fall of 1949 the British received word from the United States of a possible security leak and, subsequently, Klaus Fuchs confessed to having passed information to the Soviet Union. What connection—if any—there may have been between these two occurrences never has been established.

However, for many Americans the question of paramount interest in early 1950 was not how Klaus Fuchs had been found, but whether his confederates in the United States would be tracked down and captured. No sooner had Fuchs's arrest been announced than Representative Richard Nixon of the Un-American Activities Committee called for "a full congressional investigation" of atomic espionage "to find out who may have worked with Fuchs in this country." At the same time, a New York *World-Telegram & Sun* headline predicted: "U. S. Arrests in Spy Case Likely Soon."

Pressure to make such arrests may well have been felt within the Administration as a result of the taunts of various Republican critics of the Fair Deal. Said Senator Homer Capehart:

"There are other spies, too, and there will continue to be as long as we have a President who refers to such matters as 'red herrings' and a Secretary of State who refuses to turn his back on the Alger Hisses."

That the FBI was searching for possible American accomplices of Klaus Fuchs was made clear to Congress soon after the scientist's arrest. According to Senator Brien McMahon, J. Edgar Hoover told the Joint Committee on Atomic Energy that "Further ramifications of this matter are being worked on by the FBI here and by British intelligence in Britain."

Strong representations were made by the American government to the United Kingdom for permission for the FBI to interview Fuchs in prison. On May 11, 1950, a spokesman for the Labor government informed the House of Commons that such permission had been granted, with the proviso that Fuchs be questioned in the presence of a British prison official. Some members of Parliament were highly critical of the "unprecedented" questioning of a British prisoner by foreign police.

Finally, on May 20 (after permission had also been obtained from Fuchs), two FBI agents—Hugh Clegg, an assistant to Hoover, and Robert Lamphere—began daily questioning of Fuchs at a British prison, to seek from the scientist the information they apparently had been unable to find in his confessions—the identity of anyone who had aided him in his espionage activities in the United States.

CHAPTER 10

CAPTURE OF AN ACCOMPLICE

On May 23, 1950—three days after the first questioning of Klaus Fuchs by FBI agents at London's Wormwood Scrubs Prison—a sudden, late-evening announcement from Washington was issued jointly by the Attorney General of the United States and the Director of the FBI. The American accomplice of atom-spy Fuchs had been arrested in Philadelphia. According to J. Howard McGrath and J. Edgar Hoover, the accused man had "admitted his contacts with Dr. Fuchs and . . . given a detailed account of his activities."

In newsrooms throughout the nation, wire service tickers rattled out additional details and comments from members of Congress, who "hailed" the arrest. Reporters rushed to the Federal Building in downtown Philadelphia, as lights went on in the darkened chambers of federal Judge James P. McGranery.

At 10:45 P.M., the object of this excitement—a pudgy, sad-faced little man—was escorted into Judge McGranery's chambers by four FBI agents. He had fleshy cheeks, a trace of a double chin, a full lower lip, and prominent, heavy-lidded eyes that appeared nearly closed as he stared at the floor. His name was Harry Gold and he was a thirty-nine-year-old bachelor employed as a chemist at a Philadelphia hospital.

One of the FBI agents read aloud from a complaint stating that Gold had conspired with an unnamed individual to obtain national defense information for the Soviet Union from Klaus Fuchs.

The man against whom this complaint was directed made no comment, except to say that he had given some voluntary statements to the FBI. He asked the Judge for permission to speak with his brother and was allowed to telephone his home (where he lived with his father and younger brother). According to one account of the conversation, he was heard to say: "I'm in pretty deep now."

Then, with bail set at $100,000 and a hearing scheduled for June 12, Harry Gold, flanked by guards, was led away to his first night in prison.

For the FBI, the arrest of Gold was a tremendous coup. The importance that the FBI attached to the capture of Fuchs's accomplice has been indicated by J. Edgar Hoover. Said he:

"In all the history of the FBI there never was a more important problem than this one, never another case where we felt under such pressure. The unknown man simply had to be found."

While it would be fruitless to speculate as to the precise reasons why Hoover felt under such "pressure" regarding the apprehension of someone who might have met with Fuchs five years before, it is a fact that in the years and months prior to Gold's arrest the FBI had been subjected to considerable criticism for alleged bungling and clumsy investigative techniques in the Redin, Amerasia, Eisler, and Coplon cases. Now, praise for the FBI's successful detective work in finding Gold came from all sides.

In an editorial titled "Another FBI Triumph," the New York *World-Telegram & Sun* suggested that FBI critics "read the story of how the FBI tracked down Harry Gold. It was exciting stuff, and a convincing demonstration of efficiency."

With FBI agents known to be interrogating Fuchs in England, a natural assumption was that the Gold arrest had resulted from information provided by Fuchs. Headlined the New York *Times*: "Philadelphian Seized As Spy On Basis Of Data From Fuchs—FBI Questioning of Atom Expert in British Prison Brings About Arrest."

The story noted: "In London it was disclosed that two FBI agents questioned Dr. Fuchs Saturday [May 20] and again today [May 23]."

Thus, the story of how the FBI had found Gold seemed comparatively simple and clear-cut to readers of the *Times* on the morning after the arrest: Fuchs had named his American confederate to the two visiting agents and the FBI had promptly picked up Gold in Philadelphia. However, this easy explanation was soon shown to be erroneous when a number of publications revealed that the FBI had begun interrogating Gold some days *before* the Bureau's two agents arrived in London to interview Fuchs. Thereafter, the story became more complex and, gradually, the circumstances surrounding the capture of Gold acquired an aura of mystery. Said the *Times*: "Officials said the trail from Fuchs to Gold led F.B.I. agents through a long, painstaking quest. . . ."

As to how the FBI had gotten onto this "trail," no exact answer was offered, but all commentators agreed that Klaus Fuchs had provided the initial clues (assumedly to British police who passed them on to the FBI). Fuchs reportedly had not recalled the name of his American accomplice but had provided the authorities with a sparse physical description and—according to some accounts—a hint as to the man's possible occupation in some scientific field.

Armed with such meager descriptive details, FBI agents were said to have sifted through a list of twelve hundred persons and, eventually, to have narrowed the field down to a small group of chemists—including Harry Gold—in the New York-Philadelphia area. Just how this list of twelve hundred suspects had been compiled was the subject of much creative speculation in the press.

71

A possible reason for Harry Gold's inclusion on the list was the fact—revealed after his arrest—that he had been known to the FBI for some years, having appeared briefly before a 1947 federal grand jury investigating Elizabeth Bentley's story of Communist espionage.

Questioned by the FBI in May 1950, Gold claimed never to have met Fuchs nor been in the western United States; however, when confronted with evidence that he had visited Santa Fe, he was said to have suddenly confessed. A few hours later, Fuchs (who had previously failed to identify a still photo of Gold) was shown a movie of the Philadelphia chemist made by the FBI and reportedly then recognized his confederate.

A close reading of the many American press accounts during spring 1950 purportedly revealing how Gold was discovered by the FBI shows that no reasonably coherent account of Fuchs's role in the search was presented. Despite innumerable and often contradictory variations, however, the main point of all these stories was the same: The FBI had begun its manhunt with a rough physical description obtained from Fuchs.

The *World-Telegram & Sun*, for example, stated: "The FBI had one meager clue, a brief physical description . . . 'short, stocky build, round face.' That was how Klaus Fuchs described the nameless man. . . ."

According to *Life* magazine, Fuchs had called his contact ". . . a fat, foreign-looking American of about 40. Fuchs did not know his name. But, Dr. Fuchs remembered, the man had worn a blue pin-stripe suit."

Reported *Time:* "Fuchs tried to cooperate. . . . The go-between, he said, was a short, stocky, soft-spoken fellow with Slavic features, an oval face and a penchant for pin-striped suits. His conversation reflected scientific training."

All of these descriptions were based, of necessity, on either FBI leaks or the imaginative efforts of reporters. The assertion, for example, that Fuchs had referred to his accomplice's "penchant for pin-striped suits" may, just possibly, have stemmed from the fact that Gold was wearing such a suit at the time of his arrest. No authoritative version of Fuchs's contribution to the hunt for Gold was available until nearly a year later, when the FBI Director discussed the case in a *Reader's Digest* article, "The Crime of the Century." Said Hoover:

"Dr. Fuchs disclosed that while in the United States he had dealt with one Soviet agent only. The man's name? Fuchs had never known the agent's name. The man appeared to know chemistry and engineering but was not a nuclear physicist. Fuchs thought he was probably not an employe of an atomic energy installation.

"What did the man look like? Well, he was from 40 to 45 years of age, possibly five feet ten inches tall, broad build, round face, most likely a first-generation American. A description which might fit millions of men!"

While Fuchs's description as revealed by Hoover might, indeed, have "fit millions of men," it did not, curiously, fit little Harry Gold, who was five feet six inches tall and, at the time of meeting Fuchs, would have been thirty-three or thirty-four years old.

Thus, whatever may have occasioned the arrest of Harry Gold on May 23, 1950, his apprehension clearly did not result from a description provided by Klaus Fuchs. It would seem that the full story of the search for Gold remains untold—an impression strengthened by this cryptic statement of Hoover's regarding the manhunt: "I doubt whether it will ever be possible to disclose publicly all of the factors involved."

A source of biographical information about Harry Gold in the first weeks after his arrest was a story in *Life* that described his childhood as a poor boy brought up "on Philadelphia's grimy South Philip Street, where all the houses had false fronts and dirty narrow backyards."

Illustrating the article was a picture of Gold from his high school annual, showing an intelligent-looking and not unhandsome boy—intense and unsmiling. His classmates had captioned the picture "Silent Visage." Another picture showed the house where he was living with his father and brother at the time of his arrest—one of a row of pleasant, attached two-story brick homes on Kindred Street in Philadelphia.

Gold's arrest was said to have completely surprised his family. Said *Time:*

"That night his father, a . . . Russian-born cabinetmaker, and his brother, Joseph, 34, who had fought in the U. S. Army in World War II, heard astounding news—Harry Gold had been a spy for Russia. Cried his father: 'Harry was a good boy—maybe they gave him some drugs.' His brother angrily refused to believe that Harry Gold could possibly have led a double life. But when they went to see him, Harry said: 'I've done something that can't be rubbed off.' Why had Harry Gold done it? He could only mutter a line which a thousand sinners had muttered before: 'I must have been crazy.'"

A more ideological motivation for the crime was provided immediately after the arrest by an unnamed FBI informant who quoted Gold:

"I thought I would be helping a nation whose final aims I approved along the road to industrial strength."

Commented the *Journal-American:* "The intellectual processes by which Gold and Fuchs . . . justified to themselves their espionage in behalf of Russia were strikingly similar."

On May 31, eight days after his arrest, Gold was taken at his own request from Holmesburg Prison—where he was said to be a "self-possessed prisoner"—to the chambers of Judge McGranery. With hands folded in front of him, Gold's demeanor during this hearing was seemingly that of a meticulously polite, repentant, and self-sacrificing man, determined to cause all concerned as little inconvenience as possible; nevertheless, his various specific requests to the Court suggested a surprising firmness of purpose.

Gold informed Judge McGranery:

"I want to obtain an attorney, but the difficulty is that I do not have very much in the way of money." He explained that he had about $170 in the bank, a few hundred dollars in uncashed War Bonds, and "about $4000 that is due me from my employer in New York, back salary. It has been over two years since I left there and practically the hopes for obtaining that are pretty dim, because the firm is not in very good shape, never was."

Gold was particularly concerned about efforts by his father and brother to obtain a lawyer for him. ". . . I am very anxious not to cause them any further expense, or difficulty . . . . something of this nature could easily wreck their finances."

He then set a number of "conditions" for any attorney appointed to defend him:

". . . if an attorney is appointed I would like him to understand very clearly that I must continue to give information to the F.B.I. freely, that he is to put no restrictions whatever on that . . . regardless whether he thinks it is damaging to me or not.

"Also I would very much like that he be a man, if possible, with no radical connections whatever, no leftist or pinkish background of any kind whatsoever.

"The third thing is . . . he is to understand that I am pleading guilty; not, however, with respect to one particular matter. I did not honestly ever in my life mean any harm to the United States. Now I believe—I don't recall the charge . . . there is some phrase there which had to do with reference to intent to injure and harm the United States. Otherwise I intend to plead guilty."

Judge McGranery, stating that he agreed that Gold was entitled to speedy appointment of counsel, inquired: "And you say that in all likelihood you will be entering a plea of guilty, you think?"

When Gold replied, "Yes, I shall," the Judge reminded him that he would have to wait for the indictment to be drawn against him "and see what that looks like."

Next day, June 1, Harry Gold was again brought to Judge McGranery's chambers and the Judge was ready with a lawyer who had agreed to represent Gold, without payment, as a public service. He was John D. M. Hamilton, a former chairman of the Republican National Committee and a prominent corporation attorney. Perhaps McGranery, a stanch Democrat, thought it somewhat amusing to assign the defense of a spy to a well-known Republican. In any event, he told Gold: "Mr. Hamilton has already rendered service to his country, he has been the chairman of a great political party . . . not of my faith, but it is one of our great parties, and certainly his patriotism is above reproach. His standing at our bar is that of a partner to the dean of the Philadelphia bar, former Senator George Wharton Pepper." Gold readily accepted the appointment.

The grand jury that indicted Harry Gold on June 9 for conspiracy to commit wartime espionage—an offense carrying a possible death penalty— also named as defendants two others, identified only as "John Doe, alias 'John'" and "Richard Roe, alias 'Sam.'" The three were accused of conspiring, with Klaus Fuchs, to obtain for the Soviet Union national defense information relating to "atomic energy and nuclear fission." Omitted from the indictment, as Gold had requested, were the words "with intent and reason to believe that it was to be used to the injury of the United States."

The indictment charged that Gold had met Fuchs four times in New York City, once in Cambridge, Massachusetts, and twice in Santa Fe. The dates of the latter meetings were given as June and September 1945.

Three days later, on June 12 in Philadelphia, Gold was said by the *Times* to have "showed no signs of emotion, though he was booed by a crowd as he was led into the Federal Building by two United States marshals." The hearing was perfunctory; the government, with Hamilton's agreement, obtained a postponement until July 20.

From the very day of Gold's arrest there was widespread speculation in the press regarding possible additional arrests based on information he might provide. Representative James E. Van Zandt of the Joint Committee on Atomic Energy predicted that Gold's arrest "probably is the first of a series of arrests that may take place. We know definitely that there are others involved. It's just a question of the FBI getting them. They've been working on this for months."

Soon after, *Newsweek* summed up the thoughts of many:

". . . the announcement that Gold had been arrested and was being held in $100,000 bail raised new questions. Had he named his confederates? Would there be more arrests?"

The public did not have to wait long for answers.

CHAPTER 11

MORE ARRESTS

The decade of the Fifties began in America with a season of fear. Nineteen fifty was the year Americans learned of the decision to build a bomb a thousand times more powerful than the one that destroyed Hiroshima; the year a bloody "police action" in Korea threatened to escalate into World War III; the year McCarthyism became a force in the land; the year the press referred openly and often approvingly to the possibility of mass roundups of subversives for incarceration in already prepared detention camps; the year school officials soberly drew up plans for protecting pupils from Soviet A-bombs by teaching them to crouch beneath their wooden desks—each child wearing around his neck a metal name tag as a kind of atomic age amulet. Paradoxically, 1950 was also a year of full employment and economic boom.

During the late spring, summer, and early fall of that year, a series of nine arrests—all apparently connected with Soviet atomic espionage and the confession of Klaus Fuchs—added to the national mood of near-panic. The capture of Fuchs's accomplice, Harry Gold—the first American atom spy arrested—had been announced on May 23. Fulfilling many predictions that more arrests were imminent, arrest number two occurred on June 15 in Syracuse, New York.

Headlined the *Times*: "Syracuse Chemist Seized In Spy Ring—New Arrest Linked to Fuchs—Suspect Accused of Giving Explosive Data to Gold." The accused man, Alfred Dean Slack, was described in the Syracuse *Post-Standard* as having been arrested by FBI agents "in connection with the international atomic spying case."

Slack, forty-four, was a $75-a-week assistant production superintendent at a Syracuse paint factory. At the time of his arrest, he lived with his wife and two young boys in a house he had built himself in the small rural community of Clay. Born and raised in the area, he was a worshiper at a local Methodist church and had attended a children's day service there only the previous Sunday. At his arraignment, he told reporters: "I am not now and never was a member of the Communist Party—and never will be."

According to the Department of Justice and J. Edgar Hoover, Slack had admitted turning over to Harry Gold "a sample of a powerful new explosive" and also "highly classified information on the manufacturing process" while he was employed at a Kingsport, Tennessee, ordnance works in 1943 and 1944. Contradicting this official characterization of the explosive as "new," however, were a number of newspaper stories that identified the explosive as RDX, a pre-World War I chemical discovery used in the Second World War after Allied scientists solved mass production problems.

Surprisingly, the complaint on which Slack was arrested mentioned nothing at all about any passage by him of atomic energy information, despite the fact that he had worked for a time on the Manhattan Project at Oak Ridge, Tennessee. The press ignored this unexplained element in the story and, in general, connected Slack's arrest with what *Time* magazine termed the "plot and counterplot by which Russia had stolen U.S. atomic secrets."

Held in $100,000 bail, Slack told reporters as he was taken to prison: "I believe the charges ultimately will be understood. Any charge against me with reference to the Manhattan project has no foundation. I am completely innocent of anything wrong."

The next day brought a new and more spectacular arrest, unambiguously related to atomic energy. Arrest number three, reported from the front-page lead position in the New York *Times*, was that of David Greenglass, an ex-GI who had been stationed at Los Alamos during the war. He was accused of giving data on the atomic bomb to Harry Gold in Albuquerque, New Mexico, in June or July 1945.

The motivation for Greenglass's crime was seemingly ideological: The twenty-eight-year-old New York City machinist, described as a former member of the Young Communist League, had allegedly tried to justify his act to the FBI with these arrogant words: "I felt it was gross negligence on the part of the United States not to give Russia the information about the atom bomb because she was an ally."

A heavy-set youth attired in an open-neck white shirt and windbreaker, Greenglass was arraigned before a United States Commissioner on Friday afternoon, June 16, on a complaint charging the capital offense of conspiracy to commit wartime espionage. According to the *Times*, while waiting to be arraigned, "Greenglass appeared unconcerned, laughing and joking with an F.B.I. agent. When he appeared before Commissioner McDonald . . . he paid more attention to reporters' notes than to the proceedings.

"United States Attorney Irving H. Saypol told the commissioner that Greenglass had said that but for his wife and two children, he had considered 'running away or committing suicide' after Gold's arrest."

When Saypol requested bail of $100,000, Greenglass's attorney, O. John Rogge, called the amount unreasonable, explaining that his client always had lived in the United States and was a married man with children.

Greenglass thereupon reportedly interrupted his attorney to announce: "I have to make a formula for the baby."

Noted by the *Times* was that Greenglass had been "obdurate in the beginning," but had broken down and given a statement to the FBI after several hours of questioning.

On June 24 (June 25 in Asia) a war began in Korea that would have a profound effect on American opinion and life over the next few years. Within a week, American troops were committed to the battle and the nation rallied round the President in a surge of patriotic emotion. The next nearly three months was a time of frustrating and costly defeats on the faraway battlefield and, at home, a time of mobilization for war.

Soon reflected by nearly all organs of opinion was the widespread popular feeling of increased hostility toward native Communists and left-wingers. An extreme view, expressed several days after the war began, was that of Hearst columnist Westbrook Pegler: "The only sensible and courageous way to deal with Communists in our midst is to make membership in Communist organizations or covert subsidies a capital offense and shoot or otherwise put to death all persons convicted of such."

A week after his arrest, David Greenglass appeared at a hearing concerning his possible removal to New Mexico, scene of the crime. This hearing, as reported by the New York *Journal-American*, was an "acrimonious" one in which Saypol and Rogge "clashed repeatedly." Rogge "bitterly protested" the $100,000 bail.

At Saypol's request, the hearing was postponed to await the indictment of Greenglass by a New Mexico grand jury. Rogge had subpoenaed two FBI agents who had interrogated Greenglass prior to his arrest; because of the postponement he was not permitted to question them, though they were instructed to return for the next hearing. The reported animosity between Saypol and Rogge cast some doubt on Greenglass's cooperation with the prosecution, suggested in earlier news stories.

Observed the *Journal-American*: "Greenglass swore profusely as he was led in handcuffs back to the Federal House of Detention."

On July 6, a New Mexico federal grand jury indicted David Greenglass on a charge of conspiring to commit espionage in wartime on behalf of the Soviet Union. Specifically, he was accused of meeting with Harry Gold in Albuquerque on June 3, 1945, preparing that day "a sketch of a high explosive lens mold" and "a statement concerning the Los Alamos Project," and receiving $500 from Gold.

A week later, the New York City hearing on Greenglass's extradition was postponed again, amid indications of a more amiable relationship between the defense attorney and prosecutor Saypol.

Commented the New York *Daily Mirror:*

"The possibility that alleged atomic spy David Greenglass has decided to tell what he knows about the relay of secret information to Russia was evidenced yesterday when U. S. Commissioner McDonald granted the ex-Army sergeant an adjournment of proceedings to move him to New Mexico for trial.

". . . O. John Rogge, attorney for the twenty-eight-year-old defendant, won a postponement . . . largely because of the support of U. S. Attorney Saypol. . . .

"The court appearance followed the latest of a series of conferences between Rogge and Saypol."

On July 17, shortly after this report of David Greenglass's decision "to tell what he knows," the FBI announced the arrest of Greenglass's brother-in-law, Julius Rosenberg. A *Times* headline stated: "Fourth American Held As Atom Spy." Like the previous three prisoners, Rosenberg was held in $100,000 bail.

Atom spy number four was a thirty-two-year-old native New Yorker who lived with his wife and two children in Knickerbocker Village, a housing development near the waterfront on Manhattan's lower East Side. He held a degree in electrical engineering from New York's City College, from which he had graduated in February 1939. Employed during the war as a civilian inspector for the Army Signal Corps, he had been removed from his job in early 1945 on allegations of Communist Party membership and had been unsuccessful in his attempts to gain reinstatement.

At the time of his arrest, Julius Rosenberg was an owner of a small Manhattan machine shop which apparently was not doing well financially. A New York *Daily News* reporter who visited the shop said that the three employees were all non-union workers who related that they had been paid "about" union wages, but had recently been warned by Rosenberg that there could be no vacations because the firm had made no money in the past year and a half. The employees also disclosed that at one time David Greenglass had worked at the shop as a business partner of Rosenberg.

Reporters who spoke with the prisoner's wife, Ethel, at the Rosenberg apartment learned that the FBI had first come to question her husband a month earlier on the morning of her brother David Greenglass's arrest. She said that when her husband returned home he merely told her that the FBI had made "crazy" charges, but did not elaborate.

Describing the FBI's arrest of her husband, Ethel Rosenberg was reported by the *Journal-American* to have said:

" 'We asked them for a search warrant but they never showed one. . . . They searched the apartment thoroughly, examining my clothing and record books and going through closets and cupboards. They even went through those magazines page by page.'

"She pointed to a stack of about three Parent Magazines."

Aside from such personal interviews, the source of all information on Julius Rosenberg's alleged crime was the Department of Justice and its investigative agency, the FBI. As was true in all the other spy arrests that year, the Department of Justice in Washington issued a long press release stating as unquestioned fact the allegations against Rosenberg, so that in a very real sense the crux of the government's case was presented in the press long before it was presented in a court of law or even to a grand jury.

The Department of Justice press release stated, in part:

"J. Edgar Hoover . . . said that Rosenberg is another important link in the Soviet espionage apparatus which includes Dr. Klaus Fuchs, Harry Gold, David Greenglass and Alfred Dean Slack. Mr. Hoover revealed that Rosenberg recruited Greenglass. . . .

"Rosenberg, in early 1945, made available to Greenglass while on furlough in New York City one half of an irregularly cut jello box top, the other half of which was given to Greenglass by Harry Gold in Albuquerque, New Mexico as a means of identifying Gold to Greenglass. On this occasion in June, 1945, Greenglass was paid $500 by Gold who obtained it from his Soviet superior Anatoli A. Yakovlev,* Vice Consul of the Soviet Consulate in New York City. Greenglass then turned over to Gold classified information he had secured from the Atom Bomb Project at Los Alamos, where he was stationed at the time as a soldier.

"After Fuchs and Gold were arrested in February and May, 1950, respectively, Rosenberg warned Greenglass to leave the country and supplied him with substantial funds in twenty dollar bills to do so. He instructed Greenglass to surreptitiously obtain a passport to Mexico, travel to Switzerland and thereafter report to the Soviet Embassy in Czechoslovakia. Shortly thereafter Greenglass was arrested by the FBI."

Hoover referred to "the gravity of Rosenberg's offense" and stated that Rosenberg had "aggressively sought ways and means to secretly conspire with the Soviet Government to the detriment of his own country." This damning charge by a high government official was widely noted in the press; the *Journal-American*, for example, said Rosenberg had been "branded as one of the most 'aggressive' agents in the Klaus Fuchs atomic spy ring."

The Department of Justice press release also stated:

"Investigation to date reveals that Rosenberg . . . made himself available to Soviet espionage agents so he might 'do something to directly help Russia.'"

Many newspapers assumed that the direct quotation within the latter official statement had been made by Julius Rosenberg and attributed it to him, thereby suggesting to readers that atom spy number four was cooperating with the FBI. This suggestion was soon disproved by the news that Rosenberg had laughed at the jello box top story, calling it "fantas-

* Referred to in Gold's indictment by the alias John.

tic—something like kids hear over the television on the Lone Ranger program."

Noted *Time* magazine: "Alone of the four arrested so far, Rosenberg stoutly insisted on his innocence."

Alongside the *Time* account of Julius Rosenberg's arrest was another story—headlined "Boiling Over"—that provides a fever chart of America in summer 1950. The story began:

"The nation was good and mad at Communists—home-grown as well as the U.S.S.R. and North Korean varieties—and here & there its temper not only boiled up but boiled over."

As examples, *Time* reported that in Detroit the common council had forbade sidewalk news vendors to sell "subversive literature"; in Columbus, Ohio, police juvenile officers warned teen-age clubs to be suspicious of "any new member of a group whose background is not an open book"; in McKeesport, Pennsylvania, the city council was readying an ordinance requiring registration of "anyone who engages in activities destined to promote the principles of Communism"; in Houston, Texas, a marauding gang had hurled rocks at the apartment of the state secretary of the Communist Party; in Birmingham, Alabama, a new ordinance banished from the city "anyone caught talking to a Communist in a 'non-public place,' or anyone who passed out literature that could be traced, even remotely, to a Communist hand." Pictured on the same page with a photo of Julius Rosenberg was one showing members of an impromptu Los Angeles "Crusade Against Communism" beating up surprised workers outside the gates of a local industrial plant.

On the national scene—perhaps partly to forestall such outbreaks of vigilante action—President Truman called on all police officers and citizens to be watchful for spies, sabotage, and subversive activities, but to report their suspicions to the FBI.

Added the *Times*:

"Officials said the problem of dealing with Communist subversion undoubtedly would be far more serious than the problem of dealing with any group in any previous war period. The great majority of Communists in this country are native Americans, and under present law they may be dealt with only after they have committed an overt act of subversion. In the last war, most subversive agents were aliens and thus were rounded up immediately after the outbreak of hostilities."

On July 20, two months after he had first burst upon the American scene, Harry Gold, his hands manacled in front of him, walked into Judge McGranery's courtroom in Philadelphia to enter a formal plea to the indictment charging him with conspiring with Klaus Fuchs to commit espionage in wartime in behalf of the Soviet Union. The once obscure chemist was now notorious; his alleged confederates were being picked off one by one in a seemingly unending manhunt: Slack, Greenglass, and, only three days before, Julius Rosenberg had all been arrested.

Whatever Gold's feelings as he prepared to accept guilt for a crime carrying a possible death penalty, they were well hidden. Commented the *Journal-American:*

"While waiting, the man who admitted passing U.S. atomic secrets to Russia appeared more concerned about the outcome of the baseball pennant race than in his own ultimate fate.

"Gold picked the Detroit Tigers to cop the American League flag, with the Cleveland Indians as 'a dark horse.'"

Harry Gold's only part in the short hearing that followed was to enter his plea of guilty, after which Judge McGranery postponed sentencing and declared that he would expect from the prosecution "some testimony that will fill in the grave charges."

At this, the prosecutor, Gerald Gleeson, indicated that the government might present no evidence at all in view of the guilty plea.

GLEESON: . . . I think your Honor can very well understand that there is certain information we do not want made public. . . . The same information, of course, if he pleaded not guilty, we would probably have to make public at a trial, but in view of the fact that he has entered a guilty plea it may very well be that the government does not wish to make public certain things that it has learned, for security reasons.

JUDGE MCGRANERY: Certainly, I would have a very wholesome respect for the government's position with respect to security, but there is another security which the government is struggling to preserve in its opposition to star chamber proceedings. I will want enough evidence to satisfy me beyond any doubt as to the crimes charged and for the imposition of sentence, short of giving some opening to the security of the nation.

GLEESON: We will try to comply with your Honor's wishes. It is a difficult question to determine just what might affect our security in the way of revealing evidence. . . .

JUDGE MCGRANERY: We tried eight saboteurs right in the heat of the war, and they were tried by evidence.

GLEESON: Of course, sir, may I respectfully point out that this man has entered a plea of guilty, and it is only evidence, after all, to satisfy your Honor in determining the question of sentence. We will do the very best we can.

JUDGE MCGRANERY: But it is a plea that carries with it a maximum penalty.

GLEESON: Yes, sir, I understand. We will do the very best we can.

At this point, defense attorney Hamilton—one may fairly assume with the approval of Harry Gold—affirmed his "absolute confidence" in the prosecutor, saying: ". . . I would be perfectly willing, on behalf of the defendant, to accept any statement of the crime that he [the prosecutor] might make, without supporting evidence."

On Saturday morning, July 29, a little more than a week after he had pleaded guilty to conspiring with Klaus Fuchs, Harry Gold was rushed from Philadelphia to New York to appear before a hastily convened federal grand jury. He testified for a number of hours and, according to the *Times*, looked "the picture of utter dejection when he left the grand jury room and was taken to Mr. Saypol's office. . . ."

Later that same afternoon, the FBI announced arrests number five and six: Harry Gold's former New York City employer, Abraham Brothman, a thirty-six-year-old chemical engineer, and Brothman's business associate, Miriam Moskowitz, thirty-four. Headlined the *Times*: "New Spy Round-Up Brings 2 Arrests; Others Due Soon."

Time magazine described the pair as "two more links in the Soviet atomic spy chain which the U.S. started to unreel early this year after the arrest of the British atomic scientist, Dr. Klaus Fuchs." While no information regarding Miss Moskowitz's alleged involvement in the spy ring was available, Brothman was revealed to have been named earlier by Elizabeth Bentley, self-confessed Soviet espionage courier, as a person who had supplied her with blueprints and other information.

Once again, the Department of Justice and the FBI Director attacked the accused in a public arena, months in advance of their formal trial by jury. Reported the *Times*: "The importance of the new arrests was stressed by official statements in Washington that Brothman and Gold were part of a Soviet spy apparatus under a Russian trade organization chief working to ferret out atomic secrets." *Time* magazine attributed to J. Edgar Hoover the information that "Gold, who . . . is now talking freely, said that Brothman had been commended by a Russian official for doing work that was 'equal to the efforts of one or two brigades of men.'"

Curiously, despite these extra-legal accusations, neither Brothman nor Miss Moskowitz were indicted for espionage. They were charged by the grand jury—which acted on the last possible day before a three-year statute of limitations would have made prosecution impossible—with the far less serious offense of conspiracy to obstruct justice. Each pleaded innocent and was held in $25,000 bail. Soon after, Miss Moskowitz's attorney tried unsuccessfully to have her bail reduced to $1000, reportedly asserting that the case had been presented to the public in "a grossly exaggerated and misleading fashion."

Arrest number seven occurred on August 11. Eight weeks after the arrest of her brother and twenty-five days after the arrest of her husband, Ethel Greenglass Rosenberg, thirty-four, was herself suddenly taken into custody by FBI agents as she left the U.S. courthouse at Foley Square, where she had just testified before a grand jury. Held in $100,000 bail, she too was charged—like her brother and husband—with conspiracy to commit espionage.

Mrs. Rosenberg's attorney asked the U. S. Commissioner to parole her in his custody over the weekend, so that she could make arrangements for her two young children. She had left her apartment earlier that Friday morning to appear before the grand jury with no intimation that she was going to be arrested. The request was denied.

Newspaper accounts of this latest arrest were filled out by statements to the press from the office of the U. S. Attorney. Saypol's chief assistant, Myles J. Lane, provided the information that there "is ample evidence that Mrs. Rosenberg and her husband have been affiliated with Communist activities for a long period of time."

On August 17, Julius and Ethel Rosenberg were indicted, along with the former Soviet consular official, Anatoli Yakovlev, named in absentia. They were charged with conspiring with Harry Gold, David Greenglass, and Greenglass's wife, Ruth—the latter three named as co-conspirators but not as defendants—to obtain national defense information for the Soviet Union.

Commented the *Times:*

"This was the first time that the Government had brought Mrs. Greenglass into the case since the F.B.I. began cracking down on alleged members of the spy ring. United States Attorney Irving H. Saypol said the grand jury had directed that she not be prosecuted. Thus it was indicated that she was cooperating in the investigation and might turn Government witness."

The eighth arrest came on August 18. The *Times* headline told the story succinctly: "Engineer Is Seized At Laredo As Spy For Russian Ring— Deported by Mexico To Which He is Believed to Have Gone to Get Passage to Soviet—Fled Queens On June 21—Morton Sobell, Radar Expert Who Worked for Navy, Called a Friend of Rosenberg."

Morton Sobell, thirty-three, had been a classmate of Julius Rosenberg at City College. A resident of the New York City borough of Queens, he was an electrical engineer who had been employed on military work at Reeves Instrument Company in Manhattan. Previous jobs had been with the General Electric Company in Schenectady and the Navy Bureau of Ordnance in Washington, D.C.

Stories about Sobell stressed the point that he had fled the United States with his wife and children after the arrest of Greenglass and made clear that he was still another member of the Klaus Fuchs spy ring. *Newsweek* headlined a story about Sobell "Atom Arrest No. 8," and *Time* called him "the eighth U.S. citizen arrested on spy charges since British Physicist Klaus Fuchs began spilling what he knew of the busy

Soviet espionage ring in the U.S." Returned to New York from Texas, Sobell was held in $100,000 bail.

On August 23, Julius and Ethel Rosenberg appeared in court and pleaded innocent to the espionage charges on which they had been indicted the previous week. It was the first time that Rosenberg had seen his wife since her arrest.

Recounted the *Times:*

"As they met inside the courtroom Rosenberg slipped his arm around the waist of his wife and the two walked before the bar. Throughout the proceeding the Rosenbergs whispered to one another, held hands and seemed oblivious to arguments concerning the charge. If convicted they could receive the death penalty."

The mention of a possible death penalty for the Rosenbergs was not strange, in view of the continued hardening of American opinion concerning the need for drastic action against native Communists. As the Korean fighting continued unabated, fears of a new world war grew. A sign of the times was a proposal by Senator Harley M. Kilgore, a West Virginia Democrat, that the FBI be authorized to round up all Communists whenever the President and Congress decided that national security was imperiled. According to the New York *Daily Mirror*, Kilgore was drafting a bill to "grant the FBI 'properly safeguarded' war emergency powers to throw all Communists into concentration camps."

While the public followed the growing list of arrests like a suspense story, news of the second man apprehended—Alfred Dean Slack—had been relegated to the newspapers' back pages. On September 1 Slack was indicted in Knoxville, Tennessee, charged with conspiring with Gold and a Soviet agent, Sam, to obtain for the Soviet Union information "relating to the manufacture of explosive material." Slack was alleged to have met with Gold in Kingsport, Tennessee, in 1943 and to have turned over national defense information to Gold there around spring 1944. The indictment—like the earlier complaint against Slack—made no mention at all of any effort by the conspirators to obtain atomic secrets.

Nevertheless, the *Times* story of the indictment stated that the FBI had linked Slack "with the Klaus Fuchs spy ring that passed atomic secrets to Soviet Russia."

The short sentencing hearing for Slack on September 18, 1950, received surprisingly meager attention from the press, considering that Slack was the first alleged member of the widely publicized Klaus Fuchs spy ring whose story was revealed in open court. This was particularly unfortunate because some of the facts made known at this hearing raise perplexing questions about the nature of the spy ring that was being uncovered with so much official fanfare.

No statement had appeared in the press as to how Slack intended to plead, and the actual record of the proceedings indicates that the defendant himself may not have been entirely certain up to the last minute:

THE CLERK: How say you, guilty or not guilty?
SLACK: May I confer with Mr. Jenkins [his attorney] for a minute? (Brief consultation)
SLACK: Guilty.

The prosecutor then alleged that for a number of years, during the late Thirties and early Forties, Slack had sold commercial information from the files of his employer, the Eastman Kodak Company of Rochester, to several representatives of the Soviet Union. The recipient of some of this material was Harry Gold. The prosecutor stated that these actions by Slack "did not constitute a violation of state or Federal law, and as such did not constitute the commission of a Federal crime."

During World War II, Slack was employed by an Eastman subsidiary at a Kingsport, Tennessee, plant that manufactured the military explosive RDX. Gold visited him there and allegedly demanded "that Slack furnish him a technical write-up on the methods and process of producing this potent military explosive." Refusing this request a number of times, Slack was said to have acquiesced after "Gold threatened . . . public exposure of Slack's past activities unless Slack cooperated on this last occasion."

According to the prosecutor, Slack had "freely confessed that he did furnish to Harry Gold a technical write-up on the production process" and also a sample of the explosive. Gold, in turn, was said to have admitted taking this material to New York City and passing it to a Soviet agent. Gold and Slack never saw each other again.

At the suggestion of the Department of Justice and the Attorney General, the prosecutor recommended a sentence for Slack of ten years. He said the Justice Department had "pointed out that Slack's violation was a single, isolated violation," committed reluctantly.

From the prosecutor's presentation of the government's case, a number of rather startling facts emerge: Newspaper publicity to the contrary, Slack was neither an atom spy nor a member of the Klaus Fuchs spy ring nor, in point of fact, a member of any "spy ring." He was a man whose dealings with Harry Gold, to whom he had apparently sold commercial data, were—by the admission of the prosecutor—entirely legal, with one exception. This exception, of course, was the "single, isolated violation" committed six years before.

Though Slack had worked for a time on the atomic project at Oak Ridge after leaving the RDX plant, he had never seen Gold during this period and had never passed any information on atomic energy.

Slack's court-appointed attorney was Ray Jenkins (later known for his role as special counsel to the Senate subcommittee in the Army-Mc-

Carthy hearings). Addressing the court for only about ten minutes, defense attorney Jenkins pleaded for consideration for his client in view of the crime having been committed when Russia was an ally and friendly feelings toward the Soviet Union were at a high point. He noted that Slack had cooperated fully with the FBI and that most of the information narrated by the prosecutor "is bound to have come from the lips of this very defendant. . . ."

Four days later, on September 22, Slack appeared for sentencing. Presented to the Judge by Jenkins were a number of letters written on Slack's behalf, including one from his pastor and one—signed by seventy-nine of his neighbors and friends—declaring him to be "a man of good character and a loyal citizen." Added Jenkins: ". . . they appear to be unanimously good American names." Slack himself offered no statement.

Terming Slack's offense of "national rather than local significance," Judge Robert L. Taylor said:

"It is ironical . . . from the standpoint of this defendant that he committed his crime at a time when the United States and Soviet Russia were allies, but stands before the bar of justice to receive his punishment at a time when the United States and Soviet Russia are stirred by mutual distrust, torn by the clash of opposing ideologies and face each other across the world under the threat of devastating war. The human mind changes with the winds of passion. It is a quality of justice that it does not permit itself to be swayed unduly by the shifting tides."

Then, in seeming disregard of what he had just said, Judge Taylor outdid the government's recommendation by five years and sentenced Alfred Dean Slack to a term of fifteen years in prison.

A week after Slack's sentencing, the now familiar *Times* headline announced: "Another Suspect Is Held in Spy Case." The story began: "The Federal grand jury's continuing atom spy investigation resulted yesterday in the indictment and arrest of a 52-year-old foreign-born structural engineer on a charge of perjury."

The ninth man arrested, Oscar John Vago, was described as a former business partner of Abraham Brothman in a Queens chemical engineering firm at a time when Harry Gold was employed there. Arrested on September 28, Vago was held in $50,000 bail—unusually high for a perjury case—after U. S. Attorney Saypol referred obliquely to evidence of a desire to flee the jurisdiction "in other related cases."

Like the others arrested, Vago was linked by the press to the total spy ring, often through the use of rather questionable techniques. The *Daily News*, for example, ran a photo of Vago side by side with one of Morton Sobell, under the joint caption—"Entangled in spy hunt." On another occasion, Vago was pictured in the *Journal-American*, manacled to Julius Rosenberg.

Actually, what Vago's perjury may have had to do with the spy investigation was difficult to discern; he allegedly had lied to a grand jury about the duration of a visit to Hungary twenty years before. Soon after his arrest, Vago's attorney—pleading unsuccessfully for a reduction of bail to $10,000—revealed that his client had voluntarily returned to the grand jury within a week to recant his original testimony.

On October 10, a new indictment* was voted against the Rosenbergs and Yakovlev. This time, two additional persons were included as defendants: Morton Sobell and David Greenglass. Greenglass's changed status— from co-conspirator to defendant—meant that he now was formally charged with a criminal offense in the forthcoming New York trial and faced the possibility of punishment.

On October 18, Greenglass pleaded guilty, but remained unsentenced. From numerous press accounts, it was obvious that Greenglass and his wife (still named only as a co-conspirator) would testify for the prosecution against the Rosenbergs.

During a period of about four months, nine Americans had been presented to the public—through newspaper headlines and stories inspired by official government press releases and statements—as atom spies and members of the Klaus Fuchs spy ring. In 1950, few if any Americans noticed serious inaccuracies in these characterizations; most people reacted not so much to any *individual* arrest as to the *total* impact of all nine. Like the Congressional charges of the early postwar years, each arrest followed the next so rapidly—accompanied by such a profusion of publicity—that one accusation could hardly be separated from another with any degree of analytic objectivity.

What appeared eminently clear at the time was that a Soviet-directed atomic espionage ring of substantial size—staffed by American traitors— was being diligently ferreted out by the FBI. From newspaper accounts, the evidence seemed overwhelming—even if somewhat difficult to follow.

The continuing arrests produced undisguised gloating among some of those who had long warned of the need to protect the nation's atomic secrets from Soviet spies.

Commented Hearst columnist Bob Considine:

"Haven't heard much lately from the Pinks and the sincere Liberals who once went in for heavy breast-beating in behalf of the so-called 'sanctity of the scientist.' Where are they, now that the arrests and confessions are coming in?"

The answer to Considine's question was that many of the liberals who had spoken out in behalf of Condon and others they believed unfairly attacked by the Un-American Activities Committee were mute and bewildered now. While a number of Americans had previously been accused

---

* The defendants were actually tried on a third superseding indictment, returned January 31, 1951.

by Congressional committees or the press of being atom spies, no one had ever before been legally charged with such an offense. Wild Congressional accusations might be dismissed, but nine arrests and indictments by federal grand juries could hardly be brushed aside.

Begrudingly, many liberals were ready to admit that the political right had proved its point regarding the dangers from the enemy within.

CHAPTER 12

BLUEPRINTS FROM A CELLAR CLOSET

The first actual trial of any of the nine Americans arrested during 1950 and linked with the Klaus Fuchs atom-spy ring opened in New York City's federal courthouse at Foley Square on November 8 of that year before Judge Irving R. Kaufman. The defendants were Abraham Brothman and Miriam Moskowitz, both of whom pleaded innocent. The prosecutor was U. S. Attorney Irving H. Saypol, aided by three assistants including Roy M. Cohn.

Both defendants had been labeled A-spies by the press at the time of their arrest that past summer. Now newspaper headlines unabashedly heralded the start of an atomic espionage trial (*Daily News:* "Gold Prepares To Testify Against 2 In Atom Spy Ring" and "Bail Cancelled For 2 On Trial In Atom Plot"; *Herald Tribune:* "Two Go On Trial In Atomic Spy Case, Lose Bail—Saypol Links Brothman and Miss Moskowitz to 'World Communist Conspiracy'").

However, Brothman and Miss Moskowitz were charged, not with espionage, but with conspiring with Harry Gold to impede a federal grand jury investigation in 1947. An additional charge against Brothman alone was that he had agreed with Gold on a false explanation of their associations with each other and others and had influenced Gold to tell this manufactured story to the grand jury.

In mid-June 1947, a federal grand jury had been convened in New York City to begin what proved to be a fruitless, year-long investigation of a tale of extensive espionage activity recounted to the FBI some time before by Elizabeth T. Bentley, a self-confessed Soviet spy courier.

In preparation for this grand jury investigation, the FBI had interviewed numerous people who might have had some knowledge of Miss Bentley's story. On May 29, 1947, two FBI agents called on Abraham Brothman at the office of his small Queens firm of consulting chemists and engineers called A. Brothman Associates. The agents brought along photos of Miss Bentley and a Jacob Golos, then deceased, who Miss Bentley had alleged was her espionage superior and lover.

Informing Brothman that they were investigating a matter of possible espionage, the agents showed him Golos's photo, which he said he could not identify. However, after seeing a photo of Miss Bentley, Brothman admitted that he had known both individuals about ten years before. He explained that after hearing the word "espionage" he had not wanted to get involved, for fear of harming his business.

Brothman then told the agents that between about 1938 and 1942 he had been associated by contract with Hendrick Manufacturing Co. Golos (known to him under a different name which he could not recall) had come to his New York City office, probably through ads he had placed in chemical engineering trade journals, and offered to try to get him some business with the Russian government—with which he claimed to have connections. During meetings in Manhattan restaurants with Golos and later Miss Bentley—whom he had known as Helen and believed to be Golos's secretary—he had turned over blueprints to them for the purpose of obtaining contracts. The blueprints, which were his own, sometimes were returned and sometimes were not, but he still had the originals of most of them. He showed a number of blueprints to the agents.

Asked if anyone else ever had come to his office representing either Golos or Helen, Brothman mentioned a chemist to whom he also had turned over blueprints. He had become friendly with this individual over the years and had finally hired the man, who was now employed at the firm's Elmhurst, Queens laboratory. A few hours later the agents visited the laboratory to talk with the chemist that Brothman had told them about. This was the FBI's first introduction to Harry Gold.

After interviewing Gold in New York City, FBI agents also visited him at his home in Philadelphia to inquire about any blueprints he might have there. With Gold's permission, the agents searched his house, but evidently saw nothing incriminating.

Subpoenaed before the grand jury several months later, Brothman emphasized again that his dealings with Golos and Miss Bentley had been related entirely to business. Golos was to receive a fee if, through his intervention, a contract was secured from Amtorg—the official Soviet trade agency in the United States.

At the time, Brothman asserted, the Hendrick company was exploiting a number of his inventions and he did some of his own sales work. Lacking secretarial help, he dictated explanations of the uses of his equipment to Miss Bentley. All the information he gave her subsequently appeared in some twenty to twenty-four articles he had published; he had no access to any engineering developments other than his own.

Called before the grand jury about a week after Brothman's appearance, Harry Gold generally corroborated his employer's testimony. At a Philadelphia chapter meeting of the American Chemical Society, a friend (now deceased) had introduced him to Golos, who had hired him to pick up Brothman's blueprints and evaluate the chemical processes. Gold told the grand jury an extremely detailed story regarding Golos's failure to meet with him again or remunerate him for his work, commenting that he had decided eventually that the man was a "phony."

No charges were brought against either Brothman or Gold as a result of the 1947 grand jury inquiry. Miss Moskowitz had not been involved in the investigation at all.

Some time after his arrest in May 1950, however, Harry Gold recanted the testimony he had given the grand jury three years earlier, claiming that his former employer, Brothman, had persuaded him to lie in order to conceal their espionage relationship. He now asserted that he never had known Golos and that his detailed story about him was completely untrue. According to Gold's revised account, his first meeting with Abraham Brothman was a carefully prearranged rendezvous—carried out under instructions from his Soviet espionage superior, an Amtorg official named Semen M. Semenov, alias Sam.

Ostensibly, therefore, the main issue to be decided at the Brothman-Moskowitz trial was simply whether or not the lies that Gold now said he had told the 1947 grand jury had been made at Brothman's behest. Actually, most of the trial was devoted to what U. S. Attorney Saypol termed "evidence of activities in the interests of the Russian government, of membership and affiliation and activities connected with . . . the Communist Party." The logical inference of the prosecution seemed to be that an effort to conceal such "activities" was the motive for Brothman's subornation of perjury. No motive for Miss Moskowitz's alleged participation in the conspiracy was advanced.

Defense attorney William Kleinman, on the other hand, told the jury that Gold was a man with a "very devious and distorted mind . . . . without honor, without a vestige of truth in him. . . ." Kleinman claimed that "Gold has an insane hatred against Miss Moskowitz. Whether for real or fancied reasons, he will do anything in the world to destroy her and to destroy Brothman at the present time. . . ."

The defense attorney referred to Amtorg as "a perfectly proper and legal agency doing business under the laws of our country purchasing things for Soviet Russia." He said that Brothman was never in possession of any military or atomic secrets and that his dealings with Amtorg were in pursuit of harmless business contracts.

To prove its case, the prosecution relied primarily upon the testimony of two witnesses—Elizabeth Bentley and Harry Gold. Miss Bentley, forty-two, already widely known at the time as an ex-Communist "spy queen," had testified frequently in the previous few years before several different Congressional committees and federal grand juries. This, however, was her first appearance as a witness in a court of law where—contrary to the procedures in Congressional hearings—she could be subjected to cross-examination by an attorney for the accused.

She told of being introduced to Brothman by Jacob Golos in a Manhattan restaurant in spring 1940. After dinner, "Mr. Golos explained to Mr. Brothman that it would be rather difficult for him in the future to see him each week or each two weeks, and that therefore I would take his place in order to bring him directives from the Communist Party, to collect his Communist Party dues and to collect any material that he had to be relayed to Mr. Golos."

(Brothman had sworn before the 1947 grand jury that he had never been a Communist Party member and had belonged to the Young Communist League only very briefly while a teen-ager.)

Miss Bentley said that while she knew Brothman they had met frequently at various restaurants and that she was "the representative of the Communist Party" from whom Brothman took instructions. Their meetings, as she described them, had a semi-social, semi-sinister quality:

"Usually we first had something to eat. By this time it was fairly late and then during the meal I would explain the latest Communist Party policy and theories to Mr. Brothman or he would talk a bit about himself, and then afterwards he would hand me the blueprints and sometimes he would dictate a very involved technical explanation of what the blueprints were all about."

Miss Bentley said that the blueprints, along with her transcribed and typed notes of Brothman's technical explanations, were turned over to Golos. If Brothman gave her a blueprint that he required back, she would have it copied in an "obscure" blueprint shop. Once Brothman told her "he had access to blueprints for what he termed a kettle to be made for the Edgewater Arsenal." Later she relayed to Brothman the message that Golos "would be very much interested in obtaining that particular blueprint."

On several occasions, Brothman had asked her "if the engineers in the Amtorg were satisfied with the blueprints that they were getting." Eventually, "Mr. Brothman was dissatisfied with dealing with Mr. Golos and myself. He felt that neither of us were engineers or had any technical background, and that we did not understand his explanations as to the blueprints. He began to ask if we couldn't put him in touch with an engineer with whom he could talk them over."

Inexplicably, when Brothman was told that he was being turned over to a new contact he at first refused, finally acquiescing when reminded by Miss Bentley and Golos of his obligation as a Communist to "accept new assignments uncomplainingly." Miss Bentley then informed Brothman that the new contact would slide into the right front seat of his parked car at an appointed hour, and asked Brothman to give her his automobile license number. Said she:

"Mr. Brothman objected again. He said he did not understand why he had to meet people via that very odd way, why couldn't I or Mr. Golos do the introducing? I explained to him again that this was a decision of the Communist Party and he must abide by it."

Brothman thereupon allegedly wrote down his license number, which Miss Bentley gave to Golos. The new contact was to identify himself to Brothman by bringing greetings from Helen. Miss Bentley said she did not know who the new contact was and never had met him. The last time she saw Brothman was in the early fall of 1941.

Miss Bentley's testimony, with its cloak-and-dagger overtones, clearly implied that Brothman had been a fellow spy. However, her story lacked any assertion that the material given her by Brothman had been declared to be secret or otherwise classified by any agency of the United States government. Without such proof, any characterization of Brothman's activities as espionage would obviously be completely unwarranted.

On cross-examination, defense attorney Kleinman questioned Miss Bentley repeatedly in an effort to elicit some specific information about the nature of the blueprints. She steadfastly insisted that she never had looked at them, had barely understood a word the engineer had dictated, and could not give even a general idea of what the material dealt with. As for her stenographic notes of the meetings, she had burned them.

Pressed by Kleinman as to the subject matter of the blueprints, Miss Bentley again referred to "kettles," but offered no further elaboration.

KLEINMAN: A kettle like a tea kettle—
BENTLEY: I don't know.

Asked to recall any of the engineering terms that Brothman had used, she could remember only the word "flange." Kleinman vainly persisted in attempting to obtain further information on any aspect of the material she had testified about. Were there, he asked, "any words, Miss Bentley, in the instructions that you received that you did understand, any words in common use?"

The witness replied: "There may have been a few verbs like 'is' and things of that sort, and there may have been a few articles, but I did not understand the meaning of the sentences."

Despite the fact that she did not have "the least idea" what kind of blueprints she was receiving, Miss Bentley testified that she had the "impression" that they were stolen. Questioned by Kleinman about her statement that she had had the blueprints copied in "obscure" shops, Miss Bentley said that she had been instructed by Golos to look "through the phone book and try to find places that would be obscure where they would not ask too many questions."

KLEINMAN: Can you tell by looking at a phone book whether the place is obscure?

BENTLEY: You get a hint. The black type you take for granted are larger and the smaller ones are obscure. . . .

Questioned further, she could not recall either the name or exact location of any of the "obscure" blueprint shops she had frequented.

Miss Bentley had testified to collecting Brothman's Communist Party dues while meeting him to pick up blueprints. Queried by Kleinman, she said Brothman paid his dues irregularly and "under great duress." Asked how much he gave her, she replied: "I am afraid I can't tell you."

KLEINMAN: Could you give us approximately how much it was, a large amount or a small amount?
BENTLEY: I don't know. Communist Party dues shifted so often and the scale was so varied, and I dealt with so many people, I can't tell.

About every aspect of her relationship with Brothman—other than the fact that she had received some kind of blueprints from him ten years before—Miss Bentley's vagueness was impenetrable. Asked what she had told Brothman when he inquired several times as to whether the blueprints were acceptable to Amtorg engineers, she replied: "I didn't know what to tell him because I didn't know what he was talking about." When Kleinman then inquired whether she had not known that Amtorg was a legitimate trade agency, Miss Bentley said she knew little or nothing about Amtorg at the time and "was in complete darkness as to what they did."

Queried about her testimony two years earlier before the Un-American Activities Committee, she said: "Mr. Kleinman, I have told you that unless I see that testimony I cannot tell you what I said there because I have told too many people too many things."

Equally unsuccessful was Kleinman's attempt to learn from the witness what and when she had told grand juries and the FBI about Brothman. She had already testified that she first had talked to the FBI in 1945.

KLEINMAN: Miss Bentley, when did you get through telling your story to the FBI?
BENTLEY: I am not through yet.

Kleinman thereupon asked Judge Kaufman to examine Miss Bentley's pre-trial statements about Brothman for any inconsistencies with her present testimony. The Judge refused, saying that Kleinman's cross-examination had failed to reveal—as was then required by law—any such inconsistencies. Kleinman complained that Miss Bentley's testimony was so unresponsive that it was impossible to make such a showing.

The prosecution's principal witness, Harry Gold, had been in custody nearly six months at the time of the Brothman-Moskowitz trial, but remained unsentenced. The month before, in Philadelphia, the federal prosecutor there had requested a postponement of Gold's sentencing hearing until after January 1, 1951, asserting: ". . . in a case of this importance it is much easier for the government to conduct its investigative phases if this prisoner is unsentenced."

Judge McGranery was reluctant to accede to a continuance. "I know of no case on record," he stated, "where sentence has been deferred for so long a time. . . ." Finally, at the prosecutor's continued urging, the Judge partially yielded, but set the date for December 7.

Like Miss Bentley, Harry Gold was making his first appearance as a trial witness. With the exception of information revealed at the Slack sentencing hearing, none of the espionage activities of Klaus Fuchs's accomplice had ever before been publicly detailed. Undoubtedly, expectations of sensational testimony by Gold regarding atomic spying largely accounted for the wide press coverage accorded the Brothman-Moskowitz trial.

Trial observers remarked on the appearance of Gold, who was said to have lost fifty pounds since his arrest. According to *Time* magazine, the formerly chubby Philadelphia chemist "had improved his hours in jail by dieting" and now had "the shrunken look of an underprivileged cat."

Reported by the *Times* to have testified "unhesitatingly in a precise, even voice," Gold remained on the witness stand for four trial days. After relating that he had "entered into industrial espionage for the Soviet Union" in 1935—turning over information on varnishes and lacquers to a representative of Amtorg—he described his first meeting with Abraham Brothman in 1941.

Gold's story of this meeting tallied in most respects with that of Miss Bentley, with one exception. He testified that he had journeyed to New York from Philadelphia several times to be introduced to Brothman by Sam, his Soviet espionage superior who was also a representative of Amtorg. The introduction never took place because Brothman did not show up. Finally, Sam gave Gold Brothman's automobile license number and other instructions, which Gold wrote down on a small white card.

(The prosecution produced a card, alleged to be the original one on which Gold had written the instructions, and introduced it as a trial exhibit.)

On the evening of September 29, 1941, Gold came to New York, waited at a prearranged time and place until a car came along and, after checking the license number against that on his card, got in. Gold told the driver—Abraham Brothman—"I bring regards from Helen," and introduced himself as Frank Kessler.

Gold's subsequent dealings with Brothman, as pictured in his testimony, appeared to entail enormous expenditures of time and effort by himself and Sam with astonishingly little return for their work.

At their second meeting, Gold told Brothman what industrial information was desired by the Soviet Union and also asked for "any and all information which Abe might find available to him regarding matters of military interest." Although Gold stressed that the meetings were arranged for "an exact minute," Brothman showed up two hours late for their third meeting, bringing nothing. The fourth meeting, held in downtown Manhattan "close to the waterfront," was apparently more fruitful: "This time Abe came on time and he gave me a blueprint of a piece of chemical equipment known as an esterifier."

As was true throughout his long testimony, Gold recounted each and every stage of this meeting in meticulous detail. Asked by prosecutor Saypol what he did with the blueprint of the esterifier, or chemical mixer, Gold replied:

"I put it in a manila envelope I had ready. It is sort of a plain manila envelope. It is the sort that is used to contain $8\frac{1}{2} \times 11$ sheets, and I gave it to Sam in New York City that very night. . . ."

Surprisingly, the very same blueprint of the esterifier that had been given to Sam was then introduced as evidence by the prosecution. Sam, it appeared, had returned the blueprint to Gold because it was incomplete and, over the years, Harry Gold had retained it—along with scores of other blueprints. Gold had kept these residues of his alleged espionage work at his Philadelphia home in a cellar closet so crammed with similar material that, he said, one of the FBI agents jokingly had dubbed it "Fibber McGee's closet."

Over the next few months Gold met with Brothman half a dozen more times, receiving other incomplete blueprints which he did not submit to Sam. He explained that he was "wary" about turning over "fragmentary blueprints" to Sam, because "I had had my knuckles very smartly rapped on a number of occasions." These "fragmentary" blueprints, which Gold had kept in his cellar closet, were then introduced by the prosecution as evidence.

In December 1941, Gold informed Brothman that blueprints could now be copied quickly at Amtorg and returned to him "the same night." He also reprimanded Brothman for submitting "fragmentary bits of information" and failing to keep appointments on time. Brothman replied that he was "irritated" because the Soviet Union did not "appreciate the value of the material he had submitted in the past," claiming he had given Helen and Golos plans regarding high octane gasoline, a turbine-type aircraft engine, and an early model of the jeep.

Gold testified:

"Abe told me that if it was matters of military importance that were desired, and if it were complete plans and complete descriptions of processes, that at that very minute there was on his desk at Hendrick the complete plans plus all of the descriptive material, for the operation of a military explosive plant in Tennessee; that all the blueprints, all of the descriptive material was there, and that he could turn it over to me the next time we met."

Gold then related in elaborate detail his precise plans for meeting Brothman to obtain the explosive plant data. He also told at length of his "split-second arrangements" to transfer this material to Sam.

Some newspapers, hungry for the atomic bomb revelations they had expected from the trial, seized upon this testimony by Gold. In a story headlined "Reds Knew U.S. Had A-Plans in '41, Gold Says," the New York *World-Telegram & Sun* noted that the military explosive referred to by Gold "undoubtedly was the atom bomb, the construction of which was centered in Oak Ridge, Tenn."

Quite aside from the ludicrousness of Brothman having on his desk the many tons of plans for the gigantic isotope separation plants at Oak Ridge, Tennessee, as a matter of record, the first steps by the Army to acquire the Oak Ridge site for the Manhattan Project were not taken until September 1942.

In any event, the matter is academic; Gold said Brothman never showed up for the meeting and no further mention of the "explosive plant" appears in his testimony.

At their very next meeting, however, Brothman allegedly promised Gold that on January 1, 1942, he would give him "the complete plans for a Buna-S synthetic rubber plant plus all of the descriptive material, plus all of the operating data." On New Year's Day, Brothman arrived two hours late to inform Gold that the material was not yet ready. Over the next three months, Gold met Brothman some dozen times. "There was only one matter which I kept pressing Abe about and that was the complete Buna-S report."

Gold resorted to heroic measures to obtain the promised report. Once he rented a room at the Prince George Hotel in Brooklyn where he planned to help Brothman complete the report, but the latter did not show up and Gold's repeated phone calls to his office and home failed to locate him. Another time, Gold and Brothman arranged to spend a weekend at an upstate New York hotel where they could work on the report and "even play some handball." Late as usual, Brothman arrived to say that he couldn't make the weekend because "his wife had some guests for the evening, and he would get in trouble at home if he did. So the completion of the Buna-S report was once more postponed." Finally, in early April 1942, Gold engaged a two-room suite at the Hotel New Yorker and worked with Brothman through the night until 6 A.M., collating and otherwise putting together the two-hundred-page report, which also included twenty-five or fifty blueprints.

Added to the growing pile of prosecution exhibits from Gold's cellar closet were some handwritten notes by Gold on Buna-S and some "fragmentary" Buna-S blueprints, which Gold said he received during his dozen meetings with Brothman but did not "risk" turning over to his espionage superior, Sam.

The Buna-S report, which was the first material from Brothman given to the Russians and kept by them, led to a zany hoax perpetrated by Gold. He had, he testified, lied to Brothman "that a very important Soviet dignitary, a Russian official, was soon coming to this country, that he was making a special trip here for the explicit purpose of meeting with Abe and talking to him." According to Gold, Brothman readily agreed to meet this official.

At the meeting, held in a New York hotel, Sam played the role of the fictitious "Soviet dignitary" who had traveled from the Soviet Union just to meet Brothman. Sam "gave Abe a very praiseworthy report about the Buna-S process. He stated that it was equivalent in value to two or three brigades of men to Russia." During the evening, Sam also promised Brothman stenographic help and chatted about mathematics with him.

Commented the *Times*: "The meeting at which Semenov allegedly thanked Brothman in the name of the Soviet Union, as described by Gold, was held in an atmosphere of intrigue and mystery that proved a little confusing even to Semenov."

The reason for this "confusion" was evident from Gold's testimony that he knew Semenov as "Sam" but had introduced him to Brothman as "George"; Semenov, in turn, knew Gold's real name while Brothman, at this time, knew Gold as "Frank Kessler." Despite these vaudevillian complications, Gold said that after the hotel meeting "Abe told me that I had given him a thrill that he could never forget."

In mid-1942, Brothman left the Hendrick company to become a partner in a small chemical engineering design firm. The first material Gold received from this new source was data on a nickel catalyst plant, which he said could be used for the preparation of cooking shortenings or aviation gasoline. Next, in early 1943, Brothman provided information on an aerosol insecticide "bomb" and Gold—who did not indicate whether or not he ever was reimbursed—hired a stenographer at ten dollars a session, for several months of weekly meetings on the subject at Brothman's office. Finally, from July 1943 to the end of that year, Gold met with Brothman on Sunday mornings to learn about a magnesium powder plant that could make flares or tracer bullets.

None of this material, gathered by Gold over a period of a year and a half, ever was turned over to Sam because "my Soviet superior told me they already had these processes." Thus, as testified to by Gold, the sum total of all the data from Brothman that actually had been given to the Russians and been accepted by them was the Buna-S report plus a report on various types of chemical mixing equipment.

From Gold's bulging cellar closet, the prosecution produced and introduced as evidence "fragmentary" blueprints of the nickel catalyst process, the stenographer's transcribed and typed notes on the insecticide device, and Gold's own notes from his months of futile Sunday morning meetings on the magnesium powder plant.

While all this extracurricular "industrial espionage" activity was in progress and Gold was receiving "a continual barrage of orders from Sam," the Philadelphia chemist also was holding down a regular job at the Pennsylvania Sugar Company at which, he said, he worked between sixty and seventy hours weekly. In addition, Gold frequently undertook legitimate free-lance assignments for Brothman and others, sometimes utilizing the facilities of the well-equipped Pennsylvania Sugar laboratory. Inasmuch as these assignments were performed by Gold concurrently with his alleged role as an espionage courier for Brothman, the two areas of their relationship appeared at times to merge. An example was Gold's assertion that he had done free-lance work for Brothman on a nickel catalyst process, a subject he claimed he also had pursued as part of his "industrial espionage" endeavors with Brothman.

Gold received additional free-lance assignments from Brothman when, in 1944, the latter organized a new firm, A. Brothman Associates. Brothman also offered Gold full-time employment, which he finally accepted in 1946. Pay at A. Brothman Associates became very "irregular" in April 1947, and sometimes there were no salaries for long periods. Gold left the firm in June 1948.

Cross-examined by Kleinman, Gold said most of his Soviet contacts were regular Amtorg employees, who also secured information by "illegal" means. He admitted that Amtorg had bought steel, rubber, chemicals, and other industrial products on the open market for shipment to the Soviet Union and that the information he obtained from Brothman could have been purchased by the Russians from American companies. Explaining Amtorg's need for pilfered data, Gold said some American businesses refused to deal with Soviet representatives while others deliberately sold them incomplete processes.

During his direct examination by Saypol, Gold had proved to be far less modest than Miss Bentley regarding his technical knowledge and had spouted chemical nomenclature verbosely. However, when Kleinman—probably primed by his client—interrogated Gold, the witness disclaimed any special competence concerning the subjects he had discoursed on earlier, insisting that his chemical engineering knowledge was "rudimentary"; that he could not read blueprints; and that he was not an "expert" in industrial chemistry. He had, he said, no technical knowledge of synthetic rubber and was unaware that processes for its manufacture were known long before he met Brothman or that in 1941 synthetic rubber tires were sold in the United States.

Kleinman sought to cast doubt on whether Gold had turned over even the Buna-S and mixing equipment reports to the Russians. Shown a sixty-seven-page manuscript on Buna-S by Kleinman, Gold said the manuscript appeared identical with the one he had given the Russians, but believed the latter one was thicker. Similarly, he agreed that the appearance of a looseleaf notebook of Brothman's filled with data on mixing equipment matched his earlier description of the mixing equipment report, but thought the rings were bigger on the looseleaf book he had passed to Sam.

Shown a textbook that described one of the processes he had mentioned, Gold said the Russians did not want textbook processes but "processes in actual operation in plants." Questioned further, he did not know whether any of Brothman's processes were in "actual operation," and agreed that the blueprints represented proposed processes that were submitted to prospective buyers.

Kleinman subpoenaed from the New York Public Library technical publications containing articles by Brothman. Comparing the blueprints and notes from his cellar closet with some of Brothman's published articles, Gold said there appeared to be no "salient" differences.

U. S. Attorney Saypol objected that whether or not the prosecution exhibits were the same as published articles "is wholly immaterial."

Replied Kleinman: "I think it is highly material. There was a cloak of mystery about these patents and papers—"

Bolstering the defense's contention that Brothman wanted to sell commercial processes to Amtorg was the testimony of Hendrick's New York sales manager, who had worked with Brothman in the late Thirties and early Forties. He stated that as far as he knew Hendrick did not deal with any classified or otherwise secret material during those years; that Brothman had done some of his own sales work for processes he designed himself; that the Buna-S process was Brothman's own design which he was trying to sell; and that a model of Brothman's mixing equipment had been publicly displayed at a 1940 trade show.

An editor of a McGraw-Hill engineering publication testified that his magazine had published many articles by Brothman—on mixing equipment, Buna-S, and other subjects. Regarding Buna-S, the editor said that Brothman first had brought in a long manuscript which had been held for a year, shortened considerably, and finally published in March 1942. He recalled that Brothman had been trying to interest the United States government in his Buna-S process.

Generally speaking, Kleinman's main tack was to show that the material that Gold had testified about or that had been introduced by the prosecution from the cellar closet all referred to "commonly known processes . . . well known and easily available." This strategy backfired when Judge Kaufman, with Saypol's agreement, said that the prosecution did not contend that the material was secret. The Judge stated that secrecy was not an issue, that the material from Gold's closet had been introduced merely to show "association" between Gold and Brothman.

The prosecution, however, had already devoted a major portion of its case to testimony plainly inferring espionage activities. With the prosecution now conceding that the material was not of a secret nature, any evidence produced by the defense to show that the blueprints did not violate the espionage law was immaterial.

Once again, the case was reduced to its simplest proportions: A matter of Gold's credibility vs. Brothman's. The defendants did not take the witness stand, but some of the information elicited by Kleinman during his cross-examination of Gold reflected seriously on the credibility of the prosecution's key witness.

Gold testified that he had been instructed by Sam to tell Brothman at their first meeting that he was a married man with children, but that Sam had left the details of the story to him. The reason for these instructions was "one sad experience in the past when I had shown myself as a single man and the person involved had not been very cooperative, he thought I was too unstable."

Gold admitted that after he had accepted a job with the Brothman firm in 1946, he had elaborated the fantasies about his personal life. Unable to blame his lies at that late date on Sam, he explained that he "had become so tangled up in this web of lies that it was easier to continue telling an occasional one than to try and straighten the whole hideous mess out."

Bachelor Gold had told Brothman and others that he was married to a girl named Sarah O'Ken. He had met her while courting another girl with one blue eye and one brown eye. Sarah had formerly gone with an underworld character named Nigger Nate. His mother-in-law was a slovenly woman and a poor housekeeper and his father-in-law did not have much money. He and Sarah had to postpone their wedding because of financial difficulties. After their marriage, they had lived in a small apartment and had later purchased a house. They had twin children, a girl and a boy named Essie and David. One of the twins was stricken with polio. Finally, a rift developed between him and his wife and they separated.

Among the numerous other falsehoods that Gold had told Brothman was that his very-much-alive brother, Joe, had died overseas while in the Army in Hollandia, New Guinea. (Gold himself had been 4-F because of hypertension.)

Gold exhibited considerable skill in maintaining this complicated deception—for years he had completely fooled many people, including his friend and employer, Brothman. Obviously impressed by his own imaginative powers, Gold exclaimed at one point in his testimony: "It is a wonder steam didn't come out of my ears at times."

Gold's fantasies frequently were fashioned from the lives of real people he knew. His description of his first small apartment with Sarah, for example, actually corresponded to the appearance of the apartment of a close friend who was married. Many of the stories about his wife admittedly referred to his mother.

Asked if he had told Brothman that "as a result of your being away from home . . . that Sarah resented your absences—your wife Sarah," Gold replied: "Actually it was my mother."

Kleinman inquired if he had told Brothman on declining a 1945 job offer "that you had made an excellent purchase of a house in a suburb of Philadelphia and that your wife would not like to be transplanted from that place to New York?"

Said Gold· "That was partly false but it was based on truth. My mother and I had purchased a house and I didn't want to be transplanted to New York."

In September 1947, while Gold was in New York working for Brothman, his mother died. For whatever personal reasons, afterward he was obviously troubled by guilt. Said he: "I told people that I blamed myself for my mother's death. . . ."

Some of Gold's other testimony about his ideas and motivations rivals his fantasy family life in peculiarity. The former Soviet spy courier testified that he thought Communists were "a lot of whacked-up Bohemians"; had never been a member of the Communist Party; and had always "registered as a Democrat because I believed in general what the Democratic Party was aiming for. . . ." Nevertheless, he said that—on instructions—he had tried without success to collect Brothman's Communist Party dues "in which he was in arrears to me."

He began his espionage career out of sympathy for the Soviet people and as "a debt of gratitude" to a friend, Tom Black, who had gotten him a job and was importuning him to join the Communist Party. Gold testified that he finally agreed to engage in espionage for the Soviet Union to get "Black off my neck about joining the Communist Party. I didn't want to. I didn't like them."

Gold presented a rather weirdly mechanistic description of his mental processes as a spy, curiously reminiscent of an explanation offered eight months earlier by his alleged former espionage confederate, Klaus Fuchs. In that part of his confession made public, Fuchs had characterized as "a controlled schizophrenia" the process by which he had purportedly concealed his thoughts "in two separate compartments." Said Gold: "When I went on a mission for the Soviet Union I used a one-track mind. . . . I forgot work, family, everything. When I returned I just turned the switch and I used a one-track mind in regard to my work."

It was this "one-track mind," Gold claimed, that led him to overlook his "Fibber McGee's closet" and make no attempt to hide any of the allegedly incriminating data stored there. Said he: "The huge amount of material that was found in my home represents . . . an all-too-successful attempt to obliterate all memory of my espionage activities."

By 1945, the Russians had told Gold that they "had no further use" for Brothman and "to stay away from him" because he was "hot." Gold said he "totally forgot" this warning when he went to work for Brothman in 1946.

Testifying before the 1947 grand jury, Harry Gold had identified himself as chief chemist at A. Brothman Associates, due to become a partner soon. Subsequently, this hope for advancement in the firm had not been realized. At the Brothman-Moskowitz trial, Gold commented: "When there was no money, I was a partner. When there was money, I became an employee. . . ." In 1948, Gold had spoken with an attorney regarding $4000 in back salary owed him and had tried without success to get Brothman to sign an IOU. He had left A. Brothman Associates that year after a bitter business altercation that ended with an "indignation" meeting that broke up "acrimoniously." Finally, Gold said, Brothman had changed the locks on the door of the firm's laboratory to keep him out. The next time the two men saw each other was over two years later—after Brothman's arrest.

The forgotten defendant at the trial was Miss Moskowitz. The formal charge against her, conspiring to obstruct justice, provided no details— she was not named in any of the overt acts of the indictment. The single witness against her, Harry Gold, mentioned her only infrequently and in such oblique terms that it was impossible to judge whether she had been a conscious participant in the alleged conspiracy. Gold testified that Miss Moskowitz had been present at some of the dinner and other meetings at which he and Brothman discussed their FBI interviews and grand jury appearances and indicated that she had given them her approval and encouragement, but he told almost nothing about what she had said.

Unlike Harry Gold, Miss Moskowitz had been a partner in the firm of A. Brothman Associates. Testifying about this aspect of their relationship, Gold was more explicit. He said that she had treated him badly and without sufficient dignity and was "unkind" and that he had "found her to have a violent temper" and "avoided her."

In a case with much rather confusing testimony, where the prosecution produced masses of blueprints and other technical material allegedly related to espionage activities—and then declared the secrecy of the blueprints to be immaterial—the jury was presented with but one specific item of documentary evidence to help them decide the only issue on which the verdict could be based: The obstruction of justice charge. This evidence was the small white card on which Gold allegedly wrote his instructions from Sam for his first meeting with Brothman in 1941.

The discovery of this card was described by an FBI agent who testified that on June 3 and June 6, 1950, he was assigned to search the basement of Gold's Philadelphia home and "found a large wooden box, approximately three feet square and 30 inches deep, filled with papers and blueprints. . . . There was similar material in a closet approximately four feet across, running from the floor to the ceiling and approximately two feet deep." There was at least twenty times as much material in the cellar as had been introduced in court.

The FBI agent said that on June 3 he pulled from Gold's cellar closet a folder marked "A. B. Stuff." From the folder he had extracted a small white card bearing in Gold's handwriting Brothman's automobile license number and other information, including the remark, "Give regards from Helen."

No questions were asked the agent as to whether, during what Gold called a "cursory" search of his house for blueprints in 1947, the FBI had looked into the cellar. Neither was any explanation requested from the FBI witness as to why his search of the cellar closet and discovery of the little white card had not occurred until nearly two weeks after Harry Gold's arrest.

After deliberating three hours and fifty minutes, the jury found both defendants guilty. Judge Kaufman immediately congratulated the U. S. Attorney for his "ingenuity in searching the statute books and finding the obstruction of justice statute, because there was a serious question about the statute of limitations having run on the matter of espionage itself." Actually, the statute of limitations at the time for espionage was ten years, which would seem to have been ample in this instance for prosecution of an espionage case—if evidence were available.

Judge Kaufman also had high praise for the FBI: "Their work is truly amazing, particularly their work on Mr. Gold. It is just amazing. I think that Mr. Hoover and the Bureau should be congratulated. . . ."

Later, at the defendants' sentencing, the Judge, who had stated during the trial that the secrecy of the blueprints from Gold's cellar closet was not an issue, now commented that "the obstruction of justice, serious by itself, was laid in the background of espionage."

Referring to the imposition of sentence as "almost a God-like function," Judge Kaufman expressed "regret that the law under which these defendants are to be sentenced is so limited and so restricted that I can only pass the sentence which I am going to pass, for I consider their offense in this case to be of such gross magnitude. I have no sympathy or mercy for these defendants in my heart, none whatsoever."

He sentenced both to the maximum term permissible under the statute: Brothman, seven years and a $15,000 fine*; Miss Moskowitz, two years and a $10,000 fine.

---

* On appeal, Brothman's sentence was reduced on a technical issue to two years and a $10,000 fine.

Whether the story Harry Gold originally told the 1947 grand jury of his first meeting with Brothman, or his later one—or neither—correctly represents events nine years before the Brothman-Moskowitz trial is impossible to say. What can be said, unequivocally, is that the press accusations against Brothman and Miss Moskowitz, at the time of their arrests, regarding their membership with Klaus Fuchs and others in an atomic espionage ring was shown by the trial to be so much moonshine.

At Miss Moskowitz's sentencing, Saypol stated: "There is no evidence that she engaged in espionage." As for Brothman, we cannot, of course, know what was in his mind when he gave blueprints to Miss Bentley and Gold in the early Forties. But in any event—no matter what Brothman may have believed he was doing—the only material that Harry Gold claimed to have actually turned over to the Russians was some designs for chemical mixers and the Buna-S process. The latter, despite the wide publicity given to it and Judge Kaufman's assertion regarding the "gross magnitude" of the offense, was simply a *proposed* process for making synthetic rubber that, so far as is known, never was put to any practical use.

Is it likely that Soviet technicians were so hopelessly ignorant of synthetic rubber manufacture in 1942 that they urgently required the untried process of Abraham Brothman, a twenty-seven-year-old engineer? In this connection, a comment by former AEC chairman Gordon Dean is instructive: ". . . much of the Russian work in chemistry from 1921 to 1935 was steered in the direction of synthetic rubber. Russia needed synthetic rubber, and Russia got it during that period by means of an all-out applied-research program. Independently of the rest of the world, she developed a means for producing synthetic rubber. . . ."

Ironically, and completely unmentioned in the Brothman-Moskowitz trial, during the same period that Harry Gold allegedly was filling his cellar closet with blueprints from Brothman and chasing after the coveted Buna-S report, the Soviet Union was receiving Lend-Lease shipments from the United States in the amount of $11 billion. Describing this vast outpouring of wartime aid, the Joint Congressional Committee on Atomic Energy stated:

"The shipments included basic raw materials, explosives, shells and guns, medical supplies, chemicals, combat vehicles, airplanes, and complete alcohol, synthetic rubber, and petroleum cracking plants, together with the requisite engineering drawings, operating and maintenance manuals, spare parts lists, and other pertinent documents. . . . A large volume of blueprints, documents, and papers was required for such . . . items as the oil refinery and the synthetic rubber plants shipped to Russia."

CHAPTER 13

AN "EXTRAORDINARILY SELFLESS PERSON"

On December 7, 1950—over six months after the sudden, late-evening announcement from Washington of his arrest—the American accomplice of Klaus Fuchs was escorted into the Philadelphia courtroom of federal Judge James P. McGranery to be sentenced as an atom spy.

Observed *Time* magazine: "There was something oddly inanimate about jail-pallid, soft-eyed little Chemist Harry Gold. . . . He had a strained unhealthy air and he sat almost immobile, with his eyes straight ahead."

The previous July Gold had pleaded guilty to a charge of conspiring with Fuchs and two Soviet agents—Sam (Semen M. Semenov) and John (Anatoli A. Yakovlev)—to obtain atomic energy information for the Soviet Union. At that time, the prosecutor, Gerald Gleeson, had said the government might "not wish to present any evidence at all with respect to the commission of the crime," but Judge McGranery had indicated that he would insist on "enough evidence to satisfy me beyond any doubt as to the crimes charged." However, at the sentencing hearing, Gleeson confined his presentation to the reading of a rather brief "summary of the facts from the viewpoint of the government," but presented no evidence.

According to Gleeson, in 1935, an acquaintance—who had "approached Gold in an effort to interest him in working as a Soviet espionage agent"—introduced him to a Paul Smith in New York City. From Smith, Gold learned that the Soviet Union wished to obtain "certain industrial information" from Gold's employer, the Pennsylvania Sugar Company in Philadelphia. Over the next few years, Gold furnished "Russian espionage agents" with material concerning processes being worked on in the sugar company's laboratory.

Later, while a student at Xavier University in Cincinnati between 1938 and 1940, Gold saw an employee of Wright Field in nearby Dayton in an unsuccessful effort "to develop a source of information which would be of value to the Soviet Union."

Soon after graduating from Xavier and returning to Philadelphia, Gold met an Amtorg official, Semenov, for whom he served "as a go-between in transmitting industrial information." Early in 1944, Semenov told Gold that "he was to undertake an extremely important assignment and that he would have to drop all his contacts and discontinue all work that he had been doing for the Soviet agents." The assignment was to meet Klaus Fuchs.

When Gold and Fuchs met in New York City on a Saturday afternoon in late February or early March 1944, Fuchs had identified himself as a member of the British mission to the Manhattan Engineering District, doing work "of a very confidential nature." During a total of five New York City meetings, Gold twice received from Fuchs "a packet of papers." Within a half hour, Gold turned this material over to his new contact, Anatoli Yakovlev, a Soviet consulate employee who had replaced Semenov. Once, "Gold opened this packet of papers and saw that the information contained therein concerned highly confidential information pertaining to the national defense of the United States."

Around August 1944, Fuchs failed to show up for several scheduled meetings. On instructions from Yakovlev, Gold went looking for the British scientist and, after learning that he had moved from his Manhattan apartment, traveled to Cambridge, Massachusetts—where Fuchs's sister lived. She was said to have informed Gold that Fuchs would visit her for the Christmas holidays.

Returning to the sister's home around early 1945, Gold met Fuchs, who revealed that "he was stationed at a place called Los Alamos" and briefly discussed "the nature of the work at the research project." The two arranged to meet in Santa Fe, New Mexico, in June 1945. Fuchs gave Gold "a packet of papers" which Gold delivered to Yakovlev in New York City—returning at the same time $1500 which Fuchs had refused to accept.

When Fuchs and Gold saw each other again in Santa Fe in June 1945, they held "a long discussion as to the work being done at the highly secret defense project" and planned for a September meeting. Fuchs turned over to Gold "a large packet of papers," which Gold brought to Yakovlev.

During the September Santa Fe meeting, Fuchs provided another "packet of papers" and discussed arrangements for future contacts upon his return to England. At the conclusion of this September meeting, "Gold returned to Albuquerque, New Mexico, where he stayed overnight at the Hilton Hotel and registered under his own name."

Gleeson's description of the material transmitted in these alleged meetings between Fuchs and Gold was so guarded and circumspect that he did not mention even the words "atomic bomb" or "atomic energy." In fact, the prosecutor's statement disclosed that, with one exception, Gold had not looked at the "papers" he claimed to have received from Fuchs and so could have supplied the authorities with little specific information about their contents.

Gold's distinguished defense counsel, John D. M. Hamilton—after requesting several FBI agents familiar with the case "to correct me if I make any misstatement of facts"—filled in many particulars of his client's information-gathering activities on behalf of the Soviet Union. Said Hamilton:

"Mr. Gleeson made a statement . . . that I do not disagree with factually, I disagree with the connotation. He said they approached Gold with the thought of his becoming a Russian spy. I think the word 'espionage' has a broader connotation than what was posed to him at that time. 'Espionage' usually means the transmission of information or the obtaining of information in connection with the activities of governments, and that was not true in this case in any event. . . ."

Interestingly, Hamilton's assertion that his client's early activities could not be characterized as "espionage" contradicted Gold's own testimony only three weeks before at the Brothman-Moskowitz trial, where he had stated: "I was engaged steadily in espionage for the Soviet Union from November of 1935 until February of 1946."

Hamilton enumerated the material Gold had given to his first Soviet contact, Paul Smith, concerning processes of the Pennsylvania Sugar Company:

"Now, during the time that he was engaged in meeting with Paul Smith, I want to say this to your Honor unequivocally, all the information which Gold gave to Paul Smith had to do with . . . two processes: One was a process for the production of industrial solvents, which go into the making of lacquer and paints of certain types, and the other was a process that went into the production of absolute ethyl alcohol, which is used in pharmaceuticals. There was nothing further passed between the two men."

Gold's second contact, Steve Schwartz, who replaced Smith in the fall of 1936, received information on only one additional subject, "ethyl chloride, which was used as a local anaesthesia. So that up to this point we have only three matters which he had turned over to them, although several years have now elapsed."

Hamilton then made this fascinating revelation about his client, whose lies in 1947 to the FBI and grand jury and imaginative phantasies about a nonexistent wife and twin children had already been aired at the Brothman-Moskowitz trial:

Steve Schwartz, the second contact, had "tried to get Gold to recruit. . . . Gold made one sorry attempt at it and came to the conclusion that while he was willing to do the work he was doing he was unwilling to recruit others, and he went into a process or procedure that would be amusing if it were not, in my opinion, so dramatic. He began feeding these people in New York, these Soviet agents, fictitious names, any number of them, and would report to them on what he was doing with these fictitious names."

With Gold's third contact, Fred, whom he met in September 1937, "the custom or practice of supplying . . . fictitious names was continued." Gold also furnished Fred with data on a process for "obtaining carbon dioxide from flue gases, and that too is simply an industrial process, for carbon dioxide has no more sinister use . . . than the preparation of refrigerants and the operation of such things as soda fountains."

Regarding Gleeson's reference to an effort by Gold while at Xavier University—between 1938 and 1940—"to develop a source of information" from an employee of Wright Field in Dayton, Ohio, Hamilton emphasized that Gold never had received any material from this man. "In fact, I think it was in that period that he also again resorted to fiction in that he made up trips to Dayton which he never took. . . ."

For his next contact, Semenov, Gold picked up material from two sources: Alfred Dean Slack and Abraham Brothman.

Slack, whom Gold first met in Rochester, New York, in October 1940, provided material dealing with "commercial photography" and once went to West Virginia to obtain information "with regard to nylon salts . . . again a commercial use." Whatever the nature of Slack's photographic data—and Hamilton said that some related to aerial photography and so might have "a war potential"—the government had made clear during Slack's sentencing hearing that the passage by him to Gold of this information from Eastman Kodak was not illegal, violating neither federal nor state laws.

As for the material received by Gold from Brothman, Hamilton mentioned several items that had been discussed at length in the recent trial, including the aerosol insecticide and the "manufacturing procedures for Buna-S."

From Hamilton's narration, a far clearer view of Harry Gold's "espionage" career emerges. During the years 1935 to 1944, that career would appear to have been both harmless and ineffectual, its output surprisingly meager. The alleged transmission by Gold to the Russians, over this nine-year period, of various industrial processes—obtained from the sugar company and from Slack and Brothman—could by no flight of the imagination be termed "espionage." The espionage phase of Gold's activities would seem to have been confined to 1944 and 1945, when he received RDX data from Slack and met with Fuchs and Greenglass.

Regarding Gold's alleged meetings with Fuchs—the subject of the indictment—Hamilton added little to the prosecutor's sketchy recital, other than a few picturesque details. Semenov was described as having been "in a high state of excitement" when he gave Gold the assignment in the winter of 1944. He instructed Gold to walk near the Henry Street Settlement in New York City, wearing gloves and carrying an extra pair, and "across the street at the appointed minute a man would appear who would be carrying a tennis ball in one hand and a book in another." That man was Klaus Fuchs.

According to Hamilton, Gold's last meeting with Fuchs, on September 19, 1945, in Santa Fe, was also virtually the final act of his espionage endeavors. "His whole crime came to an end with the passing of the information of September 19 a few days later in New York City." Afterward, Gold had a number of other meetings with Soviet agents, but none ever again involved any passage of information.

Noting that by the time he had come into the case Gold had already "made up his mind to plead guilty," Hamilton summarized his approach as defense counsel: ". . . I come here to explain a crime and not to excuse one . . . I come here to state a case and not to plead one."

The former Republican National Chairman had taken his responsibility as a court-appointed attorney with the utmost seriousness. The work that he and his associate, Augustus S. Ballard, had done in their effort "to explain a crime" had entailed questioning many individuals, taking numerous statements, and "above all, hours and hours of interviewing the defendant" with a recording machine. For additional material, the attorneys were able to draw on "over two hundred pages of closely written longhand accounts by the defendant himself."

Said Hamilton:

"We are confronted here, not with a question of guilt, that is admitted, we are confronted here with question of motive, and of explanation, and of intent, and if I could find motive in greed, or avarice, or any of the baser qualities of men, this would be an easy case; if Harry Gold had received money as compensation for the work he did, this would be an easy case, but Harry Gold received no money from the Soviet other than a very partial and small reimbursement for expenses. . . . So I cannot dispose of the case that easily."

Seeking the reason for his client's crime, Hamilton recounted the life history of Gold and his parents, recalling even the experiences in Czarist Russia of Gold's mother and father; their meeting and marriage in Switzerland; Harry's birth there on December 12, 1910; and the family's emigration to the United States when Harry was about three years old. He told of the poverty of the Gold family in Philadelphia; the birth of their second child, Joseph, in 1917; and Harry's education in the Philadelphia public schools. Harry's father earned modest wages and was sometimes unemployed and his mother ("she was the dominating personality of the home") brought in extra income by giving Hebrew instructions to Jewish children in the neighborhood.

In January 1929, not long after graduating from high school (third in a class of 160), Harry Gold—who had developed an interest in science—was pleased to obtain work at the Pennsylvania Sugar Company as a laboratory assistant, at first little more than a janitor's job. Working seven days a week, he managed by September 1930 to save enough money to enter the University of Pennsylvania, but was forced to withdraw for lack of funds after three and a half semesters. Returning to the sugar company in March 1932, he worked until December—when he was laid off because of the Depression.

Through a friend, Gold met a Jersey City chemist named Tom Black, who helped him to obtain a job; with this salary, Gold supported his family for the next nine months until fall 1933, when he was able to return to Pennsylvania Sugar. Enrolling in night classes at Drexel Institute (1934–36), Gold received a diploma in chemical engineering, then spent two years at Xavier ("those were the happiest days of Harry Gold's life"), where he finally received his B.S. in 1940 with high honors. With the exception of time out for education and his brief Jersey City employment, Gold had remained at the Pennsylvania Sugar Company from shortly after his high school graduation until 1946, when he was permanently laid off and went to work for A. Brothman Associates.

During this period, Gold's political views—already revealed at the Brothman-Moskowitz trial—were plainly not favorable to Communism. Said Hamilton: "One time he told me that he thought that communism as a political dogma was no more than the victory of mediocrity in Russia. . . . In any event, he never joined the Communist Party. . . . Harry Gold has never been a Communist, and is not a Communist now, nor was he in those younger days."

As to why Gold had accepted Black's request in 1935 that he turn over information from the Pennsylvania Sugar Company "for the benefit of the masses of the Russian people," Hamilton offered several explanations: His early life had developed "a sympathy for the underdog"; his gratitude to Black for getting him a job; the rise of anti-Semitism in Germany.

While these reasons might conceivably have explained Gold's willingness to give away commercial processes filched from his employer, they did not elucidate his invention of imaginary recruits about whom he provided imaginary reports, nor his willingness many years later to meet with Fuchs and Greenglass.

Perhaps sensing the inadequacy of his explanation, Hamilton claimed that, once having started, Gold "had charted a course from which . . . he was never able to withdraw." However, the single incident offered to back up this statement was one in which the contact Fred, responding to Gold's reluctance to visit a man in Dayton, threatened to inform "the Fathers of Xavier"—a Jesuit school—"that you are a Soviet agent." Unexplained by Hamilton was why Gold should have feared the revelation that he had once provided Fred with a process for obtaining carbon dioxide—useful for soda fountains—from flue gases.

By far the most striking of all the biographical details elicited by the defense attorney in his diligent probing for a motive for his client's crime were what Hamilton referred to as "certain facts which appear and reappear so consistently in his life that I think that they may be considered as definite characteristics in the man himself."

Commenting on these "characteristics," Hamilton said:

"I say to your Honor, after forty years of association with men, and

I am testifying now, that Harry Gold is the most extraordinarily selfless person I have ever met in my life."

As a puny child, Gold had adopted "a rather monastic life, in that he withdrew from a lot of the activities you would find in other boys"; became a prodigious reader; and, from an early age, undertook to help acquaintances with their schoolwork. "At one time he told me that in these early years he wrote so many essays for other boys that he did not have any subjects left for himself, when the time came to write his own. But this willingness to help others became . . . a dominating characteristic of Harry Gold's later life."

Over the years, Gold frequently had served without pay as a tutor for fellow employees and others, often with great inconvenience to himself at a time when he was working long hours and attending night school. The tutoring was done at the homes of the students, because Gold "did not want to inconvenience his friends by having them come to his home."

Further evidence of Gold's apparently selfless personality was his willingness on a job to undertake the most arduous tasks with no regard for time. Noting that he had never known "a man who was so completely lacking in interest in time," Hamilton presented as proof two appraisals of Gold by former associates at the Heart Station of the Philadelphia General Hospital.

One statement reported that Gold had "worked overtime and on weekends nearly every week, completely disregarding any time schedule"; the second, by five scientists at the hospital, read: "The time he gave not only exceeded all normal standards, but also exceeded the time which might be expected of a conscientious research worker. . . . If an experiment required that it be started at three o'clock in the morning, he was there and remained there until it was completed."

The same statement gave some indication of the extent of Gold's self-sacrificing behavior:

"While at one time or another all technicians give their blood for tests being carried on, he gave blood far in excess of what might normally be taken from any single individual. . . . Gold also subjected himself to blood sticks, which are quite painful." While searching for a therapy for a particular ailment, Gold suggested certain substances which were investigated but found to be "toxic to humans and dangerous. Nevertheless, Gold offered to have the substance tried out on him experimentally. From Gold's character the staff was quite assured the offer was made in good faith, and it was refused because of the dangers involved."

Bordering on the bizarre was Gold's practice of freely loaning money— even if he had to borrow to get it. Soon after starting work at Pennsylvania Sugar, Hamilton said, Gold had made frequent loans to fellow employees, "even though he had never even met them or knew them before, or made any examination of their needs, and he did it at a time when his own family was in distress, and he borrowed the money to make those loans at usurious rates from a man who was in the money lending business in his own plant. I am not talking of an occasional instance again, I am talking of what went on time after time, day in and day out."

A number of statements from acquaintances extolled Gold's "generosity"; however, his actions, as described by his associates at the hospital, seem more peculiar than magnanimous:

"He was solicitous to the point of fault. He loaned money not only to those with whom he was associated, but to employees who were strangers to him. Upon one occasion at least in making such a loan he was asked by one of his associates if he had any assurance the money would ever be returned to him and his reply was that it was unimportant whether he got it back or not. . . . it was almost embarrassing to return borrowed money to him because of his reticence in accepting it."

But of all the many examples of Gold's apparent lack of concern for himself, perhaps the most interesting was his strange behavior during his questioning by the FBI before his arrest. After Gold had "fenced" with the agents for several days—the interrogation having begun on May 15, 1950—there occurred what Hamilton termed "an unusual incident":

"Late on the night of May 19, 1950, the agents of the Federal Bureau of Investigation, having made no charge of crime and having no warrant issued, asked Harry Gold if he would consent to a search of his home. Now, that is Friday night. He said, yes, he would do it, with only one condition, the condition being that the search would be made when his father and brother were not there, so that they would have no information of what was going on. It was agreed that the search would be made Monday morning, May 22. Friday night went by, Saturday Harry Gold spent the day as usual with the Heart Station, that night he was with the FBI again. Sunday he went out again to the Heart Station and fulfilled his duties and spent Sunday night with the agents of the Federal Bureau of Investigation. In the three nights and the two days that he was carrying out his duties plus his time with the FBI, if your Honor please, his home was filled with incriminating documents and he took not one step to destroy them. He had had the stubs of tickets to cities that he was supposed to have never visited. He had had written cards of instructions from Soviet agents how to meet people. He had had plans and specifications that he had delivered and maybe extra copies that he had kept. He had had books that he had bought in far away cities where he was never supposed to have been. As I say, it was filled with information. He did not [do] one thing. He finally got up at six o'clock on Monday, the search was to be made at 8:30, and he started to destroy some of them, and he quit, and there isn't any reason why he quit. Harry Gold was mentally tired of carrying his deceit and intrigue in his heart and mind. And the third item that the agents of the FBI found in his home was a map of Santa Fe, where he was to meet Klaus Fuchs, and he had told them that he had never been in the West in his life, and he sat down and asked if he could smoke a cigarette. Then he said to them: Yes, I am the man who gave the atomic information to Klaus Fuchs."

While this story filled in many of the details of Gold's confession, it also left a number of questions unanswered. If the FBI agents had had any substantial evidence against Gold on May 19, would they not have obtained a warrant to search his house immediately; in any event, why did they consider it at all worthwhile to search a suspect's house after he had received three days' warning (May 19 to 22), during which time one would normally expect a criminal to seek out and destroy any incriminating material? Why, too, when Gold confessed on Monday morning, May 22, was he not arrested until late the next evening and why had the FBI, on this most important case, then apparently deferred searching the cellar of the house of the confessed spy until June 3 and June 6—as revealed at the Brothman-Moskowitz trial?

Also unanswered was perhaps the most intriguing question of all: How had the FBI found Harry Gold and what part, if any, had Klaus Fuchs played in the search?

Present at the hearing was an FBI agent, T. Scott Miller, Jr., who stated that he had been in charge of the Gold case from the beginning, had questioned Gold many times, and had had channeled through him all the information gathered by other agents working on the case.

Addressing agent Miller, Judge McGranery stated:

"I think it is very important for me to say, there has been some view that has gone abroad that this case probably was first exposed by Fuchs. That is not true. This matter was uncovered by the Federal Bureau, and Fuchs, as a matter of fact, as I understand it, had never co-operated in any way, shape or form until after the arrest of Harry Gold. Am I correct in that?"

AGENT MILLER: I think the statement is, your Honor, that the identification of Harry Gold's picture was not made until after Gold signed a confession.

JUDGE MCGRANERY: The point that I make is that Fuchs had never co-operated with the Federal Bureau. I am told that by both the Attorney General and Mr. Hoover.

AGENT MILLER: That is correct sir.

Thus Judge McGranery laid to rest with finality the myth that Harry Gold had been apprehended as a result of information obtained from Klaus Fuchs.

Interestingly, in at least one respect Gold's sentencing hearing bore a marked similarity to that of Fuchs. At the London proceedings, the interrogating officer, Skardon, had revealed that before taking the British scientist's confession there was no evidence upon which Fuchs could have been prosecuted. Evidently, Gold also had been the source of the information used against him; the story related by prosecutor Gleeson would seem to have come largely, if not entirely, from the defendant.

How then had the prosecution checked the accuracy of this story? According to Gleeson, Klaus Fuchs had been interviewed by the FBI "in the latter part of May, 1950" and had "substantially corroborated the evidence set out in this case." This assertion by the prosecutor was not commented on by the FBI's expert on the case, who said nothing whatever about any corroboration by Fuchs of the Gold confession, referring only to Fuchs's "identification of Harry Gold's picture."

If some mystery still surrounds the manner in which Harry Gold was found by the FBI and the extent to which his confession was corroborated by Fuchs or anyone else, one fact is clear: Gold had been an extremely cooperative prisoner. He had devoted, Hamilton said, not less than two hundred or three hundred hours to the task of going through literally thousands of photos to "identify the men who were associated with him in this great conspiracy." And, as further evidence of Gold's selflessness, all this had been done freely, "without the slightest bargaining of any kind."

Still searching for some understanding of his "extraordinarily selfless" client, Hamilton told the Court:

". . . I think maybe I have failed in this case in one respect at least. After Mr. Ballard and I had had three or four conferences with Gold we came very definitely to the conclusion that there was no question at all as to Gold's legal sanity, but, on the other hand, I am not so sure I should not have called in an expert here, because it is rather difficult to fill out the equation of a man whose life is so clear and free of any crime on the one side . . . and yet, on the other hand, engaged in this terrific conspiracy."

Later, Judge McGranery assured Hamilton "that among other things we did have a psychiatric examination made of the defendant, and you need have no fear as to his mental situation."

After receiving a recommendation from the prosecution for a twenty-five-year prison term for Gold, Judge McGranery adjourned the hearing to consider sentence. If the defendant had felt any resentment against the government for requesting so heavy a sentence, it would have been understandable, but he gave no indication of such feelings.

Nine months before in London's Old Bailey, Harry Gold's confederate, Klaus Fuchs, had mumbled a few words about "other crimes" and his wish to "atone" and had thanked the Judge for a "fair trial" and the prison staff "for their considerate treatment." Now it was Gold's turn. He rose and, according to the *Times*, spoke "slowly and almost as though he had rehearsed the statement many times":

"I shall be very brief.

"There are just four points, and, with one exception, all of them have been very adequately set forth in this court on the 7th of December. I am making note of them now, because they represent matters which have been uppermost in my mind for the past few months.

"First, nothing has served to bring me to a realization of the terrible mistake that I have made as this one fact, the appointment by this Court of Mr. Hamilton and Mr. Ballard as my counsel. These men have worked incredibly hard and faithfully in my behalf, and in the face of severe personal criticism and even invective, and they have done this, not for the reason that they condoned my crime, but because they believe that as a basic part of our law I was entitled to the best legal representation available.

"Second, I am fully aware that I have received the most scrupulously fair trial and treatment that could be desired, and this has been not only in this Court, but has been the case with the F.B.I., with the other agencies of the Justice Department, and with the authorities at the various prisons where I have been lodged, both here and in New York. Most certainly this could never have happened in the Soviet Union or any of the countries dominated by it.

"Third, the most tormenting of all thoughts concerns the fact that those who meant so much to me have been the worst besmirched by my deeds. I refer here to this country, to my family and friends, to my former classmates at Xavier University, and to the Jesuits there, and to the people at the Heart Station of the Philadelphia General Hospital. There is a puny inadequacy about any words telling how deep and horrible is my remorse.

"Fourth, and very last, I have tried to make the greatest possible amends by disclosing every phase of my espionage activities, by identifying all of the persons involved, and by revealing every last scrap, shred and particle of evidence.

"Your Honor, I have finished."

Stressing the "need to deter others in the future from the commission of similar offenses," Judge McGranery sentenced Gold to thirty years imprisonment, the maximum prison term possible under the law.

Reported the *Times*: "The severity of the penalty . . . came as a surprise to most of the 150 persons in the courtroom. The defendant . . . heard the penalty without any sign of emotion."

Shortly afterward Harry Gold, who had apparently provided all the evidence against himself, had cooperated fully with the FBI and prosecution, had never bargained regarding his sentence and now accepted the severe one imposed on him with his customary selfless manner, announced through his attorney that there would be no appeal.

Within a week, newspaper reports disclosed that Gold had been brought from Philadelphia to the Tombs Prison in New York City, evidently in preparation for the forthcoming atomic espionage trial, involving four more of those arrested the previous summer: The Rosenbergs, Greenglass, and Sobell.

UNITED STATES

vs.

ROSENBERGS AND SOBELL

•

CHAPTER 14
THE TRIAL

At 10:30 A.M. on Tuesday, March 6, 1951, in New York City's massive federal courthouse at Foley Square, the clerk solemnly called the case: "The United States *versus* Julius Rosenberg, Ethel Rosenberg and Morton Sobell." Irving H. Saypol rose and responded: "The District Attorney moves the case for trial and is ready to proceed." Replied one of the defense counsel: "The defendants are ready to proceed." The nation's first trial for the theft of atomic bomb secrets was under way.

Charged with conspiracy to commit espionage in wartime were five co-defendants but two, Anatoli Yakovlev, a former Soviet vice-consul in New York who had left the country some years before, and David Greenglass, who had pleaded guilty, were granted severances for purposes of the trial. Not being tried, but named in the indictment as co-conspirators, were Ruth Greenglass and Harry Gold.

The trial was being held in the building's largest courtroom, 110, scene within recent years of such celebrated cases as that of the eleven American Communist Party leaders, Judith Coplon, Brothman and Moskowitz, and William Remington. As the selection of the jury began, the spectators' benches were crowded; an extraordinary silence bespoke great expectations.

The week before, the prosecution had released its long list of potential witnesses, containing nearly a hundred names (later expanded to about 120); included were the former head of the Manhattan Project, General Leslie R. Groves, and such eminent scientists as J. Robert Oppenheimer, Harold Urey, and George B. Kistiakowski. Further heightening the dramatic potential of the trial was the prospect of a brother testifying against his sister in a capital case. The possibility of a death sentence was the subject of much speculation by the press; the *Times* went so far as to inform its readers that in the event of a death penalty the defendants "would be executed in Sing Sing Prison."

Presiding over the trial was forty-year-old Judge Irving R. Kaufman, one of the youngest federal jurists in the nation. At the prosecution table was U. S. Attorney Saypol, whose five assistants in the case included Myles J. Lane, Roy M. Cohn, and James Kilsheimer III. Seated at the defense table with their attorneys were the three defendants. All had been imprisoned since their arrests; Julius Rosenberg for nearly eight months, Morton Sobell and Ethel Rosenberg for almost seven. A small, slightly built, dark-haired woman, Mrs. Rosenberg sat between her husband and his former college classmate, both neatly attired, rather studious-looking young men of medium height.

OPENINGS Addressing a jury of eleven men and one woman, Irving Saypol opened the prosecution's case:

"The evidence will show that the loyalty and allegiance of the Rosenbergs and Sobell were not to our country, but that it was to Communism, Communism in this country and Communism throughout the world."

These remarks evoked defense objections that "Communism is not on trial here. These defendants are charged with espionage." Judge Kaufman said he would rule later if the prosecution intended to establish communism as the motive for the crime.

Saypol continued:

". . . Sobell and Julius Rosenberg, classmates together in college, dedicated themselves to the cause of Communism . . . . this love of Communism and the Soviet Union soon led them into a Soviet espionage ring. . . . You will hear how Julius and Ethel Rosenberg and Sobell reached into wartime projects and installations of the United States Government . . . to obtain . . . secret information . . . and speed it on its way to Russia."

Asserting that the Rosenbergs had persuaded David Greenglass "to play the treacherous role of a modern Benedict Arnold," Saypol said:

"We will prove that the Rosenbergs devised and put into operation, with the aid of Soviet . . . agents in this country, an elaborate scheme which enabled them to steal through David Greenglass this one weapon, that might well hold the key to the survival of this nation and means the peace of the world, the atomic bomb."

The defense moved, unsuccessfully, for a mistrial on the ground that Saypol's opening statement was "inflammatory in character."

The Rosenbergs' attorney, Emanuel Bloch (assisted by his father, Alexander Bloch) asked the jurors not to be influenced by "hysteria," emphasizing that the prosecution had to prove that the defendants had conspired to commit espionage, not "that they believed in one ism or another ism."

On behalf of Morton Sobell, Harold Phillips (his associate was Edward

Kuntz) complained that he did not know what Sobell was alleged to have done because Sobell was not mentioned in any of the overt acts of the indictment. "Any endeavor we made to find out . . . was thwarted on all sides, and we stand here before you as ignorant of what is really meant to be charged against Sobell as you. . . . We will . . . have to . . . sit here like so many children, listening, waiting. What is the Government going to do here?"

MAX ELITCHER   Next day Phillips at least partially had his answer. The first witness for the prosecution was Max Elitcher, thirty-two, who testified that he lived with his wife and two young children in Flushing, Queens in a house situated back-to-back with the Sobell house. He had met Morton Sobell at Stuyvesant High School in New York; later, between 1934 and 1938, the two studied electrical engineering at the College of the City of New York (CCNY). After graduation, both found jobs at the Navy Bureau of Ordnance in Washington, D.C. where they shared an apartment and, Elitcher claimed, belonged to the same Communist Party group. In September 1941 their paths parted: Sobell left Washington (to obtain his master's degree at the University of Michigan); Elitcher remained at his Navy job and over the next few years they saw each other infrequently.

Elitcher testified that his first knowledge of the defendants' espionage activities was acquired in June 1944, when he was phoned by Julius Rosenberg, whom he had known slightly at college and had not seen in the six years since graduation. "I remembered the name, I recalled who it was, and he said he would like to see me. He came over after supper, and my wife was there and we had a casual conversation. After that he asked if my wife would leave the room, that he wanted to speak to me in private." Rosenberg then allegedly said that many people were aiding Russia "by providing classified information about military equipments" and asked Elitcher if he could get such information and turn it over to him. Elitcher said neither yes nor no.

Elitcher required continual prompting as he told his story, raising defense objections that Saypol was "trying to put the words into his mouth." When the prosecutor had the witness repeat the story of Rosenberg's first request for "classified information," Elitcher added a previously omitted vital detail: Rosenberg had mentioned that Sobell was "also helping in this matter."

Around Labor Day 1944, Max Elitcher and his wife vacationed with Morton Sobell and the latter's fiancée. Max told his friend of Rosenberg's visit and his disclosure that "you, Sobell, were also helping in this." Sobell "became very angry and said 'he should not have mentioned my name. He should not have told you that.'"

In September 1945 Rosenberg again paid a brief visit to the Elitchers in Washington. (The two men had been together twice in New York City at purely social meetings since the time of Rosenberg's first visit in June 1944.) Julius told Max "that even though the war was over there was a continuing need for new military information for Russia." Testified Elitcher: "I said . . . I would let him know."

While on Navy business at General Electric in Schenectady in 1946, Elitcher was an overnight guest at the home of Sobell, then employed by GE. The men discussed their jobs and Elitcher said he was working on a fire (gunnery) control system. Sobell inquired if any reports had been written on it; Elitcher replied that a pamphlet on the system was not yet ready. In Schenectady later that year on another official trip, Elitcher was asked again by Sobell about the pamphlet and said it still was not finished. Sobell then suggested that Elitcher see Rosenberg. Asked by prosecutor Saypol if his friend had told him the purpose of seeing Rosenberg, Elitcher answered: "Well, he said I don't know in what words, or implied that it had to do with this espionage business, but I don't recall the exact nature of the words."

In late 1946 or early 1947, Elitcher did see Rosenberg, visiting him at his apartment. "I told him about my new work—I was perhaps in a more receptive frame of mind for him—and he then interrupted and told me that they were having some difficulty, felt that there was a leak in this espionage, and because of that there were precautions being taken by him. He told me it would be best if I don't see him . . . until he lets me know or until someone informs me."

About a year later in New York City, Sobell—then employed by Reeves Instrument Company—asked Elitcher if he "knew of any engineering students or engineering graduates who were progressive, who would be safe to approach on this question of espionage." Elitcher said he did not.

Elitcher decided in June 1948 to quit his Navy job in Washington. Sobell tried to dissuade him and so did Rosenberg, who said "he needed somebody to work at the Navy Department for this espionage purpose." When Elitcher refused to stay on, Rosenberg suggested that he get a job where military work was being done, saying money could be made available for education to improve his technical status.

One evening in late July or early August 1948, the Elitcher family arrived at the Sobells' Flushing home, where they planned to stay while house hunting in New York. Max announced that he had been "followed by one or two cars from Washington to New York." Very angry, Sobell tried to get the Elitchers to leave, though "he didn't seem to believe" the story. Then Sobell said he had some information in his house that was "too valuable to be destroyed and yet too dangerous to keep around. He said he wanted to deliver it to Rosenberg that night." Asking his friend to accompany him because he was tired and "might not be able to make the trip back," Sobell took along what Elitcher identified as a 35-millimeter film can. Near Knickerbocker Village, Sobell left the car briefly with the film can, while Elitcher parked on a nearby street—Catherine Slip. Homeward bound (Sobell drove both ways), Elitcher asked what Rosenberg had thought about his being followed and was told not to worry about it. Sobell added that Rosenberg had said "he once talked to Elizabeth Bentley on the phone but he was pretty sure she didn't know who he was and therefore everything was all right."

That October, the Elitchers moved into a house just behind the Sobells' home and Max found a job at Reeves, where Morton worked. Driving to work together one morning, Sobell again asked about engineering students "who might eventually be asked about providing military information," noting this time that they should not be involved in any "progressive" political activity because of "increased security measures." Again Elitcher said he didn't know anyone.

On cross-examination, Elitcher agreed that Sobell was always on the lookout for young engineers who might work for Reeves. Queried about this by Judge Kaufman, Elitcher explained that Sobell had asked him about engineering students for regular employment at Reeves as well as about students for espionage purposes.

Elitcher admitted that neither of his 1946 Schenectady trips to General Electric was made at Sobell's invitation. Outside of the unfinished pamphlet, Sobell had never asked him for any document. His only contact with alleged espionage material was the film can taken by Sobell on the trip to Catherine Slip in 1948. He had no idea as to the contents of this can. (His first one or two statements to the FBI had omitted the Catherine Slip incident and Rosenberg's reported remark about Elizabeth Bentley.) He never had passed any unauthorized government information to either Rosenberg or Sobell, nor had they passed any to him. However, Elitcher insisted: "I went along. I never turned over material, but I was part of it. . . . I was part of discussions concerning it until 1948."

Elitcher disclosed that in 1947 he had falsely denied Communist Party membership on a federal Loyalty Oath form. Afterward, he had been extremely fearful of possible prosecution for perjury. This fear had been a factor impelling him to tell his story when he was approached by the FBI, shortly after Rosenberg's arrest. He had not been indicted for perjury, but said he had received no promises.

DAVID GREENGLASS   The prosecution's second witness, David Greenglass, twenty-nine, was examined by Roy M. Cohn. A machinist who had learned his trade at Manhattan's Haaren Aviation High School, he was married at the age of twenty and entered the Army soon afterward. A year later, in July 1944, he was assigned to the Manhattan District and, after brief orientation at Oak Ridge, Tennessee—where he was told he was to work on a secret project—was sent to Los Alamos, New Mexico. There he received a security badge entitling him to know only enough to do his job but not the purpose of the project.

Greenglass worked in the Los Alamos Technical Area in a group—headed by George B. Kistiakowski—doing research involving high explosives. He and the four or five others in his shop machined apparatus, following scientists' verbal instructions or sketches. A T/5 corporal later promoted to T/4 sergeant, he eventually became assistant foreman of the shop, smallest in the Area, and served briefly as foreman.

Security regulations were stringent: Los Alamos could not be mentioned in letters; the address to be used was P. O. Box 1663, Santa Fe, New Mexico. Also secret were the names of well-known project scientists; however, Greenglass said he soon learned of the presence of J. Robert Oppenheimer and Niels Bohr, known by the pseudonym Baker.

Roy Cohn interrupted the witness's testimony about Los Alamos to ask him about conversations "concerning the relative merits of our form of government and that of the Soviet Union." David said he first had such talks with his sister, Ethel, at their home in 1935 (when he was thirteen or fourteen) and, beginning two years later, with her boyfriend, Julius. They had told him, he testified, that they preferred Russian socialism to capitalism.

In late November 1944, David—who had not seen his wife, Ruth, since his assignment to New Mexico—obtained a few days' leave and met her in Albuquerque on their second wedding anniversary. From her, he allegedly learned for the first time the nature of the secret project at Los Alamos. "She told me that Julius had said that I was working on the atomic bomb."

Before leaving New York for Albuquerque, Ruth had been invited to the Rosenberg apartment. Ethel had revealed to her that Julius "was giving information to the Soviet Union." Julius then informed Ruth that her husband was working on the atomic bomb project. The Rosenbergs wanted David to provide information from Los Alamos for the Russians. Reluctantly, Ruth had agreed to tell him. When David first heard this proposal from his wife, he was "frightened and worried" and refused, but next morning he told Ruth he would do it. He gave her the names of some scientists—Oppenheimer, Bohr, and Kistiakowski—and also told her "about the general layout of the . . . Project, the buildings, number of people and stuff like that."

On January 1, 1945, David came home on furlough. One morning a few days later, Julius visited him and verbally described "the atom bomb." David told his brother-in-law that he was working on high explosive lens molds at Los Alamos. (He explained to the Court that liquid high explosive was poured into a specially shaped mold which he and other machinists constructed. When the mold was removed, "you have a high explosive lens mold.") Rosenberg asked him to write up, "late at night," any information he had.

That night David prepared some sketches and a written description of lens mold experiments, a list of scientists (largely the same names given Ruth in November), and the names of "some possible recruits . . . . people who seemed sympathetic with Communism." When Julius came for this material next morning, Ruth mentioned to him that David's "handwriting would be bad . . . and Julius said . . . Ethel would type it up."

A few days later the Greenglasses came to dinner at the Rosenbergs' apartment. Present there was Ann Sidorovich, a woman David never had met though he knew her husband. After some social conversation, Mrs. Sidorovich left and Julius explained to the Greenglasses that she might come out to see them to receive atom bomb information.

During dinner and afterward, a tentative plan was evolved whereby Ruth would go to live in Albuquerque, would put "information from Los Alamos" in her purse, and would exchange purses with Ann Sidorovich or someone else in a Denver movie theater. Julius told Ruth he would give her a means of identification—in case the person who came for the information was not Mrs. Sidorovich—and went into the kitchen with her and Ethel. When they returned, David observed that Ruth had in her hand a cut jello box side and Julius was holding the other part of it. ". . . I said, 'Oh, that is very clever,' because I noticed how it fit, and he said, 'The simplest things are the cleverest.'" Julius retained one piece and Ruth put the other in her wallet to use "for identification with the person who would come out to see us." (Handed an ordinary jello box by Roy Cohn, David cut one side into two irregular parts; the box and pieces were introduced as a prosecution exhibit.) Finally, the plan for a meeting in a Denver theater was discarded in favor of David's idea for a meeting in front of a Safeway supermarket in Albuquerque.

During that evening, David talked about high explosive lens molds and Julius wanted him to meet a "Russian" to discuss the subject further. One night a few days afterward, Julius introduced him to a man who got into the car David was driving and asked him technical questions about the lenses—which he was unable to answer.

His furlough ended, David returned to Los Alamos. Several months later, Ruth came out to Albuquerque and rented an apartment there at 209 North High Street, where David spent weekends. Ann Sidorovich never visited them; however, the first Sunday in June 1945, someone else did, a man whom David now knew to be Harry Gold. David answered a knock at the door that morning, just as he and Ruth had finished breakfast, "and there was a man standing in the hallway who asked if I were Mr. Greenglass, and I said yes. He stepped through the door and he said, 'Julius sent me,' and I said, 'oh,' and walked to my wife's purse, took out the wallet and took out the matched part of the Jello box." Gold then produced the other part and he and David checked the pieces and saw that they fitted.

David did not have the information ready and asked Gold to return in the afternoon. He started to tell about a potential espionage recruit, but Gold "cut me short." He then prepared sketches of lens mold experiments with descriptive material and "a list of possible recruits for espionage." When Gold returned, David gave him this material in an envelope and received an envelope, which he "felt and realized there was money in it." He and Ruth left the house with Gold, parting at the Albuquerque USO. The Greenglasses went in briefly, then returned to their apartment and opened the envelope—which contained $500. David gave the money to his wife.

Greenglass was temporarily displaced as a witness by Walter Koski, a former Los Alamos scientist. Koski, a physical chemist, had performed experimental studies at Los Alamos on implosion—the bursting *inward* of an explosive force. His experiments required various combinations of high explosives, cast from molds in special shapes called lenses. Like all technical work at Los Alamos, this research was secret.

Koski examined three prosecution exhibits—replicas recently drawn by Greenglass from memory of lens mold sketches he allegedly had turned over to Rosenberg and Gold in January and June 1945. Testifying as an expert, the witness concurred with Saypol's formulation that the replicas were "reasonably accurate."

Under cross-examination, Koski agreed with Bloch's characterization of Greenglass as "a plain, ordinary machinist." The sketches were "rough" but did "illustrate the important principle involved." Judge Kaufman asked Koski if the substance of his testimony was that, while the sketches might omit some details useful to a foreign nation, they did reveal to an expert what was going on at Los Alamos. Koski concurred.

Resuming his testimony, David said that the atom bomb described for him by Julius during his January furlough—"so that I would be able to know what I am looking for"—was the type that was dropped on Hiroshima. Later, David had "surreptitiously" eavesdropped on conversations at Los Alamos and gathered information on a different type of atomic bomb "that worked on an implosion effect." In New York on another furlough in September 1945, he told Julius: "I think I have . . . a pretty good description of the atom bomb."

COHN: The atom bomb itself?
DAVID: That's right.

Julius asked David to write up this information immediately and gave him $200. Against Ruth's wishes, David sketched an implosion bomb and prepared, in twelve pages, a description of it and the names of some scientists and also of some possible espionage recruits. He and Ruth then brought this material to Julius, who called it "very good" and said it should be typed up at once. Working in the Rosenberg living room,

"Ethel did the typing and Ruth and Julius and Ethel did the correction of the grammar."

Roy Cohn introduced as a prosecution exhibit a replica that David had drawn of "a cross-section sketch of the atom bomb" allegedly delivered to Julius in September 1945. In a surprise move, defense attorney Emanuel Bloch asked the Judge "to impound this exhibit so that it remains secret" and suggested that David's testimony about the sketch also be impounded. Judge Kaufman did impound both David's sketch and related testimony and barred from the courtroom all spectators—except members of the press.

Subsequently, the prosecution offered the testimony of John Derry "to establish the authenticity of the information that Greenglass gave to Rosenberg." Derry, who held a B.S. in electrical engineering, had served during the war as a liaison officer between General Groves and the Los Alamos Laboratory; at the time of his testimony he was a civilian AEC employee. Bloch suggested that the witness first be asked to describe a cross-section of the atom bomb, so that the jury might compare his description with David's. Judge Kaufman refused and the impounded testimony was read to Derry, with spectators—but not the press—again barred from the court.

Derry agreed with Saypol's formulations that the Greenglass sketch and description of the atom bomb "relate to the atomic weapon which was in the course of development in 1945"; "demonstrate substantially and with substantial accuracy the principle involved in the operation of the 1945 atomic bomb"; and would enable an expert to "perceive what the actual construction of the bomb was." Asked if the Greenglass material concerned a type of atom bomb used by the United States, Derry replied: "It does. It is the bomb we dropped at Nagasaki, similar to it."

When Bloch asked Derry whether the testimony and sketch represented "a complete description of the cross-section of the atomic bomb . . . and how it works," Judge Kaufman interjected: "I don't think it was offered as a complete or as a detailed description." U. S. Attorney Saypol agreed.

During the typing of the atom bomb material in the Rosenbergs' living room, Julius told David that he had "stolen the proximity fuse" in his briefcase while working at Emerson Radio. He also advised David to accept a civilian job at Los Alamos. However, after his Army discharge in early 1946, David returned to New York City and joined his brother, Bernard, and Julius in a machine shop business.

While they were business partners, Julius disclosed other facets of his espionage activities: He was "paying students to go to school" and "the Russians" would also pay for David to attend MIT or the University of Chicago so that he might cultivate friendships with Los Alamos acquaintances and with researchers in "physics and nuclear energy"; he had secured information on "a sky platform project" from "one of the boys, as he put it"; and "he had gotten the mathematics" on the use of atomic energy for airplanes "from one of his contacts." Julius also informed David that he communicated with the Russians by leaving microfilm in a movie theater alcove; had contacts in Schenectady at GE and in Cleveland; and had received as rewards from the Russians a citation and a watch. (From Ruth, David learned that Ethel also had received a watch.) In addition, David testified: "I believe they told me they received a console table from the Russians." He had seen this console table at the Rosenbergs' apartment.

In February 1950, just after Klaus Fuchs's arrest, Julius visited David (who had quit their machine shop business some months before) and said: "You remember the man who came to see you in Albuquerque? Well, Fuchs was also one of his contacts. . . ." Julius added that "this man . . . would undoubtedly be arrested soon," and if so would lead to David. David would have to leave the country, Julius said, reassuring him that "they let other people out who are more important than you are . . . . they let Barr out, Joel Barr, and he was a member of our espionage ring." (Barr had been referred to earlier by David as a man whom Julius said had gone to Belgium in 1947 to study music.) David testified: "Well, I told him that I would need money to pay my debts back . . . to leave with a clear head. . . . I insisted on it, so he said he would get the money for me from the Russians."

In mid-April Julius repeated his warning and, in early May, told David he would have to go as soon as possible, "via Mexico." Visiting the Greenglasses later in May, he showed David a picture of Harry Gold in the *Herald Tribune,* saying, "This is the man who saw you in Albuquerque." David did not recognize the picture, but Julius assured him that "this is the man." He gave David $1000 and promised him $6000 more. (Julius said he too had to flee because he "knew Jacob Golos . . . and probably Bentley knew him.")

Julius then gave David a "certain form letter to memorize." David was to go to Mexico City and send this letter—stating something favorable to the Soviet UN position and signed "I. Jackson"—to the Secretary to the Soviet Ambassador. Three days later, holding his middle finger between the pages of a guide book, he was to look at the statue of Columbus at the Plaza de la Colón. When a man approached, David would say, "That is a magnificent statue," adding that he was from Oklahoma and hadn't seen one like it before. Replying, "Oh, there are much more beautiful statues in Paris," the man would give David his passport. Continuing to Vera Cruz and then Switzerland or Sweden, "one or the other," he was to follow a similar routine, receiving at the statue of Linnaeus in Stockholm "means of transportation" to the final destination, Czechoslovakia, where he was to write the Soviet Ambassador "and say that I was here."

David was to get his Mexican tourist card in the border area; a letter from a doctor about smallpox inoculation was required. Julius "said he went to see a doctor and a doctor told him about it and I said I would attend to that." At Julius's request, the Greenglasses obtained passport photos, five copies of each of five photos. (David ordered an extra set and "kept it in the drawer"; later he gave the FBI four of the five photos in this extra set and these were introduced as a prosecution exhibit.)

Julius picked up the passport photos on Memorial Day. Returning the following week, he "put $4000 in a . . . brown paper wrapping, on the mantle piece in the bedroom." David had given the $1000 already received from Julius to Ruth, "who paid bills with it and spent it, generally." However, his first intention with the $4000 was "to flush it down the toilet bowl." He finally gave it to a brother-in-law, Louis Abel, "to keep for me." The brown paper wrapper was introduced as a prosecution exhibit.

In early June, Julius visited David for the last time. (He said he had just returned from upstate New York and had been planning to go to Cleveland but was "not going to go there any more.") David told Julius that he was being followed and said: "I am not going to do anything. . . . I am going to stay right here."

Early in cross-examination, Emanuel Bloch asked David, described in the press as a "smiling" witness, "Are you aware that you are smiling?" David replied: "Not very." He said he still bore affection for both Ethel and Julius and was aware of the possibility of a death penalty. David, who previously had mentioned attending two schools after high school, admitted failing eight courses out of eight at Brooklyn Polytech, but "got good marks" during one semester at Pratt Institute. Asked if he had read any scientific books in prison, he replied: "Just science fiction." He never had taken any material from Los Alamos, but had relied entirely on his memory. He was not able to tell which lens mold design was an improved version. He never had seen Ethel's watch from the Russians or Julius's citation. The gift console table "was used for photography. . . . Julius told me that he did pictures on that table."

The FBI had first talked with him about Los Alamos in February 1950. He didn't "recall exactly what the whole conversation was about. It made very little effect on me. . . ." On June 15, 1950, at about 2 P.M., while he was at home, four FBI agents arrived and spent the next five hours talking with him and searching the apartment. At about 7 P.M., he accompanied the agents to their offices at Foley Square, where the questioning continued. After signing a statement at about 2 A.M., he phoned his brother-in-law, Louis Abel, and asked him to engage an attorney, O. John Rogge. (All of the $4000 had gone to pay Rogge.) David, who slept the rest of that night at the FBI offices, was visited later in the morning by an associate of Rogge's and was arraigned that afternoon, June 16. He denied having told his attorney to fight the case for him.

During his business association with Rosenberg, he had worked in the shop with several employees and Julius was the outside man who sought orders.

BLOCH: Now, weren't there repeated quarrels between you and Julius when Julius accused you of trying to be a boss and not working on machines?

DAVID: There were quarrels of every type and every kind . . . . arguments over personality . . . arguments over money . . . arguments over the way the shop was run. . . . We remained as good friends in spite of the quarrels."

Reminded of an altercation in a candy store when Bernard Greenglass had to separate him and Julius, David said: "I don't recall if I actually hit him . . . . it was some violent quarrel over something in the business."

When David finally left the machine shop in August 1949, none of the partners had drawn salaries for months. In early January 1950, David assigned his stock in the business to Julius, at the latter's urging, but maintained physical possession of the shares. "I wanted $2000 and he finally agreed he would give me $1000 and when my wife made out the note to him to sign, he didn't want to. . . . He said his word is good enough. . . ." Julius came to the Greenglass apartment a number of times for David's stock and signed resignation as a company director and "we had some heated words." Finally, on May 1, 1950, Julius received both the stock and the resignation with no immediate payment. This was also an occasion when he urged David to leave the country.

David had lost "all of the money" he had invested in the machine shop, plus several thousand dollars in salaries. "I never recovered a single penny of it." After his arrest, he had instructed his attorney, O. John Rogge, to prosecute a claim against Julius for money from the business.

RUTH GREENGLASS   The next witness, David's wife, corroborated the essentials of his story, adding many details. The mother of a boy, four, and a girl, ten months, Ruth Greenglass—described by the *Times* as a "buxom and self-possessed brunette"—looked older than her twenty-six years. She was questioned by James Kilsheimer III.

In November 1944, Julius told her of his effort "to help the Russian people more directly other than just his membership in the Communist Party" and said "that for some time he and Ethel had not been actively pursuing any Communist Party activities . . . and he went on to tell me that he knew that David was working on the atomic bomb and I asked him how he knew. . . . He said that his friends had told him. . . ."

Testifying, according to the *Times*, "in seemingly eager, rapid, fashion," Ruth told of receiving $150 "towards the expenses" of her anniversary trip to Albuquerque from Julius, who asked for "a physical description of the project . . . the approximate number of people employed, the names of some of the scientists . . . whether the place was camouflaged . . . security measures . . . and the relative distance of the project to Albuquerque and Santa Fe."

On the night in January 1945 that the jello box side was cut, Ethel told her that all Julius's "time and his energies were used in this thing . . . that he had to make a good impression; that it sometimes cost him as much as $50 to $75 an evening to entertain his friends." When Ruth expressed concern about finances, Julius said "he would take care of my expenses; the money was no object; the important thing was for me to go to Albuquerque to live."

Next month, before departing for Albuquerque, Ruth was visited by Julius, who asked her sister, Dorothy, "to take a book and go into the bathroom . . . he had something private to discuss." Alone with Ruth, he told her to go to the Albuquerque Safeway supermarket "the last week in April and the first week in May" and someone would meet her "to get information from David."

In April, Ruth—then living in Albuquerque—wrote to Ethel that she was confined to bed after a miscarriage. Ethel replied (Ruth no longer had the letter) that "a member of the family" would come out to visit her "the last weeks in May, the third and fourth Saturdays." On both Saturday afternoons, Ruth—accompanied by David the second time—waited outside the supermarket, but no one came. The next week, the first Sunday in June 1945, Harry Gold knocked on their door. David gave the $500 he received from Gold to her; she deposited $400 in an Albuquerque bank, purchased a $50 defense bond (for $37.50) and used the rest for "household expenses."

About 1946, Ruth noticed a "mahogany console table" in the Rosenbergs' apartment. Ethel said it was a "gift" and "Julius said it was from his friend and it was a special kind of table, and he turned the table on its side." A portion of the table was hollow "for a lamp to fit underneath it so that the table could be used for photograph purposes." Julius used the table to take "pictures on microfilm of the typewritten notes."

Between 1946 and 1949, Julius discussed David's education with Ruth: "He wanted David to study nuclear fission. . . . He said money was not the question . . . that if we needed $75 a week or $100 a week to live on, we would get it; that he always took care that the students got their expenses first; that it was the most important thing as far as the Russians were concerned."

On May 24, 1950, Julius arrived at the Greenglasses' apartment with a *Herald Tribune* with Harry Gold's photo (which Ruth did not recognize) and said: "The next arrest will probably take place between June 12th and June 16th; you have to get out of the country before then." He gave them $1000, saying that they had "a month to spend it" and that he would bring them more. He told them to go "to the Soviet Union." (David had testified that Czechoslovakia was their destination.) When Ruth said they could not travel with an infant, Julius replied: "My doctor said if you take enough canned milk and boil the water, the baby will be all right." He asked her if she "could get a certificate from the doctor, stating that we had all been inoculated against smallpox. I said that I would not ask the doctor for a falsified statement. He said, 'That is all right. . . . My doctor will give it to me.'"

A few days later, the Greenglasses took passport pictures "to give to Julius so that he would think we were leaving." They never really intended to go.

When Julius brought $4000 on June 4, he said more would be available in Mexico. "He told us that we would have to leave sooner than expected, that they were closing in and getting ready to make an arrest." He said he would "meet us in Mexico." Three days later Julius returned and whispered that "he was being followed and . . . was going to bring $2000 more but he didn't because he was being extra careful."

In mid-July, about a week after David's arrest, "Ethel came with pie for me and gifts for my son . . . to . . . get assurances from me that David would not talk. She said it would only be a matter of a couple of years, and in the long run we would be better off. . . ."

On cross-examination, Alexander Bloch asked Ruth to repeat her previous testimony regarding her first espionage conversation with the Rosenbergs. When she gave it again nearly word for word, he suggested that she had memorized it. Commented Judge Kaufman: "If the witness . . . left out something, Mr. Bloch would say that the witness didn't repeat the story accurately. And the witness repeats it accurately, and apparently that isn't any good."

Several hitherto unmentioned incidents relating to money were recounted by Ruth: In 1948, Julius gave David $800; she did not explain why. Julius had told her "that he didn't care whether the business was a success or not" and she was "very enraged"; he said he could always "get $10,000 or $15,000 as a front for any business for his activities." However, asked if the person who had actually invested $15,000 in the machine shop was a "legitimate business man," Ruth readily agreed that he was.

She denied that there had been arguments about the business. "There weren't arguments, there were discussions." Asked the subject of the "discussions," Ruth replied: "Well, over a period of time Ethel Rosenberg had been complaining that David and Bernie were not paying attention to the shop, that Julius was doing all the work. . . ." Julius—who "complained about so many things"—claimed that David disappeared from work to help his wife with household tasks. Ruth had told members of the family that "I didn't think my husband was being paid commensurate with the work done."

The Greenglasses had not visited the Rosenberg apartment since early 1949. Asked if this was "on account of this friction," Ruth replied: "No, Mr. Bloch, there is no friction involved." She denied any hostility toward the Rosenbergs and said she had "friendly feelings" for them and wished them well. Asked if she wasn't "a bit angry at either Mr. or Mrs. Rosenberg because they did not pay you what you think you were entitled to," Ruth replied: "I don't think I am angry. I just can't understand their actions because there was a debt due. . . . I don't understand people who do not pay their debts. . . ."

She had been interviewed by FBI agents on the day of David's formal arrest, June 16, and was not questioned again until about a month later, in mid-July. At that time, she came voluntarily for a brief conference at Saypol's office at which her husband, their attorney, and several FBI agents also were present; after several other conferences with FBI agents, she signed a statement. She denied ever telling newsmen that David was innocent. Queried about her hopes for leniency for David, Ruth said: "I am telling the story because it's true and I hope and pray that my husband will come home. That is what I want, but I am not telling the story for that, no."

PERL ARREST While Ruth's testimony was still in progress, newspapers reported the arrest of William Perl, a thirty-two-year-old physics instructor charged with perjury for denying that he knew two former CCNY classmates—Rosenberg and Sobell. The *Times* carried an account of Ruth's trial testimony on the front page side by side with the Perl story, both under a single headline: "Columbia Teacher Arrested, Linked to 2 on Trial as Spies." The *Times* attributed to U. S. Attorney Saypol a statement that Perl had been intended as a prosecution witness "in the current atomic espionage trial" to corroborate "certain statements" of David and Ruth Greenglass.

Sobell's attorney, Edward Kuntz, told Judge Kaufman: "I saw the front page of the New York *Times* this morning . . . and I suggest . . . that we have a conference . . . because I think this is a very serious matter to the defendants. . . . I have never tried a case in my life in the newspapers."

Saypol retorted: "Well, I don't care for the implication, and I have had experience with this kind of defendants before, and with what I anticipate is to be said, I have no qualms about discussing it."

Later, after an off-the-record discussion, the matter was dropped.

MINOR CORROBORATIVE WITNESSES The testimony of David and Ruth Greenglass contained the main substance of the government's case. Minor aspects of the Greenglasses' story were confirmed by five prosecution witnesses:

Ruth had testified that Julius visited her in early 1945 and, wishing to speak with her alone, had sent her sister, Dorothy, into the bathroom. Dorothy Printz Abel, twenty-three, recalled the incident. She also said that in 1944, when she was sixteen, she had gone to the movies with the Greenglasses and the Rosenbergs and heard the latter voice the opinion that "Russia was the ideal form of government, the Russian form of government."

> BLOCH: In the course of this conversation . . . did they say anything specifically about the United States form of Government?
> DOROTHY: They didn't think that it compared at all with the Russian. . . .
> BLOCH: Can you tell us specifically what criticism they made of the United States form of Government?
> DOROTHY: Well, they said that it was a capitalistic form of Government.
> BLOCH: Yes?
> DOROTHY: That is about all I can remember.

David had testified that in June 1950 he gave a brown paper package with $4000 in it to his brother-in-law, Louis Abel, to hold. Ruth added that Abel was not told the source of the money. Louis Abel testified that in early June 1950 he agreed to keep some money for David and took a brown paper package to his own home, nearby, and hid it in a hassock. At 2 A.M. on June 16, David telephoned; he had been picked up by the FBI and wanted Abel to engage an attorney, O. John Rogge. Later that morning, Abel visited Rogge's office. "Mr. Rogge went down to see David and when he got back he said that David informed me to give him the package, which I did." A secretary at the Rogge firm, Helen Pagano, testified that on the morning of June 16, 1950, Louis Abel came to the office, left about noon and returned about 1 P.M., bringing with him $3900 "in a brown wrapper."

David and Ruth had testified to largely incompatible incidents concerning a conversation with Julius about smallpox inoculation. George Bernhardt, a Knickerbocker Village physician who had treated both Julius and his children, gave testimony which tended to conform with David's version but not Ruth's.

Three weeks after Julius's arrest, Bernhardt was visited by FBI agents, who asked whether he ever had been approached by Rosenberg "to sign a certificate of vaccination for his brother-in-law without having vaccinated him." Bernhardt did not recall, but several days later remembered a conversation about Mexico and volunteered this information to the FBI:

In the latter part of May 1950, Rosenberg phoned him and asked "what injections one needs to go to Mexico," adding that "it is not for me; it's for a friend of mine." Rosenberg said the friend was a veteran and would probably go into the interior of Mexico. The doctor mentioned the need for protection against smallpox, typhoid, and typhus.

Finally, an attorney, John Lansdale, Jr., a wartime Army intelligence officer who had worked under General Groves and been responsible for Manhattan Project security, confirmed David's testimony that efforts were made to keep secret the identities of top Los Alamos scientists. As part of this effort, Niels Bohr had been given the fictitious name of Nicholas Baker.

HARRY GOLD   The only major corroboration of the Greenglasses' story came from Harry Gold. He was questioned by Myles J. Lane.

When Lane asked Gold how long he had been "engaged in Soviet activities," the defense objected, contending that Gold's "Soviet activities" had not been proven. Disagreeing, Judge Kaufman said: "The witness knows." Gold answered: "I was engaged in espionage work for the Soviet Union from the spring of 1935 up until the time of my arrest . . . . in May [1950]."

An essential requirement for the prosecution's case was proof that the Soviet Union—through its representative, Anatoli Yakovlev—had participated in the alleged espionage conspiracy. Harry Gold provided this proof. Mentioning the absent Soviet defendant for the first time in the trial, he told of meeting Yakovlev—whom he knew as John—in March 1944, in New York City and continuing "my espionage work for the Soviet Union."

Testifying, according to *Time*, "As precisely and matter-of-factly as a high-school teacher explaining a problem in geometry," Gold described at length how he had obtained information for his "new Soviet superior," Yakovlev, "from a number of sources in America," effecting meetings by "a set of recognition signals" that always included "an object or a piece of paper" and "a code phrase . . . usually used in the form of a greeting." With "all of these people," meetings were for "an exact time at an exact place and there would be an exact schedule for what was to be done." He "made payments . . . to some of the people whom I regularly contacted" and always wrote reports for Yakovlev "detailing everything that happened at every meeting."

Gold briefly recounted a number of meetings with Klaus Fuchs in New York City in summer 1944. In January 1945 he had met Fuchs in Cambridge, Massachusetts, and received "a package of papers." This he turned over in New York City to Yakovlev, reporting to him that "Fuchs was now stationed at a place called Los Alamos, New Mexico; that this was a large experimental station. . . . Fuchs told me that a tremendous amount of progress had been made. In addition, he had made mention of a lens, which was being worked on as a part of the atom bomb." Soon after, "Yakovlev told me to try to remember anything else that Fuchs had mentioned during our Cambridge meeting, about the lens. Yakovlev was very agitated and asked me to scour my memory clean so as to elicit any possible scrap of information about this lens."

During the January meeting in Cambridge, Fuchs and Gold had arranged to see each other next in Santa Fe, New Mexico, the first Saturday in June 1945. The week before (the last Saturday in May), Gold met with Yakovlev. "I was having difficulty . . . getting off from work and he wanted to make sure that I was going." Yakovlev then told Gold "to take on an additional mission besides the one to see Dr. Fuchs. He said that he wanted me to go to Albuquerque, New Mexico." When Gold "protested," he was informed that "the matter was very vital. . . . He said that a woman was supposed to go in place of me but that she was unable to make the trip." When Gold continued arguing, Yakovlev said "That is an order" and Gold "agreed to go."

Yakovlev than handed Gold a sheet of onionskin paper "and on it was typed . . . the name 'Greenglass' . . . Then a number 'High Street' . . . and then underneath that was 'Albuquerque, New Mexico.' The last thing that was on the paper was 'Recognition signal. I come from Julius.' " Yakovlev also gave Gold an odd-shaped "piece of cardboard, which appeared to have been cut from a packaged food of some sort" and said that Greenglass would have the matching piece. (Gold identified one half of the prosecution's jello box exhibit as a replica of the piece received from Yakovlev.) An envelope, which Yakovlev said contained $500, was to be given Greenglass; if he was not home, "his wife would have the information."

On Saturday afternoon, June 2, 1945, Gold met Fuchs in Santa Fe and received "a bunch of papers"; then took a bus to Albuquerque, some sixty miles away. At about 8:30 P.M., he went to the designated address on High Street and learned that the Greenglasses were out for the evening. He found a place for the night in the hallway of a rooming house and, on Sunday morning, June 3, registered at the Hilton Hotel under his own name.

About 8:30 A.M. that Sunday, Gold returned to the High Street address and saw there "a young man of about 23. . . . I said, 'Mr. Greenglass?' He answered in the affirmative. I said, 'I came from Julius,' and I showed him the piece of cardboard . . . that had been given me by Yakovlev. . . . He asked me to enter. I did. Greenglass went to a women's handbag and brought out from it a piece of cardboard. We matched the two of them."

Observed the *Times*: "By an ironic quirk of Gold's testimony, the cut-out portion of a Jello box became the first tangible bit of evidence to connect the Rosenbergs, the Greenglasses, Gold and Yakovlev."

Gold said he introduced himself "to Greenglass as Dave from Pittsburgh. . . . Mrs. Greenglass said that it was coincidence that my first name and the first name of her husband were the same." Greenglass said that Gold's visit "on this exact day was a bit of a surprise" but that "he would have the material on the atom bomb ready for me that afternoon." When Greenglass started to give him the names of possible espionage recruits, Gold "cut him very short." He gave Greenglass the envelope containing $500. "The last thing that took place that morning was that just as I was preparing to go, Mrs. Greenglass told me that just before she had left New York City to come to Albuquerque she had spoken with Julius."

Returning to the apartment later that afternoon, Gold received an envelope from Greenglass "which he said contained . . . the information on the atom bomb. . . . Mr. Greenglass told me that he expected to get a furlough sometime around Christmas, and that he would return to New York at that time. He told me that if I wished to get in touch with him then I could do so by calling his brother-in-law Julius, and he gave me the telephone number of Julius in New York City."

Gold left the apartment with the Greenglasses, walked a ways with them, and then "immediately" returned to New York. On the train to Chicago, he quickly examined the Greenglass material, noting that it "consisted of three or four handwritten pages plus a couple of sketches . . . . [that] appeared to be for a device of some kind." He turned the material from Fuchs and Greenglass over to Yakovlev. Soon after, Yakovlev reported "that the information which I had given him some two weeks previous had been sent immediately to the Soviet Union. He said that the information which I had received from Greenglass was extremely excellent and very valuable."

Gold and Fuchs had agreed to meet again in Santa Fe in September. Gold suggested to Yakovlev that he also see the Greenglasses in Albuquerque, but was told that "it would be inadvisable to endanger the trip to see Fuchs by complicating it with a visit to the Greenglasses." On September 19, 1945, Gold and Fuchs met for the second time in Santa Fe. Fuchs said he would probably return to England soon and they worked out an arrangement whereby someone would get in touch with Fuchs in London: The contact "was to be carrying a copy of a Bennett Cerf book, 'Stop me if you have heard this.'"*

Later that year, Gold mentioned to Yakovlev that Greenglass had said he might be home on furlough around Christmastime. "I told Yakovlev . . . that we ought to make some plan to get in touch with this brother-in-law, Julius, so that we could get further information from Greenglass. Yakovlev told me to mind my own business. He cut me very short."

Under the conspiracy laws, Gold was permitted to recount any conversations he allegedly had had with the absent defendant Yakovlev. He was thus able to testify at length about Klaus Fuchs, and also to mention both

---

* There is no such book by Cerf; however, there is one titled *Try and Stop Me*.

Slack and Brothman, though none of these individuals was either a defendant or a co-conspirator in the case. Similarly, he was able to mention a number of espionage incidents extraneous to the conspiracy on trial. An example was his story of a meeting with Yakovlev to devise "an arrangement whereby some Soviet agent other than himself could get in touch with me." As one facet of this arrangement, Gold wrote a few words on a piece of paper which Yakovlev then tore, giving Gold half and keeping half. (Assistant U. S. Attorney Lane handed Gold "a replica of the sheet of paper which you had on that particular occasion of your conversation with Yakovlev" and Gold wrote on the paper and tore it. The torn pieces were then entered as a prosecution exhibit.)

On December 26, 1946, Gold received a telephone call from Yakovlev at his place of employment—the laboratory of A. Brothman Associates in New York City. That evening, Gold went to the lounge of a movie theater and "was accosted by a man who showed me a torn piece of paper which Yakovlev and I had prepared." Asked by Judge Kaufman what he meant "to convey by the word accosted," Gold replied: "The man was not Yakovlev. He was tall, about 6 feet 2, had blond hair, and a very determined feature. He walked with a catlike stride almost on the balls of his feet. . . ."

Later that evening, Gold met Yakovlev, who apologized for not seeing him in nearly a year, explaining "that he had to lie low." He told Gold to plan for a mission to meet a physicist in Paris and gave him "a sheet of onionskin paper" with typed instructions. However, when Gold chanced to mention that he was working for Abe Brothman, Yakovlev "almost went through the roof of the saloon. He said, 'You fool. . . . You spoiled eleven years of work' . . . . that I should have remembered that . . . he had told me that Brothman was under suspicion by the United States Government authorities of having engaged in espionage. . . . [Yakovlev] kept mumbling that I had created terrible damage and . . . . then told me that he would not see me in the United States again. . . ."

Harry Gold was not cross-examined.

Evidence was presented that on December 27, 1946, Yakovlev, his wife, and their two young children sailed for France as first-class passengers on the S.S. *America*, with Russia as their ultimate destination. The *Times* commented that Gold's last meeting with Yakovlev "was on Dec. 26, 1946, one day before Yakovlev fled the United States by ship."* (Aside from Gold's, the only other testimony at the trial concerning Yakovlev was that

---

* Actually, the inference that Yakovlev had left the country precipitously on December 27 as a result of his December 26 conversation with Gold is refuted by the prosecution's own evidence. Prosecution exhibit 26, records of the U. S. Lines, shows that in October 1946 Yakovlev secured passage for himself and his family on a November 14 sailing to Europe. A pier strike delayed their departure until December 27.

of Lan Adomian, who identified Yakovlev from a photograph, said he had known him between 1944 and 1946, and that he was Soviet vice-consul in New York City.)

The day after Gold had concluded his testimony, Irving Saypol introduced as a prosecution exhibit a photostat of Harry Gold's registration card at the Hilton Hotel in Albuquerque. Commented the *Herald Tribune:* "The registration card, dated June 3, 1945, bore out Gold's story that he had picked up data on the atomic bomb from David Greenglass at that time." Soon after, Saypol also introduced as an exhibit photostatic copies of records of the Albuquerque National Bank, showing a deposit of $400 to the account of Ruth Greenglass on June 4, 1945.

FLIGHT TO MEXICO   Since Max Elitcher's testimony, no other witness had mentioned Morton Sobell. Now the prosecution completed its case against him, offering the testimony of eight minor witnesses as proof that a trip made by the Sobell family to Mexico in summer 1950 could be viewed as flight.

William Danziger, thirty-three, was a former high school and CCNY classmate of Sobell. In spring 1950 he moved to New York City after an absence of many years and he and his wife paid a social visit to the Sobell home. Morton mentioned that another classmate, Julius Rosenberg—whom Danziger had not seen since college days—was in the machine shop business. Danziger, employed by a firm that sometimes farmed out such work, asked for and received Rosenberg's address. (The purpose of this testimony was apparently to establish that Sobell and Rosenberg knew each other.) Subsequently, Danziger made two brief visits to Rosenberg, in June and July. On the latter occasion, he had stopped in at Rosenberg's machine shop "to look over the . . . facilities" and Julius had mentioned that "he couldn't accept any work for some months, for me to contact him some time in the future."

Danziger also testified that about June 20, 1950, he telephoned Sobell to ask for an electric drill to do a home repair and Sobell mentioned "that he was getting ready to leave for a vacation in Mexico, and that he was leaving rather shortly and if I wanted the drill, for me to come out and get it." That evening Danziger picked up the drill at Sobell's home. Present were Sobell and his wife and children and his sister-in-law, Edith Levitov. Sobell said he was flying to Mexico City. A car in the driveway had valises in it. Asked about the appearance of the house, Danziger replied: "Well, it was quite evident that there was packing going on, there were valises standing there. The rest of the house was not too disorderly."

About a week later, Danziger (who had corresponded with Sobell over the years) received at work a letter postmarked Mexico City; written on the envelope was "M. Sowell" and a Mexico City address. The letter said: "Dear Bill, had a nice trip, held the kid on my lap all the way, and located a place to stay." Enclosed were notes to Sobell's parents and sister-in-law, Miss Levitov, accompanied by a message: "Please forward the enclosures and I will explain to you when I get back." The message also asked Danziger to deliver the Mexico City address to Max Pasternak, a relative of Sobell. Danziger complied with the requests and wrote to his friend under the name "M. Sowell or Morty Sowell in Mexico City."

Sometime in mid-July, Danziger received a second letter postmarked Mexico City. On the envelope was a return address and the name "M. or Morty Levitov." A letter said: "Dear Bill, I am having a nice time. I have moved from one place to another." Enclosed was a letter for Edith Levitov and a note: "Please forward enclosure and I will explain when I get back." He forwarded the letter and did not hear from Sobell again.

Manuel Giner de los Rios was one of a number of Mexican witnesses who testified with the aid of a translator. In early July 1950 he had seen an American on the stairway of his apartment house in Mexico City and, knowing a little English, had helped the man—who had just rented an apartment—in his palavering with a caretaker over cooking gas. He learned that the man's name was Morton Sobell. Giner de los Rios invited Sobell to a party at his house and subsequently had dinner at the Sobell apartment. At times, he saw Sobell and his family "going to the terrace to take . . . a sun bath."

One day, Giner de los Rios testified, Sobell inquired "if I wanted to be a friend of his. . . . He was a little nervous, a little worried . . . . he asked me how one could leave Mexico. And I told him that there would be no trouble if one has his papers in good order. He asked me if there would be any other way and I told him no, I didn't know of any other way." Sobell said "he was worried because . . . he was afraid to return to . . . the U. S. Army since he has already seen a war." (Selective Service Records, produced by Colonel Candler Cobb—who had testified earlier that the defendant's true name was Morton Sobell—were used to show that Sobell was never in the Army, having been deferred during World War II.) Asked if Sobell had said where he wanted to go, Giner de los Rios replied: "No, he didn't mention any place in particular. . . . He didn't specify any . . . country outside of Mexico."

After this incident, he continued to see Sobell. Once "he came to my house and asked for a hammer to break open a coconut"; another time he said he wanted to go to Vera Cruz and Giner de los Rios gave him directions to the bus station. About the twentieth or twenty-second of July, Sobell left Mexico City without his family for the seaport city of Vera Cruz. While he was away, Giner de los Rios received two letters addressed to himself—one postmarked Vera Cruz; the second, Tampico. In each envelope he found a letter that began "Dear Helen," Mrs. Sobell's first name, and gave her the letters.

Minerva Bravo Espinosa, an employee of a Vera Cruz optical store, testified that on July 26 an American—she identified Sobell as the man—

had ordered glasses and filled out a card on which he called himself "M. Sand." Jose Broccado Vendrell, an administrator of a Vera Cruz hotel, produced a registration card signed "Morris Sand" by a man who left the hotel July 30. Dora Bautista, a clerk at a Tampico hotel, testified that an American whom she identified as Morton Sobell had registered on July 30 as "Marvin Salt." Glen Dennis, a Mexican airline official, produced records showing that an "N. Sand" was a passenger on a July 30 flight from Vera Cruz to Tampico and a "Morton Solt" on an August 2 flight from Tampico to Mexico City.

Through his attorneys, Sobell conceded that he had signed the name "M. Sand" at the Vera Cruz optical shop, "Morris Sand" at the Vera Cruz hotel and "Marvin Salt" at the Tampico hotel, and that he had been an airline passenger under the names "N. Sand" and "Morton Solt."

James S. Huggins, an immigration inspector in Laredo, Texas, testified that on August 18, 1950, Morton Sobell was brought into his office by Mexican Security Police and was thereafter taken into custody by U.S. authorities. Huggins had written on a card, prepared by him at the time, "deported from Mexico." He said he had made this notation on the basis of his own observation and had not obtained such information from Mexican authorities or seen any document relating to the alleged deportation.

ELIZABETH BENTLEY   Already known to the public as a self-confessed ex-Communist and former Soviet espionage courier, Elizabeth Bentley was asked first by Saypol about her membership in the Communist Party. Judge Kaufman overruled defense objections, saying that the testimony was intended to show "the causal connection . . . between the membership in the party and intending to give an advantage to . . . the U.S.S.R., as charged in the indictment." Miss Bentley said that in 1935 she had joined the American Communist Party which was "part of the Communist International and subject to its jurisdiction as such" and "only served the interests of Moscow, whether it be propaganda or espionage or sabotage."

In 1938, she had gone "underground" and that year met Jacob Golos, whom she described as "one of a three-man control commission" of the American Communist Party. Her knowledge of the Communist Party and International was based on personal observation and also on what she was told by a number of people, including Earl Browder—then head of the American Communist Party. (After Golos's death in November 1943, she testified, she had "transmitted orders from Moscow" to Earl Browder.)

Miss Bentley said she collected information for Golos "from Communists employed in the United States Government . . . for transmission to Moscow" and was known variously as Helen, Joan, and Mary. She had two "groups" in Washington—in "agencies like the OSS and the Treasury"—

and also "quite a number of isolated individuals . . . . some 30-odd altogether."

Once, in late fall 1942, she accompanied Golos when he drove to the vicinity of Knickerbocker Village and told her "he had to stop by to pick up some material from a contact, an engineer." While she waited, Golos had met the contact and "returned to the car with an envelope of material."

> SAYPOL: Subsequent to this occasion when you went to the vicinity of . . . [Knickerbocker] Village with Golos . . . did you have a telephone call from somebody who described himself as "Julius"?
> MISS BENTLEY: Yes, I did.

She said she had transmitted messages from "Julius" to Golos and had learned that "Julius" resided in Knickerbocker Village. Judge Kaufman observed that it would "be for the jury to infer . . . whether or not the Julius she spoke to . . . is the defendant Julius Rosenberg." (Earlier, both Elitcher and David Greenglass, in somewhat contradictory testimony, had referred to statements by Rosenberg regarding Miss Bentley.)

On cross-examination by Emanuel Bloch, Miss Bentley said she had received fees for lecturing on Communism, but could not recall how many times she had lectured during the previous two years, or how much money she was paid. She also had received a $3000 advance on an autobiographical book (scheduled for publication) about "how a person can become a Communist and how they can be disillusioned and get out again."

She had mentioned the telephone calls from a "Julius" in material sent her publisher, but did not have "the least idea" when she had submitted this material and had no copy in her possession. She had received five or six phone calls in 1942 and 1943 from this individual, who had called "after midnight, in the wee small hours" and "always started his conversation by saying, 'This is Julius.'"

Miss Bentley did not know how many Communist Party units were operating in New York nor how many Party members there were during any of the years from 1935 to 1947. She said she had no knowledge of the constitution of the American Communist Party and could not recall if she had ever seen one.

Shortly after Elizabeth Bentley concluded her testimony, the prosecution rested; presentation of the government's case had taken nine trial days.

JULIUS ROSENBERG The first witness for the defense was the thirty-two-year-old defendant, Julius Rosenberg, a bespectacled, serious-faced man with a trim black mustache. New York City-born, he had graduated from the lower East Side's Seward Park High School, obtaining religious training at Downtown Talmud Torah and Hebrew High

School. He received a degree in electrical engineering from CCNY in February 1939 and, a few months later—just after his twenty-first birthday —was married to Ethel Greenglass. They had two young sons.

After a year of odd jobs, in 1940 Julius was appointed a $2000-a-year Army Signal Corps "junior engineer." In spring 1942 he and Ethel—they had been living in his mother's home and furnished rooms—rented a $46-a-month, three-room apartment in an East Side housing development called Knickerbocker Village. Furniture was given them by a friend at Julius's union who was moving to another state; later, they acquired other second-hand pieces, purchasing only one new item: A $21 console table. When "separated" from his government job in February 1945, his annual pay was $3600. He secured work at Emerson Radio, making $100 weekly with overtime; late that year he was laid off when the staff was curtailed. He then became a partner in a small surplus products business and, soon after (spring 1946), in a machine shop, in which he and Ethel's brothers— David and Bernard—invested. Additional capital came from Greenglass relatives and, later, from a businessman, David Schein.

Emanuel Bloch directed Julius's attention to each incident related to the alleged espionage conspiracy and asked if he had participated in it. He answered most of these questions with roughly the same three words—"I did not"—and completely denied any espionage activities. He testified that he never had known Anatoli Yakovlev or any other Russian official. He was not aware of the existence of the Los Alamos project before it was revealed publicly. He did not give Ruth Greenglass $150 to go to Albuquerque, nor did he ever give her any money. He did not describe the atom bomb for David, nor could he have. The Greenglasses' visit to his apartment for dinner in January 1945 was entirely social; he could not recall if Ann Sidorovich was there. (Her husband was a high school acquaintance and they had been Knickerbocker Village neighbors, who later moved to Cleveland.)

Judge Kaufman frequently interrupted Bloch's chronologic rundown of the espionage charges to inquire about the defendant's political ideas:

BLOCH: Did you ever have any discussion with Ann Sidorovich or her husband at any time with respect to getting any information relating to the national defense in this country?

JULIUS: I did not.

JUDGE KAUFMAN: Did you ever discuss with Ann Sidorovich the respective preferences of economic systems between Russia and the United States?

Julius replied that he had discussed such matters in his "normal social intercourse" and believed there were "merits in both systems." He was "heartily in favor" of the Constitution and Bill of Rights and of "our system of justice." As for the Soviet government, it had improved the "lot of the underdog . . . made a lot of progress in eliminating illiteracy . . . done a lot of reconstruction work and built up a lot of resources, and . . . contributed a major share in destroying the Hitler beast who killed six million of my co-religionists." Asked by Judge Kaufman if he had approved "the communistic system of Russia over the capitalistic system in this country," Julius denied making "any such direct statement," and added that "the people of every country should decide by themselves what kind of government they want." He refused to tell the Judge whether he ever had belonged to "any group that discussed the system of Russia," saying he would not answer questions about "membership in any political organization like the Communist Party."

In addition to his general denial of all charges, the defendant specifically contested a number of Ruth Greenglass's claims:

Ruth had testified that Ethel told her about Julius spending $50 to $75 on an evening's entertainment in connection with espionage. Denying this, Julius said he had been to a night club only once in his life—at a union dinner party—and had rarely eaten in expensive restaurants. In the previous five years he had purchased about five suits at around $26 each; in ten years, Ethel had spent a maximum total of $300 on clothes.

As for Ruth's testimony about his visit to her apartment shortly before she went to Albuquerque to live, Julius said this visit had been made at Ruth's request. When he arrived, Ruth had whispered, "I would like to talk to you alone. Tell the kid to go into the bathroom." After he had sent Dorothy Printz into the bathroom, Ruth told him that she was "terribly worried. David has an idea to make some money and take some things from the Army." He told Ruth to warn David against this, saying he had read about GI's "taking parts and gasoline from the Army, and their getting themselves in trouble."

Commenting on various details of David's testimony, Julius said it was "very unlikely" that he would have suggested that David go to MIT or the University of Chicago "because he probably couldn't get into those places." Actually, Julius said, he had complained when David attended night school—leaving the shop two or three afternoons a week with no one to supervise the employees—"and finally David quit school because of that." Neither he nor Ethel had received any Russian citation, watches, or console table; he had purchased the latter himself for cash from Macy's and had it delivered. (It was at his home when the FBI came there to arrest him.) He never had been in either Schenectady or Cleveland, where David said he had espionage contacts. As for the "sky platform project," he recalled a discussion with David regarding a "suspended lens in the sky" to concentrate the sun's rays, noting that David read *Popular Mechanics* and *Popular Science* and "always talked about things like that at the shop."

In August 1949 David quit the machine shop—business was "very bad" —and Bernard Greenglass left soon after. Between January and May 1950 Julius sought possession of David's shares of stock in the firm, but refused the Greenglasses' request for cash payment or some written evidence of indebtedness. On May 1 he received the stock, after promising verbally to pay $1000. That same day, Julius contracted to purchase the stock of the remaining partner, a businessman, David Schein, giving him a $1000 check and agreeing to pay $4500 more in $160-a-month installments. This transaction, which David was aware of, left Julius with little money in his bank account. (He subsequently cashed some U.S. bonds to meet his payments to Schein.)

About mid-May, David came to the shop and requested $2000 from Julius "at once." Referring to his $1000 downpayment and monetary obligation to David Schein, Julius said, "I have no cash left. . . . I just don't have the money. What do you want it for?" Replying, "Don't ask me questions," David insisted that he needed the money. He was "very excited . . . . he said, 'Well, if you can't help me like that maybe you can do something else for me.' I said, 'What is it? If I can help you I will.' He said, 'Will you go to your doctor and ask him if he would make out a certificate for a smallpox vaccination?' I said, 'Why don't you go to your doctor?' He said, 'Don't ask me that. I can't do it.'" When Julius agreed to ask his doctor, David added: " 'Don't tell him who it is for, and also, incidentally, while you are talking to him, ask him if he knows what kind of injections are required to go into Mexico.' I said, 'Dave, are you in trouble or something?' He said, 'Don't ask me anything about it. . . . If you can't give me the money I need, at least do this for me.'" David had been "very disturbed and agitated."

When Julius related the incident to Ethel, she said, "What is the matter? Is Ruthie nagging Dave again for money?" Julius told her that it didn't "seem to be that. He must be in some trouble. I don't know what it is." Julius said he then recalled that the previous February David had told him that the FBI had come around "to visit him and question him about some uranium." He thought David's troubles might have to do with that incident or with the conversation about stealing that "Ruthie had with me many years back."

Later, Julius asked his physician, Dr. Bernhardt, about inoculations required for Mexico and also inquired if he would "make out a certificate for a smallpox injection for somebody he didn't vaccinate." The doctor said he would not. While on the way to work, Julius stopped by the Greenglass apartment—the shop was "three or four blocks" away—to tell David about the doctor's refusal "and he said he would take care of it himself."

Around the end of May, Julius went to the Greenglass apartment in response to a phone call from David, but was not admitted because

David said he had "some company." Julius told Ethel that her brother was "in some trouble" and "acting peculiar" and she "prevailed upon me to see if we can do something to help him out." Soon after, David phoned Julius again, saying it was "very urgent" that he see him. When Julius dropped in around the beginning of June, Ruth was "cool" and "Dave was very excited. He was pale and he had a haggard look on his face." While out walking, David said he was in "a terrible jam," refused any details, and asked for "a couple of thousand dollars in cash." Julius turned down David's request that he borrow the money from relatives or take it from the business. David then said, " 'Well, Julie, I just got to have that money and if you don't get me that money you are going to be sorry.' I said, 'Look here, Dave, what are you trying to do, threaten me or blackmail me?' " David "was puffing and I saw a wild look in his eyes, and I realized it was time to cut this conversation short." Telling David to go home and "take a cold shower," Julius left and made up his mind that he "wouldn't have anything to do with him."

However, Ethel was "terribly upset" about her "kid brother" and a day or two later Julius stopped by the Greenglass apartment again, found both Ruth and David "cool" to him and "saw that Davey was calmer."

The morning of June 16, just after the FBI took David into custody, Julius was visited by three FBI agents and agreed to talk with them at their Foley Square offices. "They asked me questions concerning when David Greenglass came in on furlough. I didn't remember . . . . about two hours after I was there, they said to me, 'Do you know that your brother-in-law said that you told him to supply information for Russia?' " Julius asked the agents to bring Greenglass to him and " 'I will call him a liar to his face. . . .' And I said, 'Look, gentlemen, at first you asked me to come down and get some information concerning David Greenglass. Now you are trying to implicate me in something. I would like to see a lawyer.' " After five or six hours with the FBI, Julius phoned a lawyer who advised him to ask the agents if he was under arrest and, if not, to leave. That evening he was referred to Emanuel Bloch, who became his attorney.

Julius also denied Elitcher's story. He testified that he had seen Max Elitcher between summer and fall 1944 while assigned to work for several days at the Bureau of Standards in Washington. Lonesome, he looked through the phone book for anyone he knew, found Elitcher's name, called him, and was invited over. The visit consisted entirely of an hour of social conversation. In Washington again in April 1945, to try to see his Congressman about his Signal Corps dismissal, he phoned Max and said he wanted to talk with some people at the latter's union (Federal Workers). The Elitchers were going to union headquarters and Julius came to their apartment and drove with them. As for Morton Sobell, he had not seen him between 1940 and 1946; they never had discussed

Elitcher. Since 1946, the Sobells had made a few social visits to his home and he had met with Morton once or twice a year.

On cross-examination, Saypol's first questions concerned Julius's "associates . . . at City College" and "any common . . . activities which brought this group . . . together." Julius soon invoked the Fifth Amendment, saying he would not answer questions about the Young Communist League or Communist Party.

When the defendant said he had lost his Signal Corps job in 1945 because "It was alleged that I was a member of the Communist Party," Saypol responded: "That is, the Secretary of War in the interest of national defense directed that you be separated from the service?" Specific charges of Party membership made by the Army against Rosenberg had been denied by him at that time in a letter; he refused to answer any questions about this letter at the trial.

Asked about his wartime views regarding the Soviet Union, Julius said he "felt that the Russians contributed the major share in destroying the Nazi army" and "should get as much help as possible." Judge Kaufman inquired if he had thought in 1944 and 1945 "that if Great Britain shared in all our secrets that Russia should . . . also?" Julius replied that the ultimate decision on such matters was up to the respective governments, but his "opinion was that if we had a common enemy we should get together commonly."

Questioned about the source of his earlier statement—on direct examination—that the Soviet government had improved the "lot of the underdog," Julius said he read this information in "various newspapers." Asked Saypol: "You mean, the *Daily Worker?*" Julius replied that he read the *Worker* on occasion and also the *Times, Herald Tribune,* and *World-Telegram.*

SAYPOL: The *Wall Street Journal,* perhaps?
JULIUS: No, I don't read the *Wall Street Journal.*

Julius had also said that the Russians "built up a lot of resources." Asked to tell about "the resources," he said the Russians built large dams.

SAYPOL: Dams you consider resources?
JULIUS: That's right; hydroelectric stations. That is a dam.
SAYPOL: Did you read anything about the request of Russia for the atomic bomb? Would that be perhaps a resource that you had in mind?

Queried whether he had made "contributions to the Joint Anti-Fascist Refugee Committee," Julius answered: "Yes, I believe I did." Commented Saypol: "That is known to be an organization deemed subversive by the

Attorney General." He asked if Rosenberg had gone out and collected money for the committee.

The *Times* reported: "Receiving a denial, he [Saypol] produced a collection can bearing the committee's name and set it down on the jury box rail with a loud thump."

Saypol then read the label on the can, which he said was found in the Rosenberg apartment: "Save a Spanish Republican Child, Volveremos, We will return." (The can was entered as a prosecution exhibit.) Julius said that the International Workers Order (IWO) in which he held insurance had sent him the can and he had contributed but "never solicited funds." He was then questioned about whether IWO was a Communist organization, how he had joined, and to whom he paid his insurance premiums.

Julius was asked about a number of his acquaintances. Referring to a Vivian Glassman—mentioned in newspaper accounts of the Perl arrest—Saypol inquired: "Isn't it the fact that you gave her $2000 to take out to somebody in Cleveland?" Rosenberg denied this. Asked about another acquaintance, Alfred Sarant, Rosenberg said he believed he was in Ithaca, New York. When Saypol queried: "Don't you know that he is in Mexico?" the defense moved, unsuccessfully, for a mistrial.

Some of Saypol's questions seemed rhetorical. On the console table Julius had said he purchased for $21: "Don't you know, Mr. Rosenberg, that you couldn't buy a console table in Macy's, if they had it, in 1944 and 1945, for less than $85?" On Julius's account of David's request for $2000 and a vaccination certificate: "What did you think, he had smallpox? . . . Did you think it a little fantastic for your brother-in-law to come to you and say, 'I want $2000 for a smallpox certificate?'" On Sobell's Mexican trip: "What did you have to do with sending Sobell away?"

The latter question elicited a strong objection from Sobell's attorney: "There is no testimony here that he had anything to do with sending Sobell or anybody else away." Observed Judge Kaufman: "You are excited Mr. Kuntz." Kuntz replied: ". . . I can convict anybody by that kind of question."

MINOR DEFENSE WITNESSES   John Gibbons, a *Herald Tribune* employee, produced a photo of Harry Gold published May 24, 1950. David and Ruth had testified that, when shown this newspaper picture by Julius, they did not recognize their Albuquerque visitor. The apparent purpose of the defense was to indicate that the photo was a good likeness.

Thomas V. Kelley, a Macy's representative, was asked for any records of the sale and delivery of a console table to a Julius Rosenberg of 10 Monroe Street in 1944 or 1945. He testified that sales slips and (after checking further) delivery records for both these years had been destroyed.

ETHEL ROSENBERG   The final defense witness, Ethel Greenglass Rosenberg, thirty-five, described by the *Times* as a "little woman with soft and pleasant features," was questioned by Alexander Bloch. Born at 64 Sheriff Street on the lower East Side (her mother still lived in the same house), she had three brothers of whom David was the youngest. While attending public school, Ethel also had studied Hebrew, piano, and voice —singing for a year as the youngest member of Hugh Ross's Schola Cantorum. Graduated from Seward Park High School before the age of sixteen, she took a short secretarial course, then held various clerical jobs and was an active unionist. She belonged to dramatic groups at Clark House and at Henry Street Settlement, where she had "a scholarship . . . to take dramatic courses and modern dancing." Until her marriage at the age of twenty-three, she lived with her family, turning over her entire salary to them—"except for carfare and lunches."

Since then—to help her raise her children—she had taken courses in child psychology at the New School for Social Research and in music for children at the Bank Street School; she also had studied the guitar in spring 1950. She had not seen her two boys, Michael, eight, and Robert, three—both were in a municipal children's shelter—since her arrest seven months before.

In her Knickerbocker Village apartment, she had performed all the chores of a housewife and mother, hiring help only briefly after the birth of each child and, in 1944–45, during a period of ill health. She described the apartment's second-hand furnishings and said the console table was "a very inexpensive table." She had been at home when it was delivered from Macy's.

Ethel denied all allegations regarding espionage activity. While David was in the Army, she had sent him letters from herself and also from her mother and had occasionally written to Ruth in Albuquerque. She had treated David as her "baby brother. . . . I loved him very much." David "liked us both. He liked my husband." Asked by Judge Kaufman if David's relationship with Julius had been one of "hero worship," she replied: "Oh, by no stretch of the imagination could you say that was hero worship."

Ethel testified that she never had typed anything relating to the national defense. She owned a typewriter—she had purchased it when she was eighteen—and during her courtship had typed Julius's college engineering reports; prior to the birth of her first child, she did "a lot of typing" as a member of the ladies auxiliary of her husband's union and as secretary for the East Side Defense Council, the neighborhood branch of the Civil Defense Volunteer Organization. She also had done some typing relating to Julius's business and his attempts for reinstatement in his government job. Julius had denied Communist Party membership in the latter letters and she refused, on Fifth Amendment grounds, to answer any questions about them.

Asked by Judge Kaufman what her response had been when Julius told her of David's demand for $2000 in May 1950, Ethel answered: "Well, I said to my husband . . . 'doesn't he know the kind of financial situation we are in?' . . . And then I remember saying something to the effect that 'If Ruthie doesn't stop nagging him for money, she is liable to give him another psychological heart attack like he had in the winter.'" Later, Ethel added that "it was common knowledge that Ruthie always nagged Davey about money."

Ruth Greenglass had testified that in mid-July 1950 Ethel had sought assurances from her that David would not talk. Said Ethel: "Well I had a conversation with my sister-in-law, but it wasn't like that at all." She said she had asked Ruth, "Are you and Davey really mixed up in this horrible mess?" and Ruth had "flared up," saying "we have hired a lawyer and we are going to fight this case because we are not guilty." Ruth said she was having a difficult time financially and Ethel expressed regret at being unable to aid her. Describing their parting, Ethel said she put her arms around Ruth "and kissed her. She remained rigid in my arms . . . said, 'Goodbye' coldly, turned on her heel and left."

On cross-examination, Saypol introduced as a prosecution exhibit a petition nominating Peter Cacchione as a Communist Party candidate for New York City Councilman. It had been signed by Ethel Rosenberg in 1939.

After Julius's arrest, Ethel had testified twice (on August 7 and 11) before a federal grand jury; she had been arrested a few minutes after her second appearance. Both times, she invoked her constitutional privilege against self-incrimination frequently. Much of her grand jury testimony was read in court, disclosing that many of the same questions she had refused to answer before the grand jury she later had answered at her trial. Remarked by the *Times* was that she "had claimed constitutional privilege . . . even on questions that seemed harmless." Fully half of Saypol's cross-examination was devoted to pointing this up. Denying defense moves for a mistrial, Judge Kaufman said the jury could consider the matter in evaluating the truthfulness and credibility of Mrs. Rosenberg.

Ethel gave no specific explanation for her extensive use of the Fifth Amendment before the grand jury, but noted that both her husband and brother were under arrest at the time. Julius had told her that David had "acted very hostile" when he had seen him in jail and she feared her brother might be trying to implicate her also. "At that time I didn't know what to believe or not to believe about my brother."

SAYPOL: You profess a love for your brother, don't you?
ETHEL: You mean I once had a love for my brother.
SAYPOL: You mean that has changed?
ETHEL: I would be pretty unnatural if it hadn't changed.

Ethel had said that after the birth of her second child she had stored a rickety bridge table in a closet in her apartment because "we were too crowded." Asked by Saypol if she ever put the console table in a closet, she replied: "I may have." She denied telling anyone that the console table was a present.

Saypol asked her—as he had Julius—if she and her family had gone "to a photographer's place at 99 Park Row in May or June of 1950 . . . to have passport photographs made?" Ethel and her husband both denied taking passport photos, noting that they frequently stopped into photo shops while out walking with their children and might have taken family pictures the previous May or June. Said Ethel: "We happen to be what you would call 'snapshot hounds'. . . ."

With the conclusion of her testimony, the defendants Julius and Ethel Rosenberg rested their case. The defendant Morton Sobell elected not to take the stand; his attorney stated that he "desires to rest on the record."

PROSECUTION REBUTTAL The prosecution then presented a number of rebuttal witnesses. Mrs. Evelyn Cox testified that sometime in 1944 or 1945, when she was employed as a domestic by the Rosenbergs, she noticed a new piece of furniture—a console table. She admired it and asked Mrs. Rosenberg "where it came from . . . . she said that a friend of her husband gave it to him as a gift . . . . a sort of a wedding present."

Later, Mrs. Cox noticed that the table "wasn't where it usually stayed and I asked her why she had removed it, and she said she had put it away in the closet because the place was too congested." She had seen the table in a "very large closet" several times, but did not see it outside in the living room again. Asked by Emanuel Bloch whether the table had been used for eating purposes, Mrs. Cox said: "It was never used for any purposes, so far as I know, never. . . . It was an ornament."

The prosecution's final witness was Ben Schneider, whose small photo shop—just behind the courthouse at 99 Park Row—was within easy walking distance of Knickerbocker Village. In May or June 1950, a man and woman with two children, about six and four, had visited his shop on a Saturday, ordering three dozen passport-size pictures for about nine dollars. As the man "was leaving he was telling me they were going to France; there was some property left; they were going to take care of it . . . his wife was left some property." He identified Julius and Ethel Rosenberg in court as the couple for whom he had taken the passport photos.

Schneider said he was first visited by FBI agents about the case at 11:30 A.M. the previous day. The agents had shown him photographs from which he had picked the Rosenbergs out. Schneider agreed with Saypol's formulations that he recalled the Rosenbergs by seeing them "here now" and also because he wasn't "usually open on Saturday" and "the order was unusual in size."

Bloch's first question on cross-examination was: "Where are the negatives?" Schneider said he did not keep negatives and neither did he have any sales slips or books. The Rosenbergs, he said, had visited his shop "about the middle of June," 1950. Though he had testified that he was usually not open Saturdays, he admitted that most of the year he was open for business part of the day Saturday, though "It is a very slow day."

When Bloch asked Schneider if there were not "some Saturdays when you do a rather rushing business," Saypol interjected: "Did you say 'a Russian business' or a 'rushing business'?" Judge Kaufman admonished Saypol to "Try to restrain your desire to be another Milton Berle."

SUMMATIONS   On behalf of Julius and Ethel Rosenberg, Emanuel Bloch explained to the jury that "Two kinds of evidence came out of that witness box. One kind . . . we lawyers call 'oral evidence.' That is the evidence that comes out of the mouths of people. Then we have another kind . . . that we call 'documentary evidence' . . . . and those are what we call exhibits."

Bloch reviewed the prosecution's exhibits: Copies of Los Alamos security regulations and a directive regarding Niels Bohr; replicas of David's lens mold sketches; a cut jello box; photos of the Greenglasses, Yakovlev, Gold, Fuchs, and the Sidoroviches; a replica of a torn paper allegedly used by Gold and Yakovlev as a recognition device; a photostat of Gold's registration card at the Albuquerque Hilton Hotel; photostatic records of Ruth's $400 deposit in an Albuquerque bank; a document concerning Yakovlev's official status in the U.S.; passenger ship records of the Yakovlev family's departure from the U.S.; four Greenglass passport photos; brown paper in which $4000 was wrapped; a picture of Schneider's photo shop; Sobell's Selective Service file; Mexican optical shop, hotel, and airline records, all showing Sobell's use of various aliases; an official record of Sobell's arrival in the U.S. from Mexico; pictures of tables, including a console table; a coin collection can from the Rosenberg apartment; and a 1939 Communist Party nominating petition signed by Ethel Rosenberg.

Asked Bloch: "Is there anything here which in any way connects Rosenberg with this conspiracy . . . ?" The FBI "stopped at nothing in their investigation . . . to try to find some piece of evidence that you could feel, that you could see, that would tie the Rosenbergs up with this case . . . . and yet this is the . . . . complete documentary evidence adduced by the Government . . . . this case, therefore, against the Rosenbergs depends upon oral testimony."

David Greenglass, "a self-confessed espionage agent," was "repulsive. . . . he smirked and he smiled. . . . I wonder whether . . . you have ever come across a man, who comes around to bury his own sister and smiles." The Greenglasses had "tricked" the FBI and the prosecution.

Ruth was "the smarter of the two" and "the embodiment of evil"; she had testified "like a phonograph record." David's "grudge against Rosenberg" over money was not enough to explain his testimony. The explanation was that David "loved his wife" and "was willing to bury his sister and his brother-in-law" to save her. The "Greenglass plot" was to lessen his punishment by pointing his finger at someone else. He may have reasoned that naming Yakovlev would do him no good—he had to have "somebody whom the Government can nab." Julius was "a clay pigeon" because he had been fired from his government job for alleged Communist Party membership and "was a guy who was very open and expressed his views about the United States and the Soviet Union."

Gold "told the truth. That is why I didn't cross-examine him." Gold never "had any traffic or transactions with Rosenberg." He had received his part of the jello box directly from Yakovlev and perhaps David had also.

Elitcher had "a Damoclean sword hanging over his head"; he knew he could be prosecuted for perjury for falsely swearing that he was not a member of the Communist Party. ". . . any kind of a suggestion . . . under those circumstances would necessarily gravitate a man's thinking to fall in line with what the Government would like him to say" and, "in August or late July 1950, the FBI honestly believed that Rosenberg was guilty of this crime, and Rosenberg was suggested. . . ." Elitcher's story was highly improbable.

Miss Bentley was "a professional anti-Communist. She makes money on it." She and Gold had used all kinds of false names. If the phone calls from a "Julius" ever actually occurred, isn't "it reasonable to infer . . . that Julius was a code name?"

As for the console table, Ruth said a portion "was hollowed out for a lamp to fit underneath it . . . for photograph purposes." If this were so, would not the woman who cleaned the apartment, Mrs. Cox, have noticed it? "Did you hear Mrs. Cox testify to anything of the kind? She did not."

The Schneider testimony was "the vulgar and tawdry part of this trial." The government "contends that only yesterday, at 11:30 in the morning . . . lo and behold, this witness appears." If the Greenglasses told the FBI in June 1950 that Rosenberg asked them for passport photos and said that he also was planning to leave, wouldn't the FBI have "combed every photography shop in New York . . . to ascertain whether or not Rosenberg was taking passport photos?" Any pictures the Rosenbergs may have taken were family photographs.

If David's story about the "finger in the book down before a statue in Mexico City, and then go over to Sweden" was true, why didn't Sobell —"if he were trying to get out of Mexico because of this crime"—know about the "fingers and the statue"?

The trial—originally said to require months—had "petered out in three weeks" with most of the prosecution's listed witnesses never called. Said Bloch: ". . . if you will decide this case the way you would decide an ordinary problem that comes up in your life . . . . you either will come to the conclusion that these defendants are completely innocent, or at the very, very least that you would have a reasonable doubt about their guilt."

Summing up for Morton Sobell, Edward Kuntz said the FBI and prosecution had "labored and labored and labored, and they brought forth a mouse—Elitcher." Kuntz asserted that Elitcher, the only witness to connect Sobell to the alleged conspiracy, was "a miserable liar." His story of Rosenberg's first espionage proposal did not "make sense." Elitcher had been friends with Sobell for a long time, but did not know Rosenberg well. Yet Rosenberg "enlists him for espionage and mentions casually" that Sobell is in also. Not until three months later, on vacation, does Elitcher mention the incident to Sobell.

Referring to Elitcher's account of the July 1948 car ride to Catherine Slip to deliver some material to Rosenberg, Kuntz said: "Now, let's see what that dangerous material was. Did you hear what it was? . . . All he said was that he took a tin can that might have held film. . . . What is this that anybody could defend himself against? . . . What kind of evidence is that?"

Sobell had mentioned to a friend, Danziger, that he was going to Mexico and had flown there under his own name. "So up to that point there is no flight, is there, if I go to Mexico in my own name, with my family?" They had rented an apartment in Mexico "in their own name." As for the trips to Vera Cruz and Tampico, Kuntz said he did not care "what kind of a brainstorm Sobell might have had" or "if he had read in the newspapers something about Rosenberg. . . . That is his own business." But he "did not hide his identity" because at the time of the trip "Helen Sobell and the children were right in that apartment." Saying he had read that Saypol himself had gone to Mexico "to dig this up," Kuntz said that if the prosecutor were "serving us right," he would have "gone over to that house where the Sobells lived and found out . . . that they lived openly, in their own name."

An American immigration official, Huggins, had testified that solely on the basis of personal observation he had written on a card relating to Sobell "Deported from Mexico." Kuntz inquired why Saypol "could bring here an optician's clerk from Vera Cruz" and not produce a Mexican official to testify that the alleged deportation "was the fact."

Irving Saypol opened the prosecution's summation by describing the case as "one of the most important . . . ever . . . submitted to a jury in this country. I feel most inadequate to express to you in words the enormity of the thing. . . ."

Saypol asserted that "Rosenberg's Communist espionage superior in the early 1940s was Jacob Golos . . . one of the top Soviet espionage agents. . . . We know this from the telephone calls Miss Bentley received from this engineer, from Knickerbocker Village, Julius. . . . But most important of all we know of Rosenberg's dealings with Bentley from statements made by Rosenberg himself to Max Elitcher and David Greenglass. . . . We know that after the death of Golos Rosenberg continued his espionage activities. We do not know all of the details. The identity of some of the other traitors . . . remains undisclosed. We know that such people exist because of Rosenberg's boasting to Greenglass of . . . how he had obtained information on the secret Government project concerning the Sky Platform, concerning . . . atomic power for airplanes. . . . We don't know all the details, because the only living people who can supply the details are the defendants . . . . but there is one part of the scheme that we do know about. . . . We know that these conspirators stole the most important scientific secrets ever known to mankind from this country and delivered them to the Soviet Union."

David Greenglass's "description of the atom bomb" was typed by Ethel Rosenberg. "Just so had she on countless other occasions sat at that typewriter and struck the keys, blow by blow, against her country in the interests of the Soviets."

Noting that "Mr. Bloch had a lot of things to say about Greenglass," Saypol pointed out that the story of the Albuquerque meeting "does not come to you from Greenglass alone. Every word that David and Ruth Greenglass spoke on this stand about that incident was corroborated by Harry Gold. . . .

"The history of this Jello box side, the greetings from Julius and Greenglass's whereabouts in Albuquerque come to us not only from Ruth and David, but from Harry Gold . . . a man concerning whom there cannot even be a suggestion of motive. . . . He has been sentenced to thirty years. . . . He can gain nothing from testifying as he did in this courtroom except the . . . moral satisfaction in his soul of having told the truth and tried to make amends. Harry Gold, who furnished the absolute corroboration of the testimony of the Greenglasses, forged the necessary link in the chain that points indisputably to the guilt of the Rosenbergs.

"The veracity of David and Ruth Greenglass and of Harry Gold is established by documentary evidence and cannot be contradicted. You have in evidence before you the registration card from the Hotel Hilton in Albuquerque, which shows that he was registered there on June 3, 1945. You have before you the transcript of the record of the Albuquerque Bank showing that on the morning of June 4, 1945, Ruth Greenglass opened a bank account in Albuquerque and made an initial deposit of $400 in cash—just as she and David testified they did here on the witness stand right before you."

When Fuchs confessed, "Rosenberg's position in the Soviet espionage hierarchy in this country was such that he knew that on that trip out West to see Greenglass, Harry Gold was the one that had also collected information . . . on the atom bomb from Dr. Fuchs. Rosenberg knew that when Dr. Fuchs disclosed . . . what had happened, that he must identify Harry Gold" and that Gold "might point to Greenglass."

Saypol enumerated the prosecution's flight evidence: Passport photos of the Greenglass family, "taken at Rosenberg's insistence"; Ben Schneider's testimony; the delivery to Greenglass by Rosenberg of $1000 and, later, of $4000 "wrapped in this very piece of brown paper"; the plan given David for flight via Mexico; Dr. Bernhardt's testimony "concerning vaccination for a veteran who was going to Mexico"; and the flight of Sobell and his family to Mexico "in the same month that Rosenberg gave Greenglass money for flight."

The Greenglasses had testified that the console table "was used for microfilming" and "was a present from the Soviet," while the Rosenbergs said they had purchased it at Macy's for twenty-one dollars "in 1944 and 1945, when furniture was scarce." Noting Mrs. Cox's testimony that Mrs. Rosenberg had said the table was a wedding present from a friend of her husband's, Saypol referred to "this remarkably strange behavior taking the best piece of furniture in the house and storing it in the closet—why did they have to hide it?"

In addition to the testimony of David and Ruth Greenglass about Rosenberg's espionage activities, "Elitcher has placed the brand of Soviet spy on Rosenberg. You have the documentary evidence of Gold's registration card, the bank account, the wrapping paper, the testimony of Dr. Bernhardt, Dorothy Abel, Evelyn Cox, of Schneider. . . . That is why the evidence as to the Rosenbergs' guilt is incontrovertible."

Sobell had been an "associate" of Rosenberg since City College; the two were "joined by the common bond of communism and devotion to the Soviet Union. . . . The uncontradicted evidence of Sobell's espionage activities, of his meetings with Elitcher, of the trip to deliver the can of film to Rosenberg, of the flight to Mexico using at least five different aliases, combine to make the uncontradicted proof of Sobell's guilt overwhelming."

Saypol concluded: "No defendants ever stood before the bar of American justice less deserving of sympathy than these three."

CHAPTER 15

WHILE THE JURY IS OUT

The jury retired on Wednesday, March 28, at 4:53 P.M., charged by Judge Kaufman with the heavy responsibility of being "the sole and exclusive judges of the facts of this case." Now, in the sanctum of the jury room, their task was to resolve the issues contested during fourteen trial days, determining whether the charges against Julius and Ethel Rosenberg and Morton Sobell had been proved beyond a reasonable doubt.

Unlike many criminal proceedings, the Rosenberg-Sobell case provides no relatively clear-cut basis for deciding the truth. No disinterested eyewitness was available to testify for either side; no foolproof alibi could be offered by any of the defendants. In a murder trial, a jury may be guided by damning physical evidence, such as a weapon with fingerprints or clothing stained with a victim's blood; in the Rosenberg-Sobell trial, no prosecution evidence is so conclusively incriminating. Even the equivalent of a *corpus delicti*—to prove indisputably that a crime actually occurred—is lacking.

The prosecution alleged that beginning in 1944 the defendants had criminally conspired with the Greenglasses, Harry Gold, and other unidentified accomplices to supply national defense secrets through the person of Anatoli Yakovlev to the Soviet Union. According to Judge Kaufman, the government claimed that "the venture was successful as to the atom bomb secret." In addition to the "atom bomb secret," Julius was said to have stolen a proximity fuse and to have received from Sobell a small can—possibly containing film—and from others information on a sky platform project and an atomic-powered airplane. Espionage material was typed by Ethel and microfilmed by Julius (with a device incorporated into a console table), then left for the Russians in an alcove of an unnamed movie theater.

This story was unfolded with vivid detail and considerable complexity by four of the prosecution's twenty-three witnesses. These four—David and Ruth Greenglass, Harry Gold, and Max Elitcher—who themselves had been participants in the plot, provided all the evidence at the trial regarding the crime itself. Their testimony was consistent in broad outline and in many, though by no means all, particulars. A fifth witness,

Elizabeth Bentley, had no knowledge of the crime but her testimony about phone calls from a "Julius" tended to arouse suspicion.

In the face of these accusers, the Rosenbergs did little more than deny their guilt. Sobell did not testify in his own behalf, though his plea of not guilty meant that he also denied all charges.

Under the Anglo-American system of law a defendant is, of course, presumed innocent until such time as a jury may decide that he has been proved guilty. A common sense reason for this presumption of innocence —which places the burden of proof squarely on the prosecution—is to off-set the serious disadvantages encountered by an individual defending himself against the state. Defendants must rely for their defense on their own limited resources; a federal prosecutor has at his disposal the full investigative facilities of the government. Most important, proving oneself innocent of an accusation is nearly always difficult and frequently impossible.

This legal truism is particularly meaningful in the Rosenberg-Sobell trial, where the primary acts charged against the defendants consisted of espionage conversations and transactions with friends and relatives whom they were seeing socially during the same period. If the defendants were innocent, what more—other than to deny the charges—might they have done to *prove* this? How, for example, could the Rosenbergs have offered an alibi when a principal locale of the alleged crime was their own living room and kitchen? The fact of the matter is that the accusations against the defendants were essentially irrefutable, offering them no avenue for definitive rebuttal.

Thus, the main criterion for determining the guilt or innocence of the Rosenbergs is the credibility of the five major prosecution witnesses, while the guilt or innocence of Sobell depends on the credibility of Elitcher alone. If these five told the truth, the defendants are obviously guilty.

Unfortunately, there is very little opportunity for comparing the testimony of the key government witnesses, because most of them did not know each other and did not describe the same incidents. Neither Max Elitcher nor Elizabeth Bentley ever had met any of the others; Gold and the Greenglasses claimed to have seen each other briefly in Albuquerque, but were otherwise unacquainted.

The Greenglasses and Gold corroborated* one another's stories of Gold's visit to the Greenglass apartment in Albuquerque on June 3, 1945. Elitcher and David Greenglass both roughly confirmed Elizabeth

---

* In a strictly legal sense—which is not intended here—they did not corroborate each other, since an accomplice cannot corroborate another accomplice. However, the federal government—unlike a score of states—permits a conviction based on the uncorroborated testimony of an accomplice.

Bentley's testimony that there had been some contact between her and Julius Rosenberg, but this alleged contact was not the subject of any of the prosecution's charges. With these two exceptions, the testimony of Max Elitcher, Harry Gold, and Elizabeth Bentley was entirely unsupported by any other witness.

David and Ruth Greenglass corroborated much, but by no means all, of one another's testimony. Each testified independently to many incidents unmentioned by the other. David alone, for example, provided all of the testimony about the detailed flight plan via Mexico and Sweden, as well as about the proximity fuse, sky platform project, atomic-powered airplane, and microfilm in a movie alcove. As for Ruth, a surprising amount of her unsupported testimony concerned money: The $150 received from Julius for her first Albuquerque trip; the $50 to $75 a night Julius spent for entertainment in connection with espionage; the $75 to $100 a week Julius offered David to go to college; the $800 Julius gave David in 1948; the $10,000 or $15,000 Julius said he could always get for any business as a front for his espionage activities.

In judging the credibility of the witnesses on whom the prosecution relied for proof of the crime itself, one must consider not only this sparse corroboration of their testimony, but also the fact that all were accomplices.* Accomplice testimony obviously is often less trustworthy than testimony from a disinterested witness; the courts have ruled that it must be regarded by jurors with extreme care.

This need for care would seem particularly evident when one accomplice, David, was awaiting sentence for a capital crime; a second, Ruth, had not been indicted despite an admittedly active role in the conspiracy; and a third, Max Elitcher, was vulnerable to prosecution for perjury and probably for espionage on the basis of his own story. Also, both David and Ruth had been involved in acrimonious business disputes with Julius Rosenberg.

The single accomplice witness who appears to have had no realistic self-interest in testifying is Harry Gold. Prosecutor Saypol asserted that Gold, already under sentence of thirty years, could gain nothing but the "moral satisfaction" of telling the truth. "Not one question was asked of him by any defendant on cross-examination. It was so obvious to everyone in this courtroom that he was telling the complete truth when he described his trip to Greenglass. . . ."

Defense attorney Bloch said of Gold in his summation: ". . . I didn't cross-examine him . . . . because there is no doubt in my mind that he

* Legally, an accomplice is one who can be indicted for the same offense as the defendant. Thus, David and Ruth Greenglass, Harry Gold, and probably Max Elitcher were all accomplices.

impressed you as well as impressed everybody that he was telling the absolute truth, the absolute truth."

How did it come about that Harry Gold's truthfulness was uncontested
throughout the entire trial?

Gold's widely publicized arrest and confession ten months before as
Klaus Fuchs's accomplice had firmly established his credentials as a Soviet
spy. His sentence to a long prison term had removed any suspicion that
he might be cooperating with the prosecution to lessen his own punishment. On the witness stand, he told his story in an earnest and highly
convincing manner.

Undoubtedly, all of these factors contributed to Bloch's decision not
to cross-examine him. In addition, Bloch's theory of the case was that
Harry Gold and the Greenglasses were spies who had met without the
intervention of the Rosenbergs. The defense attorney correctly pointed
out to the jury that Gold never had any "traffic or transactions" with the
Rosenbergs and he speculated that David Greenglass, like Harry Gold,
might have received his piece of the jello box directly from Yakovlev.
However, Bloch's explanation had one serious defect: It failed to account
at all for Gold's testimony that he had used the password "I came from
Julius" and had had a number of conversations—with both the Greenglasses and Yakovlev—in which David's "brother-in-law, Julius" was mentioned.

The importance of Gold's role in the trial can hardly be overempha-
sized. In addition to his corroboration of the Greenglasses, he provided
the only link between Julius Rosenberg and a Soviet agent, Yakovlev, and
was the only witness to testify to Yakovlev's participation in the conspiracy.
Without Harry Gold's testimony, there is simply no conspiracy case.

In view of some of the curious facets of Gold's personality that had
been revealed in previous court proceedings, the matter of his veracity—
never broached at the Rosenberg-Sobell trial—should have been a crucial
issue for the jury's consideration.

Finally, in evaluating the credibility of the major witnesses, one must
weigh the fact that the testimony of David and Ruth Greenglass—who
provided the bulk of the prosecution's story of the crime—raises many
perplexing questions:

The Greenglasses testified that in November 1944 Julius informed Ruth
that he had learned from "his friends" that her husband, then stationed
at Los Alamos, was working on the atom bomb. No suggestion was given
as to where Julius's "friends" had obtained this information; according to
Harry Gold, Klaus Fuchs did not reveal the existence of Los Alamos until
January 1945. Granted that Julius and his espionage associates somehow
had learned about Los Alamos, how did Julius become aware of David's
presence there—at a time when Ruth had not yet visited him and knew
his whereabouts only as P. O. Box 1663, Santa Fe, New Mexico?

For Julius, already supposedly an espionage agent, the fortuitous assignment of his brother-in-law to this vital project was an amazing piece of luck. Even more amazing, however, is that David, a twenty-two-year-old mechanic with a high school education, was able to carry out of Los Alamos in his head significant data about a vastly complex technical effort —data that, according to Gold, Yakovlev later praised as "extremely excellent and very valuable."

Equally puzzling is the inconsistent description of Julius Rosenberg that emerges from the testimony of the Greenglasses. In 1944, at twenty-six years of age, Julius was allegedly a highly placed Soviet espionage agent, one of the few people in the world who knew of the Manhattan Project. The Russians awarded him a citation for his work. Yet he frequently appears to have been less of a master spy than a prize amateur bungler and loudmouth.

To Ruth, he revealed himself as a Soviet agent and disclosed his knowledge of the top-secret atomic bomb project without even first ascertaining whether David held a job in which he might possibly render any worthwhile aid. Later, with incredible indiscretion, he engaged in boastful small talk with David about his espionage activities at a time when David's brief tenure as an agent had long since ended. Much of David's information about Julius's work as a spy was said to have derived from this gossip.

How seriously these and other improbabilities in the testimony of the Greenglasses and other major witnesses damage the prosecution's case is entirely a matter of individual judgment. What is improbable is not impossible. However, while we cannot dismiss a story out of hand because it seems unlikely; we may choose to regard it circumspectly.

At the same time, it should be pointed out that the credibility of the Rosenbergs is open to some of the same doubts as that of their accusers. Their story was entirely uncorroborated except by one another. It is evident that both had excellent motive for lying.

Unfortunately, the prosecution's exhibits, although impressive numerically—there were nearly three dozen—are not of much help in resolving the issues of the case. None provides any substantial backing for the testimony about the crime given by the Greenglasses, Gold, and Elitcher. Most —such as the cut jello box, sketch replicas, and copies of security regulations—are merely illustrative and so have no bearing whatever on the guilt or innocence of the defendants.

Two of the exhibits, however, were directly relevant to the prosecution's case: A copy of a card from the Albuquerque Hilton Hotel showing that Gold registered there on June 3, 1945, and copies of Albuquerque bank records of an account opened by Ruth Greenglass on June 4, 1945, with a $400 deposit. Even these exhibits, while extremely important because they tend to confirm the Gold-Greenglass Albuquerque meeting, do not in any way corroborate the testimony—regarding the jello box and "Julius" password—that connects the Rosenbergs to the incident.

Aside from evidence relating to the alleged crime, testimony and exhibits about flight and plans for flight probably occupied more time at the trial than any other subject. The theme permeates the entire trial: More than half of the twenty-three prosecution witnesses dealt with it to some extent. By direct statement and inference, the prosecution contended that almost all of the principal figures in the case—the Greenglasses, the Rosenbergs, Sobell, and Yakovlev—had fled or planned to flee the United States. In addition, various acquaintances of Julius—Barr, Sarant, Perl, and Glassman—were all mentioned obliquely by the prosecution in connection with flight or flight plans.

Judge Kaufman instructed the jury: "Evidence of flight does not create any presumption of guilt, although it is a legitimate ground for an inference of a guilty mind. . . ." The weakness of any flight evidence, however, is that a "guilty mind" may be engendered by many causes other than the commission of the specific crime with which a defendant is charged. Judge Kaufman cautioned that flight evidence "should not be considered alone and by itself. It must be weighed with all of the surrounding circumstances, and of course, it should be considered together with all the other evidence in the case in determining the guilt or innocence of these defendants."

Much of the flight testimony came from David Greenglass, with Ruth and several other witnesses supporting portions of his story. To further corroborate David's flight story, the prosecution presented two exhibits —passport photos and brown wrapping paper. While the photos would seem to indicate that the Greenglasses were thinking of going abroad, they hardly prove that Julius was sending them. Neither does the brown wrapping paper in any way connect Julius to the $4000 in flight money that the paper was said to have contained.

Actually, and somewhat illogically, probably nothing helped to establish the Greenglass flight story so much as the testimony and exhibits relating to Morton Sobell's trip to Mexico City and the ports of Vera Cruz and Tampico and his use of aliases. While no evidence at all was offered connecting the Sobell trip with Rosenberg or with the proposed Greenglass flight via Mexico, Vera Cruz was a city specifically mentioned by David as part of the route of his flight plan.

Julius Rosenberg denied the Greenglass flight story and, in turn, claimed that in May and June 1950 his brother-in-law had been in a panic over some unrevealed troubles and had appealed to him for money and other help. Unfortunately, it is no simple matter to choose between David's and Julius's irreconcilable stories. Both accounts have a certain unbelievable quality, possibly because they relate to events and behavior that are to some extent outside the realm of most people's experience.

Quite obviously, though, the total impact of the flight testimony strengthens the prosecution's case considerably. Against massive prosecution evidence, the Rosenbergs' unsupported denials necessarily appear insubstantial. Nevertheless, the two main flight episodes—one involving the Greenglasses and Rosenbergs, the other Sobell—are replete with disquieting improbabilities.

For example, soon after Fuchs's arrest, Julius was said to have predicted that Gold would be caught and that the trail would then lead to David. By all accounts, spies operate in highly compartmentalized fashion so that in the event of arrest one agent cannot reveal the identity of another. Basic to a belief in the Greenglass flight story, however, is the prosecution's contention that Julius was thoroughly familiar with the activities of both Fuchs and Gold—two agents with whom he never had dealt.

Julius must also, apparently, be credited with knowledge of the inner workings of the FBI. Ruth testified that Julius had told her on May 24, 1950, that David would be the next person arrested and, with uncanny accuracy, had forecast the date of his arrest as between June 12 and June 16.

Yet despite such unexcelled inside information, plentiful funds, and long advance warning—Julius allegedly first alerted David to flee in February 1950—neither the Greenglasses nor the Rosenbergs actually did leave the country. The reason, particularly as regards the Rosenbergs, is impossible to fathom.

Curious too is that during much of the same period when Julius was said to have been urging David and Ruth to flee, the two families were also engaged in a "heated" business dispute. Why, if Julius was planning to leave the country himself, was he stubbornly trying to acquire David's stock and involving himself in a long-term deal to purchase the stock of another partner? Why would he antagonize the Greenglasses—by refusing cash payment for their stock or even the signing of a promissory note—at a time when he sought their cooperation? Though they allegedly received $5000 from Julius for flight, David and Ruth remained concerned over the unpaid $1000 business debt and, after David's arrest, asked their attorney to try to collect it.

As for Morton Sobell, if he were pursuing the same plan for flight described by David, why was he still in Mexico City with his family two months after their arrival there? Also, Sobell's promiscuous use of five aliases in Vera Cruz and Tampico hardly seems the behavior of a spy following a meticulously worked out international escape route.

We have directed our attention primarily to the five major prosecution witnesses because the testimony of the other eighteen was peripheral to the main issue: None told of the commission of any crime by the Rosenbergs or Sobell. The only really significant aid they might have lent the prosecution's case, therefore, would have been to substantiate the Greenglasses' testimony in those areas where it clashed directly with an alternative story told by the Rosenbergs. However, most of these minor witnesses —Koski, Derry, Lansdale, Cobb, Danziger, the five Mexicans, Huggins, Adomian, Pagano, and the Abels—provided no clues at all for evaluating the truthfulness of the Greenglasses versus that of the Rosenbergs.

The testimony of the remaining three—Cox, Schneider, and Dr. Bernhardt—would seem to offer a possible basis for choosing between some of the conflicting stories. On closer analysis of their testimony, this expectation is not realized.

Evelyn Cox, employed as a domestic by the Rosenbergs in 1944 and 1945, testified that Mrs. Rosenberg had told her that the console table was a gift. Mrs. Cox thereby confirmed the Greenglasses and refuted the Rosenbergs on this point. (She did not, however, say that the table was a gift from the Russians.) Mrs. Cox also testified that the table was merely decorative and was not used for any purpose; she said nothing about any special features that might have fitted it for microfilming or other photographic uses, as described by the Greenglasses. On balance, therefore, Mrs. Cox's testimony is no help in deciding between the opposing stories of the console table told by the Greenglasses and the Rosenbergs.

Ben Schneider, the photographer who said he took passport pictures of the Rosenberg family, told a story which strains one's credulity. Assuming, though, that his testimony is true and his memory accurate and that the Rosenbergs did take passport photos, their possible motives for doing so cannot be deduced without first knowing *exactly when* the photos were made. If the Rosenbergs took passport photos *before* David's arrest, this action would be strong circumstantial evidence that they were considering flight in connection with the crime. If the photos were taken *after* the arrest of David, when Julius had been questioned by the FBI and been told that his brother-in-law had accused him, we could hardly infer anything more than fear on the part of the Rosenbergs.

But Schneider did not remember exactly when he allegedly photographed the Rosenbergs. He gave the date as a Saturday "about the middle of June," 1950.* For these reasons, the Schneider testimony cannot buttress either the Greenglass flight story or the Rosenbergs' denial of it.

Finally, there is Dr. Bernhardt's testimony that he had informed Julius, at the latter's request, about smallpox and other inoculations needed for Mexico. This testimony is largely in accord with stories told by both David and Julius; the matter at issue is *why* Julius had asked his physician for such information.

David's contention was that Julius had obtained data from his physician about smallpox inoculation as part of his effort to get the Greenglasses

---

* The first Saturday in mid-June 1950 fell on June 17—the day following the arrest of David Greenglass.

to flee the country. Denying this, Julius claimed that David had importuned him to find out about inoculations for Mexico. Unfortunately, Dr. Bernhardt had no knowledge of what motivated Julius's inquiry and so could not throw any light on the conflicting testimony.

However, the prosecution's smallpox inoculation story suggests a number of rather troubling questions: Why should Julius, allegedly an experienced spy, have turned to his personal physician for some elementary travel tips that he easily could have obtained anonymously from a travel guide, public health department, Mexican Tourist Office, or numerous other sources—including his own espionage organization? Surely whatever Soviet agent gave Julius the flight plans and funds could also have supplied him with this information. According to David, Julius told him that evidence of smallpox vaccination was necessary to obtain a Mexican tourist card. If so, Julius's ignorance about Mexican travel is surprising under the circumstances: *The fact is that in 1950 no inoculations of any kind were required for a tourist card to enter Mexico.*

The prosecution asserted that the motive for the defendants' crime and subsequent attempts at flight was their adherence to Communist doctrine. Max Elitcher said that ten years before the trial he and Sobell had belonged to the same Communist Party group. Several exhibits—a cardboard collection can for Spanish Republican children and a nominating petition for a Communist candidate*—related to the Rosenbergs' political beliefs. In addition, the Rosenbergs were questioned extensively about Julius's dismissal from his government job as an alleged Communist Party member, as well as about what organizations they belonged to and what they read, believed, and talked about with their relatives and friends regarding communism, capitalism, and the Soviet Union. Both frequently pleaded the Fifth Amendment. All of this evidence of the defendants' radical left-wing politics prepared the ground for the testimony of Elizabeth Bentley who —appearing as an expert witness on communism—declared that there was a causal relationship between communism and espionage.

Whatever the rationale, communism was mentioned so often during the proceedings that at times it threatened to become a separate issue. In the violently anti-Communist political climate in which the trial was conducted, it is impossible to believe that the jury could have remained entirely objective toward the Rosenbergs and Sobell in response to such testimony, despite the Judge's injunction: "I wish to caution you most strenuously that proof of Communist Party membership or activity does not prove the offense charged in this indictment, but may be considered by you solely on the question of intent. . . ."

The jury was still deliberating at 11 P.M. that night. A communication

---

* The candidate, Peter V. Cacchione, was elected to the New York City Council four times.

to the Court noted: "One of the jurors has some doubt in his mind as to whether or not he can recommend leniency for one of the defendants." Judge Kaufman informed the jurors, as he had earlier, that any decision as to penalty would be made by him and should not influence them; if they wished, they might make any recommendation they desired and he would follow or disregard it as he saw fit.

A note from the jury at some time after midnight requested sleeping accommodations: "Will you kindly make arrangements . . . due to still existent dissident vote amongst us."

Against the protest of some of the defense attorneys, Judge Kaufman inquired whether the jury had agreed with respect to any defendant or defendants. At 12:35 A.M. the jurors replied: "We have reached our verdict on two of the defendants and we prefer to reserve rendering our verdict on all these defendants until we have complete unanimity." The jury was then locked up for the night.

The strength of the case against the Rosenbergs and Sobell is its richness of detail and inner consistency—the main themes of the story were repeated and interwoven by various witnesses in persuasive fashion. Adding further weight to its case, the prosecution had indicated a motive for the crime, communism; plans for flight; and espionage rewards allegedly received from the Russians (a citation, watches, and a console table for the Rosenbergs and money for the Greenglasses).

One other factor, perhaps the most important of all, favored the prosecution: In order to accept Julius Rosenberg's assertion of innocence the jury would have to decide that all five major witnesses had committed extensive perjury—almost certainly with some degree of prosecution collusion. To acquit Ethel Rosenberg and Morton Sobell, it was necessary to believe that the brother and sister-in-law of one and the erstwhile best friend of the other had falsely accused them of a capital crime.

The weaknesses of the prosecution's case, perhaps less manifest than its strengths, were nonetheless real. Two of the defendants—Sobell and Ethel Rosenberg—were tenuously linked to the conspiracy: The former by Elitcher alone; the latter by only the Greenglasses. As related by the Greenglasses, Mrs. Rosenberg's espionage activities had consisted entirely of participating in conversations, writing a letter to Ruth, giving moral support to her husband, and typing. Furthermore, the prosecution relied on largely uncorroborated accomplice testimony—made doubly suspect by the evident self-interest of almost all the major witnesses, the improbability of some of the case's most important elements, and the absence of any documentary evidence relating directly to the crime.

Clearly one's decision as to whether the accusers or the accused told the truth cannot be premised on any single all-compelling piece of evidence or the testimony of any single witness. There is no point on which one can fasten and say with assurance—"This is it, they are guilty" or "This is it, they are innocent." Faced with testimony unverified objectively, one must form an opinion by subjectively viewing the case as a whole, influenced inescapably by one's own biases and wishes. In this sense, the prosecution case is frustrating, even unsatisfactory. For given the facts of the case as they appear on the record, honest and fair-minded persons might well arrive at differing conclusions as to whether or not the defendants had been proved guilty beyond a reasonable doubt.

On the morning of Thursday, March 29, the jury resumed deliberations; court rumor held that the one hold-out juror was uncertain about the guilt of Morton Sobell. One hour later, the jurors—the dissident vote among them resolved—returned to the courtroom.

Queried the Clerk: "Mr. Foreman, have you agreed upon a verdict? . . . How say you?" Replied the Foreman: "We the jury find Julius Rosenberg guilty as charged. We the jury find Ethel Rosenberg guilty as charged. We the jury find Morton Sobell guilty as charged."

Thanking the jurors, Judge Kaufman told them: "My own opinion is that your verdict is a correct verdict. . . . The thought that citizens of our country would lend themselves to the destruction of their own country by the most destructive weapons known to man is so shocking that I can't find words to describe this loathsome offense."

Commenting that the defendants "represented perhaps the sharpest secret eyes of our enemies," United States Attorney Saypol said: "The case itself has implications so wide in their ramifications that they involve the very question of whether or when the devastation of atomic war may fall upon this world. The case is a necessary by-product of the atomic age. Let us hope that it will serve to supply the democracies of the world with some significant lessons."

Sentencing was set for a week later.

CHAPTER 16

JUDGMENT DAY

On the morning of April 5, 1951, the three convicted prisoners made the now familiar trip from their separate jails to Foley Square. Even before they arrived, newspapermen and curious spectators had filled the courtroom for the event. Reported that day's *Times:* "Judge Kaufman has received hundreds of letters. Most of them urged the death sentence."

The law under which the three had been found guilty carried a maximum penalty of twenty years imprisonment, with this exception: "Whoever violates this law in time of war shall be punished by death or by imprisonment for not more than thirty years." Though the defendants' violation "in time of war" had involved an ally, rather than an enemy, the more stringent provision still was considered applicable. However, no death sentence had ever been imposed under the Espionage Act since its passage in 1917.

Sentencing of Julius Rosenberg, thirty-two, and his wife Ethel, thirty-five, was scheduled first. Irving Saypol addressed the Court for the prosecution. He noted: "My statement reflects the views of the Department of Justice and the Attorney General . . . and affects the question of how grave is the offense."

Although the U. S. Attorney did not specifically recommend any sentence for the Rosenbergs, his interpretation of the gravity of their crime left little doubt as to his sentiment: "I have hesitated to translate these matters into a direct issue of life and death. It would be delusion indeed to believe that the war in Korea is anything but a war inspired by Russia. It is not an *ad hominem* appeal to suggest that it is inferable that young American lives are being daily sacrificed in Korea in defense of our way of life. These defendants gave their allegiance to forces . . . allied to the real enemy in that fight. They used methods of espionage which traditionally called for severe punishment. The secrets they sought and secured were of immeasurable importance and significance. How could the life of a single individual engaged in such treasonable activities be weighed against the life of a single American soldier fighting in a distant land. . . . In terms of human life, these defendants have affected the lives, and perhaps the freedom, of whole generations of mankind. . . .

"In the light of these considerations, is there room for compassion or mercy?"

Speaking for the Rosenbergs, Emanuel Bloch told the Court that they "have always maintained their innocence; they still maintain their innocence. And they have informed me no matter what, they will always maintain their innocence." He noted that his task might be easier "If these defendants came in crying *mea culpa*," but said he himself still believed that they were innocent and felt it his duty to continue "to do everything to try to reveal the truth."

As mitigating circumstances that the Judge might consider in determining sentence, Bloch observed that in 1944 and 1945 the United States and the Soviet Union had been wartime allies and also that the importance of the alleged crime had been exaggerated. On the latter point, he quoted from a *Yale Law Journal* article in which a former AEC counsel, discussing the question of secrecy and atomic energy, wrote: ". . . there is no likelihood whatever, with all our pre-eminence in technology, that the disparity between the level of our technical competence and that of other industrialized countries . . . is such that the latter would be more than, at most, a few years behind us. Indeed, there is abundant evidence that other nations frequently develop technological methods and processes distinctly superior to ours in a variety of fields."

The husband and wife defendants declined to comment before Judge Kaufman's pronouncement of sentence. They stood side by side as the jurist, a former federal prosecutor appointed to the bench only seventeen months before, delivered his speech:

"The issue of punishment in this case is presented in a unique framework of history. It is so difficult to make people realize that this country is engaged in a life and death struggle with a completely different system. This struggle is not only manifested externally between these two forces but this case indicates quite clearly that it also involves the employment by the enemy of secret as well as overt outspoken forces among our own people. All of our democratic institutions are, therefore, directly involved in this great conflict. I believe that never at any time in our history were we ever confronted to the same degree that we are today with such a challenge to our very existence. . . .

"The competitive advantage held by the United States in super-weapons has put a premium on the services of a new school of spies—the home-grown variety that places allegiance to a foreign power before loyalty to the United States. The punishment to be meted out in this case must therefore serve the maximum interest for the preservation of our society against these traitors in our midst. . . .

"Certainly to a Russian national accused of a conspiracy to destroy Russia not one day would have been consumed in a trial. It is to America's credit that it took the pains and exerted the effort which it did in the trial of these defendants. Yet, they made a choice of devoting themselves to the Russian ideology of denial of God, denial of the sanctity of the individual and aggression against free men everywhere instead of serving the cause of liberty and freedom."

As Judge Kaufman explained the reasons for the sentence he was about to impose, the bells of nearby St. Andrew's Church loudly tolled the noon hour, the longest toll of the day. Arriving at the heart of his comments, the Judge declared:

"I consider your crime worse than murder. Plain deliberate contemplated murder is dwarfed in magnitude by comparison with the crime you have committed. In committing the act of murder, the criminal kills only his victim. The immediate family is brought to grief and when justice is meted out the chapter is closed. But in your case, I believe your conduct in putting into the hands of the Russians the A-bomb years before our best scientists predicted Russia would perfect the bomb has already caused, in my opinion, the Communist aggression in Korea, with the resultant casualties exceeding fifty thousand and who knows but that millions more of innocent people may pay the price of your treason. Indeed, by your betrayal you undoubtedly have altered the course of history to the disadvantage of our country. No one can say that we do not live in a constant state of tension. We have evidence of your treachery all around us every day—for the civilian defense activities throughout the nation are aimed at preparing us for an atom bomb attack. . . .

"I . . . assume that the basic Marxist goal of world revolution and the destruction of capitalism was well known to the defendants, if in fact not subscribed to by them, when they passed what they knew was this nation's most deadly and closely guarded secret weapon to Soviet agents.

". . . In the light of the circumstances, I feel that I must pass such sentence upon the principals in this diabolical conspiracy to destroy a God-fearing nation, which will demonstrate with finality that this nation's security must remain inviolate; that traffic in military secrets, whether promoted by slavish devotion to a foreign ideology or by a desire for monetary gains must cease.

"The evidence indicated quite clearly that Julius Rosenberg was the prime mover in this conspiracy. However, let no mistake be made about the role which his wife, Ethel Rosenberg, played in this conspiracy. Instead of deterring him from pursuing his ignoble cause, she encouraged and assisted the cause. She was a mature woman—almost three years older than her husband and almost seven years older than her younger brother. She was a full-fledged partner in this crime.

"Indeed the defendants Julius and Ethel Rosenberg placed their devotion to their cause above their own personal safety and were conscious that they were sacrificing their own children, should their misdeeds be detected—all of which did not deter them from pursuing their course. Love for their cause dominated their lives—it was even greater than their love for their children.

"What I am about to say is not easy for me. I have deliberated for hours, days and nights. I have carefully weighed the evidence. Every nerve, every fiber of my body has been taxed. I am just as human as are the people who have given me the power to impose sentence. I am convinced beyond any doubt of your guilt. I have searched the records—I have searched my conscience—to find some reason for mercy—for it is only human to be merciful and it is natural to try to spare lives. I am convinced, however, that I would violate the solemn and sacred trust that the people of this land have placed in my hands were I to show leniency to the defendants Rosenberg.

"It is not in my power, Julius and Ethel Rosenberg, to forgive you. Only the Lord can find mercy for what you have done.

"The sentence of the Court . . . is, for the crime for which you have been convicted, you are hereby sentenced to the punishment of death, and it is ordered . . . you shall be executed according to law."

A short recess was called and the Rosenbergs were led from the room to the ground floor of the courthouse, where they were held briefly in adjoining temporary detention cells. Questioned by reporters about the demeanor of the condemned couple, the U. S. Marshals who stood guard outside their cells later revealed that both had been singing. Ethel Rosenberg began with the aria from *Madame Butterfly*, "Un Bel Di Vidremo" ("One Fine Day He Shall Return"); her husband's choice was "Battle Hymn of the Republic."

Morton Sobell's attorney, Harold Phillips, next approached the bench. Earlier that morning, he had introduced a motion in arrest of judgment, based on an affidavit by Sobell stating that he had been kidnaped from Mexico—with the apparent connivance of American authorities—and not deported. The motion denied, Phillips spoke briefly in behalf of his client, noting especially that no act had been charged against Sobell during the trial "in connection with . . . the transmission of the secret of the atom bomb."

Judge Kaufman addressed the thirty-three-year-old defendant directly:

"While I have not the slightest sympathy for you or any of your associates, as a judge, I must be objective in the examination of the evidence in this case. I do not for a moment doubt that you were engaged in espionage activities; however, the evidence in the case did not point to any activity on your part in connection with the atom bomb project. I cannot be moved by hysteria or motivated by a desire to do the popular thing. I must do justice according to the evidence in this case. There isn't any doubt about your guilt, but I must recognize the lesser degree of your implication in this offense.

"I, therefore, sentence you to the maximum prison term provided by the statute, to wit, thirty years.

"While it may be gratuitous on my part, I at this point note my recommendation against parole.

"The Court will stand adjourned."

Outside the courtroom, Emanuel Bloch stated for the Rosenbergs: "I repeat that these defendants assert their innocence and will continue to assert it as long as they breathe. They believe that they are victims of political hysteria, and that their sentence was based upon extraneous political considerations. . . ."

That afternoon, a New York *Post* reporter asked Ruth Greenglass— whose husband was to be sentenced the next day—for her reaction to the Rosenbergs' penalty. Said she: "I thought that they would tell the truth in the end. I thought she would, anyway, because of her children. But I guess they are Soviet soldiers to the end. I testified against them, but it was not done maliciously or with any intent to harm them. I just told the truth."

Opening the sentencing proceedings for David Greenglass, U. S. Attorney Saypol remarked that "the sentences imposed yesterday are substantially in accord with my views." He reminisced about other "important cases" that had been tried in the same courtroom, including "the first of the cases in this business of espionage . . . before your Honor. I refer, of course, to the trials of Abraham Brothman and Miriam Moskowitz."

Then, harking back to mid-June of the previous year, Saypol recalled: "When David Greenglass was arrested . . . I remember well how at his arraignment before the Commissioner in this district Mr. Rogge protested his innocence. Through Ruth Greenglass, his wife, came the subsequent recantation of those protestations, their cooperation and the disclosure of the facts by both of them."

Saypol recommended that Judge Kaufman demonstrate "the broad tolerance of the Court in the presence of penitence, contriteness, remorse and belated truth" and sentence Greenglass to fifteen years.

O. John Rogge strongly disagreed with Saypol "as to what mercy means in this case." He variously suggested sentences for his client of a year and a day, three years, and no more than five years. Rogge told the Court that David had been "seduced" into this conspiracy by the Rosenbergs, had always been reluctant to go along, and had agreed only because of his "fuzzy thinking" on the subject of Russia. He recommended a "light" sentence and a "pat on the back" for him, so as to encourage others to come forward with information on spying.

Judge Kaufman responded: "I like to think that neither do I ever mete out a light sentence, nor a heavy sentence, but rather a just sentence. . . ." Turning to Greenglass, the Judge added: "The fact that I am about to show you some consideration does not mean that I condone your acts or that I minimize them in any respect. . . . I must, however, recognize the help given by you in apprehending and bringing to justice the arch criminals in this nefarious scheme. . . .

". . . I have to be realistic in a situation such as this, and I recognize that despite my own inclination to be more severe on your sentence due to the revolting nature of this offense, I must subordinate my own feeling. . . . It is the judgment of this Court that I shall follow the recommendation of the government and sentence you to fifteen years in prison."

To at least one person present at the proceedings, the length of the sentence apparently came as a complete surprise. Reported the *Times*: "As the last words fell, Ruth Greenglass almost toppled from her front-row seat on the left of the courtroom. After a stiffening shudder, the defendant's twenty-seven-year-old wife dropped her bare head forward to the rail and gripped hard with her right hand to steady herself."

FINAL APPEALS

•

CHAPTER 17
THE CAMPAIGN AND THE COURTS

In the week before the sentencing of the Rosenbergs and Sobell, a number of newspapers reported that the Department of Justice might recommend the death penalty for the convicted spies as a means of persuading them to divulge information. According to one such story—by Howard Rushmore in the New York *Journal-American*—capital punishment was being "carefully considered . . . because. . . . A few months in the death house might loosen the tongues of one or more of the three traitors and lead to the arrest of . . . other Americans who were part of the espionage apparatus."

The day after Judge Kaufman condemned the Rosenbergs to die, Leonard Lyons declared in his column in the New York *Post*:

"The Rosenbergs still have a chance to save their necks by making full disclosure about their spy ring—for Judge Kaufman, who conducted the trial so ably, has the right to alter his death sentence. . . ."

A few days later, Lyons added: "Their lives . . . remain in their own hands—if they talk, they still can save themselves."

Thus was introduced a theme that was to be reiterated in the press with increasing frequency over the next two years. The choice facing the Rosenbergs was a clear-cut one: Confess or die.

Less than a week after the sentencing, Ethel Rosenberg was transferred from a New York City prison to the virtual solitary confinement of the then vacant women's section of the Sing Sing death house in Ossining, New York. Protesting this move—while appeals were pending—Mrs. Rosenberg charged an attempt to "break" her into confessing a crime of which, she said, she and her husband were innocent and would "always maintain our innocence." Five weeks later, Julius Rosenberg was sent to the men's section of the death house. The couple's execution was stayed indefinitely while their attorney carried their legal fight to a higher court.

Most of the press, including some of the most eminent American newspapers, unreservedly approved the death penalty. The St. Louis *Post-*

Dispatch, for example, called the sentences "completely justified," while the Atlanta *Constitution* congratulated Judge Kaufman and expressed the hope that his "sentencing of Julius and Ethel Rosenberg to die for stealing atomic secrets for transmission to Russia marks the end of our soft treatment of those who are disloyal."

Only a few—rather oddly disparate—voices were raised in protest. Among them were the Communist *Daily Worker* and the anti-Communist *Jewish Daily Forward.* Criticism also came from journalist Dorothy Thompson, who wrote in the Washington *Star:* "The death sentence . . . depresses me . . . . in 1944, we were not at war with the Soviet Union. . . . Indeed, it is unlikely that had they been tried in 1944 they would have received any such sentence."

Much the same point was amplified by Eugene Rabinowitch, editor of the *Bulletin of the Atomic Scientists.* Noting that the Espionage Act permitted a death penalty for spying in time of war, Rabinowitch said it seemed "common sense" to him that this "enhanced penalty was provided by the law for spying *on behalf of an enemy*"; to apply the death sentence provision of the law to spying on behalf of a wartime ally was, he said, a "tenuous construction." Moreover, he believed that it was the Rosenbergs' "stubbornness" in refusing to "admit their guilt" that had brought them such severe punishment.

Rabinowitch (a scientist who had himself worked on the Manhattan Project) suggested that these aspects of the death sentences might have provoked wider comment, were it not for the public's unrealistic fears regarding the "tremendous damage" to the nation's security inflicted by atomic spies. Some insight into the prevailing mood of the times, incidentally, can be gleaned from the fact that Rabinowitch—though he in no respect questioned the actual case against the condemned couple—labeled his rather moderate remarks as "Heretical Afterthoughts."

Throughout the United States during the spring and summer of 1951, no publication expressed the view that the Rosenbergs and Sobell might conceivably be innocent—as they claimed. This apparently complete consensus as to the guilt of the convicted spies was ended in late August 1951 by the *National Guardian,* a tabloid "progressive newsweekly" published in New York City. Posing the question, "The Rosenberg Conviction: Is This the Dreyfus Case of Cold-War America?" the paper ran a series of seven articles on the trial by William A. Reuben. In a preface to the first article, the *Guardian* contended that "the very best" that could be said for the prosecution case was that it left such reasonable doubt as to entitle the Rosenbergs to acquittal and said there were "strong grounds for suspecting they are victims of an all-out political frame-up" aimed at silencing opposition "in a period of build-up for war."

As a result of interest sparked by these articles, a National Committee to Secure Justice in the Rosenberg Case was organized in October 1951, with Reuben as acting chairman. At first, efforts by the fledgling committee to publicize allegedly dubious aspects of the trial met with little success outside of radical left-wing circles. Gradually, however, some liberals interested themselves in the case, largely in connection with their opposition to the death penalty.

On February 25, 1952, eleven months after they were found guilty, the convictions of the Rosenbergs and Sobell were affirmed by the United States Circuit Court of Appeals. An opinion written by Judge Jerome N. Frank observed: "Since two of the defendants must be put to death if the judgments stand, it goes without saying that we have scrutinized the record with extraordinary care to see whether it contains any of the errors asserted on this appeal."

As Judge Frank's opinion makes clear, the role of the Court of Appeals is a highly circumscribed one, limited to passing on the validity of various legal "errors" alleged by a defendant. Federal appellate judges have no power to enter the sacrosanct realm of jurors: They are not permitted to re-examine evidence in a case and alter a jury's verdict as to the guilt or innocence of the accused. Thus, the Court of Appeals may rule on whether a defendant has been accorded a *legally* fair trial, but not on whether the witnesses who testified against that defendant told the truth.

Regarding this important point, Judge Frank explained: ". . . where trial is by jury, this court is not allowed to consider the credibility of witnesses or the reliability of testimony. Particularly in the federal judicial system, that is the jury's province."

Among the *legal* points raised by the defense attorneys' appeals briefs were several that directly challenged Judge Kaufman's conduct of the trial. For example, the Judge was said to have taken too active and biased a role in the proceedings, thus depriving the defendants of a fair trial. Ruled the appellate court: "We think the judge stayed well inside the discretion allowed him."

The defense also claimed that Judge Kaufman had erred in admitting incompetent evidence relating to the defendants' political ideas and associations. The appellate court ruled: "We think the evidence possessed relevance," but agreed that "such evidence can be highly inflammatory in a jury trial." Noting that Judge Kaufman had cautioned the jury not to regard a defendant's possible Communist affiliations as a basis for his conviction, the Court of Appeals reflected: "It may be that such warnings are no more than an empty ritual without any practical effect on the jurors. . . ."

While apparently implying that the death sentence was "unduly harsh," Judge Frank noted: "Unless we are to over-rule sixty years of undeviating federal precedents, we must hold that an appellate court has no power to modify a sentence." Because of this long precedent, he said, the Supreme Court alone was in a position to decide whether existing laws gave the courts the right to reduce an otherwise valid sentence. "As matters now stand, this court properly regards itself as powerless to exercise its own judgment concerning the alleged severity of the defendants' sentences."

Had he such power to change a sentence, Judge Frank added, he might regard "the quality of the evidence on which the verdict rests" and "take into consideration" the fact that evidence of the Rosenbergs' espionage activities "came almost entirely from accomplices."

Whereas the Rosenbergs' appeal was denied unanimously by the three-judge court, Morton Sobell narrowly missed winning a new trial. The Court of Appeals split 2 to 1 on the question of whether Sobell had been proved a member of the Rosenberg-Greenglass-Gold atomic conspiracy or of a separate and more limited conspiracy with Rosenberg alone. The majority (Thomas W. Swan and Harrie B. Chase) held that Sobell had been shown to have been a part of the larger conspiracy because he had consented to the "single unified purpose" common to all the conspirators. "It did not matter that Sobell knew nothing of the atomic episodes; he is nevertheless charged with the acts done by Greenglass, Gold and Rosenberg, in furtherance of the over-all conspiracy." Judge Frank disagreed, stating, ". . . there was error, in this respect, which requires that Sobell be given a new trial."

A request by defense attorneys for a rehearing on their arguments was turned down by the Court of Appeals a month later. The attorneys immediately announced that they would carry the appeals of the convicted spies to the United States Supreme Court. However, on October 13, 1952, the Supreme Court denied certiorari, refusing to review any of the legal questions raised on appeal by the Rosenbergs and Sobell. The single dissenter was Justice Hugo L. Black.

The defense added a number of new points to its original petition and asked the high court to reconsider. Soon after, on November 17, Black was once again the only Justice to vote for review as the Court rejected the plea for reconsideration of its initial refusal.*

The Court's only comment on the denial of certiorari came from Justice Felix Frankfurter, who issued a memorandum opinion in which he observed: "Petitioners are under death sentence, and it is not unreasonable to feel that before life is taken review should be open in the highest court of the society which has condemned them." Such a "right of review" in capital cases, Frankfurter explained, had been the law of the land for twenty years, but Congress had abolished this right in 1911 "and since then death sentences have come here only under the same conditions that apply to any criminal conviction in a federal court."

---

* The Supreme Court also denied at that time a motion to file a brief of W. E. B. DuBois and others as *amici curiae*.

As for the import of the Supreme Court's denial of certiorari, the Justice sought to correct the widely held view that such a denial implied agreement by the high court with the decision of a lower court. Said he: "Misconception regarding the meaning [of the Supreme Court's refusal to review a case] . . . persists despite repeated attempts at explanation. It means, and all that it means is, that there were not four members of the Court to whom the grounds on which the decision of the Court of Appeals was challenged seemed sufficiently important. . . ."

Finally, Justice Frankfurter stated that one point raised by the Rosenbergs on their petition for rehearing "is beyond the scope of the authority of this Court, and I deem it appropriate to say so. A sentence imposed by a United States district court, even though it be a death sentence, is not within the power of this Court to revise."

For the defense, the Supreme Court's denial of a review marked the unsuccessful conclusion of the first round of the legal fight. A few days later, Judge Kaufman issued an order setting a date for the Rosenbergs' execution (the week of January 12, 1953). Morton Sobell was transferred from New York City, where he had been held while awaiting the outcome of his appeals, to the notorious federal prison on Alcatraz Island in California to begin serving his thirty-year sentence. Commenting on her husband's incarceration in an isolated, maximum security penitentiary ordinarily reserved for incorrigible criminals, Helen Sobell said: "They want him to name innocent persons as spies and admit a crime which he never committed."

The National Committee to Secure Justice in the Rosenberg Case called for a "supreme effort" to save the condemned couple's lives. By November 1952, the Committee's campaign to influence American public opinion about the case was reaching a widening circle of people. The aim of the campaign was to attract the support of both those who believed the Rosenbergs innocent and those who were concerned primarily with the severity of the sentences.

Committee accomplishments included an *amicus curiae* brief submitted to the Supreme Court with a petition said to have been signed by fifty thousand persons; rallies in New York and other large cities; the organization of dozens of local Rosenberg committees throughout the country; the printing and sale of the verbatim trial record; and wide distribution of both the Reuben *Guardian* articles in pamphlet form and an eight-page "Fact Sheet" on the case. One charge leveled by the "Fact Sheet" was that religious, as well as political, bigotry had helped to convict the Rosenbergs. This suggestion—that anti-Semitism had played a part in the case—was denied by leading Jewish organizations.

Despite the increasing activity of the campaign, one year after its formation the Rosenberg Committee still had failed to enlist any substantial number of prominent liberals to its cause. Aside from the radical left, no American publication or organization had expressed any doubts regarding the Rosenbergs' guilt and few apparently considered the sentences excessive. The American Civil Liberties Union—a respected and influential representative of liberal opinion—found no grounds for intervening in the case, noting that "the question of commutation of the death sentences . . . raised no civil liberties issue." However, the ACLU's general counsel, Arthur Garfield Hays, in an article on the Rosenbergs, personally decried what he called the "damnable death penalty."

Meanwhile, abroad, interest in the case was growing rapidly. Months before, the *Guardian* series had been reprinted by a number of newspapers, particularly the leftist and Communist press, throughout the world. Now, the Supreme Court denial—which made the early execution of the Rosenbergs appear likely—was followed by increasing agitation for clemency. By December 1, 1952, *Time* magazine reported:

"In the fate of the American couple who sit in the death house at Sing Sing, scheduled to be electrocuted . . . Communists the world over last week had an issue they rode hard. . . . Across the front page of Paris' Communist *L'Humanité* was spread a message from Red-smocked Painter Pablo Picasso: 'The hours count. The minutes count. Do not let this crime against humanity take place.' Above it was a macabre drawing of two electric chairs in which, side by side, sat the Rosenbergs, holding hands."

In his message, Picasso urged all Frenchmen to write President Truman asking commutation of the sentences. Similar appeals were being voiced in other countries. From Jerusalem, twenty prominent Israeli rabbis and religious leaders sent a clemency plea to the White House. Movements to "Save-the-Rosenbergs" were organized in Belgium, Holland, Scandinavia, Switzerland, England, and other nations. In London, pickets paraded outside the U. S. Embassy.

Six weeks before the date set for the executions, defense attorneys took a new legal tack. They returned to the federal district court at Foley Square and requested Judge Sylvester J. Ryan to set aside all three convictions on the grounds that various actions of the prosecution—before and during the trial—had deprived the defendants of the rights guaranteed them by law.

As proof of this allegation, one claim made by the defense was that the prosecution had knowingly allowed its rebuttal witness, the photographer Ben Schneider, to testify falsely. Schneider, who operated a small photo studio—located at 99 Park Row just behind the courthouse—was said to have been discovered there by the FBI only one day before his appearance as the surprise final witness in the case. He testified that about mid-June 1950, he had made three dozen passport photos of a couple and their two young sons. In court, he identified the Rosenbergs as the couple.

Schneider was unable to furnish any documentary proof that he had made passport photos of the Rosenbergs; he said he kept no negatives, sales slips, or record books of any kind. Therefore, his ability to recognize the Rosenbergs in court may well have influenced the jurors in their evaluation of his credibility. Soon after the photographer pointed out the Rosenbergs in the courtroom, Saypol questioned him about their visit to his shop nine months earlier:

SAYPOL: Did he [Julius Rosenberg] pay you?
SCHNEIDER: That's right, sir.
SAYPOL: And is that the last time you saw him before today?
SCHNEIDER: That's right. . . .
SAYPOL: And is it seeing him here now with his wife that recalls it to your memory that they were the persons who came in?
SCHNEIDER: That's right; that's right.

However, published about a year after the trial was a book, *The Atom Spies*, by a New York newspaperman, Oliver Pilat, who had been aided in his research by prosecutor Saypol. From this book, the defense learned for the first time that Schneider had been brought into the courtroom by an FBI agent *the day before* he testified at the trial.

The FBI agent, John A. Harrington, confirmed in an affidavit that he had escorted Schneider into the courtroom the day prior to his appearance as a witness—an act that violated Judge Kaufman's explicit order excluding all prospective witnesses. The affidavit stated that U. S. Attorney Saypol had "directed" that Schneider be brought into the courtroom "to confirm the identity of Rosenberg." Special agent Harrington noted, however, that he "at no time" pointed out or indicated "who was Julius Rosenberg or the place where he was located in the courtroom to Mr. Schneider." (For most of the day in question, Julius Rosenberg was in the witness box testifying.) Another FBI agent, Walter C. Roetting, stated in an affidavit that when he interviewed Schneider at his shop the photographer had related substantially the same story as he did the next day in court.

Agent Roetting's affidavit, incidentally, revealed that Saypol's questioning of Schneider at the trial may well have implanted still another erroneous impression concerning the photographer's identification of the Rosenbergs.

SAYPOL: Now, when the agents came to visit you yesterday, did they show you photographs?
SCHNEIDER: They did.
SAYPOL: Was it from those photographs that you picked him [Rosenberg] out?
SCHNEIDER: That's right.

Conflicting with the import of this testimony is agent Roetting's statement that he "exhibited photographs of Julius Rosenberg and asked Mr. Schneider whether he had ever seen this man." There is no suggestion here of Schneider having been shown pictures of anyone other than Julius Rosenberg; thus, there was never any opportunity or need for the photographer to have "picked him out."

Another claim made by the defense attorneys in their effort to have the convictions set aside was that pretrial publicity initiated by "prosecuting officials of the United States Government" had created a "virulent and hostile climate" which made a fair trial impossible. A defense request that the prosecution produce copies of all press releases issued at the time of the defendants' arrests was denied by Judge Ryan.

Sobell's appeals attorney, Howard Meyer, argued that the rights of his client, in particular, had been unfairly prejudiced by pretrial publicity labeling him an atom spy, inasmuch as no such evidence about him was presented at his trial. Said Meyer: ". . . there existed in 1950 a creation of the organs of public sentiment, an image, a demon called the Atom Spy, which was more reprehensible, more outrageous than any type of culprit . . . that had ever been brought to the bar of justice since the beginning of the world." He charged that the FBI director, the Attorney General, and the U. S. Attorney had all made pretrial public statements falsely characterizing Sobell as an atom spy and as a member of the Klaus Fuchs spy ring at a time when Fuchs was declared to be "the most notorious spy in history."

Also cited by the defense in support of its contention that the prosecution's behavior had nullified the defendants' rights were the circumstances surrounding the arrest for perjury of William Perl—former college classmate of Rosenberg and Sobell—in the midst of the trial. Perl's arrest, for denying before a grand jury that he knew Rosenberg, Sobell, and a number of others, had been front-page news in New York dailies. The press accounts all included details—attributed to the U. S. Attorney—that were highly relevant to the trial in progress. For example, the *Times* story noted:

"Mr. Saypol said also that Perl had been listed by the Government as a potential witness in the current atomic espionage trial. His intended role on the stand, Mr. Saypol added, was to corroborate certain statements made by David Greenglass and the latter's wife, who are key Government witnesses in the trial." (At the time this story appeared, Ruth Greenglass was on the witness stand.)

Bloch told Judge Ryan that, when defense counsel had expressed concern to Judge Kaufman over this publicity accompanying Perl's arrest, "Mr. Saypol, quite irritated, stated in a peremptory way: This indictment was returned in the regular course of criminal practice. I don't like any innuendoes. . . . And Judge Kaufman said to us, 'You have the word of the United States Attorney.' "

The defense now claimed that events since the trial showed that the prosecutor had not told the truth but had indeed "timed" the arrest of Perl to generate publicity that would provide out-of-court corroboration for his case. As evidence, the defense pointed to the fact that Perl's grand jury testimony—on which the perjury indictment was based—had taken place some six months before his widely publicized arrest. Furthermore, twenty-one months after his arrest he was still untried—despite his repeated pleas for trial.

Contesting this claim, the U. S. Attorney's office asserted that Perl had been arrested only one week after he first *admitted* that he had lied to a grand jury six months earlier.* He had not yet been brought to trial, it was said, to prevent disclosures that might interfere with other prosecutions.

Assistant U. S. Attorney Kilsheimer summed up the government's reply to the various points raised by the defense application. Said he: ". . . this motion is no more than a maneuver to forestall the execution of sentence . . . . an attempt to perpetuate the myth of innocence of these defendants."

On December 10, 1952, Judge Ryan ruled against the defense motion. Noting that the petitioners had raised "no substantial question of law," he refused a stay of execution. Soon after, his decision was upheld unanimously by the Circuit Court of Appeals. The appellate court opinion (written by Judge Swan) noted: "Judge Ryan was correct in ruling that there was not the slightest evidence that Schneider's testimony was intentionally false and that in any event it was on an immaterial point. . . ."

The Court of Appeals clearly regarded the matter of the Perl arrest as the defense's strongest argument, and used harsh language to describe the conduct of prosecutor Saypol (by then a New York State judge). The assumed prosecution tactic of timing an indictment and making a statement to the press, the opinion noted, "cannot be too severely condemned . . . . *if defendants had moved for a new trial, it should have been granted*. But they did not so move. . . . They now seek to excuse the omission because when they conferred with the judge Mr. Saypol gave assurance that he had not 'timed' the Perl indictment. Such assurance they then accepted as true but they have recently concluded that it was false, because Perl has not yet been brought to trial. This is not a valid excuse. . . . Mr. Saypol's motive and 'timing' in opening the indictment are irrelevant; the wrong consisted in the statement made to the press to

---

* When Perl finally was tried for perjury in May 1953, he specifically denied having made such an admission before his arrest, and no evidence was introduced by the prosecution to refute him.

the effect that the government had expected to use Perl's testimony to corroborate the Greenglasses, and the intimation that because he had backed out he had been indicted for perjury. Such a statement to the press in the course of a trial we regard as wholly reprehensible. Nevertheless we are not prepared to hold that it vitiates the jury's verdict when there is no allegation or evidence that any juror read the newspaper story and the defendants deliberately elected not to ask for a mistrial." (Emphasis added.)

On December 30, 1952, Emanuel Bloch appeared before Judge Irving Kaufman to plead for the lives of the Rosenbergs. The law grants a trial judge the power to modify a sentence at any time within sixty days after a higher court affirms a defendant's conviction or the U. S. Supreme Court refuses to review. Now—with the scheduled execution of the Rosenbergs two weeks away—Bloch asked Judge Kaufman to exercise this right of judicial clemency by commuting the death sentences to prison terms.

Alluding to the tremendous worldwide interest in what the French called *l'affaire Rosenberg*, Bloch noted that "tens upon tens of millions of people in this country, in Europe, in Asia . . . know about this case." Judge Kaufman retorted: ". . . I have been frankly hounded, pounded by vilification and by pressurists . . . I think that it is not a mere accident that some people have been aroused in these countries. I think it has been by design. . . ." He referred to a "barrage of telegrams" that he had received the previous day.

Reminding the Judge that "in your hands, your Honor, you have the fate of two human beings," Bloch asked why, "in the shadow of death," the Rosenbergs continued to insist on their innocence. ". . . you know that they know what we have all read in the papers . . . that if they would only talk, if they would only confess, they would save themselves. . . . What is it that stops them from doing this?"

Replied Judge Kaufman: "I have pondered that question. I have pondered it over and over again, and the only solution I have to it is to answer that it is the very same thing that drove them into it. . . . I don't know the answer to that."

Bloch responded: "Your Honor, the reason they act this way is because they believe most deeply in their hearts that they are innocent. It sounds perhaps, to cynical ears, like an oversimplification. Believe me . . . they don't want to die; they are in their middle thirties."

The burden of the defense attorney's arguments was that the case against his clients was a weak and suspect one because it was based on the testimony of accomplices with ample motives for lying. Again and again, he sought to convince the Judge that there was at least some element of uncertainty regarding the Rosenbergs' guilt. "We can spout legal rules," he told Judge Kaufman. "We can talk about the jury's verdict being proper. . . . This is not the quantum of proof that I am urging upon you now. I am saying to you, if there is one little iota of doubt, your wisdom, your judgment, your conscience must give it to these defendants so that they can live."

Then, assuming for the sake of argument that the Rosenbergs were guilty, Bloch concentrated his fire on the severity of the sentences. Referring to the Judge's "serious misapprehension . . . about the importance of the alleged information transmitted," he said: ". . . I think . . . you compounded your error by making statements that I believe you probably would not make today, namely, that it was the Rosenbergs who caused the Korean War and the fifty thousand casualties."

Replied Judge Kaufman: "They were a contributing cause."

Finally, after an apparently deeply felt personal plea in which he even offered to "get on my knees," Bloch concluded: "Through you the rest of the world will either believe that we are a compassionate nation, a nation built upon the ideals of humanity and justice, or a nation that has been gripped in panic and fear and is embarked upon mad acts. Please, your Honor, don't be offended when I say this: Don't follow in the tradition of Judge Thayer."*

Speaking for the government was Myles J. Lane, who had replaced Saypol as U. S. Attorney for the Southern District of New York—generally regarded as the most important federal prosecuting post in the United States. At the time of sentencing, Saypol had not explicitly requested the death penalty. Now, however, on behalf of the Department of Justice, Lane demanded the carrying out of the executions. Said he:

"To argue that the material supplied by the Rosenbergs to the Soviets through Greenglass and Gold did not materially shorten the time when the Soviets built their first atomic bomb is to beg the question. To anyone at all who reasons sanely the Soviets obtained invaluable information in 1944, in 1945 which enabled them to master the secrets of the atomic weapons' construction and very far in advance of the time they would have done so except for this act of espionage.

"In my opinion, your Honor, this and this alone accounts for the stand which the Russians took in Korea, [which] . . . caused death and injury to thousands of American boys and untold suffering to countless others, and I submit that these deaths and this suffering, and the rest of the state of the world must be attributed to the fact that the Soviets do have the atomic bomb, and because they do . . . the Rosenbergs made a tremendous contribution to this despicable cause."

Pointing out that the Rosenbergs could, "if they wanted to cooperate . . . lead to the detection of any number of people who, in my opinion, are today doing everything that they can to obtain additional information for the Soviet Union," Lane concluded: " . . this is no time for a court

* Webster Thayer, judge at the Sacco-Vanzetti trial.

to be soft with hard-boiled spies. . . . They have showed no repentance; they have stood steadfast in their insistence on their innocence. . . ."

Judge Kaufman reserved decision. His answer came three days later. Said he: ". . . I am again compelled to conclude that the defendants' guilt . . . was established beyond doubt. . . . Their traitorous acts were of the highest degree. . . . It is apparent that Russia was conscious of the fact that the United States had the one weapon which gave it military superiority and that, at any price, it had to wrest that superiority from the United States by stealing the secret information concerning that weapon."

Remarking that "Neither defendant has seen fit to follow the course of David Greenglass and Harry Gold," the Judge observed: "Their lips have remained sealed and they prefer the glory which they believe will be theirs by the martyrdom which will be bestowed upon them by those who enlisted them in this diabolical conspiracy (and who, indeed, desire them to remain silent). . . .

"The defendants, still defiant, assert that they seek justice not mercy. What they seek they have attained."

Then, harking back to his sentencing speech twenty-one months before, Judge Kaufman concluded: "I still feel that their crime was worse than murder. . . . The application is denied."

The scheduled executions—then a week away—were stayed by the Judge at Bloch's request to enable the condemned couple to apply to the President of the United States for Executive clemency. A few days later, each of the Rosenbergs submitted substantially identical clemency petitions to President Truman. That of Ethel Rosenberg (dated January 9, 1953) stated, in part:

"My husband and I testified in our own defense. We denied, generally, and in detail, every part of the evidence introduced by the Government to connect us with a conspiracy to commit espionage. We showed that, during the years in question, we lived a steady normal existence. Even as late as May 1950, during the period when the Government claimed we were preparing for flight, my husband depleted our meager cash reserves and obligated himself, on a long term basis, to buy out the holder of the preferred stock of the business in which he was engaged, to gain absolute ownership and control.

"Upon the birth of our two sons, I ceased my outside employment, and discharged the responsibility of mother and housewife. My husband, a graduate engineer, held a regular succession of low-salaried positions until his entrance into the machine shop enterprise with David Greenglass. The modesty of our standard of living, bordering often on poverty, discredits David's depiction of my husband as the pivot and pay-off man of a widespread criminal combination, fed by a seemingly limitless supply of 'Moscow gold.'

"Our knowledge of the existence of an atom-bomb came with its explosion at Hiroshima, and David's connection with it at Los Alamos, from his revelations to us on his discharge from the Army in 1946.

"We knew neither Gold nor Yakovlev, our alleged co-conspirators, nor Bentley—facts which the Government did not controvert.

"Our relations with Sobell, our co-defendant, were confined to sporadic social visits. Following a complete six-year break, after graduation from college, our ties with Elitcher assumed similar, but even more tenuous, character.

"Our relationship with the Greenglasses, both during and after the war, was on a purely familial and social level, the cordiality becoming strained to the breaking, however, with the advent of bitter quarrels which arose in the course of our post-war business ties. . . .

"Petitioner respectfully prays that she be granted a pardon or commutation of sentence for the following reasons:

"First: The primary reason I assert, and my husband with me, is that we are innocent.

"We stand convicted of the conspiracy with which we were charged. We are conscious that were we to accept this verdict, express guilt, penitence and remorse, we might more readily obtain a mitigation of our sentences.

"But this course is not open to us.

"We are innocent, as we have proclaimed and maintained from the time of our arrest. This is the whole truth. To forsake this truth is to pay too high a price even for the priceless gift of life—for life thus purchased we could not live out in dignity and self-respect.

"It should not be difficult for Americans to understand this simple concept to be the force that gives us strength—even in the face of imminent death, knowing well that the abandonment of principle might, alone, save our lives—to adhere to the continued assertion and profession of our innocence. . . .

"Yet we have been told again and again, until we have become sick at heart, that our proud defense of our innocence is arrogant, not proud, and motivated not by a desire to maintain our integrity, but to achieve the questionable 'glory' of some undefined 'martyrdom.'

"This is not so.

"We are not martyrs or heroes, nor do we wish to be. We do not want to die. We are young, too young, for death. We long to see our two young sons, Michael and Robert, grown to full manhood. We desire with every fibre to be restored sometime to our children and to resume the harmonious family life we enjoyed before the nightmare of our arrests and convictions. . . .

"Second: We understand, however, that the President, like the courts, considers himself bound by the verdict of guilt, although, on the evidence, a contrary conclusion may be admissible.

". . . But many times before there has been too unhesitating reliance on the verdict of the moment and regret for the death that closed the door to remedy when the truth, as it will, has risen. . . .

"We say to you, Mr. President, that the character of evidence on which we were convicted, and the force of the impact of certain circumstances in our case upon the mind of the jury, cannot assure the reasonable mind that this verdict was not corrupt.

". . . in the summer of 1950 . . . the general public fear engendered by the announced mastery of the atom bomb by the Soviet Union, was aggravated by the increased international tensions occasioned by the Korean War. . . .

"When we were arrested as spies for the Soviet Union, labeled as 'Communists,' charged, in the main, with theft of atomic-bomb information from the Los Alamos Project, the mere accusation was enough to arouse deep passions, violent antipathies, and fears as profound as the instinct of self-preservation. . . .

"It was hammered home, and kept alive by a virtual avalanche of publicity which saturated the communal mind with a consciousness that our country was imminently in danger of atomic attack and devastation by the Soviet Union, which had acquired the bomb by reason of its having obtained the 'secret,' from an espionage apparatus, ideologically motivated, of which we were 'aggressive' members.

"From this community the jurors who tried us were chosen. . . .

"Should this not temper reliance—to death—on this verdict of a jury, in which the unconscious influence of the enveloping atmosphere may have overridden the overt desire to be fair and seduced it into a more ready acceptance for the prosecution's evidence as against our defense? . . .

"Third: The Government's case against us stands or falls on the testimony of David Greenglass and Ruth, his wife. . . . How firm is a verdict predicated upon the testimony of 'accomplices' . . . ? Even the rigorous canons of the law recognize that the overriding motive for falsehood requires that the accusations of a trapped criminal, testifying to mitigate or avoid his own punishment, be taken with care and caution, and brand a prosecution founded on such evidence as 'weak' and suspect.

"We have never been able to comprehend that civilized and compassionate consciences could accept a smiling 'Cain' like David Greenglass—or the 'serpent,' Ruth, his wife—who would slay not only his sister, but his sister's husband, and orphan two small children of his own blood.

"We have always said that David, our brother, knowing well the consequences of his acts, bargained our lives away for his life and his wife's. Ruth goes free, as all the world now knows; David's freedom, too, is not so far off that he will not have many years to live a life—if we should die—that, perhaps, only a David Greenglass could suffer to live. . . .

"Fourth: Only one tribunal, the sentencing court, has asserted the correctness of our sentences to death, and only one court has affirmed it: the sentencing court. In other words, only one human being in a position of power has said we ought to die.

"Although our case was appealed to the higher courts, the appellate tribunals, denying their power to review the discretion of the sentencing judge, have not, on the assumption of our guilt, ruled on the propriety of the magnitude of the sentences of death.

"You, Mr. President, are the first one who is empowered to review these sentences—and the last one. . . .

"We are told that the 'confessions' and 'cooperation' of Greenglass and Gold and others earned them more lenient sentences. While this is recognized practice, the coercive power of sentence beyond that justified by the nature of the criminal act cannot legitimately be made to substitute for the proscribed 'thumbscrew and rack' to secure confessions which cannot in truth and good conscience be forthcoming. . . .

"Scientific judgment undermines the validity of the trial judge's claim that our alleged conduct, did or could have, put 'into the hands of the Russians the A-bomb years before our best scientists predicted Russia would perfect the bomb.'

"The judge, obdurately holding to his irrational consideration . . . reaffirmed our death sentences. . . .

"The facts of our case have touched the conscience of civilization. The compassion of men sees us as victims caught in the terrible interplay of clashing ideologies and feverish international enmities. Adjudged war criminals, guilty of mass murders and the most ghastly crimes, are daily being delivered to freedom, while we are being delivered to death. . . .

"We appeal to your mind and conscience, Mr. President, to take counsel with the reason of others and with the deepest human feelings that treasure life and shun its taking. To let us live will serve all and the common good. If we are innocent, as we proclaim, we shall have the opportunity to vindicate ourselves. If we have erred, as others say, then it is in the interest of the United States not to depart from its heritage of openheartedness and its ideals of equality before the law by stooping to a vengeful and savage deed."

With the decision on clemency now up to the President, thousands throughout the world wrote or cabled the White House urging that the Rosenbergs' lives be spared. The American press generally attributed this extraordinary international display of sympathy for the convicted spies to the machinations of Communists anxious to embarrass the United States. However, while the campaign abroad probably was largely Communist led and dominated during its initial stages, before the end of 1952 the movement to save the Rosenbergs had gained the support of broad sections of political opinion in Western European and other nations.

On December 11, 1952, for example, a long article on the case in the influential Parisian daily, *Le Monde*, raised perplexing questions about the trial and sentence. The following day, the moderate Swiss newspaper, *Tribune de Geneve*, expressed concern at the possibility of "an enormous judicial error . . . in the country which prides itself on the dignity of the individual." By January 14, 1953, the New York *Herald Tribune's* Paris correspondent reported: "The vast majority of non-Communist newspapers in France continued to urge today that the death sentences of Julius and Ethel Rosenberg . . . be commuted to life imprisonment."

In retrospect, it seems fair to say that the case of the young American husband and wife—insisting on their innocence in the face of imminent death—had fired the moral imaginations of people all over the world. In Europe especially, the plight of the Rosenbergs—whether justifiably or not—had acquired a symbolic value that made their fate a matter of supreme importance for millions. Coming at a time when many European intellectuals were increasingly concerned with the growing power of McCarthyism in the United States, the case seemed to confirm the worst fears of those who believed that the leader of the Western Alliance was moving rapidly to the right—toward Fascism and war.

Around the world, American embassies were picketed and inundated with petitions and letters urging clemency. Some embassy and consulate officials were forced to spend a goodly portion of their time receiving delegations concerned with the fate of the Rosenbergs. In an effort to aid its harried diplomats, the State Department prepared a special information bulletin on the case. But no information bulletin could still the rising chorus of protests over the impending executions, particularly among America's allies. Advised Britain's *New Statesman and Nation:* "If Mr. Truman is wise, one of his last acts as President would be to commute this sentence. . . ."

In the United States—where few, if any, of the major organs of communications advocated clemency—the campaign was conducted on a far smaller scale than in some European nations, but feelings aroused by the case would appear to have been equally intense. In early January 1953, approximately twenty-five hundred clemency supporters journeyed to Washington; some maintained a twenty-four-hour vigil outside the White House while others sought out Justice and State Department officials and various Congressmen. All during the month, rallies were held in New York, Chicago, Los Angeles, and other large cities.

Not all of those who participated in these and related activities necessarily were convinced of the innocence of the Rosenbergs. A typical handbill publicizing a clemency meeting at the time read, in part: "Millions all over the world are appealing to the President to commute their death sentence! Some believe the Rosenbergs are guilty. Some believe they are innocent. Some do not know. But all agree that the death sentence should be commuted by the President."

A statement signed by one thousand Christian clergymen—asking the President "in the spirit of the love which casts out fear to mitigate a punishment of such terrible finality"—expressed no opinion on the question of guilt or innocence. In a telegram to the White House, listing the names of hundreds of additional signers, the Rev. Jesse W. Stitt commented: "This mounting response indicates a widely held belief among many responsible community leaders that it would be a serious mistake to inflict the death penalty." Eventually, about twenty-three hundred clergymen endorsed the appeal.

In January, also, the campaign for clemency gained two of its most important adherents: Nobelists Harold Urey and Albert Einstein. While other politically liberal notables in the United States had previously deplored the death sentences, Urey's stand was unique in that he expressed serious reservations regarding the Rosenbergs' guilt. "After reading the testimony of the Rosenberg case," he wrote in a letter to the *Times*, "I find that I cannot put to rest my doubts about the verdict. . . ." He had, he said, "found the Rosenbergs' testimony more believable than that of the Greenglasses." Shortly afterward, Einstein publicly announced that he had written the President requesting him to commute the death sentences for "the same reasons which were set forth so convincingly by my distinguished colleague, Harold C. Urey."

However, the overwhelming majority of the Rosenbergs' compatriots continued to view their alleged crime with horror and to insist that America show its "strength" by executing the spies. Typical were the views of a New York City minister, the Rev. John Heuss, who declared that those who had signed the clergymen's clemency appeal had been "duped" and said: "I consider the crime for which the Rosenbergs were convicted one of the worst in the annals of mankind."

Sharp criticism of those who aided the clemency campaign was contained in a statement issued by Daniel A. Poling, editor of *The Christian Herald*, on behalf of "six representatives of the three major religious groups in the United States." Among the signers were Charles E. Wilson, ex-president of General Electric; Clarence E. Manion, former dean of the College of Law of the University of Notre Dame; and Samuel I. Rosenman, an adviser to Presidents Roosevelt and Truman. The statement noted: "Appeals in regard to clemency should be directed to the Rosenbergs themselves. They have revealed no regret for the harm which they have done our nation nor any desire to assist the Department of Justice. They have failed to take steps that might warrant clemency."

Expressing similar sentiments, Hearst columnist George E. Sokolsky wrote:

"Everything has been tried by the Rosenbergs except the only step that can justify their existence as human beings: they have never confessed; they have shown no contrition; they have not been penitent. They have been arrogant and tight-lipped. . . . It is impossible to forgive these spies; it would be possible to commute their sentences, if they told the story fully, more than we now know even after these trials. . . . Klaus Fuchs confessed. David Greenglass confessed. Harry Gold confessed. The Rosenbergs remain adamant . . . . let them go to the devil."

Harry S. Truman vacated the Presidency on January 20, 1953, without acting on the Rosenbergs' clemency appeals. He had bequeathed that emotionally charged problem to his successor, Dwight D. Eisenhower. On February 11, three weeks after Eisenhower had assumed office, the White House announced his decision: Clemency was denied. Radio and television bulletins and front-page banner headlines reported the news. A Presidential statement explained:

"I have given earnest consideration to the records in the case of Julius and Ethel Rosenberg and to the appeals for clemency made on their behalf. . . .

"The nature of the crime for which they have been found guilty and sentenced far exceeds that of the taking of the life of another citizen: it involves the deliberate betrayal of the entire nation and could very well result in the death of many, many thousands of innocent citizens. By their act these two individuals have in fact betrayed the cause of freedom for which free men are fighting and dying at this very hour.

"We are a nation under law. . . . All rights of appeal were exercised and the conviction of the trial court was upheld after four judicial reviews, including that of the highest court in the land.*

"I have made a careful examination into this case and am satisfied that the two individuals have been accorded their full measure of justice.

"There has been neither new evidence nor have there been mitigating circumstances which would justify altering this decision, and I have determined that it is my duty, in the interest of the people of the United States, not to set aside the verdict of their representatives."

Commented *Time* magazine: "Dwight Eisenhower's answer all but closed the door of doom on the Rosenbergs. There are still a few desperate delaying actions to be made—and Lawyer Emanuel Bloch might succeed in winning more borrowed time—but the only real opportunity of escape lay with the Rosenbergs themselves. If they broke their long silence—if they confessed the secrets of their spy ring—then the President might consider a new appeal for clemency. But up to now the Rosenbergs have clung to their dark secrets, have shown no flicker of regret."

From abroad came renewed clamor. Reporting that President Eisenhower had received nearly fifteen thousand clemency letters—many from Western Europe—in the course of a single week, the *Nation* observed: "It is too easy to dismiss such letters as Communist-inspired when even the

---

* This is an error inasmuch as the Supreme Court had refused to review the case.

soberly conservative *Gazette de Lausanne* of Switzerland speaks of certain 'disturbing facts' in the case. . . ." The *Nation*—one of the handful of publications in the United States that had advocated "mercy"—concluded: "If the sentence is carried out, we predict that the President will live to regret his decision."*

Aside from France, the movement to save the Rosenbergs attracted the widest popular support in Italy. For many, the case resurrected memories of the execution in the United States over twenty-five years before of two fellow countrymen, Sacco and Vanzetti. The sister of Bartolomeo Vanzetti sent a message to President Eisenhower asking him to "accept the appeal of a humble woman, to whom the great pain suffered gives the strength to implore from you an act of justice." Though the outcry for clemency in Italy was by no means confined to the left, the issue acquired political overtones when leftist newspapers remarked on the failure of the Pope to speak out on the case.

Piqued by such criticism, the Vatican newspaper *L'Osservatore Romano* revealed on February 13, 1953 that Pope Pius XII already had dispatched a message to the United States government concerning clemency. In Washington, the Apostolic Delegation announced that the previous December it had "transmitted to the Justice Department . . . at the request of the Holy See, the information that Pope Pius XII had received 'numerous and urgent' appeals for his intervention in behalf of Julius and Ethel Rosenberg. . . ." The Pope was said to have acted out of motives of charity "without being able to enter into the merits of the case."

Surprisingly, both President Eisenhower and ex-President Truman were reported to have had no knowledge of the Pope's action. This was soon explained when former judge and Attorney General James P. McGranery disclosed that while head of the Justice Department he had received the message in question, orally, from the Apostolic Delegate but had not transmitted it to the President. "The matter ended there so far as I was concerned," McGranery said.

The Apostolic Delegate then sent a letter to Presidential assistant Sherman Adams informing him of the message communicated two months previously to McGranery and adding: ". . . I am directed by the Holy See to inform the competent United States authorities that many new demands are being received at the Vatican urging the Holy Father to intervene for clemency in behalf of the Rosenbergs and that Leftist newspapers insist that his Holiness has done nothing. I will be most grateful if you will kindly notify this to the President."

The interpretation of these events by most of the American press was that the Pope had not *really* intervened in the case. However, a subsequent

---

* Another leading liberal publication in the U.S. that supported clemency was the *New Republic*.

full-page explanation in *L'Osservatore Romano* made clear that the Vatican definitely considered the Pope's action as an appeal for mercy for the Rosenbergs. The Vatican newspaper commented: "There is no doubt that when history returns to this episode, it will seal with a word of highest praise the magnanimous gesture of the Supreme Pontiff."

Meanwhile, Bloch, seeking to continue his fight in the courts, requested a stay of four to eight weeks to allow time for the filing of new motions. Judge Kaufman—who remarked that the volume of telegrams and telephone calls he was now receiving was "most amazing"—refused and set the execution date for the week of March 9, 1953.

Reporting the new date and describing preparations for the executions, the *Times* noted: ". . . the Rosenbergs may escape the death penalty if they decide to talk. They have maintained throughout the two years of trial and appeal that they were innocent. . . . If they now decide to talk, that action might influence the President to grant executive clemency."

Appearing before the Circuit Court of Appeals, Bloch (and a new associate counsel, John F. Finerty*) pleaded for a longer stay than the one granted by Judge Kaufman. Bloch explained that he required additional time to seek a U. S. Supreme Court review of the motion—regarding the alleged Schneider perjury, the Perl arrest, and other matters—previously ruled on unfavorably by both Judge Ryan and the Court of Appeals.

Again the appellate judges appeared to find most merit in Bloch's argument concerning possible prejudice to his clients resulting from William Perl's arrest, in the midst of their trial, and the concomitant statement to the press by prosecutor Saypol. Judge Learned Hand said: "I would be unwilling to foreclose the possibility of taking this question to the Supreme Court," to which Judge Frank added: "There is substance to this argument, and for my part, I believe the Supreme Court should hear it. I certainly would not want to be in the position of precluding these people from presenting their arguments to the Supreme Court." Over the protests of the Department of Justice, the judges granted the Rosenbergs a stay to enable the defense attorneys to petition the Supreme Court for review.

The Supreme Court's decision came on May 25, 1953. Once again, the high court refused to consider the case. Headlined the *Times:* "Rosenberg Appeal Denied For 3D Time By Supreme Court—Stay of Execution for Spies Vacated—Mercy for Couple Hinges on Their Talking." Justice Black—who had dissented alone on the previous Supreme Court denials of a hearing—again favored review and was joined, this time, by Justice William O. Douglas.

Soon after the Supreme Court's action, the executions were set officially

* Finerty had been associated with the defense in the Mooney-Billings and Sacco-Vanzetti cases.

for 11 P.M. June 18, 1953. About two weeks before the date scheduled for their deaths, the Rosenbergs were visited at Sing Sing by James V. Bennett, Director of the federal Bureau of Prisons. The next day, through their attorney, they issued this statement:

"Yesterday, we were offered a deal by the Attorney General of the United States. We were told that if we cooperated with the Government, our lives would be spared.

"By asking us to repudiate the truth of our innocence, the Government admits its own doubts concerning our guilt. We will not help to purify the foul record of a fraudulent conviction and a barbaric sentence.

"We solemnly declare, now and forever more, that we will not be coerced, even under pain of death, to bear false witness and to yield up to tyranny our rights as free Americans.

"Our respect for truth, conscience and human dignity is not for sale. Justice is not some bauble to be sold to the highest bidder.

"If we are executed it will be the murder of innocent people and the shame will be upon the Government of the United States.

"History will record, whether we live or not, that we were victims of the most monstrous frame-up in the history of our country."

Over two years after the Rosenbergs' conviction, the events of the case had taken on a momentum of their own. It was becoming increasingly evident that the government was not prepared to relent unless the condemned spies confessed and cooperated, and increasingly certain that no such confession would be forthcoming. Thus, in early June 1953—while millions throughout the world looked on in horror—the Rosenberg case moved, inexorably, toward its grim climax.

CHAPTER 18

NEW EVIDENCE

On June 6, 1953—with the scheduled executions only twelve days away—attorneys for the condemned couple presented Judge Kaufman with "new evidence" said to prove that the principal prosecution witnesses, David and Ruth Greenglass, had lied. On the basis of this evidence, the attorneys asked the Judge to set aside the convictions and grant the Rosenbergs a new trial.

The "new evidence" included three separate items: The previously missing Rosenberg console table, which had figured in the Greenglasses' trial testimony as a gift from the Russians specially adapted for microfilming; confidential pretrial memoranda apparently pilfered from the office of O. John Rogge, counsel to the Greenglasses; and an affidavit regarding alleged theft of a sample of uranium from Los Alamos by David Greenglass, sworn to by his brother.

For more than a month, the Rosenberg committee in the United States had been trying—with almost no success—to publicize information about the console table and Rogge memos in the American press; in Europe, however, word of the "new evidence" had quickly aroused wide interest and discussion. Commented *Le Monde* in a front-page editorial:

"These two new elements are too important to be passed over in silence. It is up to American justice to evaluate them, check their accuracy, and decide in what measure they call for a new trial."

Logically, the console table occupied a relatively minor place in the total fabric of the Rosenberg-Sobell trial. Nevertheless, the evidence about the table had a simple, dramatic quality that made it easy to grasp and remember. Undoubtedly, the table's importance was enhanced greatly by extensive repetition: Six witnesses testified about it; two prosecution exhibits were related to it; both Bloch and Saypol discussed the table in their summations, the latter playing it up as a meaningful and significant aspect of his case.

When first mentioned at the trial—by David Greenglass on direct examination—the console table was the subject of one sentence of incriminating testimony. Queried about any rewards the Rosenbergs had received for their espionage work, David replied: "I believe they [the Rosenbergs] told me they received a console table from the Russians." He added that he had seen this table at the Rosenbergs' apartment after he got out of the Army.

Asked on cross-examination to describe the table, David said it was "a dark color, mahogany probably" and had one side that "lifted up so it made an 'L' if you had it against the wall."

BLOCH: And was that console table used for eating purposes?
DAVID: That console table was used for photography.
BLOCH: For photography?
DAVID: That's right. Julius told me that he did pictures on that table.
BLOCH: Were you ever at the Rosenbergs' house when food was served on that table?
DAVID: I might have been.

Ruth Greenglass corroborated her husband's testimony that the Rosenbergs had received the table as a gift; she also elaborated his rather enigmatic comment that the table was "used for photography." Recounting the first time she saw the table, in 1946, she testified:

"I admired the table and I asked Ethel when she bought a new piece of furniture; she said she had not bought it, she had gotten it as a gift and I said it was a very nice gift to get from a friend, and Julius said it was from his friend and it was a special kind of table, and he turned the table on its side to show us why it was so special. . . . There was a portion of the table that was hollowed out for a lamp to fit underneath it so that the table could be used for photograph purposes. . . . He took pictures on microfilm of the typewritten notes."

Ruth's assertion that the Rosenbergs' table had a "portion . . . that was hollowed out for a lamp to fit underneath"—a detail completely unmentioned in David's description—is very difficult to visualize. Did she actually see a lamp or only a hollow? How would a lamp *under* a table have been useful? Would a photographer have to crawl beneath the table with his microphotography equipment and "typewritten notes"?

Also hard to comprehend is Ruth's testimony that Julius had told her that "when he used the table he darkened the room so that there would be no other light and he wouldn't be obvious to anyone looking in."

Was the Rosenbergs' living room, which they also used as a bedroom, without window drapes or shades of some sort? In any event, what would be more "obvious" to anyone "looking in" the Rosenbergs' eleventh-floor apartment than a man in a dark room under a table with a single bright light on him? These and other absurdities immediately intrude when one tries to decipher Ruth's description of the table.

Prosecutor Saypol simply ignored all of these difficulties when he told the jurors: "You heard the testimony about what was done to that console table, so that it was used for microfilming."

When the Rosenbergs took the witness stand they denied that the table had been a gift from the Russians or anyone else and testified that Julius had purchased it at Macy's department store in 1944 or 1945 for "about $21." They were unable, however, to back this assertion with any documentary proof: An employee of Macy's, called as a defense witness, testified that the store's sales and delivery records for 1944 and 1945 had been destroyed.

The Rosenbergs also denied that their table had a "hollowed out" portion or any other special features to adapt it for microfilming. They asserted that their console table had been used only for decorative and eating purposes.

Cross-examined about the table, Julius said it was dark brown and "had a piano hinge in the center, and . . . could open up double. . . . the cover of the table would swing around at right angles, you could open the table double."

U. S. Attorney Saypol questioned Ethel closely about where she had kept the console table in her former three-room Knickerbocker Village apartment, inquiring if she had "ever put that table in a closet." Ethel replied: "I may have." Asked specifically by Saypol whether she ever *hid* the table in a closet, she testified:

"I never hid anything in the closet, table or anything else. . . . There were so many changes that I made in the house, with putting things in closets and taking them out of closets, that it is perfectly true what I say, that I may or may not have put it there, and I cannot recall. . . ."

One who could recall was Evelyn Cox, the Rosenbergs' part-time domestic in 1944 and 1945, who appeared for the prosecution as a rebuttal witness. She testified to having seen and admired a new mahogany-colored console table in the Rosenbergs' living room; later, Ethel Rosenberg told her that she had put the table in a large closet and Mrs. Cox observed it there several times. She said Mrs. Rosenberg had explained to her that "she had put it away in the closet because the place was too congested."

SAYPOL: Now, was the place congested? Was there a lot of furniture there filling the place up?

MRS. COX: Well, at one time it was congested and then I don't know, I think she got rid of some of the things. I am really not sure. . . .

Although this testimony of Mrs. Cox's about the closet seems generally consistent with Ethel Rosenberg's and, in any event, is not significant in itself, Saypol emphasized it in his summation, commenting on "this remarkably strange behavior taking the best piece of furniture in the house and storing it in the closet—why did they have to hide it?"

Mrs. Cox also testified that Mrs. Rosenberg had told her that the table was a gift—a belated wedding present from a friend of her husband—

thereby buttressing Ruth Greenglass's testimony on this point. (Only David Greenglass claimed to have been informed explicitly that the table was a gift from the "Russians.")

So far as she knew, Mrs. Cox said, the table had been used by the Rosenbergs solely as "an ornament," though she agreed that it also could have been opened to eat on. The former domestic—whose duties had included the dusting and polishing of furniture—described various parts of the table but said nothing at all about any unusual physical features. (Ruth Greenglass, therefore, was the only witness who told of the table's curious adaptation for microfilming.)

U. S. Attorney Saypol attempted to discredit the Rosenbergs' assertions that the table was an inexpensive one purchased at Macy's for only "about $21." Said he: "Don't you know, Mr. Rosenberg, that you couldn't buy a console table in Macy's, if they had it, in 1944 and 1945, for less than $85?" He introduced a number of illustrations of rather costly-looking console tables, querying Julius as to which picture "most closely resembles the console table you bought." Although Julius replied that his was "much plainer. . . . This has all the frills and curves in it," Saypol exhibited the pictures to the jurors and sought, by various stratagems, to identify the unseen console table under discussion with the elaborate ones shown in the illustrations. On summation, he referred with evident disbelief to the Rosenbergs' testimony that they had been able to buy the table for only $21 at Macy's during the war "when furniture was scarce."

The actual table was never presented for the jury's examination by either the defense or prosecution. The latter did not dispute Julius Rosenberg's contention that the table had been in his living room at the time the FBI came to arrest him. As for the defense, Bloch told the Court, in another context, that after the Rosenbergs were jailed "their home was abandoned. . . . I had the lease canceled and their furniture was disposed of."

When a console table alleged to be the same one the Rosenbergs had owned was located by a *National Guardian* reporter about March 1953, it fitted the general description given at the trial by various witnesses—other than Ruth. Like the console table the Rosenbergs had testified about, this one was dark brown, quite plain in design, and had a swivel-type top. No portion could in any sense be called "hollowed out." It was not a "special kind of table" but only an ordinary-looking and obviously used article of furniture with coded store markings on the under side.

Photographs of the table and its markings were submitted to a qualified Macy's employee (Joseph Fontana), who had over thirty years experience with the store and had been the buyer of "occasional furniture" in 1944 and 1945. In an affidavit, he stated that—assuming the photographs and markings to be genuine—the console table was one of Macy's "lower priced tables" and had been sold by the store for $19.97 [with sales tax the price would have been $20.37]. Although there was some question about just when Macy's had handled this particular table (because an unclear photo of the markings made it difficult to tell whether one letter was an "E" or an "F"), he thought the probable date was "sometime during or subsequent to the year 1944."

Every aspect of the Macy employee's analysis of the table and its markings is in complete accord with the trial testimony of the Rosenbergs. In the motion for a new trial based on newly discovered evidence, Emanuel Bloch (assisted by John Finerty and a professor of law at the University of Chicago, Malcolm Sharp*) submitted this affidavit to Judge Kaufman, along with photographs of the table. As for the table itself, the attorneys noted: "The console table will be produced, at the request of the Court."

Obviously, the important question before the Court was whether the table is, in fact, the *same one* which the Rosenbergs formerly had in their apartment. If so, the Greenglasses' testimony on this subject would be discredited. To establish proof of the authenticity of the table, Bloch offered additional affidavits sworn to by himself, the defendants, three members of Julius Rosenberg's family, the reporter who allegedly found the table, and a minister. Recounted by these affidavits were a series of misadventures and lost opportunities:

For several months after the arrest of Ethel Rosenberg, the Knickerbocker Village apartment had remained unoccupied and locked, but Emanuel Bloch had continued to pay the rent. By mid-October 1950—when it became apparent that neither of the Rosenbergs would be able to raise bail—members of Julius's family agreed to the prisoners' request that the apartment be relinquished and their household and personal effects be disposed of.

Julius's brother, David, met with Bloch at the apartment and, after looking over the furnishings, decided that they were "cheap, worn-out, and . . . of no value whatsoever." He told Bloch that he would arrange for everything "to be sold for 'junk.'" However, when Julius's mother and his two married sisters, Ethel and Lena, came to pack up the items a few days later, Lena kept some pots and pans and Ethel decided to store in the basement of her Queens home the console table, two children's chests of drawers, a bicycle, and some other toys. The rest, Mrs. Sophie Rosenberg, Julius's mother, personally sold for $5 to a second-hand furniture dealer on the East Side.

Afterward, Sophie Rosenberg visited Julius and Ethel at their respective

---

* Earlier, Sharp had urged clemency, but believed the Rosenbergs guilty. His opinion changed when the console table was discovered and, soon after, he joined the defense.

jails and told them that everything, except for some clothing, had been gotten rid of for junk.

When David Greenglass began testifying about the Rosenbergs' console table at the trial, the defendants believed that it had been disposed of long since. Bloch had the impression that the recipient was "some itinerant junk dealer" and so believed that the possibility of tracing the table was "extremely remote." Members of Julius's family, who knew the whereabouts of the table, said they had no idea that it had figured in the trial. They attended no trial sessions, hardly ever discussed the evidence with the defendants, and read nothing about the console table testimony in the newspapers—Mrs. Sophie Rosenberg, in fact, is illiterate. Ethel Goldberg, who actually had the table in her possession during the trial, said in her affidavit:

"I just couldn't bring myself to read the newspapers where it concerned my brother Julius, and his wife, Ethel. . . .

"Prior to and during the trial, and for some time thereafter, I was in a state of semi-hysteria because of the impact of the arrests and the implications of the charges. . . . I secluded myself as much as I could. . . . When I visited them [the Rosenbergs] during the trial, we did not talk about anything but personal matters. . . ."

In June 1951, members of Julius's family decided to set up a home for the convicted couple's sons—who were at that time housed in a municipal children's shelter—and Sophie Rosenberg rented a four-room Manhattan apartment for this purpose. Ethel Goldberg arranged for the console table, children's chests of drawers, bicycle, and toys—until then stored in her basement—to be delivered there. When Julius's brother, David, visited this apartment, he noticed the console table and then learned, for the first time, that it and several other possessions of the Rosenbergs had not been disposed of by his sisters and mother; however, he was unaware of the table's trial significance. Emanuel Bloch recalled visiting the apartment on one or two occasions to see the Rosenberg children, but said he was so intent on the boys' needs that he never had any awareness at all of the table.

About early March 1953, a *National Guardian* reporter—assigned to look into this aspect of the case—spoke with Julius's sister, Ethel, learned that the table was being used by Sophie Rosenberg and her grandsons, and went to her apartment. There he found the console table and had photographs made of it in various views. The defendants themselves and Julius's family identified these photos as "fair and accurate representations" of the console table which they said had formerly been in the Knickerbocker Village apartment.

Also shown the photographs, as well as the table itself, was the rebuttal witness, Evelyn Cox. According to the newspaperman and a minister who accompanied him on a number of visits to her home, Mrs. Cox indicated that "she was sick and tired of this case and did not want to become involved again." She refused to sign an affidavit. Her daughter was said to have told the visitors: "From the day those FBI men brought Mama home from the trial until the day you came here with the table, Mama never said one word about the Rosenbergs or what went on at the trial or what she testified. . . ." However, although Mrs. Cox would not sign anything, she allegedly told her visitors that she would be willing to "swear in any court in the land that this looks like the table the Rosenbergs had in their apartment."

Such was the story presented to Judge Kaufman by the defense in their request for a new trial. The prosecution, in turn, did not directly contest the authenticity of the table as the one that had been owned by the Rosenbergs; its response was limited to two affidavits from Macy employees. One, from the same individual who had previously analyzed the table's markings for the defense, stated that Macy's had "handled and sold several hundred such tables." The second suggested the possibility of some irregularity in the coded markings referring to price. Both employees pointed out in their affidavits that Macy's had marked tables of that type with colored crayon, rather than white chalk. However, the precise material with which the table in question was marked had not been attested to by the defense and could not be discerned from black-and-white photographs. An offer by the defense to resolve this issue at once by presenting the table in court then and there was turned down by Judge Kaufman.*

In that part of his opinion dealing with the console table, the Judge ruled: ". . . the fact that its markings indicate that it was purchased from Macy's does not resolve the conflict in the testimony with regard to whether the table was or was not a gift. . . . Certainly no sales or delivery receipts have been produced upon this hearing that might establish that this very table was the table which was sold by R. H. Macy to the Rosenbergs. . . ."

As for the defense affidavits by members of Julius Rosenberg's family "to the effect that the table is the same one as the one they saw in the Rosenbergs' apartment," Judge Kaufman appeared to dismiss them. "On the basis of the defendants' own contention," he said, "this table was an inexpensive one, handled by Macy's, and was undoubtedly mass produced and widely sold. One such table must look very much like another."

Even were he to accept both the "basic facts" and the "conclusion" of the affidavits, the Judge said, "there would still be lacking any showing that the Government *knowingly* used perjurious testimony," and such a showing was required by law for a new trial. (Emphasis added.)

Criticizing the defense for lack of "diligence" for not having taken the

---

* Attorney Malcolm Sharp later wrote: ". . . inspection has disclosed that the table was marked in crayon, not in chalk as the government affidavits insinuated."

apparently simple steps that would have been required to locate the table during the trial, Judge Kaufman added: "Or perhaps it was not done by counsel, for he realized how unimportant and insignificant this testimony was in the light of the other testimony at the trial."

The relative importance of the console table—or any other trial evidence—in determining the ultimate verdict of a jury is, of course, a matter of individual judgment. It seems only fair to point out, however, that the Judge's own words five months earlier—during a hearing on judicial clemency—do not suggest that he regarded the console table testimony as "unimportant and insignificant." On that occasion, Bloch had tried to persuade Judge Kaufman that there was a sufficient element of doubt about the Rosenbergs' guilt to warrant commutation of the death sentence.

> BLOCH: . . . How is it that the Government with thousands upon thousands of FBI agents, could not uncover one scrap of physical evidence so that you could be absolutely sure that these accusations are true?
>
> JUDGE KAUFMAN: Wasn't there evidence about the table?

Now, with the defense claiming that they had found this table and could prove that it was an ordinary one that had been purchased at Macy's, Judge Kaufman refused to look at it or grant a preliminary hearing at which both the defense and prosecution could call witnesses to establish or refute the validity of the "new evidence."

Thus, the veracity and accuracy of the defense affidavits was never considered in court. The defense contentions remained unchallenged and the table's alleged authenticity was never disproved.

In addition to the affidavits relating to the console table, the defense also submitted to Judge Kaufman as "new evidence" copies of pretrial memoranda said to prove that the Greenglasses had testified falsely. By undisclosed means, these confidential memoranda had been removed from the office files of the Greenglasses' attorney, O. John Rogge, copied, and then returned. The copies were transmitted to France, where one was reproduced in the Parisian newspaper *Combat* in April 1953. Subsequently, photostats of the memos were sent to Emanuel Bloch who, after seeking the advice of the New York Bar Association, included several of them in his application for a new trial.

The Rogge memos must be seen in the context in which they were written to be fully understood. Two of the memos relate to events during or soon after a lengthy FBI interrogation of David Greenglass that began on Thursday afternoon, June 15, 1950. According to David's trial testimony, at about 2 P.M. that day, two FBI agents—later joined by two others—arrived at the Greenglass apartment and, for the next five and a half or six hours, questioned him "on and off" and searched the place. Then David voluntarily accompanied the agents to their headquarters in the Federal Building at Foley Square, where the questioning continued throughout that evening and into the early morning hours. After signing a statement at 2 A.M., he phoned his brother-in-law, Louis Abel, and asked him to engage an attorney, O. John Rogge.* For the rest of that night, David slept in the FBI offices. No charge had been filed against him and he was not under arrest.

Early the next morning, three FBI agents came to the apartment of Julius Rosenberg, who agreed to talk with them at their Foley Square offices. At the trial, Julius testified that, after some two hours of general questioning about David Greenglass, an agent had suddenly informed him that "your brother-in-law said you told him to supply information for Russia." Julius had denied the accusation, asked to be confronted with David, and said the FBI was "trying to implicate" him in something. After about six hours with the agents, he phoned the office of an attorney connected with his former union and, on the advice of counsel, asked the agents if he was under arrest. Told he was not, he thereupon left the FBI offices.

Meanwhile, that same morning (Friday, June 16) Louis Abel went to see Rogge as David had requested in his 2 A.M. phone call. As a result, some time before noon David was visited by attorney Herbert Fabricant, of the Rogge law firm. Returning to his office, Fabricant wrote this memo:

". . . I visited the offices of the FBI on the 6th floor of the Federal Building where I spoke with . . . the Agent in charge.

"He told me that Greenglass was down the hall and that I could see him and that he had signed a statement indicating that he had met Harry Gold and that he had transferred information to Gold.

"He further told me that the matter was being taken up with the Department of Justice and that the probability is that a complaint will be filed in Albuquerque, New Mexico charging conspiracy and advised me that I could see Greenglass if I wished. . . .

"I then was taken to a room down the hall where . . . . I was told that I could see him alone if I wished but that they would prefer to have a man present. I asked Greenglass what he would prefer and he said he would rather see me alone whereupon the agents left the room but kept the door open. Greenglass confirmed that he had given a statement that he had met Gold for an hour, that he had given him some information

---

* Rogge, then a member of the law firm of Rogge, Fabricant, Gordon and Goldman, had formerly served as an Assistant U. S. Attorney General. His firm eventually represented six prosecution witnesses in the Rosenberg-Sobell case—David and Ruth Greenglass, Max Elitcher, Dorothy and Louis Abel, and Helen Pagano—as well as several other clients who had been listed as potential witnesses but never were called to testify.

concerning the names of people who would be sympathetic but he thought that Japan was the enemy and Russia was an ally and there was no reason why information could not be given. He had told the FBI that he received $500 from Gold.

"He told me that he had made a number of confusing statements purposely in order to confound the FBI and to draw attention from his wife who is in the hospital. His wife apparently originally told him that his brother-in-law, Julius Rosenberg, had suggested this (and so I fail to see how his mind operated in connection with keeping his wife out of the picture).

"He told me further that Julius Rosenberg is apparently very close to this whole situation. Julius Rosenberg had once introduced him to a man in a car somewhere in New York who apparently made this request. He does not know if the man was a Russian and told the FBI that he didn't know."

A few hours after this interview with Fabricant, David was formally arrested on the basis of a complaint filed in New Mexico, charged with the capital offense of conspiracy to commit espionage in wartime, and—unable to post $100,000 bail—was imprisoned in New York City to await disposition of his case. The next day, Saturday, June 17, he supplemented the information he had given Fabricant orally with this handwritten memo to his attorney:

"These are my approximate statements to the F.B.I.

"1. I stated that I met Gold in N.M. at 209 N. High St. my place. They told me that I had told him to come back later because I didn't have it ready. I didn't remember this but I allowed it in the statement. When he came back again I told them that I gave him the envelope with the stuff not expecting payment and then he gave me an envelope. Later I found that it contained $500.

"2. I told them that on a visit to me in Nov. 1944 my wife asked me if I would give information. I made sure to tell the F.B.I. that she was transmitting this info from my Brother in Law Julius and was not her own idea. She was doing this because she felt I would be angry if she didn't ask me.

"I then mentioned a meeting with a man who I didn't know arranged by Julius. I established the approximate meeting place but no exact date. The place was a car an Olds owned by my father-in-law, at somewhere above 42nd St. on 1st Ave. in Man. I talked to the man but I could re-call very little about which we spoke. I thought it might be that he wanted me to think about finding out about H.E. [high explosive] lens's [sic] used in experimental tests to determine data on the a bomb.

"I made a general statement on my age etc. you know the usual thing.

"I mentioned no other meeting with anyone.

"One more thing, I identified Gold by a torn or cut piece of card, but I didn't tell them where or how I got it. Also I definitely placed my wife out of the room at the time of Gold's visit.

"Also I didn't know who sent Gold to me.

"I also made [for the FBI] a pencil sketch of an H.E. mold set up for an experiment. But this I'll tell you I can honestly say the information I gave Gold maybe not at all what I said in the statement."

Particularly striking about these two accounts of David Greenglass's initial confession to the FBI is the paucity of details regarding the alleged crime. David's assertion to his attorney that he gave Harry Gold "some information concerning the names of people who would be sympathetic" is the one and only specific mention in either memo of the passage of any material. Ruth is said to have asked David, in November 1944, at Julius Rosenberg's behest, to provide information, but there is no hint in the memos as to what data was requested and no claim that any—other than names—was given. Regarding the unknown man in the automobile, David did not recall the incident clearly but believed the man might have asked him to "think" about obtaining lens mold data. (He did not know if this person was a Russian and said he had so informed the FBI; at the trial, however, he testified that Rosenberg had told him that the man was a "Russian.")

Neither memo mentions Ethel Rosenberg. As for Julius Rosenberg, although he is said to be "very close to this situation," to have persuaded Ruth to ask David for information, and to have arranged a meeting for David with a man in a car, there is no indication in the memos as to what sort of information Julius requested nor any suggestion that he had *received* any. Missing from both memos is even the slightest reference to Julius's receipt from David of atom bomb information in January and September 1945, or of the postwar incidents involving the sky platform, atomic airplane, and money for students. Nor is a word included about the then very recent events concerning flight: The plan given David to travel to Czechoslovakia, the $5000, and the passport photos taken at Julius's request.

Moreover, nothing in the memos links Julius Rosenberg to the Gold-Greenglass Albuquerque meeting. No reference is made to either the occasion in the Rosenberg apartment when the jello box was cut or the password "Julius sent me." David said in his memo that he had identified Gold with a "torn or cut piece of card" but did not tell the FBI agents "where or how I got it" and "didn't know who sent Gold to me."

The puzzling vagueness of the memos—which makes it difficult to tell just who did what—is added to by David's admission that he was uncertain of the accuracy of parts of the statement he had signed. One cannot help feeling uneasy at such remarks by David as "I didn't remember this but I allowed it in the statement" or "I can honestly say the information I gave Gold maybe not at all what I said in the statement."

These comments, coupled with the absence from the memos of so many important details of the crime, disprove David's trial assertion that he did not "conscientiously withhold" (sic) any information regarding his espionage activities from his first FBI statement. The memos show that the real question is not *whether* David withheld information from his first statement, but *why* he did so. Either he did not, for any one of a variety of reasons, choose to fill in the details of the crime at that time or—as the defense would hold—he had not yet invented these details.

A third memo submitted by the defense as "new evidence" describes a visit paid by Rogge, and an associate, Robert Goldman, to Ruth Greenglass at her home on Sunday, June 18. She was in bed, having returned—on the day of David's arrest—from a hospital where she had been treated for infected burns. Her conversation with her attorneys was recounted in a memo (written the following day by Goldman) which reads, in part:

"Mrs. Greenglass discussed her visit to New Mexico. . . . She feels that New Mexico is a very bad place to try the case since the citizens did not like GI's because of the big boom and then the big slack, because of anti-semitism and because the local citizens all felt bitter about the wives of the GI's taking jobs there. She was employed in Albuquerque by the OPA and temporarily by the Soil Conservation Office.

"As to her husband, she stated that he had a 'tendency to hysteria.' At other times he would become delirious and once when he had the grippe he ran nude through the hallway, shrieking of 'elephants,' 'Lead Pants.'

"She had known him since he was ten years old. She said that he would say things were so even if they were not. He talked of suicide as if he were a character in the movies but she didn't think he would do it. They had been under surveillance by the FBI for several weeks. . . . She was interviewed at the hospital by two FBI men. . . . They assured her that they had nothing against her. She described her stay in Albuquerque. . . . She had only been to Los Alamos to a party for a few hours one time. She had remembered no visitors at her house. . . . She knew her mail was censored. . . .

"She pointed out Dave did not ask for the job; that he was going overseas; that they have been watched constantly, and feels as if they are the object of persecution. . . .

"People in the neighborhood want to raise a petition.

"All newspapers are to be referred to her lawyer.

"People keep flocking in the house to offer support and advice including that perhaps a right-wing lawyer should be selected. The Jewish Daily Forward, which is certainly not a leftist newspaper, is very excited about the anti-semitic issue and has offered a lawyer. . . . OJR [Rogge] pointed out that if Dave was innocent he should talk; that if not it would be advisable not to talk but to let the Government prove its case. The third course was that of cooperation. That was also discussed at length.

"There was a long discussion about JR [Julius Rosenberg]."*

This memo reveals that, during her first conference with her attorneys, Ruth Greenglass did not relate to them any aspect of the story of the crime that she later told at the trial; instead, she expressed the belief that she and her husband were "the object of persecution" and asserted that David "would say things were so even if they were not." While nine months later she was to testify that Harry Gold came to her Albuquerque apartment and "bore greetings from Julius," she now advised her attorneys that she "remembered no visitors to her house."

The memo specifically contradicts Ruth's testimony at the trial when she was questioned by Emanuel Bloch regarding this same June 18 meeting with her attorneys:

BLOCH: Did you tell Mr. Rogge that you were innocent?
RUTH: No, I told him the whole truth. . . . I told him everything I could truthfully remember. . . . Mr. Rogge asked me to tell the truth. I told him the truth the way I did here today and he outlined the different courses that could be taken.

With the exception of the FBI interview at the hospital on the day of her husband's arrest, Ruth Greenglass was not—according to her trial testimony—questioned during the next month by any representative of either the FBI or prosecution staff. In mid-July, however, she went voluntarily to a conference in the U. S. Attorney's office at which were present David, attorneys Rogge and Goldman, Saypol, and several FBI agents; the next day she attended a second meeting (without her husband) and the following morning signed a typewritten statement. It would seem a reasonable deduction that it was this statement that triggered the arrest of Julius Rosenberg on the evening of July 17.

Unfortunately, no Rogge memos recording any discussions with the Greenglasses are available for this four-week June–July period during which David must have greatly augmented his story of the crime and Julius's role in it and Ruth decided on the "course . . . of cooperation" that had been "discussed at length" during her initial meeting with her attorneys. However, a number of memos from late July and August are among

---

* This comment may refer to the Greenglasses' business difficulties with Julius. Ruth testified at the trial that she had spoken with Rogge about this matter and had asked the attorney to try to secure the money owed her husband for his share of the machine shop.

those that have been made public. One, dated July 20—a few days after Julius's arrest—reports a telephone call received by Goldman:*

"Saypol called me today and I returned his call. He stated as follows:

"'I have made arrangements to have your man Greenglass transferred to the Tombs Prison, 11th Floor, where he will be more comfortable and also because it is desirable to take him away and keep him separated from Rosenberg. I assume you agree. . . .'

"Saypol requested in referring to where he is stationed, if we did refer to it, we simply mention the Tombs and not mention that it is the 11th floor."

(The eleventh floor of the Tombs was reserved for prisoners who were "cooperating" with the authorities; many special privileges were granted the inmates. Among attorneys experienced in criminal law, the place was known as the "singing quarters.")

On August 11 Ethel Rosenberg was arrested and, six days later, she and her husband were indicted for conspiracy to commit espionage. David Greenglass (already under a New Mexico indictment relating to his Albuquerque meeting with Gold) was named as a co-conspirator, as was Ruth. A memo from Goldman to Rogge on August 21 discussed Ruth's reaction to the New York indictment:

"I spoke to Ruth Greenglass this morning. She is feeling better and so is Dave apparently about the fact that they were not named as defendants. From Helen [probably the secretary, Mrs. Pagano] I learned that she may have been a little upset about it originally but now she feels the thing is moving smoothly.

"However, Dave is worried about something else which I was able to reassure him through Ruth. Some of his cellmates in the Tombs have been telling him horror stories about the treatment he will get. I . . . . assured her that Saypol would not permit any mistreatment. But the thing that impressed her most however was that I told her that you were on friendly terms with Bennett, Director of Prisons. This impressed her because she feels that Dave may not get a suspended sentence [in New Mexico] and is worried about the kind of treatment he will get. I assured her that if he does go to jail for a period of time that you would certainly not hesitate to speak to Bennett and to make sure that Dave got good and fair treatment."

However, another memo from Goldman written two days later on August 23 indicates that all was not moving as "smoothly" as Ruth apparently believed. The memo states:

"Lane, the Assistant U. S. Attorney, called me at 1:00 o'clock and told me that something important had come up with respect to New Mexico

* This memo of July 20 and the following one of August 21 were not included as exhibits in the defense appeal.

and would I and/or Fabricant see him this afternoon. I told him that I could and HJF [Fabricant] would come with me.

". . . HJF and I went over to see Lane at 4:00 o'clock. He told us that Bloch had earlier in the day argued to the judge at the arraignment of his clients that they were absolutely innocent and that from the fact that Greenglass was not indicted but merely named as a co-conspirator in the New York indictment, it looked to Bloch as if the government had made a deal with you as Greenglass's attorney. Lane felt that we would now have to consider the question of whether it was OK that Greenglass be indicted here in a superseding indictment and not merely named as a co-conspirator. He would then be a defendant and be tried here in New York but would testify against the others.

"The New Mexico District Attorney, acting on instructions from the Attorney General's office, with whom Lane had been in touch, would agree to such a procedure. Lane pointed out that he thought it was obviously advantageous for both sides for the matter to be decided in New York . . . . clearly indicating that he felt that in a small state like New Mexico they might well prefer to give a good stiff sentence. . . .

"There was no indication that Ruth is to be indicted and neither Herb [Fabricant] nor I wanted to raise the point. I had the inference that they were not planning to indict her but I could be wrong and I didn't even want to ask the question, though you may desire to do so. . . .

"I think it best not to discuss this with Ruth until you return as she might get somewhat excited about it. . . ."

Judge Kaufman ruled that the information revealed by the Rogge memos did not constitute grounds for a new trial. Rejecting the defense contention that the apparent omission of key facts from David's first FBI statement indicated that he had later perjured himself in his trial testimony, the Judge noted: "During cross-examination at the trial, David Greenglass repeatedly asserted that he had given many, as many as six or seven statements, to agents of the Federal Bureau of Investigation; that his early statements had been very general, at the request of these agents, and that he had not at the time of his earlier statements remembered fully all the details which he later supplied.

"The statement of Ruth Greenglass, made to her attorney . . . that her husband was somewhat of an hysteric, and that he would on occasion say untrue things does not establish that at the trial his testimony . . . was untruthful."

One final item of "new evidence" was submitted as part of the defense application. During the trial, both the Greenglasses testified on cross-examination that in February 1950—over three months before Harry Gold's arrest—David had been questioned by an FBI agent, who visited their apartment for about an hour; neither revealed (despite some probing by Bloch) the subject of this inquiry. However, Julius Rosenberg testified that he had been informed by David that an FBI agent had asked him about uranium. Julius claimed that when David later indicated that he was in difficulty and requested money and help in obtaining a smallpox certificate, he recalled this mention of uranium and thought that it might be related to his brother-in-law's troubles.

Julius's trial testimony that David had been questioned about uranium was confirmed in the Rogge memo reporting Ruth's June 18 conference with her attorneys. This memo notes that in early February 1950, "the FBI asked if they [the Greenglasses] had a specimen of uranium in the house in the course of what they call a routine investigation. One of their friends had a similar experience." What appears to be still another reference to uranium is contained in the following rather enigmatic statement in the same memo: "She [Ruth] would not have allowed her husband to bring anything home after Hiroshima had disclosed what the project was. She intended to raise a family and did not want *that kind of material* around." (Emphasis added.)

Presented by the defense as "new evidence" was an affidavit (signed May 31, 1953) from Bernard Greenglass which read, in part:

"Some time in the year 1946 my brother David told me he had taken a sample of uranium from Los Alamos without permission of the authorities. . . .

"Sometime later, and I don't remember whether it was a year or more later or sometime before David's arrest in June 1950, David told me that he had thrown this uranium into the East River." Bernard also noted that Ruth Greenglass recently had stated in his presence: "David took a sample of uranium but he threw it into the East River."

Regarding the affidavit from Bernard Greenglass, Judge Kaufman ruled: "Counsel for the defendants urge that this theft of uranium indicates that David Greenglass was involved in espionage, independent of the Rosenbergs. . . . It is difficult to perceive how a theft and disposal of uranium in the manner described indicates such independent espionage. . . . It is even more difficult to perceive how this espionage would provide a motive for perjury, designed to implicate innocent members of Greenglass's family in this most serious crime."

The Judge's opinion concluded:

"It is worthy of re-emphasis that no one Government witness has recanted after all these years. I have said before and I repeat, the guilt of the defendants was established overwhelmingly, and the present alleged new evidence does not in any way diminish the strength of the Government's case. The motions in behalf of the defendants Rosenberg are denied."

The Rosenbergs' request for a new trial had been dealt with by Judge Kaufman with extraordinary speed. The defense brief detailing the "new evidence" had been filed on Saturday, June 6, 1953. The following Monday, June 8, Judge Kaufman had heard three hours of oral argument and, after retiring for a fifteen-minute recess, had returned to the courtroom to deliver his opinion—obviously written earlier—that took thirty minutes to read.

The next day, Tuesday, June 9, attorneys for the Rosenbergs appeared before the Court of Appeals to request a stay of execution while they prepared their appeal from Judge Kaufman's decision. Instead they were directed, over their objections, to argue the appeal itself then and there. The following day, Wednesday, June 10, defense attorneys submitted to the Court of Appeals a list of legal points on which, they said, their research was "inadequate," as proof of their need for a stay to properly brief their appeal. However, on Thursday, June 11, the Court of Appeals affirmed Judge Kaufman's decision and denied a stay of execution.

Next day, Friday, June 12, the Rosenbergs' attorneys appealed to the U. S. Supreme Court for a stay of execution to provide time necessary to print and file a defense petition requesting a review by the high court of the motion for a new trial.* The attorneys—who noted that without a stay it would be impossible for the high court to act on their petition before the executions—protested "the indecent haste with which this serious application . . . in a capital case" already had been disposed of by the district court and Court of Appeals.

The defense application for a stay was considered by the Supreme Court at its final conference of the term on Saturday, June 13. The following Monday, June 15—just one week after the motion based on "new evidence" had first been argued before Judge Kaufman—the Court formally announced its decision: The application had been denied by a 5 to 4 vote. Voting in favor of a stay were Justices Black, Frankfurter, Jackson, and Douglas.† As the Supreme Court recessed for the summer, the execution of the Rosenbergs was three days away.

---

* The defense also sought Supreme Court review on several other motions, including two aimed at the legality of the death sentences.
† A fifth Justice, Burton, favored granting the Rosenbergs' attorney an opportunity to present oral arguments on their application for a stay but, when this recommendation was turned down, voted against the stay.

CHAPTER 19

DEATH HOUSE LETTERS

Julius and Ethel Rosenberg spent nearly three years in prison—over two years of this time in the Sing Sing death house. There, confined in different sections of the condemned block, they saw one another only at brief weekly visits and during legal consultations with their attorney. Except for this limited direct contact, they communicated with each other entirely through letters.

When the campaign on their behalf began, the Rosenbergs agreed to the publication of some of these letters, both to aid their cause and, later, to raise funds for their two young children. Today, book-length editions of the letters are available in many languages.

Original copies of the bulk of the Rosenbergs' prison correspondence, consisting of nearly four hundred letters (aggregating about nine hundred handwritten pages),* were obtained by the authors from attorney Gloria Agrin, who was associated with the defense. Handwritten on prison stationery, each letter is dated and signed by the sender and is stamped by the prison censor.

Inevitably, in the heat of the public battle fought over their case, the Rosenbergs were sometimes dehumanized by their enemies and idealized by their defenders. The letters help to restore them to life size, as ordinary mortals with a normal quota of faults, virtues, and troublesome personal problems.†

Both had been born and raised in the slum tenements of Manhattan's lower East Side, the offspring of Orthodox Jewish immigrant parents. When they met in 1936, while Julius was a student at New York's free City College, each already had been caught up in the wave of leftist

---

* This includes letters written by the Rosenbergs to each other and also to their attorney and family.

† Ethel, for example, was burdened by long-standing emotional ills and, in 1949, entered psychiatric therapy, which was terminated by her arrest. Later, her physician—a presently practicing New York City psychoanalyst—was permitted to visit her approximately every other week at the Sing Sing death house. Asked his opinion as to the guilt or innocence of his former patient, he told the authors: "I'm afraid I can't be helpful because I'm not able to be objective. I never had any reason to doubt her innocence."

thought and activities that swept America in the Depression years. They were married on June 18, 1939. The bride was twenty-three; her husband just turned twenty-one.

While employed as an engineer with the U. S. Army Signal Corps, Julius also was active as a union organizer for the Federation of Architects, Engineers, Chemists and Technicians. In early 1945, he was fired from his government job for alleged membership in the Communist Party, a charge he denied at the time. The Rosenbergs' letters make clear that both held radical left-wing political views, but do not disclose if they ever were Communist Party members.

In the summer of 1950 when they were arrested suddenly as atom spies, Julius was thirty-two; his wife, thirty-four. They still resided—together with their two sons, Michael, seven, and Robert, three—in the same Knickerbocker Village three-room apartment that they first had rented a few years after their marriage.

It was the contention of the prosecution that during much of the period that the Rosenbergs had pursued a seemingly mundane and relatively uneventful existence in Knickerbocker Village, they also had led a fantastic double life with Julius—assisted by Ethel—the leader and pay-off man of an apparently wide-ranging espionage apparatus. Obviously, the question of whether or not they did lead such a double life cannot be resolved by their letters.

In choosing excerpts from the Rosenbergs' voluminous correspondence, we have adhered strictly to the wording of the originals (except for the most minor spelling and punctuation corrections), clearly indicating deletions. Many of these excerpts have never before appeared in print; others differ somewhat from previously published versions. Where such differences occur, these excerpts can be assumed to be accurate.

Five days after they had been sentenced to death, Julius—then in the West Street prison in New York City—wrote to his wife at the nearby Women's House of Detention:

April 10, 1951

Ethel my darling . . . Tears fill my eyes as I try to put my sentiments on paper. I can only say that life has been worthwhile because you have been besides me. I firmly believe that we are better people because we stood up . . . through a very grueling trial and a most brutal sentence and all because we are innocent. It's very difficult for people who are uninformed and who have no feelings to understand our stamina. Our upbringing, the full meaning of our lives, based on a true amalgamation of our American and Jewish Heritage which to us means freedom culture and character, has made us the people we are. All the filth, lies and slanders of this grotesque political frameup . . . will not in any way deter us but rather spur us on until we are completely vindicated. We didn't ask for this . . . but the gauntlet was laid down to us and with every ounce of life in our bodies we will fight until we are free.

Honey I think of you constantly, I hunger for you. . . . It is so painful that such a great hurt can only mean that I love you with every fibre of my being. . . .

. . . I got a wonderful letter from Michael and it moved me very deeply. I promptly wrote, reassuring him of our love and answering his two questions on a level he could comprehend. I told him we were found guilty and I also explained about the appeal to the higher courts and let him know everything will finally come out all right. That we want very much to see him and we are making every effort to get permission from the court for us to have a visit. . . . I did not tell him of our sentence. . . . It all seems so unreal but yet the cold reality of the steel bars are all around me. I eat, sleep, read and walk four paces back and forth in my cell. I do a lot of thinking about you and the children. . . . I know as time goes on more and more people will come to our defense and help set us free from this nightmare. I caress you tenderly and send all my love.

On April 11, 1951, Ethel Rosenberg was transferred without warning to Sing Sing prison in Ossining, New York, while Julius remained at the West Street jail. She was the sole occupant of the women's section of the death house, save for the matrons who guarded her.

April 17, 1951

My very own dearest husband,

I don't know when I've had such a time bringing myself to write you. My brain seems to have slowed to all but a complete halt under the weight of the myriad impressions that have been stamping themselves upon it . . . since my removal here.

. . . The bars of my large, comfortable cell hold several books, the lovely, colorful cards (including your exquisite birthday greeting to me) that I accumulated at the House of Detention line the top ledge of my writing table . . . the children's snapshots are taped onto a "picture frame" made of cardboard and smile sweetly upon me . . . and within me there begins to develop the profoundest kind of belief that somehow, somewhere, I shall find that "courage, confidence and perspective" I shall need to see me through days and nights of bottomless horror, of tortured screams I may not utter, of frenzied longings I must deny! Julie dearest, how I wait upon the journey's end and our triumphant return. . . .

April 18, 1951

Dearest Ethel,

I received your wonderful letter this afternoon. Frankly, I've been impatiently awaiting news from you. . . .

. . . if our lawyers do not succeed in bringing you back to the Womens Det House . . . I will move heaven and earth to be sent to Sing Sing to be nearer you and in order to be able to see you whenever it is possible. I beg you not to try to sway me from this decision as this is what I must do. . . .

. . . It is impossible to keep the truth and facts of our case hidden from the public. . . . Many people have already expressed to our lawyers and my family their sentiments and desire to help us. Take heart and know that we are not alone. The monstrous sentence passed on us, which at first stunned the people, will as time goes on result in an avalanche of protest and this great movement coupled to our legal fight will set us free. . . .

Constantly you are in my thoughts. At times I close my eyes and see you so clearly. . . . You are ever beckoning to me and I very willingly pursue you but you seem elusive and the reality of our separation jolts me back to consciousness. . . .

Ethel, you are just my girl and nothing on earth can change that.

May 7, 1951

(Ethel to Julius):

. . . after a listless game of handball (played solo, of course), a shower, dinner and an evening of enchanting music, during which you made passionate love to me, I . . . finally succumbed to homesick tears. . . .

Oh, darling, how greedy I am for life and living.

On May 15, Julius too was transferred to the Sing Sing death house. Confined in the separate section reserved for male condemned convicts, he was approximately one hundred feet away from his wife. He wrote to her:

May 17, 1951

Hello My Love,

You are so close at hand and yet you being in a different corridor separated by so much steel, locked away from my sight and beyond my hearing range the frustration is terrific. Tonight I was able to hear your voice when a few of the high notes of one of your arias was faintly audible. . . . Physically I am fairly comfortable and already in the routine of things. . . . I read about six newspapers a day, I play chess in a numbered board by remote control with another inmate and I am reading

"The Old Country" by Sholom Aleichem. . . . With decency and justice we'll be delivered from this darkness to beautiful life and freedom.

Goodnight my wife.

May 19, 1951

. . . My dearest husband, what heaven and what hell to welcome you to monotonous days and joyless nights, to endless desire and endless denial. And yet here shall we plight our troth anew . . . here shall we roar defiance and give battle. . . .

May 20, 1951

Dearest Julie,

Today I am at such loose ends I don't know where to turn for comfort. There has been a fine intermittent rain all afternoon and I have sat in my chair at the entrance to the yard, drinking in the fragrance of flowers growing somewhere unbeknownst to me, and watching the bedraggled sparrows picking dispassionately at the bread I had scattered earlier for them. Every once in so often, the rain lets up and then I stalk disconsolately about inspecting the few green things I possess. . . . I kneel down and glumly scrutinize a crevice in the concrete, filled with earth painstakingly accumulated from the under part of moss, small, velvety clumps of which cling to the damp, cool parts of the yard where the rays of the sun seldom penetrate. In this earth, an appleseed which I had carefully planted some few days before and which I have ever since been patiently watering, is bravely sprouting. . . .

May 21, 1951

(Julius to Ethel):

. . . The hemmed in solitude that surrounds us, and the oppressive nature of this sombre tomb must not succeed in removing our strong ties to the . . . outside world. We caged here can only protest our innocence and stand up firmly but it is the task of the American people to stay the executioner's hand and see that justice is done. I gaze at the walls of my cell and contemplate the great sufferings of my wife and children and I am helpless to aid them.

Once a week a wire mesh screen was placed in front of the bars of Ethel's cell. Julius was permitted to enter the women's wing and converse with his wife through this double barrier for an hour (in their final months in Sing Sing they were allowed two visits a week).

May 25, 1951

My Precious Woman,

Ah it was so good to see you this afternoon and the hour seemed to evaporate so quickly. Honey I sat so reserved and pent up looking at you through the screen and all the time I wanted to take you in my arms. . . .

May 27, 1951

(Ethel to Julius):

Of course, you experienced the same pangs of unfulfilled hunger at the termination of our visit as I did; and yet what sweet gratification there was for us in the simple fact of our being together. Do you know how madly in love with you I am? And how utterly shameless were my thoughts as I gazed at your glowing face through the double barrier of screen and bar! Bunny dear, I wanted you so much, and all I could do was to kiss my hand at you!

June 6, 1951

Julie dear, I can't wait to see you . . . for more than the usual reasons. You see, bunny, today I received two wonderful snapshots of the children . . . that I want very badly to share with you. . . . And yet the sight of their amazingly mature features will be hurtful, too . . . the horrible idea, of which I am never completely rid, that we may never be with them ever again, drives relentlessly through me. . . .

June 9, 1951

My Dearest Ethel,

. . . Darling it is necessary for both our peace of minds that you tell me . . . your innermost feelings, as in almost all cases they are the same that are torturing me and you by expressing them so plainly give me relief from my agony. Perhaps because of my makeup I don't show my emotions as readily as you do but I too run the gamut of joy and then frustration and heartache. . . .

. . . Such powerful feelings, profound desires and deep thought all with the same thing in mind, the big Why! of this frameup and the question when will it all be over.

June 13, 1951

(Julius to Ethel):

. . . Already, just a few points and a brief outline of our circuit court appeal gives me new courage. . . . Our lives and the future of our family depends on this outcome and given an even chance under the laws of our land we must win.

June 30, 1951

(Ethel to Julius):

The intolerable loneliness of this place seems to have entered into my very bones today. . . .

July 8, 1951

(Julius to Ethel):

. . . it's Sunday morning. . . . With the increasing heat, the mosquitoes and especially a terrible lonesomeness my sleeping has been intermittent, tiresome and tortuous. . . . My mind goes back to the leisure[ly] Sunday mornings we spent together with our children. By now it seems so far away but the beauty of it all lingers. Life has such deep meaning when we can see in retrospect. . . .

July 15, 1951

(Julius to Ethel):

. . . Somehow it seems so long ago that I saw you and everything is strange and distant. An empty feeling grips me and by the time you read this letter it will be one year that I have for all intents and purposes stopped living. . . . Ethel . . . there must be an end to this misery of ours and we must be vindicated from this frameup. Many times during the day I ask myself over and over why and I have to put it out of my mind because it doesn't make sense. . . . I'm daydreaming quite a lot and you my heart are the center of my thoughts. When we are home together I will try to convey to you what you mean to me.

The Rosenbergs' sons, by then eight and four years old, had not seen either their mother or father since the previous summer. After the arrest of their parents, the children had been cared for briefly and reluctantly by Ethel's mother and then placed in a city children's shelter; later, when the Rosenbergs were found guilty, Julius's mother established a home for the boys. Now, within the walls of Sing Sing, a family reunion, watched by a prison guard, was arranged to take place in a legal consultation room. Ethel was to see the children first, then Julius.

July 25, 1951

(Julius to Ethel):

. . . Right now I'm looking forward to seeing my own sweet sons after more than a year of forced separation. Even though it's an entire week off the tension is mounting and I'm going to have to exercise a maximum of control to keep my anxiety down. . . . You know I just got a wonderful idea. . . . I'll make pages of pictures of trains, boats and buses and I'm positive Michael and especially Robbie will like them.

July 29, 1951

(Ethel to Julius):

. . . do try to lay aside some of your anxiety. . . . Believe me, I am trying to convince myself. . . .

. . . You can't make me jealous with your boats and trains; I have an envelope full of rare specimens collected with painstaking care by that intrepid hunter of wild insects, namely your wife!

August 1, 1951

(Ethel to Julius):

. . . I'm afraid I was anything but calm . . . . as I smiled and kissed the children, I was experiencing such a bewildering assortment of emotions . . . . after all, a first visit after a year's separation, can hardly be expected to do more than "break the ice." Nevertheless, I am unable to set aside my sense of let-down and frustration. . . .

And yet I am also so full of pride. . . .

August 1, 1951

(Julius to Ethel):

. . . This morning found me restless, tense and very anxious. . . . When the sound of your singing drifted down to the cell block my tensions began to vanish. Robert's shrieking was music to my ears. After lunch I went into the counsel room and the kids were hiding behind the door. When I hugged them they seemed so small and far away. I was a bit dazed. I choked up and my eyes teared and Michael kept repeating, Daddy, your voice has changed. . . . Robbie sat on my lap. His peaked thin face, ringed eyes, looked up at me and he said "Daddy why you no come home." I carefully explained. He replied "Why did you not visit us Sundays at the Shelter." Again I explained. Naturally the baby could not comprehend. . . . Michael spent most of his time drawing trucks with a pencil. . . . One thing he said stands out and that is that it would be better if he were here and not I. . . . Darling the children need us and I hope it is not much longer that we will suffer such anguish being separated from them. . . . After I left them I felt I tore out a piece of heart.

August 2, 1951

My own dearest, darling husband,

. . . I need to weep on your shoulder; I need to feel your arms about me.

The picture of my bewildered, sad-faced baby with the haunted eyes and serious mein is a sight I cannot put out of my mind; and Michael, with his deceptively cheerful demeanor and flippant chatter, doesn't exactly allay my anxiety, either.

August 5, 1951

(Julius to Ethel):
. . . Now that a number of days have passed since the visit with our dears . . . the meeting served to place me in a position to see the cold reality of our situation. . . . A trained specialist . . . should begin to see the kids. . . . Darling I've gone through all kinds of hell since last Wednesday. . . .

August 12, 1951

(Julius to Ethel):
One solid year . . . has been taken away from you. . . . It is all so unjust and unfair. . . .
. . . Now that we have already passed through a year we can clearly see ourselves. When stripped bare the mirror of life is all revealing. I am well satisfied with what I find. . . . As long as we can depend on our individual resources and maintain our principles of life we must win.
. . . as time passes the public will get to discover the truth and then we'll not be alone.

August 13, 1951

(Ethel to Julius):
. . . It is when you cross the distance that separates us and call out your cheery greeting that I come alive and know that I am still my own self and not some fantastic being from another realm.

August 30, 1951

To My Fair Flower of Ossining Manor,
. . . Who ever invented celibacy deserves to be shot. It's not for me. The news our counselor brings us continues to raise my hopes and it's better to know exactly how long these legal matters will take and what we can expect . . . . important to us is that the facts in the trial record be made public to prove our complete innocence . . . . many people including strangers are taking a personal interest in our case. . . .
Ethel . . . I'm certain we will beat this frameup and make up for all this lost time.

September 6, 1951

My Dearest Love Ethel,

. . . The day getting shorter and the approach of winter has its dimming effect on us who are isolated from the world we love. . . . To me it is remarkable that the mind and body is able to withstand such punishment. . . . Many times it seems the mortal individual cannot withstand the pressure that only steel is designed to resist. . . .

. . . I can only take comfort in my love for you and I hope that as time passes my faith in the American people and American Justice will be reaffirmed. . . .

After a second visit from the children, Julius wrote to Ethel:

September 9, 1951

. . . Robbie . . . romped around screeching and acting mischievous. I held him close kissed him and carried him around so I could talk to Michael. . . . He asked me how you die and I told him and he asked if there is an electric chair here and I said yes. He kept on asking about the appeals and what if finally we might lose then death faced us. I kept on assuring him but I could see he was terribly upset over it. He then looked at the Sgt. [a prison guard] and said you'd better watch me for I don't want my mother and father to die for if they do I'll kill Dave [Greenglass]. . . . The boy said Daddy maybe I'll study to be a lawyer and help you in your case. . . . The baby and Michael are both frightened. . . .

(The originals of letters sent over the next three months were not among those obtained by the authors, so none are reprinted here. However, a perusal of typewritten copies of these letters shows that during this period the Rosenbergs followed with intense interest the publication by the *National Guardian* of a series of articles on their case and the subsequent formation of a committee to aid them.)

December 16, 1951

(Julius to Ethel):

At the time when the snow is on the ground and the weather outside chills the marrow of the bone I look to my sweetheart to continue to inspire me and warm my spirit. . . .

The other night I had a most wonderful dream. . . . You were so real I could touch you . . . I awoke and saw the darkness and gloom of my cell with the long shadows of the bars on the wall as the faint rays of the night lamp outlined them.

December 30, 1951

My Most Adorable Wife,

By the time you get this letter a very dark year for us will have become history. We have seen ourselves put to severe tests, and learned many lessons. . . . Compared to last year a great deal of progress has been made in organizing a campaign to secure justice for us but it still is too little and too slow. . . .

1952–BEST WISHES–LOVE–HAPPINESS–FREEDOM–PEACE

January 10, 1952

(Julius to Ethel):

. . . Dearest, for us we've got to grit our teeth and bear up under the new strains while the three judges deliberate on our appeal. Darling all we need now is a fair shake and that requires a little mazol [luck]. Above all we must be prepared for a negative decision because there is no guarantee in a case of this nature that only law, facts and fair play will be the deciding factors. In spite of this I'm still confident and optimistic that we'll get a reversal.

January 20, 1952

(Julius to Ethel):

From all sides we hear of new support. The ball is really rolling now. More and more people are joining the committee, contributing funds, writing letters and increasing thousands of people are being made aware of the facts of our case and its nature. . . . We can feel proud that our faith in the American people has born fruit so soon and this is the guarantee of our eventual freedom and complete vindication.

But, oh my wife, how cruel it is to be apart from you and suffer in isolation when we are innocent.

January 27, 1952

(Julius to Ethel):

. . . Always I keep thinking of what Manny [Bloch] said, "You are two straws buffeted about by the political winds" and I keep hoping that public opinion will be sufficiently neutralized, that the judges will be able to render a decision based strictly on the legal merits of the trial and not on extraneous issues that stem from the hysterical atmosphere in our land.

February 15, 1952

(Julius to Ethel):

With the turmoil and excitement of the children's visit and the rushing developments of events in our case I didn't have time to tell you that your face was beaming, that you looked very lovely and that I love you very much. . . .

. . . Michael is doing much better and I am convinced our little baby needs a great deal of help . . . . there is too much of a burden on their minds. . . . Can people really understand that our hearts, sincerity and conscience goes into what we write, say or do . . . to those who see the truth it is good and right and to those who hate it is defiant and arrogant. We have experienced unbelievable rottenness because of this case. . . .

A valentine to Ethel my wife my lady fair. In pain, in suffering in deep hurt but not in despair.

February 17, 1952

(Julius to Ethel):

. . . I'm marking time by reading and playing chess and as the days go by I'm getting anxious. . . . I keep mulling over in my mind all the possibilities and I repeat to myself that I should expect any eventuality and be prepared to meet it emotionally and mentally. . . .

. . . Have courage we are coming closer to our final homegoing.

On February 25, 1952, the United States Circuit Court of Appeals affirmed the Rosenbergs' conviction.

7:30 A.M. *February 26, 1952*

(Ethel to Julius):

My dear one, last night at 10:00 o'clock, I heard the shocking news. . . .

My heart aches for the children; unfortunately they are old enough to have heard for themselves, and no matter what amount of control I am able to exercise, my brain reels, picturing their terror. . . .

Sweetheart, if only I could truly comfort you, I love you so very dearly.

March 2, 1952

Dearest Wife,

. . . any illusions we may have had that even a fifty-fifty chance existed that judges of the higher courts are above hysteria and politics, are completely destroyed and we must soberly realize in spite of the stark terror of the impending death sentence that our only hope rests with the people. . . . I expect that at this late hour the campaign to bring our case before the public will gather momentum. . . .

April 13, 1952

(Julius to Ethel):

. . . The possibility of peace in Korea and a lessening of world tension will contribute materially to us obtaining a review of our case in the Supreme Court on its legal merits and our chances for a reversal will be enhanced.

April 17, 1952

(Julius to Ethel):

It is now 6:30 P.M. and dusk is settling rapidly into night and a couple of late birds, chirping sparrows, are still noisily flitting back and forth in front of the window facing my cell. Yes my love summer is approaching rapidly and the half hour the sun warmed my body gave me a new desire to be free. . . . The enemy of life is not nature but the tyranny of man. . . . The more I read the newspapers the more I become convinced that there are many powerful forces that are making our society sick and the tragedy is that there are too few people ready and willing to take up the cudgels for right because they are afraid of being labeled as unorthodox in these days of conformism . . . . as the weather gets warmer and the days are longer I miss you more and more. . . .

April 19, 1952

(Julius to Ethel):

. . . It isn't easy to carry on a principled fight when your beloved wife's life and your own hangs precariously in the balance. But for us there can be no other way for we are innocent. . . . We are conscious of our social duty to our fellow man and we will not let them down. . . . We did not create these issues they exist and we take our stand with the people fighting for peace and right.

As the year progressed, letters from Ethel to her husband became more and more infrequent. Eventually, both the Rosenbergs were permitted to see their children at the same time and, after one such visit, Ethel wrote:

April 29, 1952

You were so sweet to watch on Saturday; so, for that matter, were your sons. . . .

So I just had to get at least these few lines off . . . to let you receive some tangible evidence of the deep love and yearning the sight of my beautiful family has awakened afresh.

May 29, 1952

My Sweetheart Ethel,

. . . In a couple of months it will be two complete years that the hysterical tidal wave of political prosecutions has engulfed us and made us into a case. . . .

June 15, 1952

My Charming Girl,

. . . I'm sitting opposite an open window catching the occasional breeze that wafts across my body that is only clad in shorts in season with the summer heat. I look up at the calendar and June 18th catches my eye. Immediately I think back to our preparations thirteen years ago in anxious anticipation of our coming marriage. We were so full of joie de vivre, so happy and so much in love.

June 18, 1952

My dearest, darling husband,

How could I forget our biggest day. . . . I have only one thing to say in my behalf; I live with such a nagging, blinding misery, that I grow dully indifferent to the passage of time, even to missing up on a date with as much significance as June 18!

June 29, 1952

(Julius to Ethel):

I am so completely enamored of Manny's petition for certiorari and with every additional reading I am further impressed. . . . I have very high hopes. . . . Our relationship with him is the high point of two miserable years we have spent since our arrest and helps us to maintain faith in the goodness, dignity and virtue of mankind.

July 17, 1952

(Julius to Ethel):

After such a wonderful visit with you I am in an excellent state of morale. Why do you know that some of the people here say that when I come out from the women's wing my face is all lit up and my eyes seem to sparkle? Do you know that is exactly how I feel? . . . Sweetheart it is already two years that we've been plagued with this unbelievable nightmare. Can we ever measure it in tears, heartache and endless mental anguish? Who can tell the permanent marks that this will leave on our beloved children's lives?

September 15, 1952

Sweetest Julie,

. . . My darling, more and more I tend to withdraw into the deepest recesses of myself. . . . Day by day our separation grows the more bitterly intolerable . . . . no degree of pressure will ever cause us to repudiate those principles of democracy that sit beleaguered with us behind these repugnant bars. . . .

October 2, 1952

(Julius to Ethel):

. . . This is the important month of decision darling and we must keep our feet firmly planted in reality and not allow ourselves to be stampeded into hopelessness. . . .

As yet I haven't seen any indication of the effectiveness of the campaign the committee is waging. . . . I had hoped to begin to hear some favorable comments, at least in the liberal press, on our position. . . . there is a great fear that is paralyzing many former liberals and progressives into silence. . . . I'm still optimistic but I'm prepared for any eventualities.

October 3, 1952

(Ethel to Julius):

. . . a very pleasant surprise in the form of a new dress gave my morale an unexpected boost. I shall tear myself apart until you have a chance to see . . . it really looks very lovely on me!

. . . you are so capable and so hard working and so sweet, I just simply adore you!

October 5, 1952

(Julius to Ethel):

. . . The job of carefully scrutinizing the trial record is complete. . . . Honey the immensity of the frameup that was perpetrated against us becomes more evident with each reading of the facts.

On October 13, 1952, the United States Supreme Court denied the Rosenbergs' petition for certiorari, thus refusing to review the case.

October 13, 1952

(Julius to Ethel):

Just a word of encouragement until I see you again. . . . Although I knew from hearing the news on the 12:45 radio broadcast I didn't let on to Mama [Julius's mother] because I wanted her to be home and have people near her when she hears the bad tidings. We will have to

spare her as much suffering as possible because she is just all emotions
and completely heartbroken. . . .

. . . They are trying to make haste in putting us to death before the
court of public opinion gives its answer, protesting this political frameup.

. . . The hirelings of the kept press are howling for our blood.

October 16, 1952

(Julius to Ethel):

. . . It is important not to lose heart for one moment because as soon
as the volume of public clamor reaches sizable proportions they will be
forced to grant us our day in court. I am not dismayed by the weakness
certain so-called liberals and progressives show . . . at every crucial point
where they must take a determined stand . . . . they even equivocate
when it comes to the question of peace and war.

. . . I . . . feel calmer and more determined because I have my self-
respect . . . we have consistently conducted ourselves with dignity. . . .

On November 21, Judge Kaufman set the date for the Rosenbergs' execution as the week of January 12, 1953.

November 23, 1952

Dearest Ethel,

You already know that the "honorable" Judge has ordered that we remain alive for only 50 odd more days. I'm sure we'll confound him
again. . . .

December 4, 1952

(Julius to Ethel):

The battle is raging fiercely now and the enemy has called on his reserves the fabricators, the pen prostitute. . . . I'm positive our committee
is having excellent results because all of the gutterpress claims we've
"fooled" great numbers of people. . . . It is going to get a great deal
rougher for we've got them fuming mad because they can't use us to do
their dirty work.

December 7, 1952

(Julius to Ethel):

I am amazed at the fabulous newspaper campaign organized against us.
It . . . has the earmarks of desperation. . . .

. . . we will never lend ourselves to be tools to implicate innocent people, to confess crimes we never did and to help fan the flames of hysteria
and help the growing witch hunt.

Prosecution Exhibit 9. The pictures shown here slightly smaller than those introduced at the trial.

David Greenglass.

Ruth Greenglass.

Ruth and son.

David, Ruth, and children.

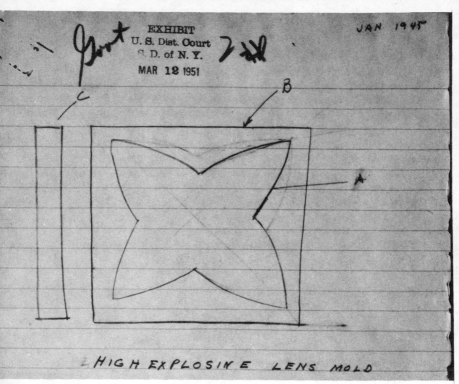

EXHIBIT
U. S. Dist. Court
S. D. of N. Y.
MAR 12 1951

JAN. 1945

HIGH EXPLOSIVE LENS MOLD

5. Prosecution Exhibit 2.

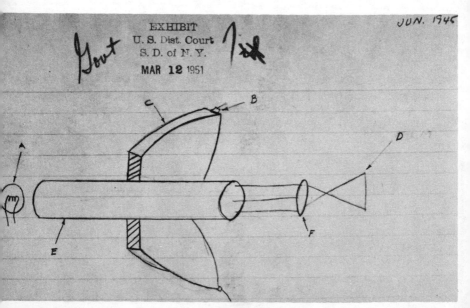

EXHIBIT
U. S. Dist. Court
S. D. of N. Y.
MAR 12 1951

JUN. 1945

6. Prosecution Exhibit 7.

7. Prosecution Exhibit 6.

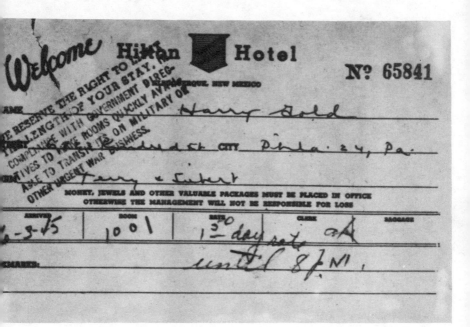

ARRIVED	ROOM	RATE	CLERK	BAGGAGE
6-3-45	1001	1⁵⁰ day rate		
REMARKS:		until 8 P.M.		

8. June card, face and reverse.

RECEIVED

JUN 4 12 36 PM '45

HILTON HOTEL
ALBUQUERQUE

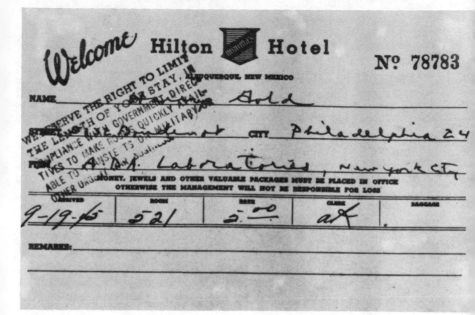

9. September card, face and reverse.

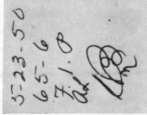

10. Klaus Fuchs, apprehended by British authorities on February 2, 1950, as a Soviet agent.

11. Harry Gold, arraigned in Philadelphia on May 23, 1950, as Fuchs' espionage accomplice.

12. Julius Rosenberg, in custody of FBI agents following his arrest on July 17, 1950, as an "atom spy."

13. Ethel Rosenberg, interviewed by reporters in the kitchen of her apartment the day after her husband was jailed. A month later she was arrested.

14. Morton Sobell, at Newark Airport on August 23, 1950, en route from Laredo, Texas, to face espionage charges.

Prosecution Witnesses
as They Appeared
at the Trial

15. David Greenglass.

16. Ruth Greenglass.

17. Max Elitcher.

18. Elizabeth Bentley.

19. Harry Gold.

20. Irving R. Kaufman, who, as a federal district judge, presided over the Rosenberg-Sobell trial.

1. Shown, left to right, U. S. Attorney Irving Saypol and his assistants Myles Lane and
.oy Cohn.

22. April 5, 1951. Ethel Rosenberg is escorted from the New York federal courthouse at Foley Square after being sentenced to die in the electric chair.

23. Washington, D.C. Clemency advocates parading near the White House.

24. Milan. Demonstrators carrying pro-Rosenberg signs picket the United States Consulate.

UNITED PRESS INTERNATIONAL PHOTO

25. Paris. Huge portraits of the Rosenbergs overlook a clemency rally in the Place de la Nation.

26. London. Marchers in Grosvenor Square, in front of the United States Embassy.

WIDE WORLD PHOTOS

27. Death house visit. Defense attorney Emanuel Bloch at Sing Sing with the Rosenbergs' sons.

28. Execution evening. On June 19, 1953, Rosenberg sympathizers fill West Seventeen Street, in New York City.

9. David Greenglass, left, leaves prison in late 1960. At right, his attorney, O. John Rogge.

30. Morton Sobell, photographed at Atlanta Penitentiary after more than a decade of imprisonment.

December 12, 1952

Dearest Ethel,

. . . It is indeed a tragedy how the lords of the press can mold public opinion by printing . . . blatant falsehoods. The pressure campaign is on in very high gear and many weak people will be scared off. . . . There is a new whipping boy in our land "the Rosenbergs" and all "respectable" people have to cleanse themselves by throwing stones at us. They are doomed to failure for the truth will out.

. . . every technique of smear is used to obscure the basic infirmities of the government's case. . . . I am still confident we'll win our freedom. But come what may I am sure that our name will eventually be cleared.

December 14, 1952

(Julius to Ethel):

The days are lonely sweetheart and the dark long nights are empty without you. There is no rest or peace when I know how great is your suffering. . . . I work hard to drown out the agony that grips me but there is no real relief.

During the month before his scheduled execution, Julius poured out his feelings in these letters to his attorney, Emanuel Bloch:

December 9, 1952

Each man is given two fifteen minute exercise periods daily. The yard is bounded on one side by the gallery of cells on the other side by the death chamber and in all is about 150 feet in circumference . . . . once in a while I play bachi-ball but in the main I have an opportunity to walk around the yard and sing the songs I like. I am not sure but I believe that I am one of the first to fill the air in the confines of this space with favorites such as "Peat Bog Soldiers," "Joe Hill" and "Freiheit." While I sing it brings back memories, inspires me and makes me think of all the other innocent political prisoners. . . .

December 27, 1952

Dear Manny,

It was cold in the yard this morning. . . . A soaring seagull was sailing upward in wide circles lifted by the strong wind and gracefully, without effort, covered the expanse of the wide open sky that my eyes could see. . . .

. . . the exercise guard gently reminded me my fifteen minutes yard period was finished. I breathed once more deeply of the fresh free air and then I went back to my cell. The steel door closed, a key turned in the lock, the padlock snapped and I was once again shut in my cubicle of concrete.

Day and night, pacing back and forth, lying on my bed and endless thoughts crowding through my mind. So little time left so much to say and live in a couple of weeks. What should be put down first? To Whom? How?

Please listen, look, see, hear, feel. . . . Each for his own defense must defend right and life.

Over and over again I began to write my sons. I wrote a few lines and tore up the paper. Then I put it off again and sent Ethel a letter and again I couldn't make it and I continue to write you dear friend. It is futile to tell a mother not to grieve for her children.

December 28, 1952

Dear good Manny in everything I've written and all that I've said I try to explain to my sons the meaning and reason for this situation. . . . One thing I feel sure of that when they are older and read the trial record and all that took place they will know that all the way through we their parents were right. . . .

January 3, 1953

Dearest Manny,

It is now Saturday afternoon the visit is over. Our children have gone home. Through the exertion of super-human efforts I have finally succeeded in reestablishing my equilibrium and I can continue to write. The love of truth and mankind demands that I make this record. . . .

Today our precious boys came and our own family lived once again for two hours. . . . I carried the baby on my back giving him a horsey ride. We looked through the barred window at the sea gulls and the tugboat pulling a string of barges on the Hudson. He zoomed through the room pretending to be an airplane as I held him in my arms tightly pressed to my heart . . . . he kissed my cheeks as he circled my neck with his little arms. My son was happy with his daddy. . . .

Michael was troubled, disturbed. . . .

I promised to play him chess. I hope to someday.

Then they had to go and as I helped Michael with his coat he suddenly clutched me with his hands and stammered as he lowered his head, "You must come home, every day there is a lump in my stomach even when I go to bed." I kissed him in a hurry for I was unable to say anything but, "everything will be all right."

When I was in the solitude of my cell once more and the door clanged shut behind me I must confess I broke down and cried like a baby because of the children's deep hurt. With my back to the bars, I stood facing the concrete walls, that boxed me in on all sides, and I let the pains that tore at my insides flood out in tears. . . .

Time is short there is but ten more days left to live. I will do my best to crowd in as much work as possible. I am raising a warning for I believe this is a test case of threatening fascism at home. Don't let them murder us.

In early January 1953, Judge Kaufman granted the Rosenbergs a stay of execution pending the President's decision on their petition for Executive clemency. By then, letters from Ethel to her husband had practically ceased, though she still corresponded with Emanuel Bloch and her children and worked on some public statements. The following excerpts are all from Julius's letters to Ethel, which he continued to write several times a week:

January 15, 1953

The press is gripped with a frenzy. . . . Always additional and newer stories are invented to take the place of the weak and unconvincing record. . . .

January 22, 1953

. . . I am confident whatever the outcome may be, for to fight for a just cause is a victory in itself.

January 25, 1953

I'm beginning to think about our boys next visit. . . . For more than 2½ years of their young lives we've been torn away from them. . . . For them . . . we can suffer in this way.

February 8, 1953

. . . From the time I left your presence this last Friday, I've been thinking about you. . . .

Honey I understand full well the deep hurts you suffer . . . . the reason for my speechlessness at that time was due to my agony reflecting your own. It is impossible to soothe you or protect you from the daily torture that is ever present here. . . .

February 12, 1953

. . . Just as we have been informed by our lawyer that it would take at least another week for Eisenhower to get the record the newspapers let the cat out of the bag and said that the Attorney General brought over the file to the President's office at 4:00 P.M. and at 5:07 P.M. the prepared statement [denying Executive clemency] was read. . . .

Like you, my beloved, I find it most difficult to think about what this new development will do to our precious sons. The heartache is just too much for it is impossible to do anything to protect them from the horrible consequences of our execution. . . . I am happy that you have made my life so meaningful.

February 19, 1953

You know honey the fact we are here still seems so unreal to me. Somewhere in the long ago I had a normal life with a sweet wife and two fine children and now all is gone and we're facing death. Yet the yearning for a wife's sweet kiss and a son's warm hug hold the promise of a return to the beautiful life I knew. . . .

February 26, 1953

. . . What we are and all that we have no one can take away from us even though they keep us apart and threaten us with death . . . . our enemies . . . can't beat us down and they will suffer to see us win regardless of the final outcome of this case.

April 16, 1953

. . . Is there any better proof of the complete bias of the press against us than by noting their . . . silence on the expose of the so-called Russian "gift" console table? . . . given time we will prove that each and every charge of the government against us is completely false. . . .

April 23, 1953

You probably recall the last scene of Maxwell Anderson's, "Mary of Scotland" where Elizabeth tells Mary that she has seen to it that the history of her reign will be written as she orders her writers to put down the events although . . . they are untrue . . . . spreading the facts about our case will ensure that history will record the truth about this miscarriage of justice and give the public a chance to right the great wrong done us.

April 26, 1953

Each succeeding time I see the children the parting becomes more difficult. It is taking a terrific toll and I've been terribly heartsick since they left. The baby's crying and Michael's parting expressions were very painful and if it affects me this way I'm much concerned for the great hardship it visits on our beloved little ones. . . .

It is appropriate on this anniversary of the heroes of the Warsaw Ghetto to recall the words "May you on the outside be blessed—where are our deliverers?"

May 3, 1953

. . . Since we are guilty of no crime we will not be party to the nefarious plot to bear false witness against other innocent progressives to heighten hysteria in our land and worsen the prospects of peace in the world. . . .
. . . Nobody welcomes suffering honey but we are not the only ones who are going through hell because of all we stand for and I believe we are, in holding our own, contributing a share in doing away with the great sufferings of many others, both at this time and in time to come.

May 21, 1953

At this moment I'm very lethargic and in a romantic mood. I guess it is the combined effect of a nice long spring day and a natural desire to be with my beloved. . . . Everything seems so unreal and out of focus. . . . It seems like we're suspended, somewhere, far off seeing everything that's being done and not being able to do anything even though we are the center of the controversy.

May 31, 1953

. . . What does one write to his beloved when faced with the very grim reality that in eighteen days on their 14th wedding anniversary it is ordered that they be put to death? The approaching darkest hour of our trial and the grave peril that threatens us requires every effort on our part to avoid hysterics and false heroics but only maintain a sober and calm approach to our most crucial problem.

June 5, 6, and 7

(Julius to Emanuel Bloch):
On Monday June 1st . . . U. S. Marshals were up to serve us with papers setting down our executions for our 14th wedding anniversary June 18 11:00 P.M. . . . They were very pleasant, but they had a job . . . to do. . . .
Tuesday, at 11:00 A.M. . . . I was ushered into the counsel room and there was Mr. Bennett, Federal Director of the Prison Bureau. Mind you this was the first time I was alone with anyone without an officer or Sing Sing official present. . . . We were alone for about an hour. . . .
Mr. Bennett opened the conversation and said: "Mr. Brownell the Attorney General sent me to see you and he wants you to know that if you want to cooperate with the government you can do so through me and I

will be able to make arrangments for you to talk with any proper officials. Furthermore if you Julius can convince these officials that you have fully cooperated with the government they will have a basis to recommend clemency." . . .

. . . I said in the first place we are innocent, that is the whole truth and therefore we know nothing that would come under the meaning of the word cooperate. . . .

You mean to tell me Mr. Bennett that a great government like ours is coming to two insignificant people like us and saying "cooperate or die." It is a terrible thing to do to offer to barter life by "talking." . . . He said "why do you know that I didn't sleep last night when I knew I had to see you and Ethel the next day and talk to you about this matter. . . ." How do you think we feel sitting here waiting for death for over two years when we are innocent. My family has gone through great suffering. My sister had a nervous breakdown. My aged ailing mother is tormented. Our children have known much emotional and mental agony. Then you talk to us about this.

. . . He then said . . . only by cooperating will there be a basis to ask for commutation. Look here Julius, he said, you didn't deny that you do not know anything about this espionage. I certainly did and furthermore did you read the [trial] record sir? He said he did not but continued by saying, you had dealings with [Elizabeth] Bentley. I never did and if you read the record she said on the stand that she did not know me and never met me. You had dealings with Gold, didn't you? Of course I didn't, he said on the stand he never knew me or met me. You should have read the record to be familiar with the facts. . . .

Listen Julius, I was just sent here but if you will agree I will bring someone to see you who is thoroughly familiar with the case and you will try to convince him you have cooperated with the government.

What do you want to do, have him convince me I am guilty when I am not . . . . you will only be satisfied when I say the things you want me to say but I will not lie about this matter. . . .

All these three years you say I am not telling the truth, then if I say what you want me to say that would be cooperating and then it would be the truth. In good conscience, I could not lend myself to this practice and . . . this pressure on us is cruel. . . . The only decent thing to do is tell Mr. Brownell to recommend clemency.

It was twelve o'clock when he went in to see Ethel for a ½ hour, and then they brought me into the women's wing and he continued to try . . . for another ½ hour till 1:00 P.M. Ethel will tell you about what took place during this hour.

Ethel wrote to her attorney about the visit:

. . . just as I was sitting down to lunch, Mr. Bennett entered the Women's Wing of the death house and announced himself. Contrary to all established practice, he was alone with me. . . .

He came right to the point. Attorney General Herbert Brownell, Jr. had directed him to inform me that he could make available to me any official to whom I might care to divulge espionage information I had hitherto withheld. If I cooperated in this fashion, the government stood ready to invalidate the death penalty. . . .

I made it short and sweet. I was innocent, my husband was innocent, and neither of us knew anything about espionage. . . .

"Well, the government claims to have in its possession documents and statements that would dispute that, so if only you were willing to cooperate, there might be a basis for commutation."

. . . "To begin with, I couldn't possibly know nor do I care what they have or don't have. Whatever it might be, it has nothing to do with me. . . . If you are persuading me to confess to activities concerning which I have solemnly sworn I have no knowledge, on the basis of evidence with which I was never confronted in court, then obviously the validity of this evidence must be strongly questioned, if it in fact exists at all. . . .

". . . Let me say to you . . . you will come to me at ten minutes of 11:00 P.M. on Thursday, June 18, and the fact of my innocence will not have changed in the slightest. . . ."

He shrugged his shoulders wearily, explained to the Warden that he was to expedite any messages we might care to send him, and bade us good-bye.

June 7, 1953

(Julius to Ethel):

. . . the latest motion for a new trial is beyond any doubt our strongest legal action . . . it contains some devastating stuff that can break this case wide open. . . .

. . . I begin to discern the general pattern of the jig-saw plot that was concocted by the Greenglasses to save themselves and frame us. . . . I have faith that we will live to be in each other's arms again.

June 10, 1953

(Julius to Bloch):

. . . The latest legal papers came with your note and I read them over carefully. . . .

The Perl situation . . . and the "uranium" set-up as divulged by papers from Rogge files and supported by Bernie's affidavit . . . . I think

. . . are the strongest points raised in our petition. Now in the context of the foregoing the "console" table further serves to nail the Greenglasses to the big lie of our involvement into espionage. Is there then any wonder why the government [is] . . . dreadfully afraid that we have our day in court to prove from the witness stand the truth of our contentions?

However, Manny, in an intelligent and adult appraisal of the many other worthy legal showings made to the courts, what can I tell myself . . . ? That as applied to us, the law has absconded into the never-never land of politics. . . .

At this point we have completed a record that for all time raises grave doubts about our guilt and the government can rectify this miscarriage of justice very simply if we are allowed to live.

June 11, 1953

(Ethel to Bloch):

No wonder you are confident, the latest stuff is terrific. Reading it has given me a good deal of comfort!

Nevertheless, I am under no illusions and am preparing myself for the worst, while remaining just as hopeful and working hard for the best. Since, however, I am a grown woman, I have to figure there might be last goodbyes to make. In this respect, I am fairly beside myself because of the tiny amount of time left in which legal matters must take precedence over personal ones. You know what's bothering me; how can you possibly be expected to continue making the necessary moves . . . and still manage to bring up the children [to Sing Sing]. . . .

I should feel so relieved, if there were a stay, so that come what might after it was used up, I should know at least that our affairs were completely in order and that we had had an ample opportunity to visit with our children.

(Julius to Bloch):

. . . It is now Thursday morning June 11th as I finish this letter and our date is set for next week. Will the people deliver us . . . or will they let us go down to our doom? The answer is in their hands.

CHAPTER 20

ELEVENTH-HOUR FIGHT

Monday, June 15, 1953 was a comparatively routine day in the nation's capital, after a Sunday-afternoon White House demonstration that Washington police called the largest in memory.* Thousands of clemency advocates from every section of the United States had paraded by 1600 Pennsylvania Avenue, carrying such signs as "New Evidence Shows Perjury" and "The Electric Chair Can't Kill the Doubts in the Rosenberg Case." Now most of the pickets had departed for home—though a few score had remained to man a round-the-clock White House "vigil."

The Supreme Court's summer recess was scheduled to begin that day. At noon, the Court announced that the pending Rosenberg petition for a stay of execution had been denied by a vote of 5 to 4. Immediately, defense attorney John Finerty arose to request permission for the filing of a habeas corpus petition. A special court term was convened that very afternoon to consider the request; at about 6 P.M., permission was denied, the brief special term ended, and the Court adjourned until October. Most of the judges prepared to start their vacations.

Justice William O. Douglas, however, was detained in his chambers by the Rosenbergs' attorneys. Like any member of the Supreme Court, he had the power to grant a stay—on grounds he deemed substantial— to provide time for a litigant to present important legal issues to a lower court. Now that the summer recess had begun, such an approach to an individual judge was the defense's last remaining avenue for obtaining a reprieve from the Supreme Court.

After hearing the attorneys' arguments for nearly an hour, Justice Douglas told them to return the following morning. Questioned by newspapermen about the Justice's reaction regarding a stay, Emanuel Bloch replied: "He did not deny it. He did not grant it."

That same day in New York City, a former corporation lawyer from Nashville, Tennessee—a newcomer to the Rosenberg case—had appeared before Judge Kaufman to argue a motion requesting a stay of execution and writ of habeas corpus. The Tennesseean, Fyke Farmer, told the press

---

* An official police estimate put the number of pickets at 6032; organizers of the demonstration placed the figure at nearly twice that.

that he had taken this action solely for humanitarian reasons. Judge Kaufman, noting that Farmer had acted without authorization by the Rosenbergs' own chosen counsel, labeled him an "intruder" and an "interloper" and denied his motion. Undaunted, the Tennessee lawyer hastened to Washington, crossing paths with Bloch, who was returning from the capital for a meeting with his clients.

Tuesday morning, June 16, Bloch brought the Rosenbergs' sons, Michael and Robert, then ten and six years old, to the death house at Ossining for what might be their last visit with their parents. Newspaper photographers caught a pose of the older boy carrying a bouquet of flowers for his mother. Emerging from the prison with the children two hours later, Bloch waved before waiting reporters a new petition for Executive clemency—just signed by the Rosenbergs. The defense attorney already had indicated that, if all his legal efforts failed, he would make a final try for clemency, seeking "an open and full hearing before President Eisenhower."

At 10:30 A.M. that same morning, in Washington, Bloch's colleagues had conferred with Justice Douglas. In addition, the Justice had agreed, shortly afterward, to see Fyke Farmer and an associate, a Los Angeles lawyer named Daniel G. Marshall. Both men represented one Irwin Edelman, whose pamphlet on the case—critical of both prosecution and defense—had provoked their efforts. After talking with Farmer and Marshall, Justice Douglas permitted the attorneys to leave with him a "next friend" brief, applying for a writ of habeas corpus, and asked them to submit additional arguments later in the day.

One of the points of the Farmer-Marshall brief was the allegation that the Rosenbergs had been tried under the wrong law. It was claimed that the 1917 espionage statute—under which the couple had been indicted and sentenced—had been superseded by the penalty provisions of the 1946 Atomic Energy Act. Under the latter act, the death sentence may be imposed only when a jury recommends it *and* the offense was committed with intent to injure the United States. Neither of these requisite conditions was fulfilled in the Rosenberg conviction.

By late afternoon, Bloch was back in Washington and had filed the Rosenbergs' second petition for Executive clemency at the Department of Justice. His understanding with Pardon Attorney Daniel M. Lyons, Bloch told reporters, was that the clemency petition would not be sent to the White House until the Rosenbergs had exhausted every possible judicial recourse.

The condemned couple's petition to President Eisenhower read, in part:

"June 16, 1953

"We, Julius Rosenberg and Ethel Rosenberg, husband and wife, are now confined in the Death House in Sing Sing Prison, awaiting electrocution on June 18, our fourteenth wedding anniversary. We address this petition to you for the exercise of your supreme power to prevent—'a crime worse than murder'—our unjust deaths.

"We appealed to you once before. Our sentences, we declared there, violated truth and the instincts of civilized mankind.

"We told you the truth: we are innocent.

"The truth does not change.

"We now again solemnly declare our innocence.

"The guilt in this case, if we die, will be America's. The shame, if we die, will dishonor this generation, and pervade history until future Americans recapture the heritage of truth, justice and equality before the law. . . .

"The highest court of the United States—its Supreme Court, enshrined in pure white marble halls—has just denied us a stay of our executions, although with death so close, it closed the doors to us to seek its review of weighty questions going to the heart of the justice of our convictions and sentences. And yet, unheard of in the annals of our law, four judges—four of the most distinguished members of that bench—had voted to let us live, at least long enough to vindicate our rights before them. Thus, the opportunity we struggled to achieve is now denied.

"Instead our accusers torture us, in the face of death, with the guarantee of life for the price of a confession of guilt. Close upon the execution date—as though to draw the last full measure of dread of death and love of life—their high negotiator came bearing this tainted proffer of life. We refuse the iniquitous bargain, even as perhaps the last few days of our young lives are slipping away. We cannot besmirch our names by bearing false witness to save ourselves. Do not dishonor America, Mr. President, by considering as a condition of our right to survive, the delivery of a confession of guilt of a crime we did not commit. . . .

"You may not believe us, because there is in the court record an undisturbed verdict of guilt. But we defended our innocence on that very record. Printed unabridged in the tens of thousands, the record itself, according to the Government the strength of its case, has convinced untold numbers of our innocence and instilled, in more, grave doubts of the correctness of the verdict. . . .

"You may not believe us, but the passage of even the few short months, since last we appealed to you, is confirming our prediction that, in the inexorable operation of time and conscience, the truth of our innocence would emerge.

"Evidence recently discovered, reveals proof positive, short of re-cantations by the Greenglasses, the prosecution witnesses-in-chief—the one, imprisoned, under the aegis of the Government; the other, free, under the constant threat of possible indictment for her admitted capital crime—that a case was constructed against us on a pyramid of lies. This new evidence should, at the very least, persuade you that doubt of our guilt is now so aggravated that good conscience demands that we live. . . .

"We submitted documentary evidence to show that David Greenglass, trapped by his own misdeeds, hysterical with fear for his own life and that of Ruth, his wife, fell back on his life-long habit of lying, exploited by his shrewd-minded and equally guilty wife, to fabricate, bit by bit, a monstrous tale that has sent us, his own flesh and blood, down a long and terrible path toward death.

"We submitted proof to show that David Greenglass stole uranium from Los Alamos, in a venture concededly unconnected with us. This fact both he and Ruth concealed at the trial, to avoid destruction of their claim that they were pawns in our hands and to cloak their independent motivation to bargain with the Government for the 'cooperation' which inculpated us and saved them.

"In fact, who knows the real crime of the Greenglasses that moved David to the dreadful penance of sending his own sister to her death. . . .

"We submitted actual physical evidence (the missing console table), never produced in court against us, to show the Greenglasses and the Government collaborated to bring into the trial false testimony that we had in our home an expensive console table, given to us by the 'Russians' and equipped for microfilming purposes. The table itself belies the Greenglass testimony. It is not a specially constructed table, but one bought by us at R. H. Macy's for about $21.00, as we testified at our trial.

"We submitted documentary evidence to show the unconscionable *quid pro quo*, for the Greenglasses' testimony implicating us. . . . The sordid 'deal,' all know, has been fulfilled: Ruth is free; David may soon be; we are in the Death House.

"We asked the courts to overturn the scandalous convictions, conceived in fraud and consummated in perjury. But the disposition we received was summary. Our right to an open trial of our proof was frustrated. We were foreclosed from the opportunity to expose the fraud and perjury. We were prevented from exhausting our appellate remedies. We were accorded only the trappings, but not the substance of justice. . . .

"If you will not hear our voices, hear the voices of the world. . . .

"Hear the great and the humble for the sake of America.

"Do not hear only our accusers in the Department of Justice whom the law makes advisers to you on our right to clemency. Does not their self-interest to secure the challenged verdict, by our deaths, tarnish their advice? . . .

"We ask you, Mr. President, the civilized head of a civilized nation to judge our plea with reason and humanity. And remember, we are a father and a mother."

The protests from abroad referred to by the Rosenbergs in their petition were by no means confined to the nations of Western Europe. For some months, clemency appeals—often signed by prominent individuals—had been arriving in increasing numbers from Canada, Mexico, Guatemala, Brazil, Argentina, Uruguay, Japan, Australia, and many other countries. Popular interest in the case also was reported to be high in some of the Communist Eastern European states.

Now, the Supreme Court's 5 to 4 denial of a stay brought the world-wide outcry over the impending executions to a new pitch. Writing from Washington, *Le Monde* correspondent Henri Pierre described the United States for his countrymen as a "disturbed community" about to rid itself of its worries and fears by a "ritual murder." Said he: "More and more the Rosenbergs seem to us like the expiatory victims of the cold war. . . ."

By Tuesday, June 16, a virtual flood of mercy telegrams and cables were pouring into the White House mail room, adding to the hundreds of thousands of messages already received.* That same day, the Polish government—stating that it was acting in response to a plea by the Polish Red Cross—extended through diplomatic channels an official offer of asylum for the Rosenbergs. State Department press officer Lincoln White termed the suggestion as "impertinence" not worthy of reply.

From France, the daughter and other relatives of Alfred Dreyfus sent President Eisenhower the following cable:

"In the name of the family of Colonel Dreyfus, to whom world protest—among others that of the people of America—and French justice assured vindication after a sentence obtained in spite of his protests of innocence, thanks to false testimony, forged documents, so-called confessions, we entreat you to prevent the irremediable in order that the Rosenbergs, alive, be permitted the inevitable review of their trial."

In the United States, some of those who favored clemency made efforts to state their case directly to the President. A few days before, Harold Urey had wired President Eisenhower: "New evidence makes even more plain what was plain enough before, that the prosecution's case has no logic in it, and that it depends upon the blowing up of patently perjured testimony." Urey, who had sought unsuccessfully to see the Attorney General, also requested an interview with the President, but received no response.

* According to the Washington *Post*, during 1953 the White House received about two hundred thousand messages on the case—most of them urging clemency—with 21,500 telegrams alone arriving between June 16 and 21.

However, on Tuesday the President did grant an interview to four clergymen (three Protestant and one Jewish) who said they represented the twenty-three hundred ministers who earlier had signed an appeal for Executive clemency. During their interview, the clergymen did not discuss the possible innocence of the Rosenbergs with the President, but instead asked him to spare the condemned couple's lives as a symbolic gesture of mercy. One of the group, Bernard M. Loomer, dean of the Divinity School of the University of Chicago, later said that the President had linked the Rosenbergs' alleged espionage activities with Korean War casualties and had expressed the view that they "did what they did for money."

That same day, President Eisenhower recorded some additional thoughts about the impending executions in a letter to his son John, then serving in Korea. He wrote:

"To address myself . . . to the Rosenberg case for a minute, I must say that it goes against the grain to avoid interfering in the case where a woman is to receive capital punishment. Over against this, however, must be placed one or two facts that have greater significance. The first of these is that in this instance it is the woman who is the strong and recalcitrant character, the man is the weak one. She has obviously been the leader in everything they did in the spy ring. The second thing is that if there would be any commuting of the woman's sentence without the man's then from here on the Soviets would simply recruit their spies from among women."

Word that the clergymen had spoken pessimistically to the press after their White House visit was received by Emanuel Bloch at the Supreme Court, where he had joined his bench-warming colleagues. In a Court anteroom, the two sets of defense attorneys were tensely awaiting Justice Douglas's decision. Their vigil had its curious aspects. Noted the *Times*: "There was no fraternizing between the Rosenbergs' lawyers and Mr. Farmer and Mr. Marshall. They sat at opposite sides of the room and exchanged no conversation. The Rosenberg group was said to oppose the activities of the 'interlopers.'"

For hour after hour that day, Justice Douglas remained in his chambers —studying the briefs left with him and seeing also a trio of government attorneys. Some time after 11 P.M., the Court clerk informed the weary lawyers that there would be no announcement that night.

On Wednesday morning, June 17, Justice Douglas made public his decision. He had before him, he observed, two applications for a stay of execution made to him after the adjournment of the Court. One (from Bloch) raised questions, concerning the fairness of the trial, that did not differ substantially from questions already considered by the Court in its rejection of review. While he disagreed with the Court majority, he could not "responsibly" grant a stay on these same grounds. The second application (a petition for habeas corpus by Farmer and Marshall), however, raised a completely new point regarding the power of the district court judge to impose the death sentence on the Rosenbergs.

Said he: "I do not decide that the death penalty could have been imposed on the Rosenbergs only if the provisions of . . . the Atomic Energy Act of 1946 were satisfied. I merely decide that the question is a substantial one which should be decided after full argument and deliberation.

"It is important that the country be protected against the nefarious plans of spies who would destroy us.

"It is also important that before we allow lives to be snuffed out we be sure—emphatically sure—that we act within the law. If we are not sure, there will be lingering doubts to plague the conscience after the event.

"I have serious doubts whether this death sentence may be imposed for this offense except and unless a jury recommends it. The Rosenbergs should have an opportunity to litigate that issue.

"I will not issue the writ of habeas corpus. But I will grant a stay effective until the question of the applicability of the penal provisions of . . . the Atomic Energy Act to this case can be determined by the District Court and the Court of Appeals. . . .

"So ordered."

At the eleventh hour, just one day before the scheduled executions, a chance for life had been won for the Rosenbergs by the "interlopers." Even if the Farmer-Marshall legal point was not upheld by the lower courts, it appeared certain that Justice Douglas's stay would remain in effect at least until the Supreme Court reconvened in early October. (In addition, the defense had now gained time to seek a Supreme Court review of their motion for a retrial based on "new evidence.")

Almost immediately after announcing his decision, Justice Douglas resumed his interrupted summer vacation, setting off in his car for the Pacific Northwest. In Washington, however, his action precipitated sharp criticism. Congressman W. McD. Wheeler (Democrat of Georgia) introduced resolutions calling for the Justice's impeachment for "high crimes and misdemeanors in office" and also requesting a House Judiciary Committee investigation of his "official conduct."

Later that same afternoon, Attorney General Herbert Brownell, Jr., filed an application with Chief Justice Fred M. Vinson asking for a special court term to review and vacate the stay of execution granted by Justice Douglas. Explained the Attorney General: "It is important in the interests of the administration of criminal justice and in the national interests that this case be brought to a final determination as expeditiously as possible."

An hour later, about 6 P.M., Chief Justice Vinson complied, ordering the Supreme Court to reconvene at noon the following day. It was the third time in the entire history of the Court that the justices ever had been summoned back to Washington during vacation recess for a special term.

Justice Douglas, hearing the news over the radio at a motel near Uniontown Pennsylvania, where he had just registered for the night, drove about fifty miles to Pittsburgh and flew to Washington. Newspapers speculated that at least six of the nine justices—a necessary quorum—would probably be able to reach the capital in time for the rare session.

However, at noon on Thursday, June 18, all nine justices were seated in the august courtroom, hurriedly prepared by cleaning crews who had removed mothproof dust covers the night before. Spectators filled every seat for the extraordinary event; a crowd of several thousand milled outside on the steps and around the building.

Argument by defense and government attorneys continued, at times rather heatedly, for about three hours with authorized counsel for the Rosenbergs sharing their time with the erstwhile "interlopers." By midafternoon, the justices retired to their conference room to debate the issues.

At Sing Sing, quiet preparations for the originally scheduled 11 P.M. executions had proceeded all that day, in the event the stay was vacated in time. The electrician who served as the executioner had been notified to be at the prison that night, the prison rabbi had visited the pair, and Julius Rosenberg had drawn up a last will and testament. Not knowing whether or not he and his wife would be executed that night, the condemned man wrote a final letter to his friend and attorney, Emanuel Bloch:

"June 18, 1953

"Dear Manny,

"I have drawn up a last will and testament so that there can be no question about the fact that I want you to handle all our affairs and be responsible for the children, as in fact you have been doing. Ethel completely concurs in this request. . . .

"Our children are the apple of our eye, our pride and most precious fortune. Love them with all your heart and always protect them in order that they grow up to be normal healthy people. That you will do this I am sure but as their proud father I take the prerogative to ask it of you, my dearest friend, and devoted brother. I love my sons most profoundly.

"I am not much at saying goodbyes because I believe that good accomplishments live on forever but this I can say—my love of life has never been so strong because I've seen how beautiful the future can be. Since I feel that we in some small measure have contributed our share in this direction, I think my sons and millions of others will have benefited by it. . . .

"Never let them change the truth of our innocence.

"For peace, bread and roses in simple dignity we face the executioner with courage, confidence and perspective—never losing faith. . . .

"P.S. All my personal effects are in 3 cartons and you can get them from the Warden. . . .

"All my love—Julie"

At 6:29 P.M., Justice Harold M. Burton left the conference room to announce that the Supreme Court had recessed until noon the following day. The Rosenbergs would not be executed that night. Sing Sing prison officials, hearing the radio news flash, quickly passed the word to the waiting couple. They were said to have been "overjoyed."

On Friday, June 19, a front-page *Times* headline reported: "Case Seen in Peril." The "peril"—from the government point of view—that the headline referred to was the near certainty that if the Atomic Energy Act were held applicable by the Court the indictment would be quashed and the Rosenbergs set free. Then, if the government still wished to press the case, it would be necessary to obtain a new indictment and to hold a new trial.

At a Cabinet meeting at the White House that morning, President Eisenhower asked the Attorney General to discuss the Rosenberg case. According to an account of that meeting provided by journalist Robert J. Donovan, Attorney General Brownell told the President that the Douglas stay seemed to be "without foundation" and that "information which corroborated the guilt of the Rosenbergs was in possession of the government . . . but could not have been used at the trial."

The Attorney General's alleged reference to the existence of extra-judicial evidence against the Rosenbergs also has been reported by former Presidential speech writer Emmet John Hughes. According to Hughes, who was present at the June 19 Cabinet meeting, the following exchange occurred:

BROWNELL: . . . I've always wanted you to look at evidence that wasn't usable in court showing the Rosenbergs were the head and center of an espionage ring here in *direct* contact with the Russians—the *prime* espionage ring in the country.*

PRESIDENT: My only concern is in the area of statecraft—the *effect* of the action.

* When former Attorney General Brownell was apprised of this statement attributed to him by Hughes, his secretary replied: "Mr. Brownell advised me that he has no recollection of the alleged incident, nor does he have any such evidence as referred to therein. . . ."

At noon Friday, after a brief morning conference, the nine judges ascended the bench. Noting that they appeared "grim," the *Times* said: "Their expressions indicated that the conferences at which the decision was hammered out might have been strenuous, perhaps bitter." Chief Justice Vinson read the majority ruling. He had convened a special term of the Court, he said, to consider the application of the Attorney General. The only matter to be decided was whether the legal point on which the stay had been granted was a "substantial question." For several minutes, listeners waited breathlessly until he came to the key words: "We think the question is not substantial. We think further proceedings to litigate it are unwarranted." By a vote of 6 to 3, the stay was vacated.

In the House of Representatives, debate on a foreign aid bill was interrupted for an announcement of the Supreme Court decision, which brought scattered applause. Commented Representative Frank L. Chelf (Democrat of Kentucky): "Praise God from Whom all blessings flow and thanks to the Supreme Court." Hearing the news, Representative Wheeler said he would still press for Justice Douglas's impeachment and suggested that the Justice be given a "one-way" visa to Russia.

As some legal historians were later to observe, the Supreme Court's action was extremely unusual. According to customary procedure, the Farmer-Marshall legal point would have been referred to the lower courts for determination, and, in time, the Supreme Court would have decided whether or not to review their decisions. What actually had occurred, however, was that the Supreme Court—which ordinarily considers such matters only on appeal—had itself made an immediate judgment on the validity of the new point and decided it was not "substantial."

The majority opinions (subscribed to by Justices Vinson, Clark, Jackson, Reed, Burton, and Minton) held that the Atomic Energy Act of 1946 does not supersede the earlier Espionage Act. Furthermore, the majority argued, the 1946 law could not be applicable because the primary overt acts in the case were committed in 1944 and 1945.

Three judges dissented: Justices Douglas, Black, and Frankfurter.

Justice Douglas observed that a considerable portion of the Rosenbergs' criminal activities—which allegedly had continued until 1950—took place after the effective date of the 1946 Atomic Energy Act. "Some say, however, that since a part of the Rosenbergs' crime was committed under the old law, the penalties of the old law apply. But it is law too elemental for citation of authority that where two penal statutes may apply—one carrying death, the other imprisonment—the court has no choice but to impose the less harsh sentence." When the motion for a stay was first presented to him, Justice Douglas said, he had spent twelve hours on "research and study" before deciding that it presented a "substantial" question. Noting that he since had had the benefit of "additional argument and additional study and reflection," he concluded: "Now I am sure of the answer. I know deep in my heart that I am right on the law. Knowing that, my duty is clear."

Justice Black declared that the legal question involved was a "substantial and serious" one because "the death penalty has been imposed for conduct part of which took place at a time when the Congress appears to have barred the imposition of that death penalty by district judges acting without a jury's recommendation." Moreover, Black questioned the power of the full Court to set aside Justice Douglas's stay, saying the action was "unprecedented" in the Court's history and he had found no statute or rule permitting it.

Justice Frankfurter, in a brief separate opinion, said the legal questions raised were "complicated and novel" and that the Attorney General's application for revocation of the stay should not be acted on without more time for study and argument (he promised to comment more fully later). Justice Black also complained that "the time has been too short to . . . give this question the study it deserves." Said he:

"It is argued [by Attorney General Brownell] that the Court is not asked to 'act with unseemly haste to avoid postponement of a scheduled execution.' I do not agree. I do not believe that Government counsel or this Court has had time or an adequate opportunity to investigate and decide the very serious question raised in asking this Court to vacate the stay. . . .

". . . Surely the Court is not here establishing a precedent which will require it to call extra sessions during vacation every time a federal or state official asks it to hasten the electrocution of defendants without affording this Court adequate time or opportunity for exploration and study of serious legal questions."

Finally, Justice Black—the one member of the high tribunal who consistently had voted to review the Rosenberg case—concluded: "It is not amiss to point out that this Court has never reviewed this record and has never affirmed the fairness of the trial below. Without an affirmance of the fairness of the trial by the highest court of the land there may always be questions as to whether these executions were legally and rightfully carried out. I would still grant certiorari and let this Court approve or disapprove the fairness of the trials."

Following the reading of the Court's ruling, Emanual Bloch moved for a further stay to provide time for President Eisenhower to act on the clemency appeal. At the same time, Fyke Farmer asked the Court to reconsider the question of its power to vacate the stay. The judges retired to deliberate, then denied both motions. Regarding Bloch's request, Justice Frankfurter commented:

"On the assumption that the sentences against the Rosenbergs are to be carried out at 11 o'clock tonight, their counsel ask this Court to stay their execution until opportunity has been afforded to them to invoke the constitutional prerogative of clemency. . . . Were it established that counsel are correct in their assumption . . . I believe that it would be right and proper for this Court formally to grant a stay with a proper time-limit to give appropriate opportunity for the process of executive clemency to operate. I justifiably assume, however, that the time for the execution has not been fixed as of 11 o'clock tonight. Of course I respectfully assume that appropriate consideration will be given to a clemency application by the authority constitutionally charged with the clemency function."

At 1:41 P.M., the Court Crier proclaimed that the special term of the Supreme Court was adjourned. The Rosenbergs' last remaining hope was Executive clemency. Presumably, the Department of Justice's Pardon Attorney would now dispatch the Rosenbergs' second clemency petition to the White House, where it would be considered by the President. At 2:09 P.M., less than a half hour after the Supreme Court had adjourned, an assistant White House press secretary told reporters: "The President declines to intervene."

According to Robert J. Donovan, at that morning's meeting at the White House, the Cabinet had talked about the "flood of propaganda" on the Rosenbergs and had agreed that the President should issue a statement "emphasizing that the free world had an interest in the proper handling of the case." It was this counterpropaganda statement—conceived earlier in the day—that was released from the White House that afternoon, shortly after the Supreme Court had announced its decision.

In his statement, President Eisenhower said:

"Since its original review of the proceedings in the Rosenberg case by the Supreme Court of the United States, the courts have considered numerous further proceedings. . . .

"I am convinced that the only conclusion to be drawn from the history of this case is that the Rosenbergs have received the benefit of every safeguard which American justice can provide. . . .

"I am not unmindful of the fact that this case has aroused grave concern both here and abroad in the minds of serious people, aside from the considerations of law. In this connection, I can only say that, by immeasurably increasing the chances of atomic war, the Rosenbergs may have condemned to death tens of millions of innocent people all over the world. The execution of two human beings is a grave matter. But even graver is the thought of the millions of dead whose deaths may be directly attributable to what these spies have done.

"When democracy's enemies have been judged guilty of a crime as horrible as that of which the Rosenbergs were convicted; when the legal processes of democracy have been marshalled to their maximum strength to protect the lives of convicted spies; when in their most solemn judgment the tribunals of the United States have adjudged them guilty and the sentence just, I will not intervene in this matter."

In a telegram to the White House, Bloch and his colleagues asked the President to grant them a clemency hearing, pointing out that the Supreme Court had never "reviewed" the Rosenberg case. Reported later by the *Times* was that the telegram was received by President Eisenhower's special counsel, Bernard Shanley, and "transmitted to the Justice Department."

Meanwhile, in New York City, an attorney representing the defense asked Judge Kaufman to stay the 11 P.M. executions because they would occur during the Jewish Sabbath, which begins approximately at sundown Friday. Denying the stay, Judge Kaufman said he already had spoken with Attorney General Brownell about the matter and had been assured that the executions would not be carried out during the Sabbath. The meaning of this assurance was made clear later that afternoon when it became known that the Attorney General had ordered the executions rescheduled for some time *before* sundown, due at 8:31 P.M. that evening.

Soon after the U. S. Marshal in charge of the executions informed the Sing Sing warden of the new hour, wooden barricades—manned by heavily armed guards and state troopers—were hastily thrown up across all roads leading to the prison. Within the death house, the Rosenbergs were together as Ethel wrote a final letter to their sons:

"*June 19, 1953*

"Dearest Sweethearts, my most precious children,

"Only this morning it looked like we might be together again after all. Now that this cannot be, I want so much for you to know all that I have come to know. Unfortunately, I may write only a few simple words; the rest your own lives must teach you, even as mine taught me.

"At first, of course, you will grieve bitterly for us, but you will not grieve alone. That is our consolation and it must eventually be yours.

"Eventually, too, you must come to believe that life is worth the living. Be comforted that even now, with the end of ours slowly approaching, that we know this with a conviction that defeats the executioner!

"Your lives must teach you, too, that good cannot really flourish in the midst of evil; that freedom and all the things that go to make up a truly satisfying and worthwhile life, must sometimes be purchased very dearly. Be comforted, then, that we were serene and understood with the deepest kind of understanding, that civilization had not as yet progressed to the point where life did not have to be lost for the sake of life; and that we were comforted in the sure knowledge that others would carry on after us.

"We wish we might have had the tremendous joy and gratification of living our lives out with you. Your Daddy who is with me in the last momentous hours, sends his heart and all the love that is in it for his dearest boys. Always remember that we were innocent and could not wrong our conscience.

"We press you close and kiss you with all our strength.

"Lovingly,

"Daddy and Mommy

"Julie   Ethel

"P.S. to Manny: The Ten Commandments religious medal and chain —and my wedding ring—I wish you to present to our children as a token of our undying love."

In Washington, Bloch and Farmer and their associates had been working desperately to forestall the now almost certain executions. Hours were expended in futile pleas for a stay to individual justices, including Black, Burton, and Frankfurter. Finally, Marshall flew to New York for a final appeal in the district court there.

Bloch and his colleagues remained at the Supreme Court Building and, at about 6 P.M., received the printed copies of the majority opinions vacating the stay. Reading them over rapidly, they suddenly noticed that —in the last two sentences of Justice Jackson's opinion—the Court majority had firmly disassociated themselves from the death sentence and appeared to imply disapproval of it.

The opinion, written by Justice Jackson and concurred in by the five other justices who voted with the majority, concluded: "Vacating this stay is not to be construed as indorsing the wisdom or appropriateness to this case of a death sentence. That sentence, however, is permitted by law and, as was previously pointed out, is therefore not within this Court's power of revision."

Immediately, Bloch informed a Justice Department official of Justice Jackson's concluding sentences and asked to be put in touch with the Attorney General. However, a few hours before, Bloch had reacted to news of the earlier execution hour with a scathing emotional attack on Brownell and the Attorney General now let it be known that he would not speak with him.

Bloch left the Supreme Court and hurried over to the White House in the hope of somehow getting to see the President. Outside the White House gates, pickets urging clemency continued to march while especially heavy police details patrolled the area. Sighting Bloch at about 6:30 P.M., the pickets let out a cheer. The defense attorney was carrying a copy of Justice Jackson's majority opinion and a letter to the President—a final plea for "mercy" which Ethel Rosenberg had written and given to Bloch on his last visit to her the previous Tuesday.

Informed by a White House police officer that he could not be admitted to the grounds without an appointment, Bloch asked to use a telephone in the guard box to call the President's assistant or press secretary, but was refused permission. Finally, he gave both the copy of the court opinion and the letter to the officer to be delivered to the President.

Then, Bloch and his associates taxied back to his hotel room, where he tried to telephone the White House to ascertain whether the Supreme Court's remarks on the death sentence had been brought to the President's attention. However, with time running out, he was unable to get through—the White House switchboard was busy.

At Sing Sing, the Rosenbergs had not talked with any visitors that day. Julius's brother had not been permitted to see him when he arrived hurriedly at 6:12 P.M.—long after the deadline for final visits to the condemned. He left a few minutes later, supported on either side by prison guards, a newspaper shielding his face from newsreel photographers.

In Paris that day, thousands had been participating in day-long rallies to "save the Rosenbergs." One youth was shot and over four hundred persons arrested as demonstrators clashed with massive police formations blocking approaches to the locked American Embassy on Place de la Concorde. Across the Channel, English supporters of the Rosenbergs made vain last-minute attempts to persuade Prime Minister Winston Churchill to intervene with President Eisenhower on behalf of the doomed pair. Thousands of clemency demonstrators roamed through London's West End.

Near Union Square in New York City, more than five thousand people congregated for a hastily called "prayer meeting." Many held aloft placards with the words "We Are Innocent."

At 6:45 P.M., attorney Daniel Marshall, who had hurried from the airport to the federal courthouse at Foley Square, asked Judge Edward J. Dimock to hear his application. However, Marshall was referred to Judge Irving Kaufman, who had remained in his chambers to deal with any last-minute legal moves in the case.

At 7:15 P.M., Marshall began his oral argument before Judge Kaufman on his plea for a writ of habeas corpus.

At 7:20 P.M., Ethel and Julius Rosenberg, who had spent their last afternoon and evening together, said farewell to each other and were separated to be prepared for the electrocutions.

At 7:25 P.M., Marshall was reminded by Judge Kaufman that the executions were set for 8 P.M. and told to "get along with your argument." Begging the Judge to order a stay until he had completed his presentation, Marshall said it would be "terrible if I could convince your Honor that you should grant the application and it would be too late."

Meanwhile, in New Haven, Connecticut, other attorneys frantically visited a number of judges of the Circuit Court of Appeals to request a stay —on the basis of their appeal of a motion turned down earlier that same day by Judge Kaufman.

At an indeterminate time that evening, Ethel Rosenberg penciled a brief final letter to Emanuel Bloch. She wrote, in part:

"Dearest person, you and ———* must see to my children—Tell him it was my last request of him. . . .

"All my heart I send to all who hold me dear—I am not alone—and I die 'with honor and with dignity'—knowing my husband and I must be vindicated by history. You will see to it that our names are kept bright and unsullied by lies—as you did while we lived so wholeheartedly, so unstintingly—you did everything that could be done—We are the first victims of American Fascism.

"Love you, Ethel"

In her letter, she noted that she was attaching to the letterhead "a few last notes." On one of these—a fragmentary message on a torn scrap of paper—she scrawled what may have been the last words she wrote: "I cry for myself as I lie dead—for shall they know all that burned my brain and breast. . . ."

At 7:32 P.M., the White House announced that President Eisenhower had read the "mercy" letter from Mrs. Rosenberg, which Bloch had left at the gate with a police officer. The President was said to have felt that the letter added nothing to his opinion on the case, expressed earlier in the day.

At 7:45 P.M., Judge Kaufman denied Marshall's motion. At about the same time, Emanuel Bloch finally managed to get a telephone call through to an assistant press secretary at the White House and inquired whether Justice Jackson's words on the death sentence had been seen by the President. According to defense attorney Malcolm Sharp, the press secretary told Bloch that "these were legal matters which did not concern the executive department."

In New York, the crowd at Union Square wept, shouted, and screamed when a woman announced over a loudspeaker that the time for the Rosenbergs' execution was near. Police turned the loudspeaker off to prevent a possible riot.

In front of the White House, some four hundred pro-Rosenberg pickets —watched belligerently from across the street by a crowd estimated by police at about seven thousand—continued their vigil until 8 P.M., the supposed moment of execution. That moment, as described in the New York *Herald Tribune*, "sounded like New Year's Eve." The paper reported: "The scene, in the midst of which President and Mrs. Eisenhower were secluded in their quarters, was unparalleled in recent White House

---

* The psychiatrist who had visited Ethel in prison.

history. . . . On the stroke of 8 there was an outbreak of cheers and honking of automobile horns. . . . Passing motorists shouted jibes at the pickets, and a few of the women in the picket line wept and had to be supported by friends."

In London's Whitehall, as Big Ben struck 1 A.M.—8 P.M. New York time—a bareheaded man knelt in prayer for two minutes, while some two hundred individuals respectfully stood still, stopping traffic.

At Sing Sing, as the evening sun went down over the Hudson River, preparations were complete for the double execution. Still connecting the prison and the Department of Justice in Washington was a direct telephone line—kept open should the Rosenbergs decide to "talk."

Julius Rosenberg, thirty-five, wordlessly went to his death at 8:06 P.M. Ethel Rosenberg, thirty-seven, entered the execution chamber a few minutes after her husband's body had been removed. Just before being seated in the chair, she held out her hand to a matron accompanying her, drew the other woman close, and kissed her lightly on the cheek. She was pronounced dead at 8:16 P.M.

The Rosenbergs went to their deaths, the New York *Times* reported, "with a composure that astonished the witnesses."

Three days after the executions, Justice Felix Frankfurter finally made public his dissenting opinion on the Attorney General's application to vacate the stay. Noting his belief that the Farmer-Marshall legal point had "substance," he decried the haste with which the matter had been decided and asked: "Can it be said that there was time to go through the process by which cases are customarily decided here?"

Then, apparently recognizing the ironically anticlimactic nature of his remarks, Justice Frankfurter concluded:

"To be writing an opinion in a case affecting two lives after the curtain has been rung down upon them has the appearance of pathetic futility. But history also has its claims."

CHAPTER 21

POST-MORTEM DIALOGUES

Not surprisingly, the death of the Rosenbergs changed the opinions of no one—neither those who had favored the executions nor those who had opposed them. What divided the two camps was not a matter of intelligence, good will, and sincerity—undoubtedly such qualities could be found on both sides of the controversy. The difference was a more fundamental one of perception: Given roughly the same set of facts, some concluded that the Rosenbergs were innocent or, at the very least, that the import of their illegal acts had been grossly exaggerated; others, that the pair had been guilty of monumental crimes. Nowhere does the irreconcilable nature of the contesting views emerge more sharply than in post-mortem statements on the case made by Frenchmen and Americans.

The day after the executions, Jean-Paul Sartre, writing in the Parisian daily *Libération*, penned a savage attack against the United States:

". . . Now that we have been made your allies, the fate of the Rosenbergs could be a preview of our own future. You, who claim to be masters of the world, had the opportunity to prove that you were first of all masters of yourselves. But if you gave in to your criminal folly, this very folly might tomorrow throw us headlong into a war of extermination. . . .

"By killing the Rosenbergs you have quite simply tried to halt the progress of science by human sacrifice. Magic, witch hunts, auto-da-fés, sacrifices—we are here getting to the point: your country is sick with fear. . . . you are afraid of the shadow of your own bomb. . . .

". . . do not be astonished if we cry out from one end of Europe to the other: Watch out! America has the rabies! Cut all ties which bind us to her, otherwise we will in turn be bitten and run mad!"

At about the same time as Sartre's article appeared in France, the New York *Times* commented:

"In the record of espionage against the United States there had been no case of its magnitude and its stern drama. The Rosenbergs were engaged in funneling the secrets of the most destructive weapon of all time to the most dangerous antagonist the United States ever confronted—at a time when a deadly atomic arms race was on. Their crime was staggering in its potential for destruction. It stirred the fears and the emotions of the American people. . . .

"The prevailing opinion in the United States . . . is that the Rosenbergs for two years had access to every court in the land and every organ of public opinion, that no court found grounds for doubting their guilt, that they were the only atom spies who refused to confess and that they got what they deserved."

French author François Mauriac, winner of the Nobel Prize for literature, made known his feelings about the executions in the conservative Parisian newspaper *Figaro:*

"After years, the long set of appeals and petitions for mercy end in this violently lighted lacquered room, furnished with a single chair.

". . . The man standing on the threshold would have only one word to say, one sign to make, not to cross it. . . .

"He did not say the word, he did not make the sign. If he had weakened, what would have been the value of his confession? Without doubt what happens nearly everywhere in the world today, and particularly these days in North Africa, would have happened. . . . The accused withdraw what has been obtained from them in ways evidently more persuasive, we agree, but certainly not less cruel than the simple telephone wire which the day before the Sabbath linked the White House and Sing Sing and which will link them forever.

"Have the Rosenbergs committed the crime for which they have been executed? That is the question. But another question obsesses and worries me: Was it of any use, and if so to whom, that even innocent they confess . . . ?"

Although Mauriac is known as a "Catholic writer," his words have nothing in common with those in an editorial published in the United States by the Catholic magazine *America.* Referring to President Eisenhower's statement that "the Rosenbergs may have condemned to death tens of millions of innocent people all over the world," the editorial declared:

"Their crime, in sober truth, must be measured by a new calculus: the megadeath, or death of a million human beings. The Rosenbergs enabled Russia, by a mere silent threat of atomic warfare, to stand up to the free world pending what may be an atomic showdown of unimaginable carnage and devastation.

"The Rosenbergs were mortal enemies, not merely of the United States, but of the entire human race. They were willing slaves of a conspiracy against humanity—unrepentant to the very end. The will to execute them was an affirmation by America, as the voice of humanity, of its will to survive. Only because they brazenly defied that will by refusing to name their accomplices did the Rosenbergs die. They died because such conspirators against humanity must either die or relent if humanity is to live."

Perhaps the fullest expression of the way some Frenchmen saw the Rosenberg case was described by Jacques Monod, a member of the

Pasteur Institute in Paris, in a long letter to the editor printed in the United States in the *Bulletin of the Atomic Scientists* (October 1953):

"Sir:

"As you may know, the execution of Ethel and Julius Rosenberg has aroused profound emotions in Europe, especially in France. It has also been the cause, or sometimes the occasion, of strong hostility and severe criticism being expressed in the press or by the public (I am referring here to the non-Communist press and public). In taking the liberty of writing to you on this subject I am urged, not by the desire to express criticism or reprobation but by my love and admiration for your country where I have many close friends.

"As a scientist, I naturally address myself to scientists. Moreover, I know that American scientists respect their profession, and are aware that it involves a permanent pact with objectivity and truth—and that indeed wherever objectivity, truth, and justice are at stake, a scientist has the duty to form an opinion, and defend it. This, I hope, will be accepted as a valid explanation and excuse for my writing this letter. In any case, whether one agrees or not with what I think must be said, I beg that this letter be taken for what it is: a manifestation of deep sympathy and concern for America.

"First of all, Americans should be fully aware of the extraordinary amplitude and unanimity of the movement which developed in France. Everybody here, in every walk of life, and independent of all political affiliations, followed the last stages of the Rosenberg case with anxiety, and the tragic outcome evoked anguish and consternation everywhere. Have Americans realized, were they informed, that pleas for mercy were sent to President Eisenhower not only by thousands of private individuals and groups, including many of the most respected writers and scientists, not only by all the highest religious leaders, not only by entire official bodies such as the (conservative) Municipal Council of Paris, but by the President of the Republic himself, who was thus obeying and expressing the unanimous wish of the French people. As your New York *Times* remarked with some irony and complete truth, France achieved a unanimity in the Rosenberg case that she could never hope to achieve on a domestic issue.

"To a certain extent these widespread reactions were due to the simple human appeal of the case: this young couple, united in death by a frightful sentence which made orphans of their innocent children, the extraordinary courage shown by Ethel and Julius Rosenberg, their letters to each other, simple and moving. All this naturally evoked compassion, but it would be wrong to think that the French succumbed to a purely sentimental appeal to pity. Public opinion, and first of all the intellectual circles, were primarily sensitive to the legal and ethical aspects of the case, which were widely publicized, analyzed, and discussed.

"If I may be allowed, I should like to review briefly the points which appeared most significant to us in forming an opinion on the whole affair.

"The first was that the entire accusation, hence the whole case of the American government, rested upon the testimony of avowed spies, the Greenglass couple, of whom David received a light sentence after turning state's evidence (fifteen years reducible to five on good behavior),* while his wife Ruth was not even indicted. The dubious value of testimony from such sources was apparent to everyone.

"Moreover, leaving the ethical and legal doubts aside, is it probable or even possible that a simple mechanic such as David Greenglass, with no scientific training, could have chosen, assimilated, and memorized secrets of *decisive* atomic importance, under the directions of the similarly untrained Julius Rosenberg? Scientists here always found this difficult to believe, and their doubts were confirmed when Urey himself clearly stated in a letter to President Eisenhower that he considered it impossible: '. . . Greenglass is supposed to have revealed to the Russians the secrets of the atomic bomb. Though the information supposed to have been transmitted could have been important, a man of Greenglass' capacity is wholly incapable of transmitting the physics, chemistry, and mathematics of the atomic bomb to anyone.' After that it was difficult for us to accept, as justification of an unprecedented sentence, the following statement of Judge Kaufman: 'I believe your conduct in putting into the hands of the Russians the A-bomb years before our best scientists predicted Russia would perfect the bomb, has already caused the Communist aggression in Korea with the resulting casualties.' The mere fact that such statements should have found their place in the text of the sentence, raised the gravest doubts in our minds as to its soundness and motivation.

"Indeed the gravest, the most decisive point was the nature of the sentence itself. Even if the Rosenbergs actually performed the acts with which they were charged, we were shocked at a death sentence pronounced in time of peace, for actions committed, it is true, in time of war, but a war in which Russia was an ally, not an enemy, of the United States. . . .

"We could not understand that Ethel Rosenberg should have been sentenced to death when the specific acts of which she was accused were only two conversations; and we were unable to accept the death sentence as being justified by the 'moral support' she was supposed to have given her husband. In fact the severity of the sentence, even if one provisionally accepted the validity of the Greenglass testimony, appeared out of all measure and reason to such an extent as to cast doubt on the whole affair, and to suggest that nationalistic passions and pressure from an inflamed

---

* Actually, the sentence could have been reduced to five years with parole or to ten years for good behavior.

public opinion, had been strong enough to distort the proper administration of justice.

"In spite of these doubts and fears, all those of us who know and love your country, followed each step in the case with anxiety, but also with hope. There were still further appeals to be made, new evidence to be presented, and in the last resort, the President would surely grant mercy where mercy was humanly and ethically called for. We thought a point would finally be reached above the level of irresponsible passions, where reason and justice would prevail.

"Above all, we counted on American intellectuals and men of science. Knowing the generosity and courage of so many of them, we felt sure they would speak, and hoped they would be heard. We constantly had in mind our own Dreyfus case, when a handful of intellectuals had risen against a technically correct decision of justice, against the Army hierarchy, against public opinion and government which were a prey to nationalist fury, and we remembered that this handful of intellectuals had succeeded, after five years of stubborn efforts, in confounding the liars, and freeing their innocent victim. We felt that you American intellectuals could similarly turn what appeared at first a denial of justice into a triumph for justice. That is why the case assumed so much importance in Europe, particularly in France. And above all, it was important to liberal intellectuals who, in contrast to Communists, had hoped to find that the most powerful nation of the free world could afford to be at once objective, just, and merciful.

"So we continued to hope through the last days of the young couple's life. . . .

"American scientists and intellectuals, the execution of the Rosenbergs is a grave defeat for you, for us, and for the free world. We do not for a moment believe that this tragic outcome of what appeared to us a crucial test-case, means that you were indifferent to it—but it does testify to your present weakness, in your own country. Not one of us would dare reproach you for this, as we do not feel we have any right to give lessons in civic courage when we ourselves have been unable to prevent so many miscarriages of justice in France, or under French sovereignty. What we want to tell you is that, in spite of this defeat, you must not be discouraged, you must not abandon hope, you must continue publicly to serve truth, objectivity, and justice. If you speak firmly and unanimously you will be heard by your countrymen, who are aware of the importance of science, and of your great contributions to American wealth, power, and prestige.

"You, American scientists and intellectuals, bear great responsibilities which you cannot escape, and which we can only partly share with you. America has power and leadership among the nations. You must, for civilization's sake, obtain moral leadership and power in your own country. Now, as never before, the world needs a free, strong, just America, turned toward social and moral as well as technical progress. Now, as never before, intellectuals the world over must turn to you American scientists to lead your country in this direction, and to help her conquer her fears and control her passions."

Two months later, a comment on Monod's letter, written by A. B. Martin, of Glen Head, New York, was published in the *Bulletin*:

"Dear Sir:

"In the October 1953 issue of the *Bulletin* is a very interesting Letter to the Editor signed by Jacques Monod and dealing with French views on the Rosenberg case. I think it would further friendship between the two countries if a small group of U.S. scientists would answer this letter, explaining why American feelings in this matter are so different from the European feelings. There are many inaccuracies in the Monod letter which need correcting—for example, to compare the case with the Dreyfus case is both ridiculous and insulting. To continually refer to the Rosenbergs as 'the young couple' is trite—Americans consider the Rosenbergs were guilty as charged, our President branded them as terrible traitors; and we are proud our country has the strength to carry out the laws of the land —we are not ashamed of the Rosenberg trial nor of its result. We are awake to the evils of communism where the French intellectual is still soft to the problem—this may explain the tragedy of the last war as far as France was concerned.

"To publish the Monod letter without editorial comment gives the reader of the *Bulletin* the feeling that editorially speaking, it is in agreement with it, which is of course false."

THE INQUEST OPENS

•

CHAPTER 22
THE CRIME IN PERSPECTIVE

The contention of the prosecution in the Rosenberg-Sobell trial was not only that David Greenglass—while employed as a Los Alamos machinist—had turned over atomic bomb information to Julius Rosenberg and Harry Gold, but that the information given was of the very *highest importance*. Ever since, those who have approved the penalties meted out in the case usually have argued that the severity of the punishment fitted the enormity of the crime.

Actually, under the conspiracy law, no evidence as to the possible significance of any national defense data secured by the defendants was essential for their conviction (and, so far as Sobell was concerned, none was offered). However, with respect to the Rosenbergs, the prosecution went far beyond the limited legal prerequisites, leveling accusations of immense implication.

In his opening to the jury, United States Attorney Irving Saypol flatly stated that the Rosenbergs, "through David Greenglass," had been able "to steal . . . this one weapon, that might well hold the key to the survival of this nation and means the peace of the world, the atomic bomb." Again, in his summation, Saypol made the government's position clear when he said: "We know that these conspirators stole the most important scientific secrets ever known to mankind from this country and delivered them to the Soviet Union."

Just before the sentencing of the Rosenbergs, prosecutor Saypol commented that "the secrets" secured by the convicted husband and wife had been of "immeasurable importance." Said he: ". . . these defendants have affected the lives, and perhaps the freedom, of whole generations of mankind." Echoing these sentiments, Judge Kaufman told the Rosenbergs—in apparent justification of the punishment he was about to impose—that, in his opinion, their spying had "already caused . . . the Communist aggression in Korea, with the resultant casualties exceeding 50,000 and who knows but that millions more of innocent people must pay the price of your treason."

The Judge added: ". . . by your betrayal you undoubtedly have altered the course of history to the disadvantage of our country."

Nearly two years later, while hearing an appeal for judicial clemency, Judge Kaufman reiterated his belief that the Rosenbergs had been a "contributing cause" of the Korean War. Voicing a similar understanding of the seriousness of the crime, U. S. Attorney Myles J. Lane said that the Soviet Union had been able "to master the secrets of the atomic weapons' construction . . . very far in advance of the time they would have done so except for this act of espionage."

When President Dwight D. Eisenhower denied Executive clemency to the condemned couple, he explained: ". . . the crime for which they have been found guilty and sentenced . . . could very well result in the death of many, many thousands of innocent citizens." In his second pronouncement on the case—issued the day of the executions—President Eisenhower declared: ". . . by immeasurably increasing the chances of atomic war, the Rosenbergs may have condemned to death tens of millions of innocent people all over the world."

Today, with the perspective afforded by the passage of over a decade, what can one say about these extraordinary statements by two U.S. attorneys, a federal district court judge, and a President of the United States? Does the trial record itself contain facts that support such terrible and—with the exception of the Nuremberg, Eichmann, and other war crimes cases—unprecedented accusations as those leveled officially against the Rosenbergs?

The source of almost all available information on the Rosenbergs' alleged atomic espionage is the testimony of David Greenglass and, to a minor extent, his wife Ruth. David, a high-school graduate employed in civilian life as a machinist, entered the Army just after his twenty-first birthday. Sent to Los Alamos about a year later, in August 1944, he was assigned there to a research division that was performing experiments with high explosives. A T/5 corporal, Greenglass was given a security badge entitling him to know only enough to accomplish his own specific job—in a machine shop—and was unaware of the over-all purpose of the secret project.

In late November of that year, David spent several days in nearby Albuquerque with his wife, who had journeyed from New York City to visit him on their wedding anniversary. From her, he learned for the first time that he was "working on the atomic bomb." This surprising news, she said, had been imparted to her shortly before she left by Julius Rosenberg, who wanted David to supply information for the Russians.

Ruth testified that she had told her husband that "Julius was interested in the physical description of the project at Los Alamos, the approximate number of people employed there, whether the place was camouflaged, what the security measures were, and the type of work that David himself did."

After hesitating briefly, David agreed and, according to Ruth, informed her "that Los Alamos had formerly been a riding academy, that it was 40 miles from Santa Fe and about 110 miles from Albuquerque, that the project itself was on the top of a hill and it was secluded; you could hardly see it until you were almost on top of it; that there was a guard at the entrance at all times, and everyone was checked going in or out. He told me the names of the scientists, Dr. Urey, Dr. Oppenheimer, Kistiakowski, Niels Bohr. David told me that he worked in an experimental shop, that he made models from blueprints that scientists brought in to him." In addition, Ruth said that her husband had estimated for her the number of people employed at Los Alamos.

Obviously, this nondescript information allegedly supplied in late November 1944 could scarcely have been of any great value to a would-be atom bomb manufacturer. At most, the names of the renowned scientists revealed by David might have provided a good clue as to the object of their research. But even this knowledge would appear to have been superfluous, for, according to the Greenglasses' version of events, Julius Rosenberg already had informed Ruth that the work at Los Alamos was aimed at developing atomic bombs.

In January 1945, while home in New York City on furlough, David gave Julius sketches and descriptive material depicting a device called a high explosive lens mold. (Such molds, made in the machine shop where David worked, were used to cast high explosives into special shapes called lenses.) He also listed the names of some scientists—the same ones disclosed by him earlier, with the addition of Hans Bethe—and of people on the project whom he regarded as potential espionage recruits. Julius then arranged for him to meet in a car with a "Russian," who asked questions about high explosive lenses that David was unable to answer.

On June 3, 1945, David was visited in Albuquerque by Harry Gold. He gave Gold sketches and explanatory material showing an experiment performed with a high explosive lens, plus another list of possible recruits for espionage. He also reported plans for what he believed, erroneously, to be a scheduled test detonation of high explosives at Alamogordo. (Gold testified that his Soviet superior, Yakovlev, later told him that "the information . . . received from Greenglass was extremely excellent and very valuable.")

Finally, in September 1945, while in New York on another furlough, David drew and turned over to Julius a sketch of an implosion type atomic bomb. Using twelve pages, he wrote out an explanation of the sketch and, once again, listed names of scientists and possible espionage recruits. (In preparing all of this information for the Soviet Union, David said that he had relied entirely on his memory; he never had stolen blue-prints, research reports, or any official papers whatsoever from Los Alamos.)

Thus, the total *technical* data that David Greenglass claimed to have provided, during his short espionage career, consisted of several sketches relating to high explosive lenses and one sketch of an implosion bomb—along with accompanying explanatory material.

The prosecution introduced as trial exhibits four sketches that Green-glass had drawn, in 1950 and 1951, while he was in custody. David identi-fied the exhibits in court as replicas of the original sketches that he had transmitted over five years earlier to Julius Rosenberg and Harry Gold.

These replica sketches and David's testimony about them represent the only available concrete information regarding the Rosenbergs' atomic espionage. As such, they must be the starting point for anyone seeking an informed estimate as to the scope of the alleged crime.

Surprisingly, no representative of the press—so far as the authors could learn—ever has seen any of the Greenglass sketches. This seeming lack of curiosity is difficult to understand, inasmuch as so many newspaper and magazine stories have ascribed supreme importance to the atom bomb secrets said to be embodied in these sketches. Morever, most trial exhibits —like trial transcripts—are matters of public record and, if kept by the court clerk after the conclusion of a case, are available to anyone.

Inquiring, the authors learned that the Rosenberg-Sobell case exhibits are today carefully retained within padlocked files at the federal court-house in Foley Square. On application, we were permitted to see and obtain photostatic copies of three of the Greenglass sketches. The repro-ductions of these sketches—prosecution Exhibits 2, 6, and 7—that appear here are the first ever published anywhere. (See second and third pages of picture section.)

During the trial, as each of these exhibits was introduced by the prose-cution, David was questioned about it by Assistant U. S. Attorney Roy Cohn. Exhibit 2, David testified, is a replica of a lens mold sketch that he gave to Julius Rosenberg in January 1945. He explained that the letters on Exhibit 2 indicate "the parts of the mold."

Asked to tell "exactly" what descriptive information he had "furnished Rosenberg along with this sketch," David replied: "'A' refers to the curve of the lens [the outside curve]; 'B' is the frame; 'C' shows approximately how wide it is. . . . It is a four-leaf clover design like; it looks something similar." He added that high explosives were poured into the mold and when the mold was removed "you had a high explosive lens."

Regarding Exhibits 6 and 7, David identified them as replicas of the two sketches he had turned over to Harry Gold in June 1945. Asked to tell the jury what Exhibit 6 "represents," David testified: "I showed a high explosive lens mold. I showed the way it would look with this high explosive in it with the detonators on, and I showed the steel tube in the middle which would be exploded [*sic*, should be "imploded"] by this lens mold."*

As for Exhibit 7, David testified that this sketch depicted "the lens mold set up for an experiment." Noting that the various parts of Exhibit 7 are marked with letters, David said that he had explained these letters on a separate sheet of paper, which he gave Gold along with the sketch.

> COHN: Now, would you tell us just what you wrote on this other sheet of paper to describe this exhibit and the letters contained thereon? . . .
> DAVID: "A" is the light source which projects a light through this tube "E," which shows a camera set up to take a picture of this light source. Around the tube it is a cross-section of the high explosive lens "C" and a detonator "B" showing where it is detonated, and the course is that when the lens is detonated it collapses the tube, implodes the tube, and the camera through the [camera] lens "F" and the film "D" shows a picture of the implosion.

In short, Exhibit 7 depicts an experiment for studying implosion whereby a specially shaped piece of high explosive, surrounding a metal tube, is detonated and a camera takes pictures through the tube to record how symmetrically the tube is imploded or squeezed together.

Certainly nothing in Greenglass's three crudely drawn sketches—or in his meager explanations of them—permits one to conclude, per se, that he had revealed matters of earth-shaking importance. In fact, David's high explosive lens data appears to be extremely rudimentary, an impression strengthened by his testimony that none of the lens sketches is drawn to scale; that he was incapable of telling which of the many types of lens molds constructed in his shop was an improvement over any other one; and that he did not know the kind, quantity, or combination of high explosives from which the lenses were made.

Further insight regarding the Greenglass lens sketches was provided by Walter S. Koski, called by the prosecution as an expert technical witness. Koski (who held a doctorate in physical chemistry) testified that at Los Alamos his work "was associated with implosion research connected with the atomic bomb."

He explained that in an "explosion" the shock waves dissipate outward while in an "implosion" the detonation waves concentrate toward a common center. Asked Saypol: "In other words, in explosion it blows out; in implosion it blows in?" The witness agreed.

---

* As the date on the bottom right of Exhibit 6 indicates, the sketch was drawn and signed by David Greenglass on June 15, 1950—the day he was apprehended and questioned at length by the FBI. Interestingly, in a report to his attorney written a few days later, David mentioned drawing this pencil sketch for the interrogating agents but did not say that he ever had given a similar sketch to Harry Gold or anyone else.

In his implosion experiments at Los Alamos, Koski had utilized various types of high explosive lenses which, he said, focused detonation waves much as an ordinary glass lens focuses light. Molds for these lenses were made by machinists, including Greenglass, who worked from designs prepared by Koski or someone under his supervision.

Koski had been present in the courtroom when David testified about the lenses. Shown the Greenglass sketches—Exhibits 2, 6, and 7—and questioned about them, he concurred with Saypol's formulation that all three sketches were "reasonably accurate" portrayals of experimental work with lens molds at Los Alamos.

What could a scientist learn from the sketches, which Koski observed were "rough" and omitted "dimensions"? Inquiring along this line, Judge Kaufman asked: "While there might have been some other details that might also have been of some use to a foreign nation which were not contained on Exhibits 2, 6 and 7, the substance of your testimony, as I understand it, was that there was sufficient . . . to reveal to an expert what was going on at Los Alamos?" Replied Koski: "Yes, your Honor."

However, if David's sketches disclosed to the Russians only "what was going on at Los Alamos," he would hardly have rendered them any signal service, since this was information they reportedly had communicated to him, months earlier, through Rosenberg.

Another part of Koski's testimony bearing on the possible significance of the sketches was his somewhat ambiguous comment on the novelty of his work at Los Alamos. Asked whether in 1944 and 1945 there had been any prior experimentation anywhere similar to what he was doing, he answered that, to the best of his knowledge, "there was no information in text books or technical journals on this particular subject."

SAYPOL: In other words, you were engaged in a new and original field?
KOSKI: Correct.

What is unclear is whether Koski was referring to the concept of high explosive lenses as "new and original" or merely to the adaptation and use of this concept in connection with the atomic bomb. For the fact is that the explosive lenses made at Los Alamos were very closely related to a far earlier development—the shaped charge—which, by 1945, had been discussed in "text books or technical journals" throughout the world for some fifty years.

In the late nineteenth century, Charles E. Munroe, an American, had discovered that the effect of cutting a cavity in the side of an explosive charge is to concentrate part of the explosive force on a particular spot. This valuable technique for converging and focusing explosive waves— known as the "Munroe effect"—soon found numerous applications, both civilian and military. A variety of shaped charges were utilized by all belligerents in World War II in many different weapons, including the bazooka.

In February 1945—during the very same period that David allegedly was passing his sketches—a detailed and profusely illustrated article on the shaped charge appeared in *Popular Science* magazine and was afterward reprinted in the July–August 1945 issue of the technical journal *Explosives Engineer.* The latter publication, incidentally, offered "grateful acknowledgement" for the many "sketches and photographs" of shaped charges supplied by the United States Army Ordnance Corps.

Thus, although the lenses devised at Los Alamos undoubtedly had unique aspects, the general idea underlying them—that the force of an explosion can be focused—certainly was nothing "new" in 1945. Moreover, David's sketches are "rough," whereas a fully effective shaped charge must be manufactured with a high degree of precision. What then might the sketches have revealed to an interested party, other than "what was going on at Los Alamos?"

According to Koski, the sketches "illustrate the important principle involved" in the experiments that he and others were performing with high explosive lenses—that is, the use of a combination of such lenses to produce an implosion. (At the time of the trial, no official data had yet been made public on the use of implosion techniques in the atomic bomb.)

The principle of implosion also figured in one other Greenglass sketch introduced at the trial as a prosecution exhibit. David testified that, in January 1945, Julius had described an atom bomb for him (so that he would know what he was looking for). Afterward, at Los Alamos, David "met people who talked of the bombs and how they operated," listened to conversations "very avidly," and asked questions "surreptitiously."

In this way, he ascertained that the bomb Julius had described was the kind dropped on Hiroshima and also learned about a different type of atomic bomb. "It was a type that worked on an implosion effect." When next he saw Julius, in September 1945, he wrote out this information for him.

COHN: Did you draw up a sketch of the atom bomb itself?
DAVID: I did.

A replica of this sketch had been prepared by David and was offered in evidence by the prosecution as Exhibit 8.

At this point, defense attorney Emanuel Bloch made a surprising and rather inexplicable move. Said he: ". . . I now ask the Court to impound this exhibit so that it remains secret to the Court, the jury and counsel."

Commenting that this was "a rather strange request coming from the defendants," Saypol acceded and Judge Kaufman received Exhibit 8 in evidence, but ordered the sketch "sealed" after it was shown to the jury.

Roy Cohn then proceeded to question David about the impounded sketch, labeled on the bottom "cross-section A bomb, not to scale."

COHN: Now, Mr. Greenglass, address yourself to that sketch and tell us, if you will, just what you wrote as best you remember of the descriptive material you gave to Rosenberg in September, 1945, the descriptive material in that sketch.

DAVID: Well, I had this sketch marked A, B, C, D, E, F, and those referred to various parts of the bomb.

COHN: Now tell us exactly what you wrote in this descriptive material.

Once again, Bloch interrupted and came to the bench to urge that David's testimony about Exhibit 8 "also be kept secret." Then, in the presence of the jury, Judge Kaufman, Bloch, and Saypol discussed the need for secrecy. A few moments before, Saypol had clearly been willing to permit both David's sketch and verbal description of "the atom bomb itself" to be made public. Now, however, the U. S. Attorney observed that the anticipated testimony was a matter "of such gravity that the Atomic Energy Commission held hearings . . . as did the Joint Congressional Committee, and representatives of the Atomic Energy Commission have been in attendance here at the trial, as your Honor knows, have been in constant consultation with me and my staff on the subject."

Finally, Judge Kaufman explained to the jury that "reluctantly, but necessarily" he was ordering all spectators to leave the courtroom while Greenglass was questioned about Exhibit 8. However, following a brief recess, the Judge informed the prosecution and defense attorneys that the press was "rather agitated" at being included in the barring order. Saypol then said he was agreeable to the reporters being present and the Judge immediately invited them back.

Whatever Bloch's original motive may have been, he now seemed thoroughly confused by the turn of events, asserting that the purpose of the barring "would be defeated, unless the press is enjoined to secrecy." Retorted Judge Kaufman: "No, they won't be enjoined to secrecy. They will be enjoined to good taste." The press then returned and heard David's testimony, after which the court stenographer's untranscribed notes were impounded.*

This curious episode may well have lent the impression to some—without a word of testimony—that a secret of vast proportions was contained in

* Excerpt from a letter to the authors written by physicist Philip Morrison: "Mr. Bloch, the counsel, told me once personally how sorry he was for the error he had made in impounding the testimony. He was eloquent in describing how lonely he was during the trial. Fear prevented anyone from helping him. . . . He knew nothing of the real story of Los Alamos."

Exhibit 8. (Most subsequent news stories failed to mention that the impounding of the exhibit and the clearing of the courtroom was first suggested by the defense and implied that the action was initiated by the Judge or prosecution.) In any event, the net effect was that, today, the only publicly available information on the impounded testimony is to be found in the contemporary press.

Recounting what was termed Greenglass's "description of the bomb," *Scientific American* reported:

"At its center, he said, was a beryllium sphere emitting neutrons; around this was a sphere of plutonium, and this in turn was enclosed in a plastic sphere. The detonating mechanism consisted of 36 'lens molds' of explosive arranged around the bomb. These shaped charges were detonated to produce an 'implosion' toward the center that collapsed the plutonium sphere and rapidly created a critical mass.

"The next day newspapers published parts of Greenglass' testimony, and news magazines followed up with diagrams of the Greenglass bomb and interpretations to clarify and fill in gaps in his testimony."

As *Scientific American* had observed, many publications that carried stories on the impounded testimony apparently found it necessary to provide their readers with "interpretations to clarify and fill in gaps." Reporters speculated on what David "may have meant" and presented widely varying and often imaginatively illustrated versions of the "Greenglass bomb." What all accounts were agreed on, however, was that David's description of the atomic bomb certainly was not a precise or fully detailed one.

Associated Press science editor Howard W. Blakeslee, for example, referred to the impounded testimony as "partly Rube Goldberg stuff." The "damaging secret" revealed by David, according to Blakeslee, was the use of lenses to produce an implosion.

Similarly, *Time* magazine noted that "Greenglass' bomb is not necessarily up to date, complete or accurate" and said that he had described the mechanism of the atomic bomb used at Nagasaki "sketchily" and "vaguely." The magazine added: "Greenglass is no scientist (at Brooklyn Polytechnic Institute he flunked eight courses out of eight), and some of his testimony made little scientific sense. He did reveal, however, the important fact that the bomb was set off by an 'implosion'. . . ."

A contrary view regarding the importance of David's revelation that "the bomb was set off by an 'implosion'" was taken by *Scientific American.* Referring to "naive newspaper readers who have gained the impression that the secret of the atomic bomb is a neat little blueprint that any mechanic could steal or even reconstruct in his basement," the publication said: "What the newspapers failed to note was that without quantitative data and other necessary accompanying technical information the Greenglass bomb was not much of a secret. *The principle of 'implosion' by means of a shaped charge has often been suggested in speculation on a possible mechanism for detonation of the atomic bomb."* (Emphasis added.)

The prosecution presented one witness, John A. Derry, an electrical engineer, to testify about the impounded evidence. In 1944 and 1945, while serving as a liaison officer for General Groves, Derry had had occasion to make regular visits to Los Alamos and to see the actual atomic bomb in the process of development. (Though employed by the AEC at the time of the trial, he did not appear as a Commission representative or spokesman.)

Prosecutor Saypol requested that Judge Kaufman "take the same precautions as have been taken heretofore, perhaps even more" and, once again, the courtroom was cleared of all spectators—with the exception of the press. Then Derry was permitted to view Exhibit 8 while the court stenographer read the impounded testimony to him.

SAYPOL: Mr. Derry, does the description as read . . . in conjunction with the sketch before you . . . relate to the atomic weapon which was in the course of development in 1945? . . .

DERRY: It does. . . .

SAYPOL: Does the knowledge as disclosed . . . demonstrate substantially and with substantial accuracy the principle involved in the operation of the 1945 atomic bomb? . . .

DERRY: It does. . . .

SAYPOL: From that testimony and from that exhibit. . . . Can a scientist, and can you, perceive what the actual construction of the bomb was?

DERRY: You can.

SAYPOL: To a substantial degree?

DERRY: You can. . . .

SAYPOL: Does the information that has been read to you, together with the sketch concern a type of atomic bomb which was actually used by the United States of America?

DERRY: It does. It is the bomb we dropped at Nagasaki, similar to it.

What, if anything, is Derry saying here about the value or significance of the impounded evidence? The fact is that the questions posed by Saypol are phrased so subjectively ("relate to," "demonstrate substantially," "perceive," "concern") as to make impossible any hard and fast judgment regarding what the witness meant to communicate when he answered them.

Cross-examined about the Greenglass sketch and testimony, Derry (like Koski) said that "the principle . . . . is what is intended here." When Bloch attempted to press the witness as to the completeness of David's description of the atomic bomb, he was interrupted by Judge Kaufman, who commented: "I don't think it was offered as a complete or as a detailed description. . . . But just as the witness has testified it is a description of a principle upon which it works."

The day after imposing the death sentences, Judge Kaufman observed that David Greenglass had "testified to the vital character of the information which he gave to Julius Rosenberg" and Koski and Derry had "attested to the tremendous importance of this information." The fact is, of course, that David never testified, nor could he have, regarding the "vital character" of his sketches and neither Koski nor Derry made any direct statement about their "tremendous importance." However, in an effort to clarify the matter once and for all, the authors obtained an interview with the witness Derry.

Today, John Derry is still a government employee—Director of the Division of Construction and Supply of the Atomic Energy Commission. One of the authors spoke with him for nearly an hour in the AEC building in Washington. (Present also was an AEC public relations man.)

Derry said he was unaware of how he had been chosen to testify, noting that there were plenty of people at Los Alamos who knew much more than he did. He was not a scientist. He was a construction man and didn't know much physics. The Greenglass sketch that he was shown, he said, demonstrated "the principle involved in the 1945 bomb."

But did the sketch reveal more than just the fact that the bomb utilized the principle of implosion, we asked. Did the sketch identify the actual components of the bomb and accurately depict their size, shape, and arrangement?

"Well," he replied, "it would have to have included some of the components." He added: "Greenglass was a mechanic and the sketch reflected what a mechanic would suppose would go into the bomb."

But was Greenglass correct in what he supposed? we asked. Derry refused to elaborate his answer.

Finally, we observed to Derry that some people had claimed that Soviet scientists would have required many additional years to make an atomic bomb without the information contained in the impounded sketch he had seen and in the three lens mold sketches (which we showed him). What did he think about this?

Derry remained silent while the question was repeated several times. At last, he offered the opinion that the information "must have helped some, but it may not have."

In the years since the Rosenberg-Sobell trial, a voluminous literature on all aspects of the Manhattan Project has come into being. Recently, this literature was augmented substantially when much long-classified data on the wartime work at Los Alamos was taken out of security wraps, making publicly available for the first time a detailed description of the development of the implosion-type atomic bomb. As a result, an unequivocal appraisal of the Rosenbergs' alleged atomic espionage now is possible.

In the spring of 1943, J. Robert Oppenheimer, charged with the task of designing and constructing atomic bombs, began gathering his distinguished scientific team at Los Alamos. By then, the main design criteria for an atom bomb had long been evident: The critical mass of uranium 235 or plutonium had to be brought together with *extreme speed*; otherwise, the lightning-fast chain reaction might begin and end before the separate pieces of fissionable material were fully and efficiently assembled. Should this happen, the fissionable core of the bomb would be blown apart with comparatively little release of energy.

The easiest solution to this problem appeared to be the use of some kind of specially adapted gun to fire one piece of fissionable material at another. A second possibility was to detonate the bomb by implosion—surrounding a sphere containing the fissionable material with a layer of explosives that would burst inward, compressing the uranium or plutonium into a critical mass. Initially, though both methods were pursued, the gun was favored because it involved relatively little new technology, as compared with implosion (which promised to be a more efficient design).

Of course the actual construction of both the gun and implosion models of the bomb—far from being simply mechanical tasks—required the interrelated efforts of the *entire* Los Alamos Laboratory. Physicists, armed with equipment that included a cyclotron and eventually an atomic reactor, performed innumerable experiments to discover the nuclear properties of uranium, plutonium, and other metals that might be used in the bomb. Figures obtained from these experiments then were utilized by mathematicians and theoretical physicists in equations aimed at calculating a host of unknowns—including the best size, shape, and velocity of assembly for each piece of fissionable material and, most important, the critical amounts of fissionable material required for a chain reaction under various conditions. Other specialists explored the chemistry, chemical engineering, and metallurgy of the fissionable metals.

The suggestion soon was advanced that some variety of shaped explosive charge, similar to the ones being used by the Armed Forces in armor-piercing weapons, might be employed in an implosion bomb. If such a spherical bomb was to implode symmetrically, each of these explosive charges surrounding it would have to be made with precision and detonated nearly simultaneously. Extensive experimentation with high explosives was required, and facilities were constructed at Los Alamos for casting large quantities of conventional explosives into a great variety of shapes and sizes.

Around July 1944 the situation at Los Alamos changed drastically: Implosion, until then assigned secondary priority as an advantageous but difficult technique for detonating the bomb, became an absolute necessity. The latest scientific findings had disclosed that the gun method of assembly would work for uranium 235 but was not rapid enough for plutonium. A *plutonium bomb would have to be detonated by implosion.*

That summer, nearly every division of the Los Alamos Laboratory was hastily reorganized to speed work on an implosion bomb. In addition, a new division to investigate and produce the high explosive components of the bomb was set up, headed by an eminent scientist and explosives expert, George B. Kistiakowski.

At this crucial juncture, Los Alamos was encountering serious shortages of civilian labor. An increasing number of soldiers with special skills were brought in to help in the explosives plant and various laboratories and shops. An August 1944 arrival was David Greenglass, assigned soon after to Kistiakowski's Explosives Division, where he was given work in a machine shop making molds for implosion experiments.

One of the scientists who brought jobs to this machine shop was Walter Koski, employed in the Explosives Division's Implosion Research group as leader of a subgroup called Flash Photography. The latter was one of the more conventional of a number of methods used at Los Alamos to record the results of the thousands of implosion experiments then being conducted. Specifically, the task of Koski's subgroup was to obtain shadow photographs of imploding cylinders.

Within seven months after implosion became a matter of extreme urgency, the main lines of development for an implosion bomb had been firmly fixed; only five months later, the first such bomb was tested at Alamogordo. Of course, this early model of an implosion bomb, quickly put together under wartime pressures, was far from perfect technically. To avoid possible delays in tight production schedules, scientists had frozen the designs of various parts of the bomb—including the explosive lenses —without taking the time to iron out all known defects.*

A long-apparent, if little noted, fact is that the Greenglass sketches do not deal with the single most costly and time-consuming aspect of the Manhattan Project's mission: The production of fissionable material in the mammoth plants at Hanford and Oak Ridge. What now can be seen from the recently declassified Los Alamos data is how ludicrously little the sketches disclose even about the complex implosion research program, within which David was a minuscule cog.

Three of the sketches roughly depict lens molds and the technique used by Koski's subgroup to photograph imploding metal cylinders. They merely show work of which David himself had personal knowledge from

---

* Referring to the "crude design" of the early implosion bomb (code named the Fat Man), two official Los Alamos historians wrote after the war: ". . . the Fat Man, as it was used at Nagasaki, could hardly be called anything more than a scientific gadget; it was certainly not a weapon."

his shop job or might have learned about routinely. (As such, David's ability to draw these replica sketches for the prosecution is no indication at all of the truth or falsity of his story of espionage.)

As for the impounded "atom bomb" sketch, David never claimed that it was derived from any *official* source to which he somehow had managed to gain access. On the contrary, he testified that the information on which he based his version of the implosion bomb was compiled by him piecemeal from conversations heard around Los Alamos.

This explanation seems plausible enough. It is, after all, reasonable to assume that, immediately after the public announcement of the atom-bombing of Japan, security strictures at Los Alamos were informally relaxed a bit. For many, the news of Hiroshima was the first indication of the nature of the project on which they had been working. A flood of gossip and rumor must have been heard around the technical area where David was employed and in the barracks where he lived during the week. Quite a number of the soldiers at Los Alamos had college educations and some scientific training and they doubtlessly speculated about the mode of operation of the bomb. Moreover, even before the Japanese surrender, the Army released the fact-crammed Smyth report with an enormous store of formerly top-secret data, including detailed information about the newly created fissionable metal, plutonium, and a description of a gun-type atomic bomb.

In addition, many elements of David's conception of the atom bomb may also have been culled by him from newspapers. For example, on August 7, 1945, a front-page story in the Santa Fe *New Mexican*—a newspaper distributed at Los Alamos—presented a whimsical explanation of the bomb and referred to "implosion." A few days later, another story, headlined "First Atomic Bomb Obsolete Even as No. 2 Hit Nagasaki," revealed that there were two models of the bomb and that the improved model had been used at Nagasaki. Soon after, the same paper carried a question and answer feature on the bomb, mentioning the long-known scientific fact that beryllium—one component of the "Greenglass bomb"—could serve as a neutron source.

During the Rosenberg-Sobell trial, the Associated Press reported that Greenglass had stated in his impounded testimony that the implosion bomb "was dropped by parachute." Later, in another context, former AEC chairman Gordon Dean wrote: "In the press of the day [1945] . . . one may find reports of how both the Hiroshima and Nagasaki bombs were dropped by parachute. Actually, neither was." Thus, the account of David's testimony about a "parachute" provides an interesting clue as to the origin of some of his information on the atom bomb—and its accuracy.

According to the prosecution's technical witnesses, the Greenglass sketches illustrate the principle of implosion, which was employed in the

Nagasaki bomb. However, implosion, as such, was no dark secret unearthed by Manhattan Project scientists. The word, denoting a "bursting inward" reaction, has long appeared in dictionaries, and the idea that this reaction could be used to assemble fissionable material rapidly was an obvious one. Furthermore, while *utilizing* an implosion reaction in a workable bomb requires a very high order of technical ability, one would certainly expect to find such a level of competence in any nation capable of the far more difficult and lengthy task of producing fissionable material.

Great Britain, whose scientists—including Fuchs—not only knew that the Nagasaki bomb was detonated by implosion but also participated in and had access to all aspects of implosion research at Los Alamos, did not test its first atomic bomb until 1952—seven years after the United States and three years after the Soviet Union. A number of nations are reported to be presently striving to develop atomic bombs. Would anyone today seriously suggest that the Greenglass sketches would advance their time-table by a *single day*?

Yet what may seem transparent nonsense now was widely accepted only yesterday. It is a melancholy commentary that in the United States of America, in the middle decade of the twentieth century, millions of citizens in all walks of life apparently agreed with Judge Kaufman that the machinist Greenglass had given away "the atom bomb secret," thus "putting into the hands of the Russians the A-bomb years before our best scientists" predicted they would perfect it.

Still, even in the period between the trial and executions, not everyone, in or out of the government, accepted this fantasy. One of the handful of publications which did not, *Scientific American*, observed:

"The relative unimportance of Greenglass' disclosure was confirmed after the trial by the Joint Congressional Committee on Atomic Energy in a report on Soviet atomic espionage." The Joint Committee report—issued long before the executions—evaluated the deeds of four alleged atom spies (Fuchs, Pontecorvo, Nunn May, and Greenglass) and concluded that ". . . Greenglass appears to have been the least effective of the four. . . ."

It is noteworthy that all of the most extravagant claims regarding the import of the Rosenbergs' crime came from the Department of Justice, the Judiciary, and the White House, but that no such statement ever has been made by the one organ of the government in the best position to know the truth—the Atomic Energy Commission. Nine months after the electrocutions, some indication of the Commission's thinking on the subject of atomic espionage was provided by a high AEC official in a speech to a meeting of industrialists in New York City. Reported the *Times:*

"The man in the Atomic Energy Commission responsible for classifying nuclear data warned here yesterday that an 'ostrich-like' attitude about atomic secrets could lead to a national catastrophe.

"Dr. James Beckerley, director of the Atomic Energy Commission Classification Office, said it was time to stop 'kidding' ourselves about atomic 'secrets,' and time to stop believing that Soviet scientists are incompetent.

". . . The atom bomb and the hydrogen bomb were not stolen from us by spies, Dr. Beckerley emphasized. Espionage played a minor role in the attainment of successful weapons by the Soviets, he said. . . .

" 'The Russians have the skills and the plants to make fission materials and bombs. . . . We must shake off our complacency and recognize the extent to which the Soviets present real competition in atomic science. . . .'

"Atom bombs and hydrogen bombs are not matters that can be stolen and transmitted in the form of information Dr. Beckerley said, in emphasizing the relative unimportance of spying in nuclear physics."

These comments acquire added relevance from the fact that they were made by a man who was thoroughly familiar with the Greenglass sketches and testimony. During the trial James Beckerley had sat at the prosecution table as an AEC representative and, prior to the court proceedings, he had personally questioned David for many hours.

Yet, in the course of the Rosenberg-Sobell trial, prosecutor Saypol repeatedly had sought to convey the impression that the AEC concurred in his assessment that the "scientific secrets" secured by the accused were "the most important . . . ever known to mankind." Referring to the presence at the prosecution table of AEC representatives (including Beckerley), the U. S. Attorney had indicated that the AEC was extremely anxious about the disclosure at the trial by Greenglass of atomic secrets. Commented Saypol during Koski's testimony about David's lens mold sketches:

"Will your Honor allow a statement for the record . . . ? The Atomic Energy Commission has declassified this information under the Atomic Energy Act and has made the ruling as authorized by Congress that subsequent to the trial it is to be reclassified."

Again, when the "atom bomb" sketch was under discussion, Saypol characterized the matter as one of "gravity" and said that he and his staff had been in "constant consultation" about it with "representatives of the Atomic Energy Commission." Describing the impounding incident, *Look* magazine noted:

"So secret was the material he [Greenglass] had passed to Rosenberg that there was a great debate within the Government as to whether it would jeopardize the security of the nation to reveal it in open court."

A severe critic of the entire impounding procedure—and particularly Emanuel Bloch's role in it—is Irwin Edelman (whose pamphlet on this and other aspects of the trial provoked attorneys Farmer and Marshall to enter the case). A few years after the executions, Edelman wrote to

Beckerley, raising questions about the propriety of the impounding. In his inquiry, Edelman also noted Saypol's remarks that the lens mold information had been "declassified" for the trial and would be "reclassified" afterward, and asked Beckerley: "Did Mr. Saypol have a basis for that statement?"

Replied the former director of the AEC's Classification Office:

"To me, the Saypol statement on 'reclassifying' was unclear. . . . Obviously we had no objection to publication of the Greenglass testimony; Mr. Bloch moved to impound the record, not us.

"The position of the AEC in this trial is not generally appreciated. We were not so much concerned with what Greenglass might reveal in the courtroom. . . . The concern was with what the prosecution's technical witnesses might reveal under cross-examination."

Since Beckerley's letter makes clear that the AEC never had any objection to the Greenglass sketch and testimony being made public, the authors asked Judge Kaufman to set aside his impounding order and release the material still locked in the vault in Room 602 at Foley Square. In 1962, over eleven years after the trial, the Judge (now a member of the United States Court of Appeals) denied the request. Citing no evidence, he declared that he has said previously and still adhered to the view that it was "in the best interests of the country that the order stand."

In addition to David Greenglass's testimony about the passage of atom bomb information, he also recounted at the trial a number of other acts of espionage allegedly committed by Rosenberg. Describing the scene at the Rosenberg apartment in September 1945 (when his implosion bomb write-up was being typed and corrected for grammatical errors), David said: "While this was going on, sometimes there would be stretches where . . . there wasn't too much changing to be made, and at this time Julius told me that he had stolen the proximity fuse when he was working at Emerson Radio. . . . He told me that he took it out in his briefcase. That is the same briefcase he brought his lunch in with, and he gave it to Russia."

According to David, in the postwar years (long after his own ten-month service as a spy had ended), Julius Rosenberg had, on occasion, related further details of his espionage exploits. Asked Roy Cohn: "Did Rosenberg mention to you any Government projects concerning which he had obtained information from any of his contacts?"

DAVID: Well, once in the presence of my brother, he mentioned a sky platform project. . . . I had a conversation with him later. I asked him in privacy. . . . I would say this was in '47, late '47.* He told

* In December 1948 Defense Secretary James Forrestal referred in a public report to an "earth satellite vehicle program" and this was discussed in the press at the time.

me he had gotten this information about the sky platform from one
of the boys, as he put it. . . .

COHN: How did he describe it?

DAVID: He said that it was some large vessel which would be suspended
at a point of no gravity between the moon and the earth and as a
satellite it would spin around the earth. . . .

COHN: Let me ask you this, did he mention any other projects, Government projects concerning which he had obtained information?

DAVID: He once stated to me in the presence of a worker of ours that
they had solved the problem of atomic energy for airplanes, and later
on I asked him if this was true, and he said that he had gotten
the mathematics on it, the mathematics was solved on this. . . . He
said he got it from one of his contacts.

Asked by the defense to clarify what he meant by "they," David replied: " 'They' meaning scientists in this country."

The foregoing excerpts are not merely a sampling from David's trial
testimony about the proximity fuse, sky platform, and atomic-powered
airplane; they constitute just about *everything* that he said on those subjects. No aspect of this brief testimony was corroborated or amplified
by any other prosecution witness.

Nearly two years after the trial, Julius Rosenberg was poring over a
transcript of the proceedings in his death house cell, searching for some
way to assist his defense. Writing to Emanuel Bloch, he added this postscript: "I've got a plan on a new investigation that I'm sure will be of
substantial help to us and prove Dave lied and I told the truth." Again,
in a letter to Bloch the next day, Julius noted: "Manny, I got a good
idea concerning the proximity fuse and an investigation to prove Dave a
liar." Finally, on February 16, 1953, Rosenberg sent his attorney a long
letter which outlined in detail the "investigation" he had in mind.*

Briefly, Rosenberg informed Bloch that his brief case at Emerson always
was crammed full of Signal Corps material essential to his job; that when
he did bring lunch from home he "always brought it in a paper bag";
that the "proximity fuse was a bulky item in size and shape and, even if
my briefcase was empty of the other material, and it never was, it would
bulk out quite a bit"; and that "whenever anyone came into the plant or
left it, armed security guards inspected the contents of the briefcase and
any packages." He concluded: "In short, even if someone wanted to commit the crime the setup at Emerson ruled out the possibility. . . ."

Far more important than Rosenberg's comments on the difficulty of
such a theft, however, was his suggestion that his attorney "could get

---

* This correspondence was among the original copies of the Rosenbergs' prison letters
seen by the authors.

positive proof from Emerson Radio that no proximity fuse was missing or stolen at any time and specifically during the time I worked there." Emphasizing the stringent inspection procedures at Emerson, Julius said: "Every subassembly and especially each complete assembly was accounted for and even the rejects were recorded and kept. . . . Never while I worked there were any units missing, lost, stolen or unaccounted for.

"A real thorough job can be done on this one single item that Greenglass slipped and said something specific [about]. . . ."

Exactly what action the defense attorney took in response to this letter is unknown to the authors; Bloch is deceased (he died at age fifty-two of a heart attack less than eight months after the executions) and a search of his files produced no pertinent information. In his letter, Rosenberg named a top Emerson official and also a number of Signal Corps officers and a civilian employee who he said could verify his statements. According to a former newspaperman who told the authors that he had assisted Bloch in this research,* the attorney did contact at least some of these individuals, seeking affidavits that might be submitted to the courts as a basis for a legal hearing on the subject. No one agreed to provide a voluntary statement and, since Bloch lacked subpoena power, the matter was dropped.

At the trial, neither the prosecution nor the defense had called anyone from the Emerson company to testify about the proximity fuse allegedly stolen from that firm. Julius's letter strongly suggests that, so far as the defense was concerned, the failure to call a witness was an oversight rather than a conscious decision.

As for the prosecution, one can only assume that prior to the trial the FBI must have followed up David's proximity fuse story by checking with Emerson to learn if a fuse had been reported missing at the time. (*Out of David's entire testimony about the crime, his account of the stolen proximity fuse was the only incident amenable to at least some objective confirmation.*) Since no evidence of a theft from Emerson was presented by the prosecution, it would seem a near certainty that no such proof ever was found.

On October 4, 1957, Americans were astounded by the news that the Soviet Union had orbited a space satellite. For some, the achievement was an educational revelation regarding the ability of Soviet scientists. Others, however, still clung tenaciously to their fond illusion that no nation on earth could possibly surpass American scientific and industrial knowhow. If the Soviet Union built an atomic bomb and a hydrogen bomb with impressive dispatch, it could have accomplished these feats only through espionage. If the Soviet Union scored the first breakthrough in

* Leon Summit.

the exploration of space, it must be that traitors in the United States were to blame.

In support of this thesis, the Chicago *Tribune* ran a front-page banner headline on October 12, proclaiming: "Bare Theft of Moon Data."

The paper's lead story elaborated:

"Russian spies stole American satellite secrets to enable the launching of the earth 'moon' now racing around the world at an 18,000 mile an hour pace.

"Evidence of Red theft of American satellite secrets was made available to THE TRIBUNE tonight from government sources in the transcript of the trial of Julius and Ethel Rosenberg. . . ."

Below pictures of David Greenglass and the Rosenbergs, the newspaper printed Greenglass's trial testimony on both the sky platform and atomic-powered airplane.

The next morning's newspapers credited former U. S. Attorney Myles Lane with having drawn the connection between David's six-year-old testimony and the Soviet space performance. Referring to the alleged transmission of American "earth satellite secrets" to Russia, Lane said: "The fact that the Soviets launched Sputnik last week did not surprise me in the least."

Several days later, a staff member of the Senate Internal Security subcommittee visited Greenglass in prison. A Senate probe into the theft of American space secrets—with Greenglass as star witness—was reported in the offing. Predicted the Chicago *Tribune* in another page one headline: "U.S. May Reopen Spy Chain Hunt; Moon Stirs Rosenberg Link Study."

The promised inquiry never was held. On November 21, 1957, at a public hearing, the Senate group's chief counsel, Robert Morris, announced that the subcommittee had sought to question Greenglass (and Gold) about "the extent to which espionage has assisted the Soviets in making their tremendous scientific progress," but the Department of Justice had refused permission for the men to leave prison to testify. Morris had therefore journeyed to Lewisburg Penitentiary, earlier that day, and had interviewed Greenglass there.

According to Morris, David Greenglass advised the United States Senate that "the Soviet Sputnik represents a tremendous sophistication of electronics development, that what they have done in electronics, that is, the equipment up in Sputnik, has been tremendous; it is prodigious." Moreover, Morris said that Greenglass had informed him that Julius Rosenberg "had been given the assignment of getting for the electronic industry in the Soviet Union every possible bit of information in the United States involving electronics."

Noting that he had "an affidavit which another subcommittee of Congress has permitted us to use, from David Greenglass, about the anti-missile missile," Morris asserted: "I was able to get some further information from Greenglass about this, as well as some information about the atomic powered airplane. . . ."

The presiding officer at the hearing, Senator John M. Butler, evinced immediate keen interest in the "antimissile missile." However, it soon developed that the affidavit in question was four years old. In it, Greenglass had mentioned to Senator McCarthy's investigators an electronic device called a "think machine," now referred to by Morris as an antimissile missile.

Next morning's *Times* headlined a story on the hearings: "Rosenbergs Cited as Missile Spies." The Philadelphia *News* reported: "Robert Morris, committee chief counsel, disclosed that executed spies Julius and Ethel Rosenberg had fed Russia our secrets on space platforms, atom-powered planes and anti-missile missiles."

However, the story never caught on. The mood and sophistication of the country were changing rapidly. With no American satellite yet launched, the Russians had again surprised the West by putting up a second and far heavier space vehicle, carrying a small dog named Laika. Then too, perhaps the long-dormant American sense of humor was reasserting itself. Poking fun at Morris, the New York *Herald-Tribune* editorialized:

"One view: Counsel Robert Morris of the Senate Internal Security Committee said convicted atom spy David Greenglass told them that Julius Rosenberg gave earth satellite secrets to the Russians shortly after World War II.

"Comment: What secrets were these? If some carbon copies of them are still left in the Defense Department files, maybe they could be dusted out from the cobwebs and put into action."

About a year later, the magazine *Aviation Week* published an unconfirmed report that the Soviet Union had developed a nuclear-powered aircraft. Predictably, attention immediately was drawn to David Greenglass's testimony on the subject. Headlined the New York *World-Telegram & Sun* on December 4, 1958: "Reds' Theft of A-Plane Data Hinted In Rosenberg Trial Record." Once again, former U. S. Attorney Lane was named as the source who had connected David's trial testimony with the rumored Soviet advance. Lane added no new information to the oft-quoted testimony; in fact, he revealed that "Greenglass had indicated in pretrial questioning that he knew nothing further about the matter."

The newspaper observed:

"If Greeenglass' testimony was accurate, it apparently took years for Soviet scientists to translate the stolen theoretical data into actual satellites and atomic planes. It is considered possible, however, that the stolen information cut years from the time which the Russians would otherwise have needed."

Actually, there is no evidence that the Soviet Union has succeeded as yet in utilizing atomic power in an operational airplane; certainly the United States has not. On March 28, 1961, in a special message to Congress on the defense budget, President Kennedy stated: "Nearly fifteen years and about $1,000,000,000 have been devoted to the attempted development of a nuclear-powered aircraft; but the possibility of achieving a militarily useful aircraft in the foreseeable future is still very remote." Announcing the cancellation of the project, the President said that this would save at least a billion dollars in additional expenditures "which would have been necessary to achieve first experimental flight."

In the years since the Rosenberg-Sobell trial, Americans have learned much about the cost, complexity, and scope of the great technological projects of our time. Such projects—particularly in the fields of atomic energy and space exploration—grow out of and express the total industrial fabric of a nation; they offer few, if any, possibilities for the theft of meaningful "secrets." The light of a new decade has revealed the executions of the Rosenbergs as a deed naked of the justification in which it was clothed.

Still, the question at hand remains unanswered. Was the crime exaggerated—or invented? Were the Rosenbergs and Sobell guilty of the legal charge of conspiring to commit espionage for the Soviet Union?

CHAPTER 23

IN SEARCH OF A SPY RING

Julius Rosenberg was presented at his trial and has since been regarded as a master spy—the chief planner, pay-off man, and recruiter for a Soviet espionage ring which had enlisted the services of a considerable number of Americans.

If this allegation is true, an investigation of it might well be expected to yield evidence corroborating the guilt of the defendants. However, such an investigation is no simple matter. Attempts to follow the spy ring story as it has evolved lead one on a circumlocutory route.

When Rosenberg was arrested by the FBI in the Korean War summer of 1950, he first was described by J. Edgar Hoover as "another important link in the Soviet espionage apparatus which includes Dr. Klaus Fuchs." By fall of that year, a total of nine so-called "links" had been apprehended and publicly identified with what the press quickly dubbed the "Klaus Fuchs spy ring."

In vaguely worded but highly incriminating news accounts, all nine* were connected with atomic espionage, Klaus Fuchs, and each other. However, after the journalistic sound and fury had subsided somewhat, subsequent courtroom proceedings showed that many of these implied connections were nonexistent.

For example, in September 1950, when Alfred Dean Slack pleaded guilty and was sentenced to fifteen years' imprisonment, he was revealed by the prosecutor to have committed only a "single, isolated violation," involving neither atomic energy nor even membership in any organized spy ring. Later, Slack moved, unsuccessfully, to withdraw his guilty plea, maintaining that he actually had violated no law because the material turned over to Gold was not secret. Asked why he had pleaded guilty, Slack replied:

"I had never been in a court of law before in my life. I did not know legal procedure. I had no idea as to what my rights were. I had written a report [on the explosive RDX] based on public information.

---

* Harry Gold, Alfred Dean Slack, David Greenglass, Julius and Ethel Rosenberg, Abraham Brothman, Miriam Moskowitz, Morton Sobell, and Oscar Vago.

It was my understanding that I had committed an offense by doing so. But I couldn't understand how it was possible.

". . . I had been accused of being a member of the Klaus Fuchs atomic spy ring, among other things . . . which was absolutely false and without foundation. . . . I had never heard of Klaus Fuchs until his name appeared in the newspapers. I certainly had no connection with any such act. But nevertheless, I was accused.

"At the same time, due to newspaper publicity, public hysteria was at a peak. It was my understanding and it was my belief that if this case went to trial in a court of law that public hysteria alone would convict me, and with that hysteria I would get the maximum sentence."

The Brothman-Moskowitz trial in November 1950 dispelled any hint of a connection between the defendants and either Fuchs or atomic espionage. In fact, quite apart from espionage, Miss Moskowitz was absolved completely of involvement in *any* kind of information passing, whether legal or not.

Similarly, Brothman's former business partner, Oscar Vago, who had been imprisoned on high bail and pictured in newspapers handcuffed to Julius Rosenberg, also was cleared eventually of any connection at all with espionage. Judge Sylvester J. Ryan, who in June 1952, at the defendant's request, heard the perjury case in lieu of a jury, criticized the prosecution for its nearly two-year delay in trying Vago and imposed a suspended sentence.

Judge Ryan said he had "the impression" that Vago, who had corrected his grand jury testimony within a week, had lied on a matter not relevant to the inquiry as a result of "poor and hasty judgment" and had done so "solely to protect himself and his wife from deportation." (Vago had overstayed a student visa when he arrived in the United States from Hungary many years before.) The Judge also pointed out that Vago had "done nothing which has warranted his indictment on any other charge, and I assume that the government made a very careful investigation . . . of his activities."

Thus, four of the nine individuals arrested in 1950 with such fanfare later were shown to have had no connection whatsoever with any atomic espionage ring, and only one, Harry Gold, ever was charged with any dealings with Klaus Fuchs. The press, aided and abetted by Department of Justice publicity releases, had distorted a number of essentially unrelated events into the semblance of a meaningful pattern. Before long, the patchwork concept of a "Klaus Fuchs spy ring" proved untenable and fell into disuse.

In March 1951, when the Rosenbergs and Sobell were tried, the prosecution described a whole new espionage network, with Julius Rosenberg as its leader. Rosenberg's pivotal role in the conspiracy was depicted graphically by Saypol, who told the jury:

"Imagine a wheel. In the center of the wheel, Rosenberg, reaching out like the tentacles of an octopus."

To whom was Rosenberg "reaching out"? The only alleged agents actually produced in court were his wife, brother-in-law, sister-in-law, and college classmate Sobell. However, the prosecution contended—with a minimum of evidence—that additional members of the "Rosenberg spy ring" were still at large.

From David Greenglass came nearly all the trial testimony regarding the existence and achievements of these other, unapprehended members of the ring. He had derived his information, he said, from conversations with Julius that took place, for the most part, during the postwar years when they were partners in the machine shop business. Though David was then no longer engaged in espionage activities, Julius allegedly had gossiped with his brother-in-law about the successes of his agents—euphemistically known as "the boys."

In these conversations, Julius had boasted about financing the higher education of various individuals with Soviet funds (David knew neither the recipients nor the schools); about securing data on a sky platform and an atomic-powered airplane from "the boys"; and about "people" in upstate New York and Ohio (Schenectady and Cleveland were mentioned) who gave him "information."*

Besides these vague references, Greenglass actually revealed the names of two alleged members of the Rosenberg spy ring who were not on trial: Ann Sidorovich and Joel Barr.

Ann Sidorovich was said by the Greenglasses to have been present at the Rosenberg apartment when they arrived for dinner in January 1945—the night the jello box side was cut in two. For about half an hour, everyone had engaged in "the usual pleasantries and playing with the child." *After Mrs. Sidorovich had left,* Julius informed his in-laws that he had arranged for her to be at the apartment so that they "would be able to recognize her" should she be the one to pick up information from them in the Southwest. (Actually, the rationale for this get-together was obscure: David had not met Mrs. Sidorovich previously, but Ruth had and the plan under discussion called for a rendezvous by the women.)

The Rosenbergs testified that they could not recollect whether or not Ann Sidorovich had visited their home at the same time as the Greenglasses. However, they described their relationship with her and her husband—a high-school acquaintance of Julius's—as entirely social, noting that, for about a year, the two families had been neighbors in the same building at Knickerbocker Village. In late 1944, the Sidoroviches had moved to Cleveland.

As for Ann Sidorovich herself, though listed as a potential prosecution

* Rosenberg testified that he never had visited either city.

witness, she did not appear at the trial. Saypol referred to her, un-equivocally, as a "woman espionage courier" and a "Soviet agent."

Joel Barr, a City College classmate of Rosenberg's, also was named by Greenglass as a member of the espionage group. David testified that, at the end of 1947, Julius had told him that "Joel Barr was leaving this country to study music in Belgium." (Rosenberg confirmed this detail, adding that Barr had stopped by the machine shop and mentioned to everyone present that he was going abroad.)

However, David testified that a subsequent conversation with his brother-in-law had put a completely different complexion on Barr's supposedly innocent trip "to study music." According to David, in February 1950, when he had complained of possible difficulties if he attempted to flee the country, Julius had said: "Oh, they let other people out who are more important than you are. . . . they let Barr out, Joel Barr, and he was a member of our espionage ring."

Though Barr had departed for Europe well over two years before Rosenberg's arrest, Saypol—without presenting any further evidence—asserted: ". . . Joel Barr fled the country. . . ."

In addition to David's meager hearsay testimony about Ann Sidorovich and Joel Barr, the prosecutor's pointed questions and press statements inferentially connected three other individuals—William Perl, Vivian Glassman, and Alfred Sarant—with the spy ring, though none was accused by any trial witness.

William Perl, a City College classmate of Rosenberg's, was first pub-licly linked with the case in the press, when he was arrested for perjury midway in the Rosenberg-Sobell trial. Newspapers quoted Saypol's re-marks that the arrested man had been slated for a role as a prosecution witness to corroborate the Greenglasses.

One of Saypol's assistants was reported by the *Times* to have "asserted that several suspects in the Soviet spy ring who associated with Perl 'have fled the jurisdiction and the Government is unaware of their where-abouts.'" Perl himself was said to have "received the offer of a 'consider-able sum' to flee the country after the arrest of Julius Rosenberg."

Additional details on this last incident were divulged in the New York *World-Telegram & Sun*, which stated: ". . . in Cleveland last summer a Miss Vivian Glassman of Manhattan offered Perl 'a substantial sum of money to flee the jurisdiction of the court.'"

Vivian Glassman's name was soon after brought into the trial by Saypol, who interrogated Julius Rosenberg about her. Miss Glassman, Julius said, had been introduced to him and his wife by Joel Barr and had been "Barr's sweetheart." After Barr went to Europe, she had con-tinued to visit the Rosenbergs' home. Julius testified that in recent years "almost every time" he had seen Miss Glassman, who was a social worker, he had discussed the emotional problems of his elder son with her and, as a result of these talks, the child had been entered into treatment at the Jewish Board of Guardians, with which she was affiliated.

SAYPOL: What else did you talk to Vivian Glassman about?
JULIUS: I had nothing else to talk to her about but that.
SAYPOL: Did you ever give her any money?
JULIUS: No, sir; never did.
SAYPOL: Did you ever send her on a trip to Cleveland?
JULIUS: No, sir; never did. . . .
SAYPOL: Isn't it the fact that you gave her $2000 to take out to somebody in Cleveland?
JULIUS: That is not the fact, Mr. Saypol.

This line of questioning—with frequent references to "money" allegedly given by Julius to Vivian Glassman—was pursued for some time by Saypol but, inexplicably, the woman in question, though listed as a witness, never was called to testify about the incident.

Alfred Sarant, a friend of Barr's, also was the subject of the prosecutor's questions:

SAYPOL: Where did you first meet him [Sarant]?
JULIUS: I met him when he was introduced to me by his friend, Joel Barr. I met him in an apartment they were sharing in Greenwich Village.
SAYPOL: Where was that?
JULIUS: I don't recall the exact name of the street. It begins with an M. It is either—
SAYPOL: 65 Morton Street, isn't it?
JULIUS: Morton, that is the place, Morton Street.
SAYPOL: You couldn't remember that, could you?
JULIUS: You just asked me and I told you.

Questioned as to Sarant's present whereabouts, Julius replied: "In Ithaca."

SAYPOL: How do you know that he is in Ithaca now?
JULIUS: Well, I saw the name of his wife on the witness list, and the address is given as Ithaca. . . .
SAYPOL: You have no other knowledge of his whereabouts, is that it?
JULIUS: No, I have no way of knowing.
SAYPOL: Don't you know that he is in Mexico?

This query by the prosecutor elicited an immediate defense motion for a mistrial. One of Sobell's attorneys pointed out that Saypol's cross-examination was "deliberately prejudicial" because Sarant "was never mentioned in this case" and "all through the trial the word 'Mexico'" had implied flight.

Thus, by one means or another, the prosecution tenuously connected five of Julius Rosenberg's friends and classmates—Mrs. Sidorovich, Barr, Perl, Glassman, and Sarant—with the alleged espionage ring and cast an aura of suspicion over a Greenwich Village apartment at 65 Morton Street. *Yet not one of the five thus "linked" with a capital crime was indicted, named as a co-conspirator, or even called as a witness.*

Summing up, Saypol declared: "The identity of some of the other traitors who sold their country down the river along with Rosenberg and Sobell remains undisclosed. We know that such people exist because of Rosenberg's boasting to Greenglass of the extent of his espionage activities. . . . We know of these other henchmen of Rosenberg. . . . We don't know all the details, because the only living people who can supply the details are the defendants."

Similar reasoning was advanced by Saypol's successor, Myles Lane, when, twenty-one months later, he spoke forcefully against granting judicial clemency to the condemned husband and wife. Said he:

"I submit that on the evidence which has been introduced to the Court, and on other material which I personally know of, that the Rosenbergs are the centers or were the centers of a real widespread network of spies, and if I am correct, the Rosenbergs have ample information which, if they wanted to cooperate, could lead to the detection of any number of people who, in my opinion, are today doing everything that they can to obtain additional information for the Soviet Union."

Soon after, when Executive clemency also was denied the Rosenbergs, *Time* magazine observed that the doomed couple's only remaining "opportunity of escape" was to confess "the secrets of their spy ring."

Yet despite the apparent certitude of Saypol, Lane, and most of the press, no alleged "other henchmen" of Rosenberg's ever have been brought to trial on espionage charges, although one of those "linked" with the spy ring, William Perl, was tried for perjury.

The trial of the former Columbia University physics instructor commenced on May 18, 1953, just one month before the Rosenbergs' deaths. Perl, then thirty-four, was charged with four counts of perjury growing out of testimony he had given over two and a half years earlier before a federal grand jury. He had denied knowing Julius Rosenberg, Morton Sobell, Helene Elitcher, or Michael and Ann Sidorovich.

In subsequent grand jury appearances, Perl partially retracted these denials, explaining that he now had "an awareness" of Rosenberg from their days as CCNY classmates and could "recall" Sobell at college and also had seen him "several times" after graduation. (However, he reiterated his previous testimony regarding Helene Elitcher and the Sidoro-viches.)

Perl's defense hinged mainly on his subjective interpretation of the word "know" in the grand jury's questions to him. He claimed that at first he honestly had forgotten "knowing" both Rosenberg and Sobell. If so, his memory may well have been influenced by his admitted eagerness to disassociate himself from his accused classmates because, as he said, "I am afraid of anything that would tend to prevent me from doing physics."

Perl testified: "In the summer of 1950, I was working extremely hard at NACA [National Advisory Committee for Aeronautics], Cleveland laboratory, winding up some aerodynamic problems and trying to get set for . . . teaching and research . . . at Columbia University. . . . Suddenly, in July . . . I became subject to a very intensive investigation by the FBI, very frequent interrogations in connection with the Rosenberg-Sobell case . . . . this sudden entrance into my life of a sort of attempted domination of my life by the FBI produced a very strange atmosphere for me. I had nothing in my experience to tie this kind of thing to. . . ."

Noting that an FBI agent had told him that "Rosenberg and Sobell were going to 'fry,'" Perl commented: "The newspaper details of the case . . . and the FBI's strong emphasis to me that Rosenberg and Sobell faced the death penalty horrified and shocked me."

Not long after this "intensive investigation by the FBI" had begun, Vivian Glassman paid a most peculiar visit to Perl at his Cleveland apartment. Perl described the visit in grand jury testimony made public at his trial:

"About noon on this Sunday afternoon [in the latter part of July 1950], while I was preparing to go out on a picnic, Vivian Glassman suddenly appeared. . . . I was quite surprised. I recognized her as a friend of Joel Barr's. I asked her to come in. She acted somewhat mysteriously. She proceeded to take some paper which I had lying around and start writing on it and motioning me to read what she had written and, well she wrote to the effect that she had instructions from a person unknown to her, in New York, to travel to Cleveland to get in touch with an aeronautical engineer to give him money and instructions to leave the country, and I believe she mentioned Mexico in that connection. . . .

"Well, I was very upset. I mentioned something about . . . I did not understand what this was all about. I believe I possibly mentioned that I thought it was a trap of some kind, words to that effect. I was feeling rather incoherent at the time. . . . Well, I told her that I thought she had better go. I ushered her out. . . . As I say, I was very upset, and I had been questioned by the FBI for the previous week or two, and this coming on top of it all, made me feel very, well, upset, so I decided that I should consult . . . a lawyer, which I. . . . tried to, the following morning. . . . I got him [the lawyer] on Tuesday, told him this whole story, and wrote out a statement regarding it and submitted it to the FBI, I think it was . . . Wednesday. . . . Of course I had been reading about the spy cases in the papers. She did mention in writing that she knew Julius Rosenberg. Well, here was something I was being asked, to flee the country for some reason. And so all I could think of was that somebody was trying to trap me into something, since I had no reason to leave."

Perl revealed that about early March 1951, shortly before the start of the Rosenberg-Sobell trial, he had been called to a meeting at Foley Square attended by various FBI agents and assistant U.S. attorneys involved in the preparation of the impending espionage case. One of those present was Roy Cohn. Perl recounted: ". . . Mr. Roy Cohn informed me that . . . if I did not confess I would be indicted." He said he had replied to Cohn that "I had nothing to confess, but whatever he or anybody else had against me, I would very much like to hear in open court."

Perl's indictment for perjury followed and, immediately afterward, prosecution spokesmen publicly disclosed details of Vivian Glassman's offer to him of instructions and money to flee the country. The obvious inference is that the prosecution, failing to gain Perl's cooperation as a witness, had timed his indictment for a moment when the resulting publicity might influence the Rosenberg-Sobell trial, then in mid-course. What the prosecution spokesmen neglected to reveal to the press, however, was the rather significant fact that Perl had immediately turned down Miss Glassman's curious offer and had himself reported it to the FBI.

For over two years after his indictment, Perl's attempts to avail himself of his constitutional right to a "speedy" trial were countered by repeated delays, requested by the government for undisclosed reasons of "security." However, the Perl perjury trial, when finally held, produced no revelations concerning espionage, though some of the testimony involved persons previously "connected" with the Rosenberg spy ring. Interestingly, this testimony indicated that, whatever else the relationship of these people may have encompassed, at least one aspect of it was purely social.

A Rosenberg-Sobell case witness, Max Elitcher, testified at the Perl trial about an evening he and his wife had spent in summer 1944 with Rosenberg, Barr, Perl, and a number of others. Questioned by Assistant U. S. Attorney Lloyd F. MacMahon, Elitcher recalled that after eating at an inexpensive Manhattan restaurant the group had gone to Joel Barr's apartment.

MACMAHON: What did you do after you got up there?
ELITCHER: . . . We played music. There was a little dancing and we had sandwiches later on. . . .
MACMAHON: Do you recall any of the subjects that were discussed that evening?

ELITCHER: Well, other than general conversation we talked about a course in music that Joel Barr was taking, and we talked about a music book that he had been using in the course, and I was interested. I subsequently bought a copy of the book.

Barr then invited the Elitchers, Rosenberg, and Perl to visit a friend of his, Alfred Sarant, who lived at 65 Morton Street in Greenwich Village.

MACMAHON: What did you do after you got there?
ELITCHER: Actually, we awakened Sarant, and we were introduced to him. We talked. . . . We played classical guitar music, and he also had some recordings of guitar music which he played for us.

About Christmas 1946, Elitcher testified, he and his wife had dined at a restaurant with Rosenberg, Barr, Perl, and the Sobells. Afterward, everyone had gone to the Rosenbergs' home, where Ethel had prepared a party. Elitcher recalled seeing a Christmas tree and a Chanukah Menorah at the apartment.

MACMAHON: Do you recall any of the subjects that were discussed that night?
ELITCHER: Well, it was Christmas time, and we talked about the religious upbringing of children, specifically Jewish and Christian children, the problems that are involved in bringing them up.

The prosecution also produced evidence at the trial showing that, in 1945, Perl had purchased a guitar through Joel Barr and, in 1947 and 1948, while studying at Columbia, he had sublet Alfred Sarant's 65 Morton Street apartment, paying rent by money order to Sarant (then at Cornell University) and using the address on his voter registration. Afterward, Perl had failed to list 65 Morton Street as one of his residences on a security questionnaire and, in a statement to a loyalty board, had sought to minimize his association with both Barr and Sarant.

By way of explanation, Perl testified that while undergoing a loyalty investigation he had been visited by FBI agents who "questioned me about Barr and Sarant and stated that they had evidence that Barr and Sarant were members of the Communist Party." He said he had no personal knowledge that either man was a Communist but had played down his relationship with them. "I was afraid I would lose my job if they [the loyalty board] got an impression that I was associated with Communists."

The Perl jury returned a verdict of not guilty on counts relating to Helene Elitcher and the Sidoroviches; guilty on counts relating to Rosenberg and Sobell, with a recommendation of clemency.

When Perl's lawyer asked the judge to continue bail pending sentence,

Assistant U. S. Attorney Robert Martin opposed this request, stating that the government had information that would "link this defendant with the Rosenberg espionage ring directly." As for the nature of the information, Martin was "sorry that we cannot make it public at this time."

The four-day Perl trial had not until then been featured prominently in the press. However, the next morning the New York *Times* ("Perl Guilty of Perjury in Spy Case; Link to Rosenbergs Now Charged") and *Herald-Tribune* ("New Atom Spy Angle, Perl Guilty of Perjury; Tied to Rosenberg Ring") lifted the Perl story from inside to page one.

When Perl appeared for sentencing a few weeks later, Assistant U. S. Attorney Lloyd MacMahon urged "a most severe sentence" because the defendant "was concealing his personal and direct knowledge of the activities of Julius Rosenberg, Morton Sobell and other persons involved in espionage on behalf of the Soviet Union."

As justification for this grave charge, MacMahon cited a number of alleged connections between Perl and various tainted persons and places. Typical was the prosecutor's assertion that Perl had been present when Alfred Sarant's apartment at 65 Morton Street, "used by Rosenberg and his associates," was vacated in January 1950, "approximately the same time as Klaus Fuchs was arrested in England." Unexplained was how Fuchs's arrest in February 1950 might have influenced the vacating of the Morton Street apartment—*the previous month.*

More to the point than this misleading juxtaposition of events was whether Perl had been involved in or had knowledge of the illegal passage of classified information. Nowhere in his presentation did the prosecutor make such a claim.

The Judge, ignoring the jury's clemency recommendation, gave Perl the maximum sentence: Five years.

Soon after, the *Times* (describing the imprisoned scientist as "one of America's foremost experts on jet propulsion")commented: "The Government has indicated that the death of the Rosenbergs will not end the story of their espionage. . . . the Justice Department says it is now in a position to link Perl to the spy network."

Newspaper publicity aside, following the Perl perjury trial the Justice Department never attempted—through legal charges tried in a court of law—to "link" Perl or anyone else with Julius Rosenberg's alleged espionage network. Nevertheless, the last had not been heard of the Rosenberg spy ring.

Four months after the Rosenbergs were electrocuted, a *Times* headline—similar to ones being carried by newspapers all over the nation—read: "Rosenberg Called Radar Spy Leader: McCarthy Says Ring He Set Up 'May Still Be in Operation' at Monmouth Laboratory." Senator Joseph R. McCarthy had launched his sensational investigation of the

United States Army Signal Corps laboratories at Fort Monmouth, New Jersey. His chief committee counsel, Roy Cohn, later noted:

"It was the Julius Rosenberg (atomic espionage) trial that sent us to Fort Monmouth. Rosenberg had worked at Fort Monmouth. We wanted to know what he did there and what and who he left behind him. We found plenty."

McCarthy was at the peak of his influence and popularity as he opened the hearings. Wrote the New York *Journal-American* on October 17, 1953, in an editorial entitled "Dig, Joe!":

". . . now it appears more than possible that the atom spy ring of Julius Rosenberg was operating also at Fort Monmouth. The executed spy worked as a civilian specialist there in 1942-'43.

"This clue is so hot that Sen. McCarthy is going today to the Federal Penitentiary at Lewisburg, Pa., to question David Greenglass. . . .

"Fantastic? So was the Rosenberg story when it broke. We are facing a fantastic, evil enemy, and the Monmouth disclosures are building up into a fantastic, evil conspiracy. We may be thankful that we can depend on Sen. McCarthy to dig it up."

McCarthy's roving aides, Roy Cohn and G. David Schine, visited Greenglass in prison and obtained from him an affidavit, in question and answer form, which Cohn read into the committee record. In allegations completely absent from his trial testimony, Greenglass had told his interviewers: "I learned that the Rosenberg ring took and obtained secrets from the Army Signal Corps and transmitted them to Russia. . . ."

COHN: Was Rosenberg the only member of the ring who committed espionage in the Signal Corps?

DAVID: No. There were others.

COHN: Would you give us details on what you know about the others?

DAVID: Yes. There was Joel Barr. He worked out at Fort Monmouth. . . . and later he worked with Sperry Gyroscope. . . . Julius had told me that Barr was one of those who had given him information on electronic apparatus. . . . [and] on the thinking machines. . . .

COHN: When did the operation of the Rosenberg ring which had as its purpose the obtaining of radar secrets for Russia stop?

DAVID: As far as I know these operations never stopped and could very possibly be continuing to this very day. . . .

COHN: Do you know Vivian Glassman?

DAVID: Yes, I do. . . . I first met Vivian Glassman after the war, around 1946. . . . at Julius' and Ethel's apartment where I was told that she worked for some kind of a board that dealt with . . . children. . . . I later learned from Julius that Joel and Vivian were keeping company together.

COHN: Did you believe Vivian Glassman to be a member of the Rosenberg spy ring?

DAVID: After Julius Rosenberg told me about Joel Barr, I knowing about the relationship between Joel Barr and Vivian Glassman, came to the conclusion that Vivian Glassman was involved in some way.

McCarthy claimed that Greenglass also had supplied other names, in addition to those in the deposition, and said that these "leads" would now be "run down." However, whatever else David Greenglass may have told the team of Cohn and Schine, the fact is that most of the "leads" utilized by the Wisconsin Senator in his Monmouth hearings came, by one means or another, from a different source: The FBI.

Observed the Washington *Post*:

"Senator Joseph R. McCarthy's investigation of Fort Monmouth indicates he has obtained access to information which originated with the FBI, but which the FBI was unable to present as legal evidence for any court case.

"McCarthy . . . has repeatedly referred to what he said witnesses told, or failed to tell, the Federal Bureau of Investigation when it was breaking the Rosenberg spy ring. . . .

"That investigation produced a mass of information, much of it not usable in the espionage trial. . . . It now appears that the Army's Fort Monmouth security suspensions—and McCarthy's inquiry—are based in large part on that residue of the FBI investigation."

In the course of the Monmouth hearings, McCarthy subpoenaed scores of present and past employees of the Fort, as well as a number of witnesses with little or no discernible relationship to the Signal Corps establishment. Among those called were Vivian Glassman, the ex-wife of Alfred Sarant, and Ann Sidorovich. (Miss Glassman and Alfred Sarant had been wartime civilian employees at Monmouth; Mrs. Sidorovich never had worked there.)*

Generally overlooked in the excitement of the hearings was a terse official comment issued by the Army, revealing that information from Fort Monmouth had been freely available to the Soviet Union while that nation was America's wartime ally. Added journalist Murrey Marder in the *Bulletin of the Atomic Scientists*: ". . . the Russians had official representatives actually in Fort Monmouth, handling classified documents, during World War II. . . . Classified communications equipment was being given to the Russians under Lend Lease; they did not have to steal it."

Some suggestion as to the manner in which the Monmouth hearings were conducted may be deduced from a query thrust by McCarthy at a

---

* The Monmouth investigation never resulted in a single indictment of any individual named or called by the committee.

witness who invoked the Fifth Amendment. Said the Senator: "Let me ask you this question: Julius Rosenberg was convicted of espionage and he has been executed. From your answers here, apparently you were engaged and still are engaged in the same type of espionage. Do you feel that you should be walking the streets of this country free, or that you should have the same fate as the Rosenbergs?"

Throughout the "investigation," McCarthy perpetrated hoax after hoax on a gullible press, with one such incident resulting in the most flamboyant headlines of the entire hearings. As described by the *Times*, McCarthy emerged from a closed-door committee session to announce to reporters a "most important development"—a close friend of Julius Rosenberg's had broken down in tears "under some rather vigorous cross-examination by Roy Cohn" and had agreed to tell all. Reporters saw a doctor and a nurse carrying medical equipment hurriedly enter a room and were informed that the witness was "shaking with fright."

Asked if the man was a member of the Rosenberg spy ring, McCarthy replied: "I don't want to say how much he participated in it." Declaring that the man would be placed in protective custody, McCarthy said: "The witness has indicated a great fear of the spy ring. . . ."

Nothing more was heard of this much-publicized "important development" until weeks later when the witness (a CCNY classmate of Rosenberg's) granted a newspaper interview to counter the persecution he said was being visited on his family by neighbors. He denied every aspect of the McCarthy story save one: He had indeed broken down under a barrage of questions—as a result of the intense stress he was under following the death of his mother two days previously.

In addition to McCarthy's frequent references to the Rosenberg-Sobell case during the Monmouth hearings, the Senator—pursuing his customary razzle-dazzle methods—was not adverse to dragging in any other available *cause célèbre* of the period. Thus, one of those interrogated was the brother of a man involved in the Hiss case, leading to such headlines as "Monmouth Figure Linked to Hiss Ring." Moreover, in the midst of his Signal Corps probe McCarthy found time to question Abraham Brothman, recently released from prison, as well as a number of "close associates" of Harry Dexter White and others, who had been accused by Elizabeth Bentley years before. Just what McCarthy was searching for in all this is difficult to surmise, unless it was a unified-field theory of espionage.

The one-man subcommittee's whirlwind investigation revealed no significant new information about members of the alleged Rosenberg spy ring, but did produce some results. Over thirty Monmouth employees were suspended from their jobs, while others were assigned to non-sensitive and often non-productive posts privately referred to as "the leper colony." Morale among scientists and technicians at the electronics research center was said to be low. Many responsible journalists who surveyed the wreckage firsthand were shocked.

Terming the situation created by McCarthy at the Monmouth laboratory "truly scandalous," Walter Millis of the New York *Herald Tribune* said the accusations leveled against the suspended employees were "an almost unbelievable farrago of guilt-by-association innuendoes." He decried the "strong elements of racial and religious bigotry and prejudice in the case."

Commented the Newark *Evening News:*

"Most of the suspended or declassified employees are graduates of City College of New York, where they studied engineering with Rosenberg and Sobell or in classes just before or after them. . . .

"Why did so many turn up at Fort Monmouth? According to some, the questioned specialists were 'depression graduates' of CCNY and took Civil Service examinations while looking for work in the late '30's. When the . . . need for engineers became acute, these same CCNY-trained men were called to Civil Service jobs at Fort Monmouth. . . ."

It was this associational link that McCarthy and his entourage had attempted to capitalize on. But the subcommittee, though armed with data whose obvious point of origin was the FBI, produced no evidence (other than the Greenglass deposition) that a Rosenberg spy ring ever had existed at Fort Monmouth. Eventually, every one of the suspended employees won back his right to his job, though for some the victory entailed long years of litigation.

For the Senator, the initial success at Monmouth turned into a debacle leading to the Army-McCarthy hearings and his deflation and censure. At the time of his death in 1957, the *Times* recalled:

"Several McCarthy investigations, including inquiries into reported spying and sabotage at the Army Signal Corps installation at Fort Monmouth . . . yielded no spies or persons of provable disloyalty."

For four years after the Monmouth hearings, the matter of the Rosenberg spy ring remained largely dormant, an extralegal mishmash of hearsay testimony, unproved allegations, and plain innuendo. Then, in October 1957, an article in *Look* magazine revealed that the Attorney General of the United States had ordered a study of the entire atomic espionage case to refute "Communist charges" of a frame-up and answer the question "many loyal citizens . . . are asking themselves: Were the Rosenbergs really guilty?"

The article, featured on the cover of *Look* as "Exclusive: The Atomic Bomb and Those Who Stole It," was authored by writer Bill Davidson. He wrote:

". . . in December, 1956, Attorney General Herbert Brownell, Jr., ordered . . . the head of the Department of Justice's Internal Security Division, to prepare a full report of the case—including previously unreleased facts. Assigned to the job was Benjamin F. Pollack, a brilliant Harvard Law School graduate and veteran Justice Department attorney. For eight months, Pollack had access to all the FBI files and to all the evidence and testimony in the case. He interviewed witnesses and the men who arrested and prosecuted the Rosenbergs and their co-conspirator, Morton Sobell. . . . This reporter . . . worked along with Pollack during much of his investigation. *Look* was given access to the extensive data that went into the Government report, of which this article is an exclusive preview."

Despite this dramatic build-up, the "exclusive preview" turns out to be somewhat less sensational than advertised. With few exceptions, the "first real story of the big atomic-bomb plot" is merely a rehash of the case derived from the trial transcript and other publicly available sources. Among those exceptions is a small amount of new information on the Rosenberg spy ring.

Attorney General Brownell's report is said to reveal that, in addition to the defendants, "there were seven other known American members of the spy ring." Regarding five of these, "the Government felt there was not enough evidence, beyond a reasonable doubt, to convict." The two others "have now disappeared behind the Iron Curtain."

The latter individuals are undoubtedly Joel Barr and Alfred Sarant, previously reported to be in Western Europe and Mexico, respectively. Though no unequivocal accusation is leveled against either man, acts of espionage by both are strongly implied.

Barr is said to have "worked on the mathematical problems of launching a 'sky-platform earth satellite.' (Some Government officials believe that Barr gave this data to Rosenberg in 1947)"* As for Sarant, the article recalls Rosenberg's alleged boasts about receiving "the mathematics of an atomic plane from one of his contacts" and claims that Sarant was "an engineer who had worked on this project."

Finally, referring to Sarant's Greenwich Village apartment previously mentioned in the Rosenberg-Sobell and Perl trials, the article states: "The FBI visited an apartment at 65 Morton Street in New York City, which they knew Rosenberg had frequented. The apartment, they discovered, contained very little furniture. It was filled, instead, with workbenches. In the kitchen, the FBI found a reflector-type flood lamp, the kind used in photography."

Immediately after the appearance of this article, a number of publica-

---

* Belying this belief is the fact that from October 1946 through October 1947 Barr was employed by Sperry Gyroscope Company on *unclassified* work aimed at determining how well radar would pick up certain missile shapes. (As reference for this job, he listed Julius Rosenberg.) He was discharged when he failed to obtain security clearance to handle classified tasks and, shortly afterward, told friends he was going to Europe to study music.

tions sought copies of the complete Department of Justice report and criticized Attorney General Brownell for his method of publicizing what was ostensibly an official study. Commented the *Nation:* "An exclusive preview of a White Paper is something of a novelty in public affairs. . . . it gives rise to an inference that the summary . . . is biased in favor of the department."

Unfortunately, the "full report of the case" (purportedly prepared at Brownell's request to still the doubts of "many loyal citizens") has never, to this day, been released by the Department of Justice.

Out of all the information—of varying authenticity—that has become available over the years about members of the alleged Rosenberg spy ring, certainly the most baffling item concerns the mysterious July 1950 visit of Vivian Glassman to William Perl's Cleveland apartment.

One possible interpretation of this visit, of course, is that Miss Glassman, serving as a courier for an espionage ring, came to Cleveland to warn Perl, a member of the ring, to flee the country.

If so, the episode would lend very powerful support to David Greenglass's uncorroborated testimony about a spy ring. It seems noteworthy, therefore, that the *Look* "preview" of the Department of Justice's report on the case contains no mention of Miss Glassman's Cleveland visit. A possible reason for this omission is that there is much about the matter which simply does not make sense.

If Miss Glassman was acting for a spy ring, she would appear to have undertaken a most hazardous, even foolhardy, mission in journeying to Cleveland about a week *after* Julius Rosenberg's arrest—at a time when almost everyone who had known Rosenberg (probably including Miss Glassman) was being interrogated or watched by the FBI. Moreover, considering the grave risks she apparently had taken on his behalf, Perl was strangely ungrateful: He turned her in, submitting a statement to the FBI about her visit and later testifying about the incident before a grand jury.

The question that cries for an answer, therefore, is why Miss Glassman, who remained in the United States, never was prosecuted.

The latter fact is particularly puzzling in the light of the FBI's disclosure, several years ago, that Miss Glassman had been interviewed by federal agents and had confirmed Perl's story regarding her visit to him. Notes an official FBI report (which, rather surprisingly, accords Miss Glassman complete anonymity): "This girl was located and on interview verified the above information [Perl's account of the visit] and stated that Perl refused to accept the sum of $2,000 which she offered him."

It is astounding, to say the least, that, following both Perl's statement to the FBI and Miss Glassman's own apparent confession of her offer to him of money to flee the country, no legal action was taken against her by the authorities. Yet she was not included in the espionage conspiracy indictment as either a defendant or co-conspirator, nor was she charged with a lesser offense such as obstruction of justice. Neither was Miss Glassman called as a witness at either the Rosenberg-Sobell trial or the Perl trial. It would seem that the whole story of her visit has not been told and the failure to question her in public regarding it does suggest some trepidation about what she might have to say.

William Perl, who professed to have been completely perplexed by Miss Glassman's visit, hinted at a possible explanation other than espionage when he told a grand jury: ". . . all I could think of was that somebody was trying to trap me into something, since I had no reason to leave." Niceties aside, might overzealous FBI agents have persuaded a frightened Miss Glassman—herself a possible suspect—to test Perl's reaction to a vague message advising him to flee the country?

In 1953, Vivian Glassman (along with her husband and sister) was summoned before the Monmouth hearings. Pregnant at the time, she suffered a miscarriage after being questioned in a closed session of the subcommittee. Her husband, a naturalized citizen, was threatened with deportation by McCarthy and, immediately after his appearance, was fired from his job as a college instructor.

The authors sought out Miss Glassman and she agreed to see us. However, when we arrived at her home, she indicated that she had had second thoughts about granting an interview. She then refused to talk about her visit to Perl or even to answer the most innocuous questions about the case. At one point, her husband told the authors: "Well, let's say for the record that we never knew of anyone who was guilty of espionage." She immediately interjected that she wouldn't say "anything" for the record.

Practically the only information she volunteered during a three-hour interview was that she had read a book once about "FBI harassment" and it was "everything it is said to be and then some." Other than that, she remained adamant in her refusal to discuss any aspect of the case.

Today, Vivian Glassman's visit to Perl remains unexplained. Additional information is required to resolve intriguing questions still outstanding. However, with the facts presently available, the episode can hardly be construed, with confidence, as firm evidence of the operation of a Rosenberg spy ring.

As for the others whose names have been mentioned publicly in connection with the alleged spy ring, Joel Barr and Alfred Sarant both are presumably living abroad. Even if they were available for questioning, one would be hard put to know what to ask them, so nebulous are the "charges" leveled against them. Similarly, William Perl (who resides in the United States) has been linked with the ring only by the vaguest innuendo.

The one alleged member of the Rosenberg spy ring who was accused of a *specific* role in the conspiracy was Ann Sidorovich, called a "Soviet agent" by Saypol. Since she was not indicted, named as a co-conspirator, or called as a witness, Mrs. Sidorovich's version of her relationship with the Rosenbergs has never been made public. The authors therefore contacted her and asked her to tell it.

Mrs. Sidorovich confirmed the trial testimony of the Rosenbergs that she had been their neighbor in the early Forties and had been introduced to them through her husband, who had attended high school with Julius. Afterward, the two families became friendly.

"Within a day or two" after the arrest of either Julius or Ethel—she was not sure which—she had first been interrogated about the case by the FBI. The agents told her that David Greenglass had said she was present at the Rosenbergs' apartment in January 1945 and that he had met her there.

Said Mrs. Sidorovich:

"Now I don't remember the occasion at all. And I have said so under oath. I do remember meeting Ruth once, but I don't remember ever meeting David at all. I can't for the life of me remember ever meeting him. But I do know that they [the FBI] told me repeatedly that he had said that he had met me there."

She emphatically denied, too, David Greenglass's testimony that she was supposed to go to Denver or Albuquerque as an espionage courier:

"I have said so under oath. I know there's no truth in it, but they have repeatedly been at me to confess to that. I had no reason to go to the West at all."

Ann Sidorovich's assertion that she had denied the Greenglass story "under oath" before the 1950 federal grand jury in New York is, of course, an entirely new piece of information, which the prosecution failed to disclose during the Rosenberg-Sobell trial. It explains why she was not called as a prosecution witness. Noting that she had not pleaded the Fifth Amendment on any question, Mrs. Sidorovich told about the grand jury proceedings:

"We [she and her husband] were at the grand jury and we gave them everything. I told them I would answer anything at all and they said I should tell them the whole story. Well, they had some sort of a story all set up—it was the Greenglass story—and if my answers didn't go along with theirs, then I was lying. No lawyer would touch the case so we had to do it all on our own. I told them everything I knew but it wasn't good enough. We were before the grand jury for about three or four consecutive days."

Mrs. Sidorovich described the activities of the FBI following her refusal to corroborate David Greenglass's story:

"Well, they kept pounding on that meeting in January which I could not remember for the life of me. That seemed to be the key point of what they wanted. I'm just obstinate enough not to tell them that, unless I remembered it myself. We were persecuted for several years. We were under 24-hour surveillance for over a year and my husband had difficulty with his job. Fortunately he's quite bright and the people he works with like him or he would have been jobless for a long time. It was really a miracle his firm kept him on. That was really a miracle.*

"In fact, a friend of ours in New York can't get any kind of executive position simply because he stood by us during the grand jury hearing and took care of our youngster. And he is a brilliant electronic engineer. This is a friend who had no connection with the case at all. He took care of my youngster while we were up there before the grand jury and after that they've hounded him."

Mrs. Sidorovich recounted her experience of being under "24-hour surveillance" by the FBI:

"Well, they park their car in front of your home and anyone who goes in or out is checked. Everybody in the apartment building was questioned and anybody who comes in contact to speak with you. Anybody at all who came in contact with you was interrogated and of course a lot of people, with the McCarthy thing on, got quite worried with their jobs and so on. We lost a great many friends. One year was sort of a 24-hour vigil and for another year after that we had to get in touch with them any time we went out of town. It was pretty rough. They would call my husband at work and get him out to their car and show him pictures and talk to him. I think simply to embarrass him. They showed us all kinds of pictures. And after a while, we'd get calls in the middle of the night and we'd answer it and nobody there. Over a long period of time. We finally either muffled the phone or left it off the hook. How long can you take that?

"I think they [the FBI] thought they had a sewed up case. We had a man from the very beginning, who felt that this case was going to push him up high in the FBI and he wanted to tie it up real quick and present it to the boss with all the short ends tied in to something else and all he needed was something from me to confirm everything else. Now, I don't know if they honestly believed it. Maybe they did at first because it was all so pat. But I think we made a couple of, well, almost friends of the FBI men who were on us. They kept with us. They got to know us better. Gradually, I think, they got a little doubtful. But the idea was: Be a good citizen and put these people where they belong. It was a loose end and they would have felt better if I had confessed to it."

Actually, whether or not Mrs. Sidorovich met David Greenglass at the Rosenberg apartment in January 1945 is of little significance. What is important is whether she could have corroborated the guilt of the Rosenbergs as spies. According to her version of events, she had absolutely no

* Michael Sidorovich died in 1962. He was caught up in the espionage investigation, despite the fact that he himself was not accused by the Greenglasses (Ruth testified that he was unaware of his wife's activities).

knowledge of any such activity on the part of the Rosenbergs and had told this to both the FBI and the grand jury. Two years of FBI pressure did not cause her to change her position.

The government could, of course, have contested Ann Sidorovich's grand jury testimony and tried her for perjury, using David and Ruth Greenglass as witnesses; it chose not to do so. Nevertheless, with no show of evidence other than the word of the Greenglasses against her denial—under oath—Saypol had labeled her an "espionage courier."*

Another possible source of information on the Rosenberg spy ring was the United States Department of Justice. The authors wrote to government attorney Benjamin Pollack, with whom *Look* writer Bill Davidson was said to have worked, requesting permission to see his report on the Rosenberg-Sobell case. Pollack replied that the report "is a confidential document for intra-departmental use and copies cannot be and have not been furnished to the public."

However, soon after, Assistant Attorney General J. Walter Yeagley agreed that we might "have access to the same information given to Mr. Davidson" and one of the authors met with Pollack at his office in Washington, D.C. (Present also during the two-hour interview was another Department of Justice employee, who took notes.) Pollack affirmed that after rather extensive research† he had written a ninety-five page report on the case for Attorney General Brownell, but he said that Davidson never had seen it. His work with the *Look* writer, he said, had consisted largely of providing him with information obtained from the trial record.

After a cordial discussion with Pollack on various aspects of the case, we noted that we were particularly interested in learning more about the alleged members of the spy ring, so that we might present the government's viewpoint on this subject as completely and accurately as possible. Pollack promised to go through his report, take out any material on the spy ring, and send it to us in a few days. The few days stretched into more than three months, during which time we wrote and telephoned reiterating our request for the data. Finally, the following letter was received from Pollack (misspelled names have been corrected):

"I regret exceedingly my inability to write to you sooner. I want you to know, though, that delay of a reply was not deliberate on my part.

"When I spoke to you in my office I had the impression that my notes taken during the course of my research on the Rosenberg case contained the facts you sought. That is why I was of the opinion that I could give

---

* The U. S. Attorney mentioned Mrs. Sidorovich's name six times in his summation.
† Pollack stated that he had interviewed neither Irving Saypol nor Roy Cohn. He said that Saypol had insisted that any questions be submitted in advance in writing and that Cohn had refused to see him at all.

you the information you wanted within a week or ten days. However, when I reviewed my notes, I found nothing of a material nature or additional to what was mentioned in the Davidson Look article. I therefore decided to go through the original files again. That took time. Moreover, illness and the necessity of performing my usual official duties and assignments, added to the delay.

"I have this day completed my review of the files and I am sorry to state that I have not discovered anything of relevance pertaining to Perl, Joel Barr . . . Sarant, Sidorovich. . . . Mr. Sarant was the occupant of Apartment 6 I at 65 Morton Street, New York. This apartment was the rendezvous of those alleged to have been members of the Rosenberg spy ring and where photographic appliances were found. Joel Barr was known to have been a close friend of Julius Rosenberg.

"I wish to assure you that Bill Davidson was not given any more information with respect to this aspect of the case. I shall be glad to confer with you at any time on any matter that I can be of help to you."

With Pollack's statement that he had reviewed the Department of Justice files on the case and had "not discovered anything of relevance" concerning Perl, Barr, Sarant, or Sidorovich (no mention was made of Miss Glassman), our search for some conclusive evidence of the operation of a Rosenberg spy ring had arrived at a dead end.

All of those who were more or less officially connected with the alleged spy ring had one thing in common: Association with Julius Rosenberg and, except for Mrs. Sidorovich, with each other. They were Rosenberg's classmates and friends and a number of them were active in the same union with him, the FAECT* (which in the postwar years came under frequent Congressional attack for its leftist leanings). They were people who were acquainted socially, dined together, visited one another's homes.

Each of these individuals who actually had associated with Rosenberg and on whom suspicion fell subsequently became himself a source of "infection" for his relatives and friends. People who never had met or heard of the Rosenbergs found themselves suspect for having associated with associates of the convicted spies. (One charge leveled against a UNESCO employee dismissed from her job in 1954 was that she had "associated with a former schoolmate" who, in turn, had associated with the Rosenbergs.) It is impossible to ascertain how many persons may have been "linked" to the spy ring by this incredible chain of guilt-by-association-once-removed, but the number may well be substantial.

One instance chanced upon by the authors—a passport proceeding involving an American cosmic ray physicist, Weldon Bruce Dayton—provides an extraordinary case history of an individual tied to the spy ring

* Federation of Architects, Engineers, Chemists and Technicians.

by remote associations and also reveals some new and illuminating information about Alfred Sarant and his apartment at 65 Morton Street.*

In late 1946, Weldon Dayton, 28, then teaching and studying for his Ph.D. at Cornell University, in Ithaca, New York, met Alfred Sarant through the latter's in-laws. Sarant, an electrical engineer, was employed in the school's physics laboratory. The Daytons and Sarants became friendly and, the following spring, when Dayton decided to build his own house in Ithaca, Sarant followed suit and purchased an adjoining lot. Dayton completed the job first and, from summer 1948 to spring 1949, the Sarants lived with the Daytons until they could move into their new home next door.

During the first half of 1950, Dayton was extremely occupied with his doctoral thesis and frequently spent long hours on experiments at the physics laboratory. In July of that year, Dayton later testified, he "became aware" that the relationship between his wife, Carol, and Alfred Sarant was "somewhat more than neighborly." Shortly afterward, an event occurred which suddenly inflamed this smoldering domestic situation.

On July 18, 1950 (one day after the arrest of Julius Rosenberg), FBI agents visited Sarant at his home. That evening, appearing haggard after a long session with the agents, Sarant told the Daytons that he had been asked about an apartment he had maintained in New York City and that the FBI "believed that this apartment had been used for espionage activities." He protested his innocence to the Daytons and "seemed outraged."

For the next four or five days, FBI cars were parked outside Sarant's house and he was interrogated daily by from two to five agents for "many, many hours." Carol Dayton took this "extremely hard." Recalled Dayton: "It is my belief that she considered Sarant to be unjustly accused. He maintained his complete innocence to us."

Dayton testified that he finally spoke with his wife about Sarant and for the first time realized the depth of her emotional involvement with their neighbor. "She was then in a bad state of turmoil." However, Carol Dayton told her husband that she had decided to break off with Sarant and would go to stay with a friend in Boston for a while. She left Ithaca and, while en route, indicated to her husband by telephone and postcard that she wanted to think things over and would not write until she had clarified her feelings. A day or so later, Sarant also left Ithaca and drove to New York City.

At the beginning of August, Dayton himself was questioned by FBI agents, who asked if he had been at 65 Morton Street in New York City in January 1950, helping to move furniture from Sarant's apartment in

---

* All of the information and quoted material that follows is contained in the testimony of Dayton that appears in the official record of Dayton vs. Dulles, Supreme Court, No. 621, October Term, 1957.

company with William Perl. He replied that he never had been to 65 Morton Street or met Perl, and agreed to confront witnesses who said he had.

Dayton then flew with FBI agents to Newark airport and was presented there with three members of a family named Elwyn (the superintendent at 65 Morton Street), all of whom he was sure he never had seen previously. However, the Elwyns claimed that they had noticed him at the apartment a number of times, including once in January 1950, and mentioned an incident in which Dayton allegedly had been seated at a table attired in pajamas.

Dayton informed the agents that he had not worn pajamas since the age of eleven and had not been in New York City at any time in January 1950. They accused him of trying to shield Sarant. He later observed: "The whole experience was so weird and this information so obviously false, that I was at a loss as to what to say."

Back in Ithaca, Dayton was able, with the aid of his thesis adviser, to assemble laboratory logbooks proving that he had been working at Cornell all during the month of January 1950—thus refuting the Elwyns. He believed the matter to be closed.

Shortly afterward, Dayton learned that his wife and Alfred Sarant had gone away together. In late July, FBI agents had seen Carol Dayton in New York City with Sarant; a few weeks later, the two had turned up in Tucson, Arizona, at the home of relatives of Carol's and had journeyed from there to Hermosillo, Mexico, after which their itinerary is unknown.

Dayton, who felt sure that his wife's desertion had no political implications, testified that neither he nor she ever had been Communists, nor was she even a politically active person. For anyone who knew her, he said, the "assumption of some kind of plot" as a reason for her departure made her conduct more, rather than less, difficult to explain. (Eventually, both Dayton and Mrs. Sarant divorced their respective spouses.)

The record of the Dayton proceedings shows that, at the time Sarant went to Mexico, Julius Rosenberg already had been in prison for weeks. Moreover, the circumstances surrounding Sarant's trip suggest that he may have undertaken it rather impulsively, motivated by his romance with his neighbor's wife and his anxiety and resentment over intensive FBI interrogation. All of this throws considerable doubt on the validity of Saypol's implication at the Rosenberg-Sobell trial that Julius was in some way responsible for Sarant's departure for Mexico.*

Speculation aside, it is a fact—never previously revealed—that Alfred Sarant, whose name has so often been mentioned as a fugitive member of the spy ring, was actually in the hands of the FBI and was not arrested

---

* Saypol also asked Rosenberg if he knew "a lady by the name of Carol Dayton." Rosenberg replied that he did not recall the name.

by them. The FBI had interrogated him at great length for about a week, and he had denied their accusations. Agents had kept him under surveillance in New York City. Not until four weeks after he first was questioned did Sarant leave the United States. It is clear that the FBI had ample opportunity to arrest Alfred Sarant—*if they had had any evidence with which to do so.* Had Sarant remained in the country (as did Mrs. Sidorovich), there is no reason to believe that he ever would have been charged with any crime.

A few weeks after the conclusion of the Rosenberg-Sobell trial, Dayton was subpoenaed before a federal grand jury in New York City. Said he: "They were investigating what you might call the second echelon of the Rosenberg spy ring." To his surprise, he was questioned once more as to whether he had been present at 65 Morton Street, which he had thought to be a dead issue. When he again denied that he ever had been there or knew anything about alleged espionage activities of Sarant, one of the assistant U.S. attorneys present was "quite intimidating." Said Dayton: "I had the helpless feeling that I really might be indicted for telling the truth."

Subpoenaed again in June 1951, he appeared before both a regular and special grand jury and also was questioned by the FBI for several days. FBI agents requested him to accompany them to 65 Morton Street, and Dayton said he did so "and was satisfied that I had never been there before." Some of the agents who interviewed him during this period were so aggressive in their questioning that he determined not to talk to the FBI any more. However, about a year later, he learned from friends that agents had again been inquiring about him and he then agreed to a further interview.

Whatever the supposed intent of such long-term and high-pressured interrogation of a prospective witness, the practical effect is clear. Afterward, when asked a question about Sarant, Dayton was unable to answer, explaining: "I have been told . . . so many things by so many FBI agents about Sarant and they have all gotten kind of melded together and congealed [so] that it is awfully hard for me to know now what I knew in the first instance."

In 1953, Dayton began to encounter "serious job worries." His contract with MIT was not renewed and every university to which he applied failed to hire him after hearing of his difficulties. He found himself unable to pursue his chosen scientific field, cosmic ray research, which, ironically, is nowhere regarded as secret work. Reluctantly, he accepted an industrial job with a glass company.

However, in 1954 he was offered a three-year appointment as a research physicist at the Tata Institute of Fundamental Research, affiliated with the University of Bombay in India. He immediately accepted and was then informed by the State Department that it was "contrary to the best interest of the United States" to give him a passport. Soon after, the Director of the Passport Office notified Dayton's attorney that "the determining factor in the case was Mr. Dayton's association with persons suspected of being part of the Rosenberg espionage ring and his alleged presence at an apartment in New York which was allegedly used for microfilming material obtained for the use of a foreign government."

This allegation—that Sarant's apartment at 65 Morton Street was "used for microfilming" by the spy ring—is, of course, a step beyond claims made by *Look* writer Bill Davidson and Justice Department attorney Benjamin Pollack. Davidson wrote that the FBI had visited the apartment and had "discovered" that it was "filled . . . with workbenches" and that in the kitchen there was "a reflector-type flood lamp, the kind used in photography." Pollack noted only that "photographic appliances were found" in the apartment.

However, information disclosed at Dayton's hearings before the State Department's Board of Passport Appeals would appear to refute both of these assertions.

According to testimony by the superintendent of 65 Morton Street, Sarant gave up his lease to his apartment in January 1950 (or late December 1949) and, at that time, all furniture was removed. Describing this furniture as dilapidated, the superintendent said it consisted of an old day bed, folding chairs, a hamper, and baskets; he mentioned nothing whatever about any "workbenches" or "photographic appliances." Furthermore, the superintendent testified that he personally had seen to it that the apartment was *completely cleared out* and, within three or four days after the removal of the furniture, it was rerented and immediately occupied by a family.

Since at the time of Rosenberg's arrest new tenants had been living in the former Sarant apartment for at least six months, it is apparent that the story of the FBI's discovery of photographic equipment there is meaningless.

(Further evidence along the same line was obtained by the authors from another new source: A memo that Helene Elitcher wrote for her attorney, O. John Rogge, describing her first interrogation by FBI agents a few days after Julius Rosenberg's arrest.* Mrs. Elitcher wrote that she had been asked about Sarant's Greenwich Village apartment, which she said she had visited in the summer of 1944. The agents had questioned her about the appearance of the place. Had she seen any tools or clocks? Any worktable? She told her attorney that she had observed none of these things, noting only that the place had been shabbily decorated and was obviously a bachelor apartment.)

* No information about this memo was obtained from any past or present member of the Rogge law firm.

Other information revealed at the Dayton passport hearings also inspires little confidence in claims that 65 Morton Street was the rendezvous of a spy ring. Sarant was shown to have sublet his supposed spy headquarters to at least two persons other than Perl, though neither of the two ever was accused of involvement in the alleged ring. Moreover, according to the superintendent, the lock on Apartment 6 I remained unchanged throughout Sarant's tenancy and could be opened with a passkey. (He said the lock had been turned over to the FBI.) It seems entirely incredible that individuals engaged in espionage would take no special security precautions regarding the place where they microfilmed stolen documents.

Eventually, Dayton won his fight. In June 1958—over four years after he first had applied for a passport—the Supreme Court ruled in his favor. Afterward, the Federation of American Scientists cited the Dayton case as one in which "long drawn-out efforts to secure a passport have drained years from the man's productive life and caused great personal anguish."

The circular reasoning of those who advance the idea of a spy ring and claim that various associates of the Rosenbergs were its members reminds one of nothing so much as a dog chasing its tail:

These suspected individuals, they say, must be guilty, they were too close to the Rosenbergs not to have been part of it; the Rosenbergs must be guilty, we know that their friends and associates were spies.

However, despite Saypol's reference to "other traitors who sold their country down the river with Rosenberg and Sobell," no proof of the existence of such people ever has been produced. The guilt or innocence of the defendants must be judged by the evidence against them alone.

A REASONABLE DOUBT

•

CHAPTER 24
ELIZABETH BENTLEY

Elizabeth Turrill Bentley never claimed to have met Julius or Ethel Rosenberg or Morton Sobell, nor did she have any knowledge of the crime charged against them. Nevertheless, her testimony—along with that of Elitcher, the Greenglasses, and Gold—constituted the heart of the government's case.

When Miss Bentley took the stand as a witness for the prosecution in the Rosenberg-Sobell trial, her name and history already were widely known among her fellow countrymen. For nearly three years, she had been prominently identified in the press as a self-confessed Communist spy, a fact which contributed enormously to the impact of her testimony and, in keeping with the prevalent logic of the Fifties, to her credibility.

Briefly, the Bentley saga, as recounted by her before various Congressional committees and courts and in her autobiography, had its unsensational inception in 1935, when the New England-born Vassar graduate, then about twenty-seven, joined the Communist Party while a student at Columbia University.

In summer 1938, still a Party member, she obtained a secretarial job in New York City at the Italian Library of Information, which she soon learned was a division of the Fascist Italian government's Propaganda Ministry. Concluding that this was a "golden opportunity to find out what propaganda the Fascists were foisting on the American people," she went, on her own tack, to national Communist Party headquarters, where a leading Italian Communist told her to "collect publications and copies of letters" from the Library.

However, the Italian Communist, "seemingly very busy," soon referred Miss Bentley to an associate, who "not only was little interested but never showed up for appointments." When she complained, she was introduced, in October 1938, to one Jacob Golos and thereafter delivered material from the Italian Library to him. Shortly, she and Golos became lovers.

Fired from her Library job, Miss Bentley earned her living as a translator and secretary and did research tasks for Golos. Later, while employed by McClure's Newspaper Syndicate, she brought him "copies of interesting documents and correspondence."

At the time Miss Bentley met him, Golos (whose legal name was Jacob Raisin) had long been an active supporter of the Soviet cause in the United States and was well known in American Communist Party circles. He ran World Tourists, a New York City travel agency "set up by the American Communist Party . . . for the dual purpose of making money and encouraging tourists to go to Russia."

In October 1939 the Department of Justice seized World Tourists' records, during a crackdown on the Communists following the outbreak of World War II. According to press reports of the time, a federal grand jury subpoenaed the records, called Golos to testify, and indicted Party leader Earl Browder for passport fraud. In March 1940 Golos himself was indicted for failing to register his firm under the Foreign Agents Registration Act. He pleaded guilty and received a four-month suspended sentence.

Throughout these well-publicized events, Miss Bentley maintained her liaison with Golos and continued to do "odd jobs" for him. One such, begun in spring 1940, was to pick up blueprints from Abraham Brothman. (Brothman's explanation—revealed at his trial—was that Golos had promised to obtain a commercial contract for him with the Soviet trade organization, Amtorg, in return for a fee.)

World Tourists' business had been seriously impaired by the Department of Justice investigation and, in early 1941, Golos arranged for the setting up of a corporate affiliate, U.S. Service and Shipping, to handle the shipment of parcels to the Soviet Union. Most of the financing was supplied, *sub rosa*, by the Communist Party, as a business venture. Miss Bentley was named vice-president of the new enterprise and was employed there for the next six years.

Without necessarily accepting every specific detail, the foregoing aspect of Elizabeth Bentley's story appears to be essentially accurate and is, in large part, amenable to verification. About the rest of her account, however, there is continuing controversy.

For Miss Bentley asserts that, as a result of her self-initiated conversation with the Italian Communist in 1938, she left the open Party and "went . . . underground"; that Golos was a member of both the three-man control commission of the American Communist Party and the Soviet secret police; and that throughout their relationship he was not only her lover but her espionage superior.

Most important, she claims that in 1941, soon after she and Golos became associated in business, she became his espionage courier to a large group of United States government employees in Washington, D.C. Jacob

Golos himself never commented on these allegations; he died in November 1943.

At the Rosenberg-Sobell trial, Miss Bentley testified that after Golos's death she "got promoted up; the rank was considerably more than a courier because I was actually acting; I had a larger group of people, more responsibility." During this period, she said, she "gave orders to Earl Browder . . . transmitted orders from Moscow to him, and he had to accept them. Sometimes he would fight against them, but he ended up by accepting them."

(Interviewed by the authors, Browder—CP Secretary from 1930 until his expulsion from the Party in 1945—characterized this claim as "nonsense." He called Miss Bentley's story a hodgepodge of fact and fancy and said his only dealings with her had concerned the Communist Party's financial investment in U.S. Service and Shipping. According to Browder's version, Golos was not a member of the Party's control commission, nor, so far as he knew, an espionage agent. Like many others, Golos sometimes had brought him research material useful in his writings and other Party work; he specifically recalled one such item that he was aware had been pilfered by Miss Bentley from McClure's.* However, he described her as "romantic and suggestible" and doubted that she ever had engaged in anything that she had considered espionage at the time she was doing it.)

Miss Bentley alleges that, eventually, in late 1944, she dealt directly with one Anatoli Gromov, First Secretary of the Soviet Embassy. Gromov ordered her to cease her espionage activities and, although she saw him a number of additional times, her career as a spy ended in December 1944.

The following year, Elizabeth Bentley took a step that was to leave its imprint on the political history of the post-World War II decade: She went to the FBI "to tell them my story." She later testified that this had occurred in New Haven, Connecticut, in August 1945. Confronted with proof that she actually had inquired at the FBI's New Haven office in August about an entirely different matter, she insisted that she also had begun her confession that month.

The date is of more than passing interest. For Miss Bentley has related that on about October 17, 1945—*while acting under the instructions of the FBI*—she met Gromov and received $2000 from him in payment for past espionage services. On the assumption that this transaction was under surveillance by FBI agents, it has been regarded by some as important corroboration for her story.

When Miss Bentley testified about this alleged mid-October meeting

---

* This was a memorandum concerning a meeting between Nazi agents and some prominent Americans. Browder said that, after first being placed with an exposé-type periodical, the memorandum was used by him in his book, Victory—and After, page 49.

with Gromov, there seemed no way to verify her claim that she had been cooperating with the FBI at the time, other than by the unlikely possibility of inspecting FBI files. Some years later, however, that possibility presented itself. At the height of a raucous political squabble growing out of unprecedented accusations by Attorney General Brownell against former President Truman, a number of FBI documents were precipitously declassified. They reveal that Miss Bentley—contrary to her testimony—did not begin recounting her tale of espionage to FBI agents until November 7, 1945, in New York City.

The next day, J. Edgar Hoover rushed a brief letter to the White House warning of an espionage ring operating within the government. The letter, marked "Top Secret," stated that information had "recently been developed" connecting fourteen individuals with possible espionage. The "highly confidential" source of this information later was identified as Elizabeth Bentley.

Though by November 8, 1945, Miss Bentley's day-old charges could have received only the most cursory study, Hoover apparently had no reservations about the basic premise of her story: That she had been an important member of a wartime espionage ring. Nor did the FBI chief doubt that the fourteen persons whose names he dispatched to the White House "were actually the source from which information passing through a Soviet espionage system was being obtained," though he noted the important qualification that "at the present time it is impossible to determine exactly how many of these people had actual knowledge of the disposition being made of the information they were transmitting."

Hoover concluded: "I am continuing vigorous investigation for the purpose of establishing the degree and nature of the complicity of these people in this espionage ring."

In less than a month, Miss Bentley's confession involved an amazing number of people. Wrote Hoover in a second communication sent to the White House in late November:

"To date over 80 individuals have been named by Miss Bentley as being connected with the Soviet espionage organization either in Washington or in New York. Of this number 37 have been identified as employees of the United States Government in Washington, D.C. Bentley has stated that each of these individuals probably obtained information from others either casually or through actual recruiting. . . ."

Having thus more or less committed himself to the Bentley story, Hoover undertook a search for corroboration. Miss Bentley says that she agreed to perform as a counterspy under FBI guidance, remaining at her job at U.S. Service and Shipping and attempting to re-establish connections with former members of the ring. Meanwhile, hundreds of FBI agents pursued various facets of her story for the next year and a half.

In the spring of 1947 a federal grand jury was convened in New York

City to hear the evidence gathered by the FBI in months of "vigorous investigation." Scores of past and present government employees, all of whom had served in the Executive branch under the New Deal, were called to testify—including some who had held rather high office. Also subpoenaed were a number of individuals, such as Abraham Brothman and a man in his employ, Harry Gold, who never had worked for the government.

The grand jury deliberated for more than a year, then abandoned its lengthy inquiry into Miss Bentley's accusations without voting a single indictment against any of the more than eighty individuals she had named.

Ordinarily, the matter would have ended there. However, those who were interested in making the Bentley story public now resorted to avenues outside the judicial system.

On July 21, 1948, hard on the heels of the FBI's grand jury fiasco, a front-page story in the New York World-Telegram, picturesquely headlined "Red Ring Bared by Blond Queen," told of widespread espionage by government employees during the New Deal administration. Further details were disclosed by the paper over the next few days, building to a climax a week later with a story, headlined "Red Spy Queen Drops Mask," that identified the "queen" as Elizabeth Bentley. Included in this same story was an announcement by Robert Stripling, chief investigator for the House Un-American Activities Committee, that Miss Bentley soon would testify at a public session of the committee.

Shortly before Miss Bentley's scheduled committee appearance, Stripling was visited by two government attorneys. One, T. Vincent Quinn, was particularly well informed about Miss Bentley because ne had participated in the presentation of evidence and testimony to the grand jury that heard her story. In Stripling's presence, the attorneys telephoned committee chairman J. Parnell Thomas, and, as Stripling later recalled, "They urged Thomas to question Miss Bentley in executive session and warned him that while the Justice Department had never been able definitely to disprove any of her allegations there was available no material evidence, and a great dearth of corroborating witnesses."

In late July, Miss Bentley's debut as a Congressional witness was launched, causing an immediate nationwide sensation. From 1948 on, she testified frequently before various House and Senate committees.

Scores of individuals publicly accused by Miss Bentley had to endure pillory—and loss of their jobs—without recourse to cross-examination of their accuser. Only very gradually did it become apparent that she never had met most of those she had named. Of the accused who had known her, several (including William Remington) testified that she had identified herself to them—under various aliases—as a researcher and that they had innocently given her routine information available to any reporter.

While Miss Bentley alleged that the material she received was intended for the Soviet Union, she was equivocal on this crucial point of whether or not those who gave her data were *aware* of its destination. In addition, her accusations were for the most part both uncorroborated and incredibly vague. When asked to describe the loot she claimed to have carried from Washington to New York in her knitting bag, she usually resorted to some loose formulation, such as "inside policy data."

Miss Bentley's sudden fame netted her many financial opportunities. She had been paid by the *World-Telegram*, which first broke the story of her espionage escapades, and, after her initial Congressional appearances, she earned money by lecturing and writing about her spy career. However, within less than two years, her reputation as a Mata Hari had become somewhat tarnished. Not one indictment had yet been obtained against any of her alleged agents. Moreover, Remington, cleared by a loyalty board and restored to his government job, had sued for libel when Miss Bentley repeated her charges on a radio program and he had received an out-of-court cash settlement from the network and program sponsor.

Herbert L. Packer, professor of law at Stanford University and author of a recent scholarly study of Elizabeth Bentley's role as a witness, suggests that by early 1950 ". . . Miss Bentley's financial future depended upon bringing her story before the public once again in a dramatic way."

Two events occurred that enabled her to do just that. First, in spring 1950 she contracted with the publishing firm of Devin-Adair to write, with the aid of a collaborator, the story of her life in the Communist underground. Subsequently, a federal grand jury in New York voted an indictment (for perjury) against Remington. An unsavory aspect of these seemingly fortuitous happenings was that Miss Bentley's literary collaborator and the foreman of the grand jury that indicted Remington were one and the same man: John Brunini.

As literary collaborator, Brunini was said by two former employees of Devin-Adair to have been named in Miss Bentley's original publishing contract—afterward destroyed—as the recipient of a share in her book profits. As grand jury foreman, Brunini had played a key role in Remington's indictment, persistently browbeating the latter's ex-wife, who eventually testified against Remington, in a manner that Judge Learned Hand later termed "beyond what I deem permissible."*

---

* Brunini: "Mrs. Remington. . . . we haven't shown our teeth, have we? Maybe you don't know about our teeth. A witness before a Grand Jury hasn't the privilege of refusing to answer a question [this, of course, is false]. You see, we haven't told you that so far. . . . Our procedure is, when we get a witness who . . . refuses to answer questions, to take them before a Judge . . . and the judge will find him in contempt . . . and sentence him to jail. . . . I don't want at this time to—I said 'showing teeth.' I don't want them to bite you."

Commenting that Remington* "was brought to book in a way that does not reflect credit on the administration of justice," Packer remarks on Miss Bentley's "inconsistent roles"—"as a pathetic witness to acts of betrayal, and as the commercial exploiter of her own story."

In March 1951, fresh from her recent courtroom appearances in the Brothman and the Remington cases, Elizabeth Bentley was called as a witness by U. S. Attorney Saypol and his special assistant, Roy Cohn, for the third time in four months. The purpose of her testimony at the Rosenberg-Sobell trial was twofold: As an "expert" on Communism, she gave testimony relating to—as Judge Kaufman expressed it—" the causal connection . . . between membership in the Party and intending to give an advantage to . . . the USSR." In addition, she also testified regarding alleged espionage activities of a man she never had met and knew only as "Julius."

Asked by Saypol if she once had accompanied Golos "to the vicinity of Knickerbocker Village," Miss Bentley recalled such an occasion over eight years before, in the fall of 1942, and recounted: "Mr. Golos said that he had to stop by to pick up some material from a contact, an engineer. . . . Mr. Golos parked the car; left me in it; went across the street to wait on the corner for his contact to appear; paced up and down for a bit. Then the contact finally arrived. Then they went three or four doors down to, I think, a candy store to carry on their business. Then Mr. Golos returned to the car with an envelope of material which he had received from the contact."

Miss Bentley testified that, following this incident, she had received some five or six telephone calls, between fall 1942 and November 1943, from a man who "always started his conversation by saying 'This is Julius.'" All of these calls came "after midnight, in the wee small hours. I remember it because I got waked out of bed." The caller instructed her to tell Golos that "he wanted to meet him." It was "considered unsafe" for her to call Golos from her own phone, so she would immediately "go out and go many blocks in the cold to get a pay telephone to call Mr. Golos." She said that she had learned that "Julius" lived in Knickerbocker Village.

Miss Bentley's account does not, of course, deal with the actual crime for which the defendants were tried. Her last telephone contact with a "Julius" was said by her to have occurred in the fall of 1943—over six months before the inception of the conspiracy alleged in the Rosenberg-

---

* When Remington's conviction was reversed on appeal, the Department of Justice took the highly unusual step of obtaining a new indictment against him for perjury allegedly committed during his first trial. Tried on this charge, he was convicted on two of five counts. The Court of Appeals sustained the verdict 2 to 1. Remington died in 1954 at the age of thirty-seven, murdered by a fellow prison inmate.

Sobell indictment. Nor was she able to identify the man she had seen with Golos or the voice of her telephone caller. Nevertheless, the inference of her story would seem to be that Julius Rosenberg, at the age of twenty-four, already was deeply involved in Soviet espionage.

Her testimony leaves a number of questions unanswered. Why, for instance, would Rosenberg have used his own first name in his dealings with Miss Bentley? She herself had employed a "collection of names," including Helen, Joan, and Mary.

Why, too, did "Julius" telephone in the "wee small hours"? Is a call in the middle of the night less likely to arouse suspicion than one in the early evening? If Miss Bentley's telephone was "considered unsafe" for calling Golos, why was it apparently safe for receiving messages from "Julius"? Finally, what about the telephone where Golos lived? Presumably Miss Bentley called Golos there, unless he slept in a phone booth. Yet there certainly was reason to suspect that Golos's phone might indeed be tapped, since he had been identified publicly with pro-Soviet activities for a number of years.

Counterbalancing these and other improbabilities is the fact that Miss Bentley's Rosenberg-Sobell trial testimony, unlike many of her other public utterances, was partially corroborated. Her story received support—albeit somewhat jumbled—from two key witnesses: Max Elitcher and David Greenglass.

Elitcher testified regarding a 1948 conversation between Rosenberg and Sobell, which he said had been recounted to him by the latter. Rosenberg reportedly had told Sobell that he had "once talked to Elizabeth Bentley on the phone" but was "pretty sure she didn't know who he was." On the other hand, Greenglass testified that, in 1950, Rosenberg had told him "that he had to leave the country himself . . . . that he knew Jacob Golos, this man Golos, and probably Bentley knew him."

This contradiction between the Elitcher and Greenglass testimony—as to whether or not Rosenberg believed that Miss Bentley "knew him"—points up a basic weakness in her account. For although Miss Bentley did not actually *know* her telephone contact, there seems little doubt that the information she claims to have learned about him in 1942 and 1943—that he was an engineer named Julius who lived at Knickerbocker Village—was ample to have led FBI agents straight to the guilty party.

Yet according to Miss Bentley, by about fall 1945—five years before Rosenberg was arrested—she had disclosed her "entire story, including Julius and the telephone calls and all to the FBI." If so, why had Rosenberg not been under surveillance by some of the hundreds of FBI agents who investigated the Bentley story and nabbed *in the act* of receiving or transmitting secret data? Why was Rosenberg never interrogated by the FBI about Golos and Miss Bentley or called before the 1947 grand jury probing her revelations?

One can only conclude either that the FBI was incredibly lax or that Miss Bentley did not tell about the "Julius" episode when she says she did.

In an attempt to discredit Miss Bentley's assertion that she had related the episode long before Rosenberg's arrest, Emanuel Bloch cross-examined her about her then unpublished book, for which she had received a $3000 advance. Had she mentioned the telephone calls in the book draft sent her publisher? Miss Bentley said she had.

BLOCH: When?
BENTLEY: I haven't the least idea. . . .

Obviously, the only definitive answer to the question of when Miss Bentley first told this aspect of her story to the authorities still remains hidden in FBI files. However, the possibility that she may have belatedly added the "Julius" incident to her confession gains substance when one is aware of her extraordinary willingness to "cooperate"—even when this means openly disregarding her previously sworn testimony.

For example, at the Brothman-Moskowitz trial, Miss Bentley testified that she and Abraham Brothman had had *long dinner meetings at public restaurants*. She also testified that she had *never met* Miriam Moskowitz or heard of her outside of the newspapers. Yet only four months later, at the Rosenberg-Sobell trial, Miss Bentley compliantly revised her story, in response to the prosecutor's leading questions:

SAYPOL: Is it not the fact that your meetings with people like Brothman *and Moskowitz* were held at odd places at night, deserted places? (Emphasis added.)
BENTLEY: Correct.
SAYPOL: And those meetings usually were brief?
BENTLEY: Yes.
SAYPOL: They took only a short time?
BENTLEY: As short as possible, yes, sir.

Since 1945, when J. Edgar Hoover dispatched the first installment of the Bentley story to the White House and assigned numerous FBI agents to its investigation, his personal prestige has, to some extent, been bound up in the story's outcome. He himself has not hesitated to accord her charges his nearly unqualified endorsement. In late 1953, Hoover declared:

"All information furnished by Miss Bentley, which was susceptible to check, has proven to be correct. She has been subjected to the most searching of cross-examinations; her testimony has been evaluated by juries and reviewed by the courts and has been found to be accurate."

Contesting this appraisal, law professor Herbert Packer, who has examined all of Miss Bentley's public testimony, concludes that Hoover's "suggestion that Miss Bentley's story has been reviewed and found accurate by operation of the judicial process is unwarranted." Packer observes: "The main outlines of her story have never been put in issue in a court trial."

As for Hoover's evaluation that all of Miss Bentley's information "which was susceptible to check, has proven to be correct," many serious inconsistencies and impossibilities in her accusations have been uncovered by persons without the investigative experience or resources of the FBI.

Probably the most extensive of such unofficial inquiries into the truth of the Bentley story was made by William Henry Taylor, a former government economist. In an early Congressional appearance, Miss Bentley named a "William Taylor" as one who had been involved in espionage and, when asked where he had been employed, replied: "William was in the Treasury." Her reference to Taylor by his first name (on another occasion she testified about a "Bill Taylor") strongly implied that she was personally acquainted with the man she was accusing; however, several years later, she admitted that she never had met him.

In 1955, William Henry Taylor, facing the loss of his job with the International Monetary Fund, sought exoneration through an all-out assault on Miss Bentley's credibility. In a lengthy brief submitted to the International Organizations Employees Loyalty Board, he and his attorney, Byron N. Scott, presented a rather thoroughgoing study of the total fabric of the Bentley story. Explaining why he had chosen so arduous and cumbersome a method to refute accusations leveled against himself, Taylor described his predicament:

"For a period of at least eight years, to my knowledge, I have been subjected to suspicion, unfavorable publicity, derision and a form of persecution. I have been questioned by FBI agents and Congressional investigators. I have been forced to appear repeatedly, always in secret, before Federal Grand Juries, Congressional Committees and now several sessions of this Loyalty Board. . . . Over the years I have been interrogated, or called for interrogation, on nineteen occasions and sometimes in a manner reminiscent of the Inquisition. Not once have I been confronted with an accuser or informer; not once have I been allowed to cross-examine. . . . Over the years I have been forced to defend myself against nebulous charges for which there is no sure defense. . . . I have suffered in silence . . . in the hope that this evil mirage would of itself dissipate and die away. But the times are such that he who refuses to answer questions under the constitutional provisions of the Fifth Amendment is adjudged by that very fact to be guilty and he who answers all questions is brought back again and again in the hope that major, or at the very least, minor discrepancies will appear in testimony spread over many pages and many years, and that thereby he who answers may be indicted and imprisoned for perjury in order to prove a major premise.

". . . As of today I am under continuing subpoena to five bodies—the House Un-American Activities Committee, the Senate Internal Security Subcommittee, the Senate Subcommittee on Government Operations, a Federal Grand Jury in New York and a Federal Grand Jury in the District of Columbia. . . .

"So vehement were the attacks upon me in late November and early December 1953 that for weeks my name was bandied about in the press, on the radio and over TV. Meantime word was reaching me from friends and acquaintances throughout this country and Canada that an intensive investigation of my life was being carried out anew by the FBI, and at its request, by the RCMP [Royal Canadian Mounted Police].

"How much of this sort of treatment must an American citizen absorb? . . . I . . . have been condemned to life in a world that is ever in twilight, subject to instant recall for repetitious questioning by anyone armed with a suspicion, a political motive and a subpoena. . . .

". . . I have come to the conclusion that there is a determination on the part of a few powerful men to render me unemployed and unemployable. . . . Who can doubt that if they are successful that I will be blackballed and blacklisted from gainful employment in my trained profession of economics for the rest of my life. I sense, however, that this is not their real motive. I happen to be the last of the many people, connected with the Government during the war years, who have been under attack as having been named by Miss Bentley, who remains in public service—though I am now with an international agency and not with the United States Government. . . . all of these people have resigned from or been forced out of public life. I, too, have been urged to resign; I, too, have been pressured to invoke the Fifth Amendment. I am now convinced that certain Government officials are not interested in me as a suspect but as a symbol—as long as I remain in Washington employed by as international agency I am a constant reminder of the failure of these same authorities to persuade a grand jury to accept the Bentley story. I am visible evidence of the weakness of their charge of twenty years of treason. . . .

"Until comparatively recently I had felt that I had almost no protection against Miss Bentley's accusations. I could put my life on display, including my service to my country during the war years and my internment in a Japanese prison camp. I could muster affidavits from friends and collect other documents. All this was done. Something, however, was lacking. I was pitting my honesty and integrity against Miss Bentley's; and Miss Bentley had become almost a national heroine. . . ."

Taylor and his attorney decided that what was "lacking" was an "intensive examination" of all of Miss Bentley's testimony and writings as well as declassified FBI documents relating to her disclosures, and they therefore undertook this task. Said Taylor: "Gradually,.there came a conviction that Miss Bentley not only had not been telling the truth in her references to William Taylor, if by that name she was referring to me, but she had not told the truth over wide areas of her story, and that these instances could be documented to a point beyond dispute."

The Taylor brief plays havoc with Miss Bentley's credibility. Some examples:

(Bentley) In July 1941, Golos informed her that "he had received from Earl Browder the name of a man working in the United States Government, who was interested in getting information to Russia and could organize a group of other government employees to help in this work." That same month, July, this man saw Golos in New York in a meeting arranged by Earl Browder.*

(Taylor brief) At the time of this incident, Browder was imprisoned in Atlanta Penitentiary, where he remained from March 1941 to May 1942.

(Bentley) William Ludwig Ullman informed her of the impending Doolittle raid on Tokyo "a week or ten days ahead of time," while he was an Air Corps officer assigned to the Pentagon.

(Taylor brief) Ullman was still at work in the Treasury Department at the time of the Doolittle raid. He was not drafted until six months later and was not stationed at the Pentagon until a full year after the Doolittle mission.

(Bentley) She collected Communist Party dues from members of the Perlo spy group and turned these over to Golos "during his lifetime."

(Taylor brief) Golos died in November 1943, and Miss Bentley has testified that she first took over the so-called Perlo group four months later, in March 1944.

(Bentley) After Golos's death, she continued his practice of showing all non-military data to Browder before passing it to the Russians.

(Taylor brief) Miss Bentley has testified that even before Golos's death she was turning over *undeveloped* microfilm to the Russians.

(Bentley) Harry Dexter White provided the spy ring with samples of Allied military currency for occupied Germany which the Russians wanted to counterfeit.

(Taylor brief) At the very same time that White allegedly was giving occupation currency samples to spies, he actually sent the Under-Secretary

* This story was altered in subsequent retellings.

of the Treasury an official memorandum in which he openly requested such samples for the British Treasury and the Soviet Ambassador—in accordance with previous high-level governmental agreements.

(Bentley) She learned the date of D-day "long before D-day happened" and passed the secret on to the Russians.

(Taylor brief) According to General Eisenhower, D-day was a variable date, left to his discretion. An invasion planned for June 5 was canceled at the last minute because of unfavorable weather, and the date of June 6 was therefore known to the Supreme Commander himself less than a day in advance. Furthermore, the date and invasion plans were not secrets from the Russian allies, who were kept posted day by day regarding timing, since the Red Army had agreed to coordinate a military offensive with D-day.

Taylor concluded:

". . . Miss Bentley has lied so often and so outrageously in her testimony to the FBI and in statements under oath that she can scarcely be looked upon longer as a creditable source. . . . that her testimony should be reexamined and reinvestigated is apparent. . . . For ten years every effort of certain investigative authorities has been taken to prove that her story is true. It should not take that long to prove that it is false, in whole or in large part."

Eventually, Taylor was cleared by the loyalty board and permitted to continue in his job. However, this vindication was won only after a further hearing in which his attorney demonstrated convincingly that a letter used as evidence against his client was a forgery.

Taylor's suggestion that the Bentley story be "reexamined" was not taken up by any governmental agency and, following his clearance, the harassment of others named by Miss Bentley continued. In 1956, one of those she had accused, V. Frank Coe, former Secretary of the International Monetary Fund, lashed back angrily when called before the Senate Internal Security subcommittee. Said Coe:

"This is no investigation; it is an attempt to keep alive the stale and discredited charges of Elizabeth Bentley. The FBI has been investigating [Harry Dexter] White and his associates for 15 years at least, grand juries for nine years, and congressional committees—about 20—have been so occupied for eight years. . . .

"But none of the eighty-odd persons investigated following their being named as spies by Elizabeth Bentley has ever been convicted or tried or indicted for espionage.

"Why? Because the charges are false, and known to this subcommittee to be false. I wish to drop the protection of the fifth amendment and to state for the record:

"I was never a spy.

"I am convinced that Harry White was not a spy, and that any notion to the contrary is unthinkable.

"I am also convinced that none of the other persons named by Bentley were spies."

Coe's rather direct challenge to the subcommittee and the Department of Justice was not followed by his indictment for perjury. One probable reason for this is that his accuser, Miss Bentley, never had met him and her hearsay allegations would be considered worthless in a court of law.

Similarly, portions of Miss Bentley's Rosenberg-Sobell trial testimony—regarding her trip with Golos to the Knickerbocker Village area to meet an "engineer"—were hearsay and were ruled inadmissible by Judge Kaufman (though what effect this legal ruling could have had on the jury that already had heard the testimony is hard to say). Miss Bentley's account of phone calls from a "Julius" was declared acceptable testimony only because of the earlier corroboration provided by Elitcher and, to a lesser extent, Greenglass. Yet this corroboration was a most slender thread on which to hang evidence in a capital case.

For Greenglass's inclusion of "Bentley" in his testimony seems strained and illogical. He claimed that Julius, while instructing him to flee the country because of the arrest of Fuchs and Gold, had remarked that he too had to leave. However, according to Greenglass, Julius's stated motive for flight was not his guilt as an atom spy but his fear that Elizabeth Bentley, whose revelations had then been public knowledge for two years, "probably . . . knew him."

As for Elitcher, he admitted that his recollection of a conversation concerning Elizabeth Bentley had been elicited from him by the FBI only after several months of pretrial interrogation. He testified: "The name Bentley was brought up by the FBI agents and I said I had nothing to do with Miss Bentley. At a much later period, I told them that the name Bentley had been mentioned to me by Sobell."

Many facets of the Bentley story still are unknown and will remain so unless an official inquiry should someday expose now secret FBI documents to public scrutiny. However, even with the information now available, it is abundantly clear that Miss Bentley's prosecution testimony at the Rosenberg-Sobell trial provides no grounds whatsoever for any firm assurance—or even well-reasoned suspicion—that the defendants were guilty.

We must look elsewhere for the answers we seek.

CHAPTER 25

MORTON SOBELL

The fate of Morton Sobell was inextricably entangled—both legally and in the popular mind—with that of the Rosenbergs. In the press, Sobell was continually labeled an "atom spy," although the prosecution made no such claim and, in fact, presented no clear-cut proof that he ever had committed any specific deed of espionage.

However, by the expedient of a joint conspiracy trial with the Rosenbergs, Sobell was made accountable for acts ascribed to his fellow defendants. To prove Sobell a member of the conspiracy, the prosecution needed only to establish that he had *agreed* to supply national defense data for the Soviet Union. A single witness, Max Elitcher, provided this essential evidence; he, alone, claimed to have any knowledge of Sobell's participation in the alleged conspiracy.

The decisive importance of Elitcher's testimony was pointed out by Judge Kaufman when he told the jury: "If you do not believe the testimony of Max Elitcher as it pertains to Sobell, then you must acquit the defendant Sobell."

At the time of the trial, Elitcher and Sobell had known each other for some twenty years. They had met, as teen-agers, at Stuyvesant High School in New York City. Later, at City College, where both studied engineering, Sobell was one of Elitcher's only friends. As Elitcher later observed about himself, he had had "almost no social relations" with his college classmates and had become friendly with "few, if any," of them. Rosenberg, also a member of his CCNY class, Elitcher knew only slightly.

After graduation, Elitcher and Sobell shared a bachelor apartment for more than two years in Washington, D.C., where both were employed by the Navy's Bureau of Ordnance. At the trial, Elitcher testified that during this period he had joined the Communist Party, claiming that he had been recruited by Sobell and had attended meetings with him.*

In 1941, Sobell went to the University of Michigan for his master's degree, while Elitcher stayed on in Washington. Despite the separation,

---

* Denying this, Sobell's wife told the authors that her husband, though a member of the Young Communist League "for a short time," never had belonged to the Communist Party.

the two maintained their close relationship. Elitcher married in 1943 and, a month afterward, took his wife to Schenectady to introduce her to his friend Sobell, then working for General Electric. When Sobell was married two years later, Elitcher was "best man" at the wedding ceremony.

In 1947, Max Elitcher made a mistake that would long haunt him: In order to retain his government employment, he falsely signed a federal loyalty oath in which he lied about his Communist Party membership. Afterward, he lived in constant fear that his perjury might be discovered. The following year, motivated largely by this anxiety, he quit the Navy Department job he had held for ten years and moved his family to New York City, where the Sobells were then living.*

The Elitchers bought a home in Flushing, Queens, on the street next to the Sobells'. The two small brick houses were located back-to-back, with easy access through unfenced abutting yards. Max obtained a job at the Reeves Instrument Company, where Morton already was employed. The two men regularly drove to work together; the women shared a jointly purchased washing machine kept in the Sobell basement.

However, the friendship between the families did not thrive in such proximity. By 1950, relations were rather strained, particularly between Morton Sobell and Helene Elitcher.

In the latter part of July, several days after the arrest of Julius Rosenberg, FBI agents visited Max Elitcher at Reeves, while other agents went to his home to talk with his wife. At the time, scores of former classmates and other associates of Rosenberg's were being questioned and were under surveillance by the FBI, so there is no reason to assume that Elitcher was regarded initially as an outstanding suspect.

However, from the first, Elitcher was well aware of his extreme vulnerability. He later commented—undoubtedly with his prejurious loyalty oath in mind—"I realized what the implications might be." For Elitcher, then thirty-one years old and the sole support of a wife and two children aged four and six months, the "implications" must have seemed serious indeed.

The FBI agents told him that they had information that he had "given material for purposes of espionage," an accusation which he promptly denied. Then the agents mentioned that they also had information that he was "a member of the Communist Party." Whether or not the FBI actually had any proof of Elitcher's Party membership is, of course, unknown. But for Elitcher, who had been "scared to death" for three years, it must have seemed certain that the moment he had dreaded for so long finally had arrived.

Elitcher decided to cooperate, apparently with the hope—if not the

---

* During his last year in Washington, Elitcher had entered psychiatric treatment at the "insistence" of his wife, who was already undergoing therapy. In New York City, he resumed treatment from 1949 to July 1950.

promise—of avoiding prosecution. He told the agents that he had been a member of the Communist Party when he signed his loyalty oath. He denied that he himself ever had turned over espionage data, but gradually confessed to a curiously circumscribed role in the alleged Rosenberg spy apparatus.

About a week after their initial interviews by the FBI, the Elitchers engaged the law firm of O. John Rogge (already representing the Greenglasses) to counsel them. In a contractual letter to the new clients, a member of the firm advised them that Max Elitcher had, in effect, admitted—in statements he said he had given the FBI—that he was guilty of the crime of perjury.

At her attorney's request, Helene Elitcher prepared a detailed account of her questioning by the FBI. She had, she wrote, been asked by the agents "how and when" she knew Rosenberg. She said that she had replied that Rosenberg had come to see them at their apartment in Washington once, sometime before the summer of 1944. He had telephoned as a school friend of her husband and visited for a few hours after dinner. The conversation, as she herself recalled it, was "banal," concerning war, jobs, and children. However, according to her husband, she had gone out of the room for a short time at Rosenberg's request and she knew nothing of what was discussed in that interval.

Helene Elitcher claimed that her husband later had reminded her of a second time that Rosenberg had visited them in Washington. She then told the FBI that there had been a second visit, although her memory of the occasion was extremely dim.

Mrs. Elitcher also stated that she and her husband had seen Rosenberg a few times in New York City. In the summer of 1944, they had dined at a restaurant with Rosenberg and several other people and had spent the evening with them. A year later, she and her husband found themselves in New York with no place to sleep for the night. Julius, whose wife and child were out of town, had invited them to stay over at his apartment at Knickerbocker Village and they had accepted. Lastly, one evening during Christmas of 1946 the Elitchers and a number of others were guests at the Rosenberg apartment.

Mrs. Elitcher concluded that this was all that she had remembered and told the agents about Julius Rosenberg.

Later, at the trial (where Helene Elitcher was listed as a witness but never called), there would be some suggestion by her husband that she "might know" about "this espionage business." However, Mrs. Elitcher's confidential report to her attorney, describing a purely social relationship with Rosenberg and making no mention of Sobell, indicates that she had no such knowledge.

The dates on which Max Elitcher told the FBI those parts of his story that connect Sobell to the alleged conspiracy are unknown. However, when Elitcher appeared before a grand jury on August 14, 1950, he related many of the main incidents involving Sobell that he subsequently testified about at the trial. Yet the indictment against the Rosenbergs handed down by the grand jury on August 17 did not include Sobell. His arrest (the following day) was based, instead, on a vaguely worded complaint sworn out by an FBI agent on August 3.

Thus, though the prosecution was interested enough in Sobell on August 3 to prepare a sealed complaint against him, two weeks later they apparently still were not certain enough of their eventual attitude toward him to request his indictment. The probable rationale for this tactic was spelled out by Saypol at the trial when he commented: "Initially, nobody knows whether an individual is a prospective witness or a prospective defendant."

Not until mid-October, when it must have been clear that Sobell was not a "prospective witness," was he named as a co-defendant of the Rosenbergs in a superseding indictment. None of the overt acts listed in this indictment mentioned or even alluded to Sobell. Thus, although he was awaiting trial for a capital offense, the only available details of the charges against him were those in the original complaint: That he "had a conversation with Julius Rosenberg" in New York City on five occasions in 1946, 1947, and 1948 (none of the dates stipulated later figured in the trial). When Sobell's attorneys petitioned the courts for a bill of particulars specifying the acts of which he was accused, the only additional information they were able to obtain was that "the approximate date when the defendant Sobell joined the alleged conspiracy is on or about June 15, 1944."

An interesting aside to the drama of one close friend testifying against another was that, in the months before the trial, Morton Sobell apparently remained unaware of the key prosecution role that Max Elitcher then was preparing to play. When the Sobell house was put up for sale to raise legal fees, Helen Sobell asked Helene Elitcher if she wanted anything for her equity in the dually owned washing machine. Mrs. Elitcher replied that she did and, soon after, she and Max accompanied their neighbor through her home, choosing various of the Sobells' possessions, including an old piano, a baby gate, and flagstones from the back yard.

At the trial, Elitcher had to be led frequently by Saypol as he told a story that was vague and improbable. He claimed that Rosenberg and also Sobell had on a number of occasions invited him to engage in espionage activities and that they had continued these requests sporadically over a four-year period—despite the fact that he never had turned over a single scrap of information to them.

Commented the New York *Daily News:* "Elitcher left trial observers with the impression that his must have been a masterpiece of equivocation and temporizing, since the first pressure was put on him in 1944.

. . . He was still resisting suggestions from Sobell and Rosenberg, he asserted . . . in 1948."

In none of his testimony did Elitcher allege that Sobell ever had sought him out for espionage purposes. Their conversations about "this espionage business" occurred only when Elitcher happened, by chance, to be visiting Sobell. In recounting the incident in which he said he had accompanied Sobell while the latter drove into Manhattan with a film can, Elitcher asserted that he did not know what, if anything, the can contained, nor had he actually seen Sobell deliver it to Rosenberg. In short, even if one believes every word of Elitcher's testimony, Sobell was not accused by him of any receipt, theft, or transmittal of information known to be secret.

The testimony of Elitcher is a classic example of the irrefutable story. The actual occurrence of most of the meetings that he told about was not disputed by the defense. The major point of contention concerned the *subject matter* of various unwitnessed conversations that he claimed took place at these meetings.

Max Elitcher was the prosecution's first witness. He had been fired from Reeves just before he testified and, once his court appearance was behind him, his attorneys turned their attention to their client's future. On March 19, 1951, while the trial was still in progress, a Rogge interoffice memo noted that Elitcher had provided the extremely important testimony connecting Rosenberg and Sobell and that it was clear he also would cooperate with the government in any forthcoming prosecutions. He had not been named as a defendant or co-conspirator in any legal action and probably never would be.

The attorney's memo further stated that Elitcher desired formal assurance from the appropriate authorities that they would help him to obtain the security clearance essential to his future employment in his specialized engineering field. It suggested that a letter addressed to Elitcher's prospective employers be secured from the Department of Justice or the FBI, stating that they would testify on his behalf at any subsequent security investigation.

It was a week after Max Elitcher stepped down from the witness stand before the name of Morton Sobell was again mentioned by the prosecution. In the interim, the jury had been occupied with the testimony of the Greenglasses and Gold and their unfolding story of atomic espionage. Now, as the prosecution's case drew to a close, the spotlight returned briefly to the bypassed defendant who sat beside the Rosenbergs at the defense table. This time, attention focused not on any accusation of criminal activity by Sobell but on his alleged flight to Mexico. This second part of the case against Morton Sobell, though of limited import legally, actually had dominated public attention from the start.

Sobell's arrest in the summer of 1950 was front-page news throughout the country and everywhere one theme, in particular, was stressed: Flight. Typical was the New York *Daily News* headline: "Fleeing Radar Expert Nabbed as Atom Spy."

The press offered details to show that the Sobell family had left their home in a hurry. Said *Newsweek* (in a story titled "Atom Arrest No. 8"): "Unopened milk bottles were aligned at the door."

Reported *Time*:

"Morton Sobell's 'vacation' trip was sudden, indeed. He locked up his house in Flushing, N.Y. one day in June, left a brand-new 1950 Buick in the garage. Without even telling his employers that he was leaving, he bundled his wife, their two children and himself into a commercial airliner, and flew to Mexico City.

"Apparently Sobell planned to travel much farther—perhaps to Russia. But last week his travel plans were altered. Picked up on a deportation order, he was whisked across the border before dawn one morning by a mysterious convoy of Mexican secret service agents and . . . arrested by waiting agents of the FBI. . . ."

At the same time, a few early accounts appeared to contradict these stories depicting Sobell's departure for Mexico as hasty, even frantic. Both the New York *Post* and the *Daily News* printed interviews with the personnel director of Reeves Instrument Company. They quoted him as saying that Sobell had requested a leave of absence from his job in June 1950, prior to his trip.

Other stories suggested some peculiarities concerning Sobell's ejection from Mexico. A *Times* account of the arrest concluded: "Mexican immigration officials in Nuevo Laredo, just across the Rio Grande, said the group that brought Sobell to the border did not report to their office. Ramon Roman Aleman, assistant immigration chief, said this was unusual."

The next day, in a story datelined Laredo, the *Times* observed: "The case was surrounded by extraordinary secrecy. The four agents who made the arrest still refused to furnish details. It was not known exactly in what manner Mexican authorities deported the instrument specialist."

Briefly, the following information about Sobell's trip to Mexico was presented by prosecution witnesses:

In the latter part of June 1950 (shortly after the arrest of Greenglass), Morton Sobell, his wife, and their two children traveled to Mexico City. From there, Sobell addressed two letters to a friend and former City College classmate, William Danziger, enclosing notes for his parents, uncle, and sister-in-law, which he asked Danziger to forward. According to Danziger's trial testimony, the first letter bore the alias "M. or Morty Sowell" on the envelope; the second, "M. or Morty Levitov."

In late July, Sobell left his wife and children in Mexico City and traveled to the seaports of Vera Cruz and Tampico. (He had previously inquired of a Mexico City neighbor, Manuel Giner de los Rios, how one might leave Mexico without papers, but had not indicated an interest in any particular country.) While on this journey to the coast, Sobell made use of five additional aliases: M. Sand, Morris Sand, Marvin Salt, N. Sand, and Morton Solt, and used false addresses as well. He also addressed letters for his wife to Giner de los Rios.

On August 18, 1950, Sobell was brought to the United States-Mexican border at Laredo, Texas, by Mexican police and was taken into custody there by FBI agents. Noted on the Sobell entry manifest card prepared by a U. S. Immigration official was the legend "deported from Mexico."

Prosecutor Saypol attempted to connect Sobell's sojourn in Mexico with the abortive plans for flight allegedly proposed by Rosenberg to the Greenglasses. He noted that in the "same month" that Rosenberg gave Greenglass money from the Russians to leave the country via Mexico, "Sobell and his family did in fact flee to Mexico." The prosecutor added that Sobell had gone to Vera Cruz, "just as Greenglass had been instructed to do."

Morton Sobell did not take the witness stand himself and no witnesses were called in his defense. The summation of his attorney, Edward Kuntz, was the only rebuttal to the flight charges heard by the jury. Kuntz claimed that Sobell had obtained a Mexican visa* and had flown "in his own name" to Mexico City, where the family had rented an apartment—"in their own name." The attorney also pointed out that Sobell's Mexico City neighbor, Giner de los Rios, had testified that he had known him by his correct name. However, he offered no explanation for Sobell's strange letters to Danziger or his trips to the Mexican seaports under aliases, observing that whatever "kind of a brainstorm Sobell might have had. . . . is his own business."

Kuntz remarked that the U. S. Immigration inspector who had written "deported from Mexico" on Sobell's entry card had admitted on cross-examination that he never had received any official notification of the alleged deportation. Commenting that "Mexico has a government; it has courts; it has Immigration officials," Kuntz challenged the prosecution as to why no Mexican official had been brought to testify that Sobell really had been deported.

The reason for this challenge became clear on the day of sentencing. Then, Sobell's attorneys brought new information into court in the form of an affidavit from their client which, if true, indicated that he had not been removed from Mexico by legal extradition proceedings but had, in fact, been kidnaped. The affidavit stated:

"On Wednesday, August 16, 1950, at about 8:00 P.M. we had just finished our dinner in our apartment in Mexico City in the United States

---

* Actually, a tourist card.

of Mexico, and while my wife and I were lingering over our coffee there was a knock on the door. My older daughter opened the door and three men burst into the room with drawn guns and bodies poised for shooting; these men did not ask my name, did not say what they wanted. I demanded to see a warrant, or some other legal process. No reply, except some vague charge that I was one 'Johnnie Jones' and that I robbed a bank in Acapulco in the sum of $15,000.00 was made. Of course, I vehemently denied the charge. . . .

". . . I insisted on calling the American Embassy but without being permitted to do so.

"They picked me up bodily and carried me down from the fourth floor to the ground floor. In the street I kept shouting for the police. A taxi was hailed and they opened the door; tried to force me into the taxi; when two more men came in and beat me over the head with blackjacks until I lost consciousness. I woke up in the taxi and I was stretched horizontally at the feet of the three men.

"When the car stopped in front of a building, they ordered me to get up; they told me to get into the building, but not to make a scene or they would plug me. . . . we went upstairs, and, we went into an office.

"They sat me down and a slim, tall, dark man came over; he looked at me. I asked him what it was all about. He slapped me in the face and told me that they were the ones that were asking questions. At that point I discovered that my head was bloody and my shirt bespattered with blood.

"However, they asked me no questions. . . . We spent in that building from approximately 8:30 P.M. till 4:00 A.M. . . .

"At 4:00 A.M. I was moved into a large four-door Packard and seated in the rear with two armed men, one on each side of me. At that moment, the same tall, thin man came to the door and spoke to my guards in English saying to them 'If he makes any trouble shoot him.'

"The driver of the car, who apparently was the leader of the expedition . . . told me that they were taking me to the Chief of the Mexican Police for further action. With a number of stops for one reason or another, we drove on until about 6:00 P.M. At that time . . . [the leader] tried to make a phone call or he did make one, and he told me that he was trying to get the chief of police. The same thing happened at about 10:00 P.M., and at midnight on August 17th, telling me that he was trying to make sure that the chief of police would be available.

"At about 1:30 A.M. we arrived at Nuevo Laredo. . . .

"We stopped at the Mexican Customs on the Mexican side of the bridge, across the Rio Grande marking the border. No examination was made of my baggage. . . . When we reached the bridge . . . our car was flagged. We stopped and the front door opened. A man entered with a badge in his hand and stated that he was a United States agent and he remained in the car. When we arrived at the United States Customs I was directed to sign a card, arrested after they searched my baggage and myself. They handcuffed me and placed me in jail where I remained for five days, after which time I was taken to New York City."*

Judge Kaufman criticized the defense for not having presented these allegations to the jury during the trial, and denied a motion for arrest of judgment based on the affidavit. He told the thirty-three-year-old Sobell: "I do not for a moment doubt that you were engaged in espionage activities; however, the evidence in the case did not point to any activity on your part in connection with the atom bomb project." Judge Kaufman thereupon imposed the maximum prison term then permitted under the espionage law—thirty years—and added: "While it may be gratuitous on my part, I at this point note my recommendation against parole."

Sobell's conviction was upheld by the Court of Appeals early in 1952 by a vote of 2 to 1. The dissenter, Judge Jerome Frank, believed that the case against Sobell should not have been tried jointly with the Rosenberg-Greenglass-Gold atom bomb conspiracy, and declared that Sobell was entitled to a new trial. Later that year, after the Supreme Court had denied certiorari, Sobell was transferred to Alcatraz Federal Penitentiary.

It would be difficult to think of any sound penological explanation for the decision of the Department of Justice to incarcerate Sobell, who had no previous criminal record, in the nation's harshest prison. However, as John Godwin noted in his book on Alcatraz, at the time of Sobell's arrival there the Rock was the jail "to which the Federal government sent prisoners it particularly disliked."

The severity of Sobell's sentence and his imprisonment in the bleak isolation of America's Devil's Island—some three thousand miles from home and family—can at least partly be accounted for by the fact that he, like the Rosenbergs, had steadfastly insisted on his innocence, refusing repeated admonitions to confess and cooperate.

In September 1953, Sobell submitted an affidavit from Alcatraz to the Court of Appeals in which he asserted:

". . . my [appeals] counsel have informed me that at every stage of this proceeding, since the trial, the United States Attorney has stressed in oral argument and affidavit, the fact that I did not take the stand in my own behalf, at the trial. It is highly inappropriate in this case that this fact be given any significance whatsoever, for the following reasons. . . .

"*I wanted to testify on my own behalf at my trial.* I did not do so because my trial attorneys insisted that I should not, because (1) of the fact that the case that the prosecution had put in against me was so weak that my innocence was clearly established; and (2) that it was so clear

---

* Sobell's wife and children were placed in another car and also driven, virtually nonstop, some seven hundred miles to the border.

A REASONABLE DOUBT

that I had nothing to do with any atomic espionage conspiracy . . . that it would necessarily follow that I would be freed. . . . I now know I should have insisted on telling my story.

"I am completely innocent of the charges made against me. The fantastic tale Max Elitcher told about a wild midnight ride to Julius Rosenberg's apartment is untrue. . . . The balance of his testimony against me, which consisted in not a scintilla more than the insinuation by him of a reference to 'espionage' in innocent and routine conversations I had had with him, is likewise untrue.

"The only other testimony concerning me at the trial related to a trip to Mexico which I made with my family, which had nothing to do with espionage, and which only after the trial did I realize was given significance by court and jury out of all proportion to what the facts actually showed. . . . to make the record clear, I want to tell the whole story now.

"My wife, daughter, infant son and I left New York in late June, 1950 for Mexico City. This was no suddenly developed plan. I had become dissatisfied with my work in the summer of 1949, but I couldn't very well leave then because I was in the middle of a big project at the Reeves Instrument Company, where I worked. I was in charge of the design and manufacture of a special radar computer known as a Plotting Board, and to have deserted it in midstream would naturally have prejudiced opportunities for future employment. During the following year I investigated several positions but couldn't find anything like what I wanted. I was really interested in getting into more basic research or an academic position.

"My project was completed by June, 1950. At about the same time my daughter's school term ended, my wife's graduate physics course at Columbia wound up, and my own course I was teaching at Brooklyn Polytechnic Institute . . . came to its summer recess. None of us had any special ties keeping us in the city, so we decided to go to Mexico. . . . we had been planning and dreaming of such a trip for several years. . . .

". . . I wrote my employer for an indefinite leave of absence, applied for and obtained necessary visas [tourist cards] from the Mexican consul in New York . . . and bought round-trip tickets at the American Airlines ticket office. On the way, I had the customs officials at Dallas examine and make a record of my foreign-made cameras, so I wouldn't have to pay duty on them when bringing them back into the country. In Mexico City, we rented an apartment for a month or two, where the family stayed all the time we were there.

"There was one aspect of the trip, however, which differentiated it from a routine vacation. I was not alone, in mid-1950, in having become apprehensive over signs of political intimidation and repression in this country. . . . Although a scientist, I was not oblivious to political developments, and in fact, in common with many other scientists, saw a danger to my future in the oppressive atmosphere in which we had to work. My wife and I talked about saving our children from the terrible things the world had seen occur in Nazi Germany, and had at least half an idea we could escape their threatened repetition here. We had both engaged in left of center political activities in college days and every day saw people, including distinguished scientists like Dr. Condon, harassed and persecuted for no more than their opinions and associations. All this, coupled with my dissatisfaction with my job anyway, and the fact that we had saved up some money meant that when we left, we just didn't know whether we would come back or not. . . .

"In Mexico, there were more typical examples of our indecision. . . . we cashed in our adult American Airlines return trip tickets that were good for only 60 days, but kept the one for our daughter that was good for six months.

"Then, in the midst of our uncertainties, the newspapers suddenly published the news of Julius Rosenberg's arrest as an alleged 'atom-spy.' To me, the charge was absurd, but nonetheless frightening in what it meant. I had known Julius in City College years before, we had been together in a number of progressive student organizations during our college days, and had seen each other infrequently since then. I felt that he was being persecuted for political reasons and that the charge was calculated to intimidate and silence political dissent in the United States. I reasoned that anybody who opposed the then new Korean war . . . would be slapped into jail on one pretext or another. But this led me to make the mistake of feeling that a dictatorship was already taking over my country.

"Then, and only then, was it that I left the family in the Mexico City apartment and traveled around Mexico—to Vera Cruz and Tampico— even using false names, and inquiring about passage to Europe or South America for all of us. It is hard to understand how I might have been led to do such a stupid thing, but it didn't take long for me to recognize how inept and pointless it was. Of course, I had no idea how it could be misinterpreted, and how dangerous it would turn out to be.

"So I went back to Mexico City, and my wife and I talked it over once again. . . .

". . . [we] decided to come back to New York, take up our lives, and join in whatever way we could in resisting the attacks on the liberties of people that were being made in the United States. We made plans for our return. . . . we then secured vaccinations in Mexico City—which we had not needed to get there, but which we did need to return to the United States.

"But then came the unheard-of attack which deprived us of the chance to return voluntarily. . . ."

Several items of documentary evidence supporting some of the assertions made by Sobell in his appeals affidavit were included in John Wexley's book, *The Judgment of Julius and Ethel Rosenberg,* published in 1955. Reproduced in a series of appendices are the following:

A May 1948 letter from Pan American Airways to Morton Sobell replying to his inquiry about "Excursion fares." This letter indicates that, two years before Sobell and his family went to Mexico, he had evidenced an interest in foreign travel. It therefore tends to confirm his contention that "we had been planning and dreaming of such a trip for several years."

Round-trip ticket stubs and a passenger list showing that Morton Sobell and his wife and two children used their own names when flying on American Airlines from New York City to Mexico City, the evening of June 22, 1950.

A letter from the school attended by the Sobells' ten-year-old daughter stating that the school term in 1950 had ended on June 21. This letter partially confirms Sobell's claim that the family had awaited the summer recess of their activities before they left New York.

A customs declaration form, made out by Sobell in his own name in Dallas, Texas (where the plane stopped en route to Mexico), proving the truth of his assertion that "I had customs officials at Dallas examine and make a record of my foreign-made cameras, so I wouldn't have to pay duty on them when bringing them back into the country."

Rent receipts for the months of July and August 1950 for a Mexico City apartment, made out to a Sr. Morton Sobell.

Various identification documents, including a social security card, birth certificate, and driver's license, issued to Morton Sobell and carried by him at the time of his arrest.

In addition, Sobell's attorneys submitted to the courts on appeal an official statement from the Mexican government indicating that the family had entered Mexico with valid tourist cards secured in their own names.

In the light of this information, which has become publicly available since the trial, how well does Saypol's claim that "Sobell and his family did in fact flee to Mexico" stand up?

The Sobells left the country openly, using genuine travel documents, and apparently made no effort to conceal their identities. That their journey began a week after the arrest of Greenglass is not necessarily significant, particularly considering the month. The end of June is the time when countless Americans embark on vacation trips.

Pretrial publicity indicated that the Sobell family had abandoned their home and activities precipitously; Sobell was said to have vanished without notifying his employer. However, the prosecution produced no witness from Reeves or elsewhere to testify to such a sudden exit. In point of fact, there is reason to believe that Sobell either had requested a leave of absence from his job or had resigned.* Furthermore, he seems to have awaited the termination of his daughter's school term before leaving.

William Danziger, who visited the Sobell home immediately before the trip, apparently perceived nothing in either the appearance of the house or the demeanor of the family to suggest flight. Several months later, when Danziger's wife met Helene Elitcher while both were testifying before a grand jury, the two women chatted about their husbands' former classmate—Sobell. Afterward, Mrs. Elitcher recounted the conversation in a memo to her attorney:

Mrs. Danziger reportedly related that her husband had visited the Sobells at their home just prior to their departure for Mexico. She said that her husband had gone there to borrow an electric drill he needed to fix his bed and that the Sobells had looked to him as though they were preparing for an ordinary vacation. However, she added, when her husband told this to the FBI, they accused him of trying to provide an alibi for Sobell.

In sum, no proof was introduced showing that Sobell's actual *departure* from the United States represented "flight," whereas abundant evidence, now available, raises the possibility that it may not have.

It was Sobell's behavior *while in Mexico*—his letters to Danziger with enclosures for his relatives† and his eleven-day trip to Vera Cruz and Tampico—that provided the bulk of the prosecution's flight evidence against him. U. S. Attorney Saypol asserted that the conduct exhibited by Sobell in Mexico "fits in the pattern of only one thing—membership in this conspiracy to commit espionage for the Soviet Union and flight from an American jury when the day of reckoning had come."

However, two seemingly irremediable flaws mar the coherence of Saypol's argument: Sobell and his family did not leave Mexico. After Morton's return from his trip to the port cities, they remained at their Mexico City apartment for the next two weeks and were living there under their own name when they were summarily taken to the border. Secondly, Sobell's "pattern" of behavior indicates that he was completely unaware of the now famous escape plan said to have been outlined for David Greenglass by Julius Rosenberg.

Central to this plan was the obtaining of false travel documents for the Greenglass family. The scheme allegedly entailed the dispatch by Greenglass of a coded letter to the Soviet Embassy in Mexico, a rendezvous several days later near a statue of Columbus in Mexico City, and

---

* A recent inquiry to Reeves elicited the reply that "Sobell's employment was terminated by his resignation."

† Regarding these letters to Danziger, Helene Elitcher noted in her memo to her attorney that Mrs. Danziger commented on how crazy Sobell must be, pointing out that he even had written to her husband from Mexico and (they later learned from the FBI) had used his actual Mexican address on the envelopes.

the receipt of forged passports, money, and instructions that would take the fugitives to Sweden and then Czechoslovakia. Yet, nearly two months after his arrival in Mexico City, Sobell was still there, and the prosecution never has alleged that, when he was arrested, any false passports or cache of Soviet flight money was found in his possession. In fact, he was said to have asked his neighbor, Giner de los Rios, how one might leave the country *without papers*.

Sobell's explanation for his trip was that it was a vacation cast against a background of apprehension over "signs of political intimidation and repression" in the United States. He claimed that he and his wife "had at least half an idea" of becoming expatriates. If so, the Sobells' views were not unique. In the summer of 1950, a belief in the imminence of war and Fascism was widespread among the American radical left. This dire prophecy may well have seemed to Sobell to be nearing fulfillment when, the day after his arrival in Mexico, the Korean War began. It was in the first weeks following the outbreak of this war that he mailed his letters with aliases to Danziger.

According to Sobell, when he read of the arrest of his classmate Rosenberg on July 17, 1950, he concluded that "a dictatorship was already taking over my country" and, five days later, traveled to the coast "inquiring about passage to Europe or South America." However, he says he soon realized "how inept and pointless" his actions were and returned to his family in Mexico City with the thought of going back to New York.

Since Sobell was forcibly removed from Mexico, there is no way of knowing if he really had intended going home of his own free will. On appeal, his attorneys contended that he had and offered evidence to prove that Mexican secret police agents—acting in collusion with the FBI—had expelled him from the country, without the knowledge of Mexican immigration authorities. These allegations have never been accorded a judicial hearing and, to this day, stand unchallenged.

Whether one assumes Sobell to have been a fugitive spy or a would-be political refugee, the fact is that many aspects of his behavior while in Mexico seem to preclude any rational motive. Why didn't Sobell write directly to his parents, uncle, and sister-in-law? Did he fear that the authorities might intercept his mail? If he believed such drastic action possible, why should he assume that letters to his friend Danziger might not also be examined? Was he trying to conceal his whereabouts? Then why did he wrote his correct address in Mexico City on the envelopes of these letters, barely hiding his identity with such thinly disguised aliases as Morty Sowell and Morty Levitov (his wife's maiden name)? If he was planning to remain in Mexico or go elsewhere, why did he write to Danziger: ". . . I will explain when I get home." What, too, can one say about the use of *five* aliases over a short period (including two different ones with the same airline in a matter of several days)?

336

It seems a fair conclusion that Sobell's letters to Danziger and, particularly, his trip to the Mexican seaports were the irrational acts of a man in panic. He himself stated: "It is hard to understand how I might have been led to do such a stupid thing." It is, of course, conceivable that his panic stemmed from his membership in the Rosenberg spy ring though, if so, it is difficult to understand why he did not follow the flight plan imparted to Greenglass. However, it is equally plausible that Sobell's explanation is at least partially correct.

Here we come to the limitations of flight testimony and the reason why, alone, it can never be taken as proof of guilt. For flight testimony can, at most, prove that a man is afraid but not what he is afraid of or even whether or not his fears are realistic.

In the belief that some significant elements of the Sobell story might still be untold, the authors conducted lengthy interviews with Helen Sobell and William Danziger and also pursued other related research paths.

William Danziger grew up in the same Bronx neighborhood with Max Elitcher and, together with him and Morton Sobell, attended Stuyvesant High School, studied engineering at CCNY, and afterward secured a job with the government in Washington. For a time, he worked "just down the hall" from Elitcher at the Navy's Bureau of Ordnance. Danziger believes Sobell innocent and has "serious doubts" about the entire Elitcher testimony, partly because of the fact that during his own years with the government he himself never was approached by Rosenberg or anyone else seeking classified data.

The authors were particularly interested in questioning Danziger about one aspect of his testimony as a prosecution witness. He had related that, in the spring of 1950, while paying a social call on Sobell, the latter had mentioned that their classmate Rosenberg was in the machine shop business. Danziger, then in private industry doing nonmilitary work, had remarked that his firm occasionally farmed out machine shop jobs. He asked Sobell for Rosenberg's address and twice, in June and July, visited his shop and spoke with him. Also in June, Danziger testified, he had gone to Sobell's home to borrow an electric drill—at which time Sobell had informed him that he was leaving "for a vacation in Mexico" and was "flying to Mexico City."

At the trial, the sequence of Danziger's meetings with Rosenberg and Sobell was not disclosed. However, Danziger told the authors that his first visit to Rosenberg had occurred a few days *before* he borrowed the drill from Sobell. Furthermore, although his present recollection is hazy, he has the impression that Rosenberg (who by then had been interrogated by the FBI following the apprehension of Greenglass) had made some general remarks to him about being investigated or harassed. Danziger remembers having communicated the substance of this conversation to Sobell while the latter was preparing for his trip to Mexico.

It was about a week later, Danziger said, that he received the first letter from Sobell in Mexico City. Seeing the name "M. Sowell" on the envelope, he thought at first that it "might be a gag"—Am so well—but finally decided that "Morty was in some kind of difficulty."

Many of Danziger's former classmates were then working, directly or indirectly, for the government, and, with the federal loyalty program becoming increasingly pervasive, they were "kept in a constant state of jitters." People he knew were being questioned by the FBI, or learning that others were being questioned about them, or worrying about some minor or major loyalty oath lie they might have committed. In this atmosphere, there was "a great deal of irrationality in people's behavior." Danziger therefore did not concern himself unduly over Sobell's use of foolish aliases or about the enclosures, which seemed innocuous when he read them. He recalls, very vaguely, that one of Sobell's notes—to his uncle, Morris Pasternak—had inquired about a "lawyer." Danziger's tentative conclusion, which he apparently still favors, was that Sobell was in some sort of loyalty oath trouble.

Helen Sobell told the authors that she feels quite sure that Danziger had mentioned to her husband an "investigation" involving Rosenberg and that this knowledge influenced his initial use of aliases. It was also a factor in her husband's note to his uncle in which, she says, he asked for the name of an attorney in Mexico conversant with American law. Not until well over a month after this note was sent, by which time she claims the family was preparing to return home, was a reply received. It came from another uncle, Louis Pasternak, and, in keeping with the surreptitious way in which the inquiry had been posed, was couched in a rather heavy-handed cloak-and-dagger style. Just why Morton Sobell had felt the need for a lawyer soon after his arrival in Mexico—other than his anxieties over the Korean War and the FBI's investigation of a classmate with whom he was friendly—was not clear to the authors. Pressed about possible fears similar to those of Elitcher's regarding a perjury prosecution, Mrs. Sobell admitted that her husband had failed to list "certain organizations" on his loyalty questionnaire, but she denied that he had felt in any "immediate danger" about this at the time.

In answer to our request for further information, Morton Sobell wrote his wife:

"I have also been trying to recall the period you spoke about—but it's not easy. One would think that such important decisions and events would stand out sharply in relief. But they don't. I can much more easily remember some seemingly insignificant trifles than these life and death matters.

"Probably the basic reason for this lies in the disjointed sequence of events and motivations. This is a big difference between novels and life.

The novelist never seems to be at a loss to explain an action. Cause and effect—like the cue stick hitting the billiard ball.

"Initially the trip involved many different considerations—and I know I had no fixed idea of what it was I was after. If I called it *exploratory* it would probably be most accurate.

"But then, once begun, events moved so swiftly that in no time we found ourselves caught up in the maelstrom of contemporary history. . . . What if there had been no Korea at that particular moment? Would I have acted as I did? (Panicked would be more accurate.). . . . In retrospect it seems I must have become frightened—the pregnant moment that might give birth to mankind's death.

"Under the circumstances was it strange that I felt the need for getting in touch with an attorney? And the letters . . . asking . . . for one. But why the impulse for an assumed name? Certainly the central reason—an attempt to avoid detection—cannot be denied. But why then? Was it what Bill had told me about Julie's trials? And my empathetic projection? What seems logical at one moment isn't necessarily so in retrospect."

The Mexican secret service police who brought Sobell to the border delivered to FBI agents there many personal effects of the prisoner's. On three or four occasions since the execution of the Rosenbergs, Sobell's attorneys have managed to secure the return of some of these items, and a number were utilized in a petition for a new trial. With Mrs. Sobell's permission, her husband's attorney provided the authors with photocopies of thirty such items not previously made public. With a single exception (a letter from Sobell to his parents), everything turned over to us had been found by police on August 16, 1950, in the Sobells' Mexico City apartment.

The largest single category of this material is various airline and passenger ship schedules to all parts of the world. All of these schedules appear to have been obtained by Sobell in Mexico.

There are also six letters exchanged by Sobell and his wife during his trip to Vera Cruz and Tampico, largely personal in content. Those from him contain a few apparent references to what he later characterized as his "inept" efforts to secure passage abroad without papers.

From Vera Cruz, he wrote: "Got here at 7:45 this morning—took a nap and looked around. . . . I walked along the docks . . .—nice harbor. . . ."

Still in Vera Cruz, a few days later: "So far I've worked up a good sun tan—and that's about all. . . . Spent the morning with a stevedore. . . . Otherwise I spend considerable time on the docks. . . . the sun is fierce."

From Tampico: "Got here about 1:30 and ate. Then looked around until 6 P.M. (this included a bus ride to the beach.)"

About a week after returning to Mexico City from the coast, Sobell sent his parents a letter, dated August 8, in which he noted: "We're really having a swell vacation and wish you could as well."

A letter received by Sobell (under an alias) in the same period was mailed from New York City on August 9 by his uncle, who commented that he had been "able to contact a top-notch doctor." (According to Mrs. Sobell, this was a guarded reference to her husband's earlier request for the name of a lawyer.)

Perhaps the most interesting item in this miscellany is a vaccination certificate made out in the name of Morton Sobell. The certificate (which has on it Sobell's correct U.S. street address) shows that he was vaccinated against smallpox on August 8, 1950, in Mexico City. Other certificates, in his wife's and daughter's names, are dated a few days later. They tend to corroborate, in part, Sobell's claim that after he got back from the coast he and his family "made plans for our return. . . . we then secured vaccinations in Mexico City—which we had not needed to get there, but which we did need to return to the United States." While the certificates really cannot prove that the Sobells were planning to "return to the United States" (vaccinations were required by many other countries), they do indicate that Sobell did not obtain this essential travel document until long after his arrival in Mexico. Moreover, the fact that Sobell's vaccination certificate is in his own name shows that, *wherever* he was planning to go, he did not expect to travel under an alias.

The authors had sought some *definitive* answer as to the source of Sobell's frightened behavior while in Mexico. In this, we were not successful. Still, we believe one can fairly dispute the claim of U. S. Attorney Saypol that Sobell's conduct "fits the pattern of only one thing." For the total picture now discernible is not that—portrayed by the prosecution—of a fugitive member of a highly organized espionage apparatus armed with a coherent flight plan. Rather Sobell appears as a fearful and confused individual who acted out of complex and at least partially obscure motives as he wandered, rather ludicrously, along the docks of Vera Cruz in the blazing August sun.

For the past decade, an amazingly persistent fight has been waged on Sobell's behalf by an organization called the National Committee to Secure Justice for Morton Sobell. Among the most active workers on its small staff are Sobell's wife and mother. Operating with modest resources from offices in New York City, the Committee has managed to spread its message widely and has gained a considerable number of adherents, including some of international eminence. Its unceasing attacks on the validity of Sobell's conviction frequently have piqued the Department of Justice.

Thus, in the spring of 1956, when Sobell's attorneys petitioned the federal district court for a hearing on motions concerning his expulsion from Mexico, the then U. S. Attorney, Paul W. Williams, charged:

"The arguments are obviously designed not so much as for legal consideration as to feed the propaganda mills of this defendant—repeatedly, ever since this trial they started to throw a deprecating and vile stream of abuse upon this court . . . Sobell's petitions are obviously designed for the consumption of those gullible people in this country and abroad—such as Bertrand Russell, who . . . said: 'I am very glad that a movement is on foot to secure justice for Morton Sobell. . . . The evidence upon which he was convicted was not such as any court of justice would have thought adequate in a case not involving hysteria.' "*

Judge Irving Kaufman, who heard Sobell's motion and denied a hearing, also scored "extralegal means resorted to in order to arouse emotions, public opinion or anything of that character. . . ."

Although it is undoubtedly true that the National Committee to Secure Justice for Morton Sobell resorted to extralegal propagandizing, the government apparently did not entirely eschew these tactics either.

In October 1957, while Sobell's petition was pending before the Supreme Court, the Rosenberg-Sobell case received prominent mention from the nation's press on at least three separate occasions within a single week.

First, former U. S. Attorney Myles Lane resurrected David Greenglass's "sky platform" testimony, thereby triggering a rash of headlines about the theft of space secrets by the Rosenberg ring. Noted the Chicago Tribune: "The Greenglass testimony was revealed as Morton Sobell . . . was making his third plea for freedom to the Supreme court."

Then, only a few days later, Sobell's wife, Helen, suddenly became the subject of banner front-page newspaper headlines. The chief government witness at the Brooklyn espionage trial of Rudolph Ivanovich Abel had injected her name into the proceedings, which were otherwise completely unconnected with the Rosenberg-Sobell case.

The witness, Finnish-born Reino Hayhanen, a self-confessed co-conspirator of Abel's, testified that in the spring of 1955 Abel had received $5000 from the Soviet Union for Helen Sobell. They had been unable to deliver the money to her, Hayhanen said, because "close to her apartment in on street corner near there was almost all the time a policeman."

Hayhanen testified that he never had seen Mrs. Sobell but had falsely reported to Moscow that "I located Helen Sobell and I gave money and told to her to spend them carefully." (He later added that he himself actually had pocketed the money which he claimed had been intended for Mrs. Sobell.) Thereafter, he allegedly was instructed to locate Helen Sobell again, give her more money, and "decide is it possible to use her as an agent." Hayhanen explained that "usually in Soviet espionage prac-

---

* Later, in a letter to the New York Times, Williams also criticized Jean-Paul Sartre for questioning Sobell's guilt and urging his release from jail.

tice they recruit husband and wife together as agents." He said it was his understanding that both Mrs. Sobell and her husband had been Soviet agents.

The New York *Times* noted that cross-examination of Hayhanen by defense attorney James B. Donovan had suggested that the witness was "a thief, a bigamist, a drunkard and a liar." Aside from the state of his morals, his tale about Mrs. Sobell strains one's credulity. That the wife of a convicted spy would be useful for espionage work hardly seems likely. Mrs. Sobell issued an immediate statement regarding Hayhanen's allegations, commenting:

"This meaningless testimony is just a way of smearing me at a time when my husband's case is before the Supreme Court in a request for a new trial."

While Hayhanen's charges were being widely reported, *Look* magazine was on the stands with its "exclusive preview" of the Department of Justice's report on the Rosenberg-Sobell case. A memorandum to the Supreme Court from Sobell's attorneys protested the government's resort to "polemics in a national magazine."

In an editorial appearing a few days after the Supreme Court refused to review the Sobell petition, the Milwaukee *Journal* criticized "the gross impropriety and indiscretion of the justice department in so obviously propagandizing just as the matter comes before the high court." Commenting that the "department rather tenuously linked" Sobell to the Rosenbergs "with less than conclusive evidence," the editorial observed that "a number of conscientious citizens, including legal scholars . . . are uneasy about many aspects of the case and have haunting doubts that the integrity of justice was fully preserved in it."

A few months later, in February 1958, Sobell's supporters won a small victory: After over five years in Alcatraz, Sobell was transferred to the more humane Atlanta Penitentiary. Among those to express pleasure at this transfer was the Rev. Peter McCormack, former Protestant chaplain at Alcatraz, who had met Morton Sobell there and had come to believe in his innocence. Rev. McCormack's efforts in Sobell's behalf had brought about his dismissal from his desolate prison pastorate.

In 1961, the newly elected President, John F. Kennedy, received a petition for Executive clemency from Morton Sobell. Many respected Americans joined in his plea. A sampling of supporting statements includes:

Lee Metcalf, U. S. Senator from Montana: ". . . Morton Sobell was convicted on very dubious evidence . . . clemency should be recommended."

Rev. Martin Luther King, Jr., Negro leader: "Morton Sobell . . . was convicted at a time when a climate of hysteria pervaded the country. . . . whether Sobell was guilty or innocent, I am firmly of the opinion that his thirty year sentence constituted a cruel and unusual punishment."

Roger Baldwin, civil libertarian: "Sobell has already served far longer than any term which would likely be imposed under normal circumstances."

Harold Urey, physicist: "In my opinion, a pardon to Morton Sobell would be correct . . . a commutation of his sentence . . . to the time already served is the minimum required to partly correct what I believe is a grave miscarriage of justice."

Rheinhold Niebuhr, theologian: "I am among those who believe that combining Mr. Sobell's trial with the Rosenberg trial was unfair to Sobell. . . ."

Maxwell Geismar, literary historian and critic: ". . . I am convinced that his trial had doubtful elements in it, and that his sentence was barbaric. . . ."

Clemency was not granted. In 1962, Sobell became eligible for parole for the first time. He had already been in prison for twelve years (time served before denial of his first appeal was not credited). Parole was denied.

One may conjecture—as some of those quoted above do—that the Rosenbergs were guilty but that Sobell probably was not (though the opposite to this proposition seems inconceivable). However, it is not possible to isolate the charges against Sobell from the total conspiracy and prove or refute them. By himself, Sobell cannot serve as a key to the ultimate mysteries of the case.

Thus, the questions raised by Morton Sobell's continuing protestations of innocence after long years of imprisonment on flimsy evidence can be resolved conclusively only through an examination of the case against his alleged fellow conspirators—the Rosenbergs.

CHAPTER 26

DAVID AND RUTH GREENGLASS

The Rosenberg-Sobell case is nearly unique among celebrated American criminal trials in one important respect: The alleged crimes of the defendants are completely invisible. No victims, recovered loot, or even missing documents could be pointed to by the prosecution as evidence of wrongdoing. The only proof that a crime actually had been committed came from the lips of prosecution witnesses—primarily David Greenglass and his wife, Ruth.

Corroborated only by Ruth, David told of handing over atomic bomb data to Julius Rosenberg. David *alone* described a Rosenberg spy ring which had gathered material on a space platform and atomic airplane; he *alone* claimed that Rosenberg had stolen a proximity fuse. Thus, not only the guilt of the Rosenbergs, but also the very reality of the crimes for which they were tried, depends largely on the memory and veracity of David Greenglass.

In view of the extent to which the entire prosecution case rests on his testimony, some of the information about David that has become publicly available over the years is, to say the least, disturbing. Newspapermen present at the June 16, 1950, arraignment of the twenty-eight-year-old machinist remarked on his peculiarly inattentive attitude, commenting that he laughed and joked with an FBI agent and appeared more concerned with reporters' notes than with the proceedings. Despite David's seemingly lighthearted demeanor, Saypol told the U. S. Commissioner that, in the weeks before his arrest, the prisoner had contemplated "running away or committing suicide" and special security precautions were taken when he was jailed.

Interviewed by David's attorneys a few days later, Ruth Greenglass reportedly asserted that her husband "talked of suicide as if he were a character in the movies," had a "tendency to hysteria," and at times "would become delirious." She recounted a bizarre incident when he had been ill and had run through the hallway nude, "shrieking of 'elephants,' 'Lead Pants.'" Ruth added that she had known David since he was ten years old and "he would say things were so even if they were not."

Some confirmation of the latter opinion was provided by David himself, when he wrote to his attorneys regarding portions of his first signed statement to the FBI: "I didn't remember this but I allowed it in the statement" and ". . . the information I gave Gold maybe not at all what I said in the statement."

At the trial, observers noted David's inappropriate smile while on the witness stand. In addition, Ethel Rosenberg testified that her brother had suffered a "psychological heart attack" in the winter previous to his arrest.

Finally, the new evidence about the console table, presented by the defense in the posttrial period, raised the possibility that both David's and Ruth's testimony on this subject may have been fabricated.

However, despite these disquieting "hints," not until after the executions of Julius and Ethel Rosenberg did the full extent of David's unreliability become evident.

In November 1953 former Assistant U. S. Attorney Roy Cohn, who had conducted the prosecution's examination of David Greenglass at the trial, had occasion to question the self-confessed spy once again. This time, Cohn was chief counsel for Senator Joseph McCarthy's investigating subcommittee and was seeking evidence of espionage at the Army's Fort Monmouth electronics research center. Curiously, although the interrogator was the same in 1953 as in 1951, the story David told was not. Adding several completely new episodes to those that he had related in his trial testimony, he accused his deceased brother-in-law of the theft of various electronics secrets—crimes he had not mentioned while on the witness stand two and a half years earlier. Declared Greenglass, in an affidavit:

". . . Rosenberg told me that the Russians had a very small and a very poor electronics industry (that is, of course, another name for the radar industry) and that it was of the utmost importance that information of an electronics nature be obtained and gotten to him. Things like electronics valves (vacuum tubes), capacitors, transformers, and various other electronic and radio components were some of the things he was interested in.

"Rosenberg also told me that he gave all of the tube manuals he could get his hands on to Russia, some of which were classified 'top secret.'

"About 1947, at a time when it was a top United States scientific secret, Julius Rosenberg told me about information he had obtained from a friend relating to a thinking machine which would send out interceptor guided missiles to knock out an enemy's guided missiles which had been detected by our radar and its course predicted by our thinking machines. Rosenberg was discussing this information with me, as I said before, when it was a top American scientific secret."

Another new claim which Greenglass made in his McCarthy committee affidavit—but had not testified about at the trial—was that Rosenberg had attempted to enlist him for an espionage assignment less than a year before his arrest (a period when David's relationship with his brother-in-

345

law, as he himself later described it, was "at a low ebb, a minimum").
Said Greenglass:

"When I was with the Arma Co. during 1949 and 1950, working in their
research and development department on various fire control gyroscopic
and radar apparatus, Julius asked me to obtain information on the projects
upon which I was working. I refused."

In the spring of 1956, David Greenglass was brought under guard from
Lewisburg Penitentiary to the nation's capital, where, before the Senate
Internal Security subcommittee, he made his first public appearance since
the trial. His propensity for enlarging and elaborating his story, demonstrated already in his affidavit for McCarthy, was displayed again during
the hearing. When a member of the subcommittee evinced particular interest in the operation of intelligence agents from Soviet embassies, David
remembered a pertinent conversation with Rosenberg—which he had not
alluded to at the trial. He stated:

". . . when we were in business together, when I had long since given
up giving information. . . . because I had been in the apparatus before
. . . he would talk about things that he should not have if he was strictly
adhering to the way espionage agents should work. But he did say that
not only are there agents in the Russian Embassies, in the satellite . . .
country embassies, but also in the embassies of the western democracies,
Russian agents. This is a direct quote."

The subcommittee's chief counsel, Robert Morris, pointedly requested
Greenglass not to "go over . . . material covered at the trial." However,
on one of several occasions when he disregarded this injunction, David
added entirely new details to the flight story that he had related as a
prosecution witness. At the trial, David had testified that Rosenberg's
first warning to him concerning the need to leave the country had been
delivered in February 1950—"a few days after Fuchs was taken in England." However, in an interchange with Morris reminiscent of an Abbott
and Costello comedy routine, Greenglass changed both the date and the
circumstances of the conversation:

DAVID: . . . one day in October [1949] he [Rosenberg] came to see
me, and he told me that I had to start thinking about leaving the
country, and I said, "Why?" And he told me, "At the present time
they are talking to the man who spoke to the courier who spoke to
you."
MORRIS: Let me see, now, because the FBI—
DAVID: No.
MORRIS: He did not say that?
DAVID: Scotland Yard.
MORRIS: Scotland Yard?
DAVID: England; in England, he said.

MORRIS: Scotland Yard was talking to the man who—

DAVID: Who had been—the man who had spoken to the man who had spoken to another man who was the man who had seen me in Albuquerque.

MORRIS: And that immediately caused you to think about your session with whom?

DAVID: As a matter of fact, I did not remember exactly who he was talking about. . . . In any case, he told me that they were speaking to him [apparently Fuchs] and that I had to think of leaving the country.

Without referring to his trial testimony describing the rather complex scheme for flight to Czechoslovakia via Mexico, Greenglass told the subcommittee of a far simpler itinerary allegedly given him by Rosenberg in October 1949:

". . . take a boat, get aboard a boat and go to France."

The flight plans described in the prosecution's case included as participants both Ruth Greenglass and Ethel Rosenberg, which was understandable on grounds of both sentiment and expediency, since both wives allegedly had been involved in espionage with their husbands. However, a completely new twist added by David for the Senate subcommittee was that Julius had considered the possible abandonment of their female partners in crime. Recounting a conversation said to have occurred in June 1950, David stated:

"He [Rosenberg] said, 'Well, you know, if I get word that it is too hot, we will just take off and leave the children and the women.'

"I said, 'Two women and four children? We are going to leave them and go? Will we ever be reunited with them?'

"He said, 'Well, I don't know. Maybe yes; maybe no.'

"I said, 'How can you think that way?'"

At the trial, David testified that in January 1945, soon after his arrival home on furlough, Julius came to see him "one morning" at the lower East Side apartment where he and his wife were staying, and requested information on the atomic bomb.

COHN: Did you say this was in the morning?

DAVID: This was in the morning. . . .

Ruth Greenglass also testified, when questioned by Assistant U. S. Attorney Kilsheimer, that Julius's visit had occurred "one morning two or three days after David had arrived in New York."

KILSHEIMER: It was in the morning?

RUTH: Yes.

However, when recounting this same first espionage meeting to the Senate subcommittee, David reversed the time of day and added details that can only be termed fantastic:

MORRIS: Now, I wonder if you would tell us of your first meeting with Julius Rosenberg when you discussed the atom bomb. . . .

DAVID: It was about 11:30 in the evening. . . . A knock came on the door, and when I opened the door, I found Julius Rosenberg standing there. He came in, and he kept his finger to his lips. I didn't say a word. He leaned close to my ear and he said, "Go next door and discover if there is a listening apparatus in the rooms next door." . . . There was an old couple living next door who must have been in bed for hours. . . . I knocked on the door, and an old woman in a bathrobe came to the door and said, "What can I do for you?" And I had to invent a lie. . . . I said, "I locked myself out and I would like to get through your window on the fire escape to my own apartment." And she said, "Well, all right." . . . I went through her bedroom to get to the fire escape. Of course, I just wanted to make sure that there was nobody there. . . . There was an old man lying in bed half asleep, her husband, and, of course, I went through the window and came into the apartment. And he said—Julius, that is, said—"Well?" I said, "No, there was nothing there." Then he felt it was all right to talk.

The year after Greenglass's Congressional appearance, the Internal Security subcommittee made strenuous efforts to recall him for further testimony. However, the Department of Justice refused to allow his removal from prison a second time. According to the New York *Times*, a Justice Department spokesman informed the Senate subcommittee that the release of Greenglass (and Gold) the previous spring had been "a mistake." Chief counsel Morris then flew to Lewisburg Penitentiary to interview Greenglass and, later that same day (November 21, 1957), reported at a public hearing on what he had learned. David had added still another new incident to his chronicle of his brother-in-law's crimes. Said Morris:

"Now another instance—and he [Greenglass] stated he only recently recalled this in trying to assist the FBI on it—was that in 1948 Rosenberg was short of money on one particular occasion, and he said that he was waiting for one of his agents who was then flying back from Egypt. He described his agent as a $200 a day consultant for the Government, an engineering consultant for the Government, a $200 a day man. He was one of Rosenberg's agents and that he was working on the Aswan Dam project in Egypt, and he was then in the process of flying back to

Egypt, that he was going to bear some money for Rosenberg which Rosenberg was going to use in his espionage operations.

"As far as we know, this man has never been exposed, and if we can follow out those leads, if we have further testimony, we may know the identity of this man who apparently occupied an important place, at least in 1948, as a $200 a day consultant. The only lead we have is the fact that he was working on the Aswan Dam."

If the subcommittee staff actually did attempt to "follow out those leads," they may well have been chagrined at their findings. A year before Greenglass told this story to Morris, the proposed high dam at Aswan on the Nile had been very much in the news (when the United States withdrew an offer of financial support; Nasser expropriated the Suez Canal; and Egypt was invaded). But *there had been no* "Aswan Dam project" *at all in 1948*, when Greenglass claimed that one of Rosenberg's agents, an "engineering consultant," had been working on it.

Thus the Greenglass story has grown. The key prosecution witness of the Rosenberg-Sobell case has appended weird, improbable, and impossible postscripts to his trial testimony, leveling new and uncorroborated accusations against the dead Julius Rosenberg. The spectacle is tawdry and highly unconvincing.

In an effort to interview David and Ruth Greenglass, the authors contacted their attorney, O. John Rogge. However, Rogge was unwilling to arrange a meeting. He said that, since David's release from prison in November 1960, the couple had been living under an alias at an undisclosed location and he did not want to disturb their anonymity. Asked to describe the Greenglasses, Rogge (author of a book on confessions that does not mention his most famous clients) called Ruth "the more stable" of the two and characterized David as the sort who could be "easily led."

Also questioned by the authors about David Greenglass was Benjamin Pollack, who had talked with him at Lewisburg Penitentiary while preparing the still-secret Justice Department report on the case for Attorney General Brownell. Pollack said that Greenglass had made a "very bad impression" on him, greeting him with a remark to the effect of, "I'm the smartest man you ever met," and boasting about the great importance of his work at Los Alamos to the development of the atomic bomb. Later, David told Ruth that Pollack had promised him parole, a claim that Pollack said he unequivocally denied when O. John Rogge phoned to check on it.

Speaking with rather astonishing candor, the government attorney offered the opinion that David was a man with "no conscience at all" and added: "If I were a judge, I wouldn't take his testimony too seriously."

However, putting aside the question of David's general credibility, one finds that most of the specific incidents he and his wife detailed at the trial about the Rosenbergs' crimes are impervious to conclusive proof or disproof. Lacking are documentary evidence and confirming testimony—except for Gold's references to the name "Julius" and a "piece of cardboard" from a jello box. What more can one say about the alleged crimes than that David claimed they took place and the Rosenbergs were responsible, Ruth corroborated many of his accusations, and the Rosenbergs —to the day of their deaths—denied any involvement?

Fortunately, there is another portion of the Greenglasses' trial testimony —one that consumed nearly as much time as the story of the crime itself—which *is* amenable to further examination: The story of the plans for flight.

The Greenglasses asserted that Julius Rosenberg had urged them to leave the country and, after the arrest of Harry Gold on May 23, 1950, had rehearsed David on procedures for following an international escape route, supplied them with funds, told them to take numerous passport photos, and advised them to secure proof of smallpox vaccination. Julius allegedly said a doctor had informed him that vaccination was necessary for admission to Mexico.

Rosenberg, on the other hand, countered that during approximately the latter half of May and early June 1950, David appeared "disturbed and agitated," stated that he was in a "terrible jam," asked for money—which Julius refused—and information on "what kinds of injections are required to go into Mexico"—which Julius obtained from his family doctor.

The doctor, George Bernhardt, testified that Julius had questioned him about inoculations needed for travel in Mexico and had noted that this information was not for himself but for a friend, who was a veteran. In general, Bernhardt's testimony is equally consistent with either David's or Julius's version. What the prosecution failed to explain, however, was why, if Julius was in contact with a Soviet espionage apparatus, he had to ask his personal physician about vaccination regulations and was unaware that no inoculations then were required for American travelers entering Mexico.

More substantial support for David's and Ruth's flight testimony was provided by documentary evidence: Prosecution Exhibit 9, the Greenglass passport photos.

David and Ruth testified that Julius had instructed them to take passport photos of themselves and their children and had requested five copies of each of five specified poses. Inexplicably, the Greenglasses ordered six copies of each pose, turning over five sets (twenty-five prints) to Julius and retaining the sixth set themselves. Four photos from this extra set comprised the prosecution's trial exhibit.

Although the four exhibit pictures obviously cannot prove whether Rosenberg asked for and received twenty-five passport photos, they are of some assistance in choosing between the Rosenberg and the Greenglass flight stories. For the very existence of this greater than usual variety of passport photos—depicting the members of the Greenglass family in four individual and group poses—strongly suggests that the pictures were to be used to meet any contingency that might arise in the forging of travel documents. As Saypol pointed out in his summation, "perhaps in perpetrating a forgery . . . mistakes might be made, pictures might be mutilated, different passports might be required, depending on the route to be taken." Exhibit 9 thus lends weight to David's account of a meticulously organized flight plan entailing the delivery of false passports through the Soviet Embassy in Mexico City, as opposed to Julius's description of his brother-in-law's "agitated" appeals for help and rather melodramatic hints about leaving the country.

Among the Rosenberg-Sobell trial exhibits seen by the authors at the federal courthouse in Foley Square were the four pictures introduced by the prosecution as evidence of the Greenglass flight story. Our first glance at them provoked an observation that was simple and perfectly clear, yet had never been made before: *They do not look like passport photos!* Closer study of Exhibit 9 only strengthened this impression.

The exhibit pictures are larger than the officially recommended size for passport photos and rectangular rather than square-shaped. In standard passport photos the head and shoulders of the subject are vignetted against a white background, while these pictures show the Greenglasses to the waist or knees against a gray background. The photographic paper on which the exhibit pictures are printed is considerably heavier than is customary for passport photos and has serrated rather than straight edges. (See reproductions of Exhibit 9 on first page of picture section.)

It is customary FBI practice for agents immediately to initial and date each item of evidence obtained in the course of an investigation. Turning the four exhibit pictures over, we read the FBI notations on the backs. Two of the pictures were dated June 15, 1950, the day of David's apprehension by the FBI. Surprisingly, the other two were dated January 26, 1951—*more than seven months* after David's arrest.*

At the trial, David's and Ruth's testimony obscured the fact that all the exhibit pictures had not come into the FBI's possession at the same time. However, the Greenglasses managed to contradict one another's testimony.

> COHN: How many, in fact, did you have taken at this passport photo shop?
> DAVID: I had six sets of pictures taken.
> COHN: How many did you give to Julius?
> DAVID: Five sets.
> COHN: What did you do with the sixth set?

---

* The FBI agents' initials on the June 15 pictures appear to be MWF, LT, LOG, and WFN; those on the January 26 pictures, WFN and JAH.

DAVID: I kept it in the drawer [presumably in his apartment].
COHN: Was that set after your arrest given to the FBI?
DAVID: *I gave it to the FBI.* (Emphasis added.)

Said Ruth from the witness stand a few days later: ". . . *I gave the sixth set to the FBI.*" (Emphasis added.)

Of course, neither David nor Ruth could have given all of the exhibit pictures to the FBI. On June 15, 1950, when the first two pictures were secured by the agents, Ruth was in the hospital. The other two pictures, initialed by FBI agents on January 26, 1951, clearly could not have been turned over by David; he was in prison then.

Moreover, since the Greenglasses testified that Julius had told them to take five different poses, the trial exhibit of four pictures is an incomplete set. The missing picture was referred to at the trial only in an aside:

COHN: By the way, I think you gave four of the five to the FBI, is that right?
DAVID: That is right.

Why there was a missing picture or what it looked like never was explained.

Another peculiarity of the Greenglass passport photo story—discernible only when one actually *sees* the exhibit—is that the pictures introduced as evidence by the prosecution are at considerable variance with the pictures described by David.

David testified that Julius had explicitly requested five poses: ". . . myself, by myself, my wife, and then my wife and the children and then myself with the children, and then I think all of us together, the family altogether." (This combination of poses would have permitted the Greenglasses the versatility of traveling either all together on a single passport or else on two passports, with a choice available as to which parent's passport would include both children.)

However, contrary to David's testimony, there is no picture of himself and the children or of Ruth and the children in the prosecution's exhibit. Furthermore, one picture that is part of the exhibit—the photo of Ruth with her son—does not correspond to any allegedly demanded by Rosenberg and, to be useful, would have required a somewhat unlikely companion photo of David with his infant daughter. In fact, Exhibit 9 contains only a single pose—that of the family all together—suitable for joint flight by the Greenglasses.

A visit to the shop where David and Ruth claimed they had passport photos taken on the last Sunday in May 1950 seemed indicated. At Foley Square, under the watchful eye of an assistant U.S. attorney, the exhibit pictures were photographed to obtain copy negatives, from which were made prints of precisely the same size as the originals. These we took with us to the Hollywood Photo Studio, at 130 Clinton Street, on the lower East Side, only a short walk from the location of the former Greenglass apartment on Rivington Street.

Today the neighborhood is still a poor one, many of whose inhabitants regard ownership of a camera as a luxury beyond their means. While we stood outside the small studio on a Sunday evening in May, eleven years after the Greenglasses had been there, groups of parents with children and young couples trooped into the shop and posed self-consciously for a few inexpensive pictures.

As soon as we told the present proprietor, Murray Deutsch, that we were inquiring about photographs relating to the Rosenberg case, he seemed aware of what we were referring to. He noted that a deceased relative, Irving Rose (listed as a prosecution witness but never called), had run the shop in those days with a partner who is now retired. Would he look at our copies of the Greenglass pictures and give us his impression? He said he would be glad to. Scrutinizing the photographs, he said that if the Greenglasses had asked for passport photos they would have received the standard size and style. These pictures, he asserted, were not passport photos, but ordinary family snapshots.

Then Deutsch disclosed to us that the FBI had picked up the negatives of the Greenglass pictures. How did he know, we asked? Well, when he had taken over the business, his relative, Irving Rose, had given him an FBI receipt for the negatives and advised him to hold onto it.

Presently, he found the receipt, saved for over a decade, and showed it to us:

> January 19, 1951
>
> Receipt is acknowledged of six photographic negatives from Irving Rose, 130 Clinton St. New York, N. Y.
>
> William F. Norton Jr.
> Special Agent, F.B.I., N.Y.

The proprietor agreed to send a letter to the FBI requesting the return of the six negatives removed by special agent Norton (whose initials appear on all four of the exhibit pictures). However, he soon after informed us that FBI agents had come to his shop and told him that a search had been made of their offices in New York City and that the negatives were not there. The agents reportedly declared that they had learned that the negatives and certain other material in the case had been sent to the Attorney General's office in Washington and destroyed.

Even without looking at the negatives, however, it is possible to reconstruct much of the history of the "passport" photos. On Sunday afternoon, May 28, 1950, David and Ruth Greenglass went for a walk with their young son and infant daughter. It was, David testified at the trial, the first day the newborn baby had been taken out of the house. They stopped in at a neighborhood photo studio and had some family pictures made. Whatever possible use David may have envisioned for these pictures, *he did not ask for passport photos*. Moreover, judging from FBI agent Norton's receipt, the Greenglasses took six—not five—different poses in all. There is no evidence as to whether they ordered more than one copy of each pose.

On June 15, 1950, when FBI agents arrived at the Greenglass apartment to question David, two of the pictures from the set were picked up and dated. Very likely, the FBI regarded these pictures (showing David alone and Ruth alone) merely as identifying photos of the suspect and his wife. About seven months later, the Greenglasses apparently "remembered" that only a few weeks before David's arrest they had taken passport photos at the behest of Rosenberg. Agent Norton then was dispatched to the photo studio and, on January 19, 1951, secured six photographic negatives. A week later, two more pictures from the set came into the possession of the FBI and were dated January 26, 1951. The source of these pictures is unknown. However, the date on which they were obtained proves that significant aspects of the Greenglasses' confessions still were being developed over half a year after David was taken into custody.

At the trial, the prosecution employed incredibly audacious tactics, akin to those of a carnival shell game, to conjure up dozens of passport photos out of the four family snapshots actually produced in court. Without testimony from the photographer in question or any other expert witness, the pictures were characterized as passport photos—merely on the say-so of the Greenglasses.* David described a variety of poses that he said Rosenberg had asked for, but the prosecution failed to mention important discrepancies between these allegedly requested poses and the real exhibit pictures. Furthermore, two pictures for which the prosecution had negatives

---

* This characterization of the pictures as "passport" photos was not contested by the defense.

(secured by Norton) were mysteriously excluded from the trial—possibly because the poses depicted were too obviously inappropriate to be passed off as passport photos.

In short, prosecution Exhibit 9, introduced by Roy Cohn, does not, when subject to close examination, support the passport photo testimony of David and Ruth Greenglass.

The only other important element in the flight story was the Greenglasses' alleged receipt from Rosenberg of thousands of dollars in Soviet funds. David testified that when Rosenberg told him he would have to leave the country—shortly after the arrest of Klaus Fuchs in early February 1950—he had asked Rosenberg for money "to pay my debts back so I would be able to leave with a clear head." Rosenberg "didn't think it was necessary" but, when David "insisted," agreed to get money for him "from the Russians." No specific sum was mentioned.

From this point on, the Greenglass flight story is studded with puzzling contradictions and logical absurdities. Julius's alleged promise of Soviet money was made while he and David already were involved in a "heated" financial dispute regarding the family-owned machine shop business. Twice more over the next three months—from February to May—Julius allegedly warned David to flee and, during this very same period, their business dispute continued unabated. Repeatedly, Julius urged David to surrender his shares of stock in the business and tender his formal resignation as a corporate officer, but refused the Greenglasses' request that he sign promissory notes for $2000. Eventually, Julius won the argument: On May 1, he received both David's stock and resignation, in return for only a verbal commitment that when he was able he would pay the Greenglasses $1000. Also on May 1, according to David, Julius advised his brother-in-law to get out of the country "as soon as possible."

The Greenglasses testified that several weeks later—on the day following the arrest of Harry Gold—Rosenberg had brought them $1000 to facilitate their flight. Both David and Ruth emphasized that this alleged payment was unrelated to the $1000 owed them from the business. (In fact, after David's arrest, they instructed their attorney to prosecute a claim against Rosenberg for the still-unpaid business debt.)

The Greenglasses accounted for the entire sum which they asserted they had obtained from Rosenberg: $500 was used to pay off installment purchases and other debts; the other $500 was saved for a while in their home —to pay for a summer cottage in the Catskills—and was used by Ruth, after her husband's arrest, for living expenses. Except for the testimony of the Greenglasses, neither the *source* nor the *existence* of any portion of this $1000 was corroborated by the prosecution.

On approximately June 4, Rosenberg allegedly carried $4000 in a brown paper wrapper to the Greenglass apartment. Since David testified that it was at his insistence that Rosenberg had agreed to obtain money for him, his reaction to the $4000—as he and his wife described it—was peculiar: He wanted to flush it down the toilet. Instead, however, the Greenglasses secreted the package of money in the chimney of their fireplace and, around June 7, gave it to a brother-in-law, Louis Abel, to hold. (Although Ruth supposedly still had $500 from the first delivery of flight money in a metal closet in her apartment,* a day or so later she apparently asked Abel to remove $100 for her from the package he had been given.)

Finally, Rosenberg was said to have visited the Greenglasses one last time and told them that he had intended to bring $2000 more but could not, because he thought he was being followed.

At the trial, Louis Abel confirmed that he had received from David, about a week before the latter's arrest, a brown paper parcel containing money and had hidden it in a hassock in his apartment. On June 16, he had turned the money over to a secretary at the law firm of O. John Rogge. The secretary testified that she had received a package of bills from Abel, counted them, and found $3900.

It seems reasonably certain that the Greenglasses actually did have this $3900 in their possession in June 1950. However, the source of these funds is another question altogether. According to Ruth, Louis Abel was not informed where the cash he was asked to hold came from. Attorney Rogge stated to the authors that on the day the $3900 was accepted from Abel, as a legal fee, his firm had no knowledge of the money's origin and no questions were asked. Following his customary office procedure, Rogge said, the $3900 had been deposited in the bank immediately—so the FBI never had seen the bills. He could not recall exactly when he first had been told that the money came from the Russians, via Julius Rosenberg, other than that it was "rather soon" after David's arrest.

The piece of brown paper in which the money had been wrapped was retained in his office by chance, Rogge said, and later was turned over to the FBI. (According to a Rogge interoffice memo, federal authorities tested the paper for fingerprints without finding anything useful.) Later, the wrapping paper was introduced as prosecution Exhibit 10, but it too revealed nothing about the source of the $3900.

The authors inspected Exhibit 10 at Foley Square and observed that the paper had been initialed and dated by various FBI personnel. The earliest date that appears on the exhibit is July 31, 1950, indicating that the wrapper did not come into the possession of the FBI until over six weeks after Abel delivered the money to the Rogge office.

Obviously, the Greenglasses did not tell anyone the story of the $3900, as it emerged at the trial, until some days or weeks after David's arrest. Aside from the word of the Greenglasses, no other prosecution evidence connected the $3900 with Julius Rosenberg.

* Ruth testified that on June 14 David deposited this $500 at the Manufacturers Trust Company, presumably in New York City.

Saypol dealt summarily with the question of the source of the alleged flight money, noting: "Certainly it is clear that Greenglass never had that much. . . ." However, despite the rather impoverished living conditions of the Greenglasses, new information has come to light which challenges Saypol's assumption.

The authors have secured copies of three receipts for money paid the Rogge law firm by Ruth Greenglass *in addition* to the initial June 16 payment of $3900. These receipts (see reproductions on this and following page) disclose that the Rogge firm received from Ruth a total of $1900 more—in cash—delivered in three installments on June 28, July 5, and July 7. (Rogge confirmed to the authors that the Greenglasses had paid him fees aggregating about $6000.)

Where Ruth got this additional cash, within three weeks after David's arrest, is unknown. Although Julius Rosenberg still was at large then, the prosecution did not allege that he gave it to her. Clearly, Ruth's possession of $1900—not attributed to Rosenberg—raises the possibility of some alternative explanation for how she and her husband acquired the $3900.

Thus, the prosecution's use of the Greenglass flight testimony and exhibits to tie Rosenberg to a Soviet espionage apparatus does not hold up. The "passport" pictures are simply four family snapshots taken at a neighborhood photo studio. They hardly constitute proof of Rosenberg's involvement in an alleged plan to spirit the Greenglasses from the United States to Eastern Europe. The $3900—like the previously unrevealed $1900—may have derived from various sources, legal or illegal.

Nevertheless, the available evidence suggests that, in May–June 1950, David Greenglass was a man in trouble. During this period, he and his brother-in-law, Julius Rosenberg, had a conversation about inoculations

June 28, 1950

Receipt is hereby acknowledged of the sum of $1,000.00 (one thousand dollars) in cash from Mrs. David Greenglass on account of fee in the matter of United States V. Greenglass.

ROGGE, FABRICANT, GORDON & GOLDMAN

By_____
O. John Rogge

hrp

July 5, 1950

Receipt is hereby acknowledged of the sum of
$400.00 in cash from Mrs. Ruth Greenglass on account
of fee in the matter of United States v. Greenglass.

ROGGE, FABRICANT, GORDON & GOLDMAN

_____
Bookkeeper

hrp

July 7, 1950

Receipt is hereby acknowledged of the sum
of $500.00 in cash from Mrs. Ruth Greenglass
on account of fee in the matter of United
States v. Greenglass.

ROGGE, FABRICANT, GORDON & GOLDMAN

By_____
Bookkeeper

---

for Mexican travel. Shortly afterward, he asked another brother-in-law, Louis Abel, to hide a package of money. These incidents, David claimed, were part of a chain of events that began in February 1950, following the arrest of Klaus Fuchs, when Rosenberg advised him he would have to flee. However, at precisely the same time as this alleged first discussion of flight, *something else*—having nothing to do with espionage—happened to David that might well have caused him to toy with the idea of leaving the country.

In early February 1950 the Greenglasses were visited by an FBI agent who questioned them about whether they had any uranium in their house. (Describing this inquiry to her attorneys, Ruth reportedly noted that, "One of their friends had a similar experience.") David did not divulge to the FBI agent what he had revealed earlier to his brother, Bernard: That he had stolen a sample of uranium from Los Alamos.

Whatever the Greenglasses' fears as a result of this initial interrogation, nothing happened for several months. Then, they became aware—exactly when is unknown—that the FBI had instituted surveillance of them. It seems a fair conjecture that David's conversations about inoculations and hiding money occurred after this discovery and may have been motivated by it.

As is apparently not uncommon, the FBI's observation of the Greenglasses was open and obvious.* Ruth informed her attorneys (during a June 18 interview) that she and David "had been under surveillance by the FBI for several weeks." She reportedly complained that they had been "watched constantly, and [she] feels as if they are the object of persecution."

On June 15, at two in the afternoon, after weeks of surveillance, David had his second face-to-face encounter with the FBI. Bill Davidson, in his *Look* magazine preview of the Justice Department's report on the case, described the scene as follows:

"On June 15, 1950, two agents visited him [Greenglass] at his apartment. He had been questioned by the FBI once before, in February, 1950, about the disappearance of some uranium from Los Alamos when he was stationed there. (Later, he admitted he had taken a piece of uranium as a souvenir but said he had become frightened about having it in his possession and had thrown it in the East River.) *The FBI men indicated that the new interview was part of the same investigation.*" (Emphasis added.)

A similar account by writer Don Whitehead, in his officially sanctioned history of the FBI, notes that one of the agents advised Greenglass: "We are trying to locate information on materials lost, misplaced or stolen at the Los Alamos project."

David permitted the agents to search his apartment and voluntarily accompanied them to their offices, where interrogation and drafting of a statement continued until 2 A.M. Some time in the twelve-hour period between the agents' arrival at the Greenglass apartment and the termination of the interview, the discussion shifted from theft of uranium (or

* Reported the New York *Daily Mirror* on June 17, 1950: "In the past three weeks, residents related, they noticed four men in a gray car watching the [Greenglass] house night and day, presumably FBI agents."

other materials) at Los Alamos to the possibility that David had had a visitor in Albuquerque—Harry Gold.

Although neither the FBI notes on the June 15 interrogation of Greenglass nor the statement signed by the suspect early the next morning has ever been made public, Greenglass himself has disclosed that the agents supplied him, in the course of the questioning, with various details of his alleged meeting with Gold. At the trial, David testified that the agents *"told me* of a man who came to see me"; *told him* that the man had visited him "in Albuquerque"; and *told him* the month the visit was said to have taken place. He also testified that he had been unable to remember the "exact sum of money" the man had given him. Later, in a written report to his attorneys, David said the FBI agents *"told me* that I had told him [Gold] to come back later because I didn't have it ready." (Emphasis added.) These indications that Greenglass's initial statement to the FBI was hardly a spontaneous or independent recollection of events naturally raise doubts as to its veracity.

Many people have shielded themselves from the fratricidal horror of the Rosenberg-Sobell case by assuming, quite illogically, that David Greenglass must have confessed truthfully—simply because he and his wife provided the sole evidence that sent his sister to her death. The question frequently is voiced: Why would he have testified against Ethel, unless she was guilty? The questioner prefers to ignore the fact that bitter animosities between brothers and sisters are by no means unknown.

One might as well ask: Why would he have testified against Ethel, whether or not she was guilty? Scripps-Howard columnist Robert Ruark, who never doubted the guilt of the Rosenbergs, finds David's testimony against his sister incomprehensible. He wrote, not long after Greenglass's release from prison:

"For some reason the thought of David Greenglass . . . has been dogging my dreams of late. . . . There is no excuse for a David Greenglass, no explanation. He helped sell the bomb secrets to the Russians, and then he sold his sister to the electric chair to avoid the death penalty. . . .

"I cannot imagine what would make a man want to live, go through all the troublous necessities of living, with his sister's ghost sitting firmly on his chest at night. . . ."

Perhaps Greenglass has suffered, feeling his "sister's ghost" on his chest at night, or perhaps Benjamin Pollack's appraisal that he is a man without conscience is nearer the truth. When Pollack saw Greenglass at Lewisburg, three years after the execution, the prisoner did not seem at all contrite. He complained about the "raw deal" he had received and said that he was "the most shocked man in the world" when, after testifying for the government against his sister, he didn't receive a suspended sentence.

Rarely questioned, but even more puzzling than David's behavior toward his sister, is the readiness with which he voluntarily implicated himself and his wife in a capital crime. Neither his meeting with Gold in Albuquerque—which he admitted to in his first FBI statement—nor his subsequent revelations that he had delivered data on the atomic bomb to the Rosenbergs probably could have been proved without his own confession.

Obviously, no simple answer can explain why a man confesses—whether truthfully or not—to an otherwise unprovable crime. However, purely in the realm of speculation, it is possible to hazard a guess as to some of the factors that may have influenced Greenglass's thinking on June 15 during his interrogation by the FBI:

He had stolen uranium from Los Alamos and may have been involved in other thefts or unlawful deeds. (Rosenberg testified at the trial that Ruth had confided to him, in early 1945, that David had "an idea to make some money and take some things from the Army." Since the FBI never examined the $3900 in bills for dating and serial numbers, the possibility cannot be precluded that the money paid Rogge on June 16 actually was obtained illicitly by the Greenglasses years earlier.)

Moreover, David had briefly belonged to the Young Communist League while a teen-ager, a fact prominently noted by the press on the day of his arrest. (New York *Daily News*, June 16: "Jail Ex-Commie Youth As A-Traitor While G.I.") If he were prosecuted for his uranium theft, this YCL membership certainly would aggravate the seriousness of the offense.* David's affiliation with a radical organization may have posed still other problems for him. Quite likely, he had filed a perjurious loyalty oath to obtain employment at Arma in 1949 and also had lied about YCL membership in 1944, when undergoing security checks prior to his assignment to Los Alamos.†

Adding to Greenglass's stresses on June 15, his wife had been hospitalized two days earlier for treatment of near-fatal burns suffered in a home accident several months before. David, who worked nights at Arma, was preparing a formula for his month-old infant daughter when the FBI agents knocked on his door.

Finally, David probably had little idea of what he was getting himself and Ruth into when he signed his first FBI statement admitting to a

---

* On August 22, 1950, another former Los Alamos enlisted man, Sanford Simons, was arrested for theft of a souvenir sample of plutonium (he had, in addition, taken uranium samples). An exonerating circumstance in his case, as pointed out by the New York *Times*, was that he had no "known link with communist or subversive organizations." Facing a possible five-year term, he was sentenced to eighteen months.
† The authors have a letter from a former Army technical instructor who says he recalls that David Greenglass and other machinists selected for Los Alamos were screened by a loyalty board of officers at Granite City, Illinois. He claims that Greenglass must have perjured himself before this board about his YCL membership.

meeting with Gold. He later testified that, while giving this statement, he was unaware of the grave charge about to be lodged against him and didn't "know sufficiently enough about the law to realize that I did involve my wife."

On the afternoon of June 16, when David was arraigned on a complaint of conspiracy to commit espionage, lawyer O. John Rogge insisted on his client's innocence and pleaded for low bail. Instead, bail was set at $100,000 and the FBI announced the arrest of a new link in the Fuchs-Gold conspiracy: David Greenglass.

At that point, Greenglass was in a net. He had embarked on a route from which he might have turned back only with the greatest difficulty. The Department of Justice had publicly committed itself to his participation in an espionage conspiracy. If he tried to retract his confession of a meeting with Gold—and there are indications that he did try*—a new problem would be added to those already facing him: He could be prosecuted for making a false declaration to the FBI.

Thus, David's early-morning statement—influenced by fear, fatigue, and ignorance and fed to him, at least in part, by FBI agents—was the root of his predicament. Whether or not this confession was the truth, the FBI apparently regarded it with the utmost seriousness. A complaint was drafted, the suspect jailed, and the press blazoned the discovery of another atom spy.

Yet one wonders what served to give the FBI such uncritical confidence in the statement signed by David Greenglass at 2 A.M. on June 16. What distinguished it from scores of confused and vague confessions given the authorities each year by unstable individuals?

When FBI agents visited Ruth Greenglass at the hospital later that morning, she did not corroborate her husband's story. Talking to David's attorneys two days later, Ruth appeared to connect his arrest with the earlier FBI inquiry about uranium and noted that she would not have allowed David to "bring anything home" after Hiroshima had revealed the nature of the project. She added that she had expected to raise a family and didn't want "that kind of material" in her house. Moreover, she said she remembered no visitors to their apartment in Albuquerque.

Thus, if any corroboration at all existed for David's confession at the time he signed his statement, only one person might have provided it: Harry Gold.

* Said Saypol at the trial: ". . . I remember well how at his [Greenglass's] arraignment . . . Mr. Rogge protested his innocence. Through Ruth Greenglass came the subsequent recantation of those protestations, their cooperation and the disclosure of the facts by both of them." Also, see page 78 for description of Saypol-Rogge clash at a June 23 hearing.

CHAPTER 27

HARRY GOLD

Not until nearly a year after his widely heralded arrest as the American accomplice of Klaus Fuchs did Harry Gold present his first public version of his alleged atomic espionage exploits. In a relatively brief appearance at the Rosenberg-Sobell trial, he told of receiving A-bomb data in 1944 and 1945 from Fuchs and, on one occasion, Greenglass, and passing it to a Soviet agent, Anatoli Yakovlev. The New York *Times* dubbed the Philadelphia chemist "Star U.S. Witness" and allotted five full columns to his testimony. Prosecutor Saypol declared that Gold had "furnished the absolute corroboration of the testimony of the Greenglasses." Noting that Gold was not cross-examined, Saypol commented: "It was so obvious to everyone in this courtroom that he was telling the complete truth. . . ."

The failure to cross-examine Harry Gold would seem to have been one of the more egregious of a number of serious errors committed by the Rosenberg-Sobell defense. Certainly, at the time, there already were ample reasons for wondering about his accuracy and reliability as a witness. A few months earlier, at the Brothman-Moskowitz trial, bachelor Gold had admitted that he had woven a series of complex fantasies about a make-believe wife and twin children and for years had successfully passed off these stories as true to his close associate Brothman and to others. At Gold's own sentencing hearing, his attorney, John D. M. Hamilton, disclosed that his client sometimes had supplied the Russians with "fictitious names, any number of them," and had delivered fabricated reports about these nonexistent contacts.

In June 1955, four years after the Rosenberg-Sobell trial, Gold was brought from Lewisburg Penitentiary to Dayton, Ohio, to testify for the prosecution in the perjury trial of one Benjamin Smilg. Searching cross-examination was conducted by defense counsel William F. Hopkins (who obviously had studied Gold's testimony at the Brothman-Moskowitz trial). Unlike the Rosenberg-Sobell jury, the Ohio jury was made aware of Gold's ability to perpetrate fantastic deceptions.

Questioned by Hopkins about his imaginary family, Gold replied: ". . . first I created this wife whom I did not have. Then there had to be children to go along with the wife, and they had to grow old, so I had to keep building one on top of the other. . . ."

HOPKINS: Did you make this statement: "It is a wonder that steam didn't come out of my ears at times"?

GOLD: That really is. . . . It really is remarkable that it didn't occur.

HOPKINS: Because of the lies you told?

GOLD: I had gotten involved into one of the doggondest tangles. . . .

HOPKINS: . . . you lied for a period of six years?

GOLD: I lied for a period of sixteen years, not alone six.

Gold also told Hopkins: "When I went on a mission for the Russians, I immediately turned a switch in my mind. . . . Just set my mind, just as if it were an automaton set to do a particular job. I just went ahead, got the information, turned it over, came back. I turned the switch again. . . . And I was once again Harry Gold . . . just a chemist. . . ."

This testimony prompted Hopkins to ask: "Have you ever, to your own knowledge, suffered from schizophrenia?"

Responded Gold: "As far as I know, I have not."

Hopkins also queried Gold about his appearance before the 1947 federal grand jury in New York City:

HOPKINS: Before that grand jury, the question came up of a man named Golos. . . .

GOLD: Yes, Jacob Golos.

HOPKINS: Before that you didn't know him?

GOLD: I didn't know him before that.

HOPKINS: Never met him?

GOLD: Never met him.

HOPKINS: Before that grand jury you faced those ladies and gentlemen, under oath, the same as you are facing these folks, and you concocted imaginary telephone conversations, even giving it word for word of what he said to you and what you said to him; is that true?

GOLD: That is true.

HOPKINS: And you didn't even know the man?

GOLD: I didn't know the man.

HOPKINS: Never had had a telephone call?

GOLD: Never had a telephone call.

HOPKINS: And you were under oath?

GOLD: And I was under oath, yes sir.

The U. S. Attorney, summing up the prosecution's case, told the jury: "To find him [Smilg] innocent. . . . You have to disbelieve Harry Gold." The jury voted Smilg's acquittal.

The following year, Harry Gold was again removed from prison and—with David Greenglass—was taken to Washington, D.C., to testify before the Senate Internal Security subcommittee. Gold devoted a substantial portion of his almost three hours under the klieg lights on April 26, 1956, to introspective rambling. An AP dispatch labeled his testimony "fiction rivaling." A Washington *Star* newspaperwoman, noting that the subcommittee's efforts to probe the self-confessed atom spy's motivations "came to naught," was moved to quote a Russian proverb: "The heart of another is a dark forest."

Gold told the subcommittee that the Russian agents "operated with me in the very manner that a virtuoso would play a violin. They did a superb job on me, now that I come to think of it." The "dreary, monotonous drudgery" of espionage work, he said, had gradually reduced "my identity and my desire to be an individual. I was becoming someone who could be told what to do and who would do it."

In the final phase of his psychological surrender to the Soviet espionage apparatus, Gold described himself as practically a robot: ". . . I came to realize . . . that I had completely lost my free will; I had actually turned over my complete personality, my complete soul, and everything. I wasn't living the life of a normal person. I wasn't married. I had been deliberately instructed not to marry, because they felt that a wife was a hindrance."

As for why he had not married after the termination of his espionage activities, Gold explained:

"I at one time considered marriage, and the girl in question told me at one time that she didn't think I was really in love with her; she felt that I was too cold. What she didn't know was that what made me cold, all over, and especially down here, what really made me cold was the thought that if we were married and we did have children, and suppose this thing came to light, what then?"

Presiding chairman of the subcommittee on the day Gold testified was Senator Herman Welker. He remarked that he first had met Harry Gold some months before during a visit to Lewisburg Penitentiary.

WELKER: Mr. Gold, at that time . . . I interrogated you with respect to certain of your activities prior to your arrest. You mentioned something to me that has been on my mind since that time about your stealing some secrets for the Russians having to do with photographing, photographing equipment.

GOLD: That is correct.

WELKER: You have not mentioned that today. I think you told me . . . that the photographic process was among the most valuable things that you had ever stolen from the United States Government? Is that true?

GOLD: Yes. It came about in this way. The material was given to me by Al Slack. But the point was this. The material could not be duplicated anywhere else in the world but in the files . . . and in the processes of Eastman Kodak. . . .

The people [at Eastman Kodak] who carried out the research on the various sensitizers and developers used in the production of these various types of color film, particularly the groups of film that are used in aerial photography for detecting camouflage, those people worked in separate departments . . . and none of this material was ever published in the literature. . . . Usually . . . firms take out patents. . . . But in this case, on certain critical materials, vital to these processes, I don't believe that Eastman took out patents.

Senator Welker inquired about Gold's observation during their earlier conversation at Lewisburg that his theft of photographic information from Kodak was "one of the most damaging things" he had done to the United States. The man who allegedly had transferred secrets of the atomic bomb from Fuchs and Greenglass to the Soviet agent Yakovlev responded: "I *consider it the most damaging*. . . ." (Emphasis added.)

A few minutes later, however, Gold told the subcommittee: "But actually, I wonder if the biggest damage, the greatest damage, wasn't the damage that I did in completely turning over myself to these people. We are free. We should be free. A person should be free. It is his right."

A verbatim transcript of Gold's Senate testimony in pamphlet form was published by the Government Printing Office in December 1956. At that time, Gold's remarks evidently came to the attention of Eastman Kodak. In a story headlined "Kodak Doubts A-Spy's Thefts Tale," the Rochester *Times Union* reported:

" 'It is difficult to understand just what film Gold refers to, for his comments are not clear technically,' said a spokesman for the firm. 'If he is referring to Kodak color aero film it should be said that the basic information about sensitizers for that type of film was available to anyone who wanted to find it, in public literature or in published patent form.' "

Unnoticed by the press at the time of the release of the record of the Senate hearing were two remarkable "exhibits" printed in the back of the same pamphlet. Each was a statement written by Gold for his attorneys in 1950—*months before* the Rosenberg-Sobell trial. The exhibits had been made a part of the official subcommittee record at the request of chief counsel Robert Morris. The latter obviously was unaware that Gold's *pretrial statements* contain a serious contradiction of his subsequent testimony about atomic espionage. The statements also cast the first glimmerings of light on the FBI interrogation of Gold during the period between his arrest and his emergence ten months later as a crucial government witness in the Rosenberg-Sobell trial.

Recounting to the Rosenberg-Sobell jury his trip to New Mexico in June 1945, to pick up data from Fuchs and Greenglass, Gold described his delivery of this material to Yakovlev in New York City. He then testified that at his very next meeting with Yakovlev, the latter had reported that "the information which I had given him some two weeks previous had been sent immediately to the Soviet Union. He said that the information which I had received from Greenglass was *extremely excellent and very valuable.*" (Emphasis added.)

This testimony about the excellence of Greenglass's information has been widely quoted in scores of books and articles about the case. It is the single instance in the entire trial of any testimony about the Russians' evaluation of the espionage data allegedly passed them. As such, the testimony may well have influenced Judge Kaufman in his determination of the significance of the crime and his imposition of the death sentence.

However, in one of his pretrial statements reprinted by the Senate subcommittee, Gold wrote:

"In June, 1945, on the occasion of my first visit to Santa Fe, I met this man [David Greenglass] at his apartment in Albuquerque and received from him information. . . . *Earlier, I have said that I believed the information to have been unimportant but I have since learned that it was highly valuable.* (Emphasis added.)

". . . Greenglass was a machinist and *I have been told* that he worked on a very important phase of the bomb assembly." (Emphasis added.)

Gold's other published pretrial statement enunciates this point again and explicitly contradicts his trial testimony:

". . . Yakovlev . . . told me that the information received [from Greenglass] was of *no value.*" (Emphasis added.)

Obviously, in his trial testimony Gold affected a complete reversal of his earlier story of his conversation with Yakovlev. After telling the investigative agents that Yakovlev had declared the Greenglass information to be of "no value," Gold soon after *was told* that he had been misled by Yakovlev—Greenglass had worked on "a very important phase of the bomb assembly" and the material he had given Gold was "highly valuable." The final step, at the Rosenberg-Sobell trial, was to put these words into Yakovlev's mouth. This Gold did, imaginatively adding the inference that the enthusiastic appraisal of Greenglass's data had come straight from Moscow.

The FBI has never disclosed precisely what information from Gold about his alleged Albuquerque meeting led the Bureau's agents to David Greenglass. However, it has been widely reported in the literature of the case that Gold clearly identified his Albuquerque contact in his confession of his atomic espionage activities and that the FBI then simply picked Greenglass up. Thus, S. Andhil Fineberg, in his book *The Rosenberg Case*, stated: ". . . Gold . . . named Greenglass in his confession." Similarly, former President Dwight D. Eisenhower wrote in his memoirs, *The White House Years:* ". . . Klaus Fuchs. . . . implicated Gold, who in turn named Greenglass."

Furthering the impression that Gold actually had "named" Greenglass was his own trial testimony. Gold testified that Yakovlev had prepared him for his Albuquerque trip by giving him "a sheet of paper; it was onionskin paper, and on it was typed the following: First, the name 'Greenglass,' just 'Greenglass.' Then a number 'High Street' . . . and then underneath that was 'Albuquerque, New Mexico.' " Gold recalled Yakovlev's "emphasis on memorizing" the contents of the paper and noted that in the course of the Albuquerque meeting he had learned that Greenglass's first name was Dave and his wife's, Ruth.

Certainly, if Gold originally related to the FBI the same story as this one to which he testified at the trial, his identification of David Greenglass is beyond dispute. That he did so has generally been assumed by most commentators on the case. *Look* magazine, for example, quoting Gold's testimony about his Albuquerque trip and Yakovlev's typed instructions containing the name "Greenglass," added:

"By the time Gold had reached this stage of his narrative, the FBI agents knew they had come across a spy case of enormous magnitude. Quickly they moved in on David Greenglass. . . ."

One of Gold's pretrial statements, however, presents a startlingly different version of his confession with respect to David Greenglass. Describing the day on which he was first taken into custody by the FBI, Gold tells how he recounted for the agents "the full story of my relationship with Klaus Fuchs in every detail . . . *the David Greenglass incident I had actually completely forgotten about.* . . . (Emphasis added.)

"Greenglass I had met . . . in Albuquerque, on the first Sunday in June of 1945. . . . As has been said before, *until some time after my arrest, all memory of this incident had fled from me.* . . . And I had forgotten the man's name completely." (Emphasis added.)

When did Gold first remember this incident and tell the FBI about it? He claims in his pretrial statement that it was more than a week after his arrest. He also gradually remembered and told the FBI, he notes, a number of details about the Albuquerque meeting and physical descriptions of the man he visited there and his wife. What about the man's name? An enigmatic footnote to the pretrial statement explains:

"But for the life of me, I could not recall David Greenglass's name. So this was done: A list of some 20 last names was selected; first we eliminated the least likely 10; then we cut the list further; finally a group of the 3 most likely was chosen, and lo, Greenglass's was at the top. For his wife's name we did likewise and again 'Ruth' headed the list."

Thus, at the time of his arrest, Harry Gold had "completely forgotten" his visit to David Greenglass five years before. He had "forgotten" the vital meeting with Yakovlev in New York, where he had received a sheet of onionskin paper with instructions and his half of the jello box side; he had "forgotten" his three separate trips to the Greenglass apartment on June 2 and 3 and the password "I come from Julius"; and he had "forgotten" turning over Greenglass's data to Yakovlev on his return to New York.

Then, more than a week later, Harry Gold "remembered" that he had met someone in Albuquerque and recalled various details about the meeting—including that Yakovlev had said the material received from this man was of "no value"—but not the man's name. At some undisclosed time later, Gold and the FBI agents identified David and Ruth Greenglass by the curious procedure of eliminating names from a list that the agents themselves had supplied.*

It is worth recalling that Gold's corroboration of the Greenglasses' espionage confession is the *only* corroboration ever presented of their claims that they were spies. Similarly, Gold was the *only* trial witness to identify the absent co-defendant, Anatoli Antonovich Yakovlev, former Soviet vice-consul in New York, as a member of the alleged espionage conspiracy.

Gold has said that all of the data he received from Fuchs in 1944 and 1945 and the material he got from Greenglass on June 3, 1945, he turned over to a Russian superior he knew only as "John" and later identified as Yakovlev. Yakovlev, he testified at the Rosenberg-Sobell trial, was between three and ten years younger than himself. In a pretrial statement, he indicated that Yakovlev was about four years his junior. However, a document entered into evidence at the trial gives Yakovlev's birth date and shows that he was only a few months younger than Gold.

Only one other personal detail about Yakovlev has ever been mentioned by Gold in any publicly available source. A pretrial statement notes that "one of the items that helped identify John as Yakovlev, was the fact that he had once let slip that he had a little boy and a girl, and that the latter was called Vicki, short for Victoria, in honor of her being born on the day that Von Poulus surrendered at Stalingrad."

But this item—allegedly used to help identify Yakovlev—does not quite check out. It is true that Yakovlev had a son and a daughter and that the girl was named Victoria. However, a prosecution exhibit consisting of documents from the United States Lines, by which Yakovlev and his family departed for Europe, shows that Victoria was five years old in October 1946. Since the surrender of the German army at Stalingrad took place on January 31, 1943, Victoria must have been over a year old at the time. It is therefore impossible that her name was inspired by that event. One wonders whether Gold had any personal knowledge of the name of Yakovlev's daughter or whether, after his arrest, he *was told* that the girl's name was Victoria and creatively supplied the confidence-inspiring detail about the Battle of Stalingrad.

---

* It seems likely that the Greenglasses—already the object of FBI interest—were under surveillance before Gold ever "recollected" visiting someone in Albuquerque.

Did Gold actually have a Soviet espionage contact called John? Gold's confession is the only basis for believing so. Was John actually the Soviet vice-consul Yakovlev? Again, only Gold's unconfirmed identification of Yakovlev supports this claim.

As for the validity of the identification of Greenglass by Gold, knowledge of the latter's prolific imagination and history as a liar—and of the FBI technique of supplying information during interrogation—does nothing to still doubts. How can we explain Gold's strange lapse of memory concerning the Albuquerque meeting and the fact that the FBI brought the name of David Greenglass to his attention *before* he ever mentioned it?

Fear of punishment, which might ordinarily deter one from falsely confessing to a capital crime, apparently did not influence Gold. An ominous hint of his perverse satisfaction at the punishment soon to be meted out to him is contained in the closing paragraphs of one of his pretrial statements:

". . . I must be punished, and punished well, for the terribly frightening things that have been done. I am ready to accept this penalty. There shall be no quivering, trembling, appeals to sympathy or fervid pleas for mercy. What was, was, and I am now prepared to pay the price."

Noting that he wanted to "indisputably establish the authenticity and the enormity of my crime," Gold clearly expressed his pleasure at the exposure of his guilt. The once obscure little chemist, suddenly catapulted to fame through his confession and the naming of his alleged fellow conspirators, wrote:

"The manner in which all of the pieces of the giant jig-saw puzzle, of which I was a part, are falling ever so gloriously into place—to reveal the whole picture—has added a tremendous zest and sense of achievement to my life."

JUNE 3, 1945

•

CHAPTER 28
THE SCENE OF THE CRIME

On the morning of June 16, 1950, the chief of the Department of Justice's Criminal Division in Washington, D.C., telephoned the Assistant U. S. Attorney in Albuquerque, New Mexico, to advise him about a crime allegedly committed in his district five years before by one David Greenglass. The Assistant U. S. Attorney was asked to authorize and prepare a complaint against Greenglass, then in voluntary custody of the FBI in New York City.

Shortly thereafter that morning, the requested complaint was filed before U. S. Commissioner Owen J. Mowrey in the Albuquerque Federal Building. Although the charges were formally sworn to by an FBI agent attached to the Bureau's New Mexico office, two agents in New York City (who had participated in the night-long interrogation of Greenglass) were named as witnesses.

The complaint accused Greenglass of conspiring with Harry Gold and Anatoli A. Yakovlev and mentioned a single overt act—a meeting between Greenglass and Gold in "June or July, 1945" for delivery of "information relating to the National Defense of the United States." The scene of the crime: Albuquerque, New Mexico.

The Albuquerque *Tribune* reported that the Assistant U. S. Attorney there had informed Saypol that he would consent if Greenglass wanted the case tried in his home state; otherwise, the prisoner was to be removed to New Mexico. Several weeks later, a New Mexico grand jury indicted Greenglass, then held under $100,000 bail in New York, for conspiracy to commit espionage.* Cited in the indictment was a meeting in Albuquerque with Harry Gold on "June 3, 1945."

When Julius Rosenberg was arrested, a month after the jailing of his

---

* Greenglass subsequently was included in a New York indictment with the Rosenbergs. However, the New Mexico indictment was kept open until May 9, 1951, remaining a potential threat to Greenglass until after the Rosenberg-Sobell trial.

brother-in-law, the complaint against him charged only one wartime overt act: a meeting with David Greenglass in New York City in January 1945. The import of this alleged meeting was immediately explained by J. Edgar Hoover in a statement released to the press. Hoover declared that in January 1945 Rosenberg had given Greenglass "one half of an irregularly cut jello box top."* Greenglass was said to have been shown the other half of this box top by Harry Gold in Albuquerque in June 1945, and to have thereupon turned over to Gold classified information "from the Atom Bomb Project at Los Alamos."

Thus, the first legal documents filed in what was to become the Rosenberg-Sobell case pertained to only one alleged crime—the Gold-Greenglass Albuquerque meeting, including Rosenberg's part in the arrangements. The FBI has since officially stated that it was the uncovering of this meeting—through the confessions of Gold and Greenglass—that brought about the discovery that the Rosenbergs were Soviet spies. At the trial, despite the addition of a number of other espionage allegations, the events of June 3, 1945, formed the core of the government's case. The matching of pieces of a jello box as a means of identification is today one of the best-known cloak-and-dagger episodes of history.

The prosecution's claim that Gold had visited the Greenglasses on a spy mission never was questioned by the defense, which limited its response solely to a denial by the Rosenbergs that they had had any part in the affair. Contesting this denial were three prosecution witnesses—David and Ruth Greenglass and Harry Gold. Bringing together their testimony, the following story emerges:

January 1945: One evening, shortly after David Greenglass arrived in New York City from Los Alamos on furlough, he and his wife went to the Rosenberg apartment, where they had been invited for dinner. Present there was a friend of the Rosenbergs, Ann Sidorovich, who departed after a brief social conversation. Julius then revealed to the Greenglasses that he had wanted them to meet Mrs. Sidorovich because she might act as a courier to pick up atom bomb information from them.

A plan was discussed whereby Ruth would move to Albuquerque to live and, on an appointed day, would travel to Denver and go to a movie theater. She would carry a purse containing data on Los Alamos and Mrs. Sidorovich, or some other courier, would meet her in the theater and the two would exhange purses.

After dinner, Ruth went into the kitchen with the Rosenbergs and Julius cut the side of a jello box into two odd-shaped pieces. He pointed out that if Ann Sidorovich were not the courier these pieces would enable the Greenglasses to identify his emissary anyway. Julius gave one half of the cut portion of the box to Ruth and kept the other half himself, saying,

* Described at the trial as the "side" of a jello box.

according to her testimony, "This half will be brought to you by another party and he will bear the greetings from me and you will know that I have sent him."

The idea of a rendezvous in a Denver theater then was abandoned and, in its stead, a new meeting place suggested by David was agreed on: In front of a Safeway supermarket in Albuquerque. The date of the proposed meeting was temporarily left in abeyance. At the end of his furlough, David returned to New Mexico, where Ruth was to join him soon.

February 1945: Early in the month, Julius came to Ruth's New York apartment and, after sending her younger sister out of the room, informed her that a courier would meet her at the designated Safeway market either the last Saturday in April or the first Saturday in May. At the end of February, Ruth left for Albuquerque.

April 1945: Ruth suffered a miscarriage and wrote Ethel about it, noting that she was confined to bed. In an answering letter, Ethel advised Ruth that "a member of the family" would visit her "the third and fourth Saturdays" in May, thus indicating that the Safeway market encounter was postponed. (The alleged letter from Ethel was not produced at the trial.)

May 1945: The third Saturday in May, in midafternoon, Ruth waited alone in front of the supermarket, but nobody met her. The following week, she and David both awaited the courier, again in vain.

However, that very same afternoon—the last Saturday in May—Harry Gold was receiving instructions to visit the Greenglasses. Meeting with Yakovlev in New York to discuss his long-scheduled mission to Santa Fe, New Mexico, to pick up data from Klaus Fuchs the next weekend, Gold was ordered to take on an additional assignment in Albuquerque as well. Yakovlev informed Gold that "a woman was supposed to go . . . but that she was unable to make the trip." From Yakovlev, Gold received typed instructions with the name of the man he was to see, his address on High Street in Albuquerque, and a recognition signal—"I come from Julius." Yakovlev also gave Gold a cut piece of a jello box and an envelope containing $500 in cash for Greenglass.

June 2, 1945: Harry Gold met with Fuchs in Santa Fe and received information from him, then took a bus to Albuquerque (about sixty miles distant). Around 8:30 P.M., Gold went to the High Street address, where he was told by an elderly man that the Greenglasses were out for the evening. He spent the night in an Albuquerque rooming house.

June 3, 1945: The next morning, a Sunday, Gold registered at the Hilton Hotel in Albuquerque in his own name. (The prosecution entered as a trial exhibit a photostat of Gold's hotel registration card.) At about 8:30 A.M., he went again to the house on High Street. When David Greenglass opened the door of his apartment, Gold spoke a recognition signal using the name "Julius"* and the two men matched pieces of the jello box. Greenglass, observing that the courier's visit on this day was unexpected, said the data was not ready and asked Gold to come back that afternoon.

Returning at about 3 P.M., Gold received an envelope with handwritten information and sketches from Greenglass and gave him the envelope with $500. (Gold's testimony described this transaction with a minor variation: He said he handed over the money during his morning visit to the Greenglasses.)

David and Ruth left their apartment with Gold and all three walked a short distance together. They parted at a USO building, which the Greenglasses entered. Gold headed back to New York.

June 4, 1945: On Monday, Ruth deposited in an Albuquerque bank $400 of the money obtained from Gold. (This deposit was documented by photostatic bank records introduced as a prosecution exhibit.)

June 5, 1945: Gold met Yakovlev in New York at 10 P.M. and turned over to him the data from Fuchs and Greenglass.

In the total fabric of the Rosenberg-Sobell trial, the significance of this Albuquerque meeting is such that, without it, the prosecution's case could not stand. For the closely meshing testimony about a cut jello box and a recognition phrase with the name "Julius" is the only prosecution evidence that connects the Rosenbergs with the self-confessed spy, Gold, and his alleged Soviet superior, Yakovlev. Even this connection is not a direct one. However, as Judge Kaufman pointed out in his charge to the jury, "The Government contends that you have a right to infer that there existed a link between Julius Rosenberg and Yakovlev in that Julius Rosenberg in some way transmitted . . . the Jello box-side to Yakovlev."

In addition to providing the prosecution with this requisite element of proof, the Albuquerque meeting also represents the major strength of the government's case. For it is the single espionage incident described by David and Ruth Greenglass that is verified by another witness—Harry Gold. Moreover, attesting to Gold's visit to the Greenglasses are two persuasive prosecution exhibits: The hotel registration card, which indicates that Gold was in Albuquerque on June 3, 1945, and the bank record, which confirms Ruth's deposit the next day and thereby lends support to the story of the $500.

Despite this seemingly incontrovertible evidential structure, we now know of Gold's startling pretrial admission to his attorneys that, at the time of his arrest, he had no recollection whatsoever of the alleged June 3

---

* Three different versions of the recognition signal were offered at the trial. David: "Julius sent me"; Ruth: ". . . he [Gold] said he bore greetings from Julius"; and Gold: "I came from Julius." (Later, before the Senate Internal Security subcommittee, Gold said the password was "I bring greetings from Julius.")

meeting. Although the unwinding of memory may follow labyrinthine pathways, it is, nevertheless, very difficult to believe that Gold could have "completely forgotten" every aspect of his Albuquerque visit—if the visit really took place. Doubts stem particularly from the fact that the details of Gold's meeting with the Greenglasses are so closely interwoven with those of his rendezvous the previous day in Sante Fe with Klaus Fuchs—from the preparatory discussion with Yakovlev in late May to the final passage of the data on June 5. Yet Gold has said that, initially, he gave the FBI agents "the full story of my relationship with Klaus Fuchs in every detail," but recalled nothing about the *entire* "David Greenglass incident."

What further proof might be marshaled to sustain or refute the prosecution's allegations regarding the Albuquerque meeting?

In 1945, Gold was employed by the Pennsylvania Sugar Company, in Philadelphia. Would his employment records there show that he had been absent from his job in early June? An inquiry along this line to the industrial relations manager of the firm* elicited a somewhat ambiguous response: "The information requested is not available, and I cannot be of further service to you." Subsequently, we learned that in 1950 one of Gold's attorneys had posed similar questions to company officials, who informed him that an up-to-date personnel system had only very recently been instituted and earlier employee records were "very skimpy." What personnel records on Gold the firm had maintained were made available to the attorney, who apparently saw no notations as to business trips, vacations, or sick leaves. It seems doubtful that any records of Gold's absences from work exist; if they do, they remain a closely guarded secret.

No plane or train ticket stubs, passenger lists, or reservations ever have been made public to document Gold's travels to and from his alleged espionage assignments in New Mexico. If any such had been known to the prosecution, they would very likely have been utilized at the trial. In his testimony, Gold did not specify his mode of transportation in June 1945 from Philadelphia to the Southwest and described only that part of his return trip from Albuquerque to Chicago. Thus, lack of adequate information precluded our undertaking any meaningful new research in this area.

In the hope that a visit to the scene of the crime might yield some useful clues, one of the authors journeyed on two separate occasions to Albuquerque and environs. The apartment that David and Ruth leased there, from early spring 1945 to February 1946, is in a two-story frame rooming house at 209 North High Street, a pleasant residential section not far from the main business district of Albuquerque. At the High Street address, we spoke with the former landlords of the Greenglasses, Mr. and

---

* Now the Pennsylvania Sugar Division of the National Sugar Refining Company.

Mrs. W. B. Freeman, who have been publicized in the local press as owners of the house where "One of the most important atomic secrets the United States possessed was passed to a Russian spy courier." They discussed their two notorious tenants with lively interest, displaying a scrapbook with newspaper and magazine stories on the case.

The Freemans noted that prior to David's arrest they had been questioned at some length by FBI agents and had aided in the investigation as best they could. In particular, the agents had asked them to try to remember anyone who had come to their house five years before to see the Greenglasses. The Freemans thought they recalled one or two visitors to the Greenglass apartment, but were unable to say whether or not Gold ever had been there. The FBI also had inquired about an elderly man who Gold said had advised him that the Greenglasses were out for the evening when he first called at the house. Mrs. Freeman suggested that this might possibly have been her aged father, and FBI agents interviewed the man, then living in California. However, according to Mrs. Freeman, her father had not been able to identify Gold either.

Gold's trial testimony is nearly barren of any description of the High Street house that might support his claim that he had been there. In one of his very few specific references to the house, he said: "I was admitted, and I recall going up a very steep flight of steps, and I knocked on a door." Actually, the stairway leading to the second floor of the Freeman house is not at all steep. (There is an outside flight in the back yard, but the Freemans assert that the entrance from these stairs to the second-floor hall was kept latched from the inside at all times. Moreover, Gold makes clear that he was "admitted" to the house before climbing the "very steep" steps.)

From Gold's testimony, one might gain the impression that when he reached the second floor of the house he saw only one apartment, that of the Greenglasses. In fact, there are five apartments on the floor and the doors have no name plates, only numbers—a detail to which Gold did not allude.

Apartment number 4, second floor rear, was occupied by Ruth Greenglass, joined by her husband on weekends. It consisted of a bed-sitting room, about thirteen feet square, and a tiny kitchen; a hall bathroom was shared with other tenants. In his testimony, Gold indicated that the Greenglasses had a kitchen, but did not otherwise describe their apartment.

The only other physical details that Gold provided about his alleged meeting with the Greenglasses appear in his account of his departure from the house. Said he: "The three of us, Mr. Greenglass, Mrs. Greenglass and myself, left the Greenglass's apartment and we walked along a slanting back street in Albuquerque, and there in front of a small building I left the Greenglasses." The building referred to by Gold was identified by the Greenglasses as the USO. However, between 209 North High Street and the former USO building (which is not particularly "small" and presently houses the Albuquerque Health Department) there is today no byway that could be described as a "slanting back street" and neither the Freemans nor any other residents of the area with whom we spoke could recall there having been one in 1945, or at any time.

Clearly, none of these fragments of information is sufficient to strengthen or weaken the prosecution's story of the Albuquerque meeting to any significant degree. What this research does indicate, however, is the likelihood that—apart from the confessions of Gold and the Greenglasses—the government's sole proof that Harry Gold was in Albuquerque on June 3, 1945, was his rather inexplicable registration at the Hilton Hotel in his own name that Sunday morning.

CHAPTER 29

THE HILTON HOTEL CARD

Summing up the prosecution's case against the Rosenbergs, U. S. Attorney Irving Saypol told the jury: "The veracity of David and Ruth Greenglass and of Harry Gold is established by documentary evidence and cannot be contradicted. You have in evidence before you the registration card from the Hilton Hotel in Albuquerque, which shows that he was registered there on June 3, 1945. You have before you the transcript of the record of the Albuquerque bank showing that on the morning of June 4, 1945, Ruth Greenglass opened a bank account in Albuquerque and made an initial deposit of $400 in cash. . . ."

In view of the importance ascribed to Harry Gold's Hilton Hotel registration by prosecutor Saypol in his summation, the card was introduced as a government exhibit at the trial with surprisingly little fanfare.

First, Gold (under direct examination by Assistant U. S. Attorney Myles Lane) provided the testimony which laid the basis for the card's admission as evidence.

> GOLD: I arrived in Albuquerque early in the evening of the 2nd of June, and about 8:30 that night went . . . to the designated address on High Street. There I was met by a tall elderly . . . man. I inquired about the Greenglasses and he told me that they were out for the evening but he thought they would be in early on Sunday morning.
> LANE: Then what did you do?
> GOLD: Then I returned to downtown Albuquerque. . . . I stayed that night—I finally managed to obtain a room in a hallway of a rooming house and then *on Sunday morning* I registered at the Hotel Hilton. (Emphasis added.)
> LANE: Now, did you register under your own name?
> GOLD: Yes, I did.

Gold then described the details of his Sunday-morning visit with the Greenglasses, to whom he introduced himself with an alias, "Dave from Pittsburgh"; his return to their apartment some hours later for the data; and his immediate departure for New York. He did not mention the Hilton Hotel again. When Gold had concluded his direct testimony, court was adjourned with no announcement by the prosecution that a copy of the Hilton registration card was available and would be produced at the trial.

The following day, Bloch waived cross-examination of Gold and the witness was excused. Two brief witnesses later, at the very end of a short court session, Saypol requested a conference at the bench with defense attorneys.

> SAYPOL: I now have some testimony which it is possible there may be a stipulation on: the fact of the registration of Harry Gold at the Hotel Hilton on June 3. I have a photostat of the registration card. I also have the original on the way, together with a witness if required. . . . May I first inquire of counsel whether they will stipulate as to the records or whether they will insist upon strict technical proof?
>
> BLOCH: . . . I am certainly not going to insist on strict technical testimony.

The U. S. Attorney thereupon repeated, this time in the hearing of the jury, his intention of introducing a copy of Gold's hotel registration card.

> SAYPOL: If counsel for the defendants are agreeable, I shall proceed to put in evidence a document, rather, a photostat of a document, relating to the witness Harry Gold's presence in Albuquerque on June 3, 1945. . . . I now inquire of the defendants whether there is any objection to the offer in evidence of this photostatic record?
>
> BLOCH: . . . the defendants have absolutely no objection to this document being used . . . and we concede that whatever the document there says, it was made in the regular course of business by the party whose records it comes from.

With this statement, the Rosenbergs' attorney completely waived the right of his clients to examine the *original* registration card and to question a hotel employee or other witness about the card's authenticity and the circumstances of its preparation and discovery. Possibly Bloch's rather limited experience as a criminal lawyer, as well as his apparent eagerness to aid his clients by not appearing obstructive, led him to err in making such a concession in a capital case. Furthermore, Bloch—with somewhat strained logic—adhered to the view that Gold's testimony about a meeting with the Greenglasses did not involve the Rosenbergs and so need not be challenged by the defense.

The fact is that Harry Gold's registration in his own name on June 3, 1945, was an exceedingly fortuitous happening for the prosecution, pro-

379

viding as it did the only documentary evidence that placed him in Albuquerque on the day of the alleged espionage meeting. From Gold's sparse testimony on this point, it is impossible to fathom his motive for taking a hotel room that day or even to know whether or not he spent any time at all in this room.

Nevertheless, his account of his registration is clear and precise: he obtained a room at the Hilton Hotel on *Sunday morning, June 3*, and later *that same day* left Albuquerque by train.

Curiously, this simple sequence has confused many writers. The first of a series of misstatements about Gold's hotel registration appeared in the New York *Times*, which reported:

"Mr. Saypol then introduced . . . a registration card for Harry Gold, confessed atomic spy, in the Hilton Hotel in Albuquerque, N.M., on the *night of June 3, 1945*." (Emphasis added.)

The same error was made by *U.S. News & World Report*:

"He [Gold] had spent the Saturday night before calling on the Greenglasses in an Albuquerque rooming house.

"After getting the material from the Greenglasses, Gold spent *Sunday night* in an Albuquerque hotel, under his own name." (Emphasis added.)

An amalgamation of Gold's testimony about the rooming-house hallway and the hotel was effected by Justin Atholl, author of a book entitled *How Stalin Knows*:

"Finding a room in war-crowded Albuquerque was not easy, but he eventually found a room in the hallway of the Hotel Hilton. Strangely, he registered in his own name. . . ."

New York *Post* reporter Oliver Pilat notes in the preface of his book, *The Atom Spies*, that he consulted with Saypol while preparing his manuscript. Nonetheless, Pilat simply disregarded Gold's testimony that he slept in a rooming house on Saturday night, and put the courier to bed at the Hilton that evening. In addition, although Gold failed to indicate that he actually had occupied his hotel room, the writer imaginatively remedied this omission.

Describing Gold's visit to the Greenglasses on Sunday morning, June 3, Pilat wrote: "Harry Gold read a mystery story for a couple of hours in his room at the Hotel Hilton, and ate his lunch there. He had registered under his right name . . . *the previous evening*, after a visit to the North High Street address. . . ." (Emphasis added.)

The surprising frequency with which this aspect of Gold's testimony has been recounted inaccurately may well be due to the fact that it is somewhat unusual to register at a hotel in the morning and leave the same day. The writers quoted distorted the incident in an apparent attempt to make it seem more reasonable to themselves and their readers.

We decided to inspect the hotel card photostat that had served as such a crucial piece of evidence in the prosecution's case; but, before we could usefully do so, it seemed necessary first to learn something about the Hilton's 1945 registration practices. At the Albuquerque Hilton, we talked with Linda Hughes, who held a responsible position at the hotel, where she had been employed for nearly twenty years. Mrs. Hughes had worked at the hotel's reception desk in 1945 and she outlined the registration procedure followed then, a fairly standard one:

Arriving at the reception desk, a guest was presented with a numbered registration card. On the top half of this card the guest filled in his name and other information; the lower part of the card was filled in by the desk clerk. Then the clerk immediately placed the card in a time-stamp machine to record the date and exact time on the back. The machine in use for this purpose in 1945 stamped the word "Received" along with the date and time, so that it could be used for incoming mail as well as registration cards.

The desk clerk also prepared a "folio," or bill, at the time of registration on which charges subsequently accrued by the guest were itemized. All registration cards and bills were retained by the Albuquerque Hilton in an attic storage area for five years.

Back in New York, at the federal courthouse in Foley Square, the authors examined prosecution Exhibit 16: The photostatic copy of Gold's hotel registration card. Written on the top half of the face of the card, in a rather small, precise hand, was "Harry Gold, 6823 Kindred St., Phila. 24, Pa."—Gold's correct address in 1945. For unknown reasons, Gold had noted as his place of business "Terry and Siebert," a firm for which he had done occasional free-lance chemical work.

The lower half of the registration card, filled in by the clerk, was dated "6-3-45." The clerk had marked the rate of the room assigned Gold as "1⁵⁰" and had added a notation: "day rate until 8 P.M." All of this tallied with Gold's testimony that he had registered at the Hilton in his own name on the morning of June 3, 1945, but had not stayed overnight at the hotel.

When we turned the card over, the time stamp captured our attention:

RECEIVED

Jun 4   12 36 PM   '45

HILTON HOTEL
ALBUQUERQUE

The dates on the front and back of the card should have been the same, but they were not! The clerk's handwritten date indicates that Gold registered at the hotel on June 3; the time stamp says June 4.

Yet, according to the prosecution's case, by June 4 Gold was already well on his way to New York City for his rendezvous with Yakovlev, and David Greenglass had returned to his Army job at Los Alamos. More-over, Gold testified that he had registered at the Hilton on Sunday *morning*, but the time stamp reads June 4, 12:36 P.M.—Monday *afternoon*. Thus, both the day and hour recorded by the time stamp conflict with Gold's statements at the Rosenberg-Sobell trial.

Whatever the explanation for this mysterious discrepancy in dating, pros-ecution Exhibit 16—the copy of the Hilton Hotel registration card—is useless as corroborative evidence of the Gold-Greenglass meeting. It simply does not prove that Harry Gold was in Albuquerque on June 3, 1945.

Clearly, our research on Exhibit 16 could not end with this discovery. What is the history of the faultily dated registration card?

A possible clue is suggested by the card itself. On the reverse side, in the upper right-hand corner, appear the initials, "FLB," which we rec-ognized as those of Fletcher L. Brumit, manager of the Albuquerque Hilton when the 1950 espionage arrests occurred. Locating Brumit,* we informed him that we had seen a copy of Gold's registration card and had observed on the back the initials FLB. Was he, we inquired, the one who actually had removed the card from the hotel's files or did he know who had?

Brumit replied that he recalled the case of Harry Gold but had no recollection at all of the circumstances under which the card was found. In fact, he had no specific memory of ever having seen or initialed the card. He could only describe his usual procedure if the FBI wanted to look at a hotel record: In such a situation, he would ask a hotel employee to obtain the requested record from the files and bring it to his office, then he would turn it over to the agents in exchange for a receipt. Generally, he initialed the card, either when he gave it to the agents or when it was returned.

We mentioned to Brumit the June 3 clerk's date on the front of Gold's card and the June 4 time stamp on the back and sought his expert opinion. He seemed perplexed. Finally, he concluded that, from all indications, the clerk had made an error; Gold probably had registered on June 4.

A similar conclusion was offered by Linda Hughes, when we spoke with her again at the Albuquerque Hilton and told her of the two different dates on the Gold card. She commented that either the clerk or the time stamp was wrong, since the dates should agree. In such a case, she would take the stamp as the valid date of registration.

Was she able to tell us anything at all about the manner in which the authorities had obtained Gold's registration card from the Hilton files? Mrs. Hughes said she remembered that in 1950 FBI agents had spent

---

* He was in Cleveland managing the Statler Hilton. He since has resumed his mana-gerial post at the Albuquerque Hilton.

several days in the hotel attic where back records were kept, apparently looking for the card.

Any such FBI search of the hotel files—as reported by Mrs. Hughes—seems difficult to account for. According to manager Fletcher Brumit, his usual procedure when the FBI requested a record was to send a hotel employee to locate it and bring it to him. Furthermore, the Hilton's filing system would seem to have obviated the need for any lengthy hunt for a registration card. (Each year's consecutively numbered registration cards were filed numerically; bills were filed alphabetically, by the guests' names.)

Nevertheless, the story that FBI agents had themselves looked through the files of the hotel for several days subsequently received substantiation from other sources. At the offices of the Albuquerque *Tribune*, news editor George Baldwin, somewhat of a buff on the atomic espionage case that had made local history, showed us his collection of press clippings on the subject. Among these was an item Baldwin had written for his own paper, which reported that in 1950 "FBI agents checked all of the Hilton records here for days. The Gold registration card they found . . . helped build the government's case. . . ."

Another clipping obtained from Baldwin suggested a new research lead. Listing those who had appeared as witnesses before the New Mexico grand jury that indicted Greenglass, this story noted that one Marc W. Neal "represented Fletcher Brumit, who had been requested to produce any registration cards and other records concerning Harry Gold."

We contacted Neal, former assistant manager at the Hilton, now an executive of another Albuquerque hotel. He confirmed that he had testified before the New Mexico grand jury and said that he had expected to come to New York to testify at the Rosenberg-Sobell trial, but had not been called.

Had he personally secured Gold's registration card from the hotel files and taken it to the grand jury session at which he appeared? Neal said he had not. His recollection was that at the time of his grand jury testimony—in early July 1950—the originals of any Albuquerque Hilton records pertaining to Gold already were in the possession of the United States Attorney for the New Mexico district. FBI agents previously had been in the hotel attic for a number of days going though the files, he said.

Informed that on Gold's registration card the clerk had written June 3 while the time machine stamped June 4, Neal exclaimed: "That *is* odd!" He observed that there obviously was some mistake, but was unable to suggest how it might have occurred. The point had not come up during his grand jury testimony.

Finally, another former Hilton executive, Coby Briehn, was located at a hotel he was managing in Texas. Briehn said that the search for Gold's card had been conducted by FBI agents, who had examined records in the hotel attic for days. He himself had spent some time with them there, answering their questions. However, he believed that, for the most part, the agents had worked in the attic alone, without any hotel employee present.

Told of the differing dates on the card, Briehn indicated that he was baffled. He guessed that the time stamp probably was the correct date of registration.

From these interviews, we concluded that there is no simple explanation for the discrepancy between the clerk's date written on the front of Gold's card and the time-stamp date imprinted on the back. In addition, we had learned that in 1950 FBI agents had direct access to the Albuquerque Hilton registration files and other records for some days.

Had Harry Gold himself ever said anything about his alleged June hotel registration in Albuquerque other than his terse mention of it at the Rosenberg-Sobell trial? Scrutinizing every publicly available source, we found that he had not. Neither in his published pretrial statements to his attorneys, his other court appearances, nor his testimony before a Congressional committee had Gold himself referred to the Hilton Hotel.

However, a reference to the hotel—though not by Gold—was made during his Philadelphia sentencing hearing, prior to the Rosenberg-Sobell trial. That proceeding was the single occasion at which the Department of Justice has let it be known that Harry Gold registered at the Albuquerque Hilton on a date *other* than June 3, 1945. The disclosure was made by U. S. Attorney Gerald Gleeson, who told federal Judge James P. Mc-Granery:

"In accordance with plans which had been made in Santa Fe in June of 1945, Gold met Fuchs in Santa Fe, New Mexico, in September of 1945. . . . When the meeting was over Gold returned to Albuquerque, New Mexico, where he stayed overnight at the Hilton Hotel and registered under his own name."

Not until 1955, with the publication of John Wexley's book on the Rosenberg-Sobell case, was Gold's September stay at the Hilton mentioned publicly again. Wexley had chanced upon the fact that the government was in possession of a copy of Gold's September registration card. We decided to have a look for ourselves.

Inasmuch as the existence of a photostat of the September card already had been revealed, the U. S. Attorney's office at Foley Square agreed to make a copy of it for us, as well as a copy of the June card photostat introduced as a trial exhibit.* (See reproductions of front and

* None of the Justice Department employees with whom the authors dealt at the U. S. Attorney's office, Southern District of New York, had been involved in the preparation or trial of the Rosenberg-Sobell case. Saypol, Cohn, and others who participated in the prosecution of the case are long since gone from Foley Square.

back of both cards on the fourth and fifth pages of the picture section.)

Gold had signed the September card with his own name, substituting a previous Philadelphia address for his actual one at the time. As his place of business, he had given "A.B.A. Laboratories, New York City"— Abraham Brothman's chemical consulting firm. (Gold was not then regularly employed by Brothman, although he had undertaken occasional freelance assignments for him.)

The room rate recorded on the September card is "5.00." Unlike the June card, there is no notation about a "day rate," so apparently Gold stayed overnight at the hotel in September.

Most important, in contrast to the June card, the date written by the clerk on the front of the September card, "9-19-45," corresponds with the time-stamp date on the back, which reads:

RECEIVED

Sep 19   12 34 PM   '45

HILTON HOTEL
ALBUQUERQUE

Rather oddly, the hour stamped on the June card, 12:36 P.M.—which is incompatible with Gold's story that he registered in the morning—is only two minutes apart from the time of day stamped on the September card.

According to the standard operating procedure of the FBI, agents identify newly discovered evidence with their initials and the date. The back of the September card, we noted, had been initialed by three agents and dated May 23, 1950. A number, "65-6," an FBI code designation for the case, also appears.

Seeing this identifying data on the September card, we suddenly were struck by the complete absence of such markings on the June card, which bears only the initials of the hotel manager, Fletcher Brumit. Why, we wondered, should two similar pieces of evidence, presumably obtained by the FBI from the same hotel record room, have been handled so differently?

This inconsistency is all the more puzzling because the FBI could simultaneously have secured Gold's two Albuquerque Hilton bills, for June and September, simply by checking the hotel's alphabetized file of 1945 bills, under "Gold." Printed on the face of every bill was the same number as on the matching registration card. Thus, both the June and September cards, filed by number, would have been located in a matter of minutes.

It is very difficult to believe, however, that FBI agents removed *both* registration cards from the Hilton files on May 23, 1950, but initialed and dated *only one*, then had the other initialed by Fletcher Brumit. Far more likely is that Gold's June and September cards were not found at the same time.

The question naturally arises as to whether the June card ever was "found" in the Hilton files by FBI agents, or was manufactured. Is the June card a counterfeit? If so, how might this be discerned?

There is little reason to doubt that Harry Gold would willingly have participated in the preparation of a fraudulent document. But what about the hotel clerk whose handwritten entries appear on the face of the card? It probably would have been necessary to forge this portion of the card.

Interestingly, the same clerk's initials—"AK"—are on both cards. We managed to identify and get in touch with this former Albuquerque Hilton desk clerk, Anna Kindernecht Hockinson, now residing in Florida. Mrs. Hockinson, who was unmarried in 1945 and whose initials were "AK," supplied us with samples of her handwriting.* These we submitted to Elizabeth McCarthy, a handwriting and document expert.

Mrs. McCarthy, an attorney, regularly examines questioned documents for the Boston Police, the Massachusetts State Police, and many others. We gave her, along with Mrs. Hockinson's handwriting samples, various samples of Harry Gold's handwriting and also copies of the June and the September registration cards. After studying these items, Mrs. McCarthy reported:

"The format of these cards as far as the printing is concerned is different. The position of the diagonally printed word 'Welcome' at the left upper corner of the card is further to the left vertically above the printed word 'NAME' beneath it on the 6/3/45 card than it is on the 9/19/45 card. This is significant because it would be most unusual to set up for one hotel two formats within a few months.

"There appears to be a slight difference in the width of the ruling of the blocks for *Arrived, Room, Date, Clerk* and *Baggage* in these two cards. . . .

"Another distinctive difference between these two cards is in the type which made the N? at their right hand upper corner. On the 6/3/45 card both the capital N and the o are defective. The capital N has a bend and a damaged portion at its right side, and the o has a chip or damaged section on its lower left curve. The 9/19/45 card has no such defect in either the capital N or the o. . . .

"Although card No. 65841 has the date 6/3/45 on its front side, it has a time stamp date of June 4 on its reverse side. Card No. 78783 has the same date written on its front and time stamped on its reverse side, namely September 19, 1945.

"It is highly probable that Harry Gold signed his name and address and

---

* We also asked Mrs. Hockinson about the two different dates on the June card. She replied: "The time stamp on the card is the governing factor."

business connections on both of the Hilton Hotel registration cards numbered 65841 and 78783.

"It is highly probable that Anna Kindernecht Hockinson wrote the date '9/19/45,' the room number '521,' the rate '5.00' and her initials 'ak' on card No. 78783. It contains all of her important, underlying, unconscious writing characteristics. These are the elements in one's writing of which he or she is not aware, and therefore cannot hide, alter or disguise. They include: handwriting system; formation arcs, angles and direction; beginning, intermediary and final strokes; proportions, relatively, of lower case, upper case and capital letters; pen pressure; lateral spacing; penscope, or number of letters written before lifting hand in horizontal progress across the page; nib-crossing in straight and curved letters; type of writing line; speed of hand; right-angled and base-line angulation; fluidity or lack of it in finger, wrist and arm motion; rhythm and balance; strength and power in hand, and over-all motion and coordination features.

"On card No. 65841 I have some very real doubts that Anna Kindernecht Hockinson wrote '6/3/45,' the room '1001,' the rate '1⁵⁰ day rate until 8 P.M.' and the initials 'ak.' Pictorially they do follow rather closely the shapes of some of her figures and letters, but there is a lot of hesitation, irregularity and slowing down in the writing line of these figures and words, and her handwriting samples display no such irregularities and hesitations. For instance, in the *ak* initial combination there are stops with the a and the k in numerous places, heavy and light pressure and a lack of coordination which is absent from her standard writing. Of course a defective pen can cause aberrations in the writing line, but these are of such a character that I would not expect that they could be explained by such a factor. A study of the connecting stroke from the a to the k in these initials shows that this is a place where Mrs. Hockinson makes a very swinging, connecting, easy motion. On card No. 65841 this is completely lacking in grace or coordination or rhythm and per contra is a shaky, jerky kind of line."

Mrs. McCarthy noted the following qualification regarding her analysis:

"It is difficult in a case of this kind for a document expert to arrive at a definite, conclusive opinion from a study of photostats or photographs alone. A detailed microscopic study of the originals is necessary before a final opinion can be reached. Therefore, I would like if possible, to have a chance to study the originals of these two registration cards."

Unfortunately, the originals of the registration cards are not a matter of public record, since they never were entered into evidence by the government in any trial. Presumably, the cards still are retained today in the FBI or other Department of Justice files, but without a court order such files are inaccessible. Nevertheless, Mrs. McCarthy's "very real doubts" about the genuineness of the clerk's handwriting on the June registration—as well as her comments about the appearance of the card itself—are in accord with all our other findings about Exhibit 16.

Our research revealed that the Hilton hotel chain had changed its official symbol, which appears at the top of all registration cards, in the years between 1945 and 1950. Therefore, anyone preparing a counterfeit June 1945 registration card in 1950 could not simply have secured an appropriately numbered card from the hotel's then current stock. Instead, a card of the type in use in 1945 would, of necessity, have been specially printed.

Consistent with the possibility that this might have been done are Mrs. McCarthy's observations that defective letters and a somewhat different format distinguish the June card from the September one, indicating that both cards were not produced from the same printing form or plate.

If a June 1945 Hilton registration card was fabricated, Gold's September registration card could have served as a convenient guide for stylistic details. But a competent forgery could not have been achieved without additional knowledge: What would be the proper number for a June 3, 1945, registration card? To what room might a guest have been assigned? (Many rooms in 1945 were permanently set aside for airlines personnel, for example.) What rates were charged for a half day's stay? Might the clerk who signed the September card "AK" also have been on duty at the reception desk in June?

Questions such as these could have been answered only after an extensive study of the Hilton's back records. The need to search out the required data may explain why FBI agents spent several days going through the files in the hotel attic.

Inasmuch as so many writers on the Rosenberg-Sobell case have reported erroneously that in June 1945 Harry Gold stayed overnight at the Albuquerque Hilton, it seems quite possible that a forger also might have been confused by Gold's story, or simply misinformed regarding hotel procedure, and made a mistake—thus, the otherwise inexplicable June 3 date on the front of the card and June 4 on the back.

As for the hour, 12:36 P.M., recorded by the time stamp on the June card, without a detailed knowledge of Gold's version of events—including his assertion that he had registered in the morning—the manufacturer of a fraudulent card may have erred in this, too. An hour similar to that stamped on the apparently authentic September card may have seemed a safe choice for the June card also—thus, 12:34 P.M. and 12:36 P.M.

Assuming that the June card is a fake, the fact that customary FBI markings are missing from it is understandable. Should the forgery have been detected, the card itself—neither initialed nor dated by any FBI agent—would have provided little help in tracing the perpetrators. The only initials that are on the back of the June card, "FLB," may have been put there at some time by manager Fletcher Brumit; on the other hand, when interviewed by the authors, Brumit remarked that he rarely uses his middle initial, "L."

What about the bill for Gold's alleged June stopover at the Albuquerque Hilton? It seems inconceivable that the registration card could have been found in the files without also securing the matching bill. Yet, at the Rosenberg-Sobell trial, no bill was introduced, nor did the prosecution even allude to the existence of one.

The handwriting on the guest portion of the June card is apparently that of Harry Gold, according to Mrs. McCarthy's analysis. While Gold's "selfless" cooperation would hardly be surprising, it does seem somewhat doubtful that so unreliable a character would be entrusted by the authorities with the knowledge that false evidence was being concocted. It is, therefore, noteworthy that at the Rosenberg-Sobell trial the prosecution deferred introducing the Hilton registration card exhibit until after Gold had left the courtroom.*

Unlike the June card, Gold's September registration card appears to be a genuine one. Our research turned up no suspicious features about it. Moreover, Mrs. McCarthy's study of the clerk's entries on the September card led her to conclude that "it is highly probable" that they were written by Anna Kindernecht herself.

The FBI date on the back of this card—May 23, 1950—is the day of Gold's late-evening arrest as Fuchs's accomplice, suggesting that the discovery of the September card may have triggered that event. Why then has so important a piece of evidence since been held in obscurity?

At the Rosenberg-Sobell trial, for example, Gold testified about his alleged September 1945 rendezvous with Fuchs in Santa Fe, but the prosecution did not introduce the September card as an exhibit. Even more surprising is the fact that J. Edgar Hoover, in his *Reader's Digest* account of the apprehension of Gold, omitted any reference to the September 1945 Albuquerque Hilton registration card unearthed by FBI investigators. Other sources which might have been expected to mention Gold's September registration card also fail to do so, including Don Whitehead's *The FBI Story* (with an appreciative foreword by Hoover) and *Look* magazine's quasi-official article on the atom spy cases.

It seems clear that those most familiar with the evidence decided not to publicize the existence of a September card and not to utilize it in courtroom proceedings—a decision that is quite comprehensible if the June card

* A hint that some technique may have been utilized whereby Gold's actual script appears on a card about which he knows little or nothing is contained in one of his published pretrial statements to his attorney. Describing the early phase of his interrogation by the FBI, Gold recounted: "The special agents and I were together for 9 hours . . . until 2 a.m., during which I submitted page after page of my handwriting and printing. . . ."

is spurious. For a careful comparative examination of both cards, including the clerk's handwriting on them, could readily have suggested to an alert observer that one of them is a forgery. Furthermore, the September card has on it the initials of three FBI agents, who might have been subpoenaed and questioned about the origins of both cards. To anyone with knowledge of these possibilities, the virtual suppression of the September card, despite its authenticity, may well have seemed the better part of discretion.

A similarly circumspect attitude appears to have influenced the prosecution's handling of the June card at the trial. Although by then the government would presumably have had possession of the "original" of the June card for many months, Saypol asserted, without explanation, that the card was not in his hands at the moment he chose to introduce it. He requested and obtained stipulations from the defense that no expert witness need be called to testify about the card and that a photostat would be acceptable instead of the original. The use of a photostat makes impossible the dating of the card's paper and ink and also precludes any definitive opinion from a handwriting analyst. It is ironical that, despite all of these precautions, the rather glaring time-stamp error on the June card was, in all likelihood, never noticed by the prosecution.

In sum, government Exhibit 16 is invalid as evidence because of the conflicting dates recorded on it. There is no documentary proof that Harry Gold was in Albuquerque on June 3, 1945. Moreover, the total information now known about Exhibit 16 points, with compelling logic, to a probable forgery.

But why bother to forge a June card when a genuine Albuquerque Hilton registration card, dated September 19, 1945, was available? Why couldn't the Gold-Greenglass meeting have been said to have taken place on that date—with the September card offered as proof? The answer is obvious: On September 19, 1945, David Greenglass was not in New Mexico; he was in New York City on furlough.*

But why should the date June 3 have been selected for the presumably forged card? Again, the reason is plain: On the following day, June 4, Ruth Greenglass had deposited $400 in an Albuquerque bank.

* David's furlough lasted from September 7 to September 25, 1945.

CHAPTER 30

MONEY FROM THE RUSSIANS

The prosecution's two Albuquerque exhibits derive their importance primarily from being paired with one another to document a sequence of events; together, they constitute powerful circumstantial evidence that the Gold-Greenglass meeting actually occurred.

However, with the Hilton Hotel registration card eliminated as proof of Gold's presence in Albuquerque on June 3, 1945, the significance of Ruth's bank deposit the next day is diminished considerably. For, by itself, the fact that Ruth Greenglass deposited $400 in an Albuquerque bank on June 4, 1945, throws no light at all on the really crucial question of *where* that money came from.

The contention of the prosecution, of course, is that the $400 was part of a $500 payment that Gold transmitted from his Soviet espionage superior, Yakovlev, to the Greenglasses.* But what if the money deposited by Ruth did not come from the Russians via Harry Gold? Where else might the Greenglasses have obtained it?

Ordinarily, it would not be difficult to speculate on other possible sources for the $400. One might assume, for example, that the money, deposited on the first Monday of the month, had been secured the previous Friday—payday. Judge Kaufman himself, during a hearing on judicial clemency, observed to Bloch that the Greenglasses could have explained away the $400 "very easily" if they had wished. "They could have said that they were saving this money for some time and decided to deposit it," the Judge suggested.

However, in the context of David Greenglass's trial testimony about the money, any such prosaic hypotheses seem excluded. For David repeatedly implied that he was extremely short of funds prior to the unforeseen receipt of espionage compensation from Gold. Thus, when Roy Cohn asked him if he had had "any discussion with Gold about the money," Greenglass replied:

"Yes, I did. He said, 'Will it be enough?' And I said, 'Well, it will be

---

* Ruth testified that the remaining $100 from Gold had been spent on a $50 war bond ($37.50) and for household expenses. The prosecution offered no further proof of these claims.

plenty for the present.' And he said, 'You need it. . . . I will see what I can do about getting some more money for you.'"

On cross-examination, David noted that he had turned the money from Gold over to his wife, "and she used it to live on." Later, Bloch inquired: "And that money was used for your house and the use of your wife, is that correct?" Replied David: "That's right."

The allegedly precarious financial situation of the Greenglasses at the time of the Albuquerque meeting was emphasized once again by David in this interchange:

BLOCH: . . . $500 was a big sum to you, wasn't it?

DAVID: Pretty big.

BLOCH: And it enabled you and your wife to live and have some luxuries, didn't it?

DAVID: It enabled us to live.

However, the impression thus fostered by David's testimony—that he and his wife were hard-pressed for money in June 1945—is demonstrably false.

When prosecutor Saypol introduced into evidence a copy of the ledger of the Greenglass account at the Albuquerque National Bank,* he read to the jury only the first entry: the $400 deposit. Apparently, no subsequent entries on the exhibit ledger were visible, for Bloch requested and was granted permission to see "the rest of the transcript of this account" if the defendants should require it. (There is no indication in the trial record that he ever availed himself of this right.)

At the federal courthouse in Foley Square, the authors were able to see *all* of the entries on the exhibit ledger sheet. What the full ledger shows is that Ruth Greenglass's initial deposit of $400 on June 4 remained practically untouched in the bank for about eight months. There were few additional transactions and, when the account was closed out (shortly before the Greenglasses departed from New Mexico), the final balance was $402!

Clearly, the Greenglasses had possessed sufficient other funds to enable them to *save* most of the money that they alleged Gold had brought them. David's testimony that his wife had used this money "to live on"—a point he reiterated three times on the witness stand—was untrue. What money had the Greenglasses lived on while they were in Albuquerque?

At the trial, this important question never was asked. Neither David nor Ruth disclosed any specific information about their earnings during this period. However, the authors have ascertained that David's Army pay, after allotment deductions, would have approximated $40 to $50 a

* Known in 1945 as the Albuquerque Trust & Savings Bank.

month.* As the wife of a soldier, Ruth received an Army allotment of $50 a month. In addition, Ruth worked as a typist for the Office of Price Administration for most of the time she resided in Albuquerque; a story in the Albuquerque *Tribune* dates her employment there from April 1945.† Depending on her civil service grade, her net monthly salary in June 1945 would have ranged between $110 and $140.

The Greenglasses' total income in the late spring of 1945 was, therefore, at least $200 to $240 a month. Their probable expenses at the time were extremely modest. They had no children; David's clothing, as well as his food (except for weekends), was supplied by the Army. Rent on their furnished one-room kitchenette apartment was about $32 a month, including gas and electricity. At 1945 price levels, their regular income from salaries and allotment could have supported them amply and even supplied excess funds for saving.

It occurred to us that the Greenglasses might have dealt with another Albuquerque bank, in addition to the one in which the $400 was deposited. We subsequently learned that they had. Two previously unrevealed Greenglass accounts (at the First National Bank of Albuquerque) provide further proof of David's and Ruth's financial well-being in 1945.

A Greenglass savings account was opened at the First National Bank on March 20, 1945, and was closed six weeks later on April 30, with the withdrawal of a balance of about $100. That same day, in the same bank, the Greenglasses opened a joint checking account with $200, in cash.

The account opened with $200 was an active one that never was overdrawn. Every seven to nine days, week after week, a deposit of $50 was made, varying no more than fifty cents from this amount. Also every week, four or five small checks, totaling about $50, were cashed at local businesses. On February 25, 1946, most of the balance was withdrawn with a $150 check made out to cash. (David was discharged from the Army on the last day of February.)

How were the Greenglasses able to deposit $50 a week at the First National Bank for ten months? Where did the money come from? Where did it go? An easy answer would be that David and Ruth simply banked their regular income and then drew checks for living expenses. However, this theory encounters serious obstacles. First, none of the Greenglasses' regular income was received weekly. To have made a $50 deposit each week, they would have had to cash their salary and allotment checks, then deposit this money piecemeal during the month in four equal installments—a pointless, inconvenient, and unlikely procedure. Second, the

---

* The amount would vary, depending on whether or not David had contributed toward an allotment for his mother, and also on his rank, which changed from corporal to sergeant.
† She also worked briefly for Soil Conservation Service.

$50 deposits remained constant over a ten-month period, while Ruth's income increased (by nearly 20 per cent) when a nationwide raise in federal civil service salaries became effective in July 1945.

If the weekly deposits of $50 did not come from the Greenglasses' regular income, what was their source? At the trial, Julius Rosenberg testified that Ruth had informed him in February 1945 (about a month before the initial Greenglass bank account at First National was opened) that her husband had a plan to make some money by stealing from the Army. Might David, who commuted between Los Alamos and Albuquerque nearly every weekend, have carried on a trade in stolen Army merchandise?

Any serious attempt to pursue this and similar conjectures would require the power to subpoena financial records. Lacking such power, the authors were unable to discover whether, in 1945-46, there were still other Greenglass bank accounts—in Albuquerque or elsewhere. Thus, the presently available information on the finances of the Greenglasses is fragmentary.

What is known, however, is that over a ten-month period the Greenglasses deposited about $2200 in the First National Bank and $470* in the Albuquerque National Bank and that much or all of this money probably came from some source other than the regular salaries and Army allotment that they were receiving at the time. What is unknown is their total assets when they left Albuquerque and returned to New York City early in 1946. (Some or all of the fee paid the Rogge law firm four years later, in 1950, may well have been money acquired and saved by the Greenglasses during their relatively lucrative wartime sojourn in New Mexico.)

When the records of the June 4 deposit were introduced at the Rosenberg-Sobell trial as government Exhibit 17, U. S. Attorney Saypol stated: ". . . I offer in evidence a photostatic copy of a ledger sheet together with a credit [deposit] slip of the Albuquerque National Bank . . . relating to the account of Ruth Greenglass. . . ."

Thus, Exhibit 17 consists of two documents: A ledger sheet and a deposit slip. However, at the Albuquerque National Bank the authors were informed by a high bank official of the existence of a third relevant document—a signature card—never produced by the prosecution at the trial.

With this hitherto undisclosed signature card in front of him on his desk, Paul H. Barnes,† vice-president of the Albuquerque National Bank, observed that it had been signed by *both* Ruth and David. (Thus, the $400 had not been deposited to "the account of Ruth Greenglass"—as Saypol

---

* In addition to Ruth's initial deposit of $400, there were several subsequent deposits, aggregating $70.

† Barnes testified before the New Mexico federal grand jury that indicted David Greenglass in July 1950.

had informed the jury—but to the *joint account* of David and Ruth Greenglass.) The signature card clearly indicates that the account was a joint one from its inception, Barnes stated; David had signed either on or before June 4, 1945.

Since David Greenglass could not have been at the Albuquerque National Bank when the account was opened on Monday, June 4, he must have signed the card earlier. (According to his testimony, he was in Albuquerque only on weekends, arriving Saturday and leaving Sunday night or very early Monday morning—long before banking hours—so as to be back on duty at Los Alamos on time.) The inescapable conclusion is that prior to the weekend of Gold's arrival—at the latest Friday, June 1— Ruth Greenglass had stopped by the bank and picked up a signature card, with the intention of having her husband sign it when he came home.

Evidently, the Greenglasses were making plans to open an account at the Albuquerque National Bank some days before Gold's Sunday visit—a fact that is incompatible with their story. For both David and Ruth explicitly indicated that the $500 allegedly delivered by Gold had come as a complete surprise; nowhere in their testimony do they suggest that they had any inkling that the courier would bring them money.

On the contrary, Ruth Greenglass was most emphatic that she had not been aware beforehand that she would be paid. Asked by Alexander Bloch whether she had accepted the money from Gold knowing it was "compensation for spy work," she answered:

"That was the first time I knew it. . . . I was under the impression at first that Julius said it was for scientific purposes we were sharing the information, but when my husband got the $500, I realized it was just C.O.D.; he gave the information and he got paid."

Similarly, David noted in a pretrial letter to the Rogge law firm that he had given the data to Gold "not expecting payment."

Was the prosecution ignorant of the joint account and its implications?

We asked Paul Barnes, the Albuquerque bank official, what the ledger sheet shows about the joint account. His answer: Contrary to normal bank practice, the ledger has only Ruth's name on it. From the ledger alone, one could not tell that the Greenglasses had a joint account. He emphasized, however, that the signature card is the governing document in the matter.

The unusual and unexplained absence of David's name from the ledger might be thought to indicate that the government had no knowledge of the troublesome fact of the joint account. But we were able to learn that the FBI was well aware of the signature card signed by both the Greenglasses. The card, along with the original of the ledger sheet,* had been sent to the FBI Laboratory in Washington and both items still bear

---

* At the trial, the ledger, like the Hilton Hotel card, was introduced as a photostat— at the request of the prosecution and with the agreement of the defense.

FBI Laboratory tags. (These tags, undated, are numbered D-117773 AX Q10 for the signature card and D-117773 AX Q1 for the ledger.)

Whatever the full story of the Greenglasses' financial transactions, it is bound to be far more complex than the oversimplified version presented to the jury at the trial.

The bank account that Ruth Greenglass opened on June 4, 1945—with a signature card secured several days earlier—was not her first in Albuquerque, but at least her third in as many months. Her deposit on June 4 was one of scores of bank deposits, totaling thousands of dollars, that she made while in Albuquerque. To single out any one of these many deposits and assert that this one, alone, was in payment for espionage services because it was made the day after Gold was in Albuquerque—with no documentary proof that Gold really was in Albuquerque on that date—is not very convincing evidence.

Nor was the June 4 deposit Ruth's only large one during this period; another Albuquerque account, also a joint one, had been opened by her previously with $200. Although the prosecution never alleged that this $200, deposited on Monday, April 30, had anything to do with espionage activities, the $400, deposited exactly five weeks later on Monday, June 4, was cited at the trial as "proof" of Harry Gold's spy mission to the Greenglasses.

Actually, of course, the $400 provides no such proof. For the more one learns about the Greenglasses' finances, the more apparent it becomes that the June 4 deposit could have come from innumerable non-espionage sources.

CHAPTER 31

VOICES FROM THE PAST

In early December 1950, at a federal court hearing in Philadelphia preparatory to the sentencing of Harry Gold, the latter's attorney, John D. M. Hamilton, mentioned to the presiding judge that he had employed a recording machine while interviewing his client.

Over a decade later, when the authors met with Hamilton in his Philadelphia office, the prominent corporation counsel disclosed to us that the phonograph records of these pretrial prison interviews had been preserved over the years and still were in his possession, along with a number of lengthy handwritten statements by Gold and other related data. Hamilton explained that all of this material was Gold's property and that Gold alone could grant permission to use it.

Heretofore, Hamilton noted, the recordings and statements had been made available to only one writer and that was in connection with a proposed series of syndicated articles about Gold.* In addition, representatives of both the FBI and the Senate Internal Security subcommittee had been afforded access to the information, with Gold's consent.

We carefully framed a letter to Gold at Lewisburg Penitentiary, asking that he allow us to listen to the recorded interviews—in order "to hear your story in your own words"—and to look at the other data in Hamilton's files. Through Augustus S. Ballard, who served as Hamilton's associate in the spy case and still is a member of the same law firm, our message was relayed to Gold. Shortly, we were notified by Ballard that he had received word "directly from Harry Gold" authorizing him to fulfill our request. What inspired Gold's affirmative response we never learned, but Ballard informed us when we saw him in Philadelphia that the prisoner had specified that we were to have "carte blanche" with the material.†

---

* The writer was Bob Considine, of International News Service, which eventually abandoned plans for the series. (Several years later, Considine was an official press witness at the execution of the Rosenbergs.)

† In addition to over fourteen hours of recordings (on small Sound Scriber disks) and long handwritten statements, we obtained hundreds of pages of correspondence relating to the Gold case, including many letters from Gold to his attorneys; also, Gold's Selective Service file and much miscellaneous data on his bank accounts and loans, schooling, employment, and social acquaintances.

We already were aware of Gold's disclosure to his attorneys that for over a week following his arrest he had had no memory at all of his alleged visit to the Greenglasses. But what had Gold said about the Albuquerque meeting in the period between his "recollection" of the encounter and the interrogation of David Greenglass by the FBI?

Perusing the mass of newly obtained data lent us by Ballard, we found that Gold had not written anything about his mission to Albuquerque prior to the time that Greenglass signed his initial FBI statement at 2 A.M., June 16.* Thus, the recordings offered us the only possibility of hearing Gold's Albuquerque story *before* he could have been influenced by Greenglass's account.

Hamilton and Ballard first interviewed their client at Holmesburg County Prison on June 6, 1950. Listening to the recording of their talk that day, we heard Gold relate to them in a flat, emotionless voice copious details of his family history and personal life. Two days later, the attorneys visited Gold again. This time, Gold recounted at great length his experiences with various Soviet contacts, starting in the mid-Thirties.

When this interview was terminated, Gold had just begun to describe preparations for his June 1945 trip to New Mexico, which he referred to only as an assignment to meet Klaus Fuchs in Santa Fe. He informed his attorneys that his next recording would "contain all the details of my trip West, my meeting with Dr. Fuchs, my return to the East, and the transfer of the information to John [Yakovlev]." No plan for a rendezvous with anyone in Albuquerque was mentioned.

After a hiatus of six days, Gold's lawyers returned to the prison. The date was June 14—only one day before FBI agents would arrive at the Greenglasses' East Side apartment.

Gold opened the June 14 interview with the immediate announcement that he would "like to take up first" the matter of a meeting in New York City with Yakovlev "just prior to my first trip to Santa Fe in June. . . . The principal purpose of the meeting as I first recalled it when I told it to the investigating agents was apparently to make certain that I was going and to make certain that there were arrangements for meeting John [Yakovlev] as soon as possible on my return so as to turn the information over to him. However, there was an additional purpose and this I found out to my surprise included the picking up of information from another person in addition to Klaus Fuchs. This matter I believe had best

---

* One of the statements written by Gold for his attorneys, entitled "Chronology of Work for the Soviet Union," later was reprinted in a Senate Internal Security subcommittee report, where it was dated "June 15, 1950." However, when the authors inspected the original of this statement, we found that Gold had dated each page separately and the last three pages—the only portion that mentions Greenglass—were dated June 16.

be told separately but I would like to mention here or to emphasize here that it occurred on the first trip and that the person from whom the information was picked up was a GI . . . and that the transfer of the information from him to me occurred in Albuquerque, New Mexico."

After completing the narrative of his meetings with Fuchs, Gold was reminded by Hamilton that he had still "left up in the air the episode of the GI." Replied Gold:

"Yes. This event, as I said, was—I'm not being—I'm being deadly serious when I say it was an extra added attraction. I use the term, as I said, not in any joking manner—because this is no joking matter—but simply because I believe it best describes the affair."

Gold then proceeded with his presentation of the "extra added attraction."

We knew that what we were about to hear could not be regarded as a really early or spontaneous report by Gold of the Albuquerque events. By June 14, 1950, he had been in FBI custody for over three weeks. He had already been questioned by FBI agents (both before and after his arrest on May 23) for a total of 102 hours.* Nevertheless, the June 14 recording makes available for the first time a version of Gold's Albuquerque story that antedates—if only just barely—the FBI interrogation of David Greenglass and the subsequent development of the Rosenberg-Sobell case.

At the trial, Harry Gold testified that on being assigned the mission to Albuquerque, he "told Yakovlev that I did not wish to take on this additional task. Yakovlev told me that the matter was very vital and that I had to do it. He said that a woman was supposed to go in place of me but that she was unable to make the trip. . . . Yakovlev told me that . . . this was an extremely important business, that I just had to go to Albuquerque . . . he said, 'That is an order;' and that was all. I agreed to go."

With this testimony, Gold emphasized the great significance that Yakovlev attached to the Albuquerque assignment and also, by alluding to a "woman" who was "supposed to go," corroborated the Greenglasses regarding Mrs. Sidorovich's intended role as a courier.

But in his recorded interview with his attorneys nine months before the Rosenberg-Sobell case, Gold said nothing whatever about any woman who was scheduled to make the trip in his stead and portrayed the tenor of his conversation with Yakovlev quite differently:

"He [Yakovlev] told me that . . . after I had seen Klaus Fuchs I was to see another man. . . . He said that the Klaus Fuchs matter was para-

---

* One of the documents obtained from Hamilton was a handwritten compilation by Gold of the dates and lengths of his sessions with FBI interrogators.

mount but that if I had the—but if it were possible I should endeavor to obtain information."

In his testimony at the trial, Gold asserted that while he was in Albuquerque to see the Greenglasses he had stayed overnight at a rooming house and then, on Sunday morning, had registered at the Hilton Hotel. In his pretrial recorded interview, Gold mentioned no such hotel stay in June.* The probability that the June card is a forgery is raised to a near certainty by this omission and by Gold's remark to his attorneys that on the morning in question, after leaving the rooming house, he had "checked my bags in the railroad station."

At the trial, Gold claimed that Yakovlev had given him a piece of paper with the name "Greenglass" and an Albuquerque address on "High Street." Pinning down the identification of his Albuquerque contacts even more concretely, Gold testified: ". . . I introduced myself to Greenglass as Dave from Pittsburgh; that was all. Greenglass introduced me to . . . his wife Ruth. Mrs. Greenglass said that it was coincidence that my first name and the first name of her husband were the same."

This testimony of Gold's, implying as it does that he had independently remembered the Greenglasses' names and address, is completely misleading. For Gold revealed in one of his handwritten statements to his attorneys that the names of David and Ruth Greenglass never were recalled by him but were, in fact, first brought to his attention by FBI agents. As for the Albuquerque address of the Greenglasses (referred to throughout the recordings only as "the GI" and "his wife"), Gold specifically remarked during the June 14 interview: "I don't remember the name of the street. . . ."

Moreover, the important point about Gold's coincidental use of the first name "Dave" as an alias is absent from the recorded interview. On the contrary, Gold informed his attorneys that he had introduced himself to the GI by "the name of Mr. Frank, possibly Raymond Frank, possibly Frank [indistinct]."

According to Gold's trial testimony, during his brief Sunday-morning visit to the Greenglasses' apartment, David had informed him "that there were a number of people at Los Alamos that he thought would make very likely recruits . . . people who might be willing to furnish information on the atom bomb to the Soviet Union."

However, Gold's description of his morning conversation at the Greenglasses, as reported to his attorneys in the June 14 recording, contained no reference to "recruits" and was, in all probability, unique in the annals of espionage. Said Gold:

---

* Gold did tell his attorneys that he had registered at the Albuquerque Hilton in his own name on the occasion of his *September* trip to New Mexico to meet Fuchs.

". . . I think that their principal talk . . . concerned the difficulty of getting Jewish food, delicatessen, in a place like Albuquerque and a mention by the man that his family or possibly her family regularly sent them packages including salami."

Gold's recorded interview (like his handwritten pretrial statements) completely nullifies his trial testimony that the Russians had praised David Greenglass's data as "extremely excellent and very valuable." He noted to his attorneys, instead, that he had returned to New York* and "turned the information over to John [Yakovlev]; John never mentioned anything about it."

Nothing in Harry Gold's Rosenberg-Sobell trial testimony, however, was more vital to the prosecution's case than his references to the cut jello box and the "Julius" password. As Saypol stressed to the jury, this testimony of Gold's "forged the *necessary link* in the chain that points indisputably to the guilt of the Rosenbergs." (Emphasis added.) What had Gold said of this "necessary link" in his report to his attorneys one day before David drew his brother-in-law's name into the espionage investigation?

At the trial, Gold asserted that Yakovlev had given him a sheet of onionskin paper with typed instructions for the Albuquerque meeting. Gold testified: "The last thing that was on the paper was 'Recognition signal. I come from Julius.' In addition to this, Yakovlev gave me a piece of cardboard, which appeared to have been cut from a packaged food of some sort. It was cut in an odd shape and Yakovlev told me that the man Greenglass, whom I would meet in Albuquerque, would have the matching piece of cardboard."

But on June 14 Gold had said nothing of the sort. In the version of his story that he related then, he claimed only that Yakovlev gave him the name and address of the man he was to meet "but gave me no other indication beyond that I was to obtain some information from him."

While on the witness stand, Gold mentioned the jello box and the name "Julius" a second time when he told of his arrival at the Greenglass apartment on a Sunday morning. He testified: "I said, 'I came from Julius,' and I showed him the piece of cardboard . . . that had been given me by Yakovlev. . . . Greenglass went to a women's handbag and brought out from it a piece of cardboard. We matched the two of them."

No such recognition ritual was recounted by Gold in his recorded interview. In fact, it was attorney Hamilton who finally raised the question of Gold's means of identifying himself to the GI.

HAMILTON: I want to interpolate something at this point. Didn't you have some recognition sign as between the two of you?

* Gold told his attorneys that his complete return trip route had been: Train from Albuquerque to Chicago, plane to Washington, and train to New York.

GOLD: Yes, we did, and while this is not the exact recognition sign I believe that it involved the name of a man and was something on the order of Bob sent me or Benny sent me or John sent me or something like that.

Describing his visit to the Greenglass apartment in his trial testimony, Gold noted: "The last thing that took place that morning was that just as I was preparing to go, Mrs. Greenglass told me that just before she had left New York City to come to Albuquerque she had spoken with Julius." In his prison interview with his attorneys, Gold related no similar comment by the GI's wife.

Again, in telling of his leave-taking from the Greenglasses, Gold testified: "Mr. Greenglass told me that he expected to get a furlough some-time around Christmas, and that he would return to New York at that time. He told me that if I wished to get in touch with him then I could do so by calling his brother-in-law Julius, and he gave me the telephone number of Julius in New York City."

However, the pretrial version of this incriminating testimony was quite different. Said Gold:

". . . he [the GI] told me that he expected to have a furlough about Christmas of 1945* and he gave me the name, or and the address, or much more likely just the name and the telephone number, of I think his father-in-law, or possibly an uncle of his, who lived somewhere in the Bronx of New York. Unfortunately, I have been unable to recall the name and the telephone number, though there are several possibilities that we have selected."

Gold's final mention of the name "Julius" in his trial testimony—his sixth—occurred during his recounting of an alleged November 1945 conversation with Yakovlev. Gold testified:

"I told Yakovlev . . . that Greenglass would be possibly coming home on a furlough about Christmas time. I told Yakovlev the time was drawing near to Christmas and that we ought to make some plan to get in touch with this brother-in-law, Julius, so that we could get further information from Greenglass. Yakovlev told me to mind my own business. He cut me very short."

But in Gold's earlier version of this alleged conversation with Yakovlev, there is no reference to a "brother-in-law, Julius." As for the GI, Gold informed his attorneys that Yakovlev had said "we could forget all about him. . . . apparently the information received had not been of very much consequence at all and that they believed that the risk attendant upon seeing him did not make any such effort worthwhile."

Clearly, on June 14, 1950, Harry Gold's evolving story of an alleged

---

* David Greenglass did not have a furlough in Christmas 1945.

Albuquerque meeting with a "GI" and "his wife" still was in a highly unfinished state. Missing from the recorded interview is any mention of the "Julius" password or cut jello box that was to serve as the prosecution's "necessary link" at the Rosenberg-Sobell trial.

After a long period of complete forgetfulness, Gold had gradually conjured up recollections of a visit to Albuquerque in June 1945. During weeks of FBI interrogation, various shifting details filled out the story—some to be retained and elaborated; others to be dropped by the time of the trial. Many elements of the developing account undoubtedly *were told* to Gold by FBI agents (including the names and address of the persons he had met); others were probably his own creations or the later contributions of David Greenglass. Among the last details to be appended to the story were those that implicated Julius Rosenberg.

The fact that Gold's version of the Albuquerque events, as related by him before the apprehension of David Greenglass, differed substantially from his subsequent trial testimony destroys his usefulness as a corroborative witness. With this discovery—added to the total evidence previously adduced—one can fairly conclude that the June 3 episode did not take place. There is not the slightest reason to believe that Gold and the Greenglasses ever met each other prior to their arrests.

Not only were Julius and Ethel Rosenberg—and Morton Sobell—unjustly convicted, they were punished for a crime that never occurred.

SUMMATION

•

CHAPTER 32
PUTTING THE PIECES TOGETHER

In early September 1949 a report was laid on the desk of J. Edgar Hoover which, the FBI director has since guardedly revealed, contained "conclusive information" that "the secrets of atom-bomb construction had been acquired by a foreign power." Later that same month, President Harry Truman announced to the American people that an atomic explosion had taken place in the Soviet Union "within recent weeks." It seems likely that the report received by Hoover was a preliminary notice to high government officials of this Soviet atomic test, which had been detected from radioactive fallout samplings.

Immediately following the President's public announcement, many in Congress and the press ascribed the Soviet accomplishment to espionage. Statements along this line were issued by such figures as Senators Karl Mundt, Styles Bridges, and Bourke Hickenlooper and Representatives Harold Velde and Richard Nixon. Their comments were based on the then widely accepted assumption that Soviet science and industry were incapable of developing nuclear weapons in the foreseeable future; it therefore followed that if Russia had an atomic bomb, she could have obtained it only by rifling America's "secrets."

The head of the Federal Bureau of Investigation evidently jumped to the same conclusion. According to author Don Whitehead,* when Hoover read the report indicating that America no longer had a monopoly on the atomic bomb, he reacted with "shock and anger." Wrote Whitehead:

"Hoover reached for the intercom telephone. He gave a series of orders to his key subordinates and soon the vast machinery of the FBI was in high gear. In essence, Hoover's orders were: 'The secret of the atomic bomb has been stolen. Find the thieves!'"

A few months later, in early February 1950, physicist Klaus Fuchs

---

* In a foreword to Whitehead's book, *The FBI Story*, Hoover lauded the author for his "accurate portrayal."

was taken into custody in England. The extent to which this action may have resulted from information provided by the FBI remains a matter of dispute. Fuchs was charged with divulging atomic information to "unknown" persons in Britain and the United States. The sole proof of his guilt offered during brief court proceedings was his own confession. The principal government witness was a special agent of British intelligence who testified that he had elicited this confession from Fuchs, while the latter was still at liberty, after several lengthy interviews conducted over a period of weeks. No other evidence against Fuchs ever has been disclosed or alluded to by British authorities. Even his confession has, for the most part, been treated as a secret document.*

The excerpts from Fuchs's confession that have been made public are remarkable principally as a demonstration of confused thought processes. These passages suggest an emotional instability which, in fact, the scientist had displayed, unambiguously, on previous occasions. British writer Alan Moorehead reports that, long before Fuchs's arrest as a spy, he sometimes suffered "morbid fits" of deep depression when he would "lie for hours, even days, on end with his face turned to the wall, eating next to nothing, saying nothing, reading nothing." After his arrest, Fuchs allegedly never inquired about what sentence he might receive and is said to have been convinced that he would be put to death until informed by his lawyer that the maximum penalty for the offense under British law was fourteen years.

Not surprisingly, Fuchs's long-time friend and colleague Rudolph Peierls thought immediately of possible psychological factors when he heard of Fuchs's espionage confession. Peierls had served as head of the British wartime scientific mission at Los Alamos, of which Fuchs was a member. He stated in a letter to the authors that, on learning of Fuchs's arrest, he had considered the possibility "that his confession might not be based on fact, that perhaps he had had a nervous breakdown and was imagining incidents or was exaggerating insignificant facts." Later, however, Peierls spoke with Fuchs in prison and became convinced that his story was "substantially correct."

According to Hoover, Fuchs disclosed that while in the United States he had dealt with "one Soviet agent only," but the scientist did not know the man's name and could describe him only in the vaguest terms. Nevertheless, Hoover decided that Fuchs's accomplice "simply had to be found." This self-appointed goal would seem to have been virtually unattainable,

---

* Klaus Fuchs dictated his confession in two parts: A technical statement and a general statement. The authors applied to the United States Atomic Energy Commission for permission to see both documents. The AEC, after reviewing the material, declared that the technical statement still is considered classified. Decision on the release of the general statement was deferred to the British, who were said to have turned down our request.

in view of the scant information Fuchs had provided about his alleged contact in the United States and the warning that the apprehension of the British scientist would have given the man.

Yet, less than four months later—and exactly eight months after the public disclosure of the first Soviet bomb test—the FBI brought about the seemingly miraculous arrest of Harry Gold, who had confessed to having acted as Fuchs's courier. After years of rumor and extra-legal accusations, an American who apparently had served as an atom spy for the Soviet Union had been caught. It was a signal achievement for Hoover's organization.

Just how the FBI managed to ferret out Harry Gold has never been made public. Hoover wrote a piece for the *Reader's Digest* in which he ostensibly detailed the manhunt for Fuchs's alleged confederate; actually, on close reading, his account proves to be little more than a recital of leads that did not work out. Moreover, even the meager physical description of the courier that Fuchs is said to have provided definitely does not fit Harry Gold.

One may speculate, therefore, that the single most important reason that the FBI chose to question Gold on the Fuchs matter may have been the fact that the name of the Philadelphia chemist was already in their files. He had come to the Bureau's attention in 1947, by chance, during the FBI investigation of Elizabeth Bentley's tale of spying. (Ironically, Miss Bentley and Gold were unacquainted and never had heard of one another.)

In any event, Gold had been known to the FBI for at least three years when agents approached him in Philadelphia on May 15, 1950, and asked him to submit to questioning. Gold's attitude was cooperative. Although no legal charges had been filed against him, he participated in some eighteen hours of interrogation over the next week without consulting an attorney; he permitted himself to be photographed; and he agreed to a search of his home without a warrant. But he denied any connection with Soviet atomic espionage.

According to Hoover, on the morning of May 22, 1950, when FBI agents arrived to search the Philadelphia house where the bachelor chemist lived with his father and brother, Gold suggested that they start in his bedroom. They did so and soon found behind a bookcase a chamber of commerce folder containing a street map of the city of Santa Fe, New Mexico. This discovery is said to have brought about a sudden admission from Gold that he was the man who had met with Klaus Fuchs. However, Gold has since noted that he was fully aware at the time of the FBI search that the tourist map "was not in itself too damning" and might have been explained away innocently. Whatever may have motivated Gold's decision to confess, his capitulation was so complete that, still without consulting an attorney, he placed himself in the legal limbo of voluntary custody and signed a statement that very day.

Did the FBI make an effort to test Gold's convenient admission objectively or did they merely accept it gratefully and uncritically? Even with a scrupulous regard for justice, it would have been difficult to distinguish Fuchs's true American accomplice from an impostor. So much about Fuchs's personal history and career had been published in the American press following the physicist's arrest that a hoaxer might easily have learned enough to construct a generally plausible story. So little was known about the alleged meetings between Fuchs and the unknown courier in America that a false confession might have been considerably embellished without seriously contradicting Fuchs's version of events.

Allegedly, shortly after Gold's confession, word was received from England that Fuchs, who previously had failed to identify a photo of Gold, had now reversed himself after seeing a movie of the Philadelphia chemist. But this fact, like the Santa Fe map, was little more than an interesting clue; the Department of Justice obviously did not dare to arraign Gold on such flimsy grounds. The next day, May 23, FBI agents secured Gold's September 1945 Albuquerque Hilton hotel registration card. Like the map, the card did not establish a link between Fuchs and Gold; it merely proved that Harry Gold had been in the city of Albuquerque, New Mexico, at a time when Klaus Fuchs was employed at Los Alamos, over one hundred miles distant. Nevertheless, that very night the Attorney General of the United States and the head of the FBI announced the arrest of Fuchs's American partner in crime.

Little is known specifically about what transpired between Gold and his FBI interrogators in the days immediately after he went into voluntary custody. By Gold's own accounting, he was interviewed for forty-five hours between May 22 and May 30. On May 31, however, when Gold finally asked federal Judge James McGranery to appoint counsel for him, his course was already firmly fixed: He instructed the Court that any attorney assigned to his case must allow him to "continue to give information to the F.B.I. freely . . . regardless whether he thinks it is damaging to me," and must "understand that I am pleading guilty."

Gold's court-appointed attorney, former Republican National Chairman John D. M. Hamilton, first visited his client in prison on June 6, 1950. The recording of their talk that day reveals the astonishing fact that, after over two weeks in custody, Gold still had not been informed that the maximum penalty for the crime to which he had been confessing was death. Hamilton read him the section of the U. S. Code under which he was charged, and asked: "Now I take it . . . that you knew generally what that provision was. . . . Is that correct?"

GOLD: I didn't know the sentence that was involved.

HAMILTON: You didn't?

GOLD: I didn't realize what sentence was involved.

HAMILTON: Well, now, before I got into this matter I saw in the newspapers that you had stated that you were going to plead guilty. . . .
Now, having had this matter explained to you . . . do you have any
change of heart in that connection?

GOLD: No, I do not.

Apparently, his own fate had become a matter of utter indifference to
Gold. Imprisonment, or even the possibility of execution, would seem to
have meant little to him. In the ensuing months, he manifested the same
disinterest in the fate of others, even those whom he formerly had
counted as friends. One can only speculate as to what smoldering angers
and frustrations, what secret guilts, what dreams of glory and nightmares
of worthlessness drove him. His espionage story became his consuming interest and he channeled his total energy, as well as his considerable
imaginative talents and intelligence, to the task of establishing "the authenticity and the enormity of my crime."

The Hamilton-Gold phonograph recordings disclose that, as the self-
confessed spy poured forth his narrative, he frequently revised it. People,
places, dates, meetings, conversations appear vividly in one session with
his lawyer, only to be denied or altered beyond recognition in another.

For example, Gold told Hamilton that he once had passed information from Alfred Dean Slack, the Syracuse chemist, to a man he had met
for two or three minutes on a dark street in Buffalo. Later, he claimed
there had never been a meeting in Buffalo and "there was no such man."

Gold also told his attorney that he had met his Soviet superior, Yakovlev, one evening "in the lounge at the Earl Theater." He said that
Yakovlev "came by me very swiftly and merely whispered, 'Third Avenue
bar in an hour, or as quick as you can get there.'" Subsequently, Gold
completely revised this story, claiming: ". . . the man whom I met at the
Earl Theater was not Yakovlev but a confederate of his. . . . I recall him
very distinctly. He was at least six foot—possibly six foot one and was—had
an extremely savage . . . and tough-looking face. . . . in general, gave the
appearance of what might be called a plug ugly."

Gold appears to have made such changes in his story largely out of
the sheer joy of creativity. One has the impression that his runaway
imagination could not be constrained in the mold of a single version of
an event. It would seem that the FBI agents who questioned him throughout the summer of 1950 could hardly have avoided realizing that they
were dealing with a thoroughly unreliable individual.

In addition to these more or less capricious alterations, many changes
that were obviously more meaningful occurred in Gold's story. Gold's

statements to his attorney make clear that his FBI interviewers were not at all silent bystanders to this development. As described by Gold, the agents frequently briefed him with information and implied the direction in which they were interested in having his story move.

Thus, in first discussing the possible information-gathering activities of a friend who had done work for the Russians, Gold was vague and noted only that his friend had been "extremely secretive." Later, however, he added that he and the FBI agents had been "going into great detail" on this individual and that he had "succeeded in recalling many things," including "glimmerings" of conversations about the transmission of data "on penicillin and other biochemicals." In addition, he knew that this friend had made "several trips to New Castle, Delaware, and the FBI tells me that the Bellanca Aircraft, a commercial aircraft firm, is located there."

This gratuitous offering of potentially incriminating information about Bellanca Aircraft to a highly suggestible suspect certainly seems designed to push him toward a more and more accusatory story.

A similar instance involved a young junior engineer, whom Gold said he had approached *unsuccessfully* for information while studying at Xavier University in Cincinnati. Gold first said in a conversation with Hamilton that he had gone to Xavier because he had been accepted there after applying to "at least fourteen" other schools in various parts of the country. He afterward altered this story, telling his attorney: ". . . I told a deliberate falsehood . . . I did not go to Cincinnati or the Midwest merely by chance." Gold's new version was that the Russians had *ordered* him to go to school in this area, specifically so that he might contact the engineer. In addition, he now noted that the FBI agents "think that it does not seem quite logical that the sole purpose for which I was placed in Cincinnati was to contact [the engineer]. . . . They claim that Cincinnati is close to other vital places—such as Detroit and Akron, Cleveland and so on."*

An honest endeavor to unravel the life of so deviously complex a man as Harry Gold and to arrive at even an approximation of truth would obviously be an awesome undertaking. The FBI evidently did not attempt this difficult task, choosing instead simply to accept what Gold said whenever it was expedient to do so and, when it was not, to subtly encourage him to revise and add to his story. Gold's eagerness to please,

---

* Though Gold did not respond to this tacit suggestion, he did eventually expand the story of the engineer, one Benjamin Smilg, considerably. Five years later, testifying at a perjury trial against Smilg—who was acquitted—Gold detailed more than a dozen encounters with him. In Gold's original story to Hamilton, however, he had numbered their meetings as four or five. Moreover, although he initially had described his first words with Smilg as an ordinary salutation, he testified at Smilg's trial that it was an "exactly worded message . . . a recognition signal" that included the phrase " 'greetings from Stan.' "

excellent memory, and inventiveness were invaluable tools in this process. The net result was a story wherein the boundaries of truth are nearly hopelessly obscured.

However, armed with Gold's voluminous account to his attorney of his activities, related while numerous parts of the story were still in a state of transition, the authors have tried to reach for an understanding of the career of the Philadelphia chemist.

As he described it to Hamilton, Gold's relationship with representatives of the official Soviet trade agency, Amtorg, in the Thirties and early Forties, consisted of the desultory collection and passage by him of rather commonplace information. Some of the data he transmitted he obtained from the files of the sugar company where he worked and from the public library. Other data was obtained from Alfred Dean Slack (who was paid for passing commercial information on several occasions) and from Abraham Brothman (who kept trying through Gold to interest the Russians in legitimately purchasing some of his engineering designs). Gold has made it clear that no military secret and probably no spy-worthy secret changed hands during this period. In short, it was not espionage.

Just when Gold's work for Amtorg terminated cannot be determined with any precision. Gold has indicated that he last received commercial photographic data from Slack sometime in 1941. As for Brothman, the date would seem to be about early 1942. (Although Gold continued to importune Brothman for technical information throughout 1943, these activities were almost certainly undertaken by Gold on his own initiative and he himself has asserted that none of this material was turned over to the Russians. In fact, a stenographer who assisted in preparing Brothman's data during this later period was actually paid by Gold out of his own pocket.)

In a larger context, it seems perfectly consistent that Gold's collecting of industrial information for Amtorg would have ceased soon after Germany attacked Russia in June 1941 and Lend-Lease goods, in enormous variety, were supplied to the Soviet Union. Thus, when Gold remarked to Hamilton that his Russian contact had advised him in the fall of 1941 that, due to the war, his continued assistance was particularly essential, the lawyer instantly recognized the incongruity of his client's statement.

"Don't you recall," Hamilton asked abruptly, "that the Lend-Lease bill had been passed . . . and that Russia automatically became a recipient of benefits when she entered the war?"

Gold, momentarily nonplussed, answered: "Yes. I am very glad that you brought up that matter, Mr. Hamilton, because it brings to mind something which I have neglected to emphasize to the investigating agents . . . I shall . . . make a note of it now." Gold went on to explain, lamely, that his Soviet contact had said the flow of material through Lend-Lease was "exceedingly slow, exceedingly poor."

Following on with Gold's narrative, it appears that his activities subsequently entered a new phase; from about late 1943 to late 1945 he allegedly was engaged in true deeds of espionage, trafficking in secret military information. The second part of Gold's career included three separate episodes: Receipt of RDX data from Alfred Dean Slack; the passing of information from Klaus Fuchs; and a single transmittal of material from David Greenglass. From the oral and written statements Gold gave his attorney, one may conjecture that not only the David Greenglass incident but even the RDX account and the story of his relationship with Klaus Fuchs may have been, partly or wholly, fabricated. In other words, Gold's activities on behalf of the Soviet Union may have consisted of nothing more than his early commercial jobs for Amtorg.

There is no reason to doubt that Gold actually received what he himself termed "sketchy" information on RDX and an inert sample of the explosive.* However, one may well ask, as did an attorney for Slack:

"Who says that Russia ever got this article? Who says it was ever delivered to a foreign power?"

Indeed, Gold's story to Hamilton of just how and when he transmitted the RDX information is unusually muddled, even for him. He first said that he had "turned the material over to Sam [an Amtorg contact]." Then, a few days later, Gold wrote to his attorney that he had "probably" given the RDX data "to John [Yakovlev] . . . probably in April 1944." At the same time, Gold contradictorily claimed that in early January 1944, just before his first meeting with Fuchs, he was warned by the Russians to discontinue all other work for them and was specifically instructed to have "nothing to do with Slack."

It seems a likely possibility that the RDX data never was requested by or delivered to any Soviet agent but, instead, was simply filed away in Gold's crowded cellar closet, along with dozens of blueprints of Brothman's which Gold admittedly collected and never gave to the Russians. Describing the "huge mass" of papers FBI agents found there when they searched his house, Gold informed his attorney that it included "material which was given to me by Al [Slack] which I did not turn over."

In a seventy-five-page autobiographical statement prepared for Hamilton, Gold spoke of the "pleasure" he had derived throughout his life from daydreaming. "I definitely did spend a great deal of time in the very enjoyable pastime of imagining Harry Gold . . . always of course in a

---

* RDX, known by a number of names, first was reported in the world chemical literature around the turn of the century. In an appeal, Slack claimed that the RDX write-up given Gold had been derived entirely from public library research and that the sample, although obtained from the plant where he worked, disclosed nothing new and could have been made in his "kitchen."

stern and self-sacrificing role."* It does not seem farfetched to picture Gold, bored with his drab existence after the excitement and sense of importance his prewar dealings with the Russians had imparted, evolving a Walter Mitty fantasy of foreign intrigue. He possibly assigned *himself* the mission of seeking out Slack after a two-year hiatus in their relationship.

Similarly, when Gold read of Klaus Fuchs's arrest some years later, these fantasies may have been reactivated. He may literally have been unable to resist confessing to an association with a man whom he considered a "genius." As he told Hamilton, "I am absolutely fascinated by a person with ability. . . . And therefore I was fascinated by—or rather, attracted to—Klaus." J. Edgar Hoover has said that Gold gave the FBI a statement in which he claimed that he and Fuchs "never engaged in any idle conversation or small talk." But Gold boasted to Hamilton that he and the British physicist "were somewhat kindred souls. . . . we were as good friends as it is possible for two men to be."

Gold's prodigious ability to lie convincingly nearly hides the amazing fact that there is no publicly known evidence which directly connects him with Fuchs. The tourist map of Santa Fe found in Gold's bedroom and Fuchs's belated identification of Gold from pictures obviously do not prove their alleged relationship. As for the registration card that Gold filled out at the Albuquerque Hilton on September 19, 1945, bits and pieces of Gold's pretrial statements obtained from Hamilton suggest that the September trip to New Mexico may not have involved a rendezvous with Fuchs—but a completely different purpose.

Gold possibly left Philadelphia in September 1945 on a business trip to the Chicago area, then impulsively decided on a sight-seeing excursion to New Mexico. The pertinent details:

The journey that Gold undertook in September 1945 did not take him directly to New Mexico; he stopped off first in Chicago, where he registered in his own name at the Palmer House Hotel.

Gold mentioned to Hamilton—without disclosing a date—that he and a co-worker at the Pennsylvania Sugar Company's distillery had visited two alcohol distilleries not far from Chicago† on what he described as "purely

---

* Gold also related to his attorney that as a boy he played "simulated games of football, baseball and boxing which I invented . . . played . . . with a single deck of Casino cards. In baseball, for example, I used a league of eight teams . . . which played a full schedule of games throughout the entire season, not forgetting doubleheaders on the weekends; the teams each had pitching staffs with imaginary hurlers, whose records and mound characteristics I carefully noted. I did a similar job with boxing, employing the various weight classifications and with special ring traits (fancy boxer, crude slugger, etc.)."

† The Hiram Walker Distillery in Peoria, Illinois, and the American Distilling Company in Pekin, Illinois.

business."* Elsewhere, Gold testified that he and this same co-worker had made business trips together for the Pennsylvania Sugar Company—in 1945.

It seems a reasonable hypothesis, therefore, that the aim of the trip Gold made to Chicago in September 1945 was to visit the nearby Illinois distilleries.

From Chicago, Gold traveled on to New Mexico. There is evidence suggesting that he may have had no plans for this second leg of his journey at the time he left Philadelphia. For Gold informed his attorney that he had "neglected" to bring along with him enough money to cover "the cost of travel from Chicago to Santa Fe." As a result, he said, he had to wire a friend from Albuquerque to ask for money for his return trip.

At the Albuquerque Hilton, Gold not only registered in his own name, he listed as his place of employment "A.B.A. Laboratories, New York City"—a most unlikely action if he were on a spy mission. For this was the firm owned by Abraham Brothman, Gold's alleged associate in his earlier information-gathering activities for the Soviet Union.

A number of clues hint that Gold might have gone to New Mexico as a tourist. In statements to his attorney, Gold referred to the "famous museum" in Santa Fe and to his genuine historical "interest in the South-west and in the well-known books of J. Frank Dobie." In fact, Gold noted that there was a volume by Dobie, who wrote on the Southwest, "on that very shelf of the sectional bookcase" where the FBI found the chamber of commerce folder with a map of Santa Fe.

While an espionage meeting with Fuchs in Santa Fe during this trip cannot be ruled out, it is apparent that there may be other explanations for Gold's travels in September 1945.

It is perhaps significant that, insofar as one can learn from available sources, September 1945 never was mentioned as the date of an espionage rendezvous by Fuchs or the FBI prior to the discovery that Gold had been in Albuquerque at that time. Interestingly, the former Director-General of the British security services, Percy Sillitoe, who was in charge of the Fuchs investigation, wrote in a book which discusses the case that the physicist turned over atomic bomb data to a Soviet agent in Santa Fe in the latter half of July 1945—a date absent from Gold's account.

J. Edgar Hoover has stated that when he determined that "the basic secrets of nuclear fission had been stolen," he "immediately mobilized every resource" of the Federal Bureau of Investigation to "find the guilty men." Describing this FBI mobilization, Don Whitehead wrote:

"Hoover's men swarmed into the Los Alamos atomic plant near Santa Fe, New Mexico, and other plants. They dug into records and personnel

---

* Queried about the matter, the former co-worker confirmed that he had made this trip with Gold, but referred the authors to the FBI for all details.

files of the Atomic Energy Commission, and interviewed hundreds of people who might have some clue."

One of the many former Manhattan Project employees questioned during this dragnet operation was David Greenglass. In early February 1950 an FBI agent came to his apartment and asked whether he had pilfered a specimen of uranium. No legal charge was made against Greenglass then, but subsequently, about May 1950, he and his wife noticed that they were under surveillance. Perhaps the FBI's renewed interest in the suspect was due to the discovery that he once had been a member of the Young Communist League, that his sister and brother-in-law had long been associated with radical left-wing politics, and that in 1945 the Greenglasses had made bank deposits not readily explicable in terms of their income.

It thus came about that, at the same time that Harry Gold was confessing to the FBI about alleged meetings with Fuchs in Santa Fe, there *already was in progress* an investigation of a former GI who had been stationed at Los Alamos during the war and whose wife had maintained an apartment in Albuquerque.

We may hazard a guess that—just as FBI agents suggested to Gold that while a student in Cincinnati he might have dealt with Soviet contacts in other nearby cities such as Cleveland or Detroit—he also was encouraged to remember meeting someone besides Fuchs elsewhere in New Mexico. Gold probably went along with this idea in as casual a fashion as he concocted—and afterward denied—a rendezvous with a man in Buffalo.

Gold's pre-Greenglass-arrest version of the Albuquerque meeting gradually came into being over a two-week period. During scores of hours with FBI agents, Gold nimbly picked up details essential for the construction of his story; other, less crucial elements of his account he improvised according to his own whims. Information that Gold learned from these talks with the agents apparently was later echoed back as his own, often in slightly altered form. Thus, it is likely that knowledge of the Greenglasses' $400 bank deposit was communicated to Gold by his interrogators, while the actual figure of $500 as the sum given the GI was invented by him.

In addition, a variety of techniques was used by the FBI to help refresh Gold's memory. When Gold could not recall the address in Albuquerque where the meeting had taken place, the FBI assisted with maps and movies. Gold informed his attorney: "I have looked at maps of Albuquerque. We—I have looked at dozens of reels of motion pictures . . . going all the way past undoubtedly the street where this G.I. lived." It was naturally not long before he had "succeeded in picking out . . . the correct house."

Similarly, when Gold could not recall the names of the GI and his wife, the FBI agents helped him to select the names of David and Ruth Greenglass from a list that they provided. By June 14, Gold was able to announce to Hamilton: ". . . I believe that we have succeeded in identifying the person who was this G.I."

As for the crime itself—the data allegedly transmitted in the Albuquerque meeting—here Gold was exceptionally cautious and vague. During the June 14 interview with Hamilton, he noted equivocally that the material he had received from the GI was "mostly typewritten, possibly handwritten." It consisted of "several sheets" and "one very small rough sketch."

HAMILTON: . . . did it refer to atomic activities?
GOLD: It referred certainly to some activity at Los Alamos.

Greenglass, already thoroughly alarmed by the open surveillance to which he was being subjected, was visited by FBI agents on June 15. At this point, the agents still had not filed a complaint against him or even secured a search warrant. Nevertheless, he agreed to submit to questioning and a search of his apartment. No legal adviser was present while the twenty-eight-year-old machinist talked with the agents that afternoon and evening and for half the night.

The method of interrogation employed seems to have been to tell Greenglass the gist of the story already arrived at with Gold, then to seek his concurrence. Thus, the agents informed Greenglass during this interview that a man had come to see him in Albuquerque in June 1945, that he had not had the information ready for his visitor, and that the exact sum of money given him by the man was $500.

Had Greenglass adamantly denied this story, there would never have been a Rosenberg-Sobell case. But, in David Greenglass, the FBI had chanced upon another highly suggestible individual—a foolish, boastful man—who, although he lacked Gold's intelligence and literary flair, was an experienced and rather accomplished liar. After long hours with the agents, he finally subscribed to the account proposed to him, added some details of his own, and signed a statement at 2 A.M. on June 16.

Later that very day, Gold was interviewed by FBI agents who must have briefed him on the results of the interrogation of Greenglass. For he immediately incorporated into his version of the Albuquerque meeting one of the items that Greenglass had just contributed to the story. Greenglass had mentioned turning over "some information concerning the names of people [at Los Alamos] who would be sympathetic." Gold therefore noted in a report that he then was preparing for Hamilton: "I believe he [Greenglass] also gave written information on possible recruits."

Two days before, on June 14, in an interview with his attorney, Gold had depreciated the work done by the GI at Los Alamos, and had observed that the material received from him "had not been of very much consequence at all." Now, under FBI tutelage, he drastically revised his account. "I have been told," he advised his attorney on June 16, "that he [Greenglass] worked on a very important phase of the bomb assembly." He now had "learned," Gold added, that the information received from Greenglass was "highly valuable."

It was in David Greenglass's initial statement to the FBI that the name of Julius Rosenberg was injected into the growing story of the Albuquerque meeting. David's relationship with his brother-in-law and former business partner had been strained by deepening animosity in the months preceding his arrest. He wrote to his lawyer that he had "made sure to tell the F.B.I." that when his wife, Ruth, asked him if he would supply information she had done so at the suggestion of Julius.

For their part, the FBI agents undoubtedly were not reluctant to seize on Rosenberg as a suspect. His FBI dossier showed that he had been ousted from government employment in early 1945 on a charge of Communist Party membership. Moreover, Rosenberg, a graduate engineer, had more technical background than did Greenglass.

On the morning of June 16, Julius Rosenberg accompanied several FBI agents to their offices, where he was questioned for some six hours. In his trial testimony, Rosenberg said of his FBI interrogators: "They were asking me questions . . . but they were also trying to direct my attention to an answer they might want." In the course of this interview, Rosenberg was told by the agents that his brother-in-law had accused him of having requested information for the Soviet Union. He denied the allegation. Learning that he was not under arrest, he walked out of FBI headquarters, still a free man. A formal complaint was not brought against him for another month.

In that month, David Greenglass made an abortive effort to recant his 2 A.M. statement to the FBI, then embarked on a hazardous course: He decided to cooperate fully with the authorities in the hope that he would be rewarded by immunity from punishment—both for the serious crime to which he was confessing falsely and for one or more lesser offenses, such as uranium theft, of which he actually was guilty. In this desperate enterprise, Ruth Greenglass joined and encouraged her husband. Together, they pointed accusing fingers at Julius Rosenberg, apparently seeing in him their best chance of extricating themselves from their predicament. It was Rosenberg, they swore, who had led them astray; they had merely been pawns.

As for Harry Gold, in the month preceding Rosenberg's arrest FBI agents interviewed him on eighteen separate occasions for a total of sixty-three hours. It was during this period that Gold added to his story the few extra details needed to implicate Rosenberg.

Julius Rosenberg now emerged as the mastermind of the Albuquerque meeting. The new version of events was arrived at easily by inserting the name "Julius" into Gold's account that he had identified himself to the

GI with a phrase such as "Benny sent me," and combining this with Greenglass's account that his visitor had carried "a torn or cut piece of card." With the manufacture of the June 3 Hilton Hotel registration in Gold's name, the basic framework was complete.

Nevertheless, there are indications that the government had no inalterable plan to prosecute the unknown East Side engineer as the chief of a Soviet atom spy ring, much preferring, instead, to gain his cooperation in naming alleged higher-ups—possibly even someone from the Communist Party's leadership against whom a spectacular show trial might be mounted. However, Rosenberg's intractability was absolute; even after his arrest on $100,000 bail, he derisively termed the jello box story "something like kids hear over the television."

It therefore became necessary for the FBI to develop a case against Rosenberg sufficiently so that he might be tried and convicted. Large numbers of agents fanned out all over the country, bringing to bear their finely honed techniques of investigation and interrogation in an effort to find prospective trial witnesses.

In Cleveland, for example, agents questioned Ann Sidorovich and William Perl. The former repeatedly denied that she ever had met David Greenglass in Rosenberg's apartment, as the agents insisted, and said she knew nothing of any espionage activities; as a result, she and her huband were "persecuted" for several years. As for Perl, he was subjected to such grueling interrogation that it seemed to him "a sort of attempted domination of my life by the FBI." His punishment for non-cooperation was a perjury indictment. One man among the hundreds whom this investigation reached was Weldon Bruce Dayton, a friend of a friend of Rosenberg's. Unable to obtain a passport or employment in his field for years after his refusal to agree to a story that the FBI had presented him with, Dayton later said: "I have been told . . . so many things by so many FBI agents . . . that it is awfully hard for me to know now what I knew in the first instance."

It is remarkable that of all those thus approached by the Bureau's agents following Rosenberg's arrest, only one person—the vulnerable and frightened Max Elitcher—subsequently supplied information in court at all relevant to the substance of the charge. Moreover, even Elitcher did not confirm the existence of the alleged atomic espionage conspiracy.

Clearly, in apprehending Rosenberg as a Soviet spy entirely on the say-so of his in-laws, the FBI had climbed far out on a limb. A search of the Rosenberg apartment when Julius was taken into custody yielded but one item that was afterward introduced as a prosecution exhibit at his trial: A cardboard coin collection container with the printed legend "Save a Spanish Republican Child." (The FBI agent who came upon this extraordinary "evidence" of an espionage plot soberly marked it with his initials and the date, hour, and minute of discovery, as well as with the precise notation: "Found in closet opposite bathroom.")

In subsequent weeks, FBI agents hunting for some physical proof to substantiate the crime charged against Rosenberg encountered no better luck. Their search produced no tangible evidence indicating that Julius Rosenberg had, indeed, been a Soviet spy. No short-wave radios, microfilming equipment, miniature cameras, receptacles for drops, stolen documents, code books, false identification cards, forged or real passports, or hidden caches of funds—in short, none of the paraphernalia of espionage—were uncovered by the intensive investigation.

This lack of witnesses and documentary proof to back up the government's headlined accusations would seem to have goaded the FBI into a number of utterly reckless maneuvers.

Firstly, Ethel Rosenberg was arrested, in what was plainly an attempt to move her husband from his refusal to cooperate. At her arraignment, government attorneys contested pleas that she be afforded some opportunity to make provision for her two young children, three and seven, and, instead, demanded and secured her immediate incarceration on $100,000 bail. Yet, in thus jailing the thirty-four-year-old housewife and publicly labeling her as an atom spy, the Department of Justice did not even have the "corroboration" of a Harry Gold; the sole evidence against her was the flimsy accusations of her brother and sister-in-law. (Other than these, the prosecution eventually produced at the trial only a former maid who said Ethel once had referred to a new table as a gift; a photographer, without records, who said she and her family had ordered passport photos; and an electoral petition nominating a Communist Party candidate for the New York City Council, which she had signed in 1939. Such was the total proof on which Ethel Rosenberg was condemned and put to death.)

Finally, the FBI arranged for the abduction from Mexico City of Morton Sobell, apparently in the expectation that he might be pressured into testifying against his former college classmate Julius Rosenberg. However, Sobell persistently denied any knowledge of Rosenberg's alleged spying, precluding the possibility of the government's using him as a witness, and he was thereupon thrown into a superseding indictment as a defendant.

The failure of the FBI to gather conclusive information corroborating the Greenglasses or to break Rosenberg's morale resulted in the elevation of Harry Gold's role in the forthcoming atomic espionage trial. He and the suspect's brother-in-law, together, would have to supply the major proof for the prosecution's case.

Gold's state of mind by that time was such that he was superbly fitted for the part he would be called on to play. He had long since decided to plead guilty and had given no indication that he had any interest in what his penalty might be. Almost daily he saw his name and picture in newspapers and magazines and read of the arrests of those whom he had named as partners in crime. One whom he had never met, David Greenglass, had actually confessed! Little wonder that his slim grasp on reality was rapidly attenuating. In a grandiose mood, he penned a twenty-five-page statement which he intended to read in court at his sentencing hearing. Gold's undelivered speech began:

"Your Honor, I feel that an explanation is due to the people of the United States . . . all of whom I have besmirched by my crime. . . . and a horrible and heinous one it is. . . . For in the end, a far more terrible weapon than any Atomic Bomb was created, namely, Harry Gold, Soviet courier, a name . . . now an anathema to all decent people."

Between the arrests and trial of the Rosenbergs, more than half a year was available to fashion Gold into a key prosecution witness, who might well be sharply cross-examined. During this period, the interminable reshaping of Gold's story continued, with many of his more improbable claims deleted or amended.

Not the least of these concerned the question of how he had financed his alleged espionage career. For reasons best known to himself, Gold was particularly insistent that he never had taken any money at all from the Soviet Union. In early June 1950 he advised Hamilton: "I would like to state here now, absolutely and categorically, that I have never accepted a cent from the Soviets for any work that I have done in connection with them, either in the form of payment or for expenses." Testifying in early August before the federal grand jury in New York City that indicted the Rosenbergs, Gold reiterated this assertion.

Perhaps at this point Gold was informed by his interrogators that his bank and other financial records did not account for the expenditures that his alleged espionage trips would have entailed.* In any event, one week after his grand jury appearance, Gold blandly told his attorney that his sworn testimony before that body had been "inaccurate." Said he: "Actually, from the first time that I had contact with the Soviets . . . I received partial payment from them."

Hamilton, seemingly innocent of the fact that his client was privileged to change his story as often as necessary with complete impunity, interjected: "Your false story to the grand jury . . . is perjury. . . . Now, what has been done to get rid of that possible perjury charge? Have you told the FBI . . . of the true facts?"

Replied Gold: "Yes, I have."

* Gold later prepared for Hamilton an elaborate twelve-page "Money Accounting of My Espionage Work," a document so replete with arithmetical errors and illogical calculations as to be useless. However, in enumerating extra sources of income that he had available to finance his spying activities, Gold did include one intriguing entry: "Bootlegging—$600–1 can/week at $6 each for two years." Apparently, he had been stealing alcohol from the Pennsylvania Sugar Company distillery, where he worked.

With Gold's consent, Hamilton addressed a letter that very day, August 9, 1950, to Arthur Cornelius, Jr., special agent in charge of the Philadelphia office of the FBI, summarizing Gold's perjurious grand jury testimony and requesting that "the corrections in this matter" be "forwarded to the United States District Attorney of the proper District," Irving Saypol.

Thus, once again it was made eminently clear, to any who cared to see, that Gold's word—even when he said "absolutely and categorically"—was literally worthless.

As the Federal Bureau of Investigation labored to build a case against the Rosenbergs, the continued absence of any tangible proof of the commission of a crime focused increasing attention on a peripheral theme: Flight. FBI agents eagerly sought any bit of information—no matter how tenuous or distorted—that might be construed as evidence of flight or plans for flight. In Philadelphia, agents questioning Gold encouraged him to expand his story in line with this requirement.

Initally, Gold had indicated that the Russians never had asked him to leave the United States. However, as he afterward explained to Hamilton, the FBI agents found this "incredible." Eventually, Gold partially acceded to the agents' importuning, obligingly recalling a number of hitherto unmentioned rendezvous with a Soviet agent in late 1949 during which the subject of flight had been discussed.* Gold declared that his Soviet contact had advised him that "it might be necessary for me to leave the country should any suspicion be attached to me." It had been "somewhat of a jolt" to hear "their insistence on my at least thinking of the possibility of having to leave home. This I could never do and leave my family."

Gold then constructed still another new espisode for his spy chronicle, asserting that there had been two further New York City meetings arranged for late 1949 and early 1950 for the purpose of his being "under surveillance by the Soviets to see whether I were being followed." Moreover, he now recollected that at one of these meetings "it had seemed to me at that time that no one had appeared. That is what I had thought. But actually someone had appeared and when I saw the picture in the paper . . . I was struck by the fact that I had seen Julius Rosenberg before, though I didn't know who he was. Julius, smoking a cigar, went by on the same side of the street where I was . . . and looked at me very closely . . . obviously he had been sent to observe me. . . ."

Gold subsequently embroidered this tale, adding that the cigar Julius had been smoking was an "agreed-upon recognition signal (I was smoking

---

* Some idea of the extreme care Gold took to cover his tracks can be seen from the fact that, on thus expanding his basic story, he immediately asked his attorney for an opportunity to add these new details to the written "Chronology of Work for the Soviet Union," which he had prepared two months earlier. This was done, with no indication that it was a belated addition.

a curved-stem pipe, also a previously arranged item). However, these were only a part of the details employed as a means of mutual identification." (Years later, when Gold was interviewed in prison by a staff member of the Senate Internal Security subcommittee, he remembered still another occasion on which he had seen Rosenberg. He stated that in 1949, while walking by a New York City restaurant that he had been instructed to pass, a man, whom he now realized had been Julius Rosenberg, had watched him through the restaurant's window.)

Not surprisingly, Gold was not asked about any of these incredible incidents during his testimony at the Rosenberg-Sobell trial.

In the fall of 1950, Gold was transferred to the eleventh floor of the Tombs Prison in New York City, known as the "singing quarters," where David Greenglass already was incarcerated. There Gold worked with the FBI and U.S. attorneys to prepare his testimony in first the Brothman-Moskowitz trial and then the Rosenberg-Sobell trial. By this time, Gold's feelings of self-importance were such that he seems to have regarded himself more a part of the prosecution staff than a prisoner. Corresponding with his lawyer in Philadelphia, he conveyed messages from Irving Saypol, commented that he found assistant U. S. Attorney Myles Lane to be "an exceedingly fine gentleman," and requested that Hamilton "make inquiry of . . . the Attorney General in Washington" regarding the proposed publication of Gold's story by International News Service.

As for David Greenglass, his fond illusion of August that he would be a witness against the Rosenbergs without being indicted along with them was rudely shattered in October, when a superseding indictment drew him firmly into the case as a defendant. The culmination of his piecemeal self-entrapment was his plea of guilty to a capital offense for which he himself had supplied the main evidence. He remained unsentenced—pending his testimony at the Rosenberg-Sobell trial—and his wife, although named only as a co-conspirator, might be similarly indicted if the government so chose. Under the circumstances, the prosecution could well feel secure regarding the Greenglasses' total cooperation.

It would be fascinating to know what Harry Gold and David Greenglass talked about during their daily association in the Tombs Prison. Perhaps they discussed the fantastic hoax in which each played a crucial part, but, more likely than not, they maintained the deception even between themselves and polished the details of their stories in circumspect collaboration.

Utilizing the dramatic techniques of a playwright, including foreshadowing and repetition of key themes, the prosecution gradually constructed a trial script of considerable scope. As finally presented to the jury, the government case included material about the Communist International, the economic system of the U.S.S.R., the American Communist Party, the *Daily Worker*, Elizabeth Bentley's alleged espionage dealings with employees of the OSS and the U. S. Treasury, the Attorney General's list of subversive organizations, left-wing groups such as the Joint Anti-Fascist Refugee Committee and the International Workers Order, and the propriety of using the Fifth Amendment—all of these highly charged subjects being, of course, completely extraneous to the issue of the defendants' guilt or innocence for a specific crime. In short, the trial—staged against a backdrop of national anxiety over the Korean War and a possible atomic conflict with the Soviet Union—was a product of its times, displaying in microcosm many of the prevalent sociopolitical assumptions and preoccupations of the day.

Harry Gold's day of glory, for which he had so long been in training, came on March 15, 1951. On the witness stand, Gold delivered his lines in what the *Times* called a "forthright" manner. Those who heard him could hardly have suspected that his testimony was the end product of a system of pretrial preparation in which interrogation had become indoctrination lasting hundreds of hours.*

Through a kind of legal legerdemain, Gold's credentials as a Soviet espionage agent had been incontestably established by his guilty plea and sentencing in Philadelphia several months before, despite the fact that the government had not produced one bit of evidence against him other than his own confession. When defense attorney Emanuel Bloch endeavored to challenge Gold's characterization of himself as a Russian spy, he was barred from doing so by Judge Irving Kaufman, who asserted: "The witness knows," and remarked to Gold: "The fact of the matter is that you did plead guilty to . . . espionage for the Soviet Government; is that correct?"

Gold's principal task at the trial was to convince the jury that the June 3, 1945, meeting in Albuquerque, about which David and Ruth Greenglass already had testified, had in fact occurred and that he had been assigned this mission by a Soviet representative, Anatoli Yakovlev.

In court, Gold identified a picture of David and Ruth Greenglass without indicating in any way that he originally had forgotten the entire incident of the Albuquerque meeting, never had independently remembered the Greenglasses' names, and had not known where in Albuquerque they had lived. He testified that the Greenglasses' address had been on High Street and pretended that he was struggling to recall the number of the house: ". . . it was a low number . . . the second figure was 'o' and the last figure was either 5, 7 or 9. . . ." Gold's testimony reached a high point of farce when he earnestly studied two cut pieces of a jello box held

---

* Gold was interrogated by FBI agents prior to the Rosenberg-Sobell trial for a total of approximately four hundred hours. In addition, he spent numerous hours with government attorneys.

out to him by prosecutor Myles Lane and indicated which fragment resembled the one he had received from Yakovlev.

In addition, the prosecution employed Gold in an effort to create the impression that David Greenglass's lens mold data was enormously significant, perhaps even represented the so-called "secret" of the atomic bomb. To accomplish this, Gold effected a brazen metamorphosis of his pretrial claim that the information received from Greenglass had been of "no value" and that Yakovlev's interest in it had been most casual. Gold, with characteristic flourish, also invented for the prosecution a whole new incident—unmentioned in his pretrial account—to bolster the point. He told the jurors that in January 1945 he had reported to Yakovlev a conversation with Fuchs which included mention of "a lens, which was being worked on as a part of the atom bomb." At their next meeting, Gold testified, Yakovlev had asked him to "try to remember anything else that Fuchs had mentioned . . . about the lens. . . . to scour my memory clean so as to elicit any possible scrap of information about this lens."

Finally, Gold helped the prosecution to draw the termination date of the conspiracy well into the Cold War period, a practical necessity if there were to be a maximum sentence for spying on behalf of a wartime ally. In November 1950, at the Brothman-Moskowitz trial, Gold had testified: "I was engaged steadily in espionage for the Soviet Union from November of 1935 until February of 1946." However, several months later at the Rosenberg-Sobell trial, held in the same courtroom, before the same judge, with the same U. S. Attorney, Gold extended his spying activities by over four years. He testified: "I was engaged in espionage work for the Soviet Union from the spring of 1935 up until the time of my arrest. . . . This arrest took place in May [1950]."

Time magazine understandably interpreted this testimony to mean that "Gold said he kept filching U.S. secrets for Russia until he was finally arrested." On reading this, Hamilton immediately wrote to Gold that it was "completely at variance with the facts as I got them for you. . . . It was my understanding that the information you received from Fuchs in September of 1945 was the last which you passed on to the Soviet agents." Gold responded contritely that the wording he had used at the trial "was the direct result of various conversations I had had with the U. S. Attorneys here in New York."

Some eighteen months after President Truman's public announcement of the detection of an atomic bomb test in the Soviet Union, Julius and Ethel Rosenberg stood before a federal judge in New York City and were sentenced to death for having made that test possible.

David Greenglass and Harry Gold—their Kafkaesque adventure ended —were immured together at Lewisburg Penitentiary. For Gold, prison was less a torment than a refuge. In a letter to Hamilton in late 1953, he expressed an unmistakable tone of well-being. He wrote:

"I am well: my weight is still at a normal 140 lbs. and I don't ever intend to become 'sloppy fat' again. . . .

"Also, a great source of satisfaction has been my work assignment here [medical research]. . . . A friend once said, with much truth, 'Just put Harry in a laboratory, and he's happy.' . . . I've been reviewing my mathematics, systematically and intensively—as I've intended for many years.

"I heard some of the World Series games on the radio here; and we get football broadcasts over the weekend: lately 'my cup runneth over,' since Penn beat Penn State. . . ."

Unlike Gold, David Greenglass—who had bargained so dearly for his freedom and lost—had strong ties to the outside world. He had lied to escape punishment; not to court it. When Greenglass was released from prison, after ten years behind bars, his appearance bespoke a suffering in dramatic contrast to Gold's apparent contentment. The *Times* described him as "Mute and Bewildered," adding: "At 38 years old he looked 48. . . . His face, once full, was thinner and sallow. His blue eyes looked at nothing."

J. Edgar Hoover, who in the fall of 1949 flashed the word to his agents that thieves had stolen the "basic secrets of nuclear fission," has since remained immutable in his views. "Who, in all good conscience, can say," Hoover declared in June 1961, "that Julius and Ethel Rosenberg, the spies who delivered the secret of the atomic bomb into the hands of the Soviets, should have been spared when their treachery caused the shadow of annihilation to fall upon all of the world's peoples?"

For the majority of Americans, however, the decade that spawned two folk demons called the Rosenbergs is irretrievably over. Now, perhaps, the time of reappraisal is about to begin.

EPILOGUE

As François Mauriac pointed out just after the executions, we live in an age when the false confession, wrung from the accused by one means or another, is no novelty. The Rosenbergs and Sobell, pressured by a vast state apparatus to tell a story they knew to be untrue, stood firm. In a period of expediency and cynicism, they refused to cooperate, refused to save themselves at the expense of others. Faced with a profound moral choice, involving for them the question of life or death, they unhesitatingly chose. In this, the final triumph was theirs.

"We have experienced unbelievable rottenness," Julius wrote to his wife. And again: "There is a new whipping boy in our land 'The Rosenbergs' and all 'respectable' people have to cleanse themselves by throwing stones at us." Yet they could not be cast into despair. Surrounded by madness, they never abandoned their belief in the eventual resurrection of human rationality, even when hope for their own lives waned.

"I am still confident we'll win our freedom," wrote Julius. "But come what may I am sure that our name will eventually be cleared." And Ethel, in words penciled minutes before her death: ". . . I die 'with honor and with dignity'—knowing my husband and I must be vindicated by history."

One would like to pretend that all of this happened in another country, another century. But it did not. Today, in a federal prison cell, Morton Sobell still waits, as he has waited since the summer of 1950, for the nightmare to end.

POSTSCRIPT—1967

Shortly before the publication of the first edition of *Invitation to an Inquest*, we made available to Morton Sobell's attorneys whatever newly discovered information we had that might be of value to them in seeking relief in the courts for their long-imprisoned client.

The attorneys, Marshall Perlin and William M. Kunstler, studied the new material with an eye to the legal requirements—not necessarily identical with the requirements of truth and logic—for filing a motion under Section 2255 of Title 28 United States Code. This statute provides that a prisoner who presents evidence that his Constitutional rights may have been violated shall be granted a hearing before a federal judge in the district in which he was convicted. At such a hearing, the prisoner's attorney is given an opportunity to prove his charges and, to this end, is accorded the vital power to subpoena both witnesses and records.* The judge may then free the prisoner, order a new trial, reduce sentence, or determine that no action is warranted.

Sobell's attorneys concluded that a 2255 motion citing recently acquired evidence of fraud surrounding the alleged Gold-Greenglass June 3, 1945, Albuquerque meeting should be submitted to the courts. And so, in the summer of 1965, the time-consuming work of drawing up the necessary petition was begun.

Ironically, it thus fell to Sobell to launch a legal assault against the core episode of the entire conspiracy trial, although the government's case against himself had consisted only of the testimony of Elitcher and the evidence concerning "flight." However, the Court of Appeals, in sustaining Sobell's conviction, had ruled by a vote of 2 to 1 that the defendants were all part of a single espionage conspiracy, thereby making Sobell accountable for all the crimes charged against his alleged fellow conspirators. The Court of Appeals majority clearly stated: "It did not matter that Sobell knew nothing of the atomic episodes; he is nevertheless charged with the acts done by Greenglass, Gold and Rosenberg, in furtherance of the overall conspiracy."

An important part of the Sobell motion would concern the charge that

---

* No post-trial evidentiary hearing ever has been granted in the Rosenberg-Sobell case, despite repeated requests by the defendants on various grounds.

Harry Gold's June 1945 Hilton Hotel registration card—a photostatic copy of which was introduced as a key prosecution exhibit—is a forgery. Sobell's attorneys therefore dispatched a letter to FBI Director J. Edgar Hoover observing that "a serious question has arisen as to the authenticity of the June 3rd card." The letter asked that a handwriting expert be permitted to examine the *originals* of both Gold's June and September Hilton cards "if they are in the possession of your agency, and, if not, that we be informed as to their exact whereabouts."

Hoover's brief reply noted: "Due to the passage of time, these cards are no longer available."

Sobell's attorneys again queried Hoover about the cards, asking: "Have they been destroyed and, if so, when, where, how and at whose orders? Do you have a receipt in your files for these cards and, if so, when was such receipt signed and by whom? When was each card originally acquired by your agency and what are the names and current addresses of the special agent or other persons who obtained them?"

Hoover refused to answer any of these questions. The attorneys had indicated in both their letters that their inquiry was being made pursuant to the filing of a 2255 motion. Although Hoover had said nothing about this in his first letter, he now mentioned the prospective motion and commented that "since this is a legal matter, your letter has been referred to the Internal Security Division of the Department of Justice."

Sobell's attorneys thereupon posed the questions that Hoover had declined to answer to the Internal Security Division. A response from Assistant Attorney General J. Walter Yeagley amplified Hoover's vague statement regarding the unavailability of the registration cards:

"The original card dated June 3rd was returned to the hotel on August 4, 1951, and it is our information that it was destroyed by the hotel, together with all cards dated prior to 1957, in the ordinary course of business.

"The original card dated September 19th was destroyed in the normal course of operations, by the Federal Bureau of Investigation, on February 11, 1960."

This reply from Assistant Attorney General Yeagley, while stating definitely that both cards had been destroyed, raised more questions than it answered. The FBI was said to have returned the original of the June card to the Hilton Hotel only four months after the conclusion of the trial, prior even to the argument of the initial appeals of the Rosenbergs and Sobell. If the higher courts had reversed the conviction on any grounds and had ordered a new trial—hardly a farfetched possibility—the defense might well have insisted that the prosecution produce the original card rather than a photostat. (In addition, an indictment still was outstanding against the alleged fugitive defendant, Yakovlev.) It would therefore seem to have been ordinary prudence for the government to have retained the original of the June card in its possession. Moreover, there was no particular reason to return the card to the Hilton, since the hotel did not maintain a permanent file of registrations and could be expected to destroy any card more than five years old.

Regarding the FBI's destruction of the September card, one is hard put to suggest an innocent rationale. The September card is probably the only piece of documentary proof tending to corroborate Gold's confession of a New Mexico meeting with Klaus Fuchs. Surely Hoover would be aware of the historical value of the September card in a case that he himself has termed the "crime of the century."

Anyone who has taken the official tour of FBI headquarters in Washington knows that the Bureau retains large numbers of clues and curiosities from all its most famous cases. Hoover and his officially authorized chroniclers have made clear that he rates the Fuchs-Gold and Rosenberg-Sobell cases high among the FBI's outstanding accomplishments. Yet Hoover apparently was unable to find permanent space in his voluminous files for two crucial items of evidence in each of these cases—the original September and June Albuquerque Hilton cards of Harry Gold.

For Sobell's attorneys, study of the original registration cards by experts —who might date the paper and ink and apply other scientific techniques for the examination of questioned documents—appeared to be foreclosed.

The attorneys now directed further questions to the Department of Justice. Regarding the June card, they asked: "Upon whose orders was it returned to the Albuquerque Hilton? If a letter of transmittal accompanied it, is it possible to obtain a copy thereof? If the Department received a receipt or letter of acknowledgement from the Albuquerque Hilton for it, is it possible to obtain a copy thereof? How did the Department learn of its destruction and, if by writing, is it possible to receive a copy thereof?" Regarding the original September card, the attorneys asked: "Upon whose orders was it destroyed? Who actually destroyed it and how was such destruction effected? If the order of destruction was in writing, is it possible to obtain a copy thereof?"

The letter from Assistant Attorney General Yeagley had concluded:

"From the nature of your letters to the Federal Bureau of Investigation we assume that your interest in the aforementioned registration cards springs from the baseless accusations set forth in the book entitled *Invitation to an Inquest*. We find it difficult to believe that you would seriously consider the fantastic hypothesis that the Federal Bureau of Investigation would either instigate, or, be a party to, a conspiracy to manufacture or falsify evidence."

Replied Sobell's attorneys: "With reference to the last paragraph of your letter, we are sure that you will agree that a full and open hearing in connection with our contemplated motion . . . might be the best way to resolve all doubts as to the authenticity of the June 3rd card."

The attorneys sent another letter to Hoover requesting the names of the

FBI agents whose initials appear on the back of the September card, as well as "the names of all FBI agents who participated in the investigation of the files of the Hilton Hotel, Albuquerque, New Mexico during the year 1950." Once again Hoover declined to answer all questions, saying that the inquiry pertained to a motion about to be filed and had been referred to the Internal Security Division. Once again the Internal Security Division also refused to provide answers, noting in a letter from Yeagley that the Department of Justice would not furnish any of the requested information unless "ordered by the Court."

Finally, the attorneys attempted to elicit an answer to a more general question. Letters were directed to Hoover and the Department of Justice asking for a copy of "your standard operating procedures with reference to the receipt of documentary evidence procured by your agency for potential use in criminal trials and the preservation and destruction thereof. If no copy is available but there are written or unwritten standards, instructions or procedures relating to the above, we would be grateful for a summary thereof." Both the FBI and the Department of Justice turned down the request. (When members of the press and the authors made a similar request to officials at the Department of Justice, answers also were refused.)

According to Assistant Attorney General Yeagley, the original of Gold's June 1945 registration card was returned to the Hilton soon after the trial in 1951 and was destroyed by the hotel "together with all cards dated prior to 1957, in the ordinary course of business." Normally, the Albuquerque Hilton retains registration cards for five years and therefore presumably would have destroyed the 1945 card immediately upon its return in 1951. If Gold's card was saved by the hotel after 1951, as the Department of Justice asserts, it obviously was not handled in an "ordinary" or routine fashion.

Just when was the original of the June card destroyed? It is impossible to ascertain the date from Yeagley's first communication with its ambiguous reference to "all cards dated prior to 1957." However, in a subsequent letter the Assistant Attorney General flatly stated that the June card had been destroyed "by the hotel in 1957."

If we accept this 1957 date, another highly interesting avenue for research is indicated. For it was in December 1956 that the then Attorney General, Herbert Brownell, Jr., ordered the Department of Justice's Internal Security Division to prepare a full report on the Rosenberg-Sobell case to refute charges of a frame-up. During 1957, the Department attorney assigned this task, Benjamin Pollack, had access to all the government's evidence in the case; his investigation included a trip to Albuquerque. *Look* magazine (on Oct. 29, 1957) carried what was described as an "exclusive preview" of Pollack's never since released government report.

The *Look* article was in large part an attack on a book by John Wexley,

The Judgment of Julius and Ethel Rosenberg, which declared the Rosenbergs and Sobell to be innocent. Though he lacked evidence to back his claim adequately, Wexley deduced that the June 3 meeting never had occurred and reasoned that the Hilton exhibit was a forgery.

Now it has been revealed by Assistant Attorney General Yeagley that the June card was destroyed in 1957 during the very same period that this charge regarding its authenticity was being officially probed by the Department of Justice.

With this new disclosure in mind, the authors contacted the Justice Department's Director of Public Information, Jack Rosenthal, and asked for a copy of the ten-year-old report. He replied that he had had similar requests recently from a number of newspapermen, but that the report could not be made public because it mentioned "living people" who presumably had to be protected. This was a completely new reason for withholding the report, one never previously cited by the Department. Asked if the names of these "living people" could be deleted and the rest of the report released, Rosenthal explained that this was impossible since the report was based almost entirely on this sort of material. When we expressed doubt at this statement, based on our knowledge of the case and conversations with Pollack, Rosenthal admitted that he had in fact never seen the report and that it was available to very few people in the Deparment of Justice. Asked if just that part of the report, if any, that dealt with the Hilton card could be released, he said that it could not.

There seemed no possibility of penetrating the official evasiveness on the case, unless the courts should order a hearing for Sobell at which the defense could subpoena documents out of concealment and call otherwise reluctant witnesses to testify.

Meanwhile, Sobell's attorneys decided to undertake research on another of the trial exhibits: Exhibit 8. This was David Greenglass's impounded sketch which had been described at the trial as a drawing of "the atom bomb itself." The lawyers hoped that the declassification in recent years of much data on the Los Alamos project, coupled with the freer political climate in the United States, might now make it feasible to obtain evaluations of Greenglass's sketch from competent scientists who had been unwilling or unable to comment before.

In spring 1966, the government agreed to supply the lawyers with a copy of Exhibit 8 along with Greenglass's explanatory testimony, which also had been impounded at the trial. However, Assistant U.S. Attorney John S. Martin, referring vaguely to a consultation with representatives of the Atomic Energy Commission, asked that the secret status of the documents be retained. Federal Judge Edmund L. Palmieri ordered the defense lawyers to hold the material in strict confidence, except for submission to scientists and use in papers filed in court.

It was not long before defense attorney Marshall Perlin found it necessary to file an affidavit in court describing preliminary results of his consultations with scientists. Attached to his affidavit, as supporting exhibits, were the impounded sketch and testimony. Once Perlin's affidavit was formally filed it would become a matter of public record and the press could obtain and publish Greenglass's sketch and testimony. To prevent this possibility, the U.S. Attorney's office set in motion an extraordinary series of hastily convened *in camera* proceedings. In the next few days, the intensity of the Justice Department's desire to prevent public disclosure of the material the Rosenbergs allegedly had transmitted 20 years before was dramatically demonstrated.

Perlin, arguing that the impounded data should be made part of the public record, reminded the Court of the history of Exhibit 8: The prosecution had been prepared to introduce it into evidence at the trial; it had been impounded only at the suggestion of defense counsel Emanuel Bloch. He told the Judge that his recent conversations with scientists who had been closely involved with the creation of the atomic bomb had revealed that the sketch which had been under lock and key for so long was inaccurate and contained nothing at all secret.

Assistant U.S. Attorney Robert L. King moved that the Perlin affidavit with the Greenglass material attached be sealed. He claimed that he had a letter from the Director of Classification of the AEC, C. L. Marshall, stating that information "comparable" to that contained in Exhibit 8 was "still classified" and that it was "desirable" to preclude further dissemination of such information. Judge Palmieri thereupon sealed Perlin's affidavit and directed the government to suggest more stringent restrictions on the use of the Greenglass material by Sobell's attorneys.

However, the action of a *New York Times* reporter, Sidney E. Zion, interrupted these plans. Zion reported that the AEC's Director of Classification had told him in a telephone conversation that the Greenglass material was "declassified" and could be published. The government attorney denounced the *Times* story as a "distortion" but, when pressed by Perlin to produce his correspondence with Marshall, he did not do so. His only response was to say that he resented Perlin's inference that the "government has in any way misrepresented the terms of that correspondence."

Perlin replied that defense counsel at his client's trial "did rely upon a representation and that resulted in an unfair conviction. . . . I will not rely upon any representation. If you have a letter, I want it produced. . . ."

Judge Palmieri now advised the government that "more cogent proof" of the alleged classified status of the Greenglass material would have to be produced. Finally, the government was forced to admit in open court that the AEC had issued a statement declaring that the Greenglass material "is unclassified and there is no legal basis for limiting its dissemination." All objections to making the information public were withdrawn.

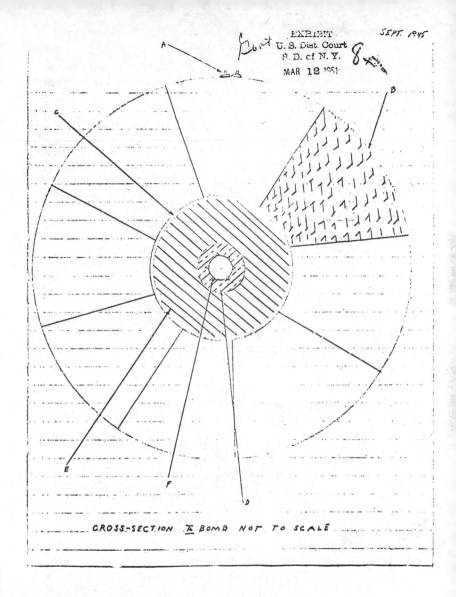

SEPT. 1945

A

B

C

E

F

D

CROSS-SECTION A BOMB NOT TO SCALE

Obviously, the government had been bluffing in an unprincipled effort to preclude disclosure of the material, not for reasons of national security but simply because it seemed the wiser course politically.

The following is David Greenglass's previously impounded explanation of his sketch of the Nagasaki implosion bomb. He testified that he had given both the drawing and this descriptive material to Julius Rosenberg:

"I have 'a', which points to two detonators, each mold. Each high explosive lens, there were 36 of them, that I have pointed to as 'b' had two detonators on them; that is, two detonators connected to capacitators which were charged by suitable apparatus and was set to go off by a switch that would throw all 72 condensers at once. There were two detonators on each lens so in case of failure of one, the other would go off. And beneath the high explosive lens there was 'c', I have marked, a beryllium plastic sphere, which is a shield for the h.e., the high explosive. Then I have 'e', which is the plutonium itself, which is fissionable material. That is also a sphere. Inside that sphere is a 'd', is beryllium. Inside the beryllium there are conical shaped holes 'f', marked 'f'.

"Now, the beryllium shield protects the high explosive from the radiation of the plutonium. This is to prevent the h.e. from deteriorating and not go off until it is set off. At the time of the discharge of the condensers the high explosive lens implode, giving a concentric implosion to the plutonium sphere on the inside. This in turn does the same to the beryllium, and the beryllium is the neutron source which ejects neutrons into the plutonium, which is now at a super or hypercritical stage because of the high pressure heat, and nuclear fission takes place. . . . The switch that set it off was set off by a barometric pressure device, and the bomb itself was on a parachute."

The final version of Sobell's 2255 petition was submitted to Judge Edward Weinfeld in late August 1966.* The petition asked the Court to grant a hearing to Sobell and, pending the hearing, requested: Sobell's release on bail; immediate authorization to take the deposition of Harry Gold;** a copy of the confession of Klaus Fuchs; and all pretrial statements of Harry Gold and the Greenglasses in the possession of the government.

The petition charged that the prosecution had "by false statements, testimony and evidence and by other deceptive and fraudulent devices"

_____

* The petition had been prepared by defense counsel Marshall Perlin and William Kunstler, assisted by attorneys Arthur Kinoy, Malcolm Sharp, Benjamin Dreyfus and Vern Countryman. A number of other attorneys, though not counsel of record, had provided aid and advice, notably Eleanor Jackson Piel.

** Gold had been paroled from Lewisberg Penitentiary on May 18, 1966, after serving about half of his 30-year sentence. He had been eligible for parole for over five years. According to the New York *Times*, on the day of his release, he talked freely with reporters except when the questioning got around to *Invitation to an Inquest*. Then Gold, "with rapid prompting by his lawyer, declined to answer."

established in the minds of the jurors, judge and defense counsel that the defendants had stolen the so-called secret of the atomic bomb. This belief was said to have so prejudiced and awed the jurors as to make them completely receptive to the testimony of Greenglass and Gold.

Specifically, the petition cited Exhibit 8 and Greenglass's descriptive testimony as false and known by the government to be false. The prosecution was said to have "compounded this fraud" by presenting John A. Derry, an AEC employee, as an "expert witness" to establish the "substantial accuracy" of Greenglass's sketch and description of the Nagasaki bomb. Lengthy affidavits in support of these charges by scientists Philip Morrison and Henry Linschitz were submitted.*

Morrison, a probable co-holder of the patent on the Nagasaki bomb, assisted in the actual assembly of both the implosion bomb tested at Alamogordo as well as the one dropped over Japan. He called the Greenglass sketch a "caricature" and termed Greenglass's testimony "confused and imprecise." He pointed out that "the cross-section and its description are not factually correct and, therefore, give a false depiction. . . . The testimony and the drawing itself entirely omit two important spherical components of that bomb, without which it could not operate." Furthermore, the component called by Greenglass a "beryllium plastic" shield is incorrectly described by him as to its construction, function and location.

As for the government's "expert" witness, John Derry, with whom Morrison had been acquainted at Los Alamos, "he had neither the scientific background to equip him with knowledge of the design and construction of the atomic bomb, nor was he closely associated with the technical aspects of the project."

Henry Linschitz served at Los Alamos in the Explosives Division as head of one of the research sections that carried out lens experiments; he also was one of the small group of scientists who assembled the Alamogordo and Nagasaki bombs. Linschitz described the Greenglass sketch and testimony as "garbled" and "highly incomplete" and pointed out that Greenglass's description "displays some naïve misunderstandings . . . such as the bizarre notion that the explosives required shielding from a radioactive center." Linschitz, like Morrison, commented on Greenglass's "evident lack of comprehension of the function of the beryllium components," complete omission of two key bomb components, and the entirely false statement that the bomb was dropped by parachute. "It is not possible in any technologically useful way," he summarized, "to condense the results of a two-billion-dollar development effort into a diagram, drawn by a high-school graduate machinist on a single sheet of paper."

* A third affidavit was submitted by physicist Robert F. Christy, who while at Los Alamos proposed the specific implosion design incorporated in the Nagasaki bomb. He expressed "general and detailed agreement" with Morrison's statements.

The claim of the prosecution's "expert," Derry, that Greenglass's sketch and description of the Nagasaki bomb revealed with "substantial accuracy" the "principle" of the bomb's operation was sharply disputed by Linschitz. "The drawing . . . leaves a basic ambiguity," he said, "in even establishing what the 'principle' of the bomb was, at least so far as the dynamics of the plutonium core are concerned and the actual mechanism of detonation."

Sobell's petition also charged that the prosecution had "falsely represented" that Greenglass's sketch and testimony had the "imprimatur of authenticity and accuracy" of representatives of the Atomic Energy Commission who were seated at the prosecution table. Moreover, in reading to the prospective jurors a list of witnesses who would be called to testify that included the names of Harold Urey and J. Robert Oppenheimer, the prosecution was said to have falsely insinuated that these eminent scientists "had expressed to the government their agreement with the prosecution's case and willingness to testify against the defendants." Both scientists gave statements to Sobell's attorneys averring that they never were asked to testify and had been unaware that their names were on the witness list.

On February 14, 1967, Judge Edward Weinfeld issued his decision on Sobell's petition for a hearing. With respect to the government's allegedly fraudulent presentation of scientific evidence at the trial, the Judge decided that the prosecution had not misled jury, Court or defense counsel as to what the Greenglass material represented. "Greenglass never claimed that he had obtained definitive documents" from Los Alamos, wrote Weinfeld. The young machinist had "readily acknowledged" that he was not a scientific expert. Exhibit 8 was clearly labeled "not to scale" and was referred to at the trial as a "schematic sketch." Both Irving Saypol and Judge Kaufman at several points in the proceedings had described Greenglass's material as not necessarily complete or accurate in every detail.

In this context, claimed inaccuracies in Greenglass's drawing and explanatory testimony were "irrelevant" to the consideration of a hearing for Sobell. "Were there a complete consensus of all the learned atomic scientists in the world that his description was deficient," the Judge ruled, "it would not draw in issue the truthfulness of his version of what he then transmitted to Rosenberg."

John Derry's credibility "was for the jury and not a panel of experts, who sixteen years after the event seek to undermine it." The trial defense had been "free to call witnesses to contradict Derry, but failed to do so." In fact, it was the Judge's opinion that the scientists consulted by Sobell had not "contradicted" the "essence" ·of Derry's testimony.

Neither the inclusion of the names of Oppenheimer and Urey in the list of witnesses read to prospective jurors nor the presence of AEC representatives at the prosecution table was improper. Finally, the present charge was repetitious of allegations made in previous petitions and should have been raised earlier; the impounded material could have been secured by the defense any time they requested it.

Whatever the legal validity of the Judge's opinion, it ignores the main thrust of the Sobell argument: The trial record clearly shows that the government repeatedy urged the view that the Greenglass material encompassed the then widely believed in "secret of the atomic bomb." Judge Weinfeld apparently decided that these repeated assertions by the prosecution should be discounted, since Kaufman and Saypol also had indicated on a number of occasions that Greenglass's sketch might contain inaccuracies.

Clearly, the prosecution was playing both sides of the street in its presentation. But one has only to read Judge Kaufman's speech sentencing the Rosenbergs to death to know that he believed (or pretended to believe) that the couple had, in effect, handed the Soviet Union the atomic bomb. This same idea is unambiguously expressed in the prosecution's opening and closing statements as well as in the Judge's charge to the jurors.

In fact, in the government's brief to the U.S. Court of Appeals opposing the initial appeal of the Rosenbergs and Sobell, the U.S. Attorney provided the following summary of Derry's testimony:

"With the [Greenglass] descriptive material and sketch, a scientist could proceed with the actual construction of the atom bomb itself."

The second part of Sobell's petition charged that the government had knowingly permitted Gold to testify falsely, as evidenced by his recently discovered pretrial statements, and had corroborated this perjury with a forged Hilton Hotel registration card. The present defense position on the entire case was summarized as follows:

"Petitioner does not claim that Fuchs and Gold never met, nor does he acknowledge that they ever did, or that Gold did or did not meet Fuchs on September 19, 1945. Petitioner does affirmatively state that Gold neither met Greenglass on June 3, 1945, nor registered at the Hilton Hotel on June 3, 1945, after allegedly seeing Fuchs in Santa Fe on June 2, 1945."

Attached to the petition were copies of the June and September Hilton Hotel cards and a new report on them from handwriting and document expert Elizabeth McCarthy. When we had consulted Mrs. McCarthy some years earlier regarding the authenticity of the Hilton registration cards, we had provided her with photostatic copies of the government's photostats and also samples of the writing of former Albuquerque Hilton desk clerk Anna Kindernecht Hockinson. On the basis of her study of this material, Mrs. McCarthy gave us her opinion—qualified because of the difficulty of working with photostats—that she had "very real doubts" that Mrs. Hockinson had written the clerk's portion of the June card.

However, Mrs. McCarthy's second consideration of the cards (arranged by Sobell's attorneys) was carried out in the Federal Courthouse at Foley Square, where she was able to work with the government's photostats directly. The photostatic copies she had examined previously, she observed, had been "much dimmer, more poorly focused." She now stated that, in her opinion, the former Albuquerque Hilton registration clerk (samples of whose writing were again made available) definitely had not written either the initials "AK" or any other writing or figures on the June card, although she had initialed and filled in the clerk's portion of the September card.*

The handwriting expert's unequivocal statement regarding the June card appeared to make a hearing mandatory. For a judge considering a 2255 motion is required to grant a hearing except if he decides that the petition and records of the case conclusively show that the prisoner is not entitled to one. In reaching his decision, the judge must accept provisionally all of the petitioner's statements of fact as true.

Defense attorney William Kunstler, addressing Judge Weinfeld during oral argument on September 12, 1966, advocated this view:

"I think, your Honor, we do not have to convince you that that is a forgery now. . . . I think, your Honor, this petitioner is at least entitled to a hearing on that alone, on that issue. Your Honor or whoever hears it would have to be the determining factor as to whether this is a forgery or it is not a forgery. . . . I do not think your Honor can decide it on the basis of counsel's argument, on the basis of government's argument, on the basis of anything except a hearing.

"I think the issue is posed by Miss McCarthy. . . . I would just like to indicate, just in conclusion, that I think we present a fundamental factual issue that in any ordinary 2255 situation would call at least for a hearing."

The Sobell petition also noted that the date-time stamp on the back of the card was not in accord with either the handwritten date on the front or with trial testimony. This point was raised by the Judge during the oral argument. "What is the explanation for the fact that the stamp on the reverse side . . . is dated June 4th and the face of the exhibit indicates a registration on June 3rd?" he asked government counsel Robert King. King responded that, if there should be a hearing, "the government will establish that all the June 3rd cards of the Hotel Hilton were stamped June 4th. . . ."

WEINFELD: Don't you think it would be desirable, since inferences are being suggested, whether properly warranted or not, to clarify the atmosphere, if that is the fact? Is that not a perfectly simple thing to dispose of? . . . If the explanation is as you say, I would think that you would want to come forward with it and dispose of it out of hand be-

---

* Mrs. McCarthy also reported that, in the course of her detailed microscopic study of the government's photostats, she had detected various erasures and evidence of eradicated writing on both cards. The significance of this finding is presently unknown.

cause it would in some measure give an indication of how wild the charges have been, which is what your contention is. . . . I am referring, unless I misunderstood you, to your statement that there is a means of proving that all the June cards, all the June 3rd cards—

KING: . . . None of the cards prior to 1961 are presently available. . . .

WEINFELD: In other words, you are saying that this would be a matter of oral testimony?

KING: It would, your Honor. We cannot go back and get those cards. . . .

King indicated that the oral testimony would be provided by FBI agents who had picked up the card.

It is rather difficult to accept the explanation that a large hotel would continue throughout an entire day to use a date-time stamp which was malfunctioning to the extent that it stamped both the wrong date and the wrong time on every card for that day. Why stamp the cards at all, in that case? Surely it would have been unnecessarily confusing to have all the cards incorrectly dated when guests who had checked in on that day had to be billed.

Moreover, does it seem possible that FBI agents—discovering that this situation had occurred unluckily on the very date when Harry Gold checked into the Hilton—simply would secure the erroneously dated piece of evidence without any additional proof that the date written by the clerk, rather than the date-time stamp, was the correct one? Such proof could, for example, have consisted of other cards of that date and affidavits from hotel employees. Yet, according to U.S. Attorney King, no documents to prove this contention are available.

(As has been noted previously, four former Hilton employees asked by the authors about the discrepancies in dates on the card concluded that, in their opinions, the machine-stamped June 4 date was the governing factor. More recently, Sobell's attorneys obtained an affidavit from the présent Albuquerque Hilton manager, John M. Arnhart, who stated, in part: "Since a similar date-time stamp is still in use at the Hilton and registration cards are stamped on their reverse side, as they apparently were in 1945, I am of the opinion that Mr. Gold probably registered on June 4 and not June 3.")

Commenting further on this difference in dates on the card, the government declared: "The fact that the card bears a different date on front and back, if it proves anything, proves its genuineness. Even those with the frame of mind to accuse the FBI of dishonesty do not accuse it of being completely incompetent. . . ." The authors have no special knowledge of the FBI's general competence in the field of forgery or other illegal practices, except as reported in the press.* However, it is difficult to accept

* The government attorney's reference in the summer of 1966 to "those with the frame of mind to accuse the FBI of dishonesty" may strike some as a bit disingenuous

the view that a serious inconsistency on a document—at variance with normal procedures—only serves to prove its genuineness.

The one new piece of information about the cards provided by the government was the acknowledgement that they were "obtained by the FBI on different dates." * No explanation is offered as to why two cards from the Albuquerque Hilton—whose filing system should have insured their simultaneous discovery—were obtained separately. It is worth noting that this circumstance is completely consistent with a theory of forgery, in which the apparently authentic September card was removed from the hotel files at the time of Gold's arrest and the June card was manufactured some time afterwards to serve as corroboration for the developing story.

In addition to the material on the Hilton Hotel cards, Sobell's petition alleged that the recently discovered pretrial version of Gold's Albuquerque story differs significantly from his trial testimony. The defense attorneys made available to Judge Weinfeld a transcript of all of Gold's recorded interviews and copies of relevant pretrial handwritten statements.

Not mentioned by the attorneys in the appeal papers were several other questionable aspects of the prosecution case, including the failure to disclose Mrs. Sidorovich's denial, before a grand jury, of espionage activities; the Greenglass "passport photos"; and the Greenglasses' testimony regarding their financial affairs. The attorneys felt that all of these matters could be brought up later at a hearing, since all were related, in one respect or another, to the alleged June 3 espionage meeting.

Regarding the Hilton Hotel card, Judge Weinfeld ruled that no inference of perfidious conduct could be drawn from the return of the original June card to the hotel shortly after the trial, since the photostat, which had been designated the trial exhibit, was still in existence.

Likewise, the Judge said that the absence of FBI markings on the June card does not support a claim of forgery. He pointed out that another trial exhibit, a photostat of a bank record, has no FBI initials either. (Actually, the original of this exhibit was examined by the authors in an Albuquerque bank, which retains its files permanently. We found that it does bear an FBI Laboratory tag.)

The Judge, as he was required to do, accepted Mrs. McCarthy's opinion that the clerk's portion on the June and September cards were not written by the same person, and added: "The fact is that it hardly needed an expert to make this observation." However, Judge Weinfeld commented that the conclusion that the two cards are in different handwritings does

---

in that, only a few months before, the Solicitor General of the United States, Thurgood Marshall, had notified the Supreme Court of the FBI's illegal activities involving electronic bugging.

* The authors had suggested this on the basis of observation of the cards. See pages 385–86.

not warrant the "inference that the June 3 card was not kept in the regular course of the business of the Hotel Hilton."

He also stated: "The circumstance that at a public and busy hotel the same initials appear on the two cards and they . . . are in different handwriting does not, in one fell swoop, permit the inference that it was 'forged.' . . ."

However, he did not spell out what alternative explanations for the differing handwritings this bustling atmosphere at the Hilton might suggest.

The Judge strongly criticized the defense for not submitting an affidavit from Anna Kindernecht Hockinson. "She is one person still available who can testify with respect to the June 3 card, whether it was kept in the regular course of the hotel's business, whether it is authentic, and the practice with respect to the preparation of registration cards by the hotel clerks."

Judge Weinfeld failed to explain why he believed that Mrs. Hockinson would be qualified to comment on the authenticity of the photostatic copy of the June card. Surely she could not seriously be expected to have any recollection of a registration allegedly prepared more than 20 years before. In a hearing, however, the defense had planned to call the former room clerk to testify on peripheral matters, such as standard hotel procedure.

Judge Weinfeld dismissed the matter of a June 4 date time stamp on a card introduced to prove a June 3 meeting, as follows: "Both sides of Exhibit 16 [the June card] were read to the jury. The difference in dates was evident. Just why an inference of corrupt conduct should now flow from this circumstance is not clear. . . ."

Thus, although the disputed government exhibit contains a clerk's notation not in the handwriting of the individual whose initials appear on it; a date-time stamp entirely at variance with testimony; and a complete lack of any FBI identification or information as to the date of its alleged discovery, the Judge concluded that there is "not a word of direct evidence" to support the charges of forgery.

Gold's pretrial statements submitted to Judge Weinfeld contain an intermediate version of his Albuquerque story, related to his attorneys after more than three weeks in FBI custody and over 100 hours of interrogation. Judge Weinfeld found that this pretrial version of the New Mexico meeting "closely parallels his trial testimony." He cited various similarities between Gold's statement to his lawyers and his later testimony.

The Judge noted that Gold's pretrial account did not mention the use of a Jello box as a means of identification; the recognition signal, "Julius"; the name of Julius Rosenberg; registration at the Hilton in June; or the name and address of the Greenglasses. These omissions Judge Weinfeld termed "details" and "of no special significance." He refused to permit

Sobell to see pretrial FBI statements given by Gold and the Green-glasses.

By analogy, it is as if A and B had confessed a murder and implicated C as the mastermind of the crime. Now, pretrial statements have been discovered showing that, in an account to his attorney a month after his arrest, A never mentioned C. The judge, however, says that this is of no consequence.

The one specific direct contradiction cited in the petition was Gold's pretrial statement that Yakovlev had declared the Greenglass material to be of "no value" and his later testimony that Yakovlev had called the Green-glass material "extremely excellent and very valuable." In an extended footnote, tortuously worked out, Judge Weinfeld postulated two different conversations between Gold and Yakovlev on the subject of the Greenglass material (although Gold, of course, testified to only one such conversation). He then theorized that Yakovlev might have made both remarks to Gold at different times, intending to mislead him. Thus, there was really no contradiction, only a possible "inconsistency."

Judge Weinfeld concluded his opinion with the observation that "no act or conduct on the part of the government" had deprived Sobell of "a fundamentally fair trial."

Whatever else one may say of Judge Weinfeld's decision, it displays a startling lack of curiosity. One searches in vain through the Judge's opinion for any sign of the questioning attitude he displayed during oral argument when, for example, he asked government counsel: "What is the explanation for the fact that the stamp on the reverse side . . . is dated June 4th . . . ?"

In denying a hearing to Sobell, Weinfeld followed in the sorry tradition of his predecessors on this case in the federal judiciary, all of whom have consistently refused the defendants the chance to air their charges of inequities in open court armed with subpoena power.

Fortunately, this ostrich-like attitude toward the more unpleasant realities of recent domestic history is not universal. Since the appearance of *Invitation to an Inquest*, the Rosenberg-Sobell case has been widely discussed in the press; many American publications, without necessarily believing in the innocence of the defendants, have concluded that the cause of justice would best be served by reopening the whole affair.

Writing in the Chicago *Daily News*, lawyer Elmer Gertz called for an "inquest. . . . The fact that the Rosenbergs are dead is no reason to shrink from a thorough inquiry. . . ." In the Cleveland *Plain Dealer*, Wes Lawrence asserted that, if the defendants were guilty, "the government should welcome a new hearing as an opportunity to prove them wrong and put an end to all reasonable doubts. To oppose reopening the case will increase rather than allay the suspicions. . . ." The St. Louis *Post*

Dispatch asked if the Rosenbergs were "victims of an era," and replied that "the question needs to be answered." The Indianapolis *News* called for a "detailed and specific answer" from J. Edgar Hoover, while the Denver *Post* editorialized that the "issues raised in the new court action . . . deserve a thorough airing."

Fred J. Cook in the *Nation* asked for an investigation of the case by "a commission appointed by Congress or the President." An editorial in the Des Moines *Register* suggested that "the Justice Department might find it advisable to answer the allegations"; the Los Angeles *Times* felt the Sobell case "is worth review again at this time"; the New York *Post* asserted that the questions raised deserve "response by the Justice Department"; and the Washington *Star* concluded that there was "sufficient evidence to warrant a reopening of the case." Commented *Newsweek*: "The Rosenbergs lie in an unquiet grave."

In the *Yale Law Journal*, attorney Leonard Boudin said: "It is time for a searching review of the entire group of political criminal cases in the Southern District of New York . . . a review is required—either to clear the name of the Government or to vindicate its victims. . . . The most effective device is probably that of an executive commission. . . ." Similarly, law professor Herbert L. Packer suggested in the *New York Review of Books*: ". . . one could wish that the moment had arrived for an impartial investigation of the troubling factual aspects of the case . . . it is not fanciful to suppose that an official body (like the Warren Commission) might possibly be able to get to the bottom of this murky affair."

Sobell will appeal the district court decision to the Supreme Court and may yet have an opportunity for an evidentiary hearing.* Meanwhile, despite this growing body of opinion, the questions raised by the Sobell petition remain unanswered; the secret files of the Department of Justice remain locked.

---

* Sobell's petition was denied without comment by the United States Court of Appeals for the Second Circuit on June 23, 1967. He finally was freed on January 14, 1969, by order of the Court of Appeals, which credited him with the months served prior to his sentencing. This decision and earned "good time" was the basis for his release. Denied parole repeatedly, he had been imprisoned for 18 years and five months.

SOURCES

CHAPTER 1: A CAPSULE VIEW

PAGE

1 *Columbia Law Review*, Feb. 1954, "The Rosenberg Case: Some Reflections on Federal Criminal Law," p. 219.

2 N. Y. *Post*, April 6, 1951, the Leonard Lyons column, p. 48.

4 *Partisan Review*, Winter, 1955, "The Intellectuals and the Discontented Classes," by David Riesman and Nathan Glazer, p. 64.

CHAPTER 2: THE WORLD IS HEADED FOR GRIEF

8 The quotation a "scientist's poem" is from *Literature for Our Time*, edited by Leonard S. Brown, Harlow O. Waite, and Benjamin P. Atkinson (Henry Holt & Co., N.Y., 1947), p. 1.

8ff Prof. Hans Thirring was quoted by William Cahn, *Einstein: A Pictorial Biography* (The Citadel Press, N.Y., 1955), p. 28.
Vernadskii was quoted by Arnold Kramish in the RAND Corporation study *Atomic Energy in the Soviet Union* (Stanford University Press, Stanford, Calif., 1959), p. 6.

11 The excerpt from the Hahn-Strassmann report appeared in Ralph E. Lapp, *Atoms And People* (Harper & Brothers, N.Y., 1956), p. 15. The original report in German was reprinted in *Foundations of Nuclear Physics*, edited by Robert T. Beyer (Dover Publications, Inc., N.Y., 1949), pp. 87–91.

12 Bohr's reaction to the Hahn-Strassmann discovery was recounted by William L. Laurence, *Men and Atoms* (Simon & Schuster, N.Y., 1959), p. 30.

12 Laura Fermi, *Atoms in the Family* (University of Chicago Press, Chicago, Ill., 1954), p. 155.

13 Szilard's letter to Joliot-Curie was quoted by Robert Jungk, *Brighter than a Thousand Suns: A Personal History of the Atomic Scientists* (Harcourt, Brace & Co., N.Y., 1958), pp. 75–76.

13 Szilard was quoted by William L. Laurence, *op. cit.*, p. 37.

CHAPTER 3: WHY THE UNITED STATES WAS FIRST

AND

CHAPTER 4: THE MANHATTAN PROJECT

A basic source for the administrative and technical history of the American atomic bomb project is Henry De Wolf Smyth, *Atomic Energy for Military Purposes* (Princeton University Press, Princeton, N.J., 1948). Also see Arthur Holly Compton, *Atomic Quest* (Oxford University Press, N.Y., 1956), particularly for a description of the work of the Metallurgical Laboratory. Miscellaneous information on the production of atomic bombs and on science in the Soviet Union and other nations was provided by Gordon Dean, *Report on the Atom* (Alfred A. Knopf, N.Y., second edition, 1959). The most detailed account of the background and development of the Manhattan Project is that of Richard G. Hewlett and Oscar E. Anderson, Jr., *The New World, 1939/1946, Volume 1, A History of the United States Atomic Energy Commission* (The Pennsylvania State University Press, University Park, Pa., 1962).

14 The Navy letter was quoted by William L. Laurence, *Men and Atoms* (Simon & Schuster, N.Y., 1959), p. 55.

14ff The full Einstein letter was reprinted by Gordon Dean, *op. cit.*, pp. 247–49.

16 The intelligence mission that investigated Nazi Germany's atomic research program was reported on by Samuel A. Goudsmit, *Alsos* (Henry Schuman, Inc., N.Y., 1947).

17 The RAND Corporation statement is from the study by Arnold Kramish, *Atomic Energy in the Soviet Union* (Stanford University Press, Stanford, Calif., 1959), p. 29.

17 The Kapitza speech was quoted by Arnold Kramish, *op. cit.*, p. 41.

22 Compton's telephone call to Conant was described by Arthur Holly Compton, *op. cit.*, p. 144.

26 Groves's top-secret memo to Gen. Marshall was reprinted by Fletcher Knebel and Charles W. Bailey II, *No High Ground* (Harper & Brothers, N.Y., 1960), pp. 88–89.

CHAPTER 5: A FEELING OF PROFOUND RESPONSIBILITY

27 Arthur Holly Compton, *Atomic Quest* (Oxford University Press, N.Y., 1956), p. 116.

27 The quotation "collection of crackpots" was reported by Laura Fermi, *Atoms in the Family* (University of Chicago Press, Chicago, Ill., 1954), p. 226.

28 Groves's statement on Russia is from his testimony before the U. S. Atomic Energy Commission Personnel Security Board, *In the Matter of J. Robert Oppenheimer* (Government Printing Office, Washington, 1954), p. 173.

28 Groves's statement on collaboration with the British is from the AEC Personnel Board hearings on the Oppenheimer matter, *op. cit.*, p. 175.

29 The full text of Bohr's memo to FDR was reprinted by Robert Jungk, *Brighter than a Thousand Suns: A Personal History of the Atomic Scientists* (Harcourt, Brace & Co., N.Y., 1958), pp. 344–47.

29 Excerpts from Szilard's memo to FDR were printed in the *Bulletin of the Atomic Scientists*, Dec. 1947, pp. 351–53.

29 Harry S. Truman's memoirs, vol. 1, *Years of Decisions* (Doubleday & Co., N.Y., 1955), p. 10.

29ff The Franck memo of April 21, 1945, was quoted in the *Bulletin of the Atomic Scientists*, Oct. 1958, "Behind the Decision to Use the Atomic Bomb: Chicago 1944–45," by Alice Kimball Smith, p. 294.

[30] Stimson's memo to the President of April 25, 1945, was reprinted by Henry L. Stimson and McGeorge Bundy, *On Active Service in Peace and War* (Harper & Brothers, N.Y., 1947), p. 635.

[31] Langmuir testified before the Special Senate Committee on Atomic Energy, *Hearings on Senate Resolution No. 179*, Nov. 30, 1945, pp. 113–14.

[31ff] Dr. Szilard's version of his meeting with Byrnes was related in *U.S. News & World Report*, Aug. 15, 1960, pp. 68–71.

[32] The May 31 meeting of the Interim Committee was described by Arthur Holly Compton, *op. cit.*, pp. 219–21 and 236–39. Recommendations adopted by the committee on June 1 were reported in *Harper's*, Feb. 1947, "The Decision to Use the Atomic Bomb," by Henry L. Stimson, p. 100.

[32] Harry S. Truman's memoirs, *op. cit.*, p. 419.

[32] Rabinowitch was quoted by Robert Jungk, *op. cit.*, p. 184.

[32ff] The Franck report was published by the *Bulletin of the Atomic Scientists*, May 1, 1946, p. 2. It was also reprinted by Robert Jungk, *op. cit.*, pp. 348–60.

[33] Groves's and Farrell's reports to Potsdam were reprinted by Herbert Feis, *Between War and Peace: The Potsdam Conference* (Princeton University Press, Princeton, N.J., 1960), pp. 165–71.

CHAPTER 6: SECURITY THROUGH SECRECY

[35] For a discussion of the scientists' efforts to disseminate information, see the *Bulletin of the Atomic Scientists*, Sept. 1947, "The Scientists as Public Educators: A Two Year Summary," by John A. Simpson, pp. 243–46.

[36] *Newsweek*, Dec. 3, 1945, p. 42.

[36] Henry De Wolf Smyth, *Atomic Energy for Military Purposes* (Princeton University Press, Princeton, N.J., 1948), p. 226.

[36ff] *Bulletin of the Atomic Scientists*, June 1947, "A Japanese Scientist Describes the Destruction of His Cyclotrons," by Yoshio Nishina, p. 145.

[37] The incident regarding McMillan's synchrotron was told in the *Bulletin of the Atomic Scientists of Chicago*, March 1, 1946, "Secrecy in Science," by Louis N. Ridenour, p. 3. See also Arnold Kramish, *Atomic Energy in the Soviet Union* (Stanford University Press, Stanford, Calif., 1959), p. 199.

[37ff] Selig Hecht, *Explaining the Atom* (Viking Press, N.Y., 1954; first edition published in 1947), pp. 167–69.

[38] The Bush-Conant estimate regarding a Soviet A-bomb was reported by Richard G. Hewlett and Oscar E. Anderson, Jr., *The New World, 1939/1946, Volume 1, A History of the United States Atomic Energy Commission* (The Pennsylvania State University Press, University Park, Pa., 1962), pp. 329, 354.

[38] Robert M. Hutchins's statement appeared in the *Bulletin of the Atomic Scientists of Chicago*, March 1, 1946, "Peace or War with Russia?", p. 1.

[38] Bernice Brode's statement is from her "Tales of Los Alamos," printed in the LASL (Los Alamos Scientific Laboratory) *Community News* in nine installments from June 2, 1960, to Sept. 22, 1960. The excerpt quoted appeared in the issue of Sept. 8, 1960, p. 7.

[39] *Bulletin of the Atomic Scientists*, Feb. 1947, "The Atomic Secrets," by Eugene Rabinowitch, p. 33.

[40] *Bulletin of the Atomic Scientists of Chicago*, March 14, 1946, "An Appeal to Reason," by E. U. Condon, pp. 6–7.

CHAPTER 7: A BLURRING OF VISION

[41] The quoted portion of the Canadian statement apeared in the N.Y. *Times*, Feb. 16, 1946, p. 1.

[41ff] The Soviet reply was reprinted in *The Report of the Royal Commission*, June 27, 1946 (Edmond Cloutier, Printer to the King's Most Excellent Majesty Controller of Stationery, Ottawa, Canada, 1946), pp. 627–29.

[42] Joint Congressional Committee on Atomic Energy, *Soviet Atomic Espionage*, April 1951 (Government Printing Office, Washington, 1951), pp. 2–3.

[42ff] May's confession was reprinted in the official Canadian report, *op. cit.*, pp. 455–56 and in the Joint Committee report on *Soviet Atomic Espionage*, *op. cit.*, pp. 58–59; an account of May's arraignment was carried by the London *Times*, March 20, 1946, and reprinted in the Joint Committee report, pp. 49–50.

[43] N.Y. *Times*, March 8, 1946, p. 3.

[43] *Newsweek*, April 8, 1946, "Russian Bear Trap," p. 22.

[43] Hoover's announcement of Redin's arrest was quoted in part in *Time*, April 8, 1946, "Don't Go Near the Water," p. 19.

[43] N.Y. *Times*, March 27, 1946, p. 1.

[43ff] N.Y. *Times*, March 31, 1946, Section IV, p. 8.

[44] The trial of U.S. *vs.* Redin was held at the federal courthouse in Seattle, Wash., June 25, 1946 (Cr. No. 46932 and 46970). The quotation from the prosecutor's summation is on p. 62.

[44] *Newsweek*, July 29, 1946, "Red Acquittal," p. 21.

[44] Thomas's statement regarding transfer of the atomic bomb back to the military appeared in the House Committee on Un-American Activities *Hearings on H.R. 1884 and H.R. 2122*, March 24–28, 1947 (Government Printing Office, Washington, 1947), p. 281.

[44] Thomas's program was outlined in House Committee on Un-American Activities *Annual Report*, Dec. 31, 1948 (Government Printing Office, Washington, 1949), pp. 2–3.

[44] Washington *Times-Herald* stories on Condon were reported by Robert K. Carr, *The House Committee on Un-American Activities: 1945–1950* (Cornell University Press, Ithaca, N.Y., 1952), p. 132. Carr dated the newspaper stories as March 1947.

[44] *American*, June 1947, "Russia Grabs Our Inventions," by J. Parnell Thomas, p. 16.

[44] *Liberty*, June 21, 1947, "Reds in Our Atom-Bomb Plants," by J. Parnell Thomas (as told to Stacy V. Jones), p. 15.

[45] The Washington *Times-Herald's* later attack on Condon was dated July 17, 1947, by Robert K. Carr, *op. cit.*, p. 132.

[45] N.Y. *Times*, Oct. 31, 1947, p. 1.

[45] N.Y. *Times*, July 10, 1947, p. 1.

[45ff] Thomas's statement appeared in the N.Y. *Journal-American*, July 10, 1947, p. 1.

[46] Condon was called the "weakest link" in the House Committee on Un-American Activities *Report to the Full Committee of the Special Subcommittee on National Security*, March 18, 1948 (Government Printing Office, Washington, 1948), p. 1.

[46] Rep. Holifield's comment appeared in the *Congressional Record*, vol. 94, March 9, 1948, p. 2435.

[46] The statement about Dr. Condon and Soviet espionage is from the House Committee on Un-American Activities *Report to the Full Committee, op. cit.*, p. 7. This report was published by the House Committee on Interstate and Foreign Commerce, House Report No. 1753, April 19, 1948, Appendix A.

[46] Condon's own statement was reported in the N.Y. *Times*, March 2, 1948, p. 1.

[46ff] N.Y. *Mirror*, Aug. 2, 1948, p. 3.

[47] The Washington *Post* report of the House Committee on Un-American Activities announcement of forthcoming atomic espionage investigations was quoted by Robert K. Carr, *op. cit.*, p. 398, and was dated by him Sept. 18, 1948.

[48ff] House Committee on Un-American Activities *Report on Soviet Espionage Activities in Connection with the Atom Bomb*, Sept. 28, 1948 (Government Printing Office, Washington, 1948), "The Chapin-Hiskey Case," p. 167; "The Scientist X Case," pp. 179–81; "The Kamen Case," pp. 181–82.

[49] Joint Committee report on *Soviet Atomic Espionage, op. cit.*, pp. 163–72.

CHAPTER 8: THE MONOPOLY ENDS

[52] For the story of the detection of the first Soviet atomic explosion see N.Y. *Times*, June 1, 1960, p. 1, and the *Times* editorial "Telltale Rainwater," June 2, 1960. Also see *Journal of Chemical Education*, June 1959, "Atmospheric Radioactivity Studies at the U. S. Naval Research Laboratory," by L. B. Lockhart, Jr., R. A. Baus, P. King, and I. H. Blifford, Jr., p. 291.

[52ff] Truman's statement appeared in the N.Y. *Times*, Sept. 24, 1949, p. 1; Eisenhower's, on p. 2. The quoted *Times* editorial, "Russia and the Bomb," appeared Sept. 24, 1949.

[53] *Atomics*, Sept. 1949, "The Russians Have It," by Andrew W. Kramer, p. 2.

[53] N.Y. *Times* editorial, Sept. 25, 1949, "Thunder on the Left."

[53] Sen Mundt's statement appeared in the N.Y. *Times*, Sept. 24, 1949, p. 3.

[53] Rep. Nixon's remarks were reported in the N.Y. *Journal-American*, Sept. 24, 1949, p. 1.

[54] Karl T. Compton's remarks are from his testimony before the U. S. Atomic Energy Commission Personnel Security Board, *In the Matter of J. Robert Oppenheimer* (Government Printing Office, Washington, 1954), p. 258.

[54] *The Forrestal Diaries*, edited by Walter Millis and E. S. Duffield (Viking Press, N.Y., 1951), pp. 495–96.

[54] John Foster Dulles, *War or Peace* (Macmillan, N.Y., 1950), p. 111.

[54] Joseph and Stewart Alsop, *We Accuse!* (Simon & Schuster, N.Y., 1954), p. 29.

[54ff] Arthur Holly Compton, *Atomic Quest* (Oxford University Press, N.Y., 1956), pp. 128–29.

[55] The Fermi quotation is from AEC Personnel Security Board hearings on the Oppenheimer matter, *op. cit.*, p. 395.

[55] George Racey Jordan (with Richard L. Stokes), *From Major Jordan's Diaries* (Harcourt, Brace & Co., N.Y., 1952), p. 236.

[56] The Joint Congressional Committee on Atomic Energy reported its findings in the Jordan matter in *Soviet Atomic Espionage*, April 1951 (Government Printing Office, Washington, 1951), pp. 184–92.

[56] Nixon's statement appeared in the *Congressional Record*, vol. 96, Jan. 26, 1950, p. 1007.

[57] Truman's statement on the super-bomb was reported in the N.Y. *Times*, Feb. 1, 1950, p. 1.

CHAPTER 9: KLAUS FUCHS CONFESSES

[59] The headline reporting Fuchs's arrest appeared in the N.Y. *Times*, Feb. 4, 1950, p. 1.

[59] Hoover's Senate appearance was reported in the N.Y. *Times*, Feb. 4, 1950, p. 1.

[59] Sen. Bridges was quoted by *Newsweek*, Feb. 13, 1950, "Hydrogen Age . . . Whither America?", p. 18.

[60] *U.S. News & World Report*, Feb. 17, 1950, "How Russia Got U.S. Secrets: 10,000 Spies in Key Places," p. 11.

[60] *Time*, Feb. 13, 1950, "Shock," p. 24.

[60] Arthur Krock's comments appeared in the N.Y. *Times*, Feb. 5, 1950, Section IV, "Some Wheels Within Wheels," p. 3.

[60ff] *Newsweek*, Feb. 20, 1950, "Red Shadows on a Worried World," p. 19.

[61] McCarthy's Wheeling, W. Va., speech was described by Richard H. Rovere, *Senator Joe McCarthy* (Harcourt, Brace & Co., N.Y., 1959), pp. 123–27.

[61ff] Portions of the testimony at Fuchs's Bow Street hearing were reported in the N.Y. *Times*, Feb. 11, 1950, and reprinted by the Joint Con-

gressional Committee on Atomic Energy, *Soviet Atomic Espionage,* April 1951 (Government Printing Office, Washington, 1951), pp. 30–33.

[64ff] The portion of Fuchs's confession quoted here is as published by the N.Y. *Times,* Feb. 11, 1950, p. 2. The same version was reprinted in the Joint Committee report on *Soviet Atomic Espionage, op. cit.,* pp. 16–17. A slightly different version of the portion of his confession read in court was printed in the London *Times,* March 2, 1950, p. 2. Other sources, Alan Moorehead, *The Traitors* (Hamish Hamilton, Ltd., London, 1952) and Rebecca West, *The Meaning of Treason* (The Reprint Society Ltd., London, 1952), contain alleged quotations from Fuchs's confession not available elsewhere. The authors were unable to obtain an official transcript of the court hearings in the Fuchs matter.

[66] Fuchs's father was quoted in the N.Y. *Times,* Feb. 14, 1950, p. 14.

[66] *Life,* March 13, 1950, "14 Years for 'Grossest Treachery'," p. 42.

[66] Portions of the Attorney General's speech at the Fuchs trial were quoted in the Joint Committee report on *Soviet Atomic Espionage, op. cit.,* p. 34.

[66] The efforts of Fuchs's defense counsel on behalf of his client were described in the London *Times,* March 2, 1950, p. 2; and *Newsweek,* March 13, 1950, "14 Years for Fuchs," p. 35.

[67] Fuchs's own statement at his trial, as quoted here, appeared in the N.Y. *Times,* March 2, 1950, p. 1.

[67] *Time,* March 13, 1950, "Thank You, My Lord," p. 27.

[67] The Tass comment on the Fuchs case was quoted in *Scientific American,* April 1950, "Science and the Citizen."

[67] The explanation of the Joint Committee on Atomic Energy regarding its decision not to release Fuchs's confessions appeared in *Soviet Atomic Espionage, op. cit.,* p. 15.

[67ff] *Time,* March 19, 1951, "Problem in Security," p. 74.

[68] The appearance of Fuchs's name in Halperin's notebook was discussed in the Joint Committee report on *Soviet Atomic Espionage, op. cit.,* pp. 34–35. See also Alan Moorehead, *op. cit.,* p. 80.

[68] Prime Minister Attlee's statement was reprinted in the Joint Committee report on *Soviet Atomic Espionage, op. cit.,* p. 28.

[68] Rep. Nixon's comments were reported by the N.Y. *Post,* Feb. 2, 1950, p. 2. The quoted *World-Telegram & Sun* headline appeared Feb. 4, 1950, p. 2.

[69] Sen. Capehart was quoted in the N.Y. *Times,* Feb. 5, 1950, Section IV, p. 3.

[69] Sen. McMahon's account of Hoover's Congressional testimony appeared in the N.Y. *Times,* Feb. 7, 1950, p. 3.

[69] The FBI's efforts to question Fuchs were described in the Joint Committee report on *Soviet Atomic Espionage, op. cit.,* p. 35.

CHAPTER 10: CAPTURE OF AN ACCOMPLICE

70 Gold's arrest was reported in the N.Y. *Times*, May 24, 1950, p. 1. An official account of the May 23 hearing is typed on the stationery of Judge McGranery, dated May 26, 1950, and filed at the U. S. District Court for the Eastern District of Pennsylvania, in Philadelphia (Cr. No. 15769).

70 Gold's telephone conversation was reported by *Life*, June 12, 1950, "The Making of a Spy," by Dean Brelis, p. 7.

70ff *Reader's Digest*, May 1951, "The Crime of the Century," by J. Edgar Hoover, p. 159.

71 N.Y. *World-Telegram & Sun*, May 26, 1950, p. 26.

71 The headline and quotation from the N.Y. *Times* appeared on May 24, 1950, p. 1.

71 N.Y. *Times*, May 25, 1950, p. 1.

72 N.Y. *World-Telegram & Sun*, May 26, 1950, p. 26.

72 *Life*, June 12, 1950, p. 7.

72 *Time*, June 5, 1950, "The Man with the Oval Face," p. 20.

72 *Reader's Digest*, May 1951, p. 159.

73 *Life*, June 12, 1950, p. 7.

73 *Time*, June 5, 1950, p. 20.

73 The FBI informant was quoted by the N.Y. *Journal-American*, May 24, 1950, p. 1.

73 The quotation "self-possessed prisoner" is from the N.Y. *Times*, May 25, 1950, p. 1.

73ff The transcripts of Gold's May 31 and June 1 appearances before Judge McGranery are filed at the U. S. District Court in Philadelphia. Also available there is the June 9 indictment voted against Gold in the Eastern District of N.Y.

75 N.Y. *Times*, June 13, 1950, p. 14.

75 Rep. Van Zandt was quoted in the N.Y. *Times*, May 24, 1950, p. 1.

75 *Newsweek*, June 5, 1950, "Good Boy Gone Wrong," p. 20.

CHAPTER 11: MORE ARRESTS

76 The headline reporting Slack's arrest appeared in the N.Y. *Times*, June 16, 1950, p. 1.

76 Syracuse *Post-Standard*, June 16, 1950, p. 1.

76 Slack's comment at his arraignment appeared in the N.Y. *Times*, June 16, 1950, p. 1; also in the same story were excerpts from the Department of Justice's announcement of Slack's arrest.

77 *Time*, June 26, 1950, "The Smaller Ones," p. 15.

77 Slack's statement to reporters concerning the charges appeared in the N.Y. *Herald Tribune*, June 16, 1950, p. 1.

77ff Greenglass's arrest and arraignment were reported by the N.Y. *Times*, June 17, 1950, p. 1.

[78] Greenglass's June 23 hearing was described in the N.Y. *Journal-American*, June 23, 1950, p. 4.

[78] Westbrook Pegler's column appeared in the N.Y. *Journal-American*, June 29, 1950, p. 3.

[78] Greenglass's July 6, 1950, indictment is on file at the U. S. District Court, Albuquerque, N.M. (Cr. No. 15938).

[78ff] Greenglass's July 12 hearing was reported by the N.Y. *Mirror*, July 13, 1950, p. 17.

[79] Julius Rosenberg's arrest was reported in the N.Y. *Times*, July 18, 1950, p. 1.

[79] The story on Rosenberg's machine shop appeared in the N.Y. *Daily News*, July 19, 1950, p. 6.

[79] The interview with Ethel Rosenberg appeared in the N.Y. *Journal-American*, July 18, 1950, p. 8.

[80] The quoted Department of Justice press release (dated July 17, 1950) is attached as an exhibit to an appeal made under Section 2255 on behalf of the Rosenbergs and Sobell on Nov. 24, 1952. These appeal papers are filed at the U. S. District Court for the Southern District of N.Y., at Foley Square (Cr. No. 134–245).

[80] N.Y. *Journal-American*, July 18, 1950, p. 1.

[80ff] Rosenberg's remarks on the jello box were quoted in the N.Y. *Times*, July 20, 1950, p. 18.

[81] *Time*, July 31, 1950, "Espionage: No. 4" and "Boiling Over," pp. 12–13.

[81] N.Y. *Times*, July 25, 1950, p. 1.

[81ff] Gold's July 20 court appearance was described by the N.Y. *Journal-American*, July 20, 1950, p. 1. The official transcript is on file at the U. S. District Court for the Eastern District of Pennsylvania, in Philadelphia (Cr. No. 15769).

[83] Gold's July 29 grand jury appearance and the arrests of Brothman and Moskowitz were reported in the N.Y. *Times*, July 30, 1950, p. 1.

[83] *Time*, Aug. 7, 1950, reported the Brothman-Moskowitz arrests in a story, "Two More Links," p. 15.

[83] Brothman's and Moskowitz's arraignment was reported in the N.Y. *Times*, Aug. 3, 1950, p. 10.

[83ff] The arrest of Ethel Rosenberg was reported in the N.Y. *Times*, Aug. 12, 1950, p. 1.

[84] The Aug. 17 indictment is on file at the U. S. District Court at Foley Square. It was reprinted in the trial transcript published by the Committee to Secure Justice for Morton Sobell, p. 4.

[84] The Aug. 17 indictment was reported in the N.Y. *Times*, Aug. 18, 1950, p. 7.

[84] N.Y. *Times* reported Sobell's arrest Aug. 19, 1950, p. 1.

[84ff] *Newsweek*, Aug. 28, 1950, "Atom Arrest No. 8," p. 30, and *Time*, Aug. 28, 1950, "Detour," p. 14, reported Sobell's arrest.

[85] The Rosenbergs' Aug. 23 hearing was reported in the N.Y. *Times*, Aug. 24, 1950, p. 20.

85 Sen Kilgore's proposal was reported in the N.Y. *Mirror*, Sept. 3, 1950, p. 23.

85ff The indictment against Slack and other records in the Slack case are stored at the Federal Records Center in Chicago (Cr. No. 5593, in the U. S. District Court for the Eastern District of Tenn.). The authors also have a copy of Slack's complete court record.

85 The N.Y. *Times* reported Slack's indictment, Sept. 2, 1950, p. 8.

87 Vago's arrest was reported in the N.Y. *Times*, Sept. 29, 1950, p. 17.

87 A story linking Vago to the spy ring appeared in the N.Y. *Daily News*, Oct. 11, 1950, p. 4.

87 A picture of Rosenberg and Vago was printed in the N.Y. *Journal-American*, Dec. 5, 1950, p. 21.

88 Both superseding indictments voted in the Rosenberg-Sobell case are available at Foley Square or in the published trial transcript, pp. 2–4 and 6–7.

88 Considine's column appeared in the N.Y. *Journal-American*, June 21, 1950, "On the Line," p. 31.

CHAPTER 12: BLUEPRINTS FROM A CELLAR CLOSET

The Brothman-Moskowitz trial record is on file at the U. S. District Court for the Southern District of N.Y., at Foley Square (Cr. No. 133-106).

90 N.Y. *Daily News* headlines, Nov. 8, 1950, p. 10, and Nov. 9, 1950, p. 10.

90 N.Y. *Herald Tribune*, Nov. 9, 1950, p. 5.

90ff An FBI agent, Donald E. Shannon, who participated in the 1947 interrogations of Brothman and Gold, testified for the prosecution at the Brothman-Moskowitz trial.

91ff Brothman's and Gold's testimony before the 1947 grand jury was read into the record at the Brothman-Moskowitz trial.

96 The hearing regarding postponement of Gold's sentencing took place Oct. 19, 1950; the transcript is filed at the U. S. District Court for the Eastern District of Pennsylvania, in Philadelphia (Cr. No. 15769).

96 *Time*, Nov. 27, 1950, "Man on the Fringe," p. 17.

96 N.Y. *Times*, Nov. 16, 1950, p. 1.

98 N.Y. *World-Telegram & Sun*, Nov. 16, 1950, p. 16.

99 N.Y. *Times*, Nov. 17, 1950, p. 16.

106 Gordon Dean, *Report on the Atom* (Alfred A. Knopf, N.Y., second edition, 1959), p. 299.

106 Joint Congressional Committee on Atomic Energy, *Soviet Atomic Espionage*, April 1951 (Government Printing Office, Washington, 1951), p. 185.

CHAPTER 13: AN "EXTRAORDINARILY SELFLESS PERSON"

The transcript of Gold's sentencing hearing is filed at the U. S. District Court for the Eastern District of Pennsylvania, in Philadelphia (Cr. No. 15769).

107 *Time*, Dec. 18, 1950, "Remorse & Punishment," p. 22.

116 N.Y. *Times*, Dec. 10, 1950, p. 1.

CHAPTER 14: THE TRIAL

The Rosenberg-Sobell trial is on file at the U. S. District Court for the Southern District of N.Y., at Foley Square (U. S. *vs.* Rosenbergs, Sobell, Yakovlev, and David Greenglass, Cr. No. 134–245). The complete trial transcript was published by and can be purchased from the Committee to Secure Justice for Morton Sobell, 150 Fifth Ave., N.Y.

119ff N.Y. *Times,* March 7, 1951, p. 1.

130 N.Y. *Times,* March 15, 1951, p. 1.

133 Perl's arrest was reported in the N.Y. *Times,* March 15, 1951, p. 1.

135 *Time,* March 26, 1951, "My Friend, Yakovlev," p. 25.

136 Harry Gold's testimony was reported in the N.Y. *Times,* March 16, 1951, p. 1.

138 N.Y. *Times,* March 16, 1951, p. 1.

139 N.Y. *Herald Tribune,* March 17, 1951, p. 22.

148 N.Y. *Times,* March 23, 1951, p. 1.

148ff N.Y. *Times,* March 8, 1951, p. 1.

150 N.Y. *Times,* March 28, 1951, p. 18.

CHAPTER 16: JUDGMENT DAY

168 N.Y. *Times,* April 5, 1951, p. 60.

172 Bloch's statement outside the courtroom was reported in the N.Y. *Times,* April 6, 1951, p. 1.

172 N.Y. *Post,* April 6, 1951, p. 5.

173 N.Y. *Times,* April 7, 1951, p. 1.

CHAPTER 17: THE CAMPAIGN AND THE COURTS

175 The story by Howard Rushmore was printed in the N.Y. *Journal-American,* April 3, 1951, early edition, p. 6.

175 Leonard Lyons's columns appeared in the N.Y. *Post,* April 6, 1951, p. 48, and April 9, 1951, p. 26.

175 Ethel Rosenberg's comments on her transfer to Sing Sing were quoted in the N.Y. *Daily Compass,* April 12, 1951, and the N.Y. *Times* of the same date, p. 21.

175ff The editorials in the St. Louis *Post-Dispatch* and Atlanta *Constitution* both were printed on April 6, 1951.

176 Denunciations of the death penalty appeared in the *Daily Worker* and the *Jewish Daily Forward* during the first few days after the sentencing.

176 Dorothy Thompson's statement appeared in the Washington *Star,* April 12, 1951, p. A-23.

176 *Bulletin of the Atomic Scientists,* May 1951, "Atomic Spy Trials: Heretical Afterthoughts," by Eugene Rabinowitch, p. 139.

176 The *National Guardian* criticism of the verdict began Aug. 8, 1951. The

first article of William Reuben's seven-part series ran on Aug. 22, 1951.

177ff The Court of Appeals opinion affirming the convictions of the Rosenbergs and Sobell was appended to the trial transcript published by the Committee to Secure Justice for Morton Sobell. It is also on file at Foley Square.

178ff Justice Frankfurter's comments are from his memorandum opinion of Nov. 17, 1952 (Supreme Court of the U.S., Oct. Term, 1952, No. 111). Portions were published in contemporary newspapers.

179 Mrs. Sobell's comment on the transfer of her husband to Alcatraz appeared in the *National Guardian*, Dec. 4, 1952.

180 The American Civil Liberties Union statement (dated Dec. 7, 1952) was reprinted by S. Andhil Fineberg, *The Rosenberg Case: Fact and Fiction* (Oceana Publications, 1953), p. 149.

180 Arthur Garfield Hays's remarks on the death sentence appeared in his article in the *Nation*, Nov. 8, 1952, "The Rosenberg Case," p. 422.

180 *Time*, Dec. 1, 1952, "The Rosenberg Diversion," p. 22.

180 The defense's petition before Judge Ryan was filed under Federal Section 2255 on Nov. 24, 1952, argued Dec. 2 and 5, and denied Dec. 10, 1952. The papers are on file at the U. S. District Court for the Southern District of N.Y., at Foley Square (Cr. No. 134–245).

181 Oliver Pilat, *The Atom Spies* (G. P. Putnam's Sons, N.Y., 1952), p. 287.

181ff The affidavits of special agents Harrington and Roetting were appended to the prosecution's papers submitted to Judge Ryan in opposition to the defense's Section 2255 petition. These documents are on file at Foley Square.

182 Meyer's statement is in the transcript of the defense's Dec. 2, 1952, argument before Judge Ryan, p. 116.

182 N.Y. *Times*, March 15, 1951, p. 1.

182ff Bloch's statement on the Perl arrest is in the transcript of the Dec. 2, 1952, argument before Judge Ryan, p. 78.

183 Assistant U. S. Attorney Kilsheimer's statement was made before Judge Ryan, Dec. 2, 1952, and appears in the transcript, p. 164.

183ff The decision of the U. S. Court of Appeals for the Second Circuit on the Section 2255 petition was handed down Dec. 31, 1952, and is filed at Foley Square.

184ff The judicial clemency hearing transcript is on file at Foley Square. The quoted colloquies between Bloch and Judge Kaufman appear on pp. 3–7, 24, 72, and 83.

185ff U. S. Attorney Lane's statements are quoted from the transcript of the judicial clemency hearing, pp. 91 and 93–95.

186ff A copy of the Rosenbergs' petition for executive clemency was obtained by the authors from the files of the late Emanuel Bloch. The major part of this document was reprinted in *The Testament of Ethel and Julius Rosenberg* (Cameron & Kahn, N.Y., Aug. 1954), pp. 189–216.

190 The quotation from the Swiss *Tribune de Genève* appeared in the *National Guardian*, Dec. 25, 1952.

190 N.Y. *Herald Tribune*, Jan. 14, 1953, p. 10.

190 The *New Statesman and Nation*, Dec. 6, 1952, p. 669.

191 The clergymen's clemency appeal was reported in the N.Y. *Times*, Jan. 14, 1953, p. 19; the quotation from Rev. Stitt's telegram appeared in the *National Guardian*, Jan. 15, 1953.

191 Urey's letter appeared in the N.Y. *Times*, Jan. 8, 1953, editorial page, and Einstein's on Jan. 13, 1953.

191 The Rev. Heuss was quoted by the N.Y. *Times*, Jan. 13, 1953, p. 15.

191 Poling's statement appeared in the N.Y. *Times*, Jan. 6, 1953, p. 1.

191ff Sokolsky's column appeared in the N.Y. *Journal-American*, Jan. 9, 1953, editorial page.

192 Eisenhower's statement denying clemency was printed in the N.Y. *Herald Tribune*, Feb. 12, 1953, p. 1.

192 *Time*, Feb. 23, 1953, "Mercy & Justice," p. 24.

192ff *Nation*, Feb. 28, 1953, editorial, "The Last Mile," p. 179.

193 The letter from Vanzetti's sister was quoted in the *National Guardian*, Jan. 22, 1953.

193 The Pope's action regarding the Rosenbergs was reported in the N.Y. *Times*, Feb. 14 and 15, 1953, p. 1.

194 *L'Osservatore Romano*, April 16, 1953, "The Significance of an Intervention."

194 The comment by the N.Y. *Times* about the Rosenbergs escaping death "if they decide to talk" appeared Feb. 17, 1953, p. 1.

194 The remarks of Judges Hand and Frank in granting a stay of execution were reported in the N.Y. *Times*, Feb. 18, 1953, p. 1.

194 The Supreme Court denial of a hearing was reported in the N.Y. *Times*, May 26, 1953, p. 1.

195 The Rosenbergs' statement on the Bennett visit was published in *The Testament of Ethel and Julius Rosenberg*, *op. cit.*, pp. 168–69.

CHAPTER 18: NEW EVIDENCE

196 The Section 2255 petition of June 1953 (concerning "new evidence"), with relevant papers and exhibits, is filed at the U. S. District Court for the Southern District of N.Y., at Foley Square (Cr. No. 134–245).

196 Paris *Le Monde*, April 20, 1953, p. 1.

199 *National Guardian*, April 13, 1953, "The Missing Table: The Proof That Key Rosenberg Case Witnesses Lied," pp. 4–5. Included are photographs of the table and its markings.

199ff The entire affidavit from the Macy's employee was reprinted in the *National Guardian*, April 13, 1953, and in John Wexley, *The Judgment of Julius and Ethel Rosenberg* (Cameron & Kahn, N.Y., 1955), p. 644.

200ff Other affidavits offered in connection with the Section 2255 petition of June 1953 were those of Emanuel Bloch, Julius and Ethel Rosenberg, Leon Summit, Rev. H. S. Williamson, David Rosenberg, Ethel Goldberg, and Sophie Rosenberg.

202 Prosecution affidavits from Macy's employees were discussed and reprinted in full by S. Andhil Fineberg, *The Rosenberg Case: Fact and Fiction* (Oceana Publications, 1953), pp. 83–87.

202n Malcolm Sharp, *Was Justice Done? The Rosenberg-Sobell Case* (Monthly Review Press, N.Y., 1956), dealt extensively with the "new evidence," pp. 111–37. The quoted statement appeared on p. 214 n.

202ff Judge Kaufman's adverse ruling on the Section 2255 petition on June 8, 1953, is filed at Foley Square.

203 Judge Kaufman's comment on the console-table evidence was made in the course of the Dec. 30, 1952, judicial clemency hearing, p. 53, filed at Foley Square.

203ff The events of June 15–16, 1950, were described by David Greenglass in his trial testimony.

204 Julius Rosenberg's FBI interview of June 16 was described by him in his trial testimony.

204ff The Rogge memos of June 16, 17, 19, and Aug. 23 quoted in these pages were included as exhibits to the Section 2255 petition of June 1953. All of the Rogge memos presented here were reprinted by John Wexley, *op. cit.*, pp. 637–42.

208 Ruth's pretrial meetings with the prosecution were recounted by her in her trial testimony.

210 Judge Kaufman's comments are from his adverse ruling on the Section 2255 petition, June 8, 1953.

211 Bernard Greenglass's affidavit was included as an exhibit to the Section 2255 petition of June 1953. It was reprinted by John Wexley, *op. cit.*, p. 645.

211 Judge Kaufman's statement is from his adverse ruling on the Section 2255 petition, June 8, 1953.

CHAPTER 20: ELEVENTH-HOUR FIGHT

237, n The White House demonstration was described in the N.Y. *Times*, June 15, 1953, p. 44. The *National Guardian*, June 22, 1953, estimated that thirteen thousand pickets had been present.

237ff Bloch's meeting with Justice Douglas on June 15 and Judge Kaufman's denial of Farmer's motion were reported in the N.Y. *Times*, June 16, 1953, p. 1.

238 The Rosenberg children's last visit with their parents was reported in the N.Y. *World-Telegram & Sun*, June 16, 1953, p. 2.

238 Irwin Edelman, *Freedom's Electrocution* (privately published, Nov. 1952).

238 Events in the Rosenberg case on June 16 were recounted by the N.Y. *Times*, June 17, 1953, p. 1.

239ff The second petition for Executive clemency was published in *The Testament of Ethel and Julius Rosenberg* (Cameron & Kahn, N.Y., Aug. 1954), pp. 217–22.

241 Paris *Le Monde*, June 17, 1953.

241 The offer of asylum by the Polish government was reported by the N.Y. *Times*, June 17, 1953, p. 1.

241n Washington *Post*, Dec. 6, 1953.

241 The text of the cable from the Dreyfus family appeared in *Le Monde*, June 18, 1953, p. 2.

241 Urey's June 12, 1953, telegram to the President was quoted in full by the House Committee on Un-American Activities, *Trial by Treason: The National Committee to Secure Justice for the Rosenbergs and Morton Sobell*, Aug. 25, 1956 (Government Printing Office, Washington, House Document No. 206), p. 33.

242 The clergymen's visit with the President was described in *The Progressive*, Sept. 1953, "A Mercy Call at the White House," by Bernard M. Loomer.

242 Dwight D. Eisenhower, *The White House Years: Mandate for Change, 1953–1956* (Doubleday & Co., N.Y., 1963), p. 225.

242 N.Y. *Times*, June 17, 1953, p. 1.

242ff Justice Douglas's ruling was printed by the N.Y. *Times*, June 18, 1953, p. 16.

243 Rep. Wheeler's resolutions were reported in the N.Y. *Times*, June 18, 1953, p. 1.

243 Attorney General Brownell is quoted from his "Application to Convene Court in Special Term and to Review Stay of Execution Granted by Mr. Justice Douglas or to Reconsider and Reaffirm This Court's Order of June 15, Denying a Stay."

244ff The originals of the final Rosenberg letters quoted in this chapter have been seen by the authors. They were obtained from attorney Gloria Agrin.

245 Robert J. Donovan, *Eisenhower: The Inside Story* (Harper & Brothers, N.Y., 1956), p. 45.

245 Emmet John Hughes, *The Ordeal of Power* (Atheneum, N.Y., 1963), p. 80.

245n From a letter from Leanora Layng, secretary to Herbert Brownell, May 24, 1963.

246 The Supreme Court decision vacating the stay was reported in the N.Y. *Times*, June 20, 1953, p. 1.

246 Reaction to the Supreme Court ruling in the House of Representatives was reported in the N.Y. *Herald Tribune*, June 20, 1953, p. 5.

246ff Individual opinions of the Justices (except for that of Justice Frankfurter) were printed in the N.Y. *Times*, June 20, 1953, p. 7.

247ff Justice Frankfurter's comments on the need for more time to invoke executive clemency were paraphrased in the N.Y. *World-Telegram & Sun*, June 19, 1953, p. 2, and quoted in a footnote to the Court's opinion (printed by the Court on July 16, 1953), p. 8.

248 Robert J. Donovan, *op. cit.*, pp. 45–46.

248ff The text of President Eisenhower's statement appeared in the N.Y. *Times*, June 20, 1953, p. 7.

249 The disposition of Bloch's telegram requesting an Executive clemency hearing was reported in the N.Y. *Times*, June 20, 1953, p. 8.

[249] The argument before Judge Kaufman regarding plans for the execution on the Jewish Sabbath was reported in the N.Y. *Times*, June 20, 1953, p. 6.

[250] Justice Jackson's opinion appeared in the N.Y. *Times*, June 20, 1953, p. 7.

[251ff] Daniel Marshall's argument before Judge Kaufman on June 19, 1953, was reported by the N.Y. *Times*, June 20, 1953, p. 6.

[251] The last-minute attempt by a number of attorneys, including Arthur Kinoy, to obtain a stay of execution from Court of Appeals Judges Swan and Frank was reported in the N.Y. *Times*, June 20, 1953, p. 6. The incident also was confirmed by another participant, attorney Marshall Perlin, in a conversation with the authors.

[252] Malcolm Sharp, who was with attorney Bloch during the hours prior to the executions, recounted the events in *Was Justice Done? The Rosenberg-Sobell Case* (Monthly Review Press, N.Y., 1956), pp. 168–71.

[252ff] Events in front of the White House on June 19, 1953, were described by Robert J. Donovan in the N.Y. *Herald Tribune*, June 20, 1953, p. 5.

[253] The executions were reported in the N.Y. *Times*, June 20, 1953, p. 1.

[253] Justice Frankfurter's final opinion was extensively quoted in the N.Y. *Times*, June 23, 1953, p. 16.

CHAPTER 21: POST-MORTEM DIALOGUES

[254] Portions of Sartre's *Libération* piece were published by the House Committee on Un-American Activities, *Trial by Treason: The National Committee to Secure Justice for the Rosenbergs and Morton Sobell*, Aug. 25, 1956 (Government Printing Office, Washington, House Document No. 206), p. 85; also by S. Andhil Fineberg, *The Rosenberg Case: Fact and Fiction* (Oceana Publications, 1953), p. viii; full text was published by the *National Guardian*, July 6, 1953.

[254ff] N.Y. *Times*, June 21, 1953, Section IV, p. 1.

[255] *Figaro*, June 23, 1953, "Torture by Hope," by François Mauriac.

[255] *America*, July 4, 1953, "Atomic-Age Executions," p. 353.

[256ff] *Bulletin of the Atomic Scientists*, Oct. 1953, pp. 319–20.

[259] *Bulletin of the Atomic Scientists*, Dec. 1953, p. 393.

CHAPTER 22: THE CRIME IN PERSPECTIVE

[262] The Dec. 30, 1952, judicial clemency hearing before Judge Kaufman is filed in the U. S. District Court for the Southern District of N.Y., at Foley Square (Cr. No. 134–245), p. 91.

[262] Eisenhower's statements in denial of Executive clemency were reported in the N.Y. *Herald Tribune*, Feb. 12, 1953, p. 1, and the N.Y. *Times*, June 20, 1953, p. 7.

[267] *Popular Science*, Feb. 1945, "The Bazooka's Grandfather," by Volta Torrey, pp. 65–67.

267 *Explosives Engineer*, July–Aug. 1945, "The Shaped Charge," pp. 160–63.

269ff *Scientific American*, May 1951, "Science and the Citizen," pp. 33–34.

269 The quotation "may have meant" is from *Time*, March 26, 1951, "The Greenglass Mechanism," p. 44.

269 Albuquerque *Tribune*, AP story by Howard W. Blakeslee, March 13, 1951.

269 *Time*, March 26, 1951, p. 44.

271ff *Manhattan District History: Project Y: The Los Alamos Project*, vol. 1, by David Hawkins, *Inception Until August 1945*; vol. 2, by Edith C. Truslow and Ralph Carlisle Smith, *August 1945 Through December 1946* (available from the Office of Technical Services, U. S. Dept. of Commerce, Washington, LAMS-2532).

273n Truslow and Smith, *op. cit.*, p. 97.

274 Santa Fe *New Mexican*, Aug. 7, 11, and 17, 1945.

274 The quotation regarding Greenglass's claim that the bomb was parachuted to earth comes from an AP story by Blakeslee printed in the Albuquerque *Tribune*, March 15, 1951.

274 Gordon Dean, *Report on the Atom* (Alfred A. Knopf, N.Y., second edition, 1959), p. 5.

275 *Scientific American*, May 1951, pp. 33–34.

275 Joint Congressional Committee on Atomic Energy, *Soviet Atomic Espionage*, April 1951 (Government Printing Office, Washington, 1951), p. 7.

275ff N Y *Times*, March 17, 1954, p. 5.

276 *Look*, Oct. 29, 1957, "The Atomic Bomb and Those Who Stole It," by Bill Davidson, p. 96.

276ff Irwin Edelman, *The Suppressed Facts in the Rosenberg-Sobell Case*, an unpublished manuscript. The Edelman-Beckerley correspondence is dated Oct. 29, 1955, and Nov. 17, 1955.

277 Letter to the authors from Judge Irving R. Kaufman, U. S. Court of Appeals, Second Circuit, June 15, 1962.

277n N.Y. *Times*, Dec. 30, 1948, p. 11.

280 Myles Lane quotation is from the N.Y. *Herald Tribune*, Oct. 13, 1957, p. 26.

280 Chicago *Tribune* headline appeared Oct. 18, 1957.

281 N.Y. *Times*, Nov. 22, 1957, p. 9.

281 Philadelphia *News*, Nov. 22, 1957.

281 N.Y. *Herald Tribune* editorial on satellite secrets, "Which Path Do We Choose?", appeared Nov. 23, 1957, p. 10.

282 Pres. Kennedy's Congressional message was printed in the N.Y. *Times*, March 29, 1961.

CHAPTER 23: IN SEARCH OF A SPY RING

283 Hoover's description of Julius Rosenberg is from a Department of Justice press release (dated July 17, 1950). The release is attached as an exhibit to an appeal made under Section 2255 on behalf of the Rosenbergs and Sobell on Nov. 24, 1952, and filed at the U. S. District Court for the Southern District of N.Y., at Foley Square (Cr. No. 134–245).

283ff The prosecutor called Slack's crime a "single, isolated violation" during his sentencing hearing, on Sept. 18, 1950, in Greeneville, Tenn., p. 12. Slack's statement explaining his guilty plea was made during the June 10, 1952, hearing on an appeal, in Knoxville, Tenn., p. 84. The records in the Slack case are stored at the Federal Records Center in Chicago (Cr. No. 5593, in the U. S. District Court for the Eastern District of Tenn.). The authors have a complete copy of Slack's court record.

284 The Brothman-Moskowitz trial record is on file at the U. S. District Court for the Southern District of N.Y., at Foley Square (Cr. No. 133–106).

284 Judge Ryan's opinion in the Vago case was delivered on June 20, 1952 (Cr. No. 133–236), in the U. S. District Court for the Southern District of N.Y., at Foley Square. The quoted excerpts are on pp. 20–21.

286 N.Y. Times, March 16, 1951, p. 8.

286 N.Y. World-Telegram & Sun, March 15, 1951, p. 1.

288 The Dec. 30, 1952, judicial clemency hearing before Judge Kaufman is filed at the U. S. District Court for the Southern District of N.Y., at Foley Square (Cr. No. 134–245), p. 93.

288 Time, Feb. 23, 1953, "Mercy and Justice," p. 24.

288ff The Perl trial began May 18, 1953, before Judge Sylvester J. Ryan. The transcript is filed at the U. S. District Court for the Southern District of N.Y., at Foley Square (Cr. No. 135–43).

292 N.Y. Times, June 21, 1953, Section IV.

292 N.Y. Times, Oct. 16, 1953, p. 1.

293 Roy Cohn bylined a series of articles for the N.Y. Journal-American beginning July 25, 1954. The quotation on Monmouth appeared July 27, 1954, p. 1.

293ff Greenglass's deposition to the Senate Subcommittee on Investigations of the Committee on Government Operations is appended to the transcript of the Army Signal Corps Hearings—Subversion & Espionage (Government Printing Office, Washington, 1954), part 1, Nov. 24, 1953, pp. 19–22.

294 The Washington Post article on Monmouth, by Murrey Marder, appeared Dec. 12, 1953, p. 11.

294 Bulletin of the Atomic Scientists, Jan. 1954, "The Fort Monmouth Story," by Murrey Marder, pp. 21–25.

295 The quoted excerpt from McCarthy's questioning of a witness appears in the transcript of the Army Signal Corps Hearings, op. cit., part 1, testimony of Harry A. Hyman, Nov. 25, 1953, p. 43.

295 The headline "Monmouth Figure Linked to Hiss Ring" appeared in the N.Y. Times, Oct. 27, 1953, p. 18.

295 The story headlined "Radar Witness Breaks Down; Will Tell All About Spy Ring" appeared in the N.Y. Times, Oct. 17, 1953, p. 1. The witness's rebuttal was reported in the Times, Nov. 17, 1953, p. 25.

296 N.Y. Herald Tribune, Dec. 7, 1953, "The Scandal at Fort Monmouth," by Walter Millis, p. 4.

[296] The quoted passage on CCNY graduates is from a series on Monmouth that appeared in the Newark, N.J., *Evening News* by staff correspondent John O. Davies, Jr., Dec. 21, 1953.

[296] N.Y. *Times*, May 3, 1957, p. 14.

[297n] The information about Barr's employment is from the Senate Subcommittee to Investigate the Administration of the Internal Security Act of the Committee on the Judiciary, *Hearings—Scope of Soviet Activity in the United States* (Government Printing Office, Washington, 1958), part 87, Nov. 21, 1957.

[298] *Nation*, Nov. 2, 1957, editorial, "Preview of a White Paper."

[298] The FBI report on Glassman's visit to Perl appears in a publication of the Senate Internal Security subcommittee, *Expose of Soviet Espionage*, May 1960, prepared by the FBI (Government Printing Office, Senate Document No. 114, Washington, 1960), p. 21.

[302ff] From a letter to the authors from Justice Department attorney Benjamin F. Pollack, March 22, 1962.

[303] The case of the former UNESCO employee is reviewed by the Senate Internal Security subcommittee, *Internal Security Annual Report for 1956* (Government Printing Office, Senate Report No. 131, Washington, 1956), pp. 282–83.

[303ff] All records in the Dayton case are on file at the Supreme Court in Washington (Dayton *vs.* Dulles, Supreme Court, No. 621, Oct. Term, 1957).

CHAPTER 24: ELIZABETH BENTLEY

[309] Bentley's autobiography is entitled *Out of Bondage* (Devin-Adair Co., N.Y., 1951).

[309ff] Quotations are all from Bentley's autobiography, *op. cit.*, pp. 92, 93, 111, and 113.

[310] Department of Justice actions against World Tourists and Golos were reported in the N.Y. *Times* during 1939 and 1940.

[310] A reference to Brothman and the quotation "odd jobs" appear in Bentley's autobiography, *op. cit.*, pp. 130–31.

[310] Brothman's explanation of his dealings with Bentley is contained in the record of his trial, filed at the U. S. District Court for the Southern District of N.Y., at Foley Square (Cr. No. 133/106).

[310ff] The Bentley quotations "went . . . underground" and "to tell them my story" are from her testimony at the Rosenberg-Sobell trial.

[311] Proof that Bentley's August 1945 visit to FBI offices in New Haven concerned a matter unconnected with espionage was contained in an Oct. 8, 1945, letter from a N.Y. FBI agent to Bentley. The letter was entered as an exhibit and discussed at the first (1951) Remington trial. Transcripts of both Remington trials are filed at the U. S. District Court for the Southern District of N.Y., at Foley Square (Cr. No. 132–344 and 136–289).

311ff Bentley's claims that she was under FBI instructions in meeting Gromov in Oct. 1945 are elaborated in the House Committee on Un-American Activities *Hearings Regarding Communist Espionage in the U. S. Government* (Government Printing Office, Washington, 1948), testimony of Elizabeth Bentley, p. 814.

312 Hoover's Nov. 8, 1945, letter was disclosed before the Senate Subcommittee to Investigate the Administration of the Internal Security Act of the Committee on the Judiciary, *Hearings on Interlocking Subversion in Government Departments* (Government Printing Office, Washington, 1953), part 16, testimony of Attorney General Brownell, Nov. 17, 1953, pp. 1113–14. Hoover's identification of Bentley as the "highly confidential source" referred to in the letter appears on p. 1143.

312 The quoted excerpt from Hoover's second communication regarding Bentley's accusations, dated Nov. 27, 1945, may be found in the Senate Internal Security subcommittee publication, *Report on Interlocking Subversion in Government Departments*, July 30, 1953 (Government Printing Office, Washington, 1953), p. 3.

313 The telephone call to Thomas was reported by Robert E. Stripling, *The Red Plot Against America* (Bell Publishing Co., Drexel Hill, Pa., 1949), edited by Bob Considine, p. 92.

314 Herbert L. Packer, *Ex-Communist Witnesses—Four Studies in Fact Finding* (Stanford University Press, Stanford, Calif., 1962), p. 84.

314 The testimony of the two former Devin-Adair employees occurred in the first Remington trial; see also the *Nation*, Dec. 28, 1957, "The Remington Tragedy: A Study of Injustice," by Fred J. Cook, pp. 486–500.

314n Brunini's questioning of Ann Remington was reprinted in Court of Appeals Judge Learned Hand's 1953 dissenting opinion on the case and is filed at Foley Square.

315 Herbert L. Packer, *op. cit.*, p. 90.

317 Hoover's endorsement of Bentley appears in the Senate Internal Security subcommittee *Hearings on Interlocking Subversion, op. cit.*, Nov. 17, 1953, p. 1145.

317ff Herbert L. Packer, *op. cit.*, pp. 113 and 114.

318ff The brief submitted to the International Organizations Employees Loyalty Board by William Henry Taylor on March 28, 1955, was made available to the authors by Taylor's attorney, Byron N. Scott, of Washington, D.C.

321 The allegedly forged letter used as evidence against Taylor was discussed in the *Nation*, Jan. 5, 1957, "The Letter That Nobody Wrote," by Byron N. Scott, pp. 5–11.

321ff V. Frank Coe's statement before the Senate Internal Security subcommittee may be found in *Hearings on Scope of Soviet Activity in the United States* (Government Printing Office, Washington, 1956), part 42, May 15, 1956.

322 Other comments in defense of Harry D. White appear in a volume privately printed in 1956 by his sister, Bessie White Bloom, from a manuscript, *Harry D. White—Loyal American*, by his brother, Nathan I. White.

CHAPTER 25: MORTON SOBELL

323ff Biographical information on these pages was derived primarily from trial testimony of Max Elitcher; Mrs. Morton Sobell confirmed many of the details in conversation with the authors.

325 The contractual letter from the Rogge law firm to the Elitchers was dated July 26, 1950. No information about it or about other Rogge office material referred to in this chapter was obtained from any past or present member of the law firm.

326 Max Elitcher described his testimony before the grand jury on August 14, 1950, in a report to his attorney.

326 The Aug. 3, 1950, complaint against Morton Sobell was reprinted in the published Rosenberg-Sobell trial transcript, pp. 25–26.

326 The court papers relating to Sobell's request for a bill of particulars appeared in the published trial transcript, pp. 12–24.

326 The incident regarding the Elitchers' receipt of various personal possessions from the Sobell home was recounted to the authors by Mrs. Sobell and also was mentioned in a statement from Mrs. Elitcher to her attorney.

326ff N.Y. *Daily News*, March 9, 1951, p. 3.

327 The Rogge interoffice memo relating to Elitcher's future employment appeared in John Wexley, *The Judgment of Julius and Ethel Rosenberg* (Cameron & Kahn, N.Y., 1955), pp. 643–44.

328 N.Y. *Daily News*, Aug. 19, 1950, p. 2.

328 *Newsweek*, Aug. 28, 1950, "Atom Arrest No. 8," p. 30.

328 *Time*, Aug. 28, 1950, "Detour," p. 14.

328 N.Y. *Post*, Aug. 18, 1950, p. 2.

328 N.Y. *Daily News*, Aug. 19, 1950, p. 2.

328 N.Y. *Times* stories on Sobell's arrest quoted here appeared Aug. 19, 1950, p. 1; and Aug. 20, 1950, p. 23.

329ff Sobell's affidavit alleging that he was kidnaped from Mexico was reprinted in the published trial transcript, pp. 1591–93.

331 John Godwin, *Alcatraz: 1868–1963* (Doubleday & Co., N.Y., 1963), p. 168.

331ff Sobell's Sept. 1953 affidavit was reprinted by John Wexley, *op. cit.*, pp. 652–54.

334 Some of this documentary evidence relating to Sobell's trip to Mexico was included with an appeal filed by the Sobell defense in May 1956; see also John Wexley, *op. cit.*, pp. 649–51, 655–57.

335n From a letter from Jack F. Lepre, vice-president of Reeves Instrument Co., dated Jan. 22, 1963.

335, n Mrs. Elitcher's memo to her attorney described a conversation with Mrs. Danziger of Sept. 20, 1950.

336 Sobell's May 1956 appeal charging expulsion from Mexico without knowledge of Mexican immigration authorities is filed at the U. S. District Court for the Southern District of N.Y., at Foley Square (Cr. No. 134–245).

338ff The letter from Morton Sobell quoted here was sent from Atlanta Penitentiary April 21, 1963.

340ff A printed record of the proceedings of Sobell's May 1956 petition in Federal District Court was presented by the defense to the Second Circuit Court of Appeals (Oct. 1956 Term) and is filed at Foley Square. For U. S. Attorney Paul William's quoted remarks see p. 192; Judge Kaufman's appear on p. 194.

341n N.Y. Times, June 26, 1956, editorial page.

341 Chicago Tribune, Oct. 12, 1957, p. 1.

341ff U.S. vs. Rudolf I. Abel began Oct. 15, 1957; the transcript is filed at the U. S. District Court for the Eastern District of N.Y. (Cr. No. 45094). References to Mrs. Sobell are on pp. 245-55.

342 The quoted story on the Abel trial appeared in the N.Y. Times, Oct. 18, 1957, p. 1; Mrs. Sobell's response to Hayhanen's testimony was printed in the Times, Oct. 16, 1957.

342 Sobell's attorneys' memorandum to the Supreme Court regarding the Look article was quoted in the Washington Star, Oct. 18, 1957, p. B-10.

342 Milwaukee Journal, Nov. 9, 1957.

CHAPTER 26: DAVID AND RUTH GREENGLASS

344 Greenglass's behavior at his arraignment was described by the N.Y. Times, June 17, 1950, p. 1.

344 Ruth Greenglass's interview with David's attorneys was reported in a Rogge interoffice memo dated June 19, 1950; the memo was entered as an exhibit to the Section 2255 petition of June 1953 and reprinted by John Wexley, The Judgment of Julius and Ethel Rosenberg (Cameron & Kahn, N.Y., 1955), pp. 639-40.

344ff David's report to his attorneys written June 17, 1950, was an exhibit to the June 1953 Section 2255 petition and was reprinted by John Wexley, op. cit., pp. 637-39.

345ff Greenglass's deposition to the Senate Subcommittee on Investigations of the Committee on Government Operations was read into the record of the Army Signal Corps Hearings–Subversion & Espionage (Government Printing Office, Washington, 1954), part 1, Nov. 24, 1953, pp. 19-22.

346ff Greenglass testified before the Senate Subcommittee to Investigate the Administration of the Internal Security Act of the Committee on the Judiciary, Hearings—Scope of Soviet Activity in the United States (Government Printing Office, Washington, 1956), part 21, April 27, 1956, pp. 1089-1111.

348 N.Y. Times, Oct. 27, 1957, p. 28.

348ff Robert Morris reported on his conversation with Greenglass to the Senate Internal Security subcommittee, Hearings—Scope of Soviet Activity in the United States (Government Printing Office, Washington, 1958), part 87, Nov. 21, 1957.

[349] O. John Rogge, *Why Men Confess* (Thomas Nelson & Sons, N.Y., 1959).

[356] The Rogge interoffice memo relating to fingerprint tests on the paper wrapper, dated Aug. 23, 1950, was an exhibit to the June 1953 Section 2255 petition and was reprinted by John Wexley, *op. cit.*, pp. 641–42.

[359] Ruth Greenglass's comments to her husband's attorneys about the Feb. FBI interview were reported in the Rogge interoffice memo dated June 19, 1950, cited above.

[359] *Look*, Oct. 29, 1957, "The Atomic Bomb and Those Who Stole It," by Bill Davidson, p. 90.

[359] Don Whitehead, *The FBI Story* (Random House, N.Y., 1956), p. 312.

[360] David's June 17, 1950, report to his attorneys is cited above.

[360] Robert Ruark's piece on Greenglass appeared in the N.Y. *World-Telegram & Sun*, Jan. 4, 1961, p. 29.

[360] Benjamin Pollack's remarks on Greenglass are quoted from a conversation that one of the authors held with him at his Department of Justice office.

[361n] N.Y. *Times*, Aug. 23, 1950, p. 1.

[361] N.Y. *Post* ran a story on Ruth Greenglass's accident, including an appeal for blood, on Feb. 15, 1950, p. 20.

[361n] The letter referred to was addressed to Mrs. Morton Sobell on Nov. 17, 1962, by one Leonard I. Tosi.

[362] The quotations are from the June 19, 1950, Rogge interoffice memo regarding a meeting with Ruth Greenglass, cited above.

CHAPTER 27: HARRY GOLD

[363] N.Y. *Times* headline, March 16, 1951, p. 1; excerpts from Gold's testimony, p. 9.

[363ff] The perjury trial of U.S. *vs.* Benjamin Smilg was held at the U. S. District Court in Dayton, Ohio, June 13–18, 1955. A partial transcript of the trial (including testimony of Gold and Smilg and the prosecutor's summation) is in the possession of the authors.

[365] The newspaperwoman whose comments on Gold's testimony are quoted here is Mary McGrory, Washington *Star*, April 27, 1956, p. A-3.

[365ff] Gold testified before the Senate Subcommittee to Investigate the Administration of the Internal Security Act of the Committee on the Judiciary, *Hearings—Scope of Soviet Activity in the United States* (Government Printing Office, Washington, 1956), part 20, April 26, 1956, pp. 1009–55.

[366] Rochester *Times Union*, Dec. 7, 1956.

[366] Gold's pretrial statements quoted in this chapter were reprinted as exhibits to his testimony by the Senate Internal Security subcommittee, *op. cit.*, pp. 1055–87.

[367] Gold's remarks regarding the value of the material allegedly received from Greenglass appear in his pretrial statements reprinted by the Senate Internal Security subcommittee, *op. cit.*, pp. 1058, 1085.

367 S. Andhil Fineberg, *The Rosenberg Case: Fact and Fiction* (Oceana Publications, 1953), p. 14.

367 Dwight D. Eisenhower, *The White House Years: Mandate for Change, 1953–1956* (Doubleday & Co., N.Y., 1963), pp. 223–24.

368 *Look*, Oct. 29, 1957, "The Atomic Bomb and Those Who Stole It," by Bill Davidson, p. 90.

368 Gold's pretrial admissions that he had originally forgotten all about Greenglass were published by the Senate Internal Security subcommittee, *op. cit.*, pp. 1084, 1085, and 1085 n.

369 Gold discussed Yakovlev in a pretrial statement reprinted by the Senate Internal Security subcommittee, *op. cit.*, pp. 1071 and 1076.

369 Yakovlev's age appeared on a Department of State document entered at the trial as prosecution Exhibit 15. Portions of this document were read into the trial record.

369 Records from United States Lines relating to Yakovlev and his family were introduced at the trial as prosecution Exhibit 26. Portions of the exhibit were read into the trial record; the full exhibit was examined by the authors at the U. S. Courthouse at Foley Square.

370 Gold's pretrial statement reprinted by the Senate Internal Security subcommittee, *op. cit.*, contains the quoted remarks on p. 1087.

CHAPTER 28: THE SCENE OF THE CRIME

371 The swearing out of the complaint against Greenglass in New Mexico was described in the Albuquerque *Tribune*, June 16, 1950, p. 1.

371 The complaint and indictment voted against Greenglass in New Mexico are filed at the U. S. District Court, Albuquerque, N.M. (Cr. No. 15938).

372 The complaint against Julius Rosenberg is filed at the U. S. District Court for the Southern District of N.Y., at Foley Square (Cr. No. 134–245).

372 Hoover's statement regarding Rosenberg's alleged crime is attached as an exhibit to the Section 2255 appeal motion of Nov. 24, 1952, filed at Foley Square.

374ff Gold's pretrial statement quoted here was reprinted as an exhibit to his testimony before the Senate Subcommittee to Investigate the Internal Security Act of the Committee on the Judiciary, *Hearings—Scope of Soviet Activity in the United States* (Government Printing Office, Washington, 1956), part 20, April 26, 1956, pp. 1083–84.

375 From a March 24, 1961, letter to the authors from Joseph A. Weber, industrial relations manager, Pennsylvania Sugar Division of the National Sugar Refining Co., Philadelphia, Pa.

375 Gold's attorneys made available to the authors an interoffice memo from their files, dated July 14, 1950, that relates in part to their research concerning Gold's employment records at the sugar company.

376 The quotation regarding the secrets passed at the Freemans' house appeared in the Albuquerque *Tribune*, Nov. 10, 1960, p. B-1.

CHAPTER 29: THE HILTON HOTEL CARD

[380] N.Y. *Times*, March 17, 1951, p. 6.
[380] *U.S. News & World Report*, April 6, 1951, "Spies in U.S. Told Russia All," p. 13.
[380] Justin Atholl, *How Stalin Knows* (Pocket Book edition printed by Jarrold & Sons Ltd., Norwich, England, 1951), p. 101.
[380] Oliver Pilat, *The Atom Spies* (G. P. Putnam's Sons, N.Y., 1952), p. 4.
[383] The Albuquerque *Tribune* story regarding FBI agents' search of the Hilton records appeared Feb. 28, 1959.
[383] A list of witnesses before the New Mexico grand jury that indicted Greenglass appeared in the Albuquerque *Tribune*, July 6, 1950.
[384] The transcript of Gold's Dec. 7, 1950, sentencing hearing is filed at the U. S. District Court for the Eastern District of Pennsylvania, in Philadelphia (Cr. No. 15769). For Gleeson's reference to Gold's September Hilton registration, see p. 9.
[384] Gold's September Hilton registration was discussed in John Wexley, *The Judgment of Julius and Ethel Rosenberg* (Cameron & Kahn, N.Y., 1955), pp. 407–10.
[389] Written accounts of the Gold story mentioned here are: *Reader's Digest*, May 1951, "The Crime of the Century," by J. Edgar Hoover; Don Whitehead, *The FBI Story* (Random House, N.Y., 1956); and *Look*, Oct. 29, 1957, "The Atomic Bomb and Those Who Stole It," by Bill Davidson.
[389n] Gold's mention of providing handwriting samples for the FBI is from his pretrial statement reprinted as an exhibit to his testimony before the Senate Subcommittee to Investigate the Administration of the Internal Security Act of the Committee on the Judiciary, *Hearings—Scope of Soviet Activity in the United States* (Government Printing Office, Washington, 1956), part 20, April 26, 1956, p. 1080.
[390n] The dates of Greenglass's furlough were supplied to the authors by Edward A. Connolly, Public Relations Office, University of California, Los Alamos Scientific Laboratory, Los Alamos, N.M.

CHAPTER 30: MONEY FROM THE RUSSIANS

[391] The transcript of the Dec. 30, 1952, hearing on judicial clemency is filed at the U. S. District Court for the Southern District of N.Y., at Foley Square (Cr. No. 134–245), p. 21.
[393] Albuquerque *Tribune* stories dating Ruth's OPA employment appeared on March 16 and 29, 1951.
[393] The amount of rent paid by the Greenglasses for their Albuquerque apartment was noted in the Albuquerque *Tribune*, Nov. 10, 1961, p. B-1, and confirmed to the authors by the Greenglasses' former landlords, Mr. and Mrs. W. B. Freeman, of Albuquerque, N.M.

[395] David's pretrial letter quoted here was included as an exhibit to the Section 2255 petition of June 1953. It was reprinted by John Wexley, *The Judgment of Julius and Ethel Rosenberg* (Cameron & Kahn, N.Y., 1955), p. 637.

CHAPTER 32: PUTTING THE PIECES TOGETHER

[405] The Hoover quotation is from his article in the *Reader's Digest*, May 1951, "The Crime of the Century," p. 158. The date on which Hoover received this information was revealed by Don Whitehead, *The FBI Story* (Random House, N.Y., 1956), p. 305.

[405] The Don Whitehead quotation is from *The FBI Story*, op. cit., p. 305. Don Whitehead, op. cit., Foreword.

[406] Alan Moorehead, *The Traitors* (Hamish Hamilton, London, 1952), p. 54.

[406] From a letter to the authors from Dr. Rudolph E. Peierls, Feb. 6, 1963.

[406] Hoover is quoted from the *Reader's Digest*, op. cit., p. 159.

[407] Gold described his eighteen hours of FBI interviews (between May 15 and May 21) in his Oct. 11, 1950, report to Hamilton entitled "The Circumstances Surrounding My Work as a Soviet Agent," reprinted by the Senate Subcommittee to Investigate the Administration of the Internal Security Act of the Committee on the Judiciary, *Hearings— Scope of Soviet Activity in the United States* (Government Printing Office, Washington, 1956) part 20, April 26, 1956, pp. 1079–81.

[407] Hoover described the search of Gold's bedroom in the *Reader's Digest*, op. cit., p. 166.

[407] Gold's comment about the Santa Fe map appeared in his Oct. 11, 1950, report to Hamilton, op. cit., p. 1083.

[408] Gold enumerated the hours of his FBI interrogation in a document entitled "Interviews with Agents T. Scott Miller, Jr., and Richard E. Brennan of the F.B.I." This report was among the papers received by the authors from Gold's attorneys.

[408] Gold's comments to Judge McGranery regarding appointment of counsel are from his May 31, 1950, hearing before Judge McGranery in Philadelphia, Pa., p. 3.

[409] Gold's reference to "the authenticity and the enormity of my crime" appeared in his Oct. 11, 1950, report to Hamilton, op. cit., p. 1087.

[410n] The Smilg perjury trial was held at the U. S. District Court in Dayton, Ohio, June 13–18, 1955. A partial transcript is in the possession of the authors.

[411] The reference to Abraham Brothman's interest in having the Russians legitimately purchase his engineering designs is based on Gold's statement to Hamilton in the recorded conversation of June 8, 1950.

[412] Gold termed the Slack RDX data "sketchy" in a recorded conversation with Hamilton, June 8, 1950.

[412] The quoted statement of Slack's attorney appeared in the transcript of a June 10, 1952, hearing on Slack's motion for a new trial in the U. S.

District Court for the Eastern District of Tennessee, at Knoxville (Cr. No. 15347), p. 468.

412 Gold told Hamilton that he gave the RDX to "Sam" in a recorded interview, June 8, 1950. He said "John" had been the recipient in the June 15, 1950, "Chronology of Work for Soviet Union." This "Chronology" was reprinted by the Senate Internal Security subcommittee, *op. cit.*, p. 1057.

412n Slack testified regarding the RDX information and sample he had given Gold during the 1952 hearing on his motion for a new trial, pp. 119–25.

412 Gold told Hamilton of the Russians warning him to discontinue work with Slack in the recorded interview of June 8, 1950.

412 The quotations regarding the material found in Gold's cellar are from a recorded interview with Hamilton, June 23, 1950.

412ff Gold's autobiographical statement is entitled "The Early Life of Harry Gold—A Report" and is dated Oct. 23, 1950. This report was among the papers received by the authors from Gold's attorneys. The quoted passage on daydreaming is on pp. 29–30.

413 Gold called Fuchs a "genius" in his Oct. 11, 1950, report to Hamilton, *op. cit.*, p. 1077.

413n The quoted passage is from the document "The Early Life of Harry Gold—A Report," *op. cit.*, p. 30.

413 Gold's remarks on his alleged relationship with Fuchs are from a recorded interview with Hamilton, June 14, 1950.

413 J. Edgar Hoover's quoted comment regarding the Gold-Fuchs relationship appeared in the *Reader's Digest, op. cit.*, p. 155.

413ff Gold described his Sept. 1945 stay at Chicago's Palmer House Hotel in a recorded interview with Hamilton, June 14, 1950; his trip to the Illinois distilleries was described to Hamilton in a recorded interview, June 23, 1950, and in the Oct. 11, 1950, report, *op. cit.*, p. 1080; Gold's reference to business trips he made in 1945 occurred in the Brothman-Moskowitz trial.

414 Gold referred to his lack of funds on the Sept. 1945 trip in a recorded interview with Hamilton, June 14, 1950; he told of wiring a friend for money from Albuquerque in his Oct. 11, 1950, report, *op. cit.*, pp. 1077–78.

414 Gold's interest in the Southwest was expressed by him in the Oct. 11, 1950, report, *op. cit.*, p. 1083.

414 Sir Percy Sillitoe, *Cloak Without Dagger* (Cassell & Co., Ltd., London, 1955), p. 165.

414 Hoover is quoted from his *Reader's Digest* article, *op. cit.*, p. 158.

414ff Don Whitehead, *op. cit.*, p. 305.

415 Gold told Hamilton about the FBI's use of maps and movies in the recorded interview of June 14, 1950; he told of the selection of the Greenglasses' names from a list in the Oct. 11, 1950, report, *op. cit.*, p. 1085 n.

416 Greenglass's statement that he had given Gold the names of people from Los Alamos was reported in a Rogge interoffice memo dated June 16. This memo was included as an exhibit to the Section 2255 peti-

tion of June 1953. It was reprinted by John Wexley, *The Judgment of Julius and Ethel Rosenberg* (Cameron & Kahn, N.Y., 1955), p. 637.

416ff Gold's quoted comments on the information he received from Greenglass are from his "Chronology of Work for Soviet Union," *op. cit.*, p. 1058. (The inaccurate dating of this document, as published by the Senate Internal Security subcommittee, is explained on p. 398 n of this book.)

417 Greenglass's letter to his attorney in which he remarked that he "made sure to tell the F.B.I." appeared in the Rogge memo of June 17. It was included in the 1953 Section 2255 petition and was printed by John Wexley, *op. cit.*, p. 637.

418 Gold mentioned to Hamilton the phrase "Benny sent me" in the recorded interview of June 14, 1950; Greenglass mentioned the "piece of card" in the June 17, 1950, letter to his attorney, cited above.

418 Rosenberg was quoted regarding the jello box in the N.Y. *Times*, July 20, 1950, p. 18.

418 The reference to the Sidoroviches being "persecuted" is from an interview by the authors with Ann Sidorovich.

418 William Perl's quoted remark appeared in the transcript of his trial, which began on May 18, 1953, at the U. S. District Court for the Southern District of N.Y., at Foley Square (Cr. No. 135–43).

418 Weldon Bruce Dayton's quoted remark appeared in his testimony before a 1955 Board of Passport Appeals and is filed at the U. S. Supreme Court (Dayton *vs.* Dulles, No. 621, Oct. Term, 1957).

418ff The coin collection container is among the Rosenberg trial exhibits retained at the U. S. Courthouse at Foley Square.

420 Gold's undelivered speech to the court, dated July 20, 1950, was among the papers obtained by the authors from Gold's attorneys.

420 Gold's statement to Hamilton that he never had taken any money from the Soviets is from the recorded interview of June 6, 1950.

420 Gold's admission to Hamilton that he had perjured himself before a grand jury was made during the recorded interview of Aug. 9, 1950.

420n Gold's "Money Accounting of My Espionage Work," dated Dec. 3, 1950, was among the papers obtained by the authors from Gold's attorneys.

421 Gold told how FBI agents found it "incredible" that he had not been urged to flee, and added the incidents of late 1949 and early 1950 to his narrative, in a recorded interview with Hamilton, Aug. 9, 1950.

421ff Gold's elaboration of the meeting where he allegedly had seen Julius Rosenberg appeared in his Oct. 11, 1950, report to Hamilton, *op. cit.*, p. 1085.

422 Gold's story about seeing Rosenberg through a restaurant window was recounted by him to Senate Internal Security subcommittee staff member, Ben Mandel, on Oct. 15, 1957. A memo from Mandel to Robert Morris reporting this interview with Gold is dated Oct. 16, 1957, and is reprinted in *Hearings on Scope of Soviet Activities*, part 86.

422 Gold's correspondence with John D. M. Hamilton was among the papers obtained by the authors. Gold conveyed a message from Saypol in a

letter of Nov. 30, 1950; the quoted phrases are from two separate letters Gold wrote on April 11, 1951.

423 N.Y. *Times*, March 16, 1951, p. 1.

424 *Time*, March 26, 1951, "My Friend, Yakovlev," p. 26.

424 Hamilton's letter to Gold regarding the *Time* interpretation of his trial testimony was dated March 22, 1951; Gold's reply was written March 24, 1951.

424ff Gold's letter to Hamilton from Lewisburg Penitentiary was dated Oct. 5, 1953.

425 N.Y. *Times*, Nov. 17, 1960, p. 20.

425 J. Edgar Hoover, *F.B.I. Law Enforcement Bulletin*, vol. 30, June 1961.

427 The Court of Appeals opinion was appended to the trial transcript published by the Committee to Secure Justice for Morton Sobell. The quotation about Sobell is on p. 1665. The appeal decision is also on file in the U.S. District Court for the Southern District of N.Y., at Foley Square.

428 Letter from William Kunstler to J. Edgar Hoover, Aug. 31, 1965, and reply from Hoover, Sept. 10, 1965.

428 Letter from William Kunstler to J. Edgar Hoover, Nov. 23, 1965, and reply from Hoover, Dec. 2, 1965.

428 Letter from William Kunstler to the Internal Security Division of the Department of Justice, Dec. 7, 1965, and reply from Assistant Attorney General J. Walter Yeagley (by John H. Davitt, Chief of the Criminal Section), Dec. 22, 1965.

429 Letter from William Kunstler to John H. Davitt, Jan. 19, 1966.

429 The quotation regarding *Invitation to an Inquest* appeared in Assistant Attorney General Yeagley's letter of Dec. 22, 1965.

429ff Letter to J. Edgar Hoover from William Kunstler, Feb. 16, 1966, and reply from Hoover, Feb. 25, 1966.

430 Answering letter to William Kunstler from Assistant Attorney General J. Walter Yeagley, Feb. 28, 1966.

430 Letters to J. Edgar Hoover and John Davitt from William Kunstler, June 29, 1966.

430 Letter from the Department of Justice stating that the June card had been destroyed "in 1957" was dated July 14, 1966.

430 *Look*, Oct. 29, 1957, "The Atomic Bomb and Those Who Stole It," by Bill Davidson.

431 John Wexley, *The Judgment of Julius and Ethel Rosenberg* (Cameron & Kahn, N.Y., 1955).

431 One of the authors interviewed Jack Rosenthal by telephone in Aug. 1966.

431 Attorneys Kunstler and Perlin moved the U.S. District Court for the Southern District of N.Y. at Foley Square on March 15, 1966, to unseal Exhibit 8 (Cr. No. 134–245).

[431] Judge Palmieri ordered Exhibit 8 and related Greenglass testimony unsealed on Apr. 14, 1966 (Cr. No. 134–245).

[431] Assistant U.S. Attorney Martin's reference to an AEC consultation was made during a hearing where copies of the impounded material were turned over to Sobell's attorneys, on Apr. 29, 1966. A transcript is filed at the U.S. District Court for the Southern District of N.Y. at Foley Square (66 Civ. 1328).

[431ff] Perlin's affidavit with impounded material attached was field at the U.S. District Court for the Southern District of N.Y. at Foley Square, on July 25, 1966 (Cr. No. 134–245).

[432] *In camera* proceedings referred to include a hearing before Judge David N. Edelstein (part of which was conducted in open court) on July 26, 1966, and hearings before Judge Edmund Palmieri on July 27 and 29, 1966. The transcripts of these proceedings are filed at the U.S. District Court for the Southern District of N.Y. at Foley Square (66 Civ. 1328).

[432] N.Y. *Times*, July 26, 1966, story by Sidney E. Zion, p. 17.

[432] The hearing where Perlin asked the government to produce the AEC correspondence was held on July 29, 1966, before Judge Palmieri. The transcript is filed at the U.S. District Court for the Southern District of N.Y. at Foley Square (66 Civ. 1328). Quotations cited appear on pp. 15, 18, 24–25, and 33.

[432] The government withdrew objection to the public dissemination of the impounded material in a hearing before Judge Palmieri on Aug. 3, 1966. The transcript is filed at the U.S. District Court for the Southern District of N.Y. at Foley Square (66 Civ. 1328).

[434] The Section 2255 petition on behalf of Sobell was filed at the U.S. District Court for the Southern District of N.Y., at Foley Square, on Aug. 22, 1966 (66 Civ. 1328). Attached are a number of affidavits and a copy of Exhibit 8.

[434n] N.Y. *Times*, May 19, 1966, reported Gold's release from prison.

[436] Oppenheimer's statement was contained in a letter to Eleanor Jackson Piel, Oct. 25, 1966; Urey's was given verbally to the attorneys and in a letter to the authors, Sept. 18, 1961.

[436] Judge Weinfeld's opinion of Feb. 14, 1967, is filed at the U.S. District Court for the Southern District of N.Y. at Foley Square.

[437] The government's 1951 brief to the U.S. Court of Appeals is filed at Foley Square (Cr. No. 134–245). The quotation appears on p. 11.

[438] Oral argument on Sobell's 2255 petition was held on Sept. 12, 1966, before Judge Weinfeld. The transcript is filed in the U.S. District Court for the Southern District of N.Y. at Foley Square (66 Civ. 1328). The excerpt from Kunstler's statement appears on pp. 65, 70–71.

[438ff] The quoted dialogue between Judge Weinfeld and Assistant U.S. Attorney King appears on pp. 117–20 in the transcript of the Sept. 12, 1966, oral argument.

[439] A discussion of the authors' interviews with four Hilton employees appears in the chapter on the Hilton Hotel card. See pp. 382–84 and 386n.

[439] Affidavit from Hilton Hotel manager John M. Amhart is dated Feb. 16, 1966.

[439] The government's statement regarding the "genuineness" of the June card appears in the Memorandum in Opposition to Amended Section 2255 Petition of Morton Sobell, filed in the U.S. District Court for the Southern District of N.Y. at Foley Square (66 Civ. 1328). The quotation is on p. 82.

[440n] Thurgood Marshall's disclosures to the Supreme Court were reported in the N.Y. *Times*, May 25, 1966.

[440] The statement that the hotel cards were obtained on "different dates" appears in the government Memorandum in Opposition to Amended Section 2255 Petition of Morton Sobell, p. 83.

[442] Chicago *Daily News*, Sept. 18, 1965, "History and the Rosenbergs," by Elmer Gertz.

[442] Cleveland *Plain Dealer*, Nov. 23, 1965, "Guilty or Not Guilty," by Wes Lawrence.

[442ff] St. Louis *Post-Dispatch*, Sept. 12, 1965, "The Rosenberg Case," by Harriett Woods.

[443] Indianapolis *News*, Oct. 2, 1965, " 'Inquest' into Rosenberg Case Raises some Reasonable Doubts," by Sexson Humphreys.

[443] Denver *Post*, Oct. 4, 1966, "New Look Needed in Sobell Case."

[443] *Nation*, Nov. 15, 1965, "I Come from Julius," by Fred J. Cook, p. 361.

[443] Des Moines *Register*, Sept. 1, 1965, "Doubts on Rosenberg Case."

[443] Los Angeles *Times*, Oct. 24, 1965, "Holding a Brief for Rosenbergs," by Richard G. Hubler.

[443] N.Y. *Post*, Oct. 7, 1965, "Out of the Past," by James A. Wechsler, p. 46.

[443] Washington *Star*, Aug. 19, 1965, "Were the Rosenbergs Guilty?," by Donald Mintz.

[443] *Newsweek*, Aug. 23, 1965, "Case of the 'Atom Spies,' " p. 82.

[443] *Yale Law Journal*, Vol. 76:222, 1966, book review by Leonard B. Boudin, p. 254.

[443] N.Y. *Review of Books*, Feb. 3, 1966, "The Strange Trial of the Rosenbergs," by Herbert L. Packer, p. 6.

INDEX

(R-S means Rosenberg-Sobell)

A. Brothman Associates, 90, 91, 100, 102, 104, 112, 138, 385, 414
Abel, Dorothy Printz, 131, 134, 144, 156, 164, 204 n, 373
Abel, Louis, 129, 134, 164, 204, 204 n, 356, 358
Abel, Rudolph Ivanovich, 341
Acheson, Dean, 57
Adams, Arthur, 48, 50
Adams, Sherman, 193
Adomian, Lan, 139, 164
Agrin, Gloria, 213
Alamogordo, N.M., 33, 263, 273
Albuquerque, N.M., June 3, 1945, meeting, 158, 263, 363, 371-77, 427, 431, 440; defense theory of, 153, 160, 372, 379, 437; FBI interrogation of Greenglass, D., 360-62, 415-17; FBI press release, 80, 372; flight warnings re arrests of Fuchs and Gold, 128, 131, 148, 346-47, 350, 358; Gold identification of Greenglasses, 367-69, 369 n, 370, 374-75, 400, 403, 415-16, 423; Gold planning meeting with Yakovlev, 136, 367-68, 373, 375, 398-400; Gold mentions of "Julius," 125, 136-37, 155, 160, 162, 206, 208, 350, 368, 373-74, 374 n, 401-3, 417-18, 441-42; Gold pretrial statements contrasted with R-S trial testimony, 366-69, 398-403, 423-24, 441-42; Gold R-S trial testimony, 136-37; Greenglass, D., attempt to retract confession, 78, 172, 362, 362 n, 417; in Greenglass complaint, 77, 371; in Greenglass indictment, 78, 371; in Greenglass pretrial memos, 204-8; in Greenglass, D., R-S trial testimony, 125-26; in Greenglass, R., R-S trial testimony, 131; information passed, 77-78, 126, 137, 161, 204-5, 261, 263-65, 265 n, 345, 360-72, 374, 416; payment of $500, 78, 80, 126, 131, 136-37, 139, 152, 155, 161, 205, 360, 373-74, 378, 391, 391 n, 392-95, 395 n, 396, 415-16; Rosenbergs and Greenglasses plan for, 80-81, 125, 131, 144, 149, 206, 285, 300, 372-73; in Saypol summation, 155-56; Yakovlev praise of Greenglass data, 137, 263, 367, 401-2, 424, 442. See also Hilton Hotel cards; Jello box

Albuquerque National Bank. See Bank records
Albuquerque Tribune, 371, 383, 393
Albuquerque Trust & Savings Bank, 392 n. See also Bank records of Greenglasses
Alcatraz Federal Penitentiary, 5, 179, 331, 342
Alsop, Joseph and Stewart, 54
Amerasia case, 71
America, 255
American Civil Liberties Union, 180
American Distilling Co., 413 n
American magazine, 44, 45
Amtorg Trading Corp., 91-93, 95-97, 100, 107, 310, 411, 412
Anderson, Carl, 10
Anti-missile missile. See Think machine
Anti-Semitism: Gold, motivated by, 112; Greenglass, R., comment on, 207; in Monmouth hearings, 296; Rosenberg, J., comment on, 144; in R-S case, 2, 179; scientists, flight from Nazis, 11
Arma Co., 346, 361
Army-McCarthy hearings, 86-87, 296
Army Signal Corps, U. S., 79, 143, 146-47, 214, 278-79, 293-96. See also Monmouth hearings
Army, U. S.: in atomic energy program, 18, 22, 27-28, 30-31, 33, 35-40, 43, 45, 48-49, 135
Arnhart, John M., 439
Arnold, Henry, 61, 63, 65
Aswan Dam, 348-49
Atholl, Justin, 380
Atlanta Constitution, 176
Atlanta Penitentiary, 320, 342
Atomic bomb, Soviet: first detected, 52; Fuchs's alleged contribution, 60, 67-68; predictions about, 28-30, 32-33, 38, 53-54; reactions in U.S., 52-56, 76, 188, 279, 405; Rosenbergs' alleged contribution, 170, 185, 271, 424
Atomic bomb, U.S.: design, 22, 60, gun-type, 25-26, 126, 267, 272, 274, implosion-type, 23-26, 126-27, 263-67, 269-73, 273 n, 274-75, 277, 433-35, 435 n, 436; Hiroshima bombing, 1, 33, 35, 38, 42, 50, 57, 187, 211, 274, 362; Nagasaki bombing, 23, 33, 38, 274; use on Japan debated, 30-33

Atomic bomb project, U.S., 20–26; attitude toward Russians, 28–32; British mission, 22, 25, 28, 59–60, 108; chain reaction, first sustained, 22; electromagnetic process, 24–25; gaseous diffusion, 21, 24–25, 60; secrecy, 23, 27–31, 35–40; thermal diffusion, 21. *See also* Hanford; Los Alamos; Met Lab; Oak Ridge

Atomic bomb secrets, comments on: Beckerley (AEC), 275–76; Bloch, E., 169, 185; Congressmen, 43–46, 53, 405; Eisenhower, 192, 248; Hoover, J. E., 405, 414, 425; Kaufman, 170; Lane, 185–86, 437; Marshall (AEC), 432; Saypol, 120, 155, 168; scientists, 37–40, 431–32, 435–36; Weinfeld, 436–37

Atomic Energy Act, 38–39, 46, 238, 243, 245–46, 276

Atomic Energy Commission, U. S. (AEC), 39, 45–46, 55–57, 60, 127, 169, 268, 270–71, 274–77, 406 n, 415, 431–32, 436

Atomic Energy for Military Purposes (Smyth Report), 36, 39, 42, 274

Atomic espionage alleged: before 1950, 41–50, 53, 55–56; Brothman, 83, 88, 90, 97–98, 106, 283 n, 284; Fuchs, 59–60, 64, 66–68, 75, 83, 108, 115, 135–37, 156, 283, 363, 366, 406, 406 n, 407, 413–14, 424; Gold, 75, 80, 82–83, 88, 107–8, 115, 125–26, 131, 135–37, 155–56, 185, 206, 261, 263–65, 265 n 283 n, 284, 296, 361, 363, 366–67, 372, 400–1, 407, 413–20, 424; Greenglass, D., 77–78, 80, 88, 120, 124–27, 131, 136–37, 143, 155–56, 185–86, 206, 257, 261, 262–65, 265 n, 266–77, 283 n, 296, 344, 347–48, 360–63, 366–67, 372, 400–1, 415–18, 424, 431–37; Greenglass, R., 124–27, 130–31, 136–37, 143, 155, 161, 206, 262–63, 296, 344, 347, 362, 372, 400–1, 417; Moskowitz, 83, 88, 90, 106, 283 n, 284; Rosenberg, E., 1, 83–84, 88, 120, 124–25, 127, 131, 149, 155, 157, 170, 176, 185–89, 206, 248, 254–55, 257, 261–62, 283 n, 296, 361, 372, 419, 432; Rosenberg, J., 1, 79–80, 88, 120, 124–27, 130–31, 143, 155–57, 161, 170, 176, 185–89, 206, 248, 254–55, 257, 261–77, 283 n, 296, 344, 347–48, 361, 372, 417–19, 432; Slack, 76–77, 85–86, 88, 182, 282, 283 n, 284; Sobell, 84, 88, 171, 182, 283 n, 331; Vago, 87–88, 283 n, 284

Atomic powered airplane, 127–28, 155, 159, 206, 278, 280–82, 285, 207, 344

Atomic research: Denmark, 8, 12; France, 7–8, 10, 13, 16; Germany, 7–8, 11, 14, 16; Great Britain, 8, 10, 17–19, 275; international character of, 9–10; Italy, 10–11; Japan, 16, 36–37; neutron, 10–13, 22, 274; secrecy, 9, 14, 27, 36–39; U.S., 10, 13, 15, 18, 37; U.S.S.R., 9–10, 13, 16–17, 37, 275–76; uranium fission discovered, 11–12

Atom Spies, The, 181, 380

Atomic Scientists of Chicago, 35

Atomics, 53

Attlee, Clement, 41, 68

Attorney General's list, 147–48, 423

Aviation Week, 281

Baldwin, George, 383

Baldwin, Roger, 343

Ballard, Augustus S., 111, 116–17, 397–402

Bank records of Greenglasses: Albuquerque National Bank (Exhibit 17), 152, 155–56, 161, 374, 378, 390, 391–92, 392 n, 393–94, 394 n, 395–96, 415, introduced at trial, 139, 395 n, 440; First National Bank of Albuquerque, 393–94

Barnes, Paul H., 394, 304 n, 395

Barr, Joel, 128, 162, 285–91, 293–94, 297, 297 n, 299, 303

Bartky, Walter, 31

Bautista, Dora, 141, 164

Beckerley, James, 275–77

Becquerel, Henri, 7

Bennett, James V., 195, 209, 233–35

Bentley, Elizabeth T., 309–22; biographical data, 309–10; and Brothman, 91, 96, 106, 310, 317; Brothman-Moskowitz trial testimony, 92–96; grand jury of 1947, 72, 90, 312–13, 407; government employees accused, 47, 50, 141–42, 295, 310, 312–13, 318–22, 422–23; R-S trial testimony, 141–42; and Rosenbergs, 2 n, 123, 128, 153, 155, 157–59, 165, 187, 234, 315–17, 322; Taylor brief, 318–21. *See also* Brunini; FBI; Golos; Remington

Bernhardt, George, 134, 145, 156, 164–65, 350

Bethe, Hans, 25, 263

Black, Hugo, 178, 194, 212, 246–47, 250

Black, Thomas L., 103, 112

Blakeslee, Howard W., 269

Bloch, Alexander, 120, 132–33, 149, 395

Bloch, Emanuel: attempts to reach President, 238, 249–52; charges prosecution deal, 210; commented on by Rosenberg, J., 229, 226; death, 279; impounding, 267–68, 268 n, 276–77, 432; judicial clemency plea, 184–85, 203, 391; letters

from Rosenbergs, 229–31, 233–36, 244–45, 252, 278–79; R-S trial, 120, 127, 129–30, 142–43, 146, 151–55, 159–60, 196–97, 199, 208, 270, 317, 379, 392, 423; R-S appeals, 182, 186, 192, 194, 200–1, 237–38, 242, 247, 250; on sentencing of Rosenbergs, 169, 172
Bohr, Niels, 8, 12, 14, 25, 29, 124, 152, 263
Boudin, Leonard, 443
Brecht, Berthold, 45
Bridges, Styles, 59, 405
Briehn, Coby, 383–84
British Intelligence, 69, 414
British Official Secrets Act, 43, 59
Brixton Prison, 66
Brode, Bernice, 38
Brooklyn Polytechnic Institute, 129, 269, 332
Brothman, Abraham, 87, 110, 119, 138, 172, 283 n, 284, 310, 313, 317, 363, 385, 411–12, 414; arrest and indictment, 83; bail, 83; and McCarthy Committee, 295; sentence, 105, 105 n. See also A. Brothman Associates; Brothman-Moskowitz trial
Brothman-Moskowitz trial, 90–106; references to, 109, 112, 115, 119, 172, 284, 315, 317, 363, 422, 424
Browder, Earl, 141, 310–11, 311 n, 320
Brownell, Herbert, Jr., 195, 231–35, 241, 243, 245, 245 n, 246–47, 249–50, 253, 296–98, 302, 312, 349, 430
Brumit, Fletcher L., 382, 382 n, 383, 385–86, 388–89
Brunini, John, 314, 314 n
Bulletin of the Atomic Scientists, 39, 176, 256, 259, 294
Burt, Leonard J., 61
Burton, Harold M., 212 n, 245–46, 250
Bush, Vannevar, 18, 38
Butler, John M., 281
Byrnes, James F., 31, 32

Cacchione, Peter V., 150, 165 n
Cambridge, Mass., 75, 108, 135–36
Canadian spy cases, 38, 41–43, 68
Capehart, Homer, 69
Capital punishment, 49, 78, 85, 119–20; appeals court powerless to revise, 177–79; approval of, 3–4, 168, 175–76, 191–92; Eisenhower on, 192, 242, 248–49; justified by crime, 261; Kaufman, 171, 184, 186; opposition to, abroad, xii, 180, 190, 193–94, 241, 257, in U.S., 3, 175–76, 179–80, 190–91, 241-42. See also Rosenbergs, pressure to confess
Cavendish Laboratory, 8, 9

Cerf, Bennett, 137, 137 n
Chadwick, James, 10, 17, 18, 25
Chambers, Whittaker, 47, 50
Chapin, John H., 48
Chase, Harrie B., 178
Chelf, Frank L., 246
Chicago Daily News, 442
Chicago Tribune, 280, 341
Chicago, University of, 20, 22, 29, 33, 38, 127, 144, 200, 242. See also Met Lab
Christian Herald, The, 191
Christy, Robert F., 435 n
Churchill, Winston, 251
City College of New York (CCNY), 2, 79, 84, 121, 133, 139, 143, 147, 156, 213, 286, 288, 295–96, 323, 328, 333, 337
Clark, Tom, 246
Clegg, Hugh, 69
Cleveland, Ohio, 128–29, 143–44, 148, 285, 285 n, 286–87, 289, 298, 418
Cleveland Plain Dealer, 442
Cobb, Candler, 140, 164
Cockcroft, John D., 17
Coe, V. Frank, 321–22
Cohn, Roy M., 302 n, 384 n; Brothman-Moskowitz trial, 90, 315; Monmouth hearings, 293–95, 345; Perl case, 290; Remington case, 315; R-S trial, 2, 120, 123–25, 127, 264–65, 267–68, 277–78, 290, 315, 347, 351–52, 355, 391
Cole, Lester, 45
Columbia Law Review, 1
Columbia University, 12–14, 18, 20, 37, 48, 288–89, 291, 309, 332
Combat, 203
Communism: and Bentley, 47, 92–95, 141–42, 153, 165, 309–11, 315, 320; and Brothman, 92–93; and classmates of Rosenberg, J., 291; and clemency campaign, 4, 180, 189–90, 256; Communist Party, trial of, 119; and Elitcher, 121, 123, 153, 165, 323, 323 n, 324–25; and espionage, 47–49, 53, 61, 90, 92, 125, 141, 155, 165, 309–11, 315, 320, 418; and Fuchs, 63, 63 n; and Gold, 73, 103, 112; and Greenglass, 77, 361, 361 n, 415; motive for crimes of Rosenbergs and Sobell, 1, 120, 156, 165–66, 177; public hostility toward, 78, 81, 85, 188; and Rosenberg, E., 84, 120, 124, 130, 134, 150, 152, 165, 188, 214, 419; and Rosenberg, J., 79, 84, 120, 124, 130, 134, 143–44, 147, 148, 156, 165, 188, 214, 417; R-S trial theme, 165, 177, 422; and Slack, 76; and Sobell, 120–21, 156, 165, 323, 323 n. See also Rosenberg, J., Communist Party

Communist Party. *See* Communism
Compton, Arthur H., 10, 18, 20, 22, 27, 29, 32, 54–55
Compton, Karl T., 9, 54
Conant, James B., 18, 22, 38
Condon, Edward U., 9, 31, 36, 40, 44–47, 50, 53, 88, 333
Considine, Bob, 88, 397 n
Console table, 128–29, 131, 143–44, 148–49, 151–53, 156–57, 164, 166, 196–203, 232, 236, 240, 345, 419
Cook, Fred J., 443
Coplon, Judith, 71, 119
Cornelius, Arthur, Jr., 421
Cornell University, 304 n, 305
Countryman, Vern, 434 n
Court of Appeals, U. S. Circuit: Remington case, 315 n; R-S case, 177–78, 183–84, 194, 212, 218, 224, 243, 251, 331, 427, 437, 443 n
Cox, Evelyn, 151, 153, 156, 164, 198–99, 201–2, 419
Curie, Irene, 10
Curie, Marie and Pierre, 7–8
Currie, Lauchlin, 47
Cyclotrons, Japanese, destroyed, 36–37

Daily Worker, 147, 176, 422
Danziger, William, 139–40, 154, 164, 328–29, 335, 335 n, 336–39; wife, 335, 335 n
Davidson, Bill, 296–97, 302–3, 307, 359
Dayton, Carol, 304–5, 305 n
Dayton, Weldon Bruce, 303–4, 304 n, 305–8, 418
Dean, Gordon, 106, 274
Death penalty. *See* Capital punishment
Dennis, Glen, 141, 164
Denver *Post*, 443
Derry, John, 127, 164, 270–71, 435–37
Des Moines *Register*, 443
Deutsch, Murray, 353–54
Devin-Adair Publishing Co., 314
Dimock, Edward J., 251
Donovan, James B., 342
Donovan, Robert J., 245, 248
Douglas, William O., 194, 212, 237–38, 242–47
Dreyfus, Alfred, 3, 258–59; family, 241
Dreyfus, Benjamin, 434 n
DuBois, W. E. B., 178 n
Dulles, John Foster, 54, 304 n

Eastman Kodak Co., 86, 365–66
Edelman, Irwin, 238, 276–77
Einstein, Albert, 8, 12, 14–15, 29, 191
Eisenhower, Dwight D., 52, 192–93, 231–32, 238, 241–42, 245, 247–52, 255–59, 262, 321, 367; wife, 252
Eisenhower, John, 242
Eisler, Gerhard, 71
Electronics secrets, 280, 292–93, 345
Elitcher, Helene, 121, 288–91, 307, 324, 324 n, 325–26, 335, 335 n
Elitcher, Max, 2, 5, 139, 146–47, 153–54, 156–59, 159 n, 161, 165–66, 187, 204 n, 309, 323–24, 324 n, 325–27, 332, 337, 418, 427; and Bentley, 123, 142, 155, 158–59, 316, 322; at Perl trial, 290–91; R-S trial testimony, 121–23
Elwyn family, 305
Emerson Radio Corp., 127, 143, 277–79
Espinosa, Minerva Bravo, 140–41, 164
Espionage Act, 168, 176, 238, 246
Explosives Engineer, 267

Fabricant, Herbert, 204, 204 n, 205, 210
Farmer, Fyke, 237–38, 242–43, 246–47, 250, 253, 276
Farrell, Thomas F., 33
FBI Story, The, 389, 405 n
Federal Bureau of Investigation (FBI), 75, 81, 85, 88, 105, 163, 338; atomic espionage probe, pre-R-S case, 405, 414–15; Bentley, 90–91, 95, 311–13, 316–22, 407; Brothman, 83, 90–91; Danziger, interrogation, 335, 335 n; Dayton, interrogation, 304–6, 418; Elitcher, Helene, interrogation, 307, 325; Elitcher, Max, 327, interrogation, 123, 153, 322, 324–25, 418; Fuchs arrest, role of FBI in, 59, 68, 406, interrogation, 69, 71, 116, 406; Glassman, 298–99; Gold, 108, 117, 397, 414 n, how found, 70–73, 114–16, 367–68, 407, informed of perjury, 421, interrogation (in 1947), 72, 91, 407, (1950 and after) 70–74, 114–15, 366–69, 369 n, 370, 372, 375, 389 n, 399, 399 n, 400, 403, 407–10, 413, 415–17, 420–23, 423 n, 434, 441–442, search of home (in 1947), 91, 105, (in 1950) 97, 104–5, 114–15, 407, 414; Greenglass, D., 77, 152, interrogation (in February 1950), 129, 145, 210–11, 359, 415, (in June 1950 and after) 78, 129, 134, 203–7, 210, 265 n, 344-45, 348, 359–62, 371–72, 398–99, 416–17, 434, investigation of story, 144, 153, 199, 279, 300–2, 351 n, 353, 356, 361, 395–96, 419, surveillance, 207, 359, 359 n, 369 n, 415–16; Greenglass, R., interrogation, 133, 207–8, 362; Hilton Hotel cards, 382–00, 408, 428–30, 439–40; Morton Street apartment, 304–8; passport photos (Greenglasses), 129,

351, 351 n, 352–54; Perl, 289–91, 298, 418; Redin case, 44; Rosenberg, E., 84, 419; Rosenberg, J., arrest, 79, interrogation, 79, 146, 164, 204, 337–38, 417, investigation, 144, 199, 418–19; publicity release, 80, 283; R-S case investigation, 134, 152, 154, 292–3, 294, 296–97, 324, 376, 418–19, 421; Sarant, 304–6; Schneider, 151, 153, 180–82; Sidorovich, Ann, 300–2, 418; Slack, 76, 87; Sobell, arrest, 328–29, complaint, 326, kidnaping, 336, 339, 419; souvenir thefts by GI's, 45–46. *See also* Hoover, J. E.

Federal House of Detention (West Street), 78, 208, 214–15

Federal Workers Union, 146

Federation of American Scientists, 308

Federation of Architects, Engineers, Chemists and Technicians (FAECT), 149, 214, 303

Fermi, Enrico, 10–14, 14 n, 18, 20, 22, 25, 32, 55

Fermi, Laura, 12

Fifth Amendment, 147, 149–50, 165, 295, 300, 318–19, 321, 423

Figaro, 255

Fineberg, S. Andhil, 367

Finerty, John F., 194, 194 n, 200, 237

First National Bank of Albuquerque. *See* Bank records of Greenglasses

Flerov, Georgii, 13, 17

Flight, 87, 138, 138 n, 148, 162–63, 286–90, 296–99, 305–6, 421. *See also* Greenglass, D.; Mexico; Passport photos; Schneider

Fontana, Joseph, 199–200, 202

Forrestal, James V., 54, 277 n

Franck, James, 29–30, 32 n; Report, 32–33

Frank, Jerome N., 177–78, 194, 331

Frankfurter, Felix, 178–79, 212, 246–48, 250, 253

Freeman, W. B., 375–77

Frisch, Otto, 12, 17, 25

Fuchs, Klaus, 2, 76, 103; arrest, 59; biographical data, 59–61; confession, 62–63, 63 n, 64–68, 406, 406 n, 414, 434; court proceedings, 59, 61–67; father, 61–62, 66; in Gold confession, 115; in Gold indictment, 75, 81, 83; identification of Gold, 71–73, 115–16, 406–7; information passed, nature of, 59–64, 66–68, 108, 275; in R-S trial, 128, 135–37, 152, 156, 363; sentence, 67; sister, 108. *See also* Federal Bureau of Investigation; Gold

Fuchs atomic spy ring, 80, 84–86, 88, 90, 106, 182, 283, 284

Gazette de Lausanne, 193

Geismar, Maxwell, 343

General Electric Co., 31, 84, 122–23, 128, 191, 324

Gertz, Elmer, 442

Gibbons, John, 148

Giner de los Rios, Manuel, 140, 164, 329, 336

Glassman, Vivian, 148, 162, 286–90, 293–94, 298–99, 303

Glazer, Nathan, 4

Gleeson, Gerald, 82, 96, 107–10, 116, 384

Godwin, John, 331

Gold, Harry: arrest, 70, 76, 160; arraignment, 70; attorney appointed, 73–75, 408; biographical data, 2, 70, 73, 102–3, 111–14, 397 n, 398, 425; bootlegging, 420 n; brother, 70, 73–74, 102, 114; Brothman-Moskowitz case, 83, 90–92, 106, 363; Brothman-Moskowitz trial testimony, 95–103; complaint, 70; events of 1947, 72, 90–92, 103–5, 313, 364, 407; fantasies, 102–3, 109, 363–64, 412–13, 413 n; father, 70, 73–74, 111, 114; fictitious contacts, 109–10, 112, 363; Fuchs, meetings with, 75, 108, 110–11, 135–37, 284, 363, 366–69, 373–75, 384, 389, 398–99, 400 n, 407–8, 412–15, 424, 429, 437; grand jury perjuries admitted, 90–92, 106, 109, 364, 420–21; in Greenglass N.M. indictment, 78; in Greenglass, D., R-S trial testimony, 125–26; in Greenglass, R., R-S trial testimony, 131; guilty plea, 74, 81–83, 111, 419, 423; imprisoned with Greenglass, 117, 422, 424; indictment, 75; mother, 103, 111; paroled, 434 n; pretrial recorded interviews, 111, 397, 397 n, 398–403, 408–10, 410 n, 411–16, 420–21, 437, 440–42; pretrial written statements, 111, 366–70, 374–75, 389 n, 397, 397 n, 398 n, 400–1, 411–13, 413 n, 414, 416–17, 420, 420 n, 421, 421 n, 422, 437, 440–42; in R-S indictment, 84; in R-S case, 2, 5, 80, 118–19, 157, 159 n, 160, 163, 178, 185–87, 189, 234, 322, 327, 331, 355, 363, 370, 417, 419–20, 422; in R-S trial summations, 152–53, 156; R-S trial testimony, 135–38; Santa Fe, N.M., map, 114–15, 407–8, 413–14; and Senate Internal Security subcommittee, 280, 348, 364–66, 422; sentence, 117; sentencing hearing, 107–17; Slack case, 86, 283, 365–66, 409, 411–12, 412 n, 413; Smilg case, 363–64, 410 n; Soviet contacts, 107, 109, 112, 398, 411, 421. *See also* Albuquerque June 3 meeting; Federal Bureau of

Investigation; Hilton Hotel cards; Semenov; Yakovlev

Goldman, Robert, 204 n, 207–10

Golos, Jacob, 90–94, 97, 128, 141–42, 155, 309–11, 315–16, 320, 364

Göttingen, University of, 8, 9

Gouzenko, Igor, 41–42, 68

Greenglass, Bernard, 127, 130, 132, 143, 145, 196, 211, 235, 359

Greenglass, David, 1, 2, 5; accomplice testimony, 159, 159 n; Army thefts, 144–45, 394; arrest and arraignment, 77–78, 205, 344, 362; attempt to retract confession, 78, 172, 362, 362 n, 417; bail, 77; and Bentley, 142, 155, 158–59, 316, 322; biographical data, 2, 123–24, 262, 392–93, 393 n; business partner of Rosenberg, 79, 127–28, 130, 132–33, 143–45, 159, 163, 187, 208 n, 355, 417; complaint, 204–5, 371; corroboration of story, 158, 158 n, 159, 163–65, 182–84, 207–8, 362, 419; espionage other than A-bomb, 277–81, 293, 341, 344–45; extradition, 78–79, 207, 209–10, 371; flight plans, 77, 80, 128–32, 134–35, 145–46, 148, 153, 159, 162–65, 329, 335–37, 346–47, 350–50, flight plans, money, 128–29, 131–32, 134, 145–46, 150, 156, 162–63, 186, 206, 329, 355–59, 361, 394; in Gold testimony, 135–37; in Greenglass, R., testimony, 130–33; improbabilities in testimony, 160–61; indictments, N.M., 78, 209–10, 371, 371 n, 383, N.Y., 84, 88, 210, 422; McCarthy Committee, 281, 293–94, 296, 345–46; meeting with Russian, 125, 205–6; mother, 219; named as co-conspirator, 84, 88, 209–10; Nov. 1944 meeting with Ruth, 124, 130, 143, 205, 262–63; pretrial memos, 196, 203–11, 344–45, 359–60, 362, 395; release from prison, 5, 349, 425; in Rosenberg, E., testimony, 149–50; in Rosenberg, J., testimony, 143–46, 148; Rosenberg spy ring, 285–86, 288, 293–94, 296, 298, 300–2; R-S trial summations, 152–53, 155–56; R-S trial testimony, 123–30; in Saypol opening, 120; Senate Internal Security subcommittee, 280–81, 346–49, 364; sentencing, 172–73; uranium theft, 145, 196, 211, 235, 240, 359, 361–62, 415, 417. See also Albuquerque June 3; Bank records; Communism; Console table; Federal Bureau of Investigation; Gold; Greenglasses, accusations against Rosenbergs; Hilton Hotel cards; Passport photos; Pitt Machine; Sketches

Greenglass, Ruth: biographical data, 2, 130, 392–93, 393 n, 394; in Gold testimony, 135–37; in Greenglass, D., testimony, 124–30; on husband's sentence, 133, 173, 209; improbabilities in testimony, 160–61; receipts from Rogge firm, 357–58; named co-conspirator, 5, 84, 88, 119, 159, 209–10, 240, 257, 422; in Rosenberg, E., testimony, 149–50; in Rosenberg, J., testimony, 143–46; in R-S trial summations, 152–53, 155–56; R-S trial testimony, 130–33. See also Greenglass, D.

Greenglasses, accusations against Rosenbergs. See Atomic espionage; Atomic powered airplane; Electronics secrets; Proximity fuse; Sky platform; Think machine

Gromov, Anatoli, 311–12

Groves, Leslie R., 22, 26–28, 30–33, 36, 38, 55, 119, 127, 135, 270

Hahn, Otto, 11, 12, 15, 19

Halperin, Israel, 68

Hamilton, John D. M., 74, 83, 108–14, 116–17, 363, 397–402, 408–10, 410 n, 411–13, 416, 420, 420 n, 421–22, 424

Hand, Learned, 194, 314

Hanford Engineer Works, 23–26, 33, 44, 273

Harrington, John A., 181

Harwell, 59, 61–66

Hayhanen, Reino, 341–42

Hays, Arthur Garfield, 180

Hecht, Selig, 37

Hendrick Manufacturing Co., 91, 97, 99, 101

Heuss, John, 191

Hickenlooper, Bourke B., 38, 405

High explosive lens molds: mentioned by Gold, 135–36, 424. See also Sketches; Greenglass, D., meeting with Russian

Hilton Hotel, Albuquerque, Gold registration cards: June 1945 (Exhibit 16), 136, 152, 155–56, 161, 373–74, 377, 378–90, 391, 395 n, 400, 418, 428–31, 437–38, 438 n, 439–42; introduced at trial, 139, 378–79, 390; September 1945, 108, 384–90, 400 n, 408, 413–14, 428–30, 437–38, 428 n, 440–41

Hiram Walker Distillery, 413 n

Hiroshima. See Atomic bomb, U.S.

Hiskey, Clarence F., 48, 50

Hiss, Alger, 3–4, 47, 50, 56, 61, 69, 295

Hockinson, Anna Kindernecht, 386, 386 n, 387, 389, 437–38, 441

Holifield, Chet, 46

Hollywood hearings, 45, 47, 50

Hollywood Photo Studio, 353–54
Hoover, Herbert, 44
Hoover, J. Edgar, 105, 393, 405, 405 n, 413–14, 425, 428–30, 443; announcing arrests, 2, 43, 59, 70, 76–77, 80, 83, 182, 283, 312, 317–18, 372, 408; search for Fuchs's accomplice, 69, 70–73, 115, 406–7. See also Federal Bureau of Investigation
Hopkins, Harry L., 55
Hopkins, William F., 363–64
House Judiciary Committee, 243
House Military Affairs Committee, 35–36, 44
House Un-American Activities Committee, 43–49, 53, 55, 68, 88, 95, 313, 319
Huggins, James S., 141, 154, 164
Hughes, Donald, 32 n
Hughes, Emmet John, 245, 245 n
Hughes, Linda, 381–83
Hutchins, Robert M., 38
Hydrogen bomb (H-bomb or super), 54–57, 59–60, 76, 276, 279

Impounded sketch. See Sketches, Greenglass
Indianapolis News, 443
Interim Committee, 32
International Workers Order, 148, 423
Izvestia, 17

Jackson, Robert H., 212, 246, 250, 252
Jello box, 80, 160–62, 285, 350, 372, 372 n, 373–74; Bloch, E., summation, 152–53; Gold, 136, 368, 401, 403, 418, 423–24, 441; Greenglass, D., 125, 205–6, 418; Greenglass, R., 131; Saypol summation, 155
Jenkins, Ray, 86–87
Jewish Daily Forward, 176
Joffe, Abram, 9
Johnson, Louis, 57
Joint Anti-Fascist Refugee Committee, 147–48, 423
Joint Congressional Committee on Atomic Energy, 42, 49, 56, 67, 69, 75, 106, 268, 275
Joliot-Curie, Frédéric, 10, 13, 16
Jordan, George Racey, 55–56
Journal of Physics, 9
Judgment of Julius and Ethel Rosenberg, The, 334, 431
Judicial clemency hearing. See Kaufman
June 3, 1945. See Albuquerque, June 3

Kaiser Wilhelm Institute, 11
Kamen, Martin, 49–50

Kapitza, Peter, 9, 17
Kaufman, Irving R.: Brothman-Moskowitz trial, 90, 95, 101–2, 105–6; court of appeals judge, 277; judicial clemency hearing, 184–86, 288, 391; R-S appeals, 196, 200, 202–3, 210–12, 237, 249, 251; R-S case, 1, 2, 4, 120, 123, 126–27, 132–33, 135, 138, 141–44, 147–50, 152, 157, 162, 166–68, 175–77, 179, 181, 183, 194, 228, 231, 238, 257, 261–62, 266–68, 270–71, 275, 277, 315, 322–23, 331, 341, 367, 374, 423–24, 436–37; sentencing of Greenglass, 172–73, of Rosenbergs, 169–71, of Sobell, 171–72
Kelley, Thomas V., 148, 198
Kennedy, John F., 282, 342
Khariton, Yulii, 9
Kilgore, Harley M., 85
Kilsheimer, James M., 120, 130, 183, 347
King, Mackenzie, 41
King, Martin Luther, Jr., 342
King, Robert L., 432, 438–39
Kingsport, Tenn., 77, 85–86
Kinoy, Arthur, 434 n
Kistiakowski, George, 119, 124, 263, 273
Kleinman, William, 92, 94–95, 100–3
Korean War, 76, 78, 81, 85, 168, 170, 185, 188, 225, 242, 257, 261–62, 283, 333, 336, 338–39, 423
Koski, Walter, 126, 163–65, 271, 273, 276
Krock, Arthur, 60
Kunstler, William M., 427–31, 434 n, 436, 438
Kuntz, Edward, 120–21, 133, 148, 154, 329
Kurchatov, Igor, 17

Lamphere, Robert, 69
Landau, Lev, 9
Lane, Myles J., 84, 120, 135, 138, 185–86, 209–10, 262, 280–81, 288, 341, 378, 422, 424
Langmuir, Irving, 31
Lansdale, John, Jr., 135, 164
Lardner, Ring, Jr., 45, 50
Lawrence, Ernest O., 10, 21, 32
Lawrence, Wes, 442
Le Monde, 190, 196, 241
Lend-Lease, 106, 294, 411
Lens molds. See High explosive lens molds
Levitov, Edith, 129–40
Lewisburg Penitentiary, 5, 280, 293, 346, 348–49, 360, 363, 365–66, 397, 424, 434 n
L'Humanité, 180
Libby, Willard F., 17

Liberation (Paris), 254
Liberty, 44
Life, 66, 72–73
Lilienthal, David E., 39, 47, 57
Linschitz, Henry, 435–36
Livingston, M. S., 10
Look, 276, 296–98, 302–3, 307, 342, 359, 368, 389, 430–31
Loomer, Bernard M., 242
Los Alamos, N.M., 268 n, 414; Derry, 127, 270–71, 435; development of A-bomb, 24–26, 33, 271–73, 273 n, 274, 435, 435 n; Fuchs, 60, 63, 64, 108, 135, 275, 406, 408; Greenglass, D., 2, 77-78, 80, 123–25, 131, 161, 207, 261–64, 267, 274, 349, 361 n, 372, 382,394–95, 400, 415–16, 436; Greenglass uranium theft from, 129, 196, 211, 240, 359–61; Koski, 126, 265–67; Rosenberg, J., alleged knowledge of, 124, 130, 143, 160, 187; security and secrecy, 28, 38, 135, 152; souvenir thefts, 45–46, 361 n
Los Angeles *Times*, 443
L'Osservatore Romano, 193–94
Loyalty program, 50, 123, 291, 314, 318, 324–25, 338, 361
Lyons, Daniel M., 238, 248
Lyons, Leonard, 175

McCarthy, Elizabeth, 386–89, 437–38, 438 n, 440
McCarthy, Joseph R., 61, 280–81, 292–96, 299, 301, 319, 345–46; McCarthyism, 3, 76, 190
McCormack, Peter, 342
McDonald (U. S. Commissioner), 77, 79
McGranery, James P., 70, 73–74, 81–82, 96, 107, 115–17, 193, 384, 408
McGrath, J. Howard, 70, 115
McGraw-Hill Publishing Co., 101
McMillan, Edwin, 37
McMahon, Brien, 38, 69. *See also* Atomic Energy Act
MacMahon, Lloyd F., 290–92
Macy's, 144, 148–49, 156, 198–200, 202–3, 240
Manhattan District, 22. *See also* Atomic bomb project
Manion, Clarence E., 191
Marder, Murrey, 294
Marshall, C. L., 432
Marshall, Daniel G., 238, 242–43, 246, 250–53, 276
Marshall, George C., 26
Marshall, Thurgood, 440 n
Martin, A. B., 259
Martin, John S., 431

Martin, Robert, 292
Massachusetts Institute of Technology (MIT), 37, 127, 144, 306
Mauriac, François, 255, 426
May, Allan Nunn, 42–43, 275
May, Andrew J., 35–36
Meitner, Lise, 11–12, 19
Metallurgical Laboratory (Met Lab), 20–22, 29, 32, 42, 48
Metcalf, Lee, 242
Mexico: Greenglass flight plans, 80, 128, 132, 124–35, 145, 153, 156, 159, 164–65, 347, 350–51, 358; in Perl case, 289; Sarant, 148, 287–88, 297, 305; and Sobell, 139–41, 148, 152, 154, 162–63, 171, 327–30, 332–41, 419
Meyer, Howard, 182
Michelson, A. A., 10
Michigan, University of, 121, 323
Miller, T. Scott, Jr., 115–16
Millikan, R. A., 10
Millis, Walter, 296
Milwaukee *Journal*, 342
Minton, Sherman, 246
Monmouth hearings, 292–96, 299, 345
Monod, Jacques, 255–59
Mooney-Billings case, 3, 194 n
Moorehead, Alan, 406
Morris, Robert, 280–81, 346–49, 366
Morrison, Philip, 268 n, 435, 435 n
Morton Street apartment, 287–88, 291–92, 297, 303–8
Moskowitz, Miriam, 119, 172, 283 n, 284, 317; arrest, 83; bail, 83; sentence, 105. *See also* Brothman-Moskowitz trial
Mowrey, Owen J., 371
Mundt, Karl, 53, 405
Munroe, Charles E., 266

Nagasaki. *See* Atomic bomb, U.S.
Nation, 192–93, 298, 443
National Committee to Secure Justice for Morton Sobell, 340–41
National Committee to Secure Justice in the Rosenberg Case, 176–77, 179, 196, 222–23, 227–28
National Guardian, 176, 179–80, 199, 201, 222
National Security Council, 57
Nature, 9, 12
Naval Research Laboratory, U. S., 52
Navy Bureau of Ordnance, 84, 121, 323, 337
Neal, Marc W., 383
Nelson, Steve, 48, 50
Newark Evening News, 296
New Deal, 3, 38, 47, 50, 55, 313
New Republic, 193 n

New Statesman and Nation, 190
Newsweek, 36, 43–44, 60, 64, 75, 84, 328, 443
New York City, Gold-Fuchs meeting's, 75, 108, 110, 135
New York *Daily News*, 79, 87, 90, 326, 328, 361
New York *Herald Tribune*, 90, 128, 131, 147, 148, 190, 252–53, 281, 292, 296
New York *Journal-American* 53, 73, 78–80, 82, 87, 175, 293
New York *Mirror*, 46–47, 78–79, 85, 359 n
New York *Post*, 2, 172, 175, 328, 380, 443
New York Review of Books, 443
New York *Times*, 43, 52–53, 59, 62, 66, 71, 75–79, 81, 83–85, 87, 96, 99, 116–17, 119, 130, 133, 135–36, 138, 147–48, 150, 168, 173, 182, 191, 194, 242, 245–46, 249, 253–54, 256, 275, 281, 286, 292, 295–96, 328, 341 n, 342, 348, 363, 380, 423, 425, 432, 434 n
New York *World-Telegram & Sun*, 68, 71, 72, 98, 147, 281, 286, 313–14
Nickson, J. J., 32 n
Niebuhr, Rheinhold, 343
Nishina, Yoshio, 36
Nixon, Richard M., 53, 56, 68, 405
Norton, William F., 353–55

Oak Ridge, Tenn., 24–26, 37, 48, 55, 77, 86, 98, 123, 273
Office of Price Administration, 207, 393
Old Bailey, 65–66, 116
Oppenheimer, Frank, 49
Oppenheimer, J. Robert, 9, 22, 25, 32, 36, 45, 49–50, 54–55, 119, 124, 263, 272, 436

Packer, Herbert L., 314–15, 317–18, 443
Pagano, Helen, 134, 164, 204 n, 209, 356
Palmer House Hotel (Chicago), 413
Palmieri, Edmund L., 431–32
Partisan Review, 4
Passport photos (Exhibit 9), 129, 132, 152, 156, 162, 206, 350–54, 354 n, 355, 357, 440; FBI receipt for, 353
Pasternak, Louis, 338
Pasternak, Morris (Max), 140, 338
Pauling, Linus, 9
Pegler, Westbrook, 78
Pegram, George B., 14
Peierls, Rudolph, 17, 406
Pennsylvania Sugar Co., 100, 107, 109–13, 375, 375 n, 411, 413–14, 420 n
Pepper, George Wharton, 75
Perl, William, 133, 148, 162, 182–83, 183 n, 184, 194, 235, 286, 288, 298–

99, 303, 305, 308, 418; trial of, 288–92
Perlin, Marshall, 427–32, 434 n, 436, 438
Perlo, Victor, 320
Perrin, Michael, 64–65, 67
Petrzhak, Konstantin, 17
Philadelphia General Hospital (Heart Station), 113–14, 117
Philadelphia *News*, 281
Phillips, Harold, 120–21, 171
Physical Review, 9
Picasso, Pablo, 180
Piel, Eleanor Jackson, 434 n
Pierre, Henri, 241
Pilat, Oliver, 181, 380
Pitt Machine Co., 79, 127–28, 130, 132, 139, 143–45, 163, 186, 337, 355
Planck, Max, 8
Plutonium, 15, 18, 20–23, 26, 33, 42, 44, 272–74, 361 n, 433–34
Poling, Daniel A., 191
Pollack, Benjamin F., 297, 302, 302 n, 303, 307, 349, 360, 430–31
Pontecorvo, Bruno, 275
Pope Pius XII, xii, 193–94
Popular Science, 267
Potsdam Conference, 33
Pratt Institute, 129
Pravda, 17
Proximity fuse, 127, 157, 159, 277–79, 344

Quinn, T. Vincent, 313

Rabinowitch, Eugene, 32, 39, 176
Radar. *See* Electronics secrets
Radiation Laboratory (Berkeley), 10, 21–22, 25, 37, 45, 47–49
Radium Institute (Paris), 8, 9
RAND Corporation, 17
Rayleigh, Lord, 24
RDX, 77, 86, 110, 283, 412, 412 n
Reader's Digest, 389, 407
Redin, Nicolai, 43–44, 71
Reed, Stanley F., 246
Reeves Instrument Co., 84, 122–23, 324, 327–28, 332, 334–35, 335 n
Remington, Ann, 314, 314 n
Remington, William W., 47, 119, 313–15, 315 n
Reuben, William A., 176–77, 179
Riesman, David, 4
Rochester *Times Union*, 366
Roentgen, Wilhelm, 7
Roetting, Walter C., 181–82
Rogge, O. John: attorney for Greenglasses, 77–79, 129–30, 134, 172, 204 n, 208 n, 349, 356, 361–62, 362 n, 394; pretrial

memoranda, Elitchers, 307, 307 n, 325, 327, Greenglasses, 196, 203–4, 207–11, 235, 395; receipts for fee, 357–58
Roosevelt, Franklin D., 14–15, 18, 29, 31, 191
Rose, Irving, 353
Rosenberg Case, The, 367
Rosenberg Committee. See National Committee
Rosenberg, Ethel: in Abel, D., testimony, 134; arrest, 83–84, 419; bail, 84; biographical data, 148–49, 186, 213–14; brother, David, comments on, 149–50, 187–88, 240; in Cox testimony, 152; death house, transferred to, 175; grand jury testimony, 150; in Greenglass, D., testimony, 124–29; in Greenglass, R., testimony, 130–33; mercy letter to Eisenhower, 250, 252; mother, 219; in Rosenberg, J., testimony, 143–46; R-S trial testimony, 148–51; as typist for espionage material, 125, 127, 149, 155, 157. See also Rosenberg, J.
Rosenberg, Julius: in Abel, D., testimony, 134; arrest 79–81; bail, 79; Bentley mention of "Julius," 142, 153, 155, 158, 315–17, 322; in Bernhardt testimony, 134–35; biographical data, 2, 79, 142–43, 213–14; brother, 200–1, 251; Communist Party, alleged membership in, 79, 144, 146–47, 149, 153, 165, 214, 417; complaint, 371–72; in Danziger testimony, 139; in Elitcher testimony, 121–23; in Greenglass, D., testimony, 124–30; in Greenglass, R., testimony, 130–33; how first linked to case, 417–18; mother, 200–1, 219, 234; in Perl case, 133, 287–92; in Rosenberg, E., testimony, 149–50; R-S trial testimony, 142–48; in Schneider testimony, 151–52; sisters, 200–1. See also Albuquerque June 3 meeting; Greenglass, D.; Passport photos; Pitt Machine; Rosenberg spy ring; Rosenbergs; Rosenbergs alleged crimes
Rosenbergs: appeals, 177–84, 194–212, 218, 223–27, 235–38, 240, 242–47, 251; in Bloch summation, 152–54; children, 143, 149, 170–71, 187, 200–1, 213–15, 217–26, 230–32, 234, 236, 238, 244, 249–50, 252, 256, 419; crime, summary of, 157–58, 344; execution, 1, 5, 253, 397 n; Executive clemency petitions, 186–89, 192, 231–32, 238–41, 247–48; indictments, 84, 88, 88 n, 209, 371 n; judicial clemency hearing, 184–86; pressure to confess, 2–5, 175, 184–87, 189, 192, 194–95, 233–35, 239,

253, 255, 288, 419, 426; pretrial proceedings, 85, 210; prison letters, 213–36, 244–45, 249–50, 252, 278–79, 426; in Saypol opening, 120; in Saypol summation, 154–56; verdict, 167
Rosenbergs, alleged crimes. See Atomic espionage; Atomic powered airplane; Electronics secrets; Proximity fuse; Sky platform; Think machine
Rosenberg-Sobell case: Papal intervention, xii, 193–94; pretrial publicity, 80–81, 182–84, 283–84, 328, 334, 362, 372, 419; reactions abroad, 4, 180, 184, 189–90, 192–94, 196, 241, 248, 251, 253, 254–59; reactions in U.S., 2–4, 175–76, 179–80, 190–92, 237, 242, 251–55, 259
Rosenberg-Sobell trial: co-conspirators named, 119; defendants named, 119; defense attorneys named, 120–21; defense witnesses, Gibbons, 148, Kelley, 148, Rosenberg, E., 148–51, Rosenberg, J., 142–48; indictment, 119; judge, 120; law tried under, 168; locale, 119; openings, 120–21; Perl arrest, 133; prosecution witnesses, Abel, D., 134, Abel, L., 134, Adomian, 139, Bautista, 141, Bentley, 141–42, Bernhardt, 134–35, Cobb, 140, Cox, 151, Danziger, 139–40, Dennis, 141, Derry, 127, Elitcher, 121–23, Espinosa, 140–41, Giner de los Rios, 140, Gold, 135–38, Greenglass, D., 123–30, Greenglass, R., 130–33, Huggins, 141, Koski, 126, Landsdale, 135, Pagano, 134, Schneider, 151–52, Vendrell, 141; prosecutors named, 120; sentences, Greenglass, 173, Rosenbergs, 171, Sobell, 172; sentencing speeches of judge, 169–73; summations, defense, 152–54, prosecution, 154–56; verdict, 167; witness list, 119. See also R-S trial exhibits
Rosenberg-Sobell trial exhibits, 152; brown paper wrapper, 129, 156, 162, 355–56; coin collection can, 148, 165, 418–19; Communist Party nominating petition, 150, 165, 419; miscellaneous, 138, 138 n, 140, 161, 369. See also Bank records; Hilton Hotel cards; Jello box; Passport photos; Sketches
Rosenberg spy ring, 192, 214, 242, 245, 283–308, 325, 337, 341, 344
Rosenman, Samuel I., 191
Rosenthal, Jack, 431
Ruark, Robert, 360
Rushmore, Howard, 175
Rusinov, L. I., 13
Russell, Bertrand, 341
Russell, Louis, 45

Rutherford, Ernest, 8, 17
Ryan, Sylvester J., 180, 182–83, 194, 284

Sacco-Vanzetti case, 3–4, 185 n, 193, 194 n. *See also* Vanzetti
Sachs, Alexander, 15
St. Louis *Post-Dispatch*, 175–76, 442–43
San Francisco Conference, 29–30
Santa Fe, N.M., Gold-Fuchs meetings: in June, 75, 108, 136, 367, 373, 375, 384, 398, 415, 437; in September, 75, 108, 110–11, 137, 384, 389, 400 n, 413–15, 437
Santa Fe *New Mexican*, 274
Sarant, Alfred, 148, 162, 286–88, 291, 292, 294, 297, 299, 303, 304–8
Sartre, Jean-Paul, 254, 341 n
Saypol, Irving H.: Brothman-Moskowitz case, 83, 90, 92, 97, 101, 105–6; Greenglass pretrial hearings, 77–79; R-S case, 2, 84, 87, 119–22, 127, 133, 139, 142, 147–48, 150–52, 154, 159, 167–68, 172, 181–83, 185, 194, 196–98, 208–9, 261, 265–68, 270, 276–77, 284–88, 299, 302, 302 n, 305, 305 n, 308, 315, 317, 326, 329, 334–35, 340, 344, 351, 357, 362 n, 363, 371, 378–80, 384 n, 390, 392, 394, 401, 421–22, 424, 436–37; R-S trial summation, 154–56
Schein, David, 143, 145
Schenectady, N.Y., 84, 122–23, 128, 144, 285, 285 n, 324
Schine, G. David, 293–94
Schneider, Benjamin, 151–53, 156, 164, 180–83, 194, 419
Scientific American, 269, 275
Scientist X, 48, 51
Scott, Byron N., 318
Seaborg, Glenn, 32 n
Semenov, Semen M. ("Sam"), 75, 85, 92, 96–100, 102, 107–8, 110, 412
Senate Internal Security subcommittee, 280–81, 319, 321–22, 346–49, 364–67, 374 n, 397, 398 n, 422
Senate Government Operations Committee (McCarthy Committee). *See* McCarthy, J.
Shanley, Bernard, 249
Shaped charge, 266–67, 270, 272
Sharp, Malcolm, 200, 200 n, 202 n, 252, 434 n
Sidorovich, Ann, 125, 143, 152, 285–86, 288–89, 291, 294, 299–302, 302 n, 303, 306, 372, 299, 418, 440
Sidorovich, Michael, 125, 143, 152, 285, 288–89, 291, 300–1, 301 n
Sillitoe, Percy, 414
Silvermaster, Nathan Gregory, 47

Simons, Sanford, 361 n
Sinel'kinov, Kyrill, 9
Sing Sing Prison, 120, 175, 180, 195, 213, 213 n, 215–17, 219, 233, 236, 238–40, 244–45, 249, 251, 253, 255
Skardon, William J., 62–64, 66–67, 116
Sketches, Greenglass: Exhibits 2, 6 & 7, 78, 124–26, 129, 137, 152, 161, 206, 263–65, 265 n, 266–67, 271, 273–77, 374, 416, 424; Exhibit 8 (impounded sketch), 126–27, 161, 263–64, 267–71, 273–77, 431–37
Sky platform, 127, 144, 155, 159, 206, 277, 277 n, 278, 280–81, 285, 297, 341, 344; Soviet space satellites, 279–81
Slack, Alfred Dean, 76–77, 80, 82, 85, 96, 110, 138, 283 n, 365, 409, 411, 413; appeal, 283–84, 412, 412 n; bail, 77; sentencing, 85–87
Smilg, Benjamin, 363–64, 410 n
Smith, Walter Bedell, 54
Smyth, Henry De Wolf. *See Atomic Energy for Military Purposes*
Sobell, Helen, 140, 154, 179, 291, 323 n, 326, 328, 330, 331 n, 332–34, 336–42
Sobell, Morton, 1, 87, 118–21, 151, 154, 156–58, 165–67, 175–76, 187, 261, 282, 283 n, 284–85, 288, 296–97, 308–9, 316, 322, 403, 426; Alcatraz, 5, 179, 331, 342; appeals, 177–84, 331–34, 336, 340–42, 427–43; arrest, 84–85, 329, 331; bail, 85; biographical data, 2, 323–24; children, 139, 154, 328, 330, 331 n, 332–35, 340; clemency petition, 342–43; Elitcher testimony, 121–23; "flight," 84, 139–41, 148, 152, 154, 156, 162–63, 287, 327–40; indictment, 88, 326, 419; kidnaping, 141, 171, 328–31, 333, 335, 339–41, 419; parents, 139, 340; Perl case, 133, 288–89, 291–92; pressure to confess, 5, 179, 326, 331, 419, 426; Rosenberg, J., testimony, 146–47; sentencing, 171–72
Sobell Committee. *See* National Committee
Sokolsky, George E., 191–92
Soviet Academy of Sciences, 17, 30
Soviet Atomic Espionage, 49, 275
Soviet State Radium Institute, 9
Space satellite. *See* Sky platform
Sperry Gyroscope Co., 293, 297 n
Stearns, Joyce, 32 n
Stimson, Henry L., 29–30, 32–33
Stitt, Jesse W., 191
Strassmann, Fritz, 11, 12, 15, 19
Strauss, Lewis L., 56
Stripling, Robert, 313
Stuyvesant High School, 121, 323, 337

Summit, Leon, 279
Supreme Court, U. S., 177–80, 184, 192, 192 n, 194, 212, 212 n, 225–27, 237, 239, 241, 242–51, 304 n, 308, 331, 341–42
Surratt, Mary, 5
Swan, Thomas W., 178, 183–84
Synchrotron, 37, 39
Syracuse Post-Standard, 76
Szilard, Leo, 12–15, 18, 29, 31–32, 32 n, 36

Tampico, Mexico, 140–41, 154, 162–63, 328–29, 333, 335, 337, 339
Tass, 67
Taylor, Robert L., 87
Taylor, William Henry, 318–21
Teller, Edward, 14 n, 55
Terry & Siebert, 381
Thayer, Webster, 185, 185 n
Think machine, 280–81, 293, 345
Thirring, Hans, 8–9
Thomas, J. Parnell, 44, 45, 313
Thompson, Dorothy, 176
Thomson, J. J., 17
Time, 60, 64, 66–67, 72–73, 77, 81, 83–84, 96, 107, 180, 192, 269, 288, 328, 424
Tombs Prison, 118, 209, 422
Tribune de Geneve, 190
Truman, Harry S., 29–33, 41, 44, 47, 52–54, 56–57, 59–60, 81, 180, 186, 190–93, 312, 405, 424

Ullman, William Ludwig, 320
U.S. News & World Report, 60, 380
U.S. Service & Shipping, 310–12
Uranium, 7, 11–18, 20–26, 42, 55–56, 272–73, 361 n. See also Greenglass, D., uranium theft
Urey, Harold, 10, 21, 25, 31, 36, 119, 191, 241, 257, 263, 343, 436

Vago, Oscar John, 87–88, 283 n, 284
Van Zandt, James E., 75
Vanzetti, Bartolomeo: sister of, 193
Veksler, Vladimir, 37
Velde, Harold, 405

Vendrell, Jose Broccado, 141, 164
Vera Cruz, 128, 140–41, 154, 162–63, 328–29, 333, 335, 337, 339–40
Vernadskii, V. I., 9
Vinson, Fred M., 243, 246

Wall Street Journal, 147
Wallace, Henry A., 29, 55
Walton, E. T. S., 17
Washington Post, 47, 241 n, 294
Washington Star, 176, 365, 443
Washington Times-Herald, 44–46
Weinberg, Joseph W., 48, 50
Weinfeld, Edward, 434, 436–42
Weisskopf, Victor F., 14 n
Welker, Herman, 365–66
Wexley, John, 334, 384, 430–31
Wheeler, W. McD., 243, 246
White, Harry Dexter, 47, 295, 320–22
White, Lincoln, 241
Whitehead, Don, 359, 389, 405, 405 n, 414
White House Years, The, 367
Wigner, Eugene, 14 n
Williams, Paul W., 340
Wilson, Charles E., 191
Women's House of Detention, 214–16
Wood, John S., 43
World Tourists, 310
Wormwood Scrubs Prison, 70

Xavier University, 107, 110, 112, 117, 410

Yakovlev, Anatoli A. ("John"), 80, 84, 88, 107–8, 119, 135–38, 138 n, 139, 143, 152–53, 157, 160–62, 187, 263, 366–7, 373–75, 381, 391, 398–402, 409, 412, 423–24, 428, 442
Yale Law Journal, 169, 443
Yeagley, J. Walter, 302, 428–31
Young Communist League (YCL), 77, 93, 147, 323 n, 361, 361 n, 415
Yukawa, Hideki, 16

Zeitschrift fur Physik, 9
Zinn, Walter, 13
Zion, Sidney E., 432

Some other books published by Penguin
are described on the following pages.

Norman Moss

MEN WHO PLAY GOD
The Story of the Hydrogen Bomb

The first complete account of how the hydrogen bomb was developed and how the world has come to live with it. It is written from the viewpoints of the scientists, statesmen, generals, strategists, and ordinary people who grapple with the problems caused by a weapon that can annihilate the human race. Every aspect of the story is told: the secret debate in Washington over whether to build an H-bomb; the searchings of conscience among scientists; the discovery of fall-out; the roles of the Strategic Air Command and the Soviet nuclear force; the development of intercontinental missiles; the new ideas about war and peace that emerged; and the unprecedented fear that now looms over the world. For this edition, the author, a British journalist, has added new material to cover recent developments. "A detailed and brilliant account . . . full of illumination . . . fascinating."—*The New Yorker*

Richard J. Walton

COLD WAR AND
COUNTERREVOLUTION

It is time to look at "the Kennedy of life, not the
Kennedy of legend," writes Richard J. Walton in
this eye-opening re-evaluation of President John
F. Kennedy's foreign policy. As Mr. Walton sur-
veys the available evidence—the public record,
the President's own words, the books written by
men in the Kennedy administration—a surprising
and ambivalent picture emerges. It becomes apparent that despite Kennedy's image as a man of
grace, courage, and intelligent liberalism, he was
actually a hawkish Cold Warrior and counterrevo-
lutionary whose vigorous anti-communism prevailed over his idealism and sympathy for the op-
pressed peoples of the world. Although he had
political skill and several great achievements to his
credit, Kennedy's chief legacy was the miscalcula-
tions of Cuba, Berlin, and Vietnam. As *Cold War
and Counterrevolution* makes clear, it is not too
early to subject that legacy to strict historical
scrutiny.

Leonard Downie, Jr.

JUSTICE DENIED
The Case for Reform of the Courts

An indictment of the American court system. This broadly informed, thoroughly documented report shows that speedy trial does not exist—except in assembly-line travesties; that court fees shut many poor people out entirely; and that the courts' interpretation of the law often gives those with economic power privileges not enjoyed by debtors, tenants, or consumers. Leonard Downie, Jr., traveled thousands of miles and visited scores of courtrooms in his search for the truth about the failings of the courts and about the possibilities of reform. His book is essential reading for all who want to see justice done in America. As an investigative reporter, Leonard Downie, Jr., wrote a series of articles for the *Washington Post* now credited with having led to important court reforms.